SETTLING AND UNSETTLING MEMORIES
Essays in Canadian Public History

Settling and Unsettling Memories analyses the ways in which Canadians over the past century have narrated the story of their past in books, films, works of art, commemorative ceremonies, and online. This cohesive collection introduces readers to overarching themes of Canadian memory studies and brings them up to date on the latest advances in the field.

With increasing debates surrounding how societies should publicly commemorate events and people, *Settling and Unsettling Memories* helps readers appreciate the challenges inherent in presenting the past. Prominent and emerging scholars explore the ways in which Canadian memory has been put into action across a variety of communities, regions, and time periods. Through high-quality essays touching on the central questions of historical consciousness and collective memory, this book makes a significant contribution to a rapidly growing field.

NICOLE NEATBY is an associate professor in the Department of History at Saint Mary's University.

PETER HODGINS is an assistant professor in the School of Canadian Studies at Carleton University.

Settling and Unsettling Memories

Essays in Canadian Public History

EDITED BY NICOLE NEATBY AND
PETER HODGINS

UNIVERSITY OF TORONTO PRESS
Toronto Buffalo London

© University of Toronto Press 2012
Toronto Buffalo London
www.utppublishing.com
Printed in Canada

ISBN 978-0-8020-3893-7 (cloth)
ISBN 978-0-8020-3816-6 (paper)

Printed on acid-free paper

Library and Archives Canada Cataloguing in Publication

Settling and unsettling memories : essays in Canadian public history / edited by
Nicole Neatby and Peter Hodgins.

Includes bibliographical references.
ISBN 978-0-8020-3893-7 (bound)   ISBN 978-0-8020-3816-6 (pbk.)

1. Collective memory – Canada.   2. Public history – Canada.   3. Canada –
Civilization – 20th century.   4. Canada – History – 20th century.   I. Neatby,
Nicole, 1962–   II. Hodgins, Peter, 1969–

FC95.4.S454 2012   971.06   C2011-908387-6

University of Toronto Press acknowledges the financial assistance to its publishing
program of the Canada Council for the Arts and the Ontario Arts Council.

 Canada Council   Conseil des Arts   ONTARIO ARTS COUNCIL
for the Arts   du Canada   CONSEIL DES ARTS DE L'ONTARIO

University of Toronto Press acknowledges the financial support of the Government
of Canada through the Canada Book Fund for its publishing activities.

This book has been published with the help of a grant from the Canadian Federation for the Humanities and Social Sciences, through the Aid to Scholarly Publications Program, using funds provided by the Social Sciences and Humanities
Research Council of Canada.

À la mémoire de ma mère

Contents

Acknowledgments xi–xii

Introduction 3

PART ONE: REMEMBERING THE HEROIC PAST

1 Commemorating the Woman Warrior of New France: Madeleine de
Verchères, 1690s–1920s 29
COLIN M. COATES

2 'Of Slender Frame and Delicate Appearance': The Placing of Laura Secord
in the Narratives of Canadian Loyalist Tradition 47
CECILIA MORGAN

3 Re-Membering Dead Heroes: Quebec City's Monument to Short-
Wallick 67
JASON F. KOVACS AND BRIAN S. OSBORNE

4 Dugua vs Champlain: The Construction of Heroes in Atlantic Canada,
1904–2004 94
RONALD RUDIN

PART TWO: PEDAGOGIES OF NATION

5 'If I'm Going to Be a Cop, Why Do I Have to Learn Religion and History?':
Schools, Citizenship, and the Teaching of Canadian History 135
KEN OSBORNE

6 Saving the Nation through National History: The Case of *Canada: A People's History*   188
LYLE DICK

7 Playing with 'Nitro': The Racialization of Chinese Canadians in Public Memory   215
TIMOTHY J. STANLEY

8 Democratizing the Past? Canada's History on the World Wide Web
SASHA MULLALLY   235

PART THREE: VISUALIZING AND REVISING THE PAST

9 The Art of Nation-Building: Canadian History Painting, 1880–1914   267
H.V. NELLES

10 Tricky Myths: Settler Pasts and Landscapes of Innocence   310
EVA MACKEY

11 Settler Monuments, Indigenous Memory: Dis-Membering and Re-Membering Canadian Art History   340
RUTH B. PHILLIPS

12 Ethnic Minorities and Wartime Injustices: Redress Campaigns and Historical Narratives in Late Twentieth-Century Canada   369
IAN RADFORTH

PART FOUR: CASHING IN ON THE PAST

13 'The Normandy of the New World': Canada Steamship Lines, Antimodernism, and the Selling of Old Quebec   419
JAMES MURTON

14 Cashing In on Antiquity: Tourism and the Uses of History in Nova Scotia, 1890–1960   454
IAN McKAY

15 'Leaving the Past Behind': From Old Quebec to 'La Belle Province'   491
NICOLE NEATBY

16 Peace, Order, and Good Banking: Packaging History and Memory in Canadian Commercial Advertising 538

IRA WAGMAN

PART FIVE: ENTERTAINING THE PAST

17 Why Must Halifax Keep Exploding?: English-Canadian Nationalism and the Search for a Usable Disaster 569

PETER HODGINS

18 The Past Is an Imagined Country: Reading Canadian Historical Fiction Written in English 591

RENÉE HULAN

Select Bibliography 615

Contributors List 649

Acknowledgments

Our first order of thanks must unquestionably go out to those who contributed to this collection. Through their strong commitment to the project, their willingness to present the results of their cutting edge research in ways that would speak to readers from multiple disciplinary horizons, they greatly enhanced the satisfaction that comes with putting a volume such as this one together. The long gestation period of this publication also meant that we had the great pleasure and privilege of working with scholars we had long admired but had yet to know beyond the page. It also gave us added opportunities to work in new ways with wonderful colleagues some of whom have become friends over the years. In keeping with this sentiment, my (Nicole Neatby) most heartfelt thanks go to Peter. Not only was he the spark that ignited this project but his unlimited intellectual curiosity, his unflinching optimism and his kind understanding and support made this project enriching in ways that I could not have imagined. I want to thank my parents, Blair and Jacqueline Neatby, for their enduring encouragements and kindness. Although my mother was not present during the whole life span of this project, she never stopped being there. My memories are filled with her timeless wise advice, enduring warmth, and insatiable curiosity, and these nourished me throughout. I hope that John, who has been there all along, knows how much his uplifting encouragements, his patience, and his unfailing capacity to make me laugh have meant to me.

For his part, Peter would like to thank Nicole for her friendship, sense of humor, patience, and warmth. When we started working on this book, I had just finished my PhD and I've learned much from working with Nicole about professionalism. Her tenacity, discipline, energy, enthusiasm, attention to detail, intellectual acuity, and generosity have served as a model and an inspiration for me. I would also like to thank my partner Annie for her love, her laughter, her wisdom, and her support (and, yes, her patience). I could not have done it without her. I would also like to thank my parents Peter and Gerarda Hodgins for their unwavering love throughout the years and especially my daughter, Maya, who has grown from a clever, curious (but somewhat temperamental) young girl into a smart, perceptive, cool, kind and knowledgable young woman during the time it took for this book to come into being. I'm deeply grateful that you're all in my life.

We would of course also like to extend thanks to the editors and staff at the University of Toronto Press. Len Husband in particular was invaluable throughout the process in helping guide us with his wise and always encouraging counsel. And thanks to the work of Frances Mundy and Judith Williams, with her eagle editorial eye, this manuscript was able to leave the final drawing board and make it to the production line. We gratefully thank the Federation of Social Sciences and Humanities for its generous support through its Aid to Scholarly Publication Program as well as the generosity of Dean John Osborne and Carleton University's Faculty of Arts and Social Sciences who provided additional funds to make this publication possible. Peter would also like to thank his former students Patrick Scott and Rob Ammerman for their help with research and editing.

SETTLING AND UNSETTLING MEMORIES

Introduction

In Ottawa in June 1996, Ovide Mercredi, the grand chief of the Assembly of First Nations, led a procession past the National Gallery of Canada up to Ottawa's Nepean Point. Sited there is a tall plinth topped by a one-and-a-half-times life-sized bronze statue of Samuel de Champlain, whose commanding and conquering gaze into the west is framed by an astrolabe held in his extended right arm like a cross or a sword. Less noticeable from a distance was a life-sized figure which occupied a small shelf near the base of the plinth. This was a bronze statue of a loinclothed 'Indian scout' who crouched beneath Champlain in a gesture of supplication and awe. When the procession arrived at the statue, Mercredi covered the scout with a blanket. He then told the assembled members of the press and onlookers that this representation of Aboriginal peoples was demeaning because of the figure's nakedness and subservient position. Mercredi gave the National Capital Commission one year to remove the sculpture of the scout. For its part, the National Capital Commission responded by announcing that it would remove the sculpture and place it in storage. As the art historian Susan Hart reports, this announcement raised a 'swift and mixed' public outcry: 'Within days, the NCC had received dozens of phone calls – mostly negative – and of the five hundred calls to the *Ottawa Citizen*'s touchline, about three-quarters were opposed to the statue's removal. While many callers felt that "history" should not be changed to suit the times, most also acknowledged the uneven power relationship the monument was now seen to signify.'[1] As a result of the ensuing controversy over what to do with the sculpture, the scout did not find a new home until October 1999. He was eventually relocated across the street, set, noble savage style, at ground level among shrubs and foliage in a remote corner of Major's Hill Park and renamed 'Anishinabe Scout.'[2]

The reason that we begin this collection on Canadian public memory with the story of the Anishinabe Scout is that it speaks to many of the tensions and challenges of thinking, writing, representing, and performing public or collective memory. What this story reveals, among other things, is our growing sense of the mutable, constructed, polysemic, and contested character of Canadian collective memory. The concept of collective memory emerged in the work of sociologist Maurice Halbwachs and has become common currency in social or cultural memory studies. Halbwachs was one of the first to argue that all acts of remembering are social, pluralistic, and driven by present-day concerns.[3] Even our most personal recollections, he argued, are shaped by interpretive frameworks and narrative templates drawn from our present-day social-cultural context and that 'present concerns determine what of the past we remember and how we remember it.'[4] Halbwachs's insights have since become axiomatic for contemporary memory scholars who study 'who remembers and why?' while taking into account the contextual, dynamic, and performed character of remembering.[5] They also aim to unravel how competing collective memories emerge and are strengthened, absorbed, or marginalized (or simply dissolve) in public space through time.[6] Indeed, underpinning the study of collective memories is a question raised by David Glassberg: 'with all the possible versions of the past that circulate in society, how did particular accounts of the past get established and disseminated as the public one?'[7]

While Halbwachs developed the concept of collective memory in the early twentieth century, more contemporary scholars on public or collective memory have been influenced by a general turn to culture and memory in a wide range of disciplines starting in the late 1970s. In their own disparate ways, cultural Marxist, postmodernist, and poststructuralist scholars in various fields have brought to the fore the degree to which a given representation of the past is inevitably coloured by present-day political, cultural, and aesthetic perspectives and priorities. In line with this evolution, the conventional opposition that had been established by scholars between history and memory has been blurred.[8] When remembering itself is being placed in what the cultural psychologist James Wertsch calls its 'sociocultural context,'[9] traditional criteria for defining its attributes and evaluating the reliability of recent or past memories as a source of information are fundamentally altered. Indeed, as memory becomes a subject of inquiry, debates over its accuracy as a source become less central. More to the point, it is remembering's very *unreliability*, its manifest malleability, that serves as an opportunity for scholars to provide new and valuable insights about the formation of collective memories and the shaping of historical consciousness.[10] This, among other things, means that scholars of memory are made to consider 'historians as both products and producers of the collective identities of the culture in which they are part.'[11] Indeed, they are '"vector[s] of memory" and carrier[s] of fundamental importance in that the vision [they propose] of the past may, after some delay, exert an influence on contemporary representations.'[12] In fact, many now would share historian Michael Kammen's observation that 'What history and memory share in common is that both merit our mistrust.'[13] And concomitantly, they would endorse Peter Seixas's view that 'historians become students of what others believe (or believed) was significant in the past,'[14] including cultural producers such as museum curators, heritage conservationists, tourism promoters, and archivists.

The notion of competing collective memories has in turn led scholars to think of them as 'usable.' Indeed, the study of remembering makes it apparent that 'some memories once functional, become dysfunctional.'[15] Thinking of memory as being usable has helped to account for the fact that some memories become dominant,[16] or 'institutionalized,'[17] often in the form of an 'official narrative of nation.'[18] Typically, these are memories upheld by what the American historian John Bodnar has called members of the 'official culture.' These include 'government officials, editors, lawyers, clerics, teachers, military officials and small business men.'[19] They can be activated to promote national unity or, on a smaller scale, to produce a stronger cohesion among certain groups, to buttress a common self-identity or self-representation. Conversely, scholars note that the process of memory construction is unavoidably accompanied by 'forgetting' and involves the silencing of alternate memories.[20]

Many have been inspired here by the insights of Eric Hobsbawm and Terence Ranger in their edited collection *The Invention of Tradition*[21] and of Benedict Anderson's *Imagined Communities*.[22] Hobsbawn and Ranger argued against the Herderian idea that nations are organic entities, naturally produced through common ethnicity, language, and ties of memory reflected in shared folklore and customs. Instead, they made the point that states and other social groups invent traditions in order to legitimate political projects and to 'inculcate certain values and norms of behaviour.' Far from originating in time immemorial, these traditions 'are responses to novel situations which take the form of reference to old situations, or which establish their own past by quasi-obligatory repetition.'[23] Anderson meanwhile spoke of 'imagined communities' constructed, among other things, through a combination of media technologies, the displacement of vernacular languages and dialects by an official 'vernacular.' This innovative reading of the process of identity formation whether at the state level or among other types of communities spurred scholars to investigate which traditions were being invented, which ones were being forgotten, how they were absorbed in collective memories, and what were the technological practices through which these imagined communities emerged. In short, it has led them to think in terms of *usable* pasts.

Of course, going too far in that direction is to consider the past as a 'tool box' from which various groups retrieve in order to impose a particular political and social order, suggesting Machiavellian manipulations and conspiracies. Scholars of public memory have adopted a more nuanced understanding of the uses of the past. First of all, there is a growing recognition that any given act of public remembering is usually the product of a wide variety of often contradictory motivations ranging from the ideological, the pecuniary, and the manipulative to the sincere and heartfelt to the traumatic. Secondly, there is a growing recognition that every memory text or performance is the product of a series of complex negotiations between cultural producers, their patrons, and the communities whose past they are purported to be commemorating. At the same time, producers must also grapple with the enabling and constraining technological possibilities of their chosen medium of remembrance, the codes, genres, and conventions associated with that medium, and the historical/intertexual baggage that comes with both.

Finally, producers must also negotiate the fact that their prospective audiences bring to the interpretation situation a historically conditioned and equally complex set of commonsensical assumptions about 'the way the past is,' the kinds of representations that count as 'historically accurate,' and their own cultural and political commitments. As Mikhail Bakhtin, Antonio Gramsci, Hayden White, Paul Ricoeur, James Werscht, and many others have argued, almost every time we take experience up into narrative, we insert it into pre-established narrative frameworks.[24] The use of such formulaic narrative frameworks is often a necessary condition for successful mass communication. In order to make themselves understood, spokespeople for the official culture often have no choice but to draw upon the highly conventionalized words, scripts, images, narratives, and myths that are culturally available to them and their publics. Furthermore, when faced with a new story, the only means most people have to make sense of it is to draw it back into the circle of their existing cultural expectations, assumptions, and prejudices about how a narrative should be composed, the sorts of characters and plots it should contain, and how it should end. In other words, public communication is conservative in its most profound sense: in order to be broadly accessible or legible and believed, the public communicator often has no choice but to work within the restricted vocabulary of the 'already-known' and the 'commonsensical.'

Compounding matters is the fact that public communicators are constantly confronted by the rhetorical problem of dealing with mixed audiences whose 'interpretative horizons' are often very traditional. As the debates over the 'Into the Heart of Africa' exhibition at the Royal Ontario Museum[25] or the television docudrama *The Valour and the Horror*[26] suggest, there are considerable risks for those who want to narrate the past in non-traditional ways. Monuments, museums, and open-air historical reconstructions cater to, to name a few, international tourists, national tourists, schoolchildren on field trips, community groups, and academic critics and must try to produce representations of the past that will fit within all of their respective interpretive horizons, please them, and satisfy their desires. This usually ends up with public historians following the advice of rhetorical theorists for dealing with such audiences: try to say something that resonates with each. When one cannot do the latter, speak ambiguously or remain silent.[27]

In recent years, this concern with the relationship between public memories and their audiences has coalesced around the issue of historical consciousness – the question of 'how ideas about history are … understood and change over time.'[28] As Jörn Rüsen has argued, the most conservative form of historical consciousness is 'traditional historical consciousness.' He argues that individuals or groups with a 'traditional historic consciousness' treat the past as immutable and look to it only as a means of confirming existing myths, beliefs, and identities.[29] In fact, this traditional historical consciousness is something closely akin to collective memory *per se*. Indeed, as Peter Novick has argued, memory in this perspective 'has no sense of the passage of time; it denies the "pastness" of its objects and insists on their continuing presence.'[30] On the other hand, what Hans-Georg Gadamer calls 'effective historical consciousness' involves the recognition that the apprehension of the past is always framed by the interpreter's finite, partial, and fallible 'horizon of interpretation.' In his *Truth and Method*, Gadamer argued that all attempts at understanding a new text involve readers situating it within a hermeneutic circle of inherited cultural assumptions that he called 'prejudices' – adopting the literal sense of the term. While convinced that we always make sense of the new by drawing it into the circle of the 'already-known,' he also made the point that our apparent imprisonment in the 'familiar' and 'already-known' could be counteracted through the development of an effective historical consciousness[31] – in effect, a recognition of 'the historicity of events.'[32] In order to understand the past of other cultures, Gadamer argued that we should have the interpretive dexterity to recognize that our forms of representation are equally rhetorical, political, conventional, and referential. Without marshalling the ethical and political courage to revise and reject aspects of those forms, codes, and media, we will continue to obscure our vision of the past or of others.[33]

In this collection, we have brought together a multidisciplinary group of established and emerging scholars who put to use the 'interpretative dexterity' required to study public representations of the past, bringing out as they do the diversity of Canadians' collective memories, the various ways in which they have been used, and more indirectly, the ways in which these may or may not correspond to traditional or 'effective' manifestations of historical consciousness. We solicited contributions from scholars who have turned their analytical gaze on what the French historian Pierre Nora calls 'sites of memory.' As reflected in our table of contents, we understand this concept much as he does when he states that these constitute 'any significant entity, whether material or non-material in nature, which by dint of human will or the work of time has become a symbolic element of the memorial heritage of any community.'[34] The authors in this volume study multiple sites of memory: monuments, art, various forms of cultural practices such as commemorations and parades, as well as history textbooks, websites, historical fiction, and the past as represented on the moving image. As they make clear, Canada – with its different communities and nations, various ethnic groups, and men and women living at different times and in different regions – offers them fertile ground to identify collective memories at play.[35] In terms of chronology, some authors touch on Canadian developments of the late nineteenth century, but most focus on twentieth-century acts of remembering. Not all regions of the country have been covered, nor have we attempted to compile a representative sample of what Canadian scholars of memory have published over time. Since the early 1990s, in the United States, memory studies have expanded into a well-established 'cottage industry'[36] in almost all areas of the social sciences and the humanities. In Canada, while not as fully developed, the field is rapidly expanding,[37] and this collection can serve as a signpost for the development of memory studies in this country.

At this point, there is no one collection that brings together scholars on the subject from such diverse disciplinary horizons focusing on such diverse Canadian 'sites of memory.' While a few multidisciplinary volumes have been published recently, each tends to focus on one specific aspect of collective memory.[38] We hope that including, in a single volume, both newly minted and previously published articles will make what tends to be discipline-segregated research more easily accessible to the ever-increasing number of those interested in how the Canadian past is remembered in public.

Much of the shared scholarly concern with the dynamic character of Canadian public memory represented by this volume can be understood as a collective response to what some call the memory-crisis of contemporary Canada and the West in general. Some account for this 'crisis' by pointing to the changing demographic composition of North American and European populations. Demographers, cultural theorists, and marketing researchers have noted that as the proportionally more populous generation of the so-called Baby Boomers drift into middle age and beyond, they appear to be drawn to things past in the way many will seek an elusive 'fountain of youth.' This attraction is manifested in the growing number and popularity of movies and novels set in the past, the emergence of television history channels and those devoted to reruns and of 'classic rock' radio stations, and the consumerist initiatives taken by marketers, restaurant and clothing designers, and architects to invoke the past. Needless to say, the emergence of new technologies of communication, particularly those provided by the World Wide Web, have made readily accessible, 'at the click of a mouse,' an ever-increasing number of resources for those drawn to the past.

This retreat into the reassuring comfort and security of a recognizable past can be understood as an escape from the uncertainties brought about by the seemingly rapid and destabilizing changes of the present.[39] According to Peter Seixas, the world has been undergoing a distinct period of accelerated change that 'renders traditional orientations to the past untenable.'[40] This change has simultaneously fostered a widespread urge to reread the past with new lenses and greater scrutiny. Scholars point to the recent dismantling of various political regimes, including the Soviet Union and those of the Balkans, which have led to a marshalling of the past by various groups to legitimize their nationalist aspirations.[41] Moreover, the reconfiguration of nation-states through recent waves of immigration has resulted in various ethnic groups challenging their host countries to revisit dominant national narratives. Global pressures to accommodate competing 'popular memories' promoted by a 'vernacular culture,'[42] or to give voice to silenced ones, have also come from several marginalized groups with relatively longer standing citizenship: women, gays, workers, first-wave immigrants, and Aboriginals, to name a few.[43]

The flip side to this is that several countries have witnessed, perhaps not surprisingly, the emergence of outspoken defenders of consensual traditional narrations of the past most often defined by them as 'national histories.' These advocates essentially argue that, for the sake of national unity and the training of committed and loyal citizens, those working in the public or in academia to narrate the past should shy away from incorporating what they perceive to be destabilizing, competing memories of the nation. For these advocates, a return to this so-called 'national' history would be the best defence against the divisive narrations to come out of 'popular memories' – more specifically, those of marginalized or silenced citizens. These developments further illustrate/confirm the extent to which representing the past in public can be understood as conflicting memories 'competing for influence in public'[44] – a competition that is increasingly referred to as 'history wars.'

Canadians have participated fully in these developments as they also show a growing desire to re-engage with the past. Evidence of this can be found in highly publicized attempts at presenting the past to wider audiences in the country. This has translated into wide-scale investments by either public or private institutions in the memorial apparatus. These initiatives have provided, among other things, funding for museums, art exhibits, websites, and historical documentaries. And, as elsewhere, some of these initiatives have made it loudly apparent that public history here can lead to highly charged outcries and debates. The uproar following the Royal Ontario Museum's exhibit 'Into the Heart of Africa' in 1989–90[45] and the controversy surrounding CBC's docudrama *The Valour and the Horror* in 1993[46] come to mind, while other initiatives such as CBC/Radio-Canada's *Canada: A People's History*[47] and most notably the Heritage Minutes, broadcast on CBC/Radio-Canada and in movie theatres since 1991,[48] have been closely monitored.

Such public initiatives have been accompanied by acrimonious sparring over what history should be taught in schools and in university.[49] The numerous polls conducted by the privately funded Dominion Institute in its efforts to assess Canadians' knowledge of their history (or lack thereof) have only added fuel to the fire.[50] And jumping into the fray is Canada's own contingent of 'national history' advocates, including, among others, historians J.L. Granatstein and Michael Bliss. Both warned, although in different ways, of the imminent death of a unifying Canadian national memory. Overall, such advocates have felt that the downplaying of the country's successes at overcoming obstacles and at moving towards national reconciliation in the past can only lead to a fracturing of the nation in the present.[51]

At the same time that they are responding to the Canadian memory-crisis, the essays in this collection are also the result of the emergence of the study of public memory in Canada since the 1980s. This study first took root in Quebec in the mid-1980s when Jacques Mathieu, Jocelyn Létourneau, Christian Laville, Bogumil Jewsiewicki, and other researchers associated with the CELAT (Centre interuniversitaire d'études sur les lettres, arts et traditions) began to investigate the construction of collective memory in Quebec. Mathieu played a lead role in this endeavour. In 1986, he edited a collection published by CELAT titled *Étude de la construction de la mémoire collective des Québécois au XXe siècle*. Five years later, he would co-write with Jacques Lacoursière (the historian behind the highly popular book series *Histoire populaire du Québec* and the television series *Épopée en Amérique*) *Les Mémoires Québécoises* – a book that interrogated many of the myths of Québécois culture.[52]

While Mathieu and Lacoursière studied the character of Québécois collective memories and myths and how they were propagated and disseminated, Laville and Létourneau focused their efforts on the historical consciousness of the audiences of such memories and myths. As Létourneau details in 'Digging into Historical Consciousness, Individual and Collective,' his research since the late 1980s has centred on the issue of the construction of a Québécois 'grand narrative' that emerged out of the Quiet Revolution and how this grand narrative is used by young Québécois to understand their place in the world.[53] More recently, he has become the head of a Canada-wide team of researchers that has been awarded a substantial grant under SSHRC's Community-University Research Alliance program. They are conducting a large-scale study of 'the presence of the past' in the everyday life of Canadians on the model of American and Australian studies published earlier. Titled 'Canadians and Their Pasts,' this study promises, in the words of its website, to answer outstanding questions 'about the focus of people's engagement with the past, popular perceptions of the trustworthiness of historical sources, how people reconcile conflicting narratives about past events, and the ways that people use the past to construct their individual and collective identities.'[54]

Although the study of collective memory was well underway in Quebec by the late 1980s, it was not until the mid-1990s that the field began to really establish itself in English Canada. In 1994, Ian McKay published *The Quest of the Folk* – a study of the rise of the myth of the Folk in the Maritimes. Following theoretical developments in cultural studies, McKay tracked the strategies by which various middle-class cultural entrepreneurs worked to construct the rural poor of Nova Scotia as 'the Folk,' to extract 'folk culture,' and then to cash in on their efforts at 'salvage archaeology' by forging alliances with the provincial government and the emerging tourist industry. In 1996, Jonathan Vance's *Death So Noble* analysed a wide variety of Canadian commemorative practices after the First World War. Vance critically examined the complex process by which what he called 'the Cult of Victory' was constructed and disseminated and co-opted into the service of a nascent Canadian cultural and political nationalism in the 1920s and 1930s. This theme of the co-optation of public memory by nationalist projects was reiterated in 1999 with the publication of Viv Nelles's *The Art of Nation-Building*. Nelles studied the public celebrations in 1908 of the three hundredth anniversary of Champlain's founding of Quebec. Reconstructing the elaborate historical pageant that was the centrepiece of the celebration through a sensitive reading of the remaining visual traces (photographs, paintings, posters, etc.) and documentary history of the planning of the event, Nelles demonstrated how what started as a celebration of French-Canadian heritage ended up becoming a celebration of British imperialism and 'the marriage of the two founding nations' myth of Canada. In that same year,

Eva Mackey published *The House of Difference*. In that book, Mackey studied contemporary Canadian commemorative practices such as Canada Day celebrations in order to reveal the flexible manner in which liberal multicultural discourse works at once to be 'inclusive' and protective of existing cultural, political, and economic hierarchies.[55]

Inspired by these landmark studies as well as the more general 'turn to memory' in the social sciences and the humanities, it is safe to say that by the early years of the twenty-first century, the study of public memory has become a central concern for Canadian intellectuals. One gets a good sense of how quickly this has happened when one compares the articles written in three edited collections on Canadian culture published in 1994, 2002, and 2006 respectively. In the 1994 collection *Canada: Theoretical Discourse*, only one article can be said to even vaguely deal with the issue of public memory (Pauline Greenhill and Diane Tye's 'Critiques from the Margin: Women and Folklore in English Canada'). In *Slippery Pastimes* (2002), on the other hand, six out of sixteen articles deal directly with the issue, and in *Canadian Cultural Poesis* (2006), the number is nine out of twenty-one. Furthermore, especially in the case of the latter collection, one is struck by how the scholarly interest in public memory now extends far beyond historians and anthropologists to scholars in film studies, media studies, literary studies, and art history.[56]

As many of the chapters in this collection demonstrate, every Canadian cultural group, region, and political movement seems to have its own preferred reading of the past that alternately contests, complements, or renegotiates the others. In spite of this narrative diversity, however, the official nationalist meta-narrative retains its centrality in Canadian public culture. Traditional Canadian national narratives have typically followed a 'colony to nation' storyline in which Canada's past is recounted as one of unbounded, incremental, and progressive success. Many of the authors in this collection address the relationship between their sites of memory and the nation-building interpretive framework. While making it all the more difficult to read Canada's history as inexorably marching forward, at the same time they confirm the remarkable resilience of this more traditional meta-narrative.

It should be noted as well that while these chapters do not *directly* reveal the ways in which the sites of memory under study have shaped the wider public's historical consciousness, they reveal much about the historical consciousness of a wide array of cultural producers. They also make it abundantly clear that 'certain groups and individuals have, historically, responded to the same narratives and participated in the same commemorative processes – but for different, at times, overlapping, reasons.'[57] They are part of the growing body of knowledge about representations of the past that is increasingly spurring some memory scholars to flesh out more specifically how groups and individuals come to know what they know about the past and how they engage with it.[58]

In the first section of our collection, 'Remembering the Heroic Past,' we have brought together contributions that analyse how Canadian heroes have been remembered, underscoring the notion raised by Ronald Rudin that 'heroes are made, not found.'[59] In their respective case studies of Madeleine de Verchères and Laura Secord, which were originally published in the mid-1990s,[60] Colin Coates and Cecilia Morgan reveal how these women are both taken up by popular historians who recount their lives 'as a morality tale, emphasizing elements that fit their particular didactic purpose.'[61] They alert us to the fact that a long-standing problem facing those who have chosen to commemorate heroines' bravery acts in the past has been to find ways of memorializing them – and all this without 'reject[ing] strict gender roles.' [62] Brian Osborne and Jason Kovacs open up another window onto the making of heroes by looking at the way in which societies have not only turned to the distant past to find candidates worthy of memorialization. Their textured analysis reveals how overnight heroes such as Major Charles Short and Staff Sergeant George Wallick can be put to nation-building purposes. For his part, Ronald Rudin offers a unique analysis of the ways different communities have remembered the same event and the same protagonists at a hundred-year interval. Samuel de Champlain and Pierre Dugua de Mons were commemorated on the East Coast in both 1904 and 2004. Rudin seized an opportunity rarely given to historians to witness 'memory in action.'

In the second section, 'Pedagogies of Nation,' contributors bring out the ways in which debates over public memory have always been linked to the challenges of forming citizens and loyal members of the Canadian nation in the face of the centrifugal pull of regionalism, and separatism, and American and now global popular culture. In a chapter that draws on a lifetime of work in the area, Ken Osborne contends that teachers have grappled with the challenge of making history appealing, presenting it in 'ways that non-specialists find accessible, informative, interesting, and even thought-provoking.'[63] This objective has also informed the work of those in the media, notably journalists, who seek to remember through the moving image. In his chapter, Lyle Dick points out that telling a dramatic story was clearly the guiding principle of the producers of the publicly funded *Canada: A People's History* series aired on CBC and Radio-Canada television. In *Canada: A People's History*, the nation-building, colony-to-nation narrative doubled with the intent of promoting national unity is directly served by the choice of the epic genre, in which heroes and enemies are clearly identified. This innovative and revealing reading of the series invites us to pay close attention to the literary forms in which these productions are structured as opposed to simply focusing on their content. For her part, Sasha Mullally provides a welcome examination of the challenges of presenting history on the Web. While a relatively new venue, it appears to be on its way to becoming the most frequented and relied upon 'site of memory.' She makes the thought-provoking point that history on the Web has the potential to democratize access to historical knowledge and to develop new ways of writing and thinking about history.

An important aspect of this democratization of public memory has been the challenging of the received official narrative and the demand that it be rewritten to reflect Canada's increasingly multi-ethnic character. In his contribution, Tim Stanley skilfully unravels the ways in which the Historica Minutes are weighted down with memories meant to strengthen among viewers a dearly held nation-building mythology. By focusing on the 'Nitro' minute, Stanley brings out how an ostensibly laudatory attempt to include in our narration of the past the racism experienced by marginalized Chinese immigrants in the late ninetheenth century ends up in effect serving to promote a self-congratulatory, redemptive nation-building storyline fraught with 'purposeful amnesia.'

The third set of chapters, 'Visualizing and Revising the Past,' makes clear that while there are ongoing attempts to produce a coherent vision of the nation and its pasts, that vision is often contested. Foremost among those seeking to create such a vision have been artists such as the Group of Seven. This handful of artists has been heralded as the first to have painted the Canadian nation, locating its essence in the North and finding an indigenous language in which to represent it.[64] H.V. Nelles, however, examines a less well known group of Canadian artists who painted during the late nineteenth century and up to the First World War and who were also involved in the business of nation-building through art by literally 'paint[ing] their past.'[65] The author accounts for their eventual failure 'to provide a visual vocabulary of historical identity'[66] by creating enlightening connections with larger 'historical pictures.' Similarly, in her chapter, which reworks and updates arguments made in *The House of Difference*, Eva Mackey describes the attempt by the Canadian state to use representations of Indigenous peoples and their cultural heritage to bolster what she calls 'official nationalist narrative.'[67] She convincingly demonstrates how the incorporation of Natives into the 'colony to nation' narrative forces Canadians to confront their racist past, but at the same time reassures them by reminding them of the remoteness of that past and the 'inclusive' nature of the present. Ruth Phillips, for her part, tells a different story – one pointing to art's potency. Put to use by marginalized groups, in this case the First Nations, art has proved to be a powerful language to re-remember the past and to visually inscribe 'silenced Indigenous memory'[68] into the official narrative of nationhood. Phillips's discerning analysis alerts us to the fact that the Native artists under study have not simply presented an alternative postcolonial remembering of the past. They have literally revisited and redrawn the place ascribed to them in works of settler art. Ian Radforth also provides particularly eloquent illustrations of the demand that the dominant vision of the Canadian past be revised and redrawn when he compares the recent redress campaigns organized by the Japanese, Italian, and Ukrainian Canadian communities and reveals how these campaigns sought to forge 'a social memory' for the group 'and then to have it inscribed into the national narrative.'[69]

The fourth section in the volume, 'Cashing In on the Past,' brings together scholars who have studied the ways in which the process of remembering has produced commodified memories designed to enhance the commercial value of tourist destinations or attract and retain buyers. All point to the fact that converting the past into objects of mass consumption is both the result of a self-conscious attempt at selling a tourist product that is most likely to appeal to consumers' nostalgia for an antimodernist past[70] and a reflection of what the host society itself values and wants to remember. James Murton, in a translation of an article that originally appeared in the *Revue d'histoire de l'Amérique Française*,[71] provides a thorough analysis of Canada Steamship Lines' initiatives during the 1930s to promote the province as a place of remembrance as it actively supported a handicraft revival and presented the authentic inhabitants of Quebec as rural habitants. He makes it clear that these initiatives were essentially meant to respond to the antimodernist longings of its tourist clientele. Ian McKay follows the ways in which the initiatives and objectives of multiple stakeholders in the government of Nova Scotia converged to 'cash in on antiquity.' His nuanced study documents the multiple ways in which the province used history to brand itself. Among other things, both these chapters illustrate a point made by Peter Hodgins elsewhere that 'the emphasis on material culture and folkloric traditions and the avoidance of narratives of political and cultural conflict ... reif[y] the memory of so-called "cultural communities" so that they take on a non-threatening character ... and are more marketable to tourists.'[72]

Still in Quebec, Nicole Neatby focuses on provincial government tourist promotion strategies, pointing to the ways in which shared objectives among state officials and business interests converged to produce similar readings of the host society's past. Bringing her study up to the 1960s, the years of the Quiet Revolution, the author demonstrates how a society's changing sense of identity can alter the way it will re-remember or re-commodify its past for a tourist clientele. Ira Wagman turns his attention to a very different case of 'memory at work' and a relatively unexplored theme: the use of historical narratives and imagery in corporate advertising. He makes the point that the 'elements of Canadian history are so pervasive in ad campaigns that Canadians have probably encountered their past more often through appeals to purchase beer than by attending museum exhibits or watching episodes of *Canada: A People's History*.'[73]

In the final section of our volume, 'Entertaining the Past,' Peter Hodgins and Renée Hulan investigate the renewed centrality of the Canadian past in contemporary cultural production. Peter Hodgins's comparative analysis of the made-for-television three-hour docudrama *Shattered City: The Halifax Explosion*, produced by an independent Halifax film company (Salter Street Films), and the Heritage Minute on the same event (*Halifax Explosion*) offers another telling example of recent attempts to make Canadian history more alluring to viewers. Sharing Lyle Dick's approach, he brings out the narrative mode of the program to get to the remembering taking place. His thorough analysis reveals the way in which historical dramatizations such as these make use of 'Hollywood codes, conventions, plots, and genres.'[74] Addressing yet another site of memory, this time a long-established one, Renée Hulan presents an evaluation of the changing ways in which English-Canadian novelists have produced historical fiction over the last century. Her impressive exploration reveals that, in much the same way as historians have questioned the possibility of finding the truth about the past, novelists have increasingly turned from a romantic gaze on the past to an ironic one.

While the thematic sections we have created serve to highlight some of the most obvious common themes and questions binding these chapters together, it will quickly become apparent that many other connections and echoing preoccupations can be brought out to link them together in different combinations. We hope that drawing these multiple linkages, explicit or yet to be articulated, will encourage readers to further explore the avenues of research being pursued here. At the very least, they should invite scholars to be increasingly self-reflective about what they read and what they themselves write about the past. More to the point, *Settling and Unsettling Memories* should further encourage memory scholars to be sensitive to the way in which the narrations of the past they come across influence their own historical consciousness while at the same time reminding them to better appreciate and question how their own narrations of the past shape the historical consciousness of their readers.

NOTES

1 Susan Hart, 'Lurking in the Bushes: Ottawa's Anishinabe Scout,' *Espace* 72 (Summer 2005): 14–17.

2 The story of the relocation of the scout is dealt with at greater lengths by Ruth Phillips, chapter 11 in this volume.

3 Maurice Halbwachs, *The Collective Memory*, trans. Francis J.D. Ditter, Jr, and Vida Yazdi Ditter (New York: Harper and Row, 1980) and *On Collective Memory*, trans. Lewis A. Coser (Chicago: University Press of Chicago, 1992).

4 See Peter Novick's analysis of Halbwachs in the Introduction to *The Holocaust in American Life* (Boston: Houghton Mifflin, 1999), 3.

5 Rarely do the introductory chapters or paragraphs to a study pertaining to memory omit noting Halbwachs's seminal contribution to the field. Most recently see James Opp and John C. Walsh, eds., *Placing Memory and Remembering Place in Canada* (Vancouver: University of British Columbia Press, 2010), 5.

6 For a fully articulated analysis of the challenges and pitfalls facing those who use this concept see chapter 1 in James Wertsch, *Voice of Collective Remembering* (Cambridge: Cambridge University Press, 2002). For a philosophical critique see Paul Ricoeur, *Memory, History and Forgetting*, trans. Kathleen Blamey and David Pellauer (Chicago: University of Chicago Press, 2004), 393–7.

7 David Glassberg, 'Public History and the Study of Memory,' *Public Historian* 18, 2 (Spring 1996): 11.

8 See Wertsch, *Voice of Collective Remembering*, 19–20. See also David Lowenthal, *The Past Is a Foreign Country* (Cambridge: Cambridge University Press, 1985), 193–219; Michael Kammen, *Mystic Chords of Memory: The Transformation of Tradition in American Culture* (New York: Vintage Books, 1993), 9–10; Colin Coates and Cecilia Morgan, *Heroines and History: Representations of Madeleine de Verchères and Laura Secord* (Toronto: University of Toronto Press, 2002), 4–6.

9 Wertsch, *Voice of Collective Remembering*, 7, 11.

10 For a fuller discussion of the distinction between memory and history see Pierre Nora and E.-Martin Meunier, eds., *Les impasses de la mémoire: histoire, filiation, nation et religion* (Montreal: Fides, 2007), most notably the article by François Dosse. This shift in understanding reflects recent findings in the field of memory psychology. As James Wertsch confirms, there is a growing consensus 'that memory is more a matter of reorganizing, or reconstructing, bits of information into a general scheme than it is a matter of accurate recall of isolated bits themselves.' (*Voice of Collective Remembering*, 7). See also Paul Connerton, 'Seven Types of Forgetting,' *Memory Studies* 1 (2008): 60–72.

11 Chris Lorenz, 'Towards a Theoretical Framework for Comparing Historiographies,' in Peter Seixas, ed., *Theorizing Historical Consciousness* (Toronto: University of Toronto Press, 2004), 28.

12 Henry Rousso, *The Vichy Syndrome: History and Memory in France since 1944*, trans. Arthur Goldhammer (Cambridge, MA: Harvard University Press, 1991), 4.

13 Kammen, *Mystic Chords of Memory*, 9–10. A forcefully contrary view is presented by John Tosh, who makes a distinction between historical 'awareness' and 'social memory' for historical scholarship to be undertaken. See chapter 1 in *The Pursuit of History*, 3rd edition (London: Pearson Education/Longman, 1999), 1–16.

14 Seixas, 'Heavy Baggage en route to Winnipeg: A Review Essay,' *Canadian Historical Review* 83, 3 (September 2002): 399.

15 Novick, *The Holocaust in American Life*, 5

16 Rousso, *The Vichy Syndrome*, 4.

17 Novick, *The Holocaust in American Life*, 6.

18 Eva Mackey, chapter10 in this volume.

19 John Bodnar, *Remaking America: Public Memory, Commemoration and Patriotism in the Twentieth Century* (Princeton: Princeton University Press, 1992), 13–16. Bodnar specifies also that 'vernacular culture,' on the other hand, is defended by 'ordinary people.'

20 This point has, in fact, become a leitmotiv in memory studies. See, among others, Kammen, *Mystic Chords of Memory*, and Lowenthal, *The Past Is a Foreign Country*, 204–6. For a more focused study on the concept of forgetting see Ricoeur's study *Memory, History and Forgetting*, and Connerton, 'Seven Types of Forgetting.' Several scholars have shown a particular interest in the ways in which the Holocaust has been remembered to explore the emergence of official memories. See, among others, Novick, *The Holocaust in American Life*; Jan Gross, *Neighbors: The Destruction of the Jewish Community in Jedwabne, Poland* (Princeton: Princeton University Press, 2001); Harold Marcuse, 'Memories of World War II and the Holocaust in Europe,' in Gordon Martel, ed., *A Companion to Europe, 1900–1945* (Oxford: Blackwell, 2006), 487–503; Mark Rosemen, 'Surviving Memory: Truth and Inaccuracy in Holocaust Testimony,' in Robert Perks and Alistair Thompson, eds., *The Oral History Reader*, 2nd edition (New York: Routledge, 2006), 230–43.

21 Eric Hobsbawm and Terence Ranger, eds., *The Invention of Tradition* (Cambridge: Cambridge University Press, 1983).

22 Benedict Anderson, *Imagined Communities: Reflections on the Origin and Spread of Nationalism* (London: Verso, 1983).

23 Hobsbawn and Ranger, eds., *The Invention of Tradition*, 1f. One could argue that, in fact, this understanding goes back to Ernest Renan's contention that forgetting is actually necessary, a pre-condition to nation-building.

24 Cf. Mikhail Bakhtin, 'The Problem of Speech Genres,' in *Speech Genres and Other Late Essays* (Austin: University of Texas Press, 1986); Hayden White, *Metahistory* (Baltimore: Johns Hopkins University Press, 1973); Ricoeur, *Memory, History, Forgetting*; Wertsch, *Voices of Collective Remembering*.

25 Cf. Shelley Butler, *Contested Representations: Revisiting 'Into the Heart of Africa'* (Amsterdam: Gordon and Breach, 1999); Eva Mackey, 'Postmodernism and Cultural Politics in a Multicultural Nation: Contests over Truth in the "Into the Heart of Africa" Controversy,' *Public Culture* 7, 2 (1995): 403–31.

26 See David Bercuson and S.F. Wise, eds., *The Valour and the Horror Revisited* (Montreal and Kingston: McGill-Queen's University Press, 1994); Graham Carr, 'Rules of Engagement: Public History and the Drama of Legitimation,' *Canadian Historical Review* 86, 2 (June 2005): 317–54; and Ernest Dick, 'The Valour and the Horror Continued: Do We Still Want Our History on Television?' *Archivaria* 35, 5 (Spring 1993): 253–69. In the United States, similar controversies have emerged, notably the Smithsonian Institution's National and Air Space Museum's Enola Gay exhibit of 1994 in Washington. See the December 1995 issue of the *Journal of American History*; Edward T. Linenthal and Tom Engelhardt, eds., *History Wars: The Enola Gay and Other Battles for the American Past* (New York: Metropolitan Books, 1996).

27 Cf. Chaim Perelman and Lucie Olbrechts-Tyteca, *The New Rhetoric* (Notre Dame: University of Notre Dame Press, 1975).

28 Glassberg, 'Public History and the Study of Memory,' 18; and 'Roundtable,' *Public Historian* 19, 2 (1997): 31–72.

29 Jörn Rüsën, *History: Narration, Interpretation, Orientation* (New York: Berghan Books, 2005).

30 Peter Novick, quoted in Seixas, ed., *Theorizing Historical Consciousness*, 9.

31 Hans-Georg Gadamer, *Truth and Method* (New York: Seabury Press, 1975).

32 Gabrielle Spiegel in Seixas, ed., *Theorizing Historical Consciousness*, 9.

33 Hans-Georg Gadamer, 'The Problem of Historical Consciousness,' in Paul Rabinow and William M. Sullivan, eds., *Interpretive Social Science: A Second Look* (Berkeley: University of California Press, 1987). For a fully developed, in-depth analysis of the difference between collective memory and historical consciousness see Peter Sexias's Introduction in *Theorizing Historical Consciousness*, particularly pages 8 to 11. Recent conferences have been devoted to exploring the multifaceted concept of historical consciousness. In 2001, the University of British Columbia's Centre for the Study of Historical Consciousness, established in 2001 and directed by Peter Seixas, organized a conference entitled 'Canadian Historical Consciousness in an International Context: Theoretical Frameworks.' Several papers presented at this conference have been published in Seixas, ed., *Theorizing Historical Consciousness*. See also the Centre's website, http://www.cshc.ubc .ca. Another conference organized in 2003 by historian Margaret Conrad at the University of New Brunswick (Fredericton) was entitled 'Heritage, History and Historical Consciousness: Public Uses of the Past.' See website: http://lusankya .hil.ca:800/archive/00000030. For a seminal study on the development of histori-

cal consciousness in the United States see Roy Rosenzweig and David Thelen, *Presence of the Past: Popular Uses of History in American Life* (New York: Columbia University Press, 1998).

34 Pierre Nora, dir., *Realms of Memory: The Construction of the French Past*, trans. Arthur Goldhammer (New York: Columbia University Press, 1996). More recently, *Rethinking France; les lieux de mémoire*, trans. Mary Trouille (Chicago: University of Chicago Press, 2001).

35 The philosopher Will Kymlicka, for instance, defines Canada as a 'multinational state' composed 'of three distinct national groups (English, French and Aboriginals)' and 'polyethnic (as a result of individual and familial immigration).' Will Kymlicka, *Multicultural Citizenship: A Liberal Theory of Minority Rights* (Oxford: Clarendon Press, 1995), 11–12, 17. See also chapter 8, 'Shared and Divergent Values,' in a collection of texts written by Charles Taylor and edited by Guy Lafôrest, *Reconciling the Solitudes: Essays on Canadian Federalism and Nationalism* (Montreal and Kingston: McGill-Queen's University Press, 1993), 155–86; Allan Smith, *Canada. An American Nation: Essays on Continentalism, Identity, and the Canadian Frame of Mind* (Montreal and Kingston: McGill-Queen's University Press, 1994).

36 Michael Kammen, 'Public History and the Uses of Memory,' *Public Historian* 19, 2 (Spring 1997): 52; Kerwin Lee Klein, 'On the Emergence of Memory in Historical Discourse,' *Representations* 69 (2000): 127–50.

37 Canadian history is a case in point, as the publication rate of scholarly monographs in the field has been ever increasing since the early 1990s. Consider, among others, C.T. Naylor, *Negotiating the Past: The Making of Canada's National Historic Parks and Sites* (Montreal and Kingston: McGill-Queen's University Press, 1990); Ian McKay, *The Quest of the Folk: Antimodernism and Cultural Selection in Twentieth-Century Nova Scotia* (Montreal and Kingston: McGill-Queen's University Press, 1994); Norman Knowles, *Inventing the Loyalists: The Ontario Loyalist Tradition and the Creation of Usable Pasts* (Toronto: University of Toronto Press, 1997); Beverly Boutilier and Alison Prentice, eds., *Creating Historical Memory: English-Canadian Women and the Work of History* (Vancouver: University of British Columbia Press, 1997); Jonathan Vance, *Death So Noble: Memory, Meaning and the First World War* (Vancouver: University of British Columbia Press, 1997); Patrice Groulx, *Pièges de la mémoire: Dollard des Ormeaux, les Amérindiens et nous* (Hull, QC: Vents d'Ouest, 1998); Elizabeth Furniss, *The Burden of History: Colonialism and the Frontier Myth in a Rural Canadian Community* (Vancouver: University of British Columbia Press, 1999); H.V. Nelles, *The Art of Nation-Building: Pageantry and Spectacle at Quebec's Tercentenary* (Toronto: University of Toronto Press, 1999); Franklin Bialystok, *Delayed Impact: The Holocaust and the Canadian Jewish Community* (Montreal

and Kingston: McGill–Queen's University Press, 2000); Alan Gordon, *Making Public Pasts: The Contested Terrain of Montreal's Public Memories, 1891–1930* (Montreal and Kingston: McGill-Queen's University Press, 2001); Coates and Morgan, *Heroines and History*; Ronald Rudin, *Founding Fathers: The Celebration of Champlain and Laval in the Streets of Quebec, 1878–1908* (Toronto: University of Toronto Press, 2003); K.T: Carlson, *The Power of Place, the Problem of Time: A Study of History and Aboriginal Collective Identity* (Vancouver: University of British Columbia Press, 2003); Jocelyn Létourneau, *A History for the Future: Rewriting Memory and Identity in Quebec*, trans. Phyllis Aronoff and Howard Scott (Montreal and Kingston: McGill-Queen's University Press, 2004); Ruth Sandwell, ed., *To the Past: History Education, Public Memory, and Citizenship in Canada* (Toronto: University of Toronto Press, 2006); Opp and Walsh, eds., *Placing Memory and Remembering Place in Canada.*

38 Most notably Seixas, ed., *Theorizing Historical Consciousness*, and Sandwell, ed., *To the Past*. The former focuses on 'debates about history education in the broader context of collective memory practices' (16) and the latter on the issues and challenges posed by the teaching of history. Comparable American edited collections include Peter N. Stearns, Peter Seixas, and Sam Wineburg, eds., *Knowing, Teaching and Learning History: National and International Perspectives* (New York: New York University Press, 2000); Sam Wineburg, *Historical Thinking and Other Unnatural Acts: Charting the Future of Teaching the Past* (Philadelphia: Temple University Press, 2001). For its part, Thomas Symons, ed., *The Place of History: Commemorating Canada's Past*, Proceedings of the National Symposium on the Occasion of the 75th Anniversary of the Historic Sites and Monuments Board of Canada (Ottawa: Royal Society of Canada, 1997), is a compilation of papers addressing issues of heritage preservation. Most recently, James Opp and J.C. Walsh have brought together studies that analyse 'how memory and place intersect' by looking at various locations across the country and the way they are rememberd. See Opp and Walsh, eds., *Placing Memory and Remembering Place in Canada*, 10.

39 On the contemporary nostalgia boom and marketing linked to demography, see Keith Naughton and Bill Vlasic, 'Nostalgia Boom,' *Businessweek*, 23 March 1998; M.B. Holbrook, 'Nostalgia and Consumer Preferences – Some Emerging Patterns of Consumer Taste,' *Journal of Consumer Research* 20, 2 (1993): 245–56. For more scholarly perspectives on the social causes of nostalgia, see Fred Davis, *Yearning for Yesterday: A Sociology of Nostalgia* (New York: Free Press, 1979) and Paul Grainge, *Monochrome Memories* (Wesport, CT: Praeger, 2002).

40 Seixas, 'Heavy Baggage en route to Winnipeg,' 393.

41 Along those lines see chapter 6, 'History Wars Abroad,' in Gary Nash, Charlotte Crabtree, and Ross E. Dunn, eds., *History on Trial: Culture Wars and the Teaching of the Past* (New York: Alfred A. Knopf, 1998), 128–48.

42 Bodnar, *Remaking America*, 13–16.
43 Seixas, 'Heavy Baggage en route to Winnipeg,' 394.
44 Glassberg, 'Public History and the Study of Memory.'
45 See for instance, Jeanne Cannizo, 'Exhibiting Cultures: "Into the Heart of Africa,"' *Visual Anthropology Review* 7, 1 (Spring 1991): 150–60, and her chapter 11, 'Into the Heart of Africa: Museum Pieces,' in Boholan Szuchewycz and Jeannette Sloniowski, eds., *Canadian Communications: Issues in Contemporary Media Cultures* (Scarborough, ON: Prentice-Hall and Bacon Canada, 1999); Butler, *Contested Representations*; Mackey, 'Postmodernism and Cultural Politics in a Multicultural Nation.' See M.L. Vanessa Vogel, 'The Glenbow Controversy and the Exhibition of Native American Art,' *Museum Anthropology* 14,4 (1990): 7–11 for a discussion of another exhibit under fire.
46 See note 26.
47 The 2001/2 Carleton University graduate history seminar analysed the series. See http://www.carleton.ca/historycollaborative; Lyle Dick, '"A New History for the New Millennium": *Canada: A People's History*,' *Canadian Historical Review* 85, 1 (March 2004): 85–109; 'Round Table': Gene Allen, 'The Professionals and the Public: Responses to *Canada: A People's History*'; Margaret Conrad, 'My Canada Includes the Atlantic Provinces'; Patrice Groulx, 'La meilleure histoire du monde,' all in *Histoire sociale/Social History* 34, 68 (November 2001): 381–414; Allen, '"Canadian History in Film": A Roundtable Discussion,' *Canadian Historical Review* 82, 2 (June 2001): 331–46; Lyle Dick, chapter 6 in this volume.
48 They can be viewed on www.histori.ca. See Elspeth Cameron, 'Heritage Minutes: Culture and Myth,' *Canadian Themes/Thèmes canadiens* 17 (1995): 25–36; Elspeth Cameron and Janice Dickin McGinnis, 'Ambushed by Patriotism: The Wit, Wisdom and Wimps of Heritage Minutes,' *Canadian Forum* 73, 837 (1995): 12–15; Katarzyna Rukszto, 'Up for Sale: The Commodification of Canadian Culture,' in ibid., 396–401; Nicole Neatby, 'The Heritage Project 60th Minute Commemorative Video,' *Canadian Historical Review* 81, 4 (December 2000): 668–70; Peter T. Hodgins, 'The Canadian Dream-Work: History, Myth and Nostalgia in the Heritage Minutes,' PhD thesis, Carleton University, 2003; Katarzyna Rukszto, 'The Other Heritages Minutes: Satirical Reactions to Canadian Nationalism,' *Topia* 14 (Fall 2005): 73–92; and Tim Stanley, chapter 7 in this volume.
49 Peter Seixas, 'The Purposes of Teaching Canadian History,' *Canadian Social Studies* 36, 2 (2002). For more on the relationship between historical pedagogy and citizenship, see, among others, Ken Osborne, *Teaching for Democratic Citizenship* (Toronto: Our Schools/Our Selves, Education Foundation, 1991) and his chapter 5 in this volume; Seixas, ed., *Theorizing Historical Consciousness*; Létourneau, *A History for the Future*; Sandwell, ed., *To the Past*.

50 See, for instance, Dominion Institute/Ipsos-Reid Poll, 5th Annual Canada Day History Quiz, http://www.ipsos –na.com/news/pressrelease.cfm?id+1255.

51 Jack Granatstein, *Who Killed Canadian History?* (Toronto: HarperCollins, 1998); Michael Bliss, 'Privatizing the Mind: The Sundering of Canadian History, the Sundering of Canada,' *Journal of Canadian Studies* 26 (Winter 1991–2): 5–12. Some of their colleagues have further argued that the 'new history,' generally labelled by them as 'social history,' has also threatened the historical profession *per se*. For a vigorous professional response to these claims see Linda Kealey et al., 'Teaching Canadian History in the 1990s: Whose National History Are We Lamenting,' *Journal of Canadian Studies* 27, 2 (Summer 1992): 129–31; A.B. McKillop, 'Who Killed Canadian History? A View from the Trenches,' *Canadian Historical Review* 80, 2 (June 1999): 269–99; Bryan Palmer, 'Of Silences and Trenches: A Dissident View of Granatstein's Meaning,' *Canadian Historical Review* 80, 4 (December 1999): 676–86; Timothy J. Stanley, 'Why I Killed Canadian History: Towards an Anti-Racist History in Canada,' *Histoire sociale/Social History* (May 2000): 79–103; Veronica Strong-Boag, 'Contested Space: The Politics of Canadian Memory,' *Journal of the Canadian Historical Association* 5(1994): 3–17; Robert Wright, 'Historical Underdosing: Pop Demography and the Crisis in Canadian History,' *Canadian Historical Review* 81, 4 (December 2000): 646–67. For an American perspective on comparable issues see Norman J. Wilson, *History in Crisis? Recent Directions in Historiography* (New York: Prentice-Hall, 1999). The contributors in Stearns, Seixas, and Wineburg, eds., *Knowing, Teaching and Learning History* discuss the challenges emerging from these debates facing those who teach history. See also Samuel Wineburg, 'On the Reading of Historical Texts: Notes on the Breach between School and Academy,' in S.W. Wineburg, ed., *Historical Thinking and Other Unnatural Acts* (Philadelphia: Temple University Press, 2001), 63–88, and Nash, Crabtree, and Dunn, eds., *History on Trial*, for a thoughtful analysis of these debates in other countries.

52 Jacques Mathieu, *Étude de la construction collective des Québécois au XXe siècle* (Sainte-Foy: Université Laval, Cahiers du Célat, 1986; Jacques Mathieu and Jacques Lacoursière, *Les mémoires Québécoises* (Sainte-Foy: Les Presses de l'Université Laval, 1991).

53 Jocelyn Létourneau, 'Digging into Historical Consciousness, Individual and Collective,' retrieved from http://www.cshc.ubc.ca/pwias/papers/Letourneau-Jocelyn .html.

54 'Canadians and Their Pasts' website. For more information, consult shc.ubc.ca/ Canadians_and_Their_Pasts.pdf.

55 Eva Mackey, *The House of Difference: Cultural Politics and National Identity in Canada* (London: Routledge, 1999). Other important works to emerge in this period include Naylor, *Negotiating the Past*; Knowles, *Inventing the Loyalists*;

Boutilier and Prentice, eds., *Creating Historical Memory*; Groulx, *Pièges de la mèmoire*; Furniss, *The Burden of History*; Bialystok, *Delayed Impact*; Gordon, *Making Public Pasts*; Coates and Morgan, *Heroines and History*; Rudin, *Founding Fathers* and his *Remembering and Forgetting in Acadie: A Historian's Journey through Public Memory* (Toronto: University of Toronto Press, 2009), and Opp and Walsh, eds., *Placing Memory and Remembering Place in Canada*.

56 Terry Goldie et al., eds., *Canada: Theoretical Discourse/Discours théoriques* (Montreal: Association for Canadian Studies, 1994); Joan Nicks and Jeannette Sloniowski, eds., *Slippery Pastimes: Reading the Popular in Canadian Culture* (Waterloo, ON: Wilfrid Laurier University Press, 2002); Garry Sherbert et al., eds., *Canadian Cultural Poesis* (Waterloo, ON: Wilfrid Laurier University Press, 2006).

57 Coates and Morgan, *Heroines and History*, 8.

58 The most ambitious Canadian initiative in this area is the Community-University Research Alliance project entitled 'Canadians and their Pasts,' funded by the Social Sciences and Humanities Research Council. It brings together a Canada-wide research team aiming to answer outstanding questions 'about the focus of peoples' engagement with the past, popular perceptions of the trustworthiness of historical sources, how people reconcile conflicting narratives about past events, and the ways that people use the past to construct their individual and collective identities.' 'Canadians and Their Pasts' website: http://www.canadiansandtheirpasts.ca. For more information, consult shc.ubc.ca/Canadians_and_Their_Pasts.pdf. In effect, they aim to produce a study inspired by the findings and methods of their Australian counterpart and of studies conducted in the United States. See also Rosensweig and Thelen, *Presence of the Past*, and Paula Hamilton and Paul Ashton, eds., *Australians and the Past* (St Lucia: University of Queensland Press, 2003).

59 Ronald Rudin, chapter 4 in this volume, 59.

60 Colin Coates, 'Commemorating the Woman Warrior of New France: Madeleine de Verchères, 1696–1930,' in Joy Parr and Mark Rosenfeld, eds., *Gender and History in Canada* (Toronto: Copp Clark, 1996), 120–36; Cecilia Morgan, '"Of Slender Frame and Delicate Appearance": The Placing of Laura Secord in the Narratives of Canadian Loyalist History,' *Journal of the Canadian Historical Association* 5 (1994): 195–212.

61 See Colin Coates, chapter 1 in this volume, 40.

62 Ibid.

63 Ken Osborne, chapter 5 in this volume, 135.

64 An early defender of this perspective can be found in Frederick Houser, *A Canadian Art Movement: The Story of the Group of Seven* (Toronto: Macmillan Company, 1926). However, assumptions about the Group of Seven's 'Canadianness' have of late been challenged. See Lynda Jessup, 'Bushwhackers in the Gallery:

Antimodernism and the Group of Seven,' in Lynda Jessup, ed., *Antimodernism and Artistic Experience: Policing the Boundaries of Modernity* (Toronto: University of Toronto Press, 2001), 130–52.

65 H.V. Nelles, chapter 9 in this volume, 270.

66 Ibid., 287.

67 Eva Mackey, chapter 10 in this volume, 312.

68 Ruth Phillips, chapter 11 in this volume, 341.

69 Ian Radforth, chapter 12 in this volume, 371.

70 For a discussion of antimodernism see, among others, McKay, *The Quest of the Folk*; Donald Wright, 'W.D. Lighthall and David Ross McCord: Antimodernism and English Canadian Imperialism, 1880s–1918,' *Journal of Canadian Studies/ Revue d'études canadiennes* 32, 2 (Summer 1997): 134–54; and James Murton, chapter 13 in this volume. In the American context, see Jackson Lears, *No Place of Grace: Antimodernism and the Transformation of American Culture, 1880– 1920* (New York: Pantheon, 1981); and Dona Brown, *Inventing New England: Regional Tourism in the Nineteenth Century* (Washington: Smithsonian Institution Press, 1995).

71 James Murton, 'La "Normandie du Nouveau Monde": la société Canada Steamship Lines, l'antimodernisme et la promotion du Québec ancien,' *Revue d'histoire de l'Amérique française* 55, 1 (Summer): 3–44.

72 Peter Hodgins, 'Our Haunted Present: Cultural Memory in Question,' *Topia* 12 (2004): 105.

73 Ira Wagman, chapter 16 in this volume, 539.

74 Peter Hodgins, chaper 17 in this volume, 572.

PART ONE

Remembering the Heroic Past

1 Commemorating the Woman Warrior of New France: Madeleine de Verchères, 1690s–1920s

COLIN M. COATES

Madeleine de Verchères, the child heroine of New France, was a cross-dressing woman warrior. In 1692, she led the defence of her family's fort at Verchères, near Montreal, against Iroquois attackers. In later accounts of her actions, she drew upon the long history of women warriors in the French and European traditions. Following the path laid out by such women as Joan of Arc, Jeanne Hachette, Catherine de Parthenay, and Philis de la Charce, Madeleine de Verchères tested the boundaries of gender roles in early modern society.[1]

One analysis of the phenomenon of women warriors suggests that there are various factors that allowed women to modify the link between maleness and warfare. Women assumed military roles because of their social rank or religious beliefs, or because they found themselves in the midst of revolution or rebellion.[2] Verchères clearly fulfilled the first of these criteria, stepping into her father's role as defender of the seigneury during his absence. But other elements of the woman warrior tradition were also apparent in her case. Women became warriors in emergency situations,[3] and they generally returned to the domestic sphere after the exploit. Often, the woman disguised herself as a man in order to participate in military matters.[4]

When she applied for a pension for her family in 1699, Madeleine de Verchères recognized that her previous actions had taken her beyond the usual bounds of her sex. In her lifetime and, later, as her story became a significant Canadian heroic narrative, the symbol of Madeleine de Verchères became entangled in the fact that women did not usually fill military roles. As her story was swept up in the cult of commemorating the history of New France in the late nineteenth and early twentieth centuries, the fact that she had disguised herself as a man was suppressed. But the ambiguities of the woman warrior figure persisted, as both men and women reworked her story.

The first official report of the Iroquois raid to the minister of the marine did not mention Verchères' bravery or her male disguise. The colonial governor wrote laconically that 'the enemies killed and took prisoner some people at Verchères, absconded with some livestock and scalped a soldier at St Ours.'[5] Madeleine de Verchères' own accounts were, of course, much more compelling. She gave two versions of her exploit. The first, a letter to Mme de Maurepas, the wife of the minister of the marine, in 1699, was succinct and clear, and it explicitly situated the story in the context of other woman warriors. Verchères asserted that she was following an honourable French tradition: 'I am aware ... that there have been women in France during the late war who went forth at the head of the peasants to repel the attacks of enemies invading their province.'[6] One of Verchères' first acts once she regained the seigneurial fort, after she narrowly escaped her intended rapist/assassin by leaving her scarf (mouchoir de col) in his hands, was to take off her headdress (coëffe) and don a soldier's cap. As she informed Maurepas, 'I then transformed myself by donning a soldier's helmet.'[7] Thus, Madeline de Verchères claimed that she disguised herself as a soldier. Not only did Verchères lock up all the (frightened) women, she displayed her male courage by shooting a cannon.

Decades later, Madeleine de Verchères presented a second narrative of her heroism in a much longer epistle to the king. Written at the behest of Governor Beauharnois, this version (with all its lack of verisimilitude) provides most of the details taken up in later accounts. Instead of being four hundred paces from the fort, Verchères was five arpents (about three hundred metres) away in the second telling. The forty-five Iroquois chasing her did not manage to catch her, nor when they stopped running and began shooting did they hit her. Her scarf thus intact, Verchères made it to the fort, and closed the gates, repairing some of the breaches in the defences. She stopped a scared soldier from blowing up the munitions and fort. Then, throwing off her headdress and putting on a man's hat, she assumed command. Her younger brother and two frightened soldiers used their guns, but Verchères fired the cannon. As they held off what may have been a siege (though there is little indication in the narrative of Iroquois activity after all the firing), she opened the fort's gates three times: first to save Pierre Fontaine and his family, who had arrived by canoe, second to allow the domestic animals back in, and third to recover the laundry. When Lieutenant La Monnerie (Crisafy according to the historian P.-F.-X. Charlevoix) arrived to relieve the fort, Verchères and he engaged in gallant banter:

– Monsieur, you are indeed welcome. I surrender arms to you.
– Mademoiselle ... they are in good hands.
– Better than you can imagine.[8]

Thus, the closure to the tale is realized in two ways: Verchères surrendered her arms to the 'real' soldiers, and La Monnerie, apparently unlike the Iroquois, recognized Verchères for what she was: a woman.

Two other versions of the story, written during Verchères' lifetime, invoked the image of the woman warrior. In his 1744 account, P.-F.-X. Charlevoix made the transformation even more complete: she took off her headdress, knotted her hair, and donned a hat and jerkin (juste-au-corps).[9] In his book, written in 1702 but not published until 1722, Claude-Charles de La Potherie recounted the story twice. In the initial version, which repeated Verchères' letter to Mme de Maurepas almost verbatim, he referred to Verchères as 'une véritable Amazone.'[10] The second story is essentially that of Verchères' second letter. Indeed, it is possible that La Potherie himself largely developed both versions of Verchères' exploits. He claimed to have helped her with the first letter justifying her petition for a pension, and later in life Verchères may have found La Potherie's other version suitable for her purposes.[11]

In Verchères' first version of the exploit, the cannon-shot ended the altercation with the Iroquois. Did her male disguise serve to protect the fort or was it the fire-power? Would the Iroquois have expected European women to eschew combat? Only two years previously, an undisguised Mme de Verchères had herself defended the fort. The Amerindians attacked numerous times, but Verchères' mother was always able to repulse them. According to Charlevoix, these Iroquois were 'very ashamed of being obliged to flee by a woman.'[12] The two defence narratives, fundamentally racist, probably say little of empirical value about the Iroquois. However, these stories do reveal something about gender ideology among Europeans.

Today, scholars disagree as to the broader significance of the phenomenon of cross-dressing. For some theorists, cross-dressers reinforce sex roles by their transgression. The woman warrior generally had to dress as a man in order to accomplish an act considered unsuitable for her sex. Although she momentarily allowed herself her freedoms, she did not fundamentally challenge traditional sex roles. For these reasons, the female transvestite became a stock figure in early modern European literature.[13] It is nonetheless possible to see female cross-dressers as proto-feminists, as they fulfilled their own individualistic desires for freedom.[14] For some, the phenomenon represents larger social dangers, since cross-dressing evokes the potential of sexual inversion and disorder.[15] Furthermore, transvestism serves to subvert both genders at once.[16] What if the cross-dresser belongs to neither sex? What if resuming the original clothing does not lead one fully back to one's previous sexual indentity? The treatments of Verchères' heroism suggest that, for many commentators, cross-dressing indeed represents a challenge to fixed gender roles.

As the accounts of Charlevoix and La Potherie indicate, despite the wider social anxiety about cross-dressing, men could accept, even celebrate, temporary inversions such as Verchères'. This was because they could see Verchères as a specific case, not as a social icon. Two centuries later, men tended to be more disturbed by the image of women cross-dressers.

Thus, Madeleine de Verchères and her contemporaries cast her as a woman warrior – even, given her age, hinting at the similarities to the quintessential woman warrior, Joan of Arc, a fact which late nineteenth- and early twentieth-century authors would not fail to notice. Joan of Arc and Madeleine de Verchères were both in their teens at the time of their famous exploits, and cross-dressed to achieve their aims. Both presented themselves as virgins, Verchères' dramatic action of leaving only her scarf in the Iroquois warrior's hand providing metaphorical evidence of her intact body. However, there were some important differences between the two. Unlike Verchères, Joan of Arc apparently never used her weapons. Unlike those of Joan of Arc, Verchères' actions were primarily defensive. Indeed, a few later commentators preferred to compare Verchères with Jeanne Hachette, who led the defence of Beauvais in 1472.[17] Of course, Verchères' closest Canadian counterpart was Dollard des Ormeaux, hero of the Battle of Long Sault. The cultural resonance of Dollard's story was as a narrative of 'la survivance,' and Madeleine de Verchères also fitted this mould.[18] This survival ideology appealed both to French and English Canadians.[19] However, unlike both Dollard and Joan of Arc, Verchères did not have the good historical sense to die at the time of her act of bravery, therefore making it difficult to interpret her acts as the definitive moment of her life, a fact later historians would use to discredit her.[20]

In choosing to be a woman warrior, Madeleine de Verchères acquired a reputation for testing gender roles that remained throughout her life. She later married the military officer and seigneur Pierre-Thomas Tarrieu de la Pérade, and acted in a number of court cases against local priests, habitants, and seigneurs. As legal custom had it, she could not act in her own right, but only in the name of her husband. The most notorious case occurred in 1730 when the priest of Batiscan, Gervais Lefebvre, took her to court to clear his name after she accused him of calling her a 'whore.'[21] At one point in the lengthy proceedings, the priest attempted to reassure himself that 'God fears neither hero nor heroine,'[22] which suggests that Verchères was renowned for her act of bravery. Moreover, the 'whore' epithet suggested that she, like so many other women warriors and warrior queens, experienced the other implications of gender-crossing: a presumption of wanton sexuality.[23]

In this way, the male disguise and the military action confused the issue of sex and sexuality in the person of Madeleine de Verchères during her lifetime.

After her death, her story was never forgotten, but authors in the late eighteenth and early nineteenth centuries dealt with it in summary fashion, usually basing their writing on the account of Charlevoix, and being equally, if not more, interested in her mother's heroism.[24] It was not until the late nineteenth century that Verchères fully entered the pantheon of French-Canadian heroes.

By this time, of course, the historical context was different. The dominant cultural traits in Quebec of the late nineteenth and early twentieth centuries were conservative, nationalistic, and religious. Interest in the past led to increased production of historical works, and specific attention was lavished on the lives of the heroes and heroines of New France.[25] Military and religious figures were of particular importance.

Commemoration went far beyond the production of historical treatises in attempts to reach a broader audience. Artists produced paintings, engravings, and statues. Writers penned memorials to Verchères, including plays, poems, short stories, and historical accounts. Some forty writers dedicated poems, full narratives, or chapters in larger works to Verchères' memory.

Concurrently, men and women were facing challenges to rigid gender roles. The late nineteenth and early twentieth centuries were, at least in the major metropolises of the Western world, a period of anxiety about proper gender roles and about sexual experimentation.[26] While Montreal was not London or New York and certainly provincial Quebec (or Canada for that matter) was not in these same cultural networks, the influences were spreading. Important figures in this cultural ferment, such as Sarah Bernhardt and Oscar Wilde, visited Montreal. Moreover, women had been working outside the home for decades, and women's organizations were demanding new rights, in particular the vote, and this blurring of public space frightened many men.[27] This was as true of Quebec as elsewhere in Canada. Leading (male) social commentators of the time pointed out this 'problem': Henri Bourassa reprinted a series of articles entitled 'Femmes-Hommes ou Hommes et Femmes?' in which he attacked feminism. Describing the likely results of women's suffrage, he poured out his invective on 'the woman-man, the hybrid and repugnant monster that will kill the woman-mother and the woman-woman.'[28]

Such fears about challenges to gender roles were not unique to Bourassa. As a quick illustration, we can take the views of two men who themselves played important roles in commemorating Madeleine de Verchères. Politician Rodolphe Lemieux rejected women's suffrage because elected female representatives would have to vote on military matters, an untenable position given his belief that 'Women ... are unfitted for military service.'[29] And Curé F.-A. Baillairgé wrote a pamphlet in 1925 warning of the dangers of North American modernity, including the confusion that would result if women dressed as men:

'The idea, for a woman, to become a man acts against nature ... Why make only one [sex], when God desires that there should be two?'[30] One might have expected that a cross-dressing Madeleine de Verchères would pose a problem for such commentators.

Yet even in the most conservative circles, another cross-dresser was becoming popular. Joan of Arc underwent a renaissance that culminated in her sainthood in 1920 from the same church that had burnt her at the stake. Joan was tremendously popular in France, England, and the United States, and not only because of her patriotism and religious fervour. Her heroism appealed to feminists, as much as to conservatives.[31] In Quebec, statues were raised to her memory, and streets and hospitals were named after her.[32] French-Canadian nationalists made pilgrimages to Domrémy[33] and to Orléans.[34] This virginal military figure inspired interest in Madeleine de Verchères. In 1902, a writer in the popular magazine *Le Monde Illustré* referred to her as 'la Jeanne d'Arc du Canada.'[35] The pictorial images of Madeleine de Verchères reflect the comparison to Joan of Arc in emphasizing her femininity. These portraits downplay her military actions and present her as an innocent, young child (see figure 1.1).

Most of the prose retellings of her story took details from the longer, second letter Verchères wrote to the king, although some combined elements of her first letter to Mme de Maurepas as well. By 1900, both letters had been widely reprinted and made accessible. Very few of the retellings provide originality or in-depth research; these were not the strengths of popular history. Rather, the defining traits of popular history at this time seem to have been the retelling of a familiar story, imbued with moral values that surpassed the mere details of the narrative.

In theory, the fact that Verchères' story involved the testing of gender roles might be considered a problem for conservative commentators. Authors dealt with Verchères' disguise by ignoring it. Though many mentioned that she took off her headdress and donned a hat, few indicated the maleness of the apparel. Indeed, many did not suggest that Verchères changed her clothes, or even fired any weapons. Some placed emphasis on Verchères' virginity, a fundamental element of the Joan of Arc figure. The scarf incident, with its virgin imagery, was often repeated, even though most writers relied on Verchères' second letter, which did not include the detail. Continuing the comparison to Joan of Arc, Verchères was transformed into a standard-bearer rather than a fighter.

Having made Verchères into a standard-bearer, many writers, particularly men, emphasized the virtues the heroine should embody. They could quote her own words for their patriotic resonance: 'Let us fight to the death for our country and for our holy religion.' In 1888, the editor of James LeMoine's version pointed out that the heroines of New France represented appropriate symbols

1.1 The young, innocent Madeleine de Verchères. National Archives of Canada, Gerald Hayward, C83513.

for the youth of the day: 'Like so many patterns for our young French-Canadian woman, like so many models of conjugal fidelity.'[36] Historian Charles Colby suggested that 'she remains a bright, alluring figure, perennially young, like the maidens on Keats' Grecian Urn.'[37] But English- and French-Canadian authors alike generally added contemporary nationalistic concerns. In 1916, Arthur Doughty published his study of Madeleine de Verchères in order to raise money for the Imperial Order Daughters of the Empire. Drawing a parallel between Iroquois and Germans that wartime readers could not miss, Doughty warned that 'Savage tribes who had lorded over the continent for centuries were challenging the advance of European civilisation.'[38] In a 1919 incident when some French-Canadian youths refused to answer a train conductor until he spoke to them in French, Pierre Homier applauded them. According to Homier, 'It was their only response, but what a clear echo of the voice of the child of the fort of Verchères.'[39]

Still, even with the cross-dressing episode suppressed, Verchères represented a potentially unruly female figure whom male writers had to tame. Poets
William Chapman, Rev. Aen. McD. Dawson, and William Henry Drummond
associated Madeleine de Verchères with the innocence and peacefulness of nature.[40] Curé F.-A. Baillairgé assured readers in his short study of Verchères'
life, 'Yes, Madeleine, who was strong, was nonetheless soft and sensitive.'[41] In
a collection of stories of heroism in New France, Thomas Marquis described
the young woman: 'Her delicate, active figure, soft, spiritual face – intelligent
forehead, brilliant eyes and well-cut lips – all bespoke gentle breeding.'[42]

Other writers were careful to ensure the closure to the story: the return to the
status quo. Just as in Verchères' second narrative, these stories ended with Verchères surrendering arms to La Monnerie (or Crisafy). Lionel Groulx emphasized how Dollard's heroism surpassed that of Verchères. Women's active roles
could only be fortuitous: 'They must sometimes fill in for men, but they must
render them the arms for the battles that are more appropriate to them.'[43] Other
male writers shifted the narrative to the (male) soldiers' pursuit of the Iroquois
and rescue of French prisoners.[44] Some added the apocryphal story, first apparently raised by Abbé François Daniel, that Verchères saved her future husband's
life at the time of the Iroquois attack, and thus in marrying him became his conquest.[45] And both male and female writers emphasized that Verchères resumed
her proper sex role following the incident. One journalist wrote in 1912 that
'Magdelon [sic] was a perfect woman, as good a housekeeper as a mother.'[46]

Women as well as men depicted Verchères' life in a heterosexual frame,
mentioning her future marriage to M. de La Pérade. Literary critic Carolyn
Heilbrun suggests that in the early twentieth century, female writers wanted
their subjects to fulfil the important aspects of a 'standard' woman's biography
in which women, regardless of their desire to live a different life, ultimately
placed men at the centre of their lives.[47] Nonetheless, women's versions had a
different purpose from those of men. They used the story to stake out a feminist claim on Canadian history, and in some cases to justify the contemporary
shifts in gender roles. Thus, Mary Sifton Pepper affirmed in 1901, 'Many of
them [the women of New France] would even nowadays be looked upon as
"emancipated" and "advanced."'[48] Many members of Women's Historical Societies were interested in the life of Madeleine de Verchères. Bellelle Guérin
of Montreal, Emma Curie of St Catharines, and Teresa Costigan-Armstrong
of Ottawa each presented papers on Verchères. In her address to the Women's
Historical Society of Montreal, Louyse de Bienville (Mme Donat Brodeur)
declared that she had considered speaking about early Canadian heroes, but
turned her attention to heroines: 'Since I am a woman, my sympathy turns
first to women.'[49] In a chapter of a book dedicated to Laura Secord, Emma

Curie discussed Verchères' exploits, deploring (incorrectly) that her heroism, like Secord's, had been unjustly ignored when it came to the request for a pension because she was 'only a woman.'[50] Marie-Claire Daveluy was clearest on the claim that Verchères' story permitted the insertion of women into history. In her 1920 short play, young girls at a convent school complain that 'history is mostly for boys ... because of battles and soldiers.' An older girl rebukes them, saying, 'And Madeleine de Verchères? She was not a boy ... and they talk about her in history.'[51] Finally, Marie-Louise d'Auteuil tried to make the strongest link between nationalism and feminism, in proposing a 'Journée de Madeleine de Verchères' for schoolgirls, to accompany the increasingly popular Dollard Day.[52]

It is interesting that women generally had less difficulty with Verchères' cross-dressing than did male writers. Mary Sifton Pepper judged Verchères' actions in this way: 'With a thoughtfulness that seems almost incredible in one so young, she tossed aside her woman's head-gear and placed a man's hat upon her head, so that if the Indians saw her they would take her for a man and therefore a more formidable opponent.'[53] Ethel Raymond supposed that Verchères 'often wished that she had been born a boy.'[54]

Only one early twentieth-century author explicitly interpreted Madeleine de Verchères' story as the narrative of a woman warrior. Frédéric de Kastner emphasized Verchères' noble lineage (an ancestry that the author was quick to point out he shared) and recognized Verchères as one in a line of 'femmes guerrières.' Indeed, he complained that most depictions portrayed her as too slight and wispish. He was clear, however, that she should not be seen as a burly, working-class woman.[55] His intervention is interesting, if only because it went unheeded by artists of the period.

A number of the authors complained about the lack of suitable memorials to Verchères. Some expressed the hope that a commemorative statue would be raised. In 1903, Henry James Morgan stated, 'Singularly enough ... no public statue has yet been erected by Canada to this the greatest of her heroines.'[56] Within a decade, two separate initiatives – one led by the priest of Verchères and the other by the governor-general of Canada, Lord Grey – attempted to remedy the problem. Curé F.-.A. Baillairgé wanted to erect the statue to Verchères as much to her memory as to put the parish of Verchères on the map. However, the costs of a statue were far beyond the means of even a relatively prosperous agricultural parish. Baillairgé held tombolas to obtain funds, and by July 1912 had raised over $2000 towards the statue.[57]

Meanwhile, the Montreal artist Louis-Philippe Hébert, sculptor of a number of other heroic statues, had already crafted a statuette in her honour. It was, he recalled, a difficult figure to model, since he was afraid of turning her into a woman warrior: 'Sometimes I felt that trying to translate all her beautiful energy, I would turn my young heroine into a virago.'[58] Ultimately, the inspiration came from Louis Fréchette's poem, in which Verchères is compared to Jeanne Hachette. Coiffed by the soldier's hat, which appears to be a soft, leather cowboy hat, she clutches her gun nervously, if heroically, her skirts swirling in the wind.

Lord Grey saw Hébert's bronze statuette, purchased a copy for Rideau Hall, and encouraged politicians to erect a statue to her memory. In 1910, he gave Rodolphe Lemieux the mission to inspire his political colleagues. He hoped that Lemieux would 'fire [Quebec Premier Lomer] Gouin with the desire to find such money as may be required to signify the great entrance to Canada by the erection on Verchères bluff of a figure which will tell the immigrant that the heroic virtues are the bedrock foundation of Canadian greatness.'[59] Ultimately, it was the federal government rather than the Quebec provincial government that paid to commemorate the heroine. The cabinet earmarked $25,000 for the statue, which was erected in Verchères parish in September, 1913.

Although Curé Baillairgé had been swept aside in the planning for the statue, he was the president of the inauguration committee. Special trains and boats were leased for the pilgrimage to the statue on 20 September 1913. After numerous speeches by men, the mayor's wife (the one woman with a public role in the ceremony) unveiled the statue before the almost five thousand people in attendance.[60] The speeches reflected many of the themes apparent in the (male) literature on Verchères. Mgr Gauthier wished that other French-Canadian women could emulate Madeleine de Verchères, but he was quick to specify what kind of woman this represented: 'There have been other Madeleine de Verchères lately, when French-Canadian [female] teachers preferred to lose their salaries rather than stop teaching French to their pupils.' For his part, Wilfrid Larose compared Verchères with Joan of Arc: 'If the kingdom of France was delivered and regenerated by Joan of Arc, this colony, then French in its cradle, was illustrated by Madeleine de Verchères.'[61]

Gazing upon the statue (see figure 1.2), no one would mistake her for a man: the swirling dress, the feminine facial features, the long braids dangling down her back, the pubescent breasts, all precluded misinterpretation. Only her (man's) hat and massive gun hinted otherwise. For Maurice Hodent, who saw the statue in Paris where it was cast, there was no question whatsoever concerning Verchères' sex: 'More than one Canadian seeing it as he sails up the St Lawrence will say that there is no prettier girl under the blue sky.'[62] The feminine icon apparently cloaked all traces of the cross-dressing Verchères.

Nine years later, in 1922, the first French-Canadian feature film – *Madeleine de Verchères* – premiered in Montreal. Like other contemporary commemorations, this film did not explicitly challenge gender ideologies. English-

1.2 Postcard photograph of the statue of Madeleine de Verchères in the village of Verchères. Author's collection.

Canadian and American entrepreneurs had already produced a film concerning
the quintessential French-Canadian hero, Dollard des Ormeaux, in 1913. It
is therefore not surprising that French-Canadian entrepreneurs should turn to
Verchères' story for the first French-Canadian feature film.[63] In 1922, Joseph-
Arthur Homier released the film to rather insipid critical acclaim. 'It is a good
picture,' one critic wrote, 'which should be seen as much as possible for its
good history lesson.'[64] According to a critic in *Le Devoir*, who nonetheless
encouraged the development of a French-Canadian film industry, 'One could
describe it as a man admiring an amateurish portrait of his ancestors. It is more
a patriotic than an aesthetic emotion.'[65]

After a week in Montreal, the film made a tour of parish halls throughout
the province, but its historical lustre could not compare with American silent
films. The screenplay, written by Emma Gendron, combines romantic intrigue
(involving Madeleine de Verchères and her future husband) with Verchères'
act of bravery. Verchères is more than a soldier in this film; she also takes care
of the wounded and encourages the defenders. La Monnerie finally relieves
her, saying, 'You have saved the country.' 'I have only performed my duty,'[66]
replies Verchères. Based on the remaining evidence of the film (some stills
catalogued at the Copyright Office), no one mistook Madeleine de Verchères
for a man in this movie. Becoming the Joan of Arc of Canada, she was seen to
embody a militant, feminine ideal.

Of course, Verchères could not live up to the historical virtues that she was expected to personify, if only because she outlived her exploit. About the same time that Verchères' narratives were reprinted, historians were setting the groundwork for the demolition of her reputation. The rediscovery of the court case concerning Curé Lefebvre's defamation of Verchères was particularly important in this matter. In 1900, an account of the 1730 trial appeared in the *Bulletin de recherches historiques*.[67] Lefebvre's testimony provided the necessary evidence of what the woman warrior persona suggested: wanton sexuality.

In 1922, provincial archivist P.-G. Roy launched the first explicit attack on Madeleine de Verchères in a paper given to the Société Royale du Canada. Listing the court cases that involved Madeleine de Verchères after her marriage to Pierre-Thomas Tarieu de La Pérade, Roy called her 'une plaideuse enragée.'[68] Were the court cases the result of her early heroism? Did her later actions flow logically from her military activity? What if, Roy posed in subtle fashion, Verchères had refused to return to the traditional woman's role?[69]

Thus, in the early twentieth century, at her time of greatest popularity, Madeleine de Verchères still represented a dangerous figure for some men. In momentarily choosing to be a woman warrior, Madeleine de Verchères challenged 'proper' gender roles. She defended the seigneurial fort against Iroquois attackers in late October 1692. Two centuries later, as she became the subject of historical commemoration, popular historians would retell her story as a morality tale, emphasizing elements that fitted their particular didactic purpose. For men primarily, this involved transforming her into an icon – a Joan of Arc figure – embodying nationalism and sacrifice. For women, Verchères, along with other religious and lay heroines, allowed them to enter the annals of Canadian history. This early form of women's history, the celebration of heroines, even cross-dressing ones, allowed elite women to establish an ancestry stretching back to the early colony, and helped to create a space where they could contribute their own view of history.

Madeleine de Verchères had clearly emerged as one of the most compelling female figures of the history of New France. Situating herself in the tradition of woman warriors, Madeleine de Verchères rejected strict gender roles. Her legacy was an ambiguous battleground for competing morality tales, nationalistic narratives, and gender ideologies.

NOTES

1 A slightly different version of this chapter appeared in Joy Parr and Mark Rosenfeld, eds, *Gender and History in Canada* (Toronto: Copp Clark, 1996), 120–36. The themes in this chapter are more fully developed in part 1 of Colin M. Coates

and Cecilia Morgan, *Heroines and History: Representations of Madeleine de Verchères and Laura Secord* (Toronto: University of Toronto Press, 2002).

2 Louise Anne May, 'Worthy Warriors and Unruly Amazons: Sino-Western Historical Accounts and Imaginative Images of Women in Battle,' PhD thesis, University of British Columbia, 1985, 21.

3 Megan McLaughlin, 'The Woman Warrior: Gender, Warfare and Society in Medieval Europe,' *Women's Studies* 17, 3–4 (January 1990): 196–7; Rudolf M. Dekker and Lotte C. van de Pol, 'Republican Heroines: Cross-Dressing Women in the French Revolutionary Armies,' *History of European Ideas* 10, 3 (1989): 360–1.

4 Natalie Zemon Davis, 'Women on Top,' in *Society and Culture in Early Modern France* (Stanford: Stanford University Press, 1975), 124–51; Marina Warner, *Joan of Arc: The Image of Female Heroism* (New York: Alfred A. Knopf, 1981), chapter 7; Dianne Dugaw, 'Balladry's Female Warriors: Women, Warfare, and Disguise in the Eighteenth Century,' *Eighteenth-Century Life* 9, 2 (January 1985): 1; Julie Wheelwright, *Amazons and Military Maids: Women Who Dressed as Men in the Pursuit of Life, Liberty and Happiness* (London: Pandora, 1989).

5 'Les ennemis avoient tué et pris prisonniers quelques personnes à Vercheres, emmené les bestiaux dans le bois et levé la chevelure a un soldat a St Ours…' Library and Archives Canada, Archives des Colonies, MG1 série C11A, Correspondance générale, Canada, Transcriptions, vol. 12, 'Relation de ce qui s'est passé en Canada depuis le mois de septembre 1692 jusques au depart des Vaisseaux en 1693,' 358–420.

6 'Je scay, Madame, qu'il y a eu en France des personnes de mon sexe dans cette derniere guerre, qui se sont mises a la teste de leurs paisant pour s'opposer à l'invasion des ennemis qui entroient dans leur province.' The translations of Verchères' accounts are taken from Edouard Richard, ed., *Supplement to Dr. Brymner's Report on Canadian Archives by Mr. Edouard Richard* (Ottawa: King's Printer, 1901), 6–7. All other translations are the author's.

7 'Je me métamorphosay pour lors en mettant le chapeau du soldat sur ma teste.'

8 – Monsieur, soyez vous le bien venu, je vous rends les armes.
   – Mademoiselle … elles sont en bonnes mains.
   – Meilleures que vous ne croyez.

9 P.-F.-X. de Charlevoix, *Histoire et description générale de la Nouvelle France* (Paris, 1744), 3:123–5.

10 C.-C. Le Roy de Bacqueville de La Potherie, *Histoire de l'Amérique septentrionale* (Paris, 1722), 151.

11 André Vachon discusses the strong resemblance between La Potherie's version and the second narrative in 'Marie-Madeleine Jarret de Verchères,' *Dictionary of Canadian Biography*, vol. 3 (Toronto: University of Toronto Press, 1974): 308–13.

12 'Bien honteux d'être obligé de fuir devant une Femme …'

13 Dugaw, 'Balladry's Female Warriors.'

14   Wheelwright, *Amazons and Military Maids*, 15.

15   Davis, 'Women on Top.'

16   Marjorie Garber, *Vested Interests: Cross-Dressing and Cultural Anxiety* (New York: HarperCollins, 1993).

17   Louis Fréchette, *La légende d'un peuple* (Trois-Rivières: Écrits des forges, 1989 [1887]); Jacques Cézembre, 'Les romans de la vie: Madeleine de Verchères, la Jeanne Hachette canadienne,' *Dimanche-illustré*, 14 September1930, 5.

18   Jacques Chevalier, 'Myth and Ideology in "Traditional" French Canada: Dollard, the Martyred Warrior,' *Anthropologica* n.s. 21, 2 (1979): 144.

19   Ramsay Cook, *The Maple Leaf Forever: Essays on Nationalism and Politics in Canada* (Toronto: Macmillan, 1971), chapters 8–9.

20   Marina Warner's comments on Joan of Arc's death are telling: 'It is astonishing how many of Joan's apologists like her dead. Without this badge of blood, this self-obliteration in the ideal, her glory would be the less' (*Joan of Arc*, 263).

21   I discuss this case in 'Authority and Illegitimacy in New France: The Burial of Bishop Saint-Vallier and Madeleine de Verchères vs. the Priest of Batiscan,' *Histoire sociale/Social History* 22, 43 (May 1989): 65–90.

22   'Dieu ne craint ni héros ni héroine.' Quoted Bibliothèque et archives nationales du Québec (BANQ) – Québec, ZQ27, 'Verchères-Naudière-Procès avec le curé de Batiscan,' 183.

23   Antonia Fraser, *The Warrior Queens* (New York: Alfred A. Knopf, 1989), 11–12.

24   D. Dainville (Gustave Bossange), *Beautés de l'histoire du Canada* (Paris: Bossange frères, Libraires, 1821), 179–81; Philippe Aubert de Gaspé, a descendant of Madeleine de Verchères, briefly compared his gun-wielding aunt Agathe de Lanaudière to his 'deux grand'tantes de Verchères' in *Mémoires* (Montreal: Fides, 1971 [1866]), 402–4. The discussion in F.-X. Garneau, *Histoire du Canada depuis sa découverte jusqu'à nos jours*, 2nd edition (Quebec: John Lovell, 1852), 313, is very short compared to that in the 8th edition (1944), 194–6.

25   Serge Gagnon, *Le Québec et ses historiens de 1840 à 1920: La Nouvelle-France de Garneau à Groulx* (Quebec: Les presses de l'Université Laval, 1978); Fernande Roy, 'Une mise en scène de l'histoire: La fondation de Montréal à travers les siècles,' *Revue d'histoire de l'Amérique française* 46, 1 (Summer 1992): 7–36; Jacques Mathieu and Jacques Lacoursière, *Les mémoires québécoises* (Sainte-Foy: Les presses de l'Université Laval, 1991), 319–23.

26   Elaine Showalter, *Sexual Anarchy: Gender and Culture at the fin de siècle* (Markham, ON: Penguin Books, 1990); Judith Walkowitz, *City of Dreadful Delight: Narratives of Sexual Danger in Late Victorian London* (Chicago: University of Chicago Press, 1992).

27   Susan Mann Trofimenkoff, 'Henri Bourassa and "The Woman Question,"' in Susan Mann Trofimenkoff and Alison Prentice, eds., *The Neglected Majority: Essays in Canadian Women's History* (Toronto: McClelland and Stewart, 1977), 104–15;

Susan Mann Trofimenkoff, *The Dream of Nation: A Social and Intellectual History of Quebec* (Toronto: Gage, 1983), chapter 12; Andrée Lévesque, *La norme et les déviantes: Des femmes au Québec pendant l'entre-deux-guerres* (Montreal: Les éditions du remue-ménage, 1989).

28 'Le femme-homme, le monstre hybride et répugnant qui tuera la femme-mère et la femme-femme.' Henri Bourassa, *Femmes-hommes ou hommes et femmes? Études à bâtons rompus sur le féminisme* (Montreal: Imprimerie du Devoir, 1925), 41.

29 House of Commons, *Debates*, (Session 1918), 1:655.

30 'L'idée, pour une femme, de se faire homme est contre nature ... Pourquoi ne faire qu'un, là où Dieu veut qu'il y ait deux?' F.-A. Baillairgé, PC, *Jeunesse et Folies* (Verchères: chez l'auteur, 1925), 40.

31 Eugene Weber, *Peasants into Frenchmen: The Modernization of Rural France, 1870–1914* (Stanford: Stanford University Press, 1976), 111–12; Warner, *Joan of Arc*, chapter 13; Martha Vicinus, *Independent Women: Work and Community for Single Women, 1850–1920* (Chicago: University of Chicago Press, 1985), 266; Martha Hanna, 'Iconology and Ideology: Images of Joan of Arc in the Idiom of the *Action française*, 1908–1931,' *French Historical Studies* 14, 2 (Fall 1985): 215–39; Showalter, *Sexual Anarchy*, 29; Walkowitz, *City of Dreadful Delight*, 62.

32 On Joan of Arc's cult in Quebec, see *Nova Francia* 3 (1927–8): 381; and *Nova Francia* 4 (1929): 318.

33 On 19 August 1913, Joseph-P. Archambault [Pierre Homier of *L'Action française*] wrote to Dr Gauvreau: 'J'ai prié ce matin Jeanne, la bienheureuse et la vaillante, pour ceux qui, au Canada, luttent comme elle au service des traditions françaises et catholiques.' BANQ – Montréal, CLG39, Fonds Joseph Gauvreau.

34 In 1907, Abbé Lionel Groulx visited Orléans, a city 'pleine à déborder du souvenir de Jeanne d'Arc.' *Mes Mémoires*, vol. 1 (Montréal: Fides, 1970), 128.

35 L'annaliste, 'M. Rodolphe Girard: L'homme du jour dans le domaine des lettres,' *Le monde illustré*, 1 March 1903, 1061; Frédéric de Kastner made the same comparison in *Héros de la Nouvelle France* (Quebec: La Cie d'Imprimerie Commerciale, 1902); Charles Colby began his discussion of Verchères by saying that 'New France had no Maid of Orleans.' *Canadian Types of the Old Régime, 1608–1698* (New York: Henry Holt and Co., 1908), 338.

36 'Comme autant de patrones [*sic*] pour nos jeunes canadiennes, comme autant de modèles de fidélité conjugale.' J.M. LeMoine, *Les héroines de la Nouvelle-France*, translated from the English (Lowell, MA: Raoul Renault, 1888), 23.

37 Colby, *Canadian Types*, 343.

38 Arthur Doughty, *A Daughter of New France* (Ottawa: Mortimer Press, 1916), 4.

39 'C'est leur seule réponse mais combien juste écho de la voix de l'enfant du fort de Verchères.' Pierre Homier, 'A travers la vie courante,' *L'Action française* 3, 6 (June 1919): 266.

40 BANQ – Québec, P244, Fonds Tarieu de Lanaudière, 2 May 1876, William Chap-

man, 'L'héroïne de Verchères' [copy of proposed poem]; Rev. Aen. McD. Dawson, 'The Heroine of Verchères,' *Canadian Antiquarian and Numismatic Journal* (Montreal: Henry Rose, 1878), 6:142–5; William Henry Drummond, *Phil-o-rum's Canoe and Madeleine Verchères* (New York: G.P. Putnam's Sons, 1898).

41 'Oui, Madeleine, qui était forte, n'en était pas moins douce et sensible.' F.-A. Baillairgé, *Marie-Madeleine de Verchères et les siens* (Verchères: chez l'auteur, 1913), 30.

42 Agnes Maule Machar and Thomas G. Marquis, *Stories of New France: Being Tales of Adventure and Heroism from the Early History of Canada* (Boston: D. Lothrop Company, 1890), 216.

43 'On doit suppléer quelques fois les hommes, mais leur rendre les armes pour les batailles qui leur reviennent.' Lionel Groulx, *Notre Maître, le passé*, 1st series, 2nd edition (Montreal: Librairie Granger Frères Limitée, 1937 [1924]), 61–9.

44 Chapman, 'L'héroïne de Verchères'; LeMoine, *Héroïnes de la Nouvelle-France*, 16.

45 François Daniel, *Histoire des grandes familles françaises*, (Montreal: E. Senécal, 1867), 519.

46 'Magdelon fut une femme parfaite, aussi habile ménagère que bonne mère de famille.' T.G., 'Magdelon la Canadienne,' *Le Temps*, 14 August 1912. 'Magdelon' was a nickname for Verchères.

47 Carolyn Heilbrun, *Writing a Woman's Life* (New York: Ballantyne Books, 1988).

48 Mary Sifton Pepper, *Maids and Matrons of New France* (Toronto: George N. Morang and Co., 1902), 4.

49 'Puisque je suis femme, ma sympathie doit d'abord se porter vers des femmes.' Madame Donat Brodeur, 'Deux héroïnes de la Nouvelle-France,' *Canadian Antiquarian* 3, 5 (1908): 65.

50 Emma A. Currie, *The Story of Laura Secord and Canadian Reminiscences* (St Catharines: n.p., 1913), 83.

51 'L'histoire, c'est fait surtout pour les garçons … à cause des batailles et des soldats.' 'Et Madeleine de Verchères? Ça n'était pas un garçon … Et l'on en parle dans l'histoire.' Marie-Claire Daveluy, 'Le Cours Improvisé' [1920] in *Aux Feux de la Rampe* (Montreal: Bibliothèque de l'Action française, 1927), 11–12. Corinne Rocheleau makes a similar point in her play illustrating the roles of women in New France. 'On dit que les peuples heureux n'ont pas d'histoire. Si cet épigramme s'applique aux individus, il faut croire que les premières Françaises établies en Amérique furent des femmes heureuses, car on n'en parle pas … ou si peu que c'est tout comme!' *Françaises d'Amérique: Esquisse historique* (Worcester, MA: La compagnie de publication Belisle, 1915), 3.

52 Marie-Louise d'Auteuil, 'Vos Doctrines?,' *L'Action française* 16, 6 (December 1926): 381.

53 Pepper, *Maids and Matrons*, 228–9.

54 E[thel] T. Raymond, *Madeleine de Verchères* (Toronto: Ryerson Press, 1929), 8–9.

55 Frédéric de Kastner, *Héros de la Nouvelle France*, 82–91. Another aristocratic author emphasizing Verchères' social class was Thérèse de Ferron, 'Une héroine de la Nouvelle-France: Marie-Madeleine de Verchères,' *Revue hebdomadaire*, 4 (October 1924): 89–102.

56 Henry James Morgan, ed., *Types of Canadian Women and of Women Who Are or Have Been Connected with Canada* (Toronto: William Briggs, 1903), 1:80. De Kastner and Richard made the same point.

57 BANQ à Trois-Rivières, Fonds de la famille Baillairgé, Livre de compte personnel, 96–9.

58 'Tantôt je sentais que pour vouloir traduire toute sa belle énergie, j'allais faire de ma jeune héroïne une virago.' Quoted in M. Hodent, 'Philippe Hébert [*sic*]: Le maître de la Sculpture Canadienne,' *La Canadienne* (Paris) 11, 9 (September 1913): 164.

59 Library and Archives Canada, MG27II D10, Fonds Rodolphe Lemieux, vol. 10, Lord Grey to Lemieux, 16 May 1910, 11878.

60 Women were thanked for organizing the brunch as well. The information in this paragraph comes from *Le Devoir*, 22 September 1913, 4–6.

61 'Il y en a eu d'autres Madeleine de Verchères dernièrement, alors que des institutrices canadiennes-françaises préférèrent perdre leur salaire plutôt que de ne pas enseigner le français à leurs élèves.' 'Si le royaume de France fut délivré et réhabilité par Jeanne d'Arc, cette colonie, alors française à son berceau, fut illustrée par Madeleine de Verchères.'

62 'Plus d'un canadien qui l'apercevra en remontant le fleuve dira qu'il n'est pas de plus jolie fille sous le ciel bleu' (Hodent, 'Philippe Hébert,' 164).

63 Summary information on the film is provided in Peter Morris, *Embattled Shadows: A History of Canadian Cinema, 1895–1939* (Montreal: McGill-Queen's University Press, 1978), 48–9; Marcel Jean, *Le cinéma québécois* (Montreal: Éditions du Boréal, 1991), 17–19. D. John Turner provides a more extended analysis in 'Dans la nouvelle vague des années 20: J.-Arthur Homier,' *Perspectives (de La Presse)* 22, 4 (week of 26 January 1980).

64 'C'est une belle vue, qu'il faut faire voir le plus possible à cause de la bonne leçon d'histoire qu'elle donne.' *La Presse,* 16 December 1922, 43.

65 'On dirait un homme qui admire le portrait de ses ancêtres – brossé par un artiste d'occasion. C'est une émotion plus patriotique qu'esthétique.' *Le Devoir*, 11 December 1922, 2.

66 'Vous avez sauvé le pays.'
'Je n'ai fait que mon devoir.'

67 Philéas Gagnon, 'Le curé Lefebvre et l'héroïne de Verchères,' *Bulletin de recherches historiques* 6 (1900): 340–5.

68 Pierre-Georges Roy, 'Madeleine de Verchères, plaideuse,' *Transactions de la Société Royale du Canada*, 3, 15 (1921): 63–72.

69 In 1946, after women had served in the armed forces, Jean Bruchési made a more explicit attack, using Verchères as an example, on 'le renversement des rôles assignés à l'homme et à la femme, sinon par décret divin, du moins par la nature, voire par le bon sens.' 'Madeleine de Verchères et Chicaneau,' *Cahiers des Dix* 11 (1946): 25.

2 'Of Slender Frame and Delicate Appearance':The Placing of Laura Secord in the Narratives of Canadian Loyalist Tradition

CECILIA MORGAN

To most present-day Canadians, Laura Secord is best known as the figure-head of a candy company, her image that of a young, attractive woman wearing a low-cut ruffled white gown.[1] Some may even harbour a vague memory from their high-school courses in Canadian history of her walk in 1813 from Queenston to Beaver Dams, to warn British troops of an impending American attack. From the mid-nineteenth century, the story of that walk has been told by a number of Canadian historians of the War of 1812 in Upper Canada. Its military implications in assisting the British during the War of 1812 have been the subject of some rather heated debate. Did Laura Secord actually make a valuable contribution to the war? Did her news arrive in time and was it acted upon? However, another and as yet little-discussed issue is the way in which late nineteenth and early twentieth-century historians attempted to transform Secord into a heroine, a symbol of female loyalty and patriotism in this period's narratives of Loyalist history.

As historian Benedict Anderson argues, the formation of modern national identities has involved more than the delineation of geographically defined boundaries and narrow political definitions of citizenship. Nations, Anderson tells us, are 'imagined political communities,' created by their citizens through a number of political and cultural institutions and practices: shared languages, newspapers, museums, and the census. Furthermore, as Anderson and others have emphasized, it is also within narratives of 'the nation's' history that these imagined communities are formed and national identities are created.[2] To the promoters of late nineteenth-century Canadian nationalism and imperialism, such narratives were of critical importance in understanding Canada's link to Britain and British political, social, and cultural traditions. As Carl Berger argues in *The Sense of Power*, 'history in its broadest cultural sense was the medium in which [these traditions were] expressed and history the final and ultimate argument for imperial unity.'[3] Those who wrote these historical narratives also worked diligently to create national heroes who symbolized loyalty and the preservation of the imperial link. Historians interested in early nineteenth-century Ontario history found that a cast of such figures lay conveniently close to hand: Major-General Sir Isaac Brock and the Upper Canadian militia, the colony's saviours during the American invasion of 1812.

But Brock and the militia were not the only significant figures to be commemorated and celebrated, for it was during this period that Laura Secord became one of the most significant female symbols of Canadian nationalism. As feminist historians have pointed out, the formation of imagined national communities has been frequently, if not inevitably, differentiated by gender. While Anderson's work has been extremely influential on historians' understanding of national identities, he fails to recognize 'that women and men may imagine such communities, identify with nationalist movements, and participate in state formations in very different ways.'[4] And, in their use of iconography, monuments, or written narratives of the nation's history, proponents of nationalism have frequently relied upon gender-specific symbols and their imagery.[5] Yet in these textual and visual representations of nationalities, gender as an analytic category has also varied according to its context and been influenced by other categories and relationships, particularly those of race, class, religion, and sexuality. By looking at the process whereby Secord became a national heroine and at the narratives that were written about Secord's walk, we can further our understanding of the links between gender, race, and imperialism in late nineteenth-century Canadian nationalism and feminism.[6]

Secord became part of the narratives of Loyalist self-sacrifice and duty to country and crown primarily – although not solely – because of the attempts of women historians and writers who, from the 1880s on, strove to incorporate women into Canadian history and to dislodge the masculine emphasis of the nineteenth-century Loyalist myths of suffering and sacrifice. Women such as Sarah Curzon, the feminist writer, historian, and temperance advocate, insisted that white Canadian women, past and present, had something of value to offer the nation and empire and that their contribution as women to the record of Canadian history be acknowledged and valued. Secord, she (and others like her) argued, was not outside the narrative of Canadian history and she (and other women) therefore had a place in shaping the 'imagined communities' of Canadian nationalist and imperialist discourse. Unlike that of other, potentially unruly and disruptive women in Canadian history, Laura Secord's image could be more easily domesticated to accord with late Victorian notions of white, middle-class femininity.[7] It could also be moulded by feminists to argue for a greater recognition of the importance of such femininity to Canadian society.

Moreover, Laura Secord was not an isolated figure. Ranged behind and about her was a whole gallery of women in Canadian history, from Madeleine de Verchères of New France to the anonymous, archetypal pioneer woman of the backwoods of Upper Canada; women, these 'amateur' historians insisted, who were historical figures as worthy of study as their male contemporaries.[8]

Before discussing the writing of Laura Secord into Loyalist history, however, it is crucial to outline the gendered nature of the nineteenth-century narratives of the War of 1812. Historians who have studied Upper Canadian politics have duly noted that assertions of loyalty and sacrifice during the war became the basis for many claims on the Upper Canadian state, in the competition for land and patronage appointments and for compensation for war losses.[9] Donald Akenson, for example, has pointed to the way in which claims to loyal duty during the war were used in attempts to justify the access of some residents to certain material benefits. Such claims were also made to legitimate the exclusion of others from such rewards.[10] Yet what has not been included in these historians' analysis of sacrifice in the war as a bargaining chip in the struggle for material gains in Upper Canada is the gendered nature of the narratives that were used. In Upper Canadians' commemorations of the War of 1812, the important sacrifices for country and monarch were made by Upper Canadian men, frequently in their capacity as members of the militia who risked life and limb to protect women and children, homes and hearths, from the brutal rampages of hordes of bloodthirsty Americans. During the war, and in its aftermath, women's contributions to the defence of the colony were either downplayed or ignored, in favour of the image of the helpless Upper Canadian wife and mother who entrusted her own and her children's safety to the gallant militia and British troops.[11]

Personifying the whole, of course, was the masculine figure of Isaac Brock, the British commander who made the ultimate sacrifice for the colony when he died at the Battle of Queenston Heights in 1812. Brock provided those who shaped the history of the war with a dualistic image of nationalism, one that managed to celebrate both Upper Canadian identity and colonial loyalty to Britain. He was also a Christ-like figure, a man who had given both his troops and the colony beneficent paternal guidance and wisdom but who had not spared himself from the physical dangers of war – physical dangers that really only threatened men in the military. Those who contributed to the glorification of Brock claimed that he had provided an invaluable means whereby the colonists might resist the enemy's encroachments. Brock had inspired Upper Canadian men, who might emulate his deed of manly patriotism, and he had reassured Upper Canadian women that, come what may, they could look to their husbands, fathers, sons, and brothers for protection.[12]

This kind of narrative, which emphasized masculine suffering, sacrifice, and achievements, was not unique to the War of 1812. As Janice Potter-MacKinnon argues, the history of Upper Canadian Loyalism focused on male military service and the political identification of male Loyalists with the British crown and constitution:

> Well into the twentieth century, loyalty was a male concept in that it was associated with political decision-making – a sphere from which women were excluded. The same can be said of the idea that the Loyalists bequeathed conservative values and British institutions to later generations of Canadians: women have had no role in fashioning political values and institutions. The notion that the Loyalists were the founders of a nation had obvious and unequivocal gender implications. The amateur historian William Caniff was right when he equated the 'founders' with the 'fathers.'[13]

Admittedly there was no automatic and essential connection between military activities and masculinity in Canadian history for, as Colin Coates has pointed out, the woman warrior tradition was not unknown to nineteenth-century Canada.[14] But specific female images (or images of femininity in general) as symbols of loyalty and patriotism in Upper Canada are almost completely lacking in the discourses of the period, which display a general reluctance to admit that women could have contributed to the war effort as civilians.[15] This silence about women and the feminine – except as helpless victims to which the masculine bravery of Upper Canadian men was inextricably linked – was quite the opposite of the discourses of the French Revolution, with their glorification of Marianne, or the American Patriot's figure of the republican mother, or even the more conservative use of the British figure of Britannia.[16]

The earliest efforts to call attention to Secord's contribution to the war were made by her husband James, by her son, and by Laura herself. In a petition written 25 February 1820 and addressed to Lieutenant-Governor Sir Peregrine Maitland, James Secord requested a licence to quarry stone in the Queenston military reserve. After mentioning his own wartime service – he had served as a captain in the militia – his wounds, and the plundering of his home by American troops, Secord claimed that 'his wife embraced an opportunity of rendering some service, at the risk of her own life, in going thru the Enemies' Lines to communicate information to a Detachment of His Majesty's Troops at the Beaver Dam in the month of June 1813.'[17] A second, similar petition was turned down in 1827, but Maitland did propose that Laura apply for the job of looking after Brock's monument. It is not clear whether Maitland was aware of the gendered and nationalist symbolism of a Canadian woman care-taking the memory of a British general; he did, however, have 'a favorable opinion of the character and claims of Mr. Secord and his wife.'[18] However, Maitland's successor, Sir John Colborne, was apparently not as well disposed towards the family and the job went to Theresa Nichol, the widow of militia Colonel Robert Nichol.[19]

When James died in 1841, Laura submitted two petitions to Governor Sydenham: one that asked that her son be given his father's post as customs' collector and another that asked for a pension. Both cited her poverty, her lack of support since her husband's death, and her need to support her daughters and grandchildren. While her petitions used the language of female dependency noted by Potter-MacKinnon in Loyalist women's submissions, they also featured her service to her country in 1813 and her new position as the head of a household.[20] Her son Charles's article, published in an 1845 edition of the Anglican paper the *Church*, publicized her walk, calling attention to his mother's service to her country and the British crown.[21] Eight years later Laura Secord wrote her own account of her trek to warn the British lieutenant James Fitzgibbon, in a piece that appeared in the *Anglo American Magazine* as part of a larger narrative of the war. While this article would be used and cited by others from the 1880s on, it was written in a straightforward manner, with few of the rhetorical flourishes or personal details that would characterize later accounts. And, while Secord concluded her story with the observation that she now wondered 'how I could have gone through so much fatigue, with the fortitude to accomplish it,' she did not stress her need to overcome physical frailty in reaching Fitzgibbon.[22]

Secord achieved some success in her campaign for financial recognition on the part of the state in 1860, when she presented her story to the Prince of Wales during his tour of British North America. She was also the only woman whose name appeared on an address presented by the surviving veterans of the Battle of Queenston Heights to the prince, in a ceremony attended by five hundred visitors and at which a memorial stone was laid on the site where Brock fell. Her 'patriotic services,' claimed the *Niagara Mail* in 1861, were 'handsomely rewarded' by the prince with an award of £100.[23] One of her more recent biographies argues that the prince 'provided the magic touch that transformed the "widow of the late James Secord" into the heroine, Laura Secord.'[24]

However, Secord did not become a heroine overnight. Her own efforts to draw attention to the service she had rendered to her country should not be seen as attempts to create a cult for herself, but rather as part of the Upper Canadian patronage game, in which loyal service to crown and country was the way to obtain material rewards.[25] Furthermore, she died in 1868, almost twenty years before her popularity began to spread. Still, references to Secord had begun to appear in a few mid-nineteenth-century accounts of the War of 1812. For example, the American historian Benson J. Lossing's *The Pictorial Field-Book of the War of 1812* devoted a page to Secord and the Battle of Beaver Dams. The page's caption read 'British Troops saved by a Heroine,' and Laura's own written account was the voice that supplied Lossing with his information.[26] The Canadian historian and government official William F. Coffin elaborated on her story by adding the cow, which, he claimed, she had milked in order to convince the American sentry to let her pass. While some regard Coffin's account as yet another example of a romantically inclined nineteenth-century historian playing fast and loose with the facts, his placing of Secord in a context of pioneer domesticity foreshadowed subsequent stories appearing two decades later. Secord thus was not rescued from complete obscurity by Curzon and others in the 1880s and 1890s; she was, however, given a much more prominent place in their narratives of the war and Upper Canadian loyalty.

Sarah A. Curzon has become known in Canadian women's history as a British-born suffrage activist and a founding member of the Toronto Women's Literary Society (which would later become the Canadian Woman's Suffrage Association) and the editor of a women's page in the prohibition paper, the *Canada Citizen*. But she was also an avid promoter of Canadian history and was one of the co-founders of the Women's Canadian Historical Society of Toronto (WCHS) in 1885, along with Mary Agnes Fitzgibbon, a granddaughter of Lieutenant James Fitzgibbon. Furthermore, Curzon and Fitzgibbon were supporters of Canada's 'imperial connection' to Britain, a link which they believed would benefit Canada both economically and culturally.[27] Emma Currie was another major contributor to the campaign to memorialize Secord. Indeed, her book, *The Story of Laura Secord and Canadian Reminiscences*, was published in 1900 as a fund-raiser for a monument to the 'heroine' of Upper Canada. Currie lived in St Catharines, helped found the Woman's Literary Club in that city in 1892, and would later join the Imperial Order Daughters of the Empire (IODE). She too was a supporter of the Women's Christian Temperance Union and women's suffrage.[28]

But these women were not alone in their crusade to win recognition for Secord. Other Canadian nationalist writers like Charles Mair, Agnes Maule Machar, and William Kirby praised Secord's bravery in their poetry and prose,[29] while local historical societies and those who purported to be 'national' historians, such as Ernest Cruikshank, also published papers that focused on the Battle of Beaver Dams and acknowledged Secord's role in it.[30] Much of their work, as well as that of Curzon and Currie, was part of late Victorian Canadian imperialist discourse, which perceived the past as the repository of those principles (loyalty to Britain, respect for law and order, and the capacity for democratic government) that would guide the nation into the twentieth century.[31] As Berger has argued, the local history societies that spread in the 1880s and 1890s were part of this 'conservative frame of mind' in which loyalism, nationalism, and history were inextricably linked.[32]

Tributes in ink composed the bulk of this material but they were not the only efforts to memorialize Secord. As Currie's book indicates, printed material might be used to raise funds and spread awareness in order to create more long-lasting, substantive reminders, such as monuments and statues. On 6 June 1887, W. Fenwick, a grammar school principal in Drummondville, wrote to the Toronto *World* asking for better care for the Lundy's Lane graveyard, a national monument to be erected to honour those who had died there, and a separate monument to Laura Secord. Curzon joined in a letter-writing campaign, calling for the women of Canada to take up the matter, and petitions were presented to the Ontario Legislature. When these were unsuccessful, the Lundy's Lane and Ontario Historical Societies mounted fund-raising drives for the monument, sending out circulars asking Canadian women and children to contribute 10¢ and 1¢ respectively to the cause.[33] A competition for the sculpture was held and won by a Miss Mildred Peel, an artist and sculptor who also would paint the portrait of Secord hung in 1905 in the Ontario legislature.[34] After fourteen years of campaigning, the monument was unveiled 22 June 1901 at Lundy's Lane. In 1911, the Women's Institute of Queenston and St David's felt that the village of Queenston (site of the Secord home during the War of 1812) had not done enough to honour Secord's memory and built a Memorial Hall as part of Laura Secord school. The gesture that ensconced her name in popular culture came in 1913, when Frank O'Connor chose Secord as the emblem for his new chain of candy stores.[35]

While it was not suggested that celebrating Secord's contribution was the responsibility solely of Canadian womanhood, many aspects of this campaign were shaped by gendered notions and assumptions about both past and present. The idea that women might have a special interest in supporting the subscription drive, for example, or petitioning the legislature, linked perceptions of both womanhood and nationalism, drawing upon the underlying assumptions of self-sacrifice and unselfishness that lay at the heart of both identities.[36] Groups such as the WCHS, with their 'unselfish patriotism,' were exactly what the country needed, Kirby told Mary Agnes Fitzgibbon upon being made an honorary member of the society, adding 'let women be right and the country will be might!'[37] Moreover, while male writers and historians certainly expressed an interest in Secord, it is important not to overlook the significance of the participation of Anglo-Celtic, middle- and upper middle-class women in the writing of Canadian history, a task they frequently undertook as members of local historical societies. Such women scrutinized historical records in order to find their foremothers (in both the literal and metaphorical sense).[38] However, they also were fascinated with the entire 'pioneer' period of Canadian history, both French and English, and with both male and female figures in this context. For the most part, women members of historical societies researched and presented papers on as many generals and male explorers as they did 'heroines.'[39]

There was, however, a difference in their treatment of the latter. They insisted that Canadian women's contributions to nation-building be valued, even though they had not achieved the fame and recognition of their male counterparts. To be sure, they did not offer alternative narratives of early Canadian history and tended to place political and military developments at its centre. Nevertheless, they sought to widen the parameters of male historians' definitions of these events in order to demonstrate their far-reaching effects on all Canadian society. In the meetings of organizations such as Canadian Women's Historical Societies of Toronto and Ottawa, papers were given on topics such as 'Early British Canadian Heroines' or 'Reminiscences' of pioneer women.[40] Women such as Harriett Priddis, who was active in the London and Middlesex Historical Society during this period, believed that while the history of the pioneer women of the London area

> records no daring deed ... nor historic tramp, like that of Laura Secord, yet every life is a record of such patient endurance of privations, such brave battling with danger, such a wonderful gift for resourceful adaptability, that the simplest story of the old days must bear, within itself, the sterling elements of romance. While they took no part in the national or political happenings of the day, it may be interesting to us, and to those who come after us, to hear from their own lips how these public events affected their simple lives.[41]

Their efforts were shared by male novelists and historians who not only glorified Secord but also wished to rescue other Canadian women of her era and ilk from obscurity.[42] However, as more than one honorary member of the WCHS told Fitzgibbon, Canadian women should have a special desire to preserve records of their past. According to Mair, 'the sacred domestic instincts of Canadian womanhood will not suffer in the least degree, but will rather be refreshed and strengthened' by the Society's 'rescuing from destruction the scattered and perishable records of Ontario's old, and, in many respects, romantic home life.'[43] The collection of material concerning this latter area, Mair and others felt, should be the special work of Canadian women.[44]

The extent to which this relegation of the 'social' realm to women historians set a precedent for future developments, whereby 'romantic home life' was perceived as both the preserve of women and the realm of the trivial and anecdotal, is not entirely clear.[45] Certainly it does not appear to have been Mair's intention that these areas be perceived as trivial or unworthy of male historians' attention, while women such as Mary Agnes Fitzgibbon were as eager to research battles and collect military memorabilia as they were concerned with 'primitive clothing, food cookery, amusements, and observances of festivals attending births and wedlock or the Charivari.'[46] Yet it was probably no coincidence that the first historian to seriously challenge the military value of Secord's walk was the male academic W.S. Wallace, who in 1930 raised a furor among public supporters of Secord with questions concerning the use of historical evidence in documenting her walk.[47]

This, then, was the context in which Laura Secord became an increasingly popular symbol of Canadian patriotism: one of feminism, history, patriotism, and imperialism. While many of these histories were, as Berger has pointed out, local and might seem incredibly parochial in their scope, their authors saw locally based stories as having a much wider emotional and moral significance in the narratives of the nation.[48] Hence, narratives of Secord's contribution to the War of 1812 and to the colonial link with the British Empire were marked by the interplay of locality, nationality, and gender. First, Laura and James Secord's backgrounds were explored and their genealogies traced, in order to place them within the Loyalist tradition of suffering and sacrifice. For those writers who were concerned with strict historical accuracy, such a task was considerably easier for the Secords than for Laura's family, the Ingersolls. James's male ancestors had fought in the Revolutionary war for the British crown and the many military ranks occupied by the Secord men were duly listed and acclaimed. Moreover, the Secords could claim a history of both allegiance to the British crown and a desire for the protection of the British constitution; they were descended from Huguenots who arrived in New York from LaRochelle in the late seventeenth century.[49]

But it was not only the Secord men that had served their country and suffered hardships. The Loyalist legacy inherited by both Laura and James had, it was pointed out, been marked by gender differences. As Curzon told her audiences, James Secord's arrival in Canada had been as a three-year-old refugee, part of his mother's 'flight through the wilderness, with four other homeless women and many children, to escape the fury of a band of ruffians who called themselves the "sons of Liberty." After enduring frightful hardships for nearly a month, they finally arrived at Fort Niagara almost naked and starving.' Curzon went on to comment that these were by no means 'uncommon experiences.' Frequently, she pointed out, Loyalist men had to flee 'for their lives' and leave their women and children behind (as well as their 'goods, chattels, estates, and money'). Their loved ones were then left to endure the terrors of the wilderness:

> unprotected and unsupported, save by that deep faith in God and love to King and country which, with their personal devotion to their husbands, made of them heroines whose story of unparalleled devotion, hardships patiently borne, motherhood honourably sustained, industry and thrift perseveringly followed, enterprise successfully prosecuted, principle unwaveringly upheld, and tenderness never surpassed, has yet to be written, and whose share in the making of this nation remains to be equally honored with that of the men who bled and fought for its liberties.[50]

Unfortunately for Laura's popularizers, the Ingersoll family did not fit as neatly into the Loyalist tradition. Her father, Thomas, had fought against the British in 1776 and had seen his 1793 land grant cancelled as a result of British efforts to curb large-scale immigration of American settlers into Upper Canada.[51] As J.H. Ingersoll observed in 1926, Laura's inability to claim the United Empire Loyalist pedigree 'has been commented upon.' However, some historians argued that Thomas Ingersoll came to Upper Canada at Lieutenant-Governor Simcoe's request.[52] For those poets who felt free to create Laura's Loyalism in a more imaginative manner, her patriotism was traced to a long-standing childhood attachment to Britain. They insisted that she chose Canada freely and was not forced to come to the country as a refugee.[53] Moreover, despite these historians' fascination with lines of blood and birth, they were equally determined to demonstrate that the former could be transcended by environment and force of personality. The loyal society of Upper Canada and the strength of Laura's own commitment to Britain were important reminders to the Canadian public that a sense of imperial duty could overcome other relationships and flourish in the colonial context.[54]

Accordingly, these historians argued, it should come as no surprise that both Laura and her husband felt obliged to perform their patriotic duty when American officers were overheard planning an attack on the British forces of Lieutenant Fitzgibbon.[55] However, James was still suffering from wounds sustained at the Battle of Queenston Heights and it therefore fell to Laura – over her husband's objections and concern for her safety – to walk the twenty miles from Queenston to warn the British troops at Beaver Dams. (Here the linear chronology of the narratives was frequently interrupted to explain that Laura had come to his aid after the battle when, finding him badly wounded and in danger of being beaten to death by 'common' American soldiers, she had attempted to shield him with her own body from their rifle butts – further evidence that Laura was no stranger to wifely and patriotic duty.[56]

Laura's journey took on wider dimensions and greater significance in the hands of her commemorators. It was no longer just a walk to warn the British but, with its elements of venturing into the unknown, physical sacrifice, and devotion to the British values of order and democracy, came to symbolize the entire 'pioneer woman's experience in Canadian history.'[57] Leaving the cozy domesticity and safety of her home, the company of her wounded husband and children, Secord had ventured out into the Upper Canadian wilderness with its swamps and underbrush in which threatening creatures, such as rattlesnakes, bears, and wolves, might lurk.[58] And even when Sarah Curzon's 1887 play permitted Laura to deliver several monologues on the loveliness of the June woodland, the tranquillity of the forest was disrupted by the howling of wolves.[59]

But most serious of all, in the majority of accounts, was the threat of the 'Indians' she might meet on the way. If Secord's commitment to Canada and Britain had previously been presented in cultural terms, ones that could be encouraged by the colonial tie and that might transcend race, it was at this point that her significance as a symbol of white Canadian womanhood was clearest. While her feminine fragility had been the subject of comment throughout the stories, and while her racial background might have been the underlying subtext for this fragility, it was in the discussions of the threat of Native warriors that her gender became most clearly racialized.[60] Unlike the contemporary racist and cultural stereotypes of threatening black male sexuality used in American lynching campaigns, however, her fears were not of sexual violence by Native men – at least not explicitly – but of the tactics supposedly used by Native men in warfare, scalping being the most obvious.[61]

To be sure, some stories mentioned that Secord had had to stay clear of open roads and paths 'for fear of Indians and white marauders.'[62] But even those who downplayed her fear of a chance encounter with an 'Indian' during her journey were scrupulous in their description of her fright upon encountering Mohawks outside the British camp. Secord herself had stated that she had stumbled across the Mohawks' camp and that they had shouted 'woman' at her, making her 'tremble' and giving her an 'awful feeling.' It was only with difficulty, she said, that she convinced them to take her to Fitzgibbon.[63] As this meeting with the Natives was retold, they became more menacing and inspired even greater fear in Secord. In these accounts, at this penultimate stage in her journey she stepped on a twig that snapped and startled an Indian encampment. Quite suddenly Secord was surrounded by them, 'the chief throws up his tomahawk to strike, regarding the intruder as a spy.'[64] In some narratives, he shouted at her, 'Woman! what does woman want!' Only by her courage in springing to his arm is the woman saved, and an opportunity snatched to assure him of her loyalty.[65] Moved by pity and admiration, the chief gave her a guide, and at length she reached Fitzgibbon, delivered and verified her message – 'and *faints.*'[66] Fitzgibbon then went off to fight the Battle of Beaver Dams, armed with the knowledge that Secord had brought him, and managed to successfully rout the American forces. In a number of narratives, this victory was frequently achieved by using the threat of unleashed Indian savagery when the Americans were reluctant to surrender.[67] While the battle was being fought, Secord was moved to a nearby house, where she slept off her walk, and then returned to the safety of her home and family. She told her family about her achievement but, motivated by fear for their security (as American troops continued to occupy the Niagara area) as well as by her own modesty and self-denial, she did not look for any recognition or reward. Such honours came first to Fitzgibbon.[68]

Women such as Curzon and Currie might see Secord's contribution as natural and unsurprising (given her devotion to her country), but they also were keenly aware that their mission of commemoration necessitated that their work appeal to a popular audience. These narratives were imbued with their authors' concerns with the relations of gender, class, and race and the way in which they perceived these identities to structure both Canadian society and history. For one, Secord's 'natural' feminine fragility was a major theme of their writings. As a white woman of good birth and descent, she was not physically suited to undertake the hardships involved in her walk (although, paradoxically, as a typical 'pioneer woman' she was able to undertake the hardships of raising a family and looking after a household in a recently settled area). Her delicacy and slight build, first mentioned by Fitzgibbon in his own testimony of her walk, was frequently stressed by those who commemorated her.[69] Her physical frailty could be contrasted with the manly size and strength of soldiers such as Fitzgibbon and Brock.[70] Nevertheless, the seeming physical immutability of gender was not an insurmountable barrier to her patriotic duty to country and empire. The claims of the latter transcended corporeal limitations. Even her maternal duties, understood by both conservatives and many feminists in late nineteenth-century Canada to be the core of womanly identity, could be put aside or even reformulated in order to answer her country's needs.[71] While her supporters did not make explicit their motives in stressing her frailty, it is possible to see it as a subtext to counter medical and scientific arguments about female physical deficiencies that made women, particularly white, middle-class women, unfit for political participation and higher education.[72]

Furthermore, there were other ways to make Secord both appealing and a reflection of their own conceptions of 'Canadian womanhood,' and many historians treated her as an icon of respectable white heterosexual femininity.

Anecdotes supposedly told by her family were often added to the end of the narratives of her walk – especially those written by women – and these emphasized her love of children, her kindness and charity towards the elderly, and her very feminine love of finery and gaiety (making her daughters' satin slippers, for example, and her participation as a young woman in balls given by the Secords at Newark). Indeed, they went so far as to discuss the clothing that she wore on her walk. Her daughter Harriet told Currie that she and her sisters saw their mother leave that morning wearing 'a flowered print gown, I think it was brown with orange flowers, at least a yellow tint.'[73] Elizabeth Thompson, who was active within the Ontario Historical Society and was also a member of the IODE, also wrote that Secord wore a print dress, adding a 'cottage bonnet tied under her chin … balbriggan stockings, with red silk clocks on the sides, and low shoes with buckles' – both of which were lost during the walk.[74]

For her most active supporters, the walk of Laura Secord meant that certain women could be written into the record of loyalty and patriotic duty in Canadian history, and heroines could gain recognition for the deeds they had committed. In the eyes of these historians, such recognition had heretofore been withheld simply because of these figures' gender, for in every other significant feature – their racial and ethnic identities, for example – they were no different from their male counterparts. But such additions to the narrative were intended to be just that: additions, not serious disruptions of the story's focus on the ultimate triumph of British institutions and the imperial tie in Canada. Like her walk, Secord herself was constructed in many ways as the archetypal 'British' pioneer woman of Loyalist history, remembered for her willingness to struggle, sacrifice, and thus contribute to 'nation-building.' These historians also suggested that patriotic duties and loyalty to the state did not automatically constitute a major threat to late nineteenth-century concepts of masculinity and femininity. Secord could undertake such duties, but still had to be defined by her relations to husband and children, home and family. She did not, it was clear, take up arms herself, nor did she use her contribution to win recognition for her own gain.

In the context of late nineteenth and early twentieth-century debates about gender relations in Canadian society, Secord was a persuasive symbol of how certain women might breach the division between 'private' and 'public,' the family and the state, and do so for entirely unselfish and patriotic reasons. The narratives of Laura Secord's walk helped shape an image of Canadian womanhood in the past that provided additional justification and inspiration for turn-of-the-century Canadian feminists. These women could invoke memory and tradition when calling for their own inclusion in the 'imagined community' of the Canadian nation of the late nineteenth century.[75] Furthermore, for those such as Curzon who were eager to widen their frame of national reference, Secord's legacy could be part of an imperialist discourse, linking gender, race, nation, and empire in both the past and the present.

NOTES

1 A Dorian Gray–like image that, as the company has enjoyed pointing out, becomes younger with the passage of time. See the advertisement 'There must be something in the chocolate,' *Globe and Mail*, 25 November 1992, A14.

2 This tenet has been an invaluable methodological tool in thinking about the narratives of Secord. See Benedict Anderson, *Imagined Communities: Reflections on the Origin and Spread of Nationalism*, revised edition (London and New York: Verso, 1991). See also Eric Hobsbawm and Terence Ranger, eds., *The Invention of Tradition* (Cambridge and New York: Cambridge University Press, 1983). Like Anderson's work, however, this collection does not address the complex relationships of gender. nationalism, and the 'invented traditions' it analyses.

3 Carl Berger, *The Sense of Power: Studies in the Ideas of Canadian Imperialism 1867–1914* (Toronto: University of Toronto Press, 1970), 78.

4 Catherine Hall, Jane Lewis, Keith McClelland, and Jane Rendall, Introduction, *Gender and History: Special Issue on Gender, Nationalisms, and National Identities* 5, 2 (Summer 1993): 159.

5 Recent work by historians of Indian nationalism explores the use of female images, particularly that of the nation as mother. See, for example, Samita Sen, 'Motherhood and Mother Craft: Gender and Nationalism in Bengal,' *Gender and History: Special Issue on Gender, Nationalisms and National Identities*, 231–43. See also the essays in *History Workshop Journal. Special Issue: Colonial and Post-Colonial History* 36 (Autumn 1993), and Mrinalini Sinha, 'Reading Mother India: Empire, Nation, and the Female Voice,' *Journal of Women's History* 6, 2 (Summer 1994): 6–44.

6 One of the few Canadian historians to point to these connections has been George Ingram, 'The Story of Laura Secord Revisted,' *Ontario History* 57, 2 (June 1965): 85–97. Other works tackling these questions have looked at such areas as social reform. See Angus McLaren, *Our Own Master Race: Eugenics in Canada, 1885–1945* (Toronto: McClelland and Stewart, 1990) and Mariana Valverde, *The Age of Light, Soap, and Water: Moral Reform in English Canada 1885–1925* (Toronto: McClelland and Stewart, 1991).

7 For a heroine who was not so easily domesticated, see Colin M. Coates, 'Commemorating the Woman Warrior of New France: Madeleine de Verchères, 1692–1930,' chapter 1 in this volume; also Marina Warner, *Joan of Arc: The Image of Female Heroism* (New York: Alfred A. Knopf, 1981).

8 See, for example, the *Transactions* of both the Women's Canadian Historical Society of Ottawa and the Women's Canadian Historical Society of Toronto from the 1890s to the 1920s.

9 David Mills, *The Idea of Loyalty in Upper Canada, 1784–1850* (Montreal and Kingston: McGill-Queen's University Press, 1988).

10 Donald H. Akenson, *The Irish in Ontario: A Study in Rural History* (Montreal and Kingston: McGill-Queen's University Press, 1984), 134.

11 See Cecilia Morgan, 'Languages of Gender in Upper Canadian Politics and Religion, 1791–1850,' PhD thesis, University of Toronto, 1993, chapter 2. It is interesting that, while the militia myth has been challenged by many historians, its gendered nature has received very little attention. See, for example, the most recent study of the War of 1812, George Sheppard's *Plunder, Profit, and Paroles: A Social History of the War of 1812 in Upper Canada* (Montreal and Kingston: McGill-Queen's University Press, 1994).

12 Morgan, 'Languages of Gender,' 56–60; see also Keith Walden, 'Isaac Brock: Man and Myth: A Study of the Militia Myth of the War of 18J2 in Upper Canada 1812–1912,' MA thesis, Queen's University, 1971.

13 Janice Potler-Mackinnon, *While the Women Only Wept: Loyalist Refugee Women in Eastern Ontario* (Montreal and Kingston: McGill-Queen's University Press, 1993), 158.

14 Coates, 'Commemorating the Woman Warrior of New France.'

15 Morgan, 'Languages of Gender,' chapter 2.

16 On the French Revolution, see Maurice Agulhon, *Marianne into Battle: Republican Imagery and Symbolism in France, 1789–1880*, trans. Janet Lloyd (Cambridge: Cambridge University Press, 1981). For republican motherhood, see Linda Kerber, 'The Republican Mother: Female Political Imagination in the Early Republic,' in *Women of the Republic: Intellect and Ideology in Revolutionary America* (Chapel Hill: University of North Carolina Press, 1980); for Britannia, see Madge Dresser, 'Britannia,' in Raphael Samuel, ed., *Patriotism: The Making and Unmaking of British National identity*. Volume III: National Fictions (London: Routledge, 1989), 26–49.

17 The petition is reprinted in Ruth McKenzie's *Laura Secord: The Legend and the Lady* (Toronto: McClelland and Stewart, 1971), 74–5. To date, McKenzie's book is the most thorough and best researched popular account of the development of the Secord legend.

18 Ibid., 76.

19 Ibid., 76–7; also Sheppard, *Plunder, Profit, and Paroles*, 221.

20 McKenzie, *Laura Secord*, 84–5.

21 Ibid., 49ff.

22 Ibid., 91–2; also in Benson J. Lossing, *The Pictorial Field-Book of the War of 1812* (New York, 1869), 621.

23 McKenzie, *Laura Secord*, 102.

24 Ibid., 103–4.

25 For an analysis of patronage in nineteenth-century Ontario, see S.J.R. Noel, *Patrons, Clients, Brokers: Ontario Society and Politics 1791–1896* (Toronto: University of Toronto Press, 1990).

26 Lossing, *The Pictorial Field-Book*, 621.

27 See Sarah A. Curzon, *Laura Secord, the Heroine of the War of 1812: A Drama and Other Poems* (Toronto, 1887). For biographical sketches of Curzon and Fitzgibbon, see Henry James Morgan, *The Canadian Men and Women of the Time: A Hand-Book of Canadian Biography* (Toronto, 1898 and 1912), 235–6 and 400. Curzon's work is briefly discussed in Carol Bacchi's *Liberation Deferred? The Ideas of the English-Canadian Suffragists, 1877–1918* (Toronto: University of Toronto Press, 1981), 26–7 and 44, but Bacchi's frame of reference does not take in Curzon's (or other suffragists') interest in history as an important cultural aspect of their maternal feminism and imperialism.

28 Henry James Morgan, *The Canadian Men and Women of the Time*, 288–9; see also Mrs G.M. Armstrong, *The First Eighty Years of the Women's Literary Club of St. Catharines, 1892–1972* (n.p., 1972); Emma A. Currie, *The Story of Laura Secord and Canadian Reminiscences* (St Catharines, 1913).

29 Charles Mair, 'A Ballad for Brave Women,' in *Tecumseh: A Drama and Canadian Poems* (Toronto, 1901), 147; William Kirby, *Annals of Niagara*, ed. and intro. Lorne Pierce (1896; Toronto, 1927), 209–10. Kirby had been Currie's childhood tutor in Niagara and both she and Curzon continued to look to him for advice, support, and recognition (Archives of Ontario [AO]), MS 542, William Kirby Correspondence, Reel I, Curzon and Currie to Kirby, 1887–1906). Kirby and Mair were made honorary members of the WCHS (AO, MU 7837–7838, Series A, WCHS papers, Correspondence File I, William Kirby to Mary Agnes Fitzgibbon, 11 April 1896, Charles Mair to Fitzgibbon, May 1896). For Machar, see 'Laura Secord,' in her *Lays of the True North and Other Poems* (Toronto, 1887), 35. See also Ruth Compton Brouwer, 'Moral Nationalism in Victorian Canada: The Case of Agnes Machar,' *Journal of Canadian Studies* 20, 1 (Spring 1985): 90–108.

30 See, for example, Ernest Cruikshank, 'The Heroine of the Beaver Dams,' *Canadian Antiquarian and Numismatic Journal* 8 (Montreal, 1879): 135–6. Many thanks to Colin Coates for this reference. See also Ernest Cruikshank, *The Fight in the Beechwoods* (Drummondville: Lundy's Lane Historical Society, 1889), I, 13–14, 19.

31 Berger, *The Sense of Power*, 89–90.

32 Ibid., 95–6.

33 Janet Carnochan, 'Laura Secord Monument at Lundy's Lane,' *Transactions of the Niagara Historical Society* (Niagara, 1913), 11–18.

34 Ibid., 13.

35 McKenzie, *Laura Secord*, 118–19.

36 Marilyn Lake has made a similar argument about Australian nationalist discourse during the First World War. See her 'Mission Impossible: How Men Gave Birth to the Australian Nation – Nationalism, Gender and Other Seminal Acts,' *Gender and History. Special Issue on Motherhood, Race and the State in the Twentieth Century* 4, 3 (Autumn 1992): 305–22, particularly 307. For the theme of self-sacrifice in Canadian nationalism, see Berger, *The Sense of Power*, 217. The links between the discourses of late Victorian, white, bourgeois femininity and that of Canadian racial policy have been explored by Valverde in *The Age of Light, Soap, and Water*, in the contexts of moral reform, the white slavery panic, and immigration policies. See also Bacchi, *Liberation Deferred?*, chapter 7. For gender and imperialism in the British and American contexts, see Vron Ware, *Beyond the Pale: White Women, Racism and History* (London and New York: Verso, 1992). The seminal article on imperialism and British womanhood is Anna Davin, 'Imperialism and Motherhood,' *History Workshop Journal* 5 (Spring 1978): 9–65.

37 WCHS papers, MU 7837–7838, Series A, Correspondence File I, to Fitzgibbon, 14 April 1896.

38 See, for example, Mrs J.R. Hill, 'Early British Canadian Heroines,' *Women's Canadian Historical Society of Ottawa Transactions*, 10 (1928): 93–8; Harriet Prudis, 'Reminiscences of Mrs. Gilbert Ponte,' *London and Middlesex Historical Society Transactions* (1902, pub. 1907): 62–4.

39 Harriett Priddis, 'The 100th Regiment,' *L & M H S Transactions* 5 (1912–13): n.p.; Agnes Dunbar Chamberlin, 'The Colored Citizens of Toronto,' *WCHS of Toronto Transactions* 8 (1908): 9–15; also the biography of Brock by Lady Edgar, one of the first presidents of the WCHS [*Life of General Brock* (Toronto, 1904)].

40 See note 39 above.

41 Priddis, 'Reminiscences of Mrs. Gilbert Ponte,' 62.

42 See Ernest Green, 'Some Canadian Women of 1812–14,' *WCHS of Ottawa Transactions* 9 (1925): 98–109.

43 WCHS papers, MU 7837–7838, Series A, Correspondence File I, Mair to Fitzgibbon, May 1896.

44 Ibid.; see also WCHS papers, MU 7837–7838, Series A, Correspondence File I, John H. to Fitzgibbon, 6 May 1896.

45 As Linda Kerber argues, it was precisely this relegation that women's historians of the 1960s and 1970s had to confront in their attempts to lift women's lives from the 'realm of the trivial and anecdotal.' See her 'Separate Spheres, Female Worlds, Woman's Place: The Rhetoric of Women's History,' *Journal of American History* 75, 1 (June 1988): 9–39, especially 37.

46 Mair to Fitzgibbon, 8 May 1896.

47 W.S. Wallace, *The Story of Laura Secord* (Toronto, 1932). For a response to Wallace, see 'What Laura Secord Did,' *Dunnville Weekly Chronicle* 35 (1932), reprinted from Toronto *Saturday Night*, 22 June 1932.

48 Berger, *The Sense of Power*, 96. As M. Brook Taylor has pointed out about the work of nineteenth-century writers such as John Charles Dent, Francis Hincks, and Charles Lindsey, 'National historians were essentially Upper Canadian historians in masquerade.' See his *Promoters Patriots, and Partisans: Historiography in Nineteenth-Century English Canada* (Toronto: University of Toronto Press, 1989), 231.

49 Currie, *The Story of Laura Secord*, 21–33.

50 Curzon, *The Story of Laura Secord*. 1813 (Lundy's Lane Historical Society, 25 July 1891), 6–7.

51 See Gerald M. Craig, *Upper Canada: The Formative Years 1784–1841* (Toronto: McClelland and Stewart, 1963), 49, for a discussion of this shift in policy. McKenzie also argues that Ingersoll did not fulfil his settlement obligations (*Laura Secord*, 29). See also Currie, *The Story of Laura Secord*, 38–9.

52 I.H. Ingersoll, 'The Ancestry of Laura Secord,' *Ontario Historical Society* (1926): 361–3. See also Elizabeth Thompson, 'Laura Ingersoll Secord,' *Niagara Historical Society Papers* 25 (1912): 1. Others argued that Ingersoll was urged by Joseph Brant to come to Upper Canada (Ingersoll, 363). The Brant connection was developed most fully and romantically by John Price-Brown in *Laura the Undaunted: A Canadian Historical Romance* (Toronto: Ryerson Press, 1930). It has also been pointed out that Price-Brown picked up the story, 'invented out of whole cloth' by Curzon, that Tecumseh had fallen in love with one of Secord's daughters. See Dennis Duffy, *Gardens, Covenants, Exiles: Loyalism in the Literature of Upper Canada/Ontario* (Toronto: University of Toronto Press, 1982), 61. In Price-Brown's account, Tecumseh proposes just before he is killed; Laura, however, disapproves of the match (259–69).

53 Price-Brown, *Laura the Undaunted*, 16–17, 180–2.

54 Just as French Canadians could overcome other ties (see Berger, *The Sense of Power*, 138–9).

55 Thompson, 'Laura Ingersoll Secord,' 2; Currie, *The Story of Laura Secord*, 48; Ingersoll, 'The Ancestry of Laura Secord,' 362.

56 Price-Brown's 'fictional' account is the most colourful, since one of the American officers who did not intervene to save the Secords was a former suitor of Laura's, whom she had rejected in favour of James and Canada (*Laura the Undaunted*, 252–5). See also Currie, *The Story of Laura Secord*, 53–4.

57 Norman Knowles, in his study of late nineteenth-century Ontario commemorations of Loyalism, argues that pioneer and rural myths subsumed those of Loyalism. 'Inventing the Loyalists: The Ontario Loyalist Tradition and the Creation of a Usable Past, 1784–1924,' PhD thesis, York University, 1990. To date, my research

on women commemorators indicates that, for them, both Loyalism (particularly people, places, and artefacts having to do with 1812) and the 'pioneer past' were closely intertwined; both were of great significance and inspirational power in their interpretations of the past. See Elizabeth Thompson, *The Pioneer Woman: A Canadian Character Type* (Montreal and Kingston: McGill-Queen's University Press, 1991) for a study of this archetype in the fiction of Canadian authors Catharine Parr Trail, Sara Jeannette Duncan, Ralph Connor, and Margaret Laurence.

58 The most extensive description is in Curzon's *The Story of Laura Secord*, 11–12.

59 Curzon, *Laura Secord: The Heroine of the War of 1812*, 39–47.

60 While examining a very different period and genre of writing, I have found Carroll Smith-Rosenberg's 'Captured Subjects/Savage Others: Violently Engendering the New American' to be extremely helpful in understanding the construction of white womanhood in the North American context. See *Gender and History* 5, 2 (Summer 1993): 177–95. See also Vron Ware, 'Moments of Danger: Race, Gender, and Memories of Empire,' *History and Theory* 31, 4 (December 1992): 116–37.

61 See Ware, 'To Make the Facts Known,' in *Beyond the Pale* for a discussion of lynching and the feminist campaign against it. Smith-Rosenberg points to a similar treatment of native men in Mary Rowlandson's seventeenth-century captivity narrative ('Captured Subjects/Savage Others,' 183–4). While the two examples should not be conflated, this issue does call for further analysis.

62 Cruikshank, *The Fight in the Beechwoods*, 13.

63 Secord in Thompson, 'Laura Ingersoll Secord,' 4–5.

64 See, for example, Blanche Hume, *Laura Secord* (Toronto, 1928), 1. This book was part of a Ryerson Canadian History Readers series, endorsed by the IODE and the Provincial Department of Education.

65 Ibid., 15.

66 Curzon, *The Story of Laura Secord*, 13.

67 See, for example, Cruikshank, *The Fight in the Beechwoods*, 18.

68 Currie, *The Story of Laura Secord*, 52–3. Fitzgibbon supposedly took full credit for the victory, ignoring both Secord's and the Caughnawaga Mohawks' roles (McKenzie, *Laura Secord*, 66–7). He later became a colonel in the York militia and was rewarded for his role in putting down the 1837 rebellion with a £1000 grant (89–90).

69 Fitzgibbon in Thompson 'Laura Ingersoll Secord,' 6.

70 Hume, *Laura Secord*, 4.

71 For example, in Curzon's play Secord is asked by her sister-in-law, the Widow Secord, if her children will not 'blame' her should she come to harm. She replies that 'children can see the right at one quick glance,' suggesting that their mother's maternal care and authority is bound to her patriotism and loyalty (*Laura Secord: The Heroine of the War of 1812*, 34).

72 See Wendy Mitchinson, *The Nature of Their Bodies: Women and Their Doctors in Victorian Canada* (Toronto: University of Toronto Press, 1991), especially chapter 2, 'The Frailty of Women.'

73 Currie, *The Story of Laura Secord*, 71.

74 Thompson, 'Laura Ingersoll Secord,' 3. Balbriggan was a type of fine, unbleached, knitted cotton hosiery material.

75 See Hobsbawm and Ranger, 'Introduction: Inventing Tradition,' in *The Invention of Tradition*, particularly their argument that invented traditions are often shaped and deployed by those who wish either to legitimate particular institutions or relations of authority or to inculcate certain beliefs or values (9). In this case I would argue that the Secord tradition served very similar purposes, although it was used both to legitimate and, for certain groups of women, to subvert.

3 Re-Membering Dead Heroes: Quebec City's Monument to Short-Wallick

JASON F. KOVACS AND BRIAN S. OSBORNE

Searching for Connections

The story of the erection of Quebec City's Short-Wallick memorial is a simple one in the telling, but a complex one in the analysis. The monument was prompted by the fact that 122 years ago two soldiers died while striving valiantly to save the lives and property of their fellow citizens. It was the raw material of classical heroism in a Victorian age when the tropes of self-sacrifice underpinned the imagination and ideology of Empire and the conduct expected of its servants. In this way, heroes-eidolons are incorporated into the complex narrative involving national chronicles, monuments, performed commemorations, and the construction of imperial, state, and national identities.[1] But this is where the story of the Short-Wallick memorial gets complex.

An essential part of Anthony Smith's model of the power of 'ethno-symbolism' in the construction of nations and national identities is the role of preferred heroes in the nurturing of loyalty, and even devotion, to symbolic values. These are extrapolated from the individual to the emerging collective *ethnos* in a demonstration of 'the principle of *filiation*.' That is, the greater community defines itself by these symbolic and mythologized values which are later used when encountering the problems of 'relationships and cohesion in modern, complex societies.'[2] Indeed, how heroes and their acts are 're-membered' is central to this paper. For Colin Coates and Cecilia Morgan, the relationship between actual events and how they are appropriated by a collective memory is always in a state of 'permanent evolution.' As they put it, this constant dynamic is 'subject to the dialectic of remembering and forgetting, unconscious of the distortions to which it is subject, vulnerable in various ways to appropriation and manipulation, and capable of lying dormant for long periods only to be suddenly reawakened.'[3]

The history of the Short-Wallick monument is a clear demonstration of how history as a putative record of past events can be manipulated by evolving socio-political contexts, and how the attempted elision of some of our stories can amount to the imposition of a purposeful amnesia for political effect. It also raises questions of how, in the process of public remembering, public spaces become ideological sites of conflict for populist, institutional, and state forces. For Robert Bevan, this process is 'all about the continued power struggle between memory and forgetfulness, truth and propaganda.'[4] And, in a critique of the overused and often inappropriate use of 'collective memory,' Jay Winter has shifted his attention to the process of 'collective remembering' as the approach to 'enabling us to understand what groups of people try to do when they act in public to conjure up the past'[5] and, we would add, construct a future. In particular, the bones and corpses of dead people, and especially revered people, have long been used as emotive devices to extract symbolic power through death rituals, commemoration, and remembrance. As Katherine Verdery has put it, 'dead-body politics' are often pursued through the monumentalizing of 'dead people cast in bronze or carved in stone' to extend their physical and symbolic presence, 'into the realm of the timeless or the sacred, like an icon.'[6] For Anthony Smith, the role of the 'glorious dead' in the 'new religion' of nationalism is to ensure that their sacrifices on behalf of the collective become appropriated in its 'sacred destiny.'[7]

This is what this Short-Wallick story is really about: who remembers, what, how, and why? It is a 'necrography': an account of 'post-mortem manifestations' of both hagiography and iconoclasm, the conflict between them ensuring the enduring life of the subject-heroes.[8] But let's start with the dramatic events in Quebec City in the spring of 1889 that underpin this exercise in the construction of heroes and identity-making in a young nationalizing-state as it encountered well-established regional and cultural consciousnesses.

The Facts of the Matter: A Tragic Fire

Shortly after midnight on Thursday, 16 May 1889, a 'lurid red light' appeared on the western skyline of Quebec City.[9] Church bells swiftly alerted a sleepy populace to a fire that was engulfing the adjacent village of St Sauveur, a municipality of some fifteen thousand people that was separated from the old city by the mere width of a street.[10] The fire had broken out in a vacant house on St Valier Street and it immediately drew a large gathering. Fanned by a strong east wind, the flames quickly consumed the close-packed wooden houses and spread unchecked in all directions. The repeated strident sound of the fire-alarm caused a panic and the entire population fled before the rapidly spreading inferno.

From the outset, it was clear that St Sauveur's volunteer fire brigade was unable to cope with the emergency, even with the assistance of a number of volunteers including St Sauveur's mayor and other 'prominent citizens.'[11] Simply put, other than a few cisterns, there was no water supply in this community of wooden structures.[12] Unforgivingly, Quebec City's French-language newspaper, *L'Électeur*, pointed to the cruel irony of the tragedy: the local council had only recently rejected 'le projet de l'introduction de l'eau de l'aqueduc dans cette paroisse.'[13] The far better equipped Quebec City fire brigade was dispatched to the scene but, like its volunteer counterpart, it too was 'crippled by want of water' and was unable to arrest the flames which seemingly 'jumped from one wooden building to another.'[14] Soon, it became apparent to all who were trying to fight the fire with the aid of buckets of water from a nearby well that 'it was beyond human power to arrest its progress.'[15] Without a convenient supply of water, the fire could not be contained and, within a few hours of the alarm bells being rung, several hundred houses were destroyed.

With the fire out of control, the mayor of St Sauveur telephoned the authorities at Quebec City's Citadel and requested aid from the military there. The response was immediate. By 1:30 a.m., over 130 soldiers from 'B' battery of the Royal Canadian Artillery arrived under the command of Lieutenant-Colonel Montizambert.[16] Given the immensity of the problem facing them, they introduced a new strategy. While the firemen continued to direct their efforts to 'the salvation of the already burning houses,' the artillerymen attempted to 'stop the progress of the fire by demolishing the houses in its course.'[17] To this end, the soldiers strove for several hours with axes and rope-and-tackle to clear away buildings that were fuelling the fire.[18]

Soon, however, their Herculean efforts gave way to a more effective, albeit more dangerous, method: explosives. In the dark hours before dawn, several small kegs of gunpowder were employed successfully in razing four structures. Perhaps because they were tiring at their laborious task, or because they saw the success of their use of explosives, or perhaps because they sensed the need to speed up their counter-attack, the soldiers increased the scale of their use of explosives. At 6:45 a.m., several soldiers entered a fifth building at the corner of St Gertrude and St Sauveur streets (see figure 3.1).[19] A fuse was lit on an unusually large (100 lbs) keg of gunpowder centred in the middle of the house. The soldiers quickly left the site, but the fuse failed to ignite the powder. At this point, Major Charles Short, the second in command, together with Staff-Sergeant George Wallick, entered the building to check the fuse. The two soldiers 'were hardly there a second or two' when a spark blown through an open window from a fire in an adjoining house ignited the charge. According to one horrified onlooker, the 'house was hurled intact several feet into the air' but fell as 'a chaotic mass.'[20] Major Short was killed instantly, but Sergeant Wallick was

3.1 A devastated St Sauveur. ANQ, Coll. Initiale (La Santé et L'Assistance Publique au Québec 1886–1986, p. 37).

still breathing even though his badly mutilated body had been thrown 'about two hundred feet from the place of the explosion.' He was quickly carried off to the Marine hospital, where he died later that evening.[21] The fire prevented the search for Major Short's remains for some two hours, but portions of his body were located and sent off to the Citadel.

Despite the onset of rainfall at 8 a.m., the fire continued its destructive path until the early afternoon when it reached the open fields north of the municipality.[22] By 2 p.m., the whole district of St Sauveur was described as a 'mass of smouldering ruins.'[23] Initial accounts of the destruction estimated that up to 700 houses had been destroyed, the majority of which had housed poor families with no insurance.[24] A week later, it was confirmed that 430 properties consisting of 1050 buildings had been destroyed.[25] Further, since a large number of the houses were tenements occupied by more than one family, the number of families left homeless was estimated at 900 to 1200, or approximately 4000 to 6000 individuals. Over a thousand of the homeless victims had fled the scene and encamped in the wet fields to the north and south. There, they were visited by the premier of Quebec, the Hon. Honoré Mercier, local politicians, and the mayor of Quebec City, while members of the clergy distributed hot coffee, tea, and bread to the drenched and homeless.[26] Recognizing the immediate need, the minister of militia and defence, Sir A.P. Caron, ordered the distribution of 300 tents to accommodate the victims, and granted access to the drill hall.[27] Subsequently, Premier Mercier opened up several public buildings, and, by the next day, the majority of the homeless had taken shelter in the courthouse, town hall, market hall, the convent, and schoolhouses.[28]

The aftermath of the fire was horrific. The next day, the streets of St Sauveur were littered with dead horses, pigs, and cats, and the air was full of the stench emanating from several 'smouldering heaps of fire.'[29] Pathetically, former residents sifted through the debris in hope of finding some valued possessions, while others began to stake off their properties with the aim of quickly rebuilding their homes. Some valuables had been saved from the fire, having been thrown into wells, but most were either destroyed or stolen by the 'ghouls who attend fires for purposes of pillage.'[30] Others commented on the 'many sad scenes' witnessed during the fire and the 'many victims to burns, and in some cases broken limbs,' while one evocative account merits special mention as encapsulating the material and psychic loss after such devastation:

> Here a number of pigs that had been saved from the flames were herded by a group of children, there a coffin dropped on the roadway out of a wagon load of sundries that was being rapidly driven away from the burning premises of an undertaker. Another vehicle containing a small but carefully guarded coffin was apparently removing the body of a child beyond reach of the devouring element, while the usual miscellaneous supply of household goods was piled upon the streets in indescribable confusion or similarly hurled into carts to be driven away, often, there is reason to fear, beyond reach of their owners.[31]

Truly, it was a scene of incomprehensible material destruction, personal loss, and psychological trauma.

'The Heroes of St Sauveur'

But while much journalistic attention was directed to the suffering of the community, the press did not fail to lionize the 'heroes of St Sauveur.' The very day after the fire, Quebec City's *L'Électeur*, the voice of the province's moderate Liberals, included a drawing of Major Short with the subtitle 'Mort en héros, victime de son dévouement.'[32] The editorial went on to declare that 'la mort qu'ils ont trouvée en cherchant à sauver des centaines de familles est toute aussi glorieuse que celle qu'ils auraient trouvée dans la bataille.' Such sympathetic write-ups immediately drew praise from members of Quebec's anglophone population, who sent letters of thanks to the newspaper's editor. Perhaps predictably, English-language newspaper reports played up the 'courageous' acts of the 'intrepid heroes' who had perished in an effort to save the French Catholic community.[33] Indeed, from the very first reports on the fire, the Quebec, Montreal, Toronto, Ottawa, and Kingston newspapers related the two soldiers' heroic death to the courage they had displayed over the course of their military careers. Nor was the commentary limited to the pages of the newspapers. According to several Montreal correspondents, the 'sole subject of conversation on the streets to-day was the fire at Quebec, and the sad but heroic death of Major Short and Sergeant Wallick,' who were reported to have been well known in the city and were 'general favourites.'[34] Thus, the 'gallant' Major Short, along with the 'handsome young sergeant,' were rapidly elevated into the pantheon of heroes, having sacrificed their all for others.[35]

And equally predictably given the times, less attention was devoted to the man of the ranks, Staff-Sergeant Wallick. A native of Guelph, Ontario, he had been stationed in Kingston with 'B' Battery in 1885 and had taken part in the suppression of the North-West Rebellion, where he became 'famous for his bravery' while in charge of a Gatling gun at Fort Pitt. At the time of his death, the twenty-five-year-old Wallick had served in the artillery battery for seven years, was its riding master, and was purportedly to have been married the following week. Yet, paired as he was in heroic deed and tragic death with his comrade, Wallick's story was overshadowed by that of the larger-than-life Major Short.

If little is known of Wallick,[36] much was bruited abroad about 'the overshadowing loss to the Dominion in the tragic death of the ideal Canadian soldier, Major C.J. Short, of "B" Battery.'[37] In the construction of the heroic narrative, the tropes of comradeship, sacrifice, and courage were to the fore:

… the battery men unable in most instances to maintain their soldierly bearing from excess of feeling, were compelled to stand by with idle hands while the flames cracked and hissed over the remains of their officer and companion-in-arms. Together they had braved danger with unbroken front in riots and street troubles, when blood had freely flown, without a murmur; they had suffered hardships and borne the brunt of the North-West campaign against the rebels under Riel, and now it was with tear-stained faces and tottering bent frames they stood around that blazing pyre, some in speechless horror, some with lamentations upon their lips at being so near their hero and yet so helpless.[38]

Readers were soon to learn of Major Short's impressive military career: his initial admission into Quebec's School of Artillery; his award of a first-class gunnery certificate in 1874 and immediate promotion to lieutenancy; his appointment to the rank of brevet major in the militia in 1878; his entry and appointment to the command of the Quebec 'B' Battery in 1882; and his appointment as an extra ADC to the governor-general in 1888.[39] They were further informed of how Short distinguished himself in Montreal's Orange riots in 1878, and also in the Quebec stevedore riots the following year when he had been wounded.[40]

Of some significance to subsequent events, it was Short's involvement in the North-West Rebellion of 1885 that prompted particular comment, as it was there that 'his gallantry had won him great honors.'[41] In command of the eighty men of 'B' Battery, Major Short was in Colonel Otter's column sent to the relief of Battleford. Later, he distinguished himself in the attack on Poundmaker at the Battle of Cut Knife on 2 May 1885:

> Once, when some half-breeds made a desperate attempt to capture the gun, he rushed out at the head of three or four gunners and drove them back. Unfortunately, the gun carriages for the six-pounders he had with him were unserviceable … He always regretted that he did not have his own nine-pounders with him, as he would have been able to do far more execution. When withdrawing from the hill to the open prairie Major Short worked the Gatling with his own hands, while the line of riflemen formed in rear. He was an ideal artillery officer, and on his way back to Battleford did his best to cheer the wounded.[42]

The general gist of this story was reiterated in other accounts, and it was accepted by all that Major Short had 'proved himself the *beau idéal* of an officer.'[43]

But a hero has to be more than a distant ideal. To be truly effective, he must also possess qualities that ensure his powers of leadership. Certainly, his fellow officers considered him to have been 'exceptionally popular in the military circles' and, for Lieutenant-Colonel Straubenzee, 'Charlie Short was every inch a soldier. He was reliable, gallant and brave. He was the best officer in the Canadian service.' For Major Wilson of 'A' Battery, Short 'was one of the noblest men that ever lived. Ever since he entered the regulars his military career has been a brilliant succession of daring exploits … Many and many a time he braved dangers when death seemed imminent.' Further, for Captain Drury, the major was a 'gallant' and 'good-natured leader' whose 'men always felt sure of their position while he was at their head.'[44] Others emphasized Major Short's 'chivalric spirit' and 'heroism,' which he demonstrated outside of his military duties:

> [H]e was a splendid and daring horseman, an excellent boxer, and probably the best amateur actor in the Dominion, as was shown about a year ago during the production of 'Our Regiment' in the Academy, in which he took the principal part. Being a wonderful swimmer, he once saved a man who was carried away by the current, while bathing near St. Helen's Island. At another time he jumped from the Quebec boat after one of the men of his battery, who had fallen overboard and by which he almost lost his own life, while his rescue of a boy who had fallen in near Point Lévis is still fresh in the mind of the Quebec people. These, however, are only a few of the instances where he risked his life to save that of others ...[45]

Major Short's accomplishments were particularly noted in Kingston and, in consequence, his loss was most grievously felt there. No doubt, his heroic actions in a campaign of overt Canadian expansionism were less ambivalently received there, the heartland of nineteenth-century Canadianism and empire, than in Quebec City, where Riel was seen by many to be a French-Canadian victim. Also, the biographical sketch published there on the day after his death reflected on Short's military and family connections to the community and 're-minded' Kingstonians how the thirty-eight-year-old Sherbrooke-born hero of the North-West Rebellion 'was bound to Kingston by ties of the most enduring character':

> Kingston grieves to-day over no uncommon loss. The feelings of the people have been stirred deeply and sincerely. Those who witnessed the scene upon the arrival of the news from Cut Knife Creek and knew the pride felt by the citizens in Major Short's gallantry, with their pleasure at his safety, can alone realize the sadness following the tragedy ... Major Short died a martyr to an irrepressible public spirit, coupled with the dash and self-abnegation which characterize the best type of British officer. As a representative Canadian from one of its oldest families, he was also a credit to the Dominion. For five years only a resident here, he yet became one of the city's favourites. His gallant bearing, activity and geniality were irresistible. United later to one of Kingston's most loved daughters, he was held in still higher personal regard ...[46]

In 1884, Major Short had married Miss Carruthers, the daughter of a prominent Kingston merchant, Mr John Carruthers, who had contested the Kingston seat against John A. Macdonald in three elections. Mrs Short had been visiting

Kingston with her two-year-old daughter at the time of her husband's death and had planned to return to Quebec City on the 17th. On hearing the tragic news, she directed that her husband's remains be forwarded by rail to Kingston for burial.

Honouring a Hero: Quebec City

Despite these past shadows and questionable connections, Major Short was not to leave Quebec City without being honoured by a community grateful for his sacrifice on their behalf. At 11.30 a.m. on 18 May, a hot Saturday morning, Major Short's funeral cortège began its solemn and symbolic procession from the Citadel *en route* to the city's Anglican Cathedral. It was an official day of mourning, and flags were flown at half-mast at Laval University, City Hall, the Government House, Post Office, and Court House as well as on other buildings throughout the city. Many houses were draped with mourning badges while stores along the procession route were closed.

The 'immense' procession was a colourful, if sombre, array of civic and military institutions: a detachment of fifty policemen accompanied a military firing party and regimental bands; Major Short's body was conveyed on a flag-draped gun-carriage drawn by seven horses, the coffin bearing his helmet and sword, and many handsome floral tributes; and a special carriage displayed the floral offering of Her Royal Highness the Princess Louise and the Marquis of Lorne. Of course, the military were to the fore, with senior officers from an array of distinguished regiments serving as pallbearers; some 120 officers and men of the 'B' Battery of the School of Gunnery were prominent, as were others from the Queen's Own Canadian Hussars, the Royal School of Cavalry, Quebec cavalry, and artillery, rifle, and infantry regiments. An array of prominent mourners ranged from the lieutenant-governor, to senators and members of the House of Commons, the premier and Provincial Cabinet, members of the Legislative Council and Legislative Assembly, the mayors, aldermen and councillors of Quebec City, and, perhaps most importantly, the mayor, Council, and citizens of St Sauveur.[47]

The streets from the Citadel to the Anglican Cathedral were 'lined with crowds of sympathetic citizens, whose hushed and reverent demeanor showed their respect for the gallant dead.'[48] Indeed, the reverence displayed by the citizenry elicited particular comment:

Jamais encore, de mémoire d'homme, on n'avait vu pareille affluence dans les rues de notre ville à l'occasion de funérailles. Celles de Charles John Short ont pris les proportions d'une ovation populaire à laquelle toutes les classes de la société, toutes les races et en particulier toute la population canadienne-française ont tenu à s'associer.[49]

Church bells of both the Anglican cathedral and the Catholic basilica were tolled during the solemn procession. On arrival at the cathedral, only a small part of the large cortege was able to enter the building as it was already full with mourners.

Following the service, the procession re-formed and Major Short's remains were escorted to the city's wharf. There, following the firing of three customary volleys over the coffin, the body was transferred onto the *Queen*, the largest available steamer, and moved to the Grand Trunk Railway station for conveyance to Kingston.[50]

Kingston Does Its Bit

Accompanied by various delegations from Quebec and Montreal, Major Short's body reached Kingston on the morning of 19 May and was taken to 'Annandale,' the residence of Major Short's brother-in-law, Mr J.B. Carruthers. It was a Sunday and the death of Short and Wallick was the subject of several sermons that day. Rev. Carey of St Paul's declared that 'the lives of two valuable men' had been 'sacrificed in Quebec' and that 'the little municipality of St. Sauveur was mainly responsible for [their] deaths.' He also urged the Dominion government to 'take steps to ensure the safety of the lives of those men who go among the people and try to do them good at the risk of death' and said that it was 'high time the military authorities of Canada, if the lives of her best sons are to be jeopardized, should guard against the repetition of deaths such as occurred last week.' It was concluded that the 'remarks of the reverend gentleman seemed to meet with the approval of his listeners and almost everyone here now places the blame of the death of Major Short and Sergeant Wallick on the municipality of St. Sauveur.'[51] For his part, the Rev. John Mackie of St Andrew's Presbyterian Church, who was not averse to flurries of anti-Catholicism, took a different tack.[52] Speaking in Ontario Hall as, ironically, his own church had burned down a year earlier, 'he moved many in the large audience to tears' in an excess of emotive imagery in his sympathy for a 'daughter of Kingston,' Short's widow, who had been 'smitten to the dust as by a lightening flash from heaven.'[53]

At 1.00 p.m. on the following day, crowds of Kingstonians flocked to 'Annandale' at the corner of Earl and Sydenham streets where the wreath from Princess Louise and the Marquis of Lorne was prominently displayed. The military arrived and took up their positions as the streets began to teem with life, and the military forces were out in great numbers. They were drawn up on Earl Street and presented an 'imposing sight.' A brief service at the house was conducted by Revs. B.B. Smith and A.W. Cooke of St George's Cathedral. When all was hushed, the body was carried out of the house and placed tenderly on a gun-carriage. The bands of 'A' and 'B' Batteries and the 14th Battalion struck up a mournful dirge and, shortly after 2:30 p.m., 'the cortege moved toward the city of the dead.'[54]

A 130-man strong firing party, consisting of men from the 'A' Battery and cadets from the Royal Military College, 'marched with slow and measured tread, carrying their guns reversed' ahead of the coffin draped with the royal standard.[55] Led by Rev. Messrs. Smith and Cook, the procession proceeded behind the combined bands playing the Dead March from *Saul*. The gun-carriage carrying the body was drawn by six horses, with Major Short's helmet, sword, and belt arrayed on the coffin, and accompanied by his charger, 'Tom King,' with his boots reversed in the stirrups. The long column was made up of distinguished pallbearers, politicians, the military, clergymen, and professors. Then came the general public, including such dignitaries as Sir Richard Cartwright, Hon. M. Sullivan, Judge Price, Professor Marshall, as well as 'aldermen, civic officials, gentlemen of different professions and respected citizens.'[56]

This immense cortege moved slowly down Earl Street, along Bagot Street, and then up Princess Street. At the corner of Alfred and Princess streets it halted and most of the citizens and a few of the soldiers dropped out. The line of march was then resumed and 'the soldiers and quite a few citizens, to the number probably of 1000, proceeded on foot to Cataraqui cemetery, a distance of not less than four miles.' After the 'usual three rounds were fired over the deceased's grave,' the assembled throng commenced the long journey home.

In evaluating the day, it was concluded that 'it is safe to say that never before in the history of Kingston has there been such an enormous turn out to do honor to any one man.' While the memory of that momentous day may have faded, Short's heroism and devotion to duty were recorded on his grave-memorial in Kingston's Cataraqui Cemetery: a simple marble plinth supports a column evocatively cut off at the top, as if to dramatically signify an interrupted life (see figure 3.2). The inscription reads, 'In memory of Major Charles John Short A.D.C. commanding "B" Battery R.C.A. (Royal Canadian Artillery) who lost his life in the discharge of his duty at the Great Fire at St. Sauveur, 16th May 1889, age 42.'

Contested Sites of Remembrance

At the same hour, on the same day, Sergeant Wallick's remains were buried with full military honours in Quebec City's Mount Hermon cemetery, far away

3.2 Short's memorial in Kingston's Cataraqui Cemetery. Credit: Linda Cyr.

from his home in Guelph. Although 'not quite so numerously attended' as Major Short's funeral, the ceremony was essentially similar. Following a service at the Citadel at 2.00 p.m., Sergeant Wallick's body was borne on a gun-carriage drawn by six horses, preceded by the firing party, and military bands. It was followed by a car full of floral tributes, a military contingent, and a large number of people including the mayor, the premier of the province, Dominion and Provincial politicians, leading citizens, and the public at large.[57] The procession made its way along St Ursule Street to the Methodist church, where a large congregation attended the burial service conducted by four ministers of the faith. Sergeant Wallick's body was then escorted to the cemetery. A volley was fired over the open grave and the public funeral ended. In a final gesture attempting to overcome the miles separating the victim from his home and family in Ontario, several of the floral offerings were conveyed to Wallick's mother in Guelph via his stepfather, who had attended the funeral.

With the bodies committed to their respective graves and tributes accorded to their heroic lives, others turned their attention to ensuring that their memory would not be forgotten. In an age of *statuemania*,[58] the proposition of a permanent memorial was a predictable response. Indeed, the day after the tragic St Sauveur fire, the case for a monument to Major Short turned to a remarkable precedent: 'En 1866 lors du grand incendie qui dévastait le faubourg St Roch un autre militaire, un artilleur, le lieutenant Bain perdit la vie dans des circonstances analogues. Aujourd'hui sur sa tombe au cimetière Mount Hermon, on voit un monument qui lui a été élevé par la reconnaissance des citoyens de Québec.'[59] And there seemed to be some support for this idea. As early as 18 May, it was reported that the owner of the house in which Major Short had been killed intended to erect a monument on the site in memory of the two heroes.[60] Two weeks later, another report accompanying illustrations of the devastated St Sauveur focused on 'The Spot Where Major Short and Sergeant Walleck [*sic*] Were Killed':

It is to be hoped that some memorial will mark the spot where the two valiant soldiers – a commissioned and a non-commissioned officer of the most important service in our little army – gave their lives so bravely in the cause of the public safety. No heroism of the battlefield could better deserve remembrance than that which led Major Short and Sergeant Walleck [*sic*] to an early doom.[61]

But all discussions regarding the appropriate manner of commemorating the Short-Wallick sacrifice soon became confused by another issue: the Saint-Jean-Baptiste celebration.[62] Every 24 June, the annual festivities of this nationalist-cultural celebration of identity were a highlight of the Quebec calendar.

But, out of respect for the tragic events at St Sauveur, and as an expression of sympathy for the material and human losses suffered by the people there, the Société Saint-Jean-Baptiste (SSJB) initially decided to cancel the festivities.[63] The decision was immediately challenged and the organizers decided to go ahead with their special day. It was to be a particularly momentous one, as the focal point was to be the unveiling of a tribute to two of Quebec's founding fathers, the early French explorer Jacques Cartier and the Jesuit martyr Jean de Brébeuf. Ironically, subsequent events were to ensure that Short and Wallick were not to be excluded from these festivities.

According to the Toronto *Globe*, the Saint-Jean-Baptiste festivities of 1889 constituted an 'immense display of French Canadian nationality' with some twenty-five thousand attending the unveiling of the Cartier-Brébeuf monument.[64] The soon-to-be prime minister of Canada, Wilfrid Laurier, paid tribute to these heroes of Quebec's history but then turned to another theme: his imagination of a post-Confederation Canada and the 'new duties' of the old colony in the young nation.[65] To this end, Laurier attempted to persuade the predominantly French-Canadian gathering that, henceforth, the whole of Canada was their country. And, as if to drive home this point, the remainder of Laurier's speech moved away from a rear-window memorialization of Cartier and Brébeuf and, instead, highlighted the qualities of such notable Canadian figures as John A. Macdonald, his political adversary, and Edward Blake, his close friend.[66] And, to underscore his thesis, Laurier turned to the two anglophone victims of St Sauveur who had died in an attempt to save their French co-citizens:

> Major Short did not belong to our race; but he was our fellow countryman; and I would ask which one of you, French Canadians, in the midst of the still smoking ruins of your city and the presence of the dead hero, did not feel proud of being a Canadian?[67]

While it is not known to what extent Laurier's speech was responsible, certainly, the pressure for a monument to the two soldiers moved apace. The first action was taken by Major Short's brother officers, who, in April 1890, placed a brass memorial tablet in Quebec City's Anglican Cathedral of the Holy Trinity.[68] And there were other initiatives under way. On 11 March, Quebec's city council had been petitioned for a memorial and a Short-Wallick monument committee (SWMC) was formed.[69] By early October 1890, the committee had successfully accumulated over $2915.84,[70] and, on 3 October 1890, the SWMC voted on three possible sites: the 'porte de la terrasse,' also known as the 'Dufferin' or 'Durham Terrace'; 'L'Esplanade,' in front of the Garrison

Club; and the 'Rond de Chaîne,' or Place Des Armes. The outcome of this initial proposal advanced by the SWMC was the 'terrasse,' a significant tourist site overlooking the St Lawrence.[71]

The decision to erect a monument to 'St. Sauveur's heroes' on the public promenade in the heart of the old city resulted in a spontaneous uproar. At issue was the historical significance of Dufferin Terrace, or 'terrasse Frontenac' as it was popularly called, for French-Canadian identity. For many, the site of the Chateau St. Louis was a sacred place. Consider the views of the editors of *Courrier du Canada* on this matter: 'Le monument Short-Wallick est un monument destiné à commémorer un évènement tragique, mais qui n'évoque aucun souvenir lié à notre histoire et à nos traditions.'[72] Moreover, as early as 1879, the predominantly English-dominated Literary and Historical Society of Quebec had pressed for a monument in honour of Champlain: 'a discoverer, a geographer, an undaunted leader, a man of letters, a Christian gentleman, the founder and first Governor of Quebec.'[73] And the preferred site was the iconic 'terrasse Frontenac.' But while the initial proposal was not acted on, two circumstances served to bring it back to the fore. First, the approach of the fiftieth anniversary of the founding of the Saint-Jean-Baptiste Society in Quebec prompted some to think that the unveiling of a monument to Champlain would be an appropriate device for communicating their message.[74] Secondly, the upsurge of mass-public opinion to locate the Short-Wallick monument there pricked very specific ethno-nationalistic sensitivities. Simply put, the 'terrasse Frontenac' was destined to be the site of a national pantheon and was uniquely destined to accommodate, not only a monument to Champlain, but also other historical monuments that depicted the grand figures of the *pays*.[75]

While their heroism was not in dispute, the two Anglo-Canadians, Short and Wallick, did not qualify for inclusion in what was to be a pantheon of French-Canadian heroes at this sacred site. Laurier's grand oratory aside, the Short-Wallick monument lacked nation-building significance for the people of Quebec. Rather, it had more local significance for the people of St Sauveur and, thus, should be located there, the site of their courageous sacrifice. More specifically, why not L'Esplanade or, better yet, Langelier Boulevard (St Ours Street) between St Sauveur and St Roch?[76] Such was the volatility surrounding the controversy that the SWMC and SSJB met on 18 October 1890. The SSJB proposed that the Short-Wallick monument be erected on Langelier Boulevard.[77] Clearly, the growing public opposition to the siting of the Short-Wallick monument on the Terrace could not be overlooked and, in early April 1891, the SWMC submitted a written request to the minister of militia and defence for permission to erect the statue in front of the drill hall at 'Manège Militaire,' on Grande Allée Est, opposite the National Assembly.[78] Much to the relief of many, the request was granted.

While the precise location for the Short-Wallick monument had been anything but clear-cut, the selection of the design proceeded without problem. In December 1890, the SWMC decided overwhelmingly to approve a drawing submitted by Louis-Philippe Hébert, a French-Canadian artist who was living in Paris at the time.[79] Emerging at this time as the premier sculptor in post-Confederation Canada, Hébert was as politically astute as he was talented. He was prepared to serve clients of both Liberal and Conservative persuasion, and also portray the sometimes conflicting narratives of Quebec, Canada, and Empire. His dramatic renderings of prominent figures and landmark events captured the scopic imagination of the day as he contributed to the growing pantheon of 'outdoor history' in Canada's public spaces (see figure 3.3.). His representation of Major Short and Sergeant Wallick reflected this: at the base of his monument, an allegorical figure of Quebec City pays homage to the towering busts of the two heroes; in her left hand, she holds the city's emblem while in her right hand she holds a flag that drapes the shoulders of the soldiers; a plaque located at the monument reads,

> To the memory of Major Charles Short and Staff Sergt. Geo. Wallick, B Battery Regiment Artillery, who lost their lives whilst in the performance of their duty in the great fire of St. Sauveur on Thursday, 16th of May, 1889. This monument is erected by the citizens of Quebec in grateful remembrance of their noble and heroic conduct.[80]

A year after his winning plan had been submitted, Hébert's creation arrived on the Allen Line's SS *Numidian* on 6 October 1891.[81] A month later, the installation of the tribute to Short and Wallick was nearly complete. According to one reporter, the bronze was superb while the bust of Major Short was a 'perfect resemblance' and revived his essential energy and courage.[82] With the inauguration date set for Thanksgiving Day, 12 November 1891, the event was widely advertised as an opportunity for all of Quebec's citizens to show their gratitude to the 'heroic victims.'[83]

Despite cold weather and drizzling rain, which 'marred the beauty of the display,' the unveiling ceremony of the twelve-foot-high structure in front of the drill hall on Grande Allée drew an 'enormous' crowd.[84] The ceremony commenced at 2:30 p.m. with detachments of the Montreal Garrison Artillery, Quebec 'B' Battery, Royal School of Cavalry, 8th and 9th Battalions, and the Queen's Own Hussars arrayed around the monument, which was covered with the Union Jack.[85] The immediate space surrounding the draped sculpture was,

PROFIL DU MONUMENT SHORT-WALLICK

D'après une esquisse de M. P. Hébert, sculpteur canadien à Paris

3.3 Louis-Philippe Hébert's Proposed Short-Wallick Monument. *L'Électeur*, 13 December 1890.

however, reserved for religious and military figures along with members of the SWMC and prominent civilians. Mayor Frémont addressed the large crowd in French and English and delivered a dramatic and emotional account of how Short and Wallick were victims to their own devotion to their fellow citizens.[86] At 3:00 p.m., the monument was unveiled, the honour guard presented arms, military bands played the 'Old Hundred,' and 'magnificent flower wreaths' were laid by senior officers.[87] The ceremony was closed by a speech from Quebec's Premier Mercier who related the bravery of Short and Wallick to highlight Canadian unity and commented on the emotive power of the tribute that transcended a mere bronze sculpture:

> Listen! What does it say? ... [I]t recalls two Englishmen sacrificing their young, vigorous and promising lives to rescue a French section of this city from the ravages of a disastrous fire, it suffices to read on the pedestal the name of a French-Canadian sculptor, who modeled it in the heart of France, in the ancient metropolis of this colony, conquered from it by English arms ... As long as it stands here, this monument will say to us: You are all brothers: you are all children of one and the same country! Forget the dissensions and conflicts of the past! Be united and have only one rivalry – to see who will do the most honour to the Canadian name and be the readiest, if ever reason requires, to die for the good of the flag and the country![88]

While Mercier's 'eloquent speech' was delivered in English, his message, nonetheless, resonated throughout the city. Indeed, the report observed that neither English nor French spectators could keep their hands in their pockets during the premier's eloquent appeal for the flag flying over the Citadel and for the union between the peoples.

Despite the euphoria of the unveiling of the Short-Wallick monument, and even though it was regarded as 'one of the most beautiful ornaments' of Quebec City,[89] the dispute over its siting continued. Initially, the Manège Militaire site had appeared to be unproblematic and acceptable to all: but, enter the sculptor! In June 1892, Hébert expressed disappointment over the location of his creation. He wanted his 'small monument' to be relocated to a more aesthetically appropriate site.[90] However, the matter soon moved beyond aesthetics. Hébert's interventions served to reinvigorate, yet again, French nationalist opposition to the siting of the Short-Wallick monument. On 1 March 1893, a petition for its removal was sent to the SWMC. Citing Hébert's critique, the petition suggested that the transfer of the monument to a more appropriate place would allow it to become an 'ornament for the city' while better serving its purpose in perpetuating the memory of the two soldiers. The true reasoning behind the petition, however, was clear: the Short-Wallick monument was located on part of the Plains of Abraham, a site which should be reserved solely for historical markers of French-Canadian history.[91]

On 25 May, it was reported that the increasingly problematic Short-Wallick monument was to be relocated from Grande Allée to the actual location in St Sauveur where the two soldiers had died. Responding to the considerable public reaction to this news, it was argued that the decision was based upon requests made by committee members, citizens, and the artist himself.[92] Further, the petitioners, a large number of whom had originally subscribed to the monument's construction, would cover all of the transportation costs. However, the monument was not moved.[93] It was allowed to remain in its original, if continually contentious, location on the grounds of the drill hall, close to the Grande Allée.

A Final Resting Place

For close to a century, the heroes of the St Sauveur fire were honoured at several commemorative sites. Short's grave in Kingston's Cataraqui Cemetery and Wallick's in Quebec City's Mount Hermon were splendid testimonies to their courageous self-sacrifice. Their dual monument, crafted by the *doyen* of nineteenth-century monumental portrait sculpture, Louis-Philippe Hébert, graced a prominent public space in the grounds adjacent to Quebec's National Assembly. To be sure, perhaps as befitting an officer, Major Short was the beneficiary of even more attention: a plaque had been installed in Quebec City's Anglican Cathedral of the Holy Trinity; and, on 'Gunner's Day,' 25 Saturday 1985, a replica of that plaque was installed with due ceremony on the wall of the Officers' Mess at Fort Frontenac, Kingston, donated by members of the Royal Regiment of Canadian Artillery and members of the Short and Carruthers families.[94]

As for the grand Short-Wallick monument, it aged gracefully over the years as its two heroes, bonded in bronze, gazed down over the city they had served so well. But, apparently, not all of the good citizens of that city looked back with approval. According to a City of Quebec report of the late 1980s, a proposal for its removal to St Sauveur had been presented by members of the city council in 1950.[95] Although the resolution had been approved, the project was abandoned on 24 April 1951 because of public opposition and the expense involved. Accordingly, the provocative monument with its Anglo-Canadian-Imperial connotations survived through the ensuing years of the 'Quiet Revolution.' Indeed, it appears that it had been cleaned in 1965–6 at a cost of $995. Five years later, it attracted the attention of a brief newspaper report which argued cogently that while the names Short and Wallick would not be recognized by the majority of Québécois, their monument was one of many important components of Quebec's 'petite histoire.'[96] By the late 1980s, however, the inventory report on the monument's condition said it all: it was covered with sulphate; the inscription on the plaque was faded; and the screws holding the plaque were rusted. Action was taken and the plaque was replaced in either 1987 or 1988. Thus, partly refurbished, the Short-Wallick monument stood guard over the Grande Allée into the 1990s, and then, in 1999, it disappeared![97]

But this gratuitous act of cultural lobotomy did not go unnoticed. In August 2002, an article in the Kingston *Whig Standard* posed the question, 'Where is Maj. Charles Short?' Soon, Liz Barrett and her daughter, Blythe Cronyn, descendants of Major Short, answered the question: the monument to Short-Wallick was no longer in its original place outside the drill hall on Grande Allée; it had been cut up in pieces behind the federal armoury (see figure 3.4). Distressed at her find, Liz Barrett declared, 'Why would they put it in a place like that? If they don't want it, then I'm sure Kingston would want it.'[98] Assurances were soon coming from Jacques MacKay, assistant curator of the regimental museum of Les Voltigeurs de Québec: 'These are heroes of Quebec' and 'We don't want anyone to think we don't honour our heroes.'[99] Certainly, this perspective was affirmed by no less a figure than Lieutenant-General Roméo Dallaire, of Rwanda fame. Another Canadian hero, and a 'Gunner' to boot, his intervention was commanding: 'The statue ... will be put back. It had better go back up, all cleaned up and back in shape.'[100] And it was. On 1 June 2002, in a splendid ceremony of pomp and circumstance, proud descendants of Major Short witnessed the unveiling and rededication of the monument to the heroes of the St Sauveur fire of 16 May 1889 (see figure 3.5).[101]

So, Short and Wallick are back in the Place George V, albeit displaced from the original position fronting onto Grande Allée. But why was this 'fameux monument,' this 'superbe sculpture,' ever moved?[102] The bureaucratic answer was clear: it had been a decision of the committee charged with organizing the festivities associated with the celebration of the Millennium in 2000: they needed the space for flower beds. But was there something else afoot? Are there echoes of the nationalist protests of the 1890s still in the air? There is no doubt that the very active Commission de la capitale nationale du Québec was actively furthering the 'national' memory-project in this, the centre of French-Canadian culture, and especially with the approach of 2008, the four hundredth anniversary of the founding of that culture.[103] Perhaps, yet again, there were concerns that Short and Wallick, heroes and defenders of Quebecers though they may have been, were not part of that cultural history. Indeed, once again, they may have been seen by some to have been irritating interlopers on *la terre sacrée* of the Plains of Abraham and *la capitale de la nation*, that is, as heroes not *of our race*. What is sure, however, is that the restoration of the Short-Wallick monument to its place of honour serves to demonstrate, yet again, the dynamic role of heroes in identity formation.

Conclusion

Clearly, in the final analysis, the critical issues are, how and why was the heroic

Ian MacAlpine/The Whig-Standard

3.4 Dismantled monument: 'The statue honouring Maj. Charles Short and Staff-Sgt. George Wallick is in pieces for now.' Kingston *Whig-Standard*, 5 August 2000.

3.5 Restored monument. Credit: Matthew Hatvany.

sacrifice of the Short-Wallick duo perceived at the time and then remembered and manipulated later? A recent exploration of two millennia of heroes and heroism in the Western world posed the question: 'What is a hero?' After an evaluation of heroes and heroic behaviour 'in every age and in all kinds of places,' the conclusion was that the 'chief criterion is the verdict of the public' and that this has often been 'arbitrary, eccentric and often irrational.'[104] But this is too simple and perhaps cynical. According to the doyen of the study of heroes, Joseph Campbell, a hero 'is someone who has given his or her life to something bigger than oneself.'[105] At issue in understanding the past and present constructions of the Short-Wallick case-study is determining what prompted their sacrifice: a personal sense of valour? a sense of duty? a civic sense of responsibility to their community? If these are accepted, it might be argued that the Short-Wallick monument, if seen by some as an interloper in a sacred Quebec ethno-nationalist space, certainly stands as a reminder of the values central to a civic-liberal society. Anglophone heroes from Ontario though they may have been, Major Short and Staff-Sergeant Wallick sacrificed their lives for their co-citizens and merit recognition as members of the pantheons of both Quebec and Canada.

NOTES

1 For more on this see Brian S. Osborne, 'Landscapes, Memory, Monuments, and Commemoration: Putting Identity in Its Place,' *Canadian Ethnic Studies* 33, 3 (2001): 39–77, and 'From Patriotic Pines to Diasporic Geese: Emplacing Culture, Setting Our Sights, Locating Identity in a Transnational Canada,' *Canadian Journal of Communications* 31 (2006): 147–75. See also Samuel Levinson, *Written in Stone: Public Monuments in Changing Societies* (Durham, NC, and London: Duke University Press, 1998); John Gillis, ed., *Commemorations: The Politics of National Identity* (Princeton: Princeton University Press, 1994); Sergiusz Michalski, *Public Monuments: Art in Political Bondage* (London: Reaktion Books, 1998); Anthony Smith, *Chosen People: Sacred Sources of National Identity* (Oxford: Oxford University Press, 2003).

2 Anthony Smith, *Myths and Memories of the Nation* (Oxford: Oxford University Press, 1999), 64–5.

3 Colin Coates and Cecilia Morgan, *Heroines and History: Representations of Madeleine de Verchères and Laura Secord* (Toronto: University of Toronto Press, 2002), 4–5.

4 Robert Bevan, *The Destruction of Memory: Architecture at War* (London: Reaktion Books, 2006), 211.

5 Jay Winter, *Remembering War: The Great War between Memory and History in the Twentieth Century* (New Haven: Yale University Press, 2006), 5.

6 Katherine Verdery, *The Political Lives of Dead Bodies: Reburial and Postsocialist Change* (New York: Columbia University Press, 1999), 5.

7 Smith, *Chosen Peoples*, vii-viii.

8 Alan McNairn, *Behold the Hero: General Wolfe and the Arts in the Eighteenth Century* (Montreal and Kingston: McGill-Queen's University Press, 1997), vii.

9 Ottawa *Daily Citizen*, 17 May 1889.

10 Toronto *Globe*, 17 May 1889.

11 Montreal *Daily Star*, 16 May 1889.

12 Ottawa *Evening Journal*, 17 May 1889. A week later, St Sauveur council members met to discuss their deficient water supply; a year later, the village was annexed to Quebec City.

13 Quebec *L'Électeur*, 16 May 1889.

14 Montreal *Daily Star*, 16 May 1889.

15 Montreal *Gazette*, 17 May 1889.

16 Montreal *Gazette*; Ottawa *Daily Citizen*; Toronto *Globe*, 18 May 1889.

17 Ottawa *Daily Citizen*, 18 May 1889.

18 Quebec *L'Électeur*, 16 May 1889.

19 Ottawa *Daily Citizen*, 18 May 1889.

20 Toronto *Globe*, 18 May 1889.

21 Montreal *Gazette*, 17 May 1889.

22 Toronto *Daily Mail*, 17 May 1889.

23 Montreal *Daily Star*, 16 May 1889.

24 Montreal *Gazette*; Toronto *Globe*; Quebec *L'Électeur*, 17 May, 22 May 1889. Less than half of the estimate was covered by insurance because of 'prohibitive insurance rates' and the municipality's 'labouring class' majority (Ottawa *Evening Journal,* 17 May 1889). The conflagration of St Sauveur added to a list of fires that devastated substantial portions of the city and its surroundings over the course of the nineteenth century: 1845; 1846; 1865; 1866; 1870; 1872; 1876; 1881; 1889 (Quebec *L'Électeur*, 22 May 1889).

25 Quebec *L'Électeur*, 22 May 1889.

26 Toronto *Globe*; Montreal *Gazette*, 17 May 1889.

27 Ottawa *Evening Journal*; Toronto *Daily Mail*, 17 May 1889.

28 Ottawa *Daily Citizen*, 17; Toronto *Daily Mail*, 23 May 1889.

29 Toronto *Daily Mail*, 18 May 1889.

30 Ibid.

31 Toronto *Globe*, 17 May 1889.

32 Quebec *L'Électeur*, 17 May 1889.

33 There were only four Protestant families living in St Sauveur (Quebec *L'Électeur*, 22 May 1889).

34 Toronto *Daily Mail*; Toronto *Globe*, 18 May 1889.

35 Ottawa *Evening Journal*, 17 May 1889.

36 For more on Wallick, see Jason F. Kovacs and Brian S. Osborne, 'A Fire in Quebec City, a Burning Question for Guelph: Who Was George Wallick, the Hero of St. Sauveur?,' *Historic Guelph: The Royal City* 48 (2009): 39–49.

37 Ottawa *Daily Citizen*, 18 May 1889.

38 Montreal *Gazette*; Ottawa *Daily Citizen*, 18 May 1889.

39 Montreal *Gazette*; Ottawa *Daily Citizen*, 17 May 1889.

40 Kingston *Daily Whig*, 16 May 1889.

41 Ottawa *Evening Journal*; Toronto *Daily Mail*; *Globe*; Quebec *L'Électeur*, 17 May 1889.

42 Toronto *Daily Mail*, 17 May 1889.

43 Kingston *Daily Whig*, 16 May 1889.

44 Ottawa *Daily Citizen*, 18 May 1889.

45 Montreal *Daily Star*, 16 May 1889.

46 Kingston *Daily Whig*, 17 May 1889. Reprinted in Toronto *Daily Mail*, 17 May 1889; Ottawa *Daily Citizen*, 18 May 1889.

47 Montreal *Gazette*; Toronto *Globe*, 20 May 1889.

48 Montreal *Gazette*, 20 May 1889.

49 Quebec *L'Électeur*, 20 May 1889.

50 Toronto *Globe*, 20 May 1889.

51 Kingston *British Whig*, 20 May 1889; Montreal *Gazette*, 21 May 1889.

52 Brian S. Osborne, *The Rock and the Sword: A History of St. Andrew's Presbyterian Church, Kingston* (Kingston: Heinrich Heine Press, 2004), 304–7.

53 Kingston *British Whig*, 20 May 1889.

54 Toronto *Daily Mail*, 21 May 1889.

55 Kingston *Daily Whig*, 20 May 1889.

56 Montreal *Gazette*, 21 May 1889.

57 Toronto *Daily Mail*, 21 May 1889.

58 Maurice Algulhon, 'La "statuomanie" et l'histoire,' *Ethnologie française* 8 (1978): 145–72.

59 Quebec *L'Électeur*, 17 May 1889.

60 Quebec *L'Électeur*, 18 May 1889.

61 *Dominion Illustrated*, 1 June 1890.

62 Founded in 1834 by journalist Ludger Duvernay, the Saint-Jean-Baptiste Society was a French-Canadian patriotic association concerned with stimulating a nationalist spirit and nurturing cultural and linguistic heritage. See Richard Jones, 'St-Jean-Baptiste Society,' *The Canadian Encyclopedia*, 2nd edition (Edmonton: Hurtig, 1988), 3:1913.

63 Quebec *L'Électeur*, 21 May 1889.

64 Despite its official hyphenated title, the monument was more often than not

referred to simply as the 'Cartier monument' in contemporary newspaper articles. It was erected adjacent to the St-Charles River near Lairet stream in what was then St Charles village.

65 The 28 June 1889 edition of *L'Électeur* included a transcription of Laurier's speech and judged the speech to be both 'eloquent' and 'admirable.'

66 U. Barthe, *1871–1890. Wilfrid Laurier on the platform. Collection of the principal speeches made in Parliament or before the people by the Hon. Wilfrid Laurier, P.C., Q.C., M.P., Member for Quebec East in the Commons, since his entry into active politics in 1871* (Quebec: Turcotte and Menard's Steam Printing Office, 1890), 529.

67 Ibid., 530–1.

68 *Dominion Illustrated*, 26 April 1890.

69 Mayor Fremont was the president, John C. Moore the treasurer, and Geo. R. White and Ernest Pacaud the secretaries. The committee was also symbolically composed of other prominent figures including the dean of Quebec and the prime minister.

70 Quebec *L'Événement*, 3 October 1890.

71 This was thought to be the most advantageous spot for the monument since it would be more accessible to tourists (Quebec *L'Événement*, 4 October 1890).

72 Quebec *Courrier du Canada*, 7 October 1890.

73 *Transactions of the Literary and Historical Society of Quebec, 1879–80*, quoted in Ronald Rudin, *Founding Fathers: The Celebration of Champlain and Laval in the Streets of Quebec, 1878–1908* (Toronto: University of Toronto Press, 2003), 59–60.

74 Ibid., 60.

75 Quebec *L'Événement*, 8 October 1890.

76 Quebec *Courrier du Canada*, 7 October 1890.

77 The meeting took place in St Sauveur at Saint-Pierre hall. In demonstration against the SWMC plan, St Sauveur's musical corps, Union Lambillotte, played in front of the hall. Quebec *Courrier du Canada*, 18 October 1890.

78 Quebec *L'Événement*, 6 April 1891; Quebec *Courrier du Canada*, 7 April 1891.

79 Michael Champagne, 'Hébert, Louise-Phillippe,' *The Canadian Encyclopedia*, 2:975. See also Daniel Drovin et al., *Louis-Philippe Hébert* (Quebec: Musée du Québec, 2001).

80 Quebec *L'Événement*, 3 December 1890. Although bruited as a 'superior conception,' Hébert's design was critiqued by E.E. Taché, who commented on the posture of the allegorical figure: 'elle comporte surtout un trop grand effort, peu en harmonie avec le reste du corps.' In his opinion a calmer allegorical figure constructed in the traditions of 'statuaire antique' was more in line with the monument's purpose (Quebec *L'Électeur*, 13 December 1890).

81 Quebec *L'Événement*; Quebec *Courrier du Canada*, 8 October 1891.

82 Quebec *L'Événement*, 6 November 1891.

83 Quebec *Canadien*; Quebec *L'Électeur*, 10 November 1891. A list of those who contributed to the monument fund of $3905 was given in the 12 November 1891 edition of *L'Électeur*. It also provides a summary of the expenses of the project: bronze $3000; stone pedestal $850; miscellaneous $200; total $4050.

84 Toronto *Globe*; Quebec *Canadien*, 13 November 1891.

85 Toronto *Globe*, 13 November 1891.

86 Quebec *Canadien*, 13 November 1891.

87 Montreal *Gazette*; Toronto *Globe*, 13 November 1891.

88 Quebec *L'Électeur*, 14 November 1891.

89 Quebec *L'Électeur*, 13 November 1891.

90 Quebec *Courrier du Canada*, 13 June 1892.

91 Quebec *L'Événement*, 1 March 1893.

92 Quebec *L'Électeur*, 26 May 1893.

93 According to the 26 May 1893 edition of *L'Électeur*, a petition was to be submitted to city council by some citizens. An 1896 city-guide map has the monument still standing in front of the drill hall.

94 Kingston *Whig-Standard*, 29 May 1985.

95 'Report on the Short-Wallick Monument,' City of Quebec (n.d., late 1980s). Quebec City Archives.

96 Quebec *Soleil*, 13 October 1971.

97 Quebec *Soleil*, 6 June 2001, 'Le retour du monument manquant.'

98 Kingston *Whig-Standard*, 5 August 2000.

99 Ibid.

100 Ibid.

101 Kingston *Whig-Standard*, 3 June 2002.

102 Quebec *Soleil*, 6 June 2001.

103 See 'Les monuments,' on the CCNQ website,

104 Paul Johnson, *Heroes: From Alexander the Great and Julius Caesar to Churchill and De Gaulle* (New York: HarperCollins, 2007), xvii.

105 Quoted in Bruce Meyer, *Heroes: The Champions of Our Literary Imagination* (Toronto: HarperCollins, 2007), 19.

4 Dugua vs Champlain: The Construction of Heroes in Atlantic Canada, 1904–2004

RONALD RUDIN

During the summers of 1904 and 2004, celebrations were held to mark the first effort to establish a permanent French settlement in North America. In 1604, an expedition of seventy-nine men made its way across the Atlantic, ultimately choosing Île Ste-Croix, an island that sits on the current border between New Brunswick and Maine, to establish itself. As it turned out, this would be the only winter that the Frenchmen would spend on the island. Roughly half would die, and the survivors would move on in the following spring to re-establish their settlement on the other side of the Bay of Fundy, creating Port-Royal (near present-day Annapolis Royal, Nova Scotia).

Even though the tercentenary and quadricentenary celebrations were largely conceived to mark the same events from the early seventeenth century, they were constructed in ways that differed from one another in almost every conceivable regard. The events of 1904 were managed from beginning to end by English-speaking leaders of Atlantic Canada, who had little interest in hearing the voices of either the Acadians, the French settlers in this part of the world, or the Passamaquoddy, the First Nations people who greeted the French upon their arrival at Île Ste-Croix. By contrast, the fêtes of 2004 focused upon the initial dialogue between these two people, whose voices were easily audible.[1]

Closely related to the issue of which voices could be heard on each occasion, there were also some significant differences between the two celebrations in terms of how the two leading figures from the expedition to Île Ste-Croix, Pierre Dugua de Mons and Samuel de Champlain, were presented to the public. In 1604, the former, a Huguenot, was the leader in his capacity as lieutenant-general 'of the coasts, lands and confines of Acadia, Canada, and other places in New France.'[2] As for Champlain, who as a cartographer was a fairly humble member of Dugua's entourage, his presence might well have been forgotten altogether had he not emerged as a French Catholic hero owing to his founding of Quebec City later in the decade and had he not left behind detailed accounts of his adventures.[3]

In terms of the commemorative politics that shaped both the tercentenary and quadricentenary celebrations, the actual roles played by these two men in the seventeenth century were less significant than the context that existed on each occasion. As numerous studies have persuasively shown, heroes are made, not found.[4] An individual deemed heroic at any one point in time may be deemed less heroic or heroic for an entirely different set of reasons at another moment. The deeds (imagined or real) of the candidate for heroic treatment may shape or constrain the story that can be told. Nevertheless, the key element in the construction of a hero is the context, which encourages people to invest the energy to promote the candidate's cause and largely determines which elements of his (or her) life are worth emphasizing. As we will see in terms of Dugua and Champlain, their shifting fortunes as heroes from the expedition of 1604 reflected various changes over the course of the twentieth century, most notably the shifting balance of power between English- and French-speakers in Atlantic Canada. Moreover, the dramatically different means used to present the heroes to the larger population reflected significant changes in terms of the relationship of the public with the past.

Mr Longley's Party

Although the events celebrated in 1904 had been the work of Frenchmen, the individuals who organized the celebrations, nearly all of those who participated in them, and probably most of those who attended were English-speaking Protestants. Acadians, the French Catholic inhabitants of the Atlantic provinces, did not live particularly close to the sites in Nova Scotia and New Brunswick where festivities would be held. Although they could trace their existence, in a sense, to the events of 1604, they now lived in other parts of the region, particularly in eastern and northwestern New Brunswick, as a result of their deportation in the 1750s. From this perspective, it was perhaps understandable that Acadians might have been marginal players in the celebrations of 1904, which were orchestrated by English-speakers from the various 'lieux de mémoire' (sites of memory).[5] Nevertheless, the almost complete absence of Acadians from these events remains striking given that they occurred in the midst of a period of revival in Acadian fortunes which saw a significant increase in the French-speaking population of the Maritime provinces. [6] While the economic and political power of Acadians remained limited, the late nineteenth century had seen the emergence of a national organization to advance their interests; along the way Acadian leaders selected unique flags, anthems, and holidays, all of which served to distinguish them from the much more numerous French-speakers of Quebec.

In spite of this cultural renaissance, control over the tercentenary events remained firmly in the hands of English-speakers, led by J.W. Longley, the attorney-general of Nova Scotia. Given that the expedition three hundred years earlier had had nothing to do with the territory that would later become Nova Scotia, Longley's involvement with the affair requires some explanation. A member of an old Nova Scotia family, he was born not far from Port-Royal, in Annapolis County, which he had represented in the Nova Scotia Assembly since 1882.[7] He wanted to mark the anniversary of the establishment of Port-Royal that had occurred in 1605, and might have logically waited until 1905 to celebrate the event. However, he saw an opportunity to piggyback on the anniversaries that could more logically be marked in 1904, and so he chose to link the Port-Royal anniversary with celebrations on the other side of the Bay of Fundy, to create one intricately choreographed celebration.

As president of the Nova Scotia Historical Society, Longley worked closely with his counterparts in both New Brunswick and Maine to construct a series of connected events that would begin in Annapolis Royal before moving on to Saint John, New Brunswick and then sites in both New Brunswick and Maine that were close to Île Ste-Croix. In a sense, this commemorative journey replicated the route taken by Dugua and Champlain three hundred years earlier. On that occasion, the expedition sailed along the south shore of what would become Nova Scotia, before entering the 'Baie française' (later Bay of Fundy), soon exploring the site where the settlement of Port-Royal would be established in the following year. In 1604, however, the Frenchmen kept sailing, ultimately entering, on 24 June, the mouth of a river that flowed into the bay and which was named by Champlain the 'Rivière St-Jean' in honour of St John the Baptist on his feast day. It would be some time before Saint John would be established here, but Champlain's role in christening the river justified the inclusion of New Brunswick's largest city on the tercentenary itinerary. Dugua and his crew continued west until they found an island not far from the mouth of yet another river, establishing what turned out to be the short-lived settlement on Île Ste-Croix.

Longley's concrete involvement with the tercentenary began in 1902 when, following some preliminary discussions among community leaders, he was appointed to a committee of the Nova Scotia Historical Society which was given responsibility for mounting a celebration at Annapolis Royal.[8] It soon became clear, however, that it was really Longley alone who was in charge and that he had a larger vision of the celebrations, given that the landing at Port-Royal was 'with the exception of the landing at St Augustine, the first by

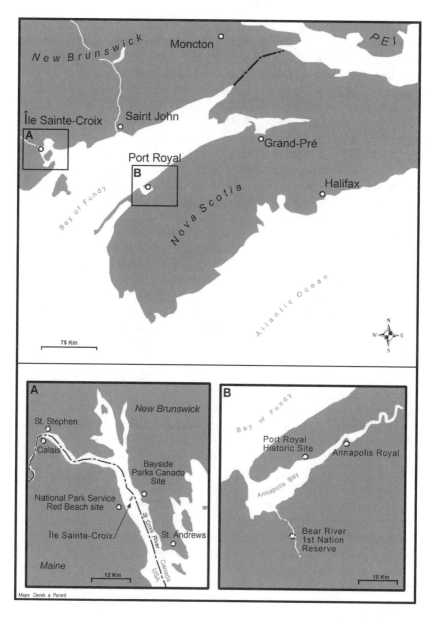

4.1 Sites of Acadian beginnings.

Europeans on the soil of North America resulting in a permanent settlement.' In making such a claim, Longley was conveniently ignoring the fact that the Île Ste-Croix settlement had predated the one at Port-Royal. The point might have been made that the former settlement had only survived for a single winter, but in fact Port-Royal fared little better. Faced with financial difficulties, Dugua lost his claim on New France in 1607, with the result that he brought most of the residents of Port-Royal back home. So that there should be no doubt that this was a short-lived colony, it was burned down by the English in 1613.[9]

These considerations aside, Longley observed that 'a mere local celebration [of the founding of Port-Royal] could easily have been arranged but the circumstances seemed of such moment as to justify an international celebration which would involve a demonstration of a some what [sic] imposing character.'[10] True to his vision for the two-day fête scheduled for June 1904, every conceivable public figure in Canada was invited, as well as the presidents of both France and the United States, and representatives of historical societies and universities from across North America.[11] Recognizing the extent of Longley's dreams, the governor-general, Lord Minto, confided to Sir Archibald Douglas, the commander of the British navy in North American waters, 'Longley asked the King and the President of the French Republic to come in person! – he may for all I know have invited the Sultan and all the crowned heads of Europe.' Minto clearly did not want to attend the events in Annapolis Royal, but felt some obligation because 'Longley is so enthusiastic about it I do not like disappointing him.' In the end, however, Minto did not attend, his sense of obligation to Longley outweighed by the fact that 'it is an enormous distance for me to go for a short ceremony and might make it difficult for me to get out of other things that would at once be proposed at St. John and elsewhere – I hardly think under the circumstances that I need go.'[12]

Minto's unwillingness to participate was matched by that of the elected officials in Ottawa. Neither Sir Wilfrid Laurier nor any cabinet minister made the trip east, claiming that they were too busy because Parliament was in session.[13] Of course, the prime minister and his colleagues could have found the time, had they wanted to. After all, representatives from France and the United States did manage to attend. While Laurier's cryptic response to Longley, claiming that he was too busy, is not particularly revealing, one has to wonder if the prime minister was not staying clear of a commemorative celebration that, as we shall see, was dominated by English-speakers such as Longley and which might have been viewed with a jaundiced eye in Quebec, where Laurier had to deal with a growing chorus of *nationaliste* opponents. Indeed, in 1908, he would do everything he could to discourage the organizers of the tercentenary in Quebec City, recognizing that someone would be inevitably alienated by reference to the past. In the end, he could not avoid the Quebec Tercentenary, although he limited his participation as much as possible. However, Annapolis Royal was far enough away that he could remain comfortably in Ottawa, delegating the local MP to represent his government.

While Longley had difficulties in delivering all the dignitaries whom he had worked so hard to attract, he did manage to line up both representatives from the United States and France, plus a commitment from those two nations, as well as England, to send military vessels to mark the occasion. Longley also brought ten thousand spectators into a town with barely more than one thousand permanent residents. This was no small achievement, given Longley's preference for events that were 'intellectual rather than spectacular.'[14] Over the course of the two-day celebration, there were numerous speeches, a visit to the site where Port-Royal had stood, and the laying of the cornerstone for a monument to Dugua, which would be completed later in the year on the grounds of Fort Anne.

In a sense, the closing of the festivities with this tribute to Dugua was appropriate, since this event had been unambiguously billed as his tercentenary, giving Champlain scant attention. In this regard, it was significant that Dugua had been a Protestant, and Champlain a Catholic, who had already achieved heroic status in Quebec. The marginalization of Champlain was strikingly evident in the speech, at the opening of the affair, by the lieutenant-governor of Nova Scotia, A.G. Jones, who placed Dugua in the company of 'other illustrious men' such as Columbus, Cabot, Cortes, and Pizzaro, not giving Champlain as much as a mention in passing. Champlain did not necessarily deserve special mention in the context of the establishment of Port-Royal, since he had been no more than a humble member of Dugua's crew. However, if Jones were prepared to recognize the larger contributions to the European occupation of North America of those such as Columbus and Cabot, one has to wonder why he could not mention any of the leading French Catholic figures such as Cartier or, closer to home, Champlain.

Invoking Champlain's name in 1904 was complicated by the heroic status that he had already achieved in Quebec, among English- and French-speakers alike. In 1898, a monument in honour of Champlain had been unveiled with great ceremony in Quebec City. While French-speakers tended to see him in rather exclusive terms, as someone who had helped build a French Catholic society, even English-speakers participated in celebrating the deeds of someone who had been the first governor of what would become Canada. In this regard, the governor-general of the day, Lord Aberdeen, unveiled the monument to someone who had been the first to occupy his office. At the time of the

4.2 Monument to Pierre Dugua, Annapolis Royal, Nova Scotia. Université de Moncton, Centre d'études acadiennes Anselme-Chiasson, Collection de photographies, PB1–215(a).

Annapolis Royal tercentenary, there were further movements afoot in Quebec to mark the tercentenary of the founding of that city, which would be held in 1908. As in 1898, there may have been differences in precisely how French- and English-speakers viewed Champlain, but both accorded him a central role in the building of Canada.

By contrast, there was little evidence that the leaders involved in organizing the Annapolis Royal events were interested in viewing Champlain as a founder of the larger Canadian nation. Given Champlain's status in Quebec, to have done so would have been an admission that Canada had been constituted by two founding nations. Instead, Longley's own writings indicate that he was more comfortable with advocating closer ties between Canada and the United States. Unlike some of his contemporaries, Longley indicated no sympathy with the integration of Canada into an Imperial Federation, and was publicly in favour of reciprocity with the United States, or even a fuller integration of the two countries to create a Commercial Union.[15] As to whether there should be some sort of political union with the Americans, Longley was evasive, observing at one point that it deserved a 'fair discussion.' Nevertheless, he had sympathy for the views of Goldwin Smith that much could be gained through 'a union of English-speaking people on this continent,' apparently writing French-speakers out of the equation.[16]

Given this view of Canada, it was little surprise that Champlain had a hard time competing for attention with Dugua, who as a Huguenot was a much more comforting figure who did not conjure up visions of a bicultural nation. Accordingly, in his own speech at Annapolis Royal, Longley ignored Champlain and referred to Dugua in terms that side-stepped the religious divisions within his crew which were embodied by the presence of noteworthy Protestant and Catholic leaders: 'The expedition headed by De Monts ... was sent out under the authority of a French king, it was commanded by a Frenchman and was composed of French colonists.' By secularizing Dugua and his colleagues, Longley avoided reference to divisions that might have been seen as presaging the creation of a country with two religious traditions that reflected, to a certain degree, the presence of two linguistic groupings.[17]

The English-speaking orators at Annapolis Royal showed little interest in viewing the 1605 expedition as anticipating the duality that would later form part of Canadian life. Nevertheless, the *Halifax Herald* made precisely this point, observing that while 'this earliest colonizing expedition was entirely French, there were in it both Catholics and Huguenots, accompanied by Catholic priests and Protestant ministers – a happy augury of the religious freedom and good will that was to prevail on this continent.' In the spirit of duality, the newspaper went on to warn that 'so much attention is likely to be paid to the leader that all others are in danger of being forgotten. Champlain, of course, must be equally honoured with De Monts.'[18]

However obvious this may have appeared to the *Herald*, it remained for the two French Canadians on the program to make that point in public. While no other province had an official delegate at Annapolis Royal, Adélard Turgeon, the Quebec minister of colonization, was delegated as its representative. Turgeon was an orator of note, and in 1908 would be asked by Laurier to speak on his behalf at one of the major public events of the Quebec Tercentenary. Even on this occasion, there was some ambiguity as to Turgeon's precise role, since Longley described him as both representing Quebec and 'in the absence of Sir Wilfrid Laurier ... speak[ing] in the name of the French population of Canada.'[19] Addressing the crowd mostly in French (so that Longley recorded none of his remarks in the 'official' account of the festivities), Turgeon remarked that he stood with those who had 'seen in the maintenance of the French element a token of greatness, of progress and even of security for our Confederation ... National dualism is not a bar to the growth of a young nation.'[20] Laurier could have said the same words had he chosen to attend, but probably recognized the risk of presenting a message that might not have been universally embraced.

The other speaker from Quebec was Charles Langelier, the sheriff of Quebec City, who was on hand to represent the Institut Canadien, a literary organization in the *vieille capitale*. Langelier, like Turgeon, would occupy a key role in the Quebec Tercentenary, playing the part of Champlain in the massive pageants that were staged on the Plains of Abraham. On this occasion, however, he stood out from the other speakers by giving Dugua a religion: 'Although De Monts was a Calvinist he brought with him Catholic priests and Protestant clergymen, showing thus that his colony was open to all, what[ever] may be their religious beliefs. Yes I proclaim it to be the honour of Nova Scotia, your Province has always shown a great religious tolerance. We have never seen among you those religious conflicts which have caused such crises in other Provinces, and which have caused dissension to endanger our national progress ... You have well understood ... that the diversity of worship is not a necessary cause of weakness of national sentiments ... If the celebration of today was only to remind us of those things, it would be sufficient to greet it with joy as a national festival.'[21]

While Champlain was not explicitly mentioned in Langelier's speech, the duality that he and Dugua had embodied was central to his message, which had its own pertinence during the summer of 1904. By that time, bitter debates had already begun regarding the rules that would be established in the soon-to-be-created provinces of Alberta and Saskatchewan regarding denominational schools. By the time of the tercentenary, Laurier had already made it clear that he felt that the Catholic minorities in the two new provinces 'were entitled to some form of separate school system.'[22] Of course, this was not the dominant view across English Canada, and to indicate his opposition to the prime minister's goals, Clifford Sifton noisily resigned from the federal cabinet early in 1905. For their part, Langelier and Turgeon, in emphasizing religious tolerance, reflected the dominant perspective from French-speaking Quebec, namely that Catholics had a historic right to recognition in the educational institutions of the country. This point of view might have been advanced by Laurier had he seen fit to travel east, but was probably not shared by the others on the podium, who chose to avoid reference to Champlain's involvement in the establishment of Port-Royal in particular, and to the presence of Catholics more generally.

While Turgeon and Langelier spoke about diversity, there were other French-speakers who might have addressed those issues with greater authority in the context of the Maritime provinces. In the end, however, Acadian leaders occupied a rather marginal part in celebrations that might have been constructed to mark the start of their existence. Although Longley invited the Société nationale l'Assomption, the leading Acadian organization of the time, to play a part in the Annapolis Royal festivities, in the end no Acadian spoke. To be fair, Senator Pascal Poirier, the president of the Société, did not participate because he was ill; and Rémi Benoit, who was there to represent Acadians living in New England, declined to speak 'owing to the lateness of the hour.'[23] Nevertheless, one can understand the frustration of L'Évangéline, which observed after the fête was over, 'Nos Acadiens étaient représentés en nombre, mais leurs principaux orateurs, ceux que nous aurions aimé voir là, manquaient dans ce concert des représentants de trois pays pour célébrer après trois longs siècles la mémoire des découvreurs du pays. La vieille province de Québec a été fièrement représentée, nous eussions voulu pouvoir en dire autant de l'Acadie.'[24] The only consolation that L'Évangéline could find in light of the Acadians' marginal status was the satisfaction that 'nous sommes au moins heureux dans la pensée que ces personnages que nous estimons étaient au milieu de nous de coeur et d'esprit.'[25] The personages in question were, of course, Champlain and Dugua, presented in that order by L'Évangéline, which seemed to embrace the Quebec reverence for the former.

This pairing of Champlain and Dugua, in whatever order, was rare in the 'official' descriptions of the celebration, but was presented graphically in the intensive coverage of the event by the Quebec City newspaper Le Soleil, whose ties to Laurier were well known. The newspaper stood apart from other newspapers by leading every report from Longley's celebration with an image of Champlain superimposed upon one of Dugua, the images ringed with the words Champlain–De Monts, 1604–1904. Whether Champlain 'deserved'

4.3 Medal: Tercentennial of Champlain's Landing at Saint John, 1604–1904. New Brunswick Museum, Saint John, NB: X6121-20.

equal, let along first, billing with Dugua at Annapolis Royal is beside the point. *Le Soleil* was trying to underscore the messages of Canadian duality that had been delivered by Turgeon and Langelier, and which might have been presented by other speakers had the Acadians had their moment on the podium. Here they were in black and white, the Catholic and Protestant 'founders' of Canada.

As soon as the festivities at Annapolis Royal were completed, most of the dignitaries boarded a steamer that would take them to the next stop along the tercentenary tour. Longley had worked with the organizers at Saint John and Île Ste-Croix to guarantee that one series of events would seamlessly blend into the next. However, at least two of the speakers from Annapolis Royal went home after that celebration was over, this in spite of the comment by Alfred Kleczkowski, the French delegate to the tercentenary, who commented to his superiors back in Paris that 'Tous les personnages ayant participé aux fêtes d'Annapolis sont invités à prendre part aux fêtes de St Jean, et aucun ne pourra s'y dérober.'[26] *Le Soleil*, which also disappeared from the scene, reported that Adélard Turgeon and Charles Langelier returned to Quebec after a series of meetings in Halifax.[27] While the two men had been invited to continue on to Saint John aboard the steamer that Longley had reserved for the occasion, one has to wonder how welcome they were after their speeches in Annapolis Royal. On 21 June, while Turgeon and Langelier would still have been at Longley's celebration, one of the leaders of the Saint John festivities wrote to a colleague that 'Hons Langelier and Turgeon will speak at our meeting if needed.'[28] Something happened, however, by the evening of the 22nd when the steamer set sail. Were they no longer needed, or had they decided that they had had enough? In either case, their departure underscored the marginal status of anyone at Annapolis Royal whose view of the founding of Canada was more complex than Longley and his associates had conceived it.

Reinforcing this point, Sir Wilfrid Laurier, who had stayed safely out of the way in Ottawa, received an angry letter early in 1905 from Judge A.W. Savary, a local leader in Annapolis Royal, who had played a bit part in the festivities there during the summer of 1904. The federal government had made a contribution towards the construction of the Dugua monument, whose cornerstone had been laid at the time of the celebrations and which was completed later in the year. Savary was shocked by the fact that the inscription that had been placed on the monument was in English only. He wrote to the prime minister: 'I am strongly of the opinion that the inscription on the monument should be in French as well as English. In this, I am sorry to say, the Honourable Mr Longley decidedly differed from me, and sent forward the inscription written by me, without instructing a French version of it to be placed on the monument … [Dugua] was a Frenchman; he founded a French colony, and a large proportion of the people of Canada speak and will always speak the French language.' In the end, Savary's was a voice in the wilderness. As even he recognized, this had been Longley's party, and the English-only inscription would survive until a French one was finally added in the 1980s.[29]

Champlain Returns to Saint John

If Champlain had largely been kept out of view at Annapolis Royal, such was certainly not the case at Saint John, New Brunswick. In fact, of the three venues for the 1904 celebrations, this was the one that unambiguously belonged to

Champlain, since the event being remembered was the cartographer's naming of the Rivière St-Jean, on the feast day of John the Baptist. Of course, while the 'facts' of the case pushed Dugua to the background, they raised an entirely new problem, as Saint John, a proudly Loyalist town, had to find the means to celebrate the exploits of a Catholic from France. A certain reluctance to celebrate Champlain too warmly was evident as the process of organizing the Saint John celebrations began with some very tentative efforts by the New Brunswick Historical, Natural History, and Loyalist societies in 1902 and 1903. While the Natural History Society was prepared to mark 'the three hundredth anniversary of the discovery of the harbour and river of St. John by Champlain,' the minutes of the meetings of the Loyalist Society consistently referred to 'the tercentenary of the discovery of the River St. John,' never mentioning the 'discoverer' by name.[30]

The three societies met both separately and collectively with some regularity, but by late 1903 it was clear that the organization of the tercentenary had stalled. This all changed, however, when the indefatigable Mr Longley became involved in what he called 'the tercentenary of De Monts' first voyage.' In his typically self-assured manner, Longley wrote to the Reverend W.O. Raymond, an Anglican minister and a local historian of note, that 'if no accident happens, the celebration at Port Royal will be one of the most memorable occasions in Canadian history. My suggestion is that the St. John celebration should be timed so as to follow instantly on the Annapolis [one] … In that way the same persons who will be induced to take part in the Annapolis celebration could be induced by special steamer accommodations to attend and take part in St. John immediately after … I have already spoken to the Admiral of the Fleet about sending one or more ships of war to Annapolis and of course, if he does so, these ships would move promptly on to St. John.'[31]

Longley subsequently came to Saint John to give his pep talk to the entire tercentenary committee, which immediately signed on. Accordingly, by the start of 1904 work was being done to give the celebration some substance, so much so that Longley, watching from the attorney-general's office in Halifax, could write: 'I am very much pleased to hear that your St. John committees are waking up.'[32] As this letter suggests, Longley viewed the Saint John organizers with some condescension, and he displayed the same attitude when he learned several months later that no invitation had been sent from Saint John to the governor-general. As we have seen, Longley felt that Lord Minto was needed to legitimize these celebrations, and so he was shocked when he found that the work had not been done: 'When I was in Ottawa the other day, I found that no invitation had yet been sent to the Governor General and so far as I learned no steps had been taken by your Society to interest him in the matter … I think it is time the St. John invitations were sent to all the Societies and Institutions of which [we] sent you the list.'[33]

Longley was even more pointed with his criticism, however, when he learned of the ambitious program that the Saint John organizers had in mind. While the Annapolis Royal celebrations avoided the sort of public spectacles that had become part of the turn-of-the-century commemorative repertoire, the Saint John people were determined to construct a carefully orchestrated affair. As a result, they were preoccupied with their finances, so much so that Longley admonished them: 'You entirely overestimate the necessity for money ... Expensive side shows are very nice from a spectacular point of view and please the masses but my idea of historical celebrations of this character is to have them intellectually commemorative and this can be done for much less money.'[34]

In the end, unlike Longley, who believed that crowds could be attracted without the use of spectacles, the Saint John leaders were in the mainstream of commemorative organizers of the time, as they found themselves investing substantial energy in lobbying governments for significant funding so that their plan could be executed. While the federal government tried to stay clear of the affair, both the municipal and provincial governments soon received demands from tercentenary organizers. While these local leaders had hoped to receive $5000 from each level of government, they were forced to settle for $2000, and within days of receiving the news most of it had been allocated to put on the big show.[35] Rather small amounts were provided for such 'intellectual' events (to use Longley's expression) as the meeting of the Royal Society of Canada in Saint John and a 'literary evening' in which speeches would be made to explain the significance of the moment. A much larger portion of the funds was set aside to stage a landing of Champlain at Saint John on 24 June, precisely three hundred years after he had first visited the site. The Neptune Rowing Club and the Royal Kennebeccasis Yacht Club received $500 each, the former so that its members could take to their canoes dressed as First Nations people who would welcome Champlain and his crew, played by the Yacht Club, aboard a reconstruction of his ship, the *Acadie*. Although one member of the rowing club claimed that 'genuine Indians could be got for the Champlain welcome,' there is no evidence, in this case or in any other part of the tercentenary events of 1904, that any serious effort was made to have Natives play themselves.[36] Similarly, there is no evidence that anyone ever considered having Acadians brought in to play the Frenchmen from the seventeenth century.

When the big day came around, spectators witnessed the arrival of Champlain and his comrades, who then made their way to Market Square, 'where they made gifts to the Indians and smoked with them the pipes of peace. They took possession of the land, with formal ceremony in the name of the King of

4.4 De Monts–Champlain Tercentenary Celebrations – The Landing, Saint John, New
Brunswick, 24 June 1904. New Brunswick Museum, Saint John, NB: X11235.

France, and their new friends danced the war dance about them.' With the close
of this ceremony, Champlain, his entourage, and the 'natives' made their way,
along with an imposing number of soldiers and sailors, to the site of a monument that had been erected in the north end of the city in honour of the soldiers
who had fought in the Boer War.[37]

There was something incongruous about the 1904 embodiment of Champlain, who had been a Catholic serving the French state, taking part in commemorating the actions of New Brunswick volunteers in a war that had been
fought to defend the interests of the British empire. Such incongruity, however,
was to be expected given the discomfort felt by some with the celebration of a
French Catholic hero. While there were those who were prepared to celebrate
Champlain, viewing him as the 'discoverer' of their town and choosing to overlook his nationality and religion, still others preferred to ignore him altogether,
or sought ways to combine his celebration with that of other, more comfortable

symbols. For instance, in the aftermath of the landing of Champlain, one Saint John newspaper remarked in a headline: 'Glorious Welcome for Champlain II, At The Spot Where First Loyalists Set Foot.'[38] Champlain could not stand on his own, but rather needed to be paired with the less threatening reference to the Loyalists. In a similar manner, over the months leading up to the two-day celebration in Saint John, the tercentenary was frequently absorbed in the local press into a week-long celebration of 'Old Home Week' which would culminate in Sunday church services. Several days after the dignitaries had left for Île Ste-Croix, thanks would be given in local churches for 'the two greatest events in the history of St. John, the landing of the Loyalists and the discovery of the St. John River by Champlain.'[39]

The reluctance to embrace Champlain too warmly was expressed in other ways as well. The appropriation of municipal funds for the tercentenary was resisted by some who felt that Champlain had been 'an ancient mariner with whose adventure we are nowise concerned.'[40] The grudging celebration of Champlain was also evident in some of the speeches that were made at the 'literary evening' on the night preceding the return of the discoverer. Attorney-General Longley, in his only public appearance, managed to avoid mentioning Champlain's name, always referring instead to 'De Monts' land[ing] at St. John.' For his part, Dr A.A. Stockton, the vice-president of the New Brunswick Historical Society, was more pointed. He began by identifying himself as 'a descendant of the Loyalists' and went on to observe: 'We do well to honour the memory of the French discoverer, but we do only half our duty unless we also honour the Loyalists who came nearly two centuries later to these shores. Beside the tablet to Champlain should be one in memory of the Loyalists.'[41]

The tablet in question was to be unveiled on 24 June, following the return of Champlain and the unveiling of the war memorial, on the occasion of the opening of the new public library. The Historical Society had considered the construction of a memorial to Champlain, which might have paralleled the one to Dugua in Annapolis Royal, but this idea was quickly pushed aside, to be replaced by the 'erection of a tablet to Champlain and De Monts' at the new library.[42] Champlain just could not stand alone in the eyes of some, and even though he had been paired with Dugua on this occasion, there were those who were bothered that the Catholic hero might be given precedence over the Huguenot. In this context, Reverend Raymond, who stood out throughout the affair as an unapologetic advocate for giving the French Catholic hero his due, felt the need to 'reply to the criticism that [the organizers] were making this a Champlain rather than a De Monts celebration.' Raymond went on to argue, undoubtedly to the displeasure of some, that 'Champlain was the greater man … He was the father of Canada and left his impress upon it, while De Monts left no memorial.' Raymond cut to the heart of the matter when he observed, 'At St. John, de Monts left absolutely nothing to show that he had ever visited it ... And yet today the Historical Society, in the tablet to be unveiled, would make the two central characters of our celebrations partners in the honours of the tercentenary.'[43]

Dugua seems to have been added to the Champlain tablet to make it more palatable to residents of Saint John who might have had trouble embracing a Catholic hero. However, even with Dugua included, there was so little enthusiasm for the project that it was difficult to raise the $160 needed to construct the tablet. Although the official tercentenary committee blessed the idea of erecting such a tablet in early May, it appropriated none of its $4000 to the effort. Instead, there was to be an appeal for funds from the general public, but these accumulated very slowly, so that by early June, two weeks before the unveiling ceremony, only $65 had been collected.[44]

In this context, the secretary of the tercentenary committee wrote to Senator Pascal Poirier, the president of the Société nationale l'Assomption, asking that Acadians pay for half the tablet. While Poirier politely responded that this might be difficult 'as we are a community destitute of worldly goods,' within days of the request for Acadian support the treasurer of the Société, Judge Pierre-Amand Landry, appealed to the 'descendants des colons acadiens de 1604 de prendre l'initiative d'une contribution volontaire au monument historique projeté; et je prends la liberté d'inviter mes compatriotes acadiens à m'adresser chacun une obole – $1.00 ou moins, selon leur bon vouloir – que je me ferai un agréable devoir de transmettre au trésorier à St-Jean.'[45] By the time of the unveiling, $50 of the $150 so far subscribed for the tablet had come from Acadians, and further contributions came in the days that followed.[46]

While tercentenary organizers needed Acadian dollars, they showed little enthusiasm otherwise for including Acadian leaders in the celebration, which was perhaps to be expected in a town in which the French presence was even less significant than had been the case in Annapolis Royal.[47] While the population of New Brunswick was roughly one-quarter Acadian, the areas of such settlement were far from Saint John, and in spite of the high-minded talk of tercentenary boosters that their fête would benefit all New Brunswickers, Acadians did not really figure in their calculations. This blind spot was reflected in the *New Brunswick Magazine*, which rather condescendingly observed, 'While there are some descendants of the earliest French settlers and many of others of more recent date the country is British, the language English, and the sentiment of the people irrespective of nationality that of loyalty to the British crown and Constitution.'[48]

Although there had been talk of planning tercentenary celebrations in Saint

John since 1902, there was not a single reference to any Acadian involvement until late May 1904 when Senator Poirier tried to interest organizers in Acadian participation.[49] However, all that Poirier's intervention seemed to achieve was the request from tercentenary leaders for Acadian contributions for the tablet for the library. Invitation lists prepared by the tercentenary organizers at the start of June did not contain the name of a single Acadian leader; nor for that matter was the Société nationale l'Assomption on a list that included societies with varied interests from across North America. One week before the start of the celebration, Senator John V. Ellis, a Laurier appointee from Saint John, sent a telegram pointing out that 'St. John NB might be wise to assign Senator Poirier or some representative Acadian place on public program.'[50] It would seem that only after this intervention from Ottawa did Judge Landry and Rémi Benoit (the representative of Acadians living in New England) receive invitations to speak at the 'literary evening' that preceded the day of Champlain's return. With the representatives from Quebec, Turgeon and Langelier, preparing to take the train back to Quebec, they were the only French-speakers on the program.

Given an opportunity to address the crowds, Landry spoke not about the legacy of Champlain, but rather the achievements of the Acadians, who had surpassed other Canadians in their ability to speak both languages. 'The Acadians were progressing educationally and asked the privilege of walking hand-in-hand with their English fellow citizens in the work of nation-building.' For his efforts, Landry received, according to the *St. John Daily Telegraph*, 'earnest applause,' this in contrast with the 'hearty and long continued applause' that greeted Commander Dillingham, the American representative who had made the journey from Annapolis Royal.[51] In the end, various voices were heard at Saint John, but some were taken more seriously than others.

The End of the Tercentenary Tour

While some continued to celebrate 'Old Home Week' at Saint John, the dignitaries made their way to Dochet Island, as Île Ste-Croix was officially known before the summer of 1904, along with the various military vessels that had been part of the journey from its start.[52] Much like the other two celebrations, this last stop on the circuit was to a considerable extent the work of a historical society, in this case the Maine Historical Society (MHS), which was only fitting since the island was in American waters. Nothing of substance had been done to stage a tercentenary event until the secretary of the MHS and Baptist minister, Rev. Henry Burrage, became involved in early 1904, corresponding with Longley, on the one hand, and with the municipal governments in the vicinity of Île Ste-Croix, on the other.[53] In the end, however, Burrage seems to have had more of an impact upon the Calais, Maine city government, which immediately moved into action, than upon that of St Stephen, New Brunswick, just across the border, which took no steps to move the tercentenary forward. When a committee with representatives from towns on both sides of the border was formed to look after the local arrangements, the Americans clearly provided most of the initiative. In the end, there were two main events that constituted the Île Ste-Croix celebration, one on the island and the other in Calais, Maine. There was an event held just across from the island on the Canadian side, but it was inexplicably staged 'while the services were in progress on the island,' so that 'the attendance was not large.'[54]

In late 1903 and early 1904, as the Annapolis Royal and Saint John organizers were scrambling to put their celebrations together, the leaders in Maine were thinking about Île Ste-Croix, but in a much broader context than their Canadian counterparts. While the historical societies in both Nova Scotia and New Brunswick were focused exclusively on 1904, the Maine Historical Society indicated a very different commitment, having already held in November 1901 an event marking the 'commemoration of the millenary anniversary of the death of King Alfred the Great.' Placing the Historical Society's interest in the past in the broadest of terms, its president, James Baxter, observed: 'It has been the practice from the earliest times for civilized people to publicly commemorate important episodes in the lives of those who have made themselves conspicuous by their achievements, not alone for the purpose of showing reverence for the mighty dead, but for the loftier one of keeping bright the memory of virtues worthy to be emulated by the living.' Alfred was particularly worthy of respect because 'of what he wrought for a great race from whose loins we sprang.'[55]

Moving closer to home, starting in 1903 and continuing to 1907, Baxter and his colleagues were involved in a series of celebrations to mark the anniversaries of various incursions by Europeans along the Atlantic coast of Maine. Perhaps reflecting the experience of the MHS in organizing such events, Henry Burrage did not seem too concerned when he wrote to Longley in February 1904, 'We have not yet fixed a date, but shall endeavour to conform to the dates of your celebrations.'[56] There was still no permanent organizing committee in place until late April, but perhaps the slow pace was possible because this was designed to be a small affair. After the fact, one local newspaper observed that the Ste-Croix celebration had been 'less varied' than the one at Annapolis Royal and 'less spectacular' than that at Saint John: 'With little money to spend, it was simple, solemn and grand.'[57]

In the end, however, what distinguished the American-run event was the equal treatment that was provided to the heroes of the moment. In a telling phrase that reflected a perspective that had not been evident at either Annapolis Royal or Saint John, Burrage reported to Longley that he and his colleagues were prepared to celebrate 'De Monts' settlement and Champlain's voyage along the coast in 1604.'[58] While there were no carefully orchestrated spectacles, just two events largely dominated by speeches, the words that were spoken at the Île Ste-Croix stop brought into relief some of the themes that had stood out at the two larger (and thoroughly Canadian) events. While there had been moments at both Annapolis Royal and Saint John when the mere mention of Champlain's name seemed unacceptable to some, there was no such reluctance on this occasion. Even though the celebration was formally referred to as the 'De Monts Tercentenary,' the tablet that was unveiled at the brief event on the island included the names of both Dugua and Champlain, given equal credit for establishing on Île Ste-Croix what was 'then the only settlement of Europeans north of Florida.' The equal treatment of the two men continued in the three main speeches that were delivered over the course of the day, the first of which dealt with Dugua, and the last with Champlain. In between the two, Professor W.F. Ganong, a professor at Smith College and a native of Saint John, went out of his way to describe the landing at Île Ste-Croix of 'two [men who] bore the unmistakable stamp of leadership.'[59]

While there had been a few English-speaking voices at Annapolis Royal and Saint John that had presented Champlain and Dugua as presaging the existence of two founding people in Canada, there had also been those, such as Longley in the former case and the leaders of the Loyalist Society in the latter, who could barely bring themselves to utter Champlain's name. They seemed to feel that in the Canadian context the parallel treatment of the two men somehow legitimized the recognition of two founding cultures. In the end, the only voices from the Canadian stops of 1904 that consistently spoke about duality in this regard were the French-speakers, and they were of course few in number.

At Île Ste-Croix, when Judge Landry was unable to attend, there were no French Canadians, but there were also few English Canadians. Instead, most of the speakers were Americans whose references to Champlain and Dugua had different political implications from what they had had at either Annapolis Royal or Saint John. When Henry Burrage referred to the presence of both Catholics and Protestants at Île Ste-Croix in 1604, he saw them, not as harbingers of Canadian biculturalism, but rather as having anticipated American freedom of worship: 'In this French colony, Protestants and Catholics were found side by side, both minister and priest being included in the personnel of the expedition.' While religious liberty suffered setbacks in France, 'it was to have a rebirth on this side of the sea ... And now to us, religious liberty is so common a thing that we fail oftentimes, Protestants and Catholics alike, to estimate aright our indebtedness for a boon of such priceless value.'[60] Champlain and Dugua were brought together as they never had been in Canada, as Burrage had no reason to focus on two founding nations, but rather a much broader acceptance of all religious persuasions.

Dugua's Moment

Following the summer of 1904, Champlain and Dugua returned to public view from time to time, receiving much the same relative attention that they had been accorded upon the tercentenary. In the case of Saint John, for instance, Champlain was granted a measure of respect with the unveiling of a monument in his honour in 1910. Nevertheless, in 1954, on the 350th anniversary of Champlain's naming of the St John River, English-speakers generally felt the need to speak of the French Catholic hero in tandem with Dugua, as had been the case fifty years earlier; and it still remained for the Acadians to insist that attention be focused upon Champlain. The only Acadian leader to speak at those festivities, Père Clément Cormier, the president of the New Brunswick Museum, made this point quite clearly, noting, 'Even though de Monts was officially in charge, the outstanding figure of the expedition was undoubtedly Champlain. He is rightly called the Father of New France.'[61] This Acadian preoccupation with Champlain would evaporate, however, when a variety of circumstances combined to make Dugua the centre of attention during the summer of 2004.

As had been the case in 1904, much of the initial enthusiasm for staging the quadricentenary events came from individuals, almost invariably English-speakers, who lived at the various sites of memory. Leading the way on this occasion was a dedicated group of citizens from both sides of the international border who wanted to seize the opportunity to mark the anniversary of the original settlement on Île Ste-Croix. Perhaps reflecting the decline of voices (at least English-speaking ones) from Atlantic Canada that could make themselves heard very far from their homes, no single individual in the mould of J.W. Longley emerged on this occasion. Instead, a group of community leaders joined together in the late 1990s, to a considerable degree to promote the celebration of 2004 with an eye towards the development of the tourist industry in the region.

Their fondest dream was the construction, on land in New Brunswick overlooking the island, of a replica of the settlement of 1604. They hoped that the quadricentenary would draw attention to the now all-but-forgotten expedition and encourage both public and private investors to help fund the enterprise. As Norma Stewart, executive director for the Ste-Croix 2004 Co-ordinating

Committee, put it: 'This whole plan, if you will, to bring Ste-Croix history to life again and to capitalize on it as a heritage resource for economic prosperity of the region is a real motivator behind why this international community of Washington County (Maine) and Charlotte County (New Brunswick) has come together to [mark the four hundredth anniversary].'[62]

At one point, Stewart and her colleagues had hoped that the reconstructed settlement would be open, or at least well underway, by the summer of 2004, but this was not to be. In fact, they experienced considerable difficulty in staging commemorative events to mark the quadricentenary, let alone in embarking upon a significant construction project. To no small degree, they perceived that their plans were stalled by a certain lack of interest that stemmed from the fact that they were English-speakers, trying to promote a moment in the past that spoke most profoundly to the Acadians, who were preparing on their own to mark 2004 as the four hundredth anniversary of their beginning as a people.

The fact that Longley and his colleagues were English-speakers had not created any difficulties in 1904, but the context was now very different as Acadians were determined to have their voices heard, but not necessarily by promoting the celebration of what had happened at Île Ste-Croix. Instead, the leading Acadian organization, the Société nationale de l'Acadie (SNA), was involved in promoting commemorative events across Atlantic Canada. Moreover, considerable resources were being invested to stage the Congrès mondial acadien, a major tourist event that would bring Acadians from all over the world to Nova Scotia. In the midst of this activity, Île Ste-Croix was not quite on the radar screen. In part, this was simply a function of the fact that, as Stewart put it, 'the bulk of Acadians don't live in this part of the province. So I understood why they didn't want to take the ownership, perhaps, because it's geographically not theirs.' This perspective was echoed by Chantal Abord-Hugon, a key organizer of 2004 events for the SNA, who found that '[Île] Ste-Croix n'est pas un lieu qui a une résonance pour les Acadiens.'[63]

More generally, Norma Stewart felt that there were linguistic considerations that worked against English-speakers securing support for what Acadians saw as 'their' anniversary. She perceived that her committee was 'swimming against the tide in order to get the recognition from the levels of government. There is no denying that this island and this river was the site of that first settling in 1604. But because we are an anglophone community, we were constantly banging our heads up against the bureaucratic wall of the francophones. And in fact there was a real sense, up until a year ago (ie 2003), that there was no assistance coming, especially because we were anglophones.'[64] This same sense of being marginal to celebrations that were essentially Acadian was also felt by some English-speakers in Nova Scotia, trying to promote events of their own. A member of the group Acadie 2003–5, which had the mandate to over-see quadricentenary events in the province, complained that the process was being driven by the SNA, which wanted to 'come in and claim ownership.'[65] For his part, Maurice Basque, a historian and director of the Centre d'études acadiennes at the Université de Moncton, confirmed that English-speaking and Acadian leaders were not always on the same wavelength: 'Il est certain que 2004 n'appartient pas exclusivement aux Acadiens mais il y a beaucoup de frustration de leur part dans les dernières années en voyant d'autres gens de l'Atlantique s'approprier cette anniversaire.'[66]

While English-speaking and Acadian leaders may have had their differenc-es, they also shared certain perspectives on the quadricentenary events, such as a profound frustration with the slowness with which the federal govern-ment provided financial support. While Longley spoke to his colleagues in 1904 about the possibility of staging events on the cheap, this was no longer possible, given the expectations that a big show needed to be held to attract large crowds. The New Brunswick government provided operating expenses to keep Norma Stewart and her colleagues afloat, but it was only the federal government that could fund a large-scale celebration. Much to the dismay of many in the Atlantic provinces, this support was slow in coming, in spite of the fact that some $18 million was provided to mark this anniversary by means of various events that would be staged in France to mark four hundred years of Canada-France relations. Ultimately, in 2002, a much smaller envelope, $10 million, was allotted to events that would be spread across the four Atlantic provinces to mark what was called 'le 400e anniversaire de l'Acadie.'[67] While the organizers at Île Ste-Croix ultimately secured roughly $500,000 from these funds to stage their celebration, the federal proclamation that 2004 marked the birth of Acadie made it clear to the English-speakers that lobbying by Acadian leaders had been crucial to the process and that their own efforts had achieved relatively little.

Questions of funding aside, all the various parties, English- and French-speakers alike, shared the view that the hero of the moment was Pierre Dugua de Mons, with barely a nod in the direction of Champlain. During the summer of 1904, each of the heroes from the seventeenth century had had his moments in the sun. Dugua took centre stage at Annapolis Royal, Champlain (however grudgingly) did the same at Saint John, and the two shared the limelight at Île Ste-Croix. However, one hundred years later, Dugua largely had the stage to himself. In a carefully choreographed affair, the 'official' start of the cel-ebration of the quadricentenary was held in the fall of 2003 at Fontainebleau, the same French château where Henri IV had provided Dugua with his com-mission four hundred years earlier. On this occasion, with numerous Acadian leaders in attendance, there was a re-enactment of that event, so that Dugua was present, while Champlain was conspicuous by his absence, a pattern that would continue throughout the quadricentenary celebrations.

Yet another Dugua re-enactor was in evidence, also in the fall of 2003, when the National Park Service, which owns Île Ste-Croix (since it is in American waters), opened a commemorative trail on dry land in Maine, in anticipation of the quadricentenary. The presence of the 'live' Dugua only reinforced his presence in bronze, as he was represented in one of six life-size statues erected to tell the story of the short-lived experience on the island. Only a few months later and just miles away in Calais, Maine, yet another likeness of Dugua, this time in a video for museum-goers, told visitors the story of the expedition to Île Ste-Croix, at the Downeast Heritage Center, which opened to mark the quadricentenary. If this were not enough, the Park Service's Dugua re-enactor figured prominently in the advertising designed to draw people to the region during the summer of 2004.[68]

When that summer finally arrived, the Dugua emphasis continued, particularly in the course of the two events staged at sites of memory that had had celebrations in 1904.[69] The first of the two was staged at Saint John, the site that most logically 'belonged' to Champlain, since legend had long had it that he named the St John River on 24 June, the feast day of St-Jean-Baptiste; and indeed considerable attention was paid to him on the quadricentenary. A dramatic walk through the early history of the site where Saint John would later emerge included a re-enactor playing the famous cartographer (although with Dugua on hand as well), and there were ceremonies held at the Champlain monument, which itself had been constructed shortly after the tercentenary. However, the most intriguing part of the celebrations focused upon the unveiling of a monument to Dugua, who had been given relatively little attention in 1904, since it was an article of faith that this was Champlain's moment. While Champlain's name had long been linked to the river, this monument overlooking the harbour moved Dugua to the centre of the story, noting that he had been responsible for naming 'la Baie française,' which later became the Bay of Fundy. Dugua was even given equal credit with Champlain for having named the St John River.

That this was Dugua's summer was also evident at the largest commemorative events of the season, the ones that marked the establishment of the settlement at Île Ste-Croix. Given the location of the island on the international border, both the Canadian and American governments were involved. In order to place the event in some context, Parks Canada observed in a press release that '2004 marks the 400th anniversary of Sainte Croix Island, site of Pierre Dugua, Sieur de Mons' first attempt at settlement in North America.' Champlain only entered the picture in this account via references to his writings about the time spent on the island.[70] In a similar manner, Marie Rust, the regional director for the National Park Service, placed the emphasis upon Dugua, only making reference to Champlain when it came to his role in founding Quebec City, and even then it was Dugua who 'sent him up the St. Lawrence River.'[71]

The prominence of Dugua and the virtual disappearance of Champlain reflected some significant social changes that had taken place since 1904. On the occasion of the tercentenary, Dugua was largely the hero of English-speakers, while Champlain was championed by francophones, Acadians and Quebecers alike, when they had the chance to speak. To no small degree, this reflected the central role of religion as a marker of identity in the early twentieth century. As Maurice Basque has put it, Dugua could not be embraced by Acadians at the time of the tercentenary because 'un Protestant ne pouvait certainement pas être le père fondateur de la Nouvelle-France.'[72] However, by the early twenty-first century, such religious matters no longer held much significance, thus making it possible for everyone in Atlantic Canada to get on the Dugua bandwagon. English-speakers had embraced him in 1904, and now Acadians were prepared to do the same. He became, in the words of Chantal Abord-Hugon of the SNA, 'un héro de l'Atlantique.'

Dugua also provided the opportunity for Acadians to distinguish themselves from their cousins in Quebec, who still maintained that Champlain was their founding father. Recognizing the desire by Acadians to come out from the shadow of Quebecers, Abord-Hugon observed that 'Cette année [2004] pour nous c'est une occasion aussi un petit peu de réhabiliter Pierre Dugua de Mons et de montrer le rôle important qu'il a joué parce que sans [Dugua] il n'y aurait pas eu Champlain ... Beaucoup d'acadiens perçoivent Champlain comme un héro québécois ... On est toujours très fier de dire ici que Pierre Dugua de Mons a fondé l'Acadie, mais c'est lui qui a envoyé Champlain fonder Québec ... Alors Pierre Dugua de Mons est en fait à l'origine de la fondation de l'Acadie et aussi du Québec.'[73]

As if to underscore Abord-Hugon's point, in the course of the numerous speeches that were made upon the quadricentenary of the settlement at Île Ste-Croix, speakers who put Champlain at the centre of the action tended to be individuals from outside the region. Quebecers were particularly conspicuous in their emphasis upon Champlain, and typical in this regard was the public statement by the Quebec minister of intergovernmental affairs, Benoît Pelletier. While giving Dugua a passing reference, he focused upon the role of Champlain. 'En effet, parmi l'équipage du sieur de Mons se trouvait Samuel de Champlain, géographe du roi, qui, quatre ans plus tard, en 1608, fondera la ville de Québec. C'est d'ailleurs Champlain qui donna à l'Acadie et à Québec leur nom respectif ... C'est enfin Champlain qui conclut les premières alliances entre la France et les peuples autochtones des Maritimes et de la vallée du Saint-Laurent en 1603, donnant ainsi naissance à une amitié profonde entre les populations francophones et autochtones en Nouvelle-France.'[74]

This effort to push Dugua to the side dovetailed with the efforts of some Quebec leaders to marginalize the significance of the events of 1604. While Adélard Turgeon and Charles Langelier, the two Quebec representatives to the 1904 celebrations, had tried to speak for the Acadians, some Quebec voices on the occasion of the quadricentenary reacted defensively to Acadian efforts to assert their own identity, as if Quebecers' own place in the French-speaking hierarchy of Canada would be threatened if the Acadians managed to prove that their part of the world, and not the St Lawrence valley, had been the site of the first French efforts to settle in North America. Leading the chorus in this regard was the mayor of Quebec City, Jean-Paul L'Allier, who, in several public statements, managed to ignore the significance of Île Ste-Croix altogether and to dismiss the settlement at Port-Royal as ephemeral. As he put it, 'J'ai beaucoup de respect pour l'Acadie, mais le Canada tel qu'on le connaît est né à Québec en 1608, tous les historiens sont d'accord là-dessus.'[75] Of course, there was no such agreement among historians on this matter, but that did not prevent L'Allier from viewing the federal government's investment of $10 million in celebrating 2004 in Atlantic Canada as having been excessive, a point of view that was not shared in that region. However, the mayor was prepared to be philosophical about that contribution, if Ottawa were to provide $100 million for Quebec City in 2008. As L'Allier put it, 'Il faut nous réjouir de l'ampleur de l'effort qui est fait à Port-Royal parce que c'est un peu comme dans un menu: ils (le gouvernement fédéral) mettent beaucoup d'efforts sur l'entrée et quand viendra le plat principal, et bien, il devrait être proportionnel.'[76]

This competition between two branches of the same family might be dismissed as trivial if it did not point to the very reason why Acadian leaders invested so much energy, sometimes to the annoyance of their English-speaking neighbours, in using the quadricentenary as a vehicle that would present them as a dynamic people. This celebration was designed to mark, above all else, 'le quatre centième anniversaire de l'Acadie,' and towards that end Dugua was a symbol of a people marked by their perseverance and dynamism.[77] In the process they pushed to the side their deportation, *le grand dérangement*, which had heretofore been the defining moment in the Acadian experience.

Throughout much of the twentieth century, the most significant moments of public remembrance of the Acadian past focused upon Grand-Pré, immortalized by Henry Wadsworth Longfellow as the site from which the stoic Evangeline had been deported along with her beloved Gabriel. Pilgrimages were held there, and in 1955 there was a solemn commemoration of the bicentenary of the deportation, watched over by the Société nationale l'Assomption, itself heavily influenced by the Catholic church.[78] As a consequence of this bicentenary, the federal government committed itself to establishing Grand-Pré as a national historic park, in a sense institutionalizing the place of the *grand dérangement* in Acadian memory. On another level, however, the bicentenary marked the last hurrah for the Société nationale l'Assomption, which in 1957 was reborn as the Société nationale des Acadiens (which itself would become the Société nationale de l'Acadie that exists to this day). As its name suggests, the new organization was secular and reflected the profound changes that were bringing a 'Quiet Revolution' to Acadie, just as profound as the one about to transform Quebec. The transformation of Acadie was symbolized by the rapid growth of the Acadian population, especially in New Brunswick, where French-speakers constituted nearly 40 per cent of the population by the start of the 1960s, a far cry from the roughly 25 per cent of the New Brunswick population that would have been Acadian at the time of the 1904 tercentenary.[79] This demographic growth was, in turn, reflected politically in the election of Louis Robichaud, who became the first Acadian to be elected premier of New Brunswick in 1960. Robichaud's rise to power subsequently led to the creation of the Université de Moncton, the province's only French-language university, in 1963 and to the passage of legislation that made the province officially bilingual in 1969. Parallel to this new-found political power, there was also the flourishing of the Acadian presence in the arts, marked, among other distinctions, by Antonine Maillet's winning of the Prix Goncourt in 1979.

Ultimately, however, there was something incongruous about a people who were increasingly distinguishing themselves by their vitality maintaining a historical memory whose defining moment was one of loss. While the story of the deportation could be told in terms of the survival of a people, it served to truncate Acadian history and to put the Acadian chronology on a different path from that of other societies in the Americas (the Quebecers included) whose beginnings could be traced back to the initial encounter between Europeans and Aboriginal people. Although the deportation would still form part of the narrative of Acadian history, the quadricentenary of the founding of the short-lived settlement on Île Ste-Croix provided Acadian leaders with the opportunity to construct a different starting point and, in the person of Dugua, to provide themselves with a founding father of their own.

Moreover, by normalizing the Acadian past and moving the focus away from the deportation and its consequences, reconceptualizing the Acadian past allowed the more modern aspects of the culture to be presented.[80] The newsletter produced by the Société nationale de l'Acadie on the occasion of the quadricentenary observed: 'Le 400e [est] une occasion unique pour se remémorer la fondation de l'Acadie, le moment où les Français ont foulé le sol de ce pays. Célébrer les premiers pas permet de se voir autrement, et cette re-création de l'image de soi aura des répercussions à long terme sur notre perception de l'histoire acadienne.'[81] In particular, there was the opportunity to move away from folkloric representations of the Acadian past, what Maurice Basque described as a preoccupation with such images as Evangeline and Gabriel, and to focus upon the modern. As Chantal Abord-Hugon put it, the quadricentenary provided 'une occasion pour nous de finalement repasser toute l'histoire de l'Acadie, du début jusqu'à l'Acadie d'aujourd'hui. Donc [nous ne voulons] pas seulement présenter l'Acadie historique mais de présenter l'Acadie moderne.'[82] In this endeavour, Dugua was a useful symbol, an alternative to Evangeline, as he spoke to a history that extended from 1604 to 2004, and which was not confined by a preoccupation with the events of 1755.

Packaging the Past

Alongside the dramatic emergence of Dugua as the hero of the quadricentenary, there were also some significant shifts in terms of how the past was presented to the public in 2004, when compared with what had been done one hundred years earlier. The tercentenary events fell in the midst of the heyday of public celebration of the past. Across the Western world, leaders – both lay and clerical – were busy staging spectacles and erecting monuments designed to close the gap between the past and the present, hopeful that messages from a not so distant past might provide guidance for the future. These leaders presumed that they were playing to a public which understood, and would take the time to appreciate, carefully choreographed public events such as the re-enactment in Saint John of the arrival of Champlain in 1904. While he was not an 'ordinary' member of the public, Professor W.F. Ganong, whom we saw earlier as a participant in the celebrations at Île Ste-Croix, reacted as organizers might have hoped to this event, expressing a certain sense of awe: 'All this part of the ceremony was extremely effective. In fact, so well was it done that I quite forgot for a time that it was a show ... I had some momentary impulse to approach Champlain and ask him the truth as to certain ambiguous passages in his narratives!'[83] Ganong's sentiments were also reflected by some of those who observed the intricately staged historical pageants presented at the Quebec tercentenary of 1908. As Viv Nelles has indicated, 'The therapy of theatre, especially in the form of the mass participatory re-enactment, taught lessons in different ways, reached new audiences by making them actors, and potentially reshaped public consciousness.'[84] In both of these cases, the past was performed in a way that made the lessons of the past seem close at hand.

By contrast, during the summer of 2004, when re-enactors were trotted out to make the past come alive, the public treated them more as objects of curiosity, or even amusement, than as figures capable of transporting an audience back in time. This was particularly clear when the United States National Park Service (NPS) decided to dress up one of its employees to play Dugua (there was no Champlain) as part of the opening ceremonies in October 2003 for a commemorative trail on the Maine coast, overlooking Île Ste-Croix. There was no sense of wonderment about this Dugua, who had no illusions about the role that he was playing, frequently falling out of character and talking about Dugua's exploits from the seventeenth century as if they were the acts of someone else (which of course they were). As for the audience, it could not help but view the re-enactor as one of them, often referring to him by his 'real' name.[85] While the re-enactors from the early twentieth century managed to make spectators such as Professor Ganong feel that they had been brought closer to the past, this one only drew attention to the distance between past and present.

In addition to the presentation of spectacles, the early twentieth-century packaging of the past also included the erection of elaborate monuments. In this regard, the tercentenary saw the construction at Annapolis Royal of a relatively austere monument for the time, not much more than a column topped with Dugua's bust, instead of the statues that frequently crowned such structures. Although the monument lacked the various allegorical figures that were then common, a bas-relief depicting Dugua's landing at Port-Royal was designed to communicate the heroic actions of the past that might influence the present. On the occasion of the quadricentenary, Dugua was presented very differently by the NPS, which created a series of life-size bronzes on its commemorative trail in Maine. This Dugua was literally not on a pedestal, so that observers could look straight into his eyes, making them feel as if they were in the presence of an accessible figure, not entirely unlike the NPS's own Dugua re-enactor, who posed next to the bronze statue at the unveiling ceremonies for the trail. Much like the re-enactor, this Dugua seemed to be little different from those who gazed at him. These observers may have been engaged by the 'great man' who was presented on a human scale. However, in the absence of reference to heroic values that might have linked the early seventeenth and early twenty-first centuries, this Dugua was an object to be contemplated, but not emulated. As Maurice Agulhon has put it, monuments such as the latest version of Dugua lacked the overt instructional qualities of the turn-of-the-twentieth-century structures. [86]

The causes for these changes in historical packaging are complex and per-

4.5 Two Duguas: Opening of Red Beach Trail, Maine, October 2003. Photograph by Robert Thayer.

tain to both the creators of commemorative events and the audiences to which they were appealing. Without viewing the First World War as having entirely transformed public representation of the past, there was a new questioning, more evident after the war, about the inevitability of progress. By and large, in the late nineteenth and early twentieth centuries, leaders in Atlantic Canada and across the Western world were prepared to view the past as providing guidance in the present for an even better future. However, following the carnage of the First World War and the other horrors of the twentieth century, such faith was shaken, and the presentation of the past started to take on new forms. The pageantry of pre-war years gave way to reconstructed historical villages where the past was frozen in time. There were frequently messages for the present embedded in such reconstructions, but there was no suggestion – as had been the case in terms of the pageants – that the gap between past and present could somehow be bridged. In the context of the French settlements of early seventeenth-century Acadie, the reconstruction of the Port-Royal Habitation by the

Canadian government in 1939 was in the mainstream of what David Glassberg has described as the movement to show how the 'past was receding from the present and the future, rather than leading to it.'[87]

The newer forms of historical representation were, in their own right, influenced by the exposure of the population over the course of the twentieth century to movies, television, and the internet. While audiences in the early twentieth century, only recently exposed to silent films, may have been prepared to suspend disbelief when exposed to historical re-enactments or classically inspired statuary, such was no longer the case by 2004, when there were expectations that representations of the past should somehow look 'real,' much like the various versions of the past that can readily be seen on the popular media of our time. Stories about the past could be told in each context, in the process engaging audiences, albeit in different ways. By 2004, Dugua had supplanted Champlain, particularly among Acadians, as the preferred hero from 1604. However, the past to which he belonged could no longer be made as immediate as had been the case in 1904.

NOTES

1 I have discussed the 1904 events in more detail in both 'The Champlain–De Monts Tercentenary: Voices from Nova Scotia, New Brunswick and Maine, June 1904,' *Acadiensis* 33 (Spring 2004): 3–26; and *Remembering and Forgetting in Acadie: A Historian's Journey through Public Memory* (Toronto: University of Toronto Press, 2009). While this essay does not deal with the Aboriginal voices heard in 2004, they are addressed at length in both *Remembering and Forgetting in Acadie* and in the documentary film: Leo Arisitimuno (director) and Ronald Rudin (producer), *Life after Île Ste-Croix*, National Film Board of Canada, 2006, DVD.

2 George MacBeath, 'Pierre Du Gua de Monts,' *Dictionary of Canadian Biography*, 1:291–4. While the leader of the expedition was generally referred to as de Monts in the early twentieth century, I will refer to him as Dugua to follow the practice of the early twenty-first century.

3 C.-H. Laverdière, ed., *Œuvres de Champlain* (Quebec, 1870).

4 In the Canadian context, see, for instance, Colin Coates and Cecilia Morgan, *Heroines and History: Representations of Madeleine de Verchères and Laura Secord* (Toronto: University of Toronto Press, 2002); or Patrice Groulx, *Pièges de la mémoire: Dollard des Ormeaux, les Amérindiens et nous* (Hull: Vents d'Ouest, 1998).

5 Pierre Nora, 'Between Memory and History: Les lieux de mémoire,' *Representations* 26 (1989): 7–24.

6 The Acadian population of the three provinces increased from roughly 90,000 in the 1870s to over 140,000 in the early twentieth century; while Acadians account- ed for 11 per cent of the region's population in 1871, this figure had increased to 16 per cent by 1901. The growth was most noticeable in New Brunswick, where the Acadian share of the larger population increased from 15 per cent (1871) to 24 per cent (1901), in the process allowing Acadians to take the place of the Irish as the most important Roman Catholic group in the province. These demographic issues are discussed in Muriel Roy, 'Settlement and Population Growth in Acadia,' in Jean Daigle, ed., *The Acadians of the Maritimes: Thematic Studies* (Moncton: Université de Moncton, Centre d'études acadiennes, 1982), 166–70.

7 James Wilberforce Longley (1848–1922) represented Annapolis County (with only a short absence) as a Liberal member from 1882 to 1905, at which time he was named to the Supreme Court of Nova Scotia. He served as the province's attorney-general from 1886 to 1905.

8 Town of Annapolis Royal, Minutes of Town Council, 29 December 1902. A resolution was passed indicating that 'the Town Council is in sympathy with the movement to celebrate the ter-centenary of the founding of Annapolis Royal, and that the Council most respectfully request that the Nova Scotia Historical Society take the initiative and carry out the programme in connection with the celebration.' I am most grateful to Leah Butler for her research assistance in the town council minutes.

9 The trials and tribulations of Port-Royal are described in John Reid, *Acadia, Maine and New Scotland: Marginal Colonies in the Seventeenth Century* (To- ronto: University of Toronto Press, 1981), 18–19.

10 J.W. Longley, 'Demonts Tercentenary at Annapolis, 1604–1904,' *Collections of the Nova Scotia Historical Society* 14 (1910): 107–8.

11 In spite of the wide net cast by Longley, there is no evidence that he invited any women, nor did women figure in the organization of the festivities at Annapo- lis Royal, or for that matter at Saint John or Île Ste-Croix. The only time that a woman emerged from the shadows in the Nova Scotia celebration came via the publication by Isabella Owen of her recollections of her role as a hostess in her home to several of the dignitaries who were in town (*Halifax Chronicle Herald*, 20 August 1921). One striking change by the time of the quadricentenary was the central role of women in positions of leadership.

12 Paul Stevens and J.T. Saywell, eds., *Lord Minto's Canadian Papers* (Toronto: Champlain Society, 1981), 2:462. For his part, Longley later observed that 'many there are who think that [Minto] both could and should have attended on such an important occasion.' Longley, 'De Monts' Tercentenary,' *Acadiensis* 5 (1905): 7.

13 Library and Archives Canada (hereafter LAC), Laurier Papers, Laurier to Longley, 23 May 1904, p. 85955.

14 New Brunswick Museum (hereafter NBM), Champlain Tercentenary Fonds, Longley to D.R. Jack, 11 April 1904. In this regard, Longley stood apart from a contemporary commemorative event promoter, Earl Grey, who played a pivotal role in shaping the Quebec tercentenary of 1908. On this and other matters related to the Quebec Tercentenary, see H.V. Nelles, *The Art of Nation-Building: Pageantry and Spectacle at Quebec's Tercentenary* (Toronto: University of Toronto Press, 1999); and Ronald Rudin, *Founding Fathers: The Celebration of Champlain and Laval in the Streets of Quebec, 1878–1908* (Toronto: University of Toronto Press, 2003).

15 For Longley's support for closer economic ties with the Americans, see *Commercial union between the United States and Canada: Speech by J.W. Longley; delivered in the House of Assembly of Nova Scotia, May 2, 1887* (s.l., s.d.). Regarding his biographies, see *Joseph Howe* (Toronto, 1906), and *Sir Charles Tupper* (Toronto, 1916).

16 Longley, *The Future of Canada* (s.l., s.d.), 15.

17 Longley, 'Demonts Tercentenary at Annapolis, 1604–1904,' 118; 115.

18 *Halifax Herald*, 21 June 1904. From its founding in the 1870s, the *Herald* had been a staunch supporter of the 'Liberal-Conservative Party.' In fact, shortly after the conclusion of the tercentenary festivities, it enthusiastically supported the Conservatives, led by the native son, Robert Borden, in the federal election that took place in November. In its support for Borden during the election, the *Herald* characterized Laurier's Liberals as pro-American, in the process trying to view the Conservatives as the party of Canadian nationalists. From this perspective, it would have had little interest in supporting Longley's narrower vision of the country.

19 Nova Scotia Archives and Records Management, Nova Scotia Historical Society Records, MG 20, vol. 687, S.-N. Parent to Longley, 14 January 1904; Longley, 'De Monts Tercentenary at Annapolis, 1604–1904,' 122.

20 *Halifax Morning Chronicle*, 22 June 1904. Turgeon concluded his remarks in French, but did not repeat this sentiment.

21 Ibid. Like Turgeon, Langelier also appears to have spoken in both languages (*L'Évangéline*, 30 June 1904). His speech was reprinted in its entirely in *Le Trois-Centième Anniversaire de l'Arrivée de M. DeMonts à Port-Royal: Discours prononcé par l'Honorable Chs. Langelier, le 21 juin 1904* (Quebec, 1904).

22 H.B. Neatby, *Laurier and a Liberal Quebec* (Toronto: McClelland and Stewart, 1973), 153.

23 *L'Évangéline*, 30 June 1904; *Halifax Morning Chronicle*, 23 June 1904.

24 *L'Évangéline*, 30 June 1904

25 Ibid.

26 LAC, Fond du ministère des affaires étrangères (Paris), Kleczkowski to Minister, 10 May 1904 (microfilm F-2180).

27 *Le Soleil*, 25 June 1904.

28 NBM, Champlain Tercentenary Fonds, telegram from W.C. Gaynor to D.R. Jack, 21 June 1904.

29 LAC, Laurier Papers, A.W. Savary to Laurier, 20 January 1905, p. 93902. The information on the addition of the French text was provided by Theresa Bunbury, Operations Superintendent, National Historic Sites, Southwest Nova Scotia.

30 NBM, Natural History Society, Minutes of General Meeting, 3 June 1902; NBM, Alice Fairweather Fonds, Minutes of the Loyalist Society (F16), 13 January 1903. The events at Saint John in 1904 have also been discussed, from a slightly different perspective, in Greg Marquis, 'Celebrating Champlain in the Loyalist City: Saint John, 1904–10,' *Acadiensis* 33 (2004): 27–43.

31 NBM, Champlain Tercentenary Fonds, Longley to Raymond, 11 November 1903. Raymond was active in the New Brunswick Historical Society and the author of numerous works, many of which dealt with the history of the St John Valley.

32 Ibid., Longley to D.R. Jack, 10 February 1904.

33 Ibid., 8 April 1904.

34 Ibid., 11 April 1904. While Longley thought the Saint John organizers went too far in presenting a spectacle for the public, the *New Brunswick Magazine* found that the celebration 'was largely of a literary character and was not signified by parades and pageants that were not unnaturally looked for by the general public, though this feature was not altogether lacking.' *New Brunswick Magazine* 4 (September 1904): 9.

35 Provincial Archives of New Brunswick, Executive Council Records (RS9), T.H. Bullock to L.J. Tweedie, 26 March 1904; Minutes of the Common Council, City of Saint John, 4 April and 2 May 1904.

36 NBM, White Scrapbook #19: Tercentenary, 1904; shelf 37a; clipping from 12 February 1904. It is tempting to speculate why the organizers of the three events eschewed Native participation, but they left behind no explanations in this regard.

37 W.F. Ganong, 'A Visitor's Impression of the Champlain Tercentenary,' *Acadiensis* 5 (1905): 21. While it was customary for local newspapers to trumpet the size of the crowds at such events, no such estimate was published in this case. It is impossible to know if this was a result of careless reporting or if it suggested that the crowds were less than the promoters might have wished.

38 *St. John Daily Telegraph*, 25 June 1904.

39 Ibid., 4 June 1904.

40 Ibid., 29 April 1904.

41 Ibid., 24 June 1904. The Loyalist Society repeated this demand for a tablet in honour of their ancestors shortly after the tercentenary. NBM, Alice Fairweather Fonds, Minutes of the Loyalist Society (F16), 15 July 1904. Although proposed, this tablet was never erected. Nor was any action taken on the proposal to have

two tablets alongside the one to Champlain, one in honour of the Loyalists and the other in honour of the 'men who made St. John the centre of trade for the Maritime Provinces before the Loyalists came here.' *New Brunswick Magazine* 4 (September 1904): 12.

42 NBM, New Brunswick Historical Society, Regular meeting, 3 May 1904. A statue to Champlain would ultimately be constructed in 1910. Although it was first proposed in the early 1900s, the slow construction of the monument, its rather marginal location, and the tributes to Dugua on the occasion of its unveiling all suggested some of the reluctance to embrace Champlain that had been evident in 1904. See Marquis, 'Celebrating Champlain,' 41–3.

43 *St. John Daily Telegraph*, 24 June 1904; *New Brunswick Magazine* 4 (September 1904): 29.

44 NBM, New Brunswick Historical Society, Meeting, 7 June 1904.

45 NBM, Champlain Tercentenary Fonds, Pascal Poirier to D.R. Jack, 5 June 1904; *Le Moniteur Acadien*, 16 June 1904.

46 *St. John Daily Telegraph*, 25 June 1904; *Le Moniteur Acadien*, 30 June 1904.

47 According to the 1911 census, while roughly 5 per cent of the population of Annapolis Royal was of French origin, this figure was only 2 per cent for Saint John.

48 *New Brunswick Magazine* 4 (September 1904): 14.

49 NBM, Champlain Tercentenary Fonds, letters from Pascal Poirier, 22 May and 31 May 1904.

50 Ibid., Champlain Tercentenary Fonds, John V. Ellis to D.R. Jack, 15 June 1904.

51 *St. John Daily Telegraph*, 25 June 1904. A longer and more assertive text was published in *Le Moniteur Acadien*, 7 July 1904. Since other speeches in French were signalled as such by the *St. John Daily Telegraph*, it seems likely that Landry spoke in English and then published a fuller French text for Acadian consumption.

52 The history of the name of the island is discussed in 'Tercentenary of the Landing of De Monts at St Croix Island,' *Collections of the Maine Historical Society* 3rd series, 2 (1906): 108–9.

53 Nova Scotia Archives and Records Management, Nova Scotia Historical Society Records, MG 20, vol. 687, Henry Burrage to Longley, 1 February 1904; Calais (Maine) Municipal Archives, City Council Minutes, 8 February 1904.

54 *St Croix Courier*, 30 June 1904.

55 *Collections of the Maine Historical Society*, 3rd series, 1 (1904): 2.

56 Nova Scotia Archives and Records Management, Nova Scotia Historical Society Records, MG 20, vol. 687, Henry Burrage to Longley, 1 February 1904.

57 *St Croix Courier*, 30 June 1904.

58 Nova Scotia Archives and Records Management, Nova Scotia Historical Society Records, MG 20, vol. 687, Henry Burrage to Longley, 1 February 1904.

59 'Tercentenary of the Landing of De Monts at St Croix Island,' 112.

60 Ibid., 80.

61 *Saint John Evening Times Globe*, 24 June 1954.

62 Interview by the author with Norma Stewart, 28 May 2004.

63 Ibid.; interview by the author with Chantal Abord-Hugon, 25 May 2004. Abord-Hugon worked for the Société nationale de l'Acadie as 'Coordonnatrice du 400e anniversaire de l'Acadie.'

64 Interview with Norma Stewart.

65 Minutes of meeting of Acadie 2003–5, 22 August 2000. Document secured via access to information request to Canadian Heritage, 232-ATH-03/04–093. The frustration that English-speakers were marginal players was similarly felt in Annapolis Royal, which wanted to stage a celebration of the four hundredth anniversary of the founding of Port-Royal in 1605. While Longley had been prepared to mark this event in 1904, David Kern, president of the Port-Royal 400 Society, wanted to mark the establishment of the settlement in 2005. However, his group was unable to secure financial support because it was constructing an event that was outside the limits set in order to focus upon 2004 as the anniversary of the birth of Acadie. Kern's concerns were chronicled in a series of articles in the [Annapolis Royal] *Spectator*, 5 August–2 September 2003. This matter is dicussed at length in my *Remembering and Forgetting in Acadie*.

66 Interview by the author with Maurice Basque, 26 May 2004.

67 Government of Canada press release, 'Le gouvernement du Canada est fier de participer à la commémoration du 400e anniversaire de l'Acadie,' 15 August 2002.

68 New Brunswick Official Travel Guide, 2004, p. 5. The same re-enactor is depicted on the Parks Canada website, superimposed upon Île Ste-Croix, http://www.pc.gc.ca/voyage-travel/pv-vp/itm4-/page7_e.asp (accessed 26 February 2005). The Park Service's Dugua is depicted below, along with the bronze of the hero of 2004. It should be noted that the NPS prefers to claim that the bronze in question was only a 'French gentleman.' In fact, however, this life-sized figure is shown next to a plaque that features the exploits of Dugua, thus making it hard for the observer to avoid concluding that he was in fact the subject of the statue.

69 As we saw above, the leaders of Annapolis Royal chose to stage their own quadricentenary celebrations in 2005.

70 Parks Canada press release in advance of ceremonies, 26 June 2004.

71 National Parks Service, 'Notes for Marie Rust at the 400th Anniversary of Saint Croix,' distributed 26 June 2004. The list of Dugua-dominated activities could go on at some length. He was featured in speeches which marked the founding of the Île Ste-Croix settlement, and was the subject of postage stamps issued in both Canada and France. As for the recognition of Dugua in France, the four hundredth anniversary celebrations saw both the publication of Guy Binot, *Pierre Dugua de Mons* (Royan, France: Éditions Bonne Answe, 2004) and the production of the

film *Sur les pas de Pierre Dugua de Mons,* by Marie-Claude Bouchet and Michel Gemon.

72 Interview with Maurice Basque.

73 Interview with Chantal Abord-Hugon.

74 'Notes pour une allocution du ministre délégué aux Affaires intergouvernementales canadiennes et aux Affaires autochtones, M. Benoît Pelletier, à l'occasion d'une cérémonie commémorative soulignant le 400e anniversaire de la fondation de l'Acadie et du premier établissement français en Amérique du Nord, le samedi 26 juin 2004, au site historique international de l'Île Sainte-Croix, Bayside, Nouveau-Brunswick.' This emphasis upon Champlain was also found during other moments of the 2004 celebrations when the control of Acadians was not evident. The federal government, as part of a program to raise the visibility of Canada in France upon the quadricentenary, invested in the creation of a Maison Champlain in Brouage, the site of his birth. Outside governmental circles, Historica created the website 'Champlain and Acadia,' http://www.histori.ca/champlain/index.do (accessed 15 February 2005), which is dedicated to celebrating 'the 400th anniversary of the arrival of Samuel de Champlain in Acadia in 1604'; and the CBC created the site 'Champlain Anniversary,' http://www.cbc.ca/news/background/ champlainanniversary/ (accessed 15 February 2005), which similarly pushed Dugua to the side. There was also the lavish book in honour of Champlain published under the direction of Denis Vaugeois (a former Quebec cabinet minister) and Raymonde Litalien (of the Canadian embassy in Paris). See *Champlain: The Birth of French America* (Montreal: McGill-Queen's University Press, 2004).

75 Cited in Carol Doucet, 'Encore une polémique sur le premier établissement français au Canada? Le Québec a peur de quoi au juste?' www.capacadie.com/ chroniquedumonde/detail.cfm?id=101149 (accessed 24 February 2005).

76 Cited by Radio-Canada, 7 August 2003: http://www.radio-canada.ca/regions/ atlantique/nouvelles/200308/07/002-doute-qc-2004.shtml (accessed 25 February 2005).

77 There was also a second theme, a recognition of the role that First Nations people had played in the establishment of Acadie. Space limitations prevent discussion of that question, which I have addressed at length in both *Life after Île Ste-Croix* and *Remembering and Forgetting in Acadie.*

78 The role of Grand-Pré as a lieu de mémoire for Acadians is discussed in Barbara Le Blanc, *Postcards from Acadie: Grand-Pré, Evangeline and the Acadian Identity* (Kentville, NS: Gaspereau Press, 2003).

79 While the population with French as its mother tongue increased numerically in the other Atlantic provinces up to the 1960s, this growth as a percentage of each province's population was rather modest compared to the situation in New Brunswick. Since the 1960s, however, while the French mother-tongue population

stayed rather stable in New Brunswick, it declined as a percentage of the provincial population, standing at roughly one-third in 2001. Accordingly, while the population has shown considerable vitality, Acadian leaders were also aware of its fragility, and so had a further motivation for advancing its specific identity in the context of the events of 2004.

80 There were parallels between the redefinitions of the self-image of Acadians and Quebecers. In the latter case, Jocelyn Létourneau has described the transformation of the understanding of the past from one that saw the French Canadian, who had been 'vaincu, humilié et démoralisé,' replaced in the historical record by the Québécois, 'accompli, entreprenant et ambitieux.' 'La production historienne courante portant sur le Québec et ses rapports avec la construction des figures identitaires d'une communauté communicationnelle,' *Recherches sociographiques* 36 (1995): 12.

81 *Les Mots de la Fête* no. 7 (May 2004): 2.

82 Interview with Maurice Basque, 26 May 2004.

83 Ganong, 'A Visitor's Impression of the Champlain Tercentenary,' 21.

84 Nelles, *The Art of Nation-Building*, 163.

85 These observations are derived from film footage collected at the event.

86 See Maurice Agulhon, 'La "statuomanie" et l'histoire,' *Ethnologie française* nos 2–3 (1978): 145–72.

87 David Glassberg, 'History and the Public: Legacies of the Progressive Era,' *Journal of American History* 73 (1984): 974.

PART TWO

Pedagogies of Nation

5 'If I'm Going to Be a Cop, Why Do I Have to Learn Religion and History?': Schools, Citizenship, and the Teaching of Canadian History

KEN OSBORNE

Introduction

One of public history's responsibilities is to present specialized historical research in ways that non-specialists find accessible, informative, interesting, and even thought-provoking. It bridges the gap that often exists between history as practised by researchers and people's general interest in the past, between analytical history and celebratory (or nostalgic) heritage. As a result it is necessarily concerned with the discovery and organization of information, with its presentation, and with pedagogy. Viewed in these terms, the history that is taught in schools is a form of public history. It represents a sustained attempt not only to teach people, in this case children and adolescents, about the past, but also to interest them in it and to lead them to think about it. For many people school is the first, and often the only, place where they encounter history, not as a grab-bag of miscellaneous information, but as a formal subject of study, and in the best classrooms a form of disciplined inquiry. We all have our personal sense of the past, but it is in school that we are systematically introduced to a past that is not part of our direct experience. Indeed, one of the purposes of public schooling is to make us feel that this impersonal past is part of our own, personal history, that the people and events described in our textbooks belong to us and are in some way our ancestors and forebears.

In addition, of course, school history is not just any history, or a comprehensive survey of the whole of the known past, but rather the study of those aspects of the past that someone, somewhere, has decided that children need to know, either for their own good or, more often, for the good of the society in which they are growing up to become citizens. More than perhaps any other subject, history is supposed to teach citizenship, broadly defined as a combination of a sense of national identity, patriotic spirit, civic engagement, and more or less critical acceptance of societal norms and values. Above all, school history has been expected to buttress that collective memory and strengthen those mnemonic bonds that are believed to hold society and the nation-state together.

In what follows I examine the ways in which schools in Canada have used Canadian history as a vehicle for citizenship education. In doing so, I suggest that history education in Canada falls into three stages: first, a period of entrenchment and consolidation stretching from the 1890s to the 1960s; second, the charting of a new direction, beginning in the 1970s and continuing through the 1990s and beyond; and, third, a period of challenge and critique in the 1990s that contributed to the beginnings of a fundamental rethinking of the nature and purpose of history education in the schools.

The Entrenchment of History, 1890s–1960s

In the second half of the nineteenth century, in Britain and the United States, history had to struggle to find a place in school and university curricula. Defenders of the traditional curriculum saw it as an undeserving interloper, a soft option that demanded nothing more than an agile memory and that lacked the intellectual rigour of such established subjects as Latin, Greek, and mathematics. Proponents of the new natural sciences saw it as an unwelcome competitor for space in an already crowded curriculum. However, when Canadian governments created systems of compulsory public schooling in the late nineteenth and early twentieth centuries, these battles had been largely fought and won. In Canada provincial policy-makers accepted without question that history should be one of the core subjects of the school curriculum. By the turn of the century English-Canadian nationalists saw it as axiomatic that school history should instil in students their particular version of Canadian identity. As Vincent Massey put it in 1926, 'In a country with so scattered a population as ours and with a vast frontier exposed to alien influences, the task of creating a truly national feeling must inevitably be arduous. But this is the undertaking to which our educational systems must address themselves, for by true education alone will our problems be solved.'[1]

It is not difficult to see how history was expected to help in this process. Through a sense of shared history, students in all parts of Canada, including those of immigrant parentage, would learn to see themselves as Canadians first and foremost. History was the inspirational story of the building of the Canadian nation, usually against heavy odds, whether in the shape of internal doubters or external enemies, and always in the context of a harsh and forbidding natural environment. History demonstrated the national character in action. In the words of a 1905 textbook: 'Every boy and girl of Canada likes to read the story of our past. It is a tale of discovery and adventure, of the deeds of heroes, of fierce struggles with enemies, of bravely facing death and suffering in many forms. This record of the deeds of heroic men and brave women, who suffered and toiled to carve from the wilderness homes that are fitted to nourish a sturdy race, will help to form the life and character of the children who grow up to fill their place.'[2] This conception of history and its purpose prompted Ontario's minister of education, George Ross, in 1892 to dismiss the textbooks of his day as mere 'provincial histories, without reference to our common country.' As he went on to ask, posing a question that was to be asked many times over the next hundred years: 'Can't we agree upon certain broad features common to the whole of this Dominion with which we can indoctrinate our pupils, so that when a child takes up the history of Canada he feels that he is not simply taking up the history of Canada such as the old Canada was, but that he is taking up the history of a great country?'[3] Twenty years later, Manitoba's minister of education echoed the same call, telling teachers that 'A teacher should be a teacher, not for one province only but for all Canada. Our schools should not be Manitoba schools, but Canadian schools located in Manitoba.'[4]

Ross exaggerated when he accused history textbooks of being 'merely provincial histories.' Such books did exist, especially in Atlantic Canada, which was understandably concerned lest its long pre-Confederation history disappear in national history textbooks that emphasized the formation of the Canadian state, and in Quebec, where textbooks emphasized the importance of the Roman Catholic religion and the historical development of French North America.[5] However, such regional histories did not exclude the use of more broadly 'national' histories, and in Atlantic Canada school curricula included both. Indeed, textbook authors largely shared Ross's sentiments. In the words of Andrew Archer, author of the authorized textbook in New Brunswick schools, writing in 1877, 'Separate histories of the British North American Provinces have, from time to time, been written for the use of schools; but these, viewed from the stand-point of the Dominion under Confederation, are incomplete.'[6] In other words, contrary to Ross's allegations of excessive provincialism, textbook authors saw themselves as writing the history of the Dominion as a whole. To quote the New Brunswick textbook once more, 'In the present book an endeavour has been made to give a general view of the history of the country now known as Canada, from the earliest to the latest times.'[7] The textbook used in Ontario and Manitoba in the 1880s made a similar point: 'The History of Canada … tells us how each province began and grew in numbers, extent, and wealth; and how they all came afterwards to form the Union called the Dominion of Canada.'[8] Moreover, textbook authors justified the study of history in terms of its pan-Canadian value as training in 'the duties of citizenship' and the shaping of an 'intelligent patriotism.'[9]

It was not so much that textbooks, at least before the 1890s, celebrated the creation of the new Dominion, but rather that they accepted it as an unavoidable reality, perhaps even a necessary evil. The creation of the new Canadian state at some point demanded the construction of a new pan-Canadian history. If Nova Scotians, New Brunswickers, and the residents of all the other provinces were now obliged to think of themselves as Canadians, and thereby add to their existing sense of colonial/imperial (and now provincial) identity a new identification with Canada as a whole, then it followed that they needed to know what being Canadian entailed. And this, inevitably, meant knowing something about Canada's history. It was not so much a matter for celebration, but rather the recognition of a new reality. The precise relationship between the new Canadianism and existing regional loyalties remained to be worked out – indeed, in many ways it became one of the defining features of Canada's continuing existence, hence the repetitious debates over the teaching of Canadian history in the schools which seem to occur about once each generation.

All of which leaves one wondering what Ross was getting at. As G. Laloux-Jain suggests, he might have been flying the nation-building flag in order to protect his political credentials against Ontario critics who were accusing him of authorizing textbooks that failed to imbue young Ontarians with sufficient loyalty to 'the Union Jack, the beaver, and the maple leaf.'[10] His attack on provincialism might also have been a veiled criticism of French-language textbooks in Quebec, which took an explicitly Quebec-centred line and praised Confederation and the British connection, not for creating a united Canada, but for providing an umbrella under which Quebec could control its own affairs. As a widely used Quebec text noted in 1882, 'Aujourd'hui, les Canadiens-Français sont maîtres de leur destinée, tant est imaginaire la tutelle britannique.' At the same time, however, this text urged its young readers to take advantage of the wider opportunities that Canada offered them (albeit in an attempt to discourage them from emigrating to the United States): 'Il ne s'agit plus de guerroyer contre un ennemi envahisseur, ou de s'opposer à une souveraineté qui veut imposer des lois arbitraires. Maintenant, c'est la joute des talents entre les membres de la famille canadienne, joute pacifique, mais la plus grandiose qui fut jamais.'[11] It is equally possible that Ross was attempting to tell his audience what he assumed they wanted to hear. It was presumably no coincidence that he voiced his call for a national vision of history during the course of his Presidential Address to the Dominion Education Association at the very time that the Association was organizing its campaign for a single national history textbook to be used in all Canadian schools.

Above all, Ross wanted textbooks to present a more explicitly nation-building narrative, both to give coherence to an otherwise fragmented story and to instil a pan-Canadian patriotism in the young. As things stood, the need to keep textbooks cheap at a time when parents had to pay for them, together with the desire to avoid accusations of religious or political partisanship, meant that textbooks became short catalogues of facts devoid of rhetorical distinction or stylistic elegance, primers rather than books. In New Brunswick, Andrew Archer's first version of his Canadian history text, for example, ran to some 470 pages and was full of dramatic incident and purple prose, but his abridged and much cheaper version, designed for use as a school primer, was dramatically different: less than half the length and written in much flatter language. In the case of another widely used school textbook, Jeffers compressed his three-hundred-plus-page history of Canada into a mundane primer less than half as long, while in Quebec Toussaint explicitly called his book a summary ('abrégé').[12]

These textbooks took their central theme as the creation of the Dominion of Canada. They treated Canadian history as primarily the history of Quebec and Ontario, with very little attention to the West, which was judged to have had virtually no history prior to the entry of Manitoba and British Columbia into Confederation, and a few chapters or parts of chapters devoted to the Atlantic provinces. In the words of a New Brunswick textbook, Canadian history 'centres on the Provinces now called Quebec and Ontario which long alone bore the name of Canada, but though these necessarily occupy the greatest space, the course of events in Nova Scotia, New Brunswick, and the other Provinces, is in this book treated in the order of their relative importance.'[13] The problem was, of course, that this conception of Canadian history marginalized the pre-Confederation histories of provinces other than Quebec and Ontario, and indeed their post-Confederation histories also insofar as these had no direct bearing on the development of the Canadian state. In effect, Ontario and Quebec became Canada, and all other provinces became peripheral 'regions.'

Ross saw 1867 as the key event in the historical trajectory of Canadian nationhood, both the culmination of the developments of the previous centuries and a foundation for the future. Maritime authors, by contrast, in the 1870s and 1880s saw it as a terminus, the point at which their local histories ended and a new history of Canada began. Provincial history textbooks, for example, took 1867 as their end-point, usually ending with a brief survey chapter on the constitution of the new Dominion. They did not celebrate it. Nor did they use it as an occasion for rhetorical celebration of a new national future. This began to happen only towards the end of the 1890s, no doubt as a consequence of the national textbook contest that was launched in 1892. Until then, Maritime textbooks described Confederation very matter-of-factly as a political arrangement among provincial governments to which public opinion was largely opposed. In the words of an 1878 text, 'There was a storm of opposition in the maritime provinces. Prince Edward Island turned her back upon confederation with utter scorn. New Brunswick rejected it by electing a strong anti-confederate House. In Nova Scotia, there were murmurings of dissatisfaction, but the people had no opportunity of expressing their views at the polls.'[14]

In the 1890s the immediate result was that the history of Canada appeared, not so much as a coherent unity, but rather an assemblage of selected pieces of provincial histories. In contrast, Ross wanted a historical narrative that would 'declare to the world that Canada is not divided into provincial ideas, but that the sentiments of the provinces are united into one harmonious whole.'[15] In this regard, Ross and the Dominion Education Association spoke as one, calling for a new kind of textbook that would be written from 'a Dominion and not from any provincial stand-point' in which the 'purely provincial shall be repressed, and what is of Dominion interest made prominent.'[16] However, this Dominion standpoint was not designed to supersede provincial identities but somehow to integrate them in order to incorporate 'the histories of all the provinces as nearly as possible concurrently and show, too, the points of historical contact and similarity between the provinces from their earliest period.'[17] Needless to say, there is considerable ambivalence here, though it is an ambivalence that has marked the writing of Canadian history ever since 1867. Ross and his colleagues were trying to reconcile two incompatible conceptions of Canada. One saw (and sees) Canada as a national entity distinct from and superior to the provinces that compose it. The other saw (and sees) Canada as the aggregate of its provincial parts, a community of communities, to use a later phrase, or an articulation of 'limited identities,' to use the term made famous by Ramsay Cook and Maurice Careless in the 1960s.[18] These competing definitions of Canadian identity are the subject of a long-standing Canadian debate and one that is central to the understanding of Canadian federalism. Since the 1890s it has also been central to both the theory and the practice of Canadian history education.

To promote its vision of a nation-building history, the Dominion Education Association in the 1890s organized a contest to produce a truly national textbook, acceptable in all provinces. Though the evidence is tacit on this point, it was probably no coincidence that this initiative began with the anglophone, Protestant teachers of Quebec, who might well have seen in national history a way of compensating for, and even overcoming, their minority status in the province. Whatever the case, a winner was duly selected and, though it did not in fact command universal acceptance, it pioneered a nation-building narrative, while also establishing an explicit link between the study of history and

Canadian nationhood, that quickly became the textbook norm.[19] In contrast to their dour descriptions of Confederation in the 1870s and 1880s, by the early 1900s Maritime authors had begun to adopt a much more celebratory tone, as in this 1905 example, revealingly headed 'Growth of a National Spirit': "'Dominion Day," July 1st, 1867, was observed throughout Canada with rejoicings. Separate colonies had become a Dominion, still under the protection of the British Crown, but enjoying the fullest measure of self-government ... A third of a century ago, the country we are now proud to call Canada was made up of colonies or provinces with separate interests and with few ties to bind them together. Now they are joined, with a growing ambition to become knit more closely as a Dominion and more closely united to the great British Empire, of which they form an important part.'[20] By the 1920s, at least outside francophone Quebec, there existed a de facto national history curriculum. Provincial curricula gave particular attention to those episodes of the Canadian past that affected them most directly, but otherwise presented a fairly uniform view of Canadian history which, in turn, set the pattern that was followed by textbooks.

For the most part, the persistent theme was endurance and success, usually against discouraging odds: Champlain's refusal to admit defeat; Frontenac defying the English in 1690; explorers and fur traders coping with distance and hardship; Loyalists overcoming their problems; Van Horne building the Canadian Pacific Railway; pioneers settling the Prairies; and so on. These success stories were interspersed with inspirational accounts of heroic sacrifice and even failure: Hudson's abandonment by his crew; Dollard des Ormeaux going down to defeat at the Long Sault; Isaac Brock's death at Queenston Heights. In Quebec, textbooks had a different list of successes and failures, and concentrated more on the history of New France and the place of Quebec in Canada, but in all textbook narratives, whether written in French or English, some cardinal virtues stood out, notably tenacity, survival, pragmatism, courage, and endurance.[21]

By and large, English-language textbooks organized their narrative around four topics: the European settlement of Canada and its territorial expansion; the shaping of political institutions, with an emphasis on federalism and parliamentary democracy; the achievement of national sovereignty from the winning of responsible government in the 1840s to the Statute of Westminster of 1931; and the political, economic, and demographic consolidation of the Canadian federation after 1867. All four topics were firmly anchored in a discourse of nation-building, as 1940s textbook titles made clear: *From Colony to Nation*; *Building the Canadian Nation*; *Canada – A Nation and How It Came to Be*, and others. Textbooks and curricula alike, at least in English-speaking Canada, saw Canada, not as a nation that was already built, but rather as one in the process of formation, and they saw the teaching of history as preparing young Canadians to take their part in that process. In their view, the future of Canada depended, at least in part, on how well young Canadians learned and understood this nation-building vision of their common history.

This nation-building narrative had its blind spots. It downplayed the existence of social conflict within Canada, except when it could not be ignored, as in the case of the 1837 rebellions or the Métis uprisings in the West. Like its academic counterpart, school history before the 1970s totally ignored class conflict, or indeed any mention of social class. By today's standards, little was said about Aboriginal people. Before the 1970s, most textbooks contained a quasi-anthropological chapter describing traditional Aboriginal life and culture, awarding high marks for such qualities as courage, endurance, and ingenuity, while commenting adversely on what they saw as Aboriginal 'barbarism,' and rejoicing that, under the paternal eye of the Canadian government, 'civilization' was making its presence felt. This done, textbooks then largely ignored the Aboriginal presence in Canadian history, save for a sometimes lurid description of Iroquois pressures on New France, some discussion of Pontiac's activities in the 1760s, and passing mention of Aboriginal participation in the fur trade and the War of 1812. Women similarly received very short shrift, except for brief mention of a few exceptional individuals such as Marie de l'Incarnation, Jeanne Mance, and Laura Secord, and some passing tributes to the virtues of pioneer women. Ethnic and racial minorities were either ignored or described in stereotypical terms, to the extent that an analysis of history texts in the late 1960s concluded that they were teaching, not history, but 'prejudice.'[22] Other critics pointed to the historiographical deficiencies of school history, accusing it of being at least a generation behind developments in the discipline. Most fundamentally of all, this version of national history took the concepts of nation and nationhood for granted. By focusing on the historical formation of the Canadian nation-state, it ignored all those aspects of the past that did not contribute to its evolution. It treated some people and events as historically significant, and therefore worthy of remembrance, to the extent that they contributed to a particular conception of the nation, and ignored everything and everyone else. To adapt an analogy used recently by an Irish historian in another context, history became a railway train, moving along prescribed tracks towards a set destination, passing clearly marked stations (Cartier, Champlain, Frontenac, Wolfe, the Quebec Act, and so on) along the way.[23]

As early as the 1920s, and certainly by the 1930s, critics were complaining that the nation-building grand narrative of school history failed to grip students. To quote the textbook publisher Lorne Pierce, no doubt drawing on his own extensive contacts with schools and teachers, it was 'nothing short of a tragedy, that such a large percentage of our boys and girls heartily dislike the story of their own country as it is now largely written.'[24] The Women's International League for Peace and Freedom undertook a survey of Canadian textbooks in the early 1930s, looking for evidence of militarism and chauvinism. It reported that the books were in fact reasonably balanced, but were irredeemably dull and uninteresting.[25] This judgment was repeated twenty years later when another investigation reported that Canadian history curricula were 'factualized to the point of boredom' producing a 'desiccated form of treatment ... quite sufficient to remove from the Canadian story any kind of interest or glamour which it may have possessed.'[26]

Some commentators blamed historians for this state of affairs, criticizing them for turning history into an arid story of political and constitutional developments that were, by definition, beyond the grasp of most school-age students, while at the same time robbing the Canadian past of its inherent romance and excitement. They called for less attention to political history and more to the social history of everyday life, which they assumed would be more intelligible and more interesting to school-age students.[27] The literary critic W.A. Deacon turned this into a more general argument, rebuking Canadian historians for relying on European models of dynastic history rather than exploring that distinctively Canadian theme, the conquest of the wilderness. As he saw it, 'All historians of Canada err in their approach to the drama of this land's early story. Being university men, they have been trained in a purely European method of looking at national events. They naturally think in terms of dynasties, wars, treaties, and the doings of officialdom ... Yet our great Battle of the Wilderness, in which long-enduring hearts have scored their glorious victories over nature, is too commonplace a thing for the academic historian to notice, though it began with Cartier and its end is not now in sight.'[28] Some critics, among them many school inspectors, blamed teachers for sticking too closely to their textbooks and treating history as a catalogue of poorly understood dates and events, though more perceptive commentators conceded that teachers faced what a 1923 report called 'a hopeless task,' themselves often minimally trained and educated, faced with unsympathetic school boards, lacking resources, and overwhelmed by adverse working conditions. Others blamed what this same 1923 report described as 'the cast-iron examination system by which pupils are more often than not encouraged to memorize verbally large sections of a text which they do not understand and in which they are quite uninterested.'[29]

These complaints that history failed to grip students, combined with the appeal of American-style progressive education, with its emphasis on a more innovative pedagogy that was designed to make students more active agents of their own learning, led most provinces in the 1930s to drop history from the early grades. Before the 1930s, even in the early grades children were taught history, not in any formal or systematic way, but in the form of stories, biographies, poetry, music, and drama. In this way, educationists hoped to teach children the essentials of the national narrative, while also teaching them to read and write, inculcating valuable moral lessons along the way, and laying the foundation for the later, more systematic study of history. In the 1930s, however, many educationists concluded that history was not a suitable subject for the early grades. Educational psychologists claimed that children had a very limited sense of time and chronology and understood the here and now concreteness of their immediate environment much better than they did the abstractions of the past. In addition, to the extent that citizenship was seen as an important goal of schooling, a persuasive case could be made for studying the local community rather than the exotica of ancient Rome or the Renaissance. Moreover, by the 1930s educationists were increasingly, though not unanimously, agreed that education was not so much a matter of instilling knowledge as of developing students' innate powers, so that subject-matter became a means to an end rather than an end in itself.

As a result, history increasingly lost ground to an interdisciplinary, community-centred social studies. This new subject had the further advantage of offering pedagogical opportunities that educationists and teachers found very attractive. Even the defenders of history worried about the limitations of the teacher-centred, textbook-dominated instruction that they saw taking place in many history classrooms. By contrast, the new social studies seemed to offer a real possibility of turning classrooms into 'laboratories' in which students engaged in the first-hand investigation of problems. For many so-called progressive educationists, both citizenship and pedagogy would be better served by having students investigate a local problem such as garbage disposal, care for the infirm, or beautifying the school, than by forcing them to remember the dates of battles and the terms of treaties or to study the lives of the great and famous people of the past.

The result was that by the late 1930s many provinces had eliminated history from the early grades and were contemplating replacing it with interdisciplinary social studies at all grade levels. Indeed, in the Depression years of the 1930s, social studies, with its emphasis on the present rather than the past, seemed to offer the possibility that schools could become agents of social reform, turning students into activist citizens equipped to tackle society's problems. Less ambitiously, its activity-based pedagogy seemed to offer an alternative to the frustrations of trying to interest students in the past, while also promising a more effective education for citizenship. In the event, thanks to a combination of lack of resources and the onset of the Second World War, most provinces refrained from making any fundamental change to their curricula beyond the early grades. Though they considered replacing history with social studies at all grade levels, only Alberta actually did so, thanks in large part to the influence of a few strategically placed advocates of progressivism in the province's education system, and to a general climate of agrarian radicalism that saw history as an outdated relic of academic elitism and favoured instead a curriculum more closely attuned to community needs and the training of citizens.[30] It was not until the 1970s that social studies began to displace, or in some cases absorb, history in most provincial curricula beyond the early grades.

The obvious exception to the nation-building narrative that was the norm in English-speaking Canada was to be found in francophone Quebec. The concern of Quebec educationists was for national survival, not nation-building. In their view, Quebec did not need to build a nation since it already was one. It existed within the Canadian federation and they feared that its survival would be threatened by English Canada's emphasis on building a new Canadian nation that, by definition, would comprise an English-speaking majority. Before the 1970s, history education in Quebec followed the line laid down by Lionel Groulx with his emphasis on the survival of Roman Catholic, French culture in North America. Like their English-speaking colleagues, Quebec educationists saw history as a national story, but in their case the nation of choice was Quebec, or, perhaps more accurately, Quebec-in-Canada. They saw English Canada's nation-building version of the past as a threat to Quebec's distinctive identity – which, indeed some of their anglophone counterparts intended it to be, especially in the Western provinces where there was scant support for French-language rights and considerable sympathy for the unilingual nationalism embodied by the United States. Few English-Canadian educationists shared Henri Bourassa's vision of a bi-national Canada, though some of them endorsed the historians' *bonne ententiste* view of two founding peoples living side by side within the Canadian tent – that is, when they thought about the question at all. The British historian Raphael Samuel once suggested that there are two ways to view history.[31] One sees the past as prologue to the present, the foundation of the contemporary world. The other sees the past as the world we have lost and values it for what it tells us about directions not taken. School history in English-speaking Canada was of the first type. In francophone Quebec, it tended towards the second, looking at the pre-conquest past of New France with regret, always wondering what might have happened had Wolfe not defeated Montcalm. Recalling his schooling in the Saguenay in the 1950s, Lucien Bouchard remembered that 'We spent so much time – years and years – on the French regime before the Plains of Abraham defeat. It was like a golden age for us. Some kind of Arcadia ... Then, very late in our teaching, there was the battle of Wolfe and Montcalm. That was the big thing. We spent weeks on that. The battle, before the battle, during the battle, after the battle.'[32]

In the late 1930s the Laval historian Arthur Maheux accused French-language history texts of teaching hatred of the English. His critics replied that to describe the injustices perpetrated by English-speaking Canada against Quebec and French Canadians was not to peddle hatred but to recite historical fact. André Laurendeau examined the texts in question and reported that, in their catalogue-like presentation of the past, they were too dull to teach anything, whether hatred of the English or love of Quebec.[33] The debate stirred up by Maheux and his critics entered the political arena and in 1943 the Quebec government investigated the textbooks at issue. The resulting report absolved them of teaching hatred but faulted both English-language and French-language books alike for failing to pay sufficient attention to the place of both groups in Canada's past and present. The problem, it concluded, was not hatred but mutual ignorance.[34]

In effect, two mutually opposed versions of the past were on offer. A whole series of key events was seen differently by the two language groups, most obviously the British conquest of Quebec, the 1837 rebellion, the Durham Report, the Act of Union of 1840, Confederation, the Riel rebellions, the Manitoba Schools Question and other language disputes, and conscription in the two World Wars. More broadly, what English-speaking Canada celebrated as the building of the Canadian nation, Quebec saw as the growing threat of assimilation to the English-speaking majority. In this context, Quebec educationists turned to the past to instil in the young a sense of solidarity with and commitment to the survival of the nation of Quebec. In the words of the Laval educationist Charles Bilodeau: 'Sous la plume de nos auteurs, l'histoire enseigne à conserver le mode de vie française et catholique, donne des exemples de courage et de tenacité qui constituent toujours une inspiration.'[35]

This issue came to a head (though not to a resolution) in a 1944 Senate debate that ended with a call for a national history textbook containing those facts – and nothing but those facts – that all Canadians, French and English alike, should know. The debate was initiated and virtually monopolized by a group of Quebec senators concerned that wartime tensions were creating a rift between Quebec and the rest of Canada. They concluded that the real problem was that French and English Canada did not know enough about each other and that what they did know was tendentiously selective. Their solution was to ask historians to identify those facts that all Canadians should know so that a single national text could be produced. Taking a simplistically empiricist view of history, and creating a rigid barrier between what they called 'history' (facts) and the 'philosophy of history' (interpretations), the senators maintained that such a book would be unobjectionable since it would contain nothing but agreed facts whose significance was vouched for by expert historians.[36]

Not surprisingly, historians steered well clear of this particular minefield, though in 1952 the then president of the Canadian Historical Association, Jean Bruchési, observed that the fact that applicants for citizenship had to pass a basic test in history suggested that someone, somewhere, had been able to decide what historical facts Canadians should know.[37] Moreover, in 1945 a committee of the Canadian and Newfoundland Education Association, including such luminaries as Arthur Maheux, Arthur Lower, and Richard Saunders, published a model history curriculum, covering grades 7 to 12.[38] It seems to have had little impact, since it took no notice of provincial plans and priorities and was in any case judged to be too ambitious for the students for whom it was intended.

Historians overwhelmingly rejected the idea of a single national textbook, and, by implication, a single national curriculum, which they saw as unachievable in practice and undesirable in principle. In their view, a single national textbook, containing only approved facts, would be a travesty of history. As the University of Saskatchewan's Hilda Neatby noted, 'At the present stage of our history and of our historiography, a text that would suit the two cultural groups and the four great geographic and historic sections of Canada would be a featureless mass of facts.'[39] Groulx himself pointed out that the very selection of facts and deciding how to order and describe them were themselves a matter of judgment and interpretation. Even the task of deciding how many textbook pages to allocate to New France and how many to the rest of Canada was, he insisted, a matter of values, not of facts. Other historians feared that a single national text embodying an approved list of facts, and backed by some kind of political or professional imprimatur, would too easily become a form of propaganda, whether for some version of national identity or, as Manitoba's W.L. Morton feared, for a Laurentian version of history that would legitimize the hegemony of central Canada over the rest of the country. Other historians took a more pedagogical line, fearing that the spurious prestige of an official national textbook would only encourage teachers to become even more textbook-based in their teaching than they already regrettably were. In this view, what was needed was not a single national textbook, but a greater variety of better textbooks than those currently in existence.[40]

Historians' objections to a single national textbook, and to treating history as a catalogue of facts, were the visible manifestation of a much deeper question. Was teaching history as a form of citizenship education, whether defined in terms of national identity, pan-Canadian understanding, democratic values, political literacy, or some other attributes, a subversion of history as a form of disciplined inquiry and a negation of its contribution to a genuinely liberal education? Did it turn what should be a disinterested investigation of the past into a form of political propaganda, no matter how noble the cause? As the University of Toronto historian C.N. Cochrane observed in 1923, taking aim at both the rising Canadian nationalism and the burgeoning appeal of internationalism that emerged after the First World War, 'There are grave dangers in assuming too readily that history is a natural medium for teaching either patriotism or internationalism.'[41]

In their capacity as educators, historians were torn between their commitment to history as an intellectual discipline and their belief that an understanding of Canadian history would and should strengthen Canadians' sense of national identity and common purpose, especially in the face of regional and ethnic loyalties and Americanizing pressures. As a result, their textbooks often steered an uncertain course between history as an objectively neutral description of the events of the past and mythistory as a narrative that embodied and demonstrated the national character in action. As a leading textbook author, the University of Toronto historian George Brown, put it in the early 1940s, Canadian history displayed 'a persistent tendency toward nationhood.'[42] This came dangerously close to saying that the nation was somehow immanent in its developing past and that, by definition, historians were its high priests. If this were indeed the case, then it followed that textbook narratives should focus on and celebrate whatever helped build the Canadian nation and ignore whatever did not. As a result, when historians wrote school textbooks, as many of them did before the 1960s, they left out the evidential and interpretative uncertainties that were the stock in trade of the university lecture room, partly because they believed that school-age children were too young to handle interpretative history and partly because they thought it would not be good for them. Lionel Groulx, for example, drew a sharp distinction between historians as researchers, where he believed their work should be governed by the norms of scientific objectivity, and historians as teachers, especially in the schools, where their work should be governed by national and moral imperatives.[43] English-Canadian historians did not speak so explicitly, but their textbooks suggest they shared Groulx's views. To take a familiar example, McGill's E.R. Adair first published his demolition of the conventional heroic story of Dollard des Ormeaux at the Long Sault in 1932, but no textbook, including those written by historians, so much as mentioned it before the 1960s. The subtext of textbooks was that history was a descriptive account of the significant events of the past and that significance was itself a matter, not of interpretation, but of objective assessment.

Pedagogically, this rendered students powerless, largely confining them to the memorization of what their teachers and textbooks told them. Even when teachers wanted to teach against the textbook, as some certainly did, their freedom of manoeuvre was restricted by the pressure of textbook-based provincial examinations which emphasized the memorization of factual information. In mathematics, languages, science, and other subjects, there were problems to be solved and activities to engage in; in history, there were only facts to regurgitate. The teaching method of choice was the 'recitation.' As a British educationist observed in 1910, 'It is difficult to devise preparation for the boy other than the learning from a text-book of the facts of the lesson that is to be given or the revising of the facts of a lesson that has been given ... The limits of change appear to be the short lecture, the lecture interspersed with questions, the expansion of the textbook, the occasional setting of problems and the essay.'[44] The advent of educational films and radio in the 1920s and 1930s did little to change this state of affairs, since, like textbooks, they treated history as the authoritative recital of facts, albeit suitably tailored to their student audience and the imperatives of the classroom. Some teachers sought to escape from this stalemate by turning to a more innovative pedagogy, for example by using drama, poetry, music, and historical novels, by incorporating local or family history into their lessons, or by assigning research-based projects to their students, though this was most easily done in the elementary grades which were not subject to the pressures of provincial examinations. More often, teachers tried to add some interest to their lessons by drawing on such lurid and colourful episodes as the Iroquois tortures of the missionaries, John A. Macdonald's drinking habits, and other such exotica, thereby turning history into what one early historian called a form of police gazette, whose 'intrinsic interest appears to vary in direct ratio to its gruesomeness.'[45]

At a more routine level, students were offered a view of history that saw it as a series of noteworthy occurrences, connected by little more than chronological sequence, each of which could most usefully be described in terms of causes, events, results, and, perhaps, historical importance. This view of history gained added force by being embodied in provincial examinations which, for ease and uniformity of marking on a province-wide basis, relied almost exclusively on questions that called for factual recall of information. On these examinations, despite the conventional defence of history as important for national identity and citizenship, the nature of the questions indicated that history consisted of the memorization of factual information in order to write short descriptive essays. There was no reference to either national identity or citizenship in questions such as these:

> Draw a line about six and a half inches long. At the left of the line write the date 1763, when British rule began in Canada. At the right end write 1928. Let this

represent the period of British rule in Canada, each inch representing about 25 years. Several acts were passed during this time changing the form of government.

(a) Divide the line into parts, each part to represent approximately the time each act was in force.
(b) Under each division mark, write the name of the Act that came into force at that time.
(c) Write the date under the same point, one for each Act.
(d) Underneath the date write the name of one person who was prominent in the public life of Canada at that time. (Manitoba Department of Education, normal school and university entrance examination, 1928)

Outline the history of Manitoba since 1871. (Manitoba Department of Education, grade 11 examination, 1931)

List the terms of the Constitutional Act 1791. (Manitoba Department of Education, grade 11 examination, 1966)

Even more than textbooks, provincial examinations exerted a powerful influence on the way teachers taught, if only because teachers' professional reputations depended to a considerable extent on their students' performance on examinations. The causes-events-results approach to history had the added advantage of providing a pedagogically practicable, no matter how historiographically deficient, method of teaching which, for the most part, was equated, not with introducing students to the ambiguities of history and historical method, but with preparing them to write the provincial examinations. The result was that in the actually existing world of the classroom, teachers said little about either nation-building or citizenship. From a student's point of view, history became, not a narrative of nation-building or an induction into the national past, but simply one of the many hurdles to be jumped in order to graduate from high school. If students were learning anything about citizenship, it was to complete pointless tasks and do what they were told.

In effect, though they do not appear to have discussed it publicly and perhaps were not always aware of it themselves, historians found themselves facing something of a dilemma. For obvious reasons, ranging from professional self-interest to concern for the public good, they wanted history to be taught in schools. However, if, as historians believed, history as an academic discipline and subject of study consisted of the painstakingly difficult reconstruction and interpretation of the past through the investigation of primary sources, then by definition it was beyond the reach of school-age students. Indeed, many historians saw it as beyond the reach even of university undergraduates, which is why they typically reserved the study of historiography and historical method to graduate level studies. To some extent, narrative history and biography bridged this divide. The story-telling approach to Canadian history seemed to offer a way out of the historians' dilemma. History-as-story – and the more dramatic the story, the better – could easily be adapted for school use. Thus, by the 1920s textbook writers had enriched the austerely factual primer approach they had adopted in the 1890s by combining it with descriptions of dramatic events and larger-than-life characters. In 1929, for example, three of Canada's most eminent historians, George Wrong, Chester Martin, and Walter Sage, wrote a school textbook that was explicitly designed to present Canadian history as an adventure story 'written in a simple, vivid, narrative and dramatic style, emphasizing at all times the romance of incident and character.'[46]

The story-telling approach to history offered some obvious pedagogical advantages. One, it promised to make history interesting to students. Two, it would lay a foundation for later, more sophisticated, study for those who chose to pursue it. Three, it would create the cultural literacy and stock of shared knowledge that was thought to be essential for informed citizenship. Four, it offered a way of adapting the exigencies of historical study to the capacities of an immature audience. However, while story-telling history taught students the basic findings of the historical discipline, it taught them nothing about its methods of inquiry. As early as the 1890s some historians argued that, even in schools, history was best taught through the investigation of primary sources, but they were never more than a small minority of the profession.[47] Before the 1970s such approaches were rare, though not unknown, in Canada and were in any case precluded by the demands of fact-based provincial examinations. Until then, most educationists and historians distinguished between the kind of history taught in schools (and even in undergraduate courses) and that taught in graduate school. The former was knowledge-based and narrative-centred. Its favoured pedagogy was the lecture, the reading of assigned texts, and the essay or, in some cases, the oral report. The latter emphasized methodology and the investigation of problems. Its favoured pedagogy was the analysis of sources, the seminar, and the research paper. In terms of history as an intellectual discipline, the former was seen as the essential foundation for the latter. Thus, what was taught in schools could still be described as 'history' despite its disciplinary shortcomings.

In their treatment of school history, historians largely ignored the tension between the critically detached nature of historical study and the celebratory socialization inherent in education for citizenship. In their view, an objectively descriptive account of Canadian history, even when tailored to the demands of curricula and textbook publishers, and even when romanticized to whet the appetites of children and adolescents, would in and of itself stimulate patriotism in the young. In effect, to know Canada was to love it. In the words of a 1926 textbook:

> The prime need of the student is for an unbiassed account of how Canada came to be what she is today, and the main object of writing this book has been to provide such an account. In so doing, the author hopes to instil into those who read it a thorough-going spirit of patriotism which, while not wholly ignorant of the mistakes of the past, may yet express itself in a proper and predominant love of country, based on a healthy pride in its past record and a firm belief in its future greatness.[48]

Needless to say, by today's standards this 1926 text had its share of sexist, racist, and other biases, but what is notable about it is its assumption that what, at least by the standards of the 1920s, was a mainstream account of Canadian history (albeit one that did not dwell unduly on the 'mistakes' of the past) would automatically be a stimulus to patriotic feeling. The result, as W.L. Morton noted in 1953, was that there was often a conspicuous gap between the preamble to a program of studies and its contents. The first spoke of citizenship and other such virtues; the second simply recited the events of the past. Morton explained this dichotomy by noting that educationists usually wrote the preambles while historians and their teacher allies (who were often their former students) wrote the programs of study.[49]

A New Direction for History Education, from the 1970s to the 1990s

Between the 1970s and the 1990s history education took a new direction. It did not totally abandon the traditional nation-building approach but it certainly offered an alternative to it that some textbooks and curricula adopted. More often, the result was a hybrid that eclectically, and sometimes incoherently, combined elements of the old and the new approaches. At the very least, however, this new direction presented an alternative conception of history education that served as a model of what could be. Not the least of its attractions for teachers was that, whatever its implications for the traditional linkage between history education and the nation-state, it offered a way out of the pedagogical impasse that had for so long confined history to a narrowly didactic, recitation-based, form of teaching.

This new direction gained some of its appeal from a widespread conviction that the status quo was no longer tenable. In 1965 in Quebec the Parent Commission on educational reform rejected any use of history for patriotic purposes and urged that it be taught as a critical study of the past. A 1968 report on the teaching of Canadian history, bearing the pessimistic title *What Culture? What Heritage?*, described history curricula as outmoded and worthless, textbooks as stodgy and boring, teachers as barely competent, and universities and ministries of education as indifferent and uncaring. Only 7 per cent of Canadian history classrooms won a passing grade. At a time when some commentators were speculating that Canada's first hundred years might also be its last, the nation-building narrative seemed to have failed. A century of nation-building history had resulted in the rise of Quebec separatism, increasing provincial assertiveness, and accelerating Americanization. According to the report, Canada desperately needed a new civic education designed to promote pan-Canadian understanding, but the only thing students were learning from Canadian history was to dislike both it and Canada.[50]

This was not the first report to decry the teaching of history in the schools. It had been preceded by others over the years and it itself referred to 'thirty futile years' of discussion of the problems it revealed.[51] It was, however, the first report to be based on visits to classrooms all across Canada as well as on a wide variety of other data. Perhaps more to the point, its publication in the immediate aftermath of the celebration of the 1967 centenary of Confederation, with its concentration of fears for the future of Canada, gave it a unique newsworthiness and influence. Ironically, however, its call for a reinvigoration of Canadian history education led, not so much to an improvement in history teaching, as to the replacement of history by an interdisciplinary, present-oriented, Canadian Studies, promoted by the influential Canada Studies Foundation that was created in 1970. As a 1970 symposium on Canadian Studies was told, it was time to organize the curriculum around 'continuing Canadian concerns,' thereby freeing it from 'the dead hand of the past' so that it would become 'something more than an unproductive and unscientific form of story-telling.'[52] This particular appeal was intended as a call for a new approach to history based on the persisting themes of the Canadian experience, but, in the event, it opened the curriculum to a presentist emphasis on contemporary Canada and its problems that drew heavily on the social sciences. It was as if history's reformers had decided that history could not meet their expectations and so turned to something new.

In broad terms, the new conception of history education that began to gain ground in the 1970s consisted of eight related innovations. One, it reduced the time and emphasis devoted to political and constitutional history in order to incorporate the findings of the new social history that were beginning to appear by the 1970s. Two, as a result, curricula and textbooks began to include hitherto ignored, and often previously unknown, aspects of the Canadian past, notably in the form of women's history, Native history, labour history, and the history of minorities more generally. Three, it sought to make the study of history more demanding by introducing students to what curriculum designers called 'the structure of the discipline,' defined as the methods of inquiry and conceptual frameworks used by historians. Four, it paid less attention to chronological narrative and history-as-story, and more to the analysis of concepts, issues, and themes – for example, power, decision-making, federalism, and the like. Five, it explicitly subordinated the past to the needs of the present, treating history as valuable only to the extent that it addressed contemporary problems and concerns, and, in some instances, adopting a reverse chronology that began with the issues of the present and then followed them backwards into the past. Six, it was less concerned with the coverage of a wide range of subject-matter and more with the in-depth examination of a select number of topics. Seven, it favoured a pedagogy in which students were seen as researchers and investigators, as constructing their own meaning of the past rather than absorbing whatever their textbooks and teachers told them. Eight, and as a natural consequence of all these developments, the new conception of history education broke with many of the assumptions of the nation-building narrative that had hitherto characterized history education, notably by defining citizenship, not as an initiation into an essentialized narrative of the past, but as the ability to analyse, and in its more utopian versions perhaps even resolve, the public issues of the present.[53]

At the same time, the 1970s saw a marked decline in university-based historians' influence over history education in the schools. The first generation or two of Canadian historians had taken a keen interest in the state of history in schools. As well as writing textbooks, they sat on and advised curriculum committees, helped prepare and mark provincial examinations, spoke at teachers' meetings, and generally acted as academic gatekeepers for curricular matters. In addition, the most influential teachers had often been their students and maintained personal and professional relations with them. By the 1960s, however, Canadian history was becoming more and more specialized and historians had to devote more time and attention to keeping abreast of it. At the same time, university reward structures became more formal, with contracts and collective agreements spelling out terms and conditions of service and criteria for promotion. Historians increasingly had to meet disciplinary and institutional criteria of performance in which research and scholarship were seen as more prestigious than teaching or service. As a result, historians' academic and professional success came to depend on their contribution to the discipline of history, not on their involvement with the schools. At the same time, education had begun to establish itself as a university-based discipline with its own professors and researchers, housed in their own university departments and faculties, possessing their own specialized journals and jargon, and applying their own disciplinary standards and criteria. As a result, by the 1960s education specialists in the expanding faculties of education increasingly assumed the educational role once occupied by historians as shapers of curricula and examinations and writers of textbooks. Meanwhile, in the schools increasingly well qualified teachers displayed a new confidence and moved to take control of their own affairs, especially once traditional curriculum controls were relaxed and provincial examinations were abolished, thus giving them room to experiment and innovate with new courses and teaching methods.

The elimination of provincial examinations in the 1970s removed one avenue by which historians had exercised considerable influence over the high schools through their influence on examination committees. On provincial curriculum committees, historians found themselves at best only one voice among many, and a voice that was often out of sympathy with the new language of teachers and educationists, with their talk of entering behaviours, taxonomies of objectives, organizing concepts, and the like. In the 1960s a new discipline of curriculum studies emerged in Canada, posing questions that historians were unused to answering. Most historians more or less took it for granted that history should hold, as it long had, a privileged place in the curriculum. The new curriculum specialists, with backgrounds in education or the social sciences rather than history or the humanities, were more sceptical. Faced with designing a new curriculum, they asked whether history was even necessary. What were the goals that had to be achieved? What was the most effective way of attaining them? How could their attainment be measured? These specialists spoke not of subjects but of 'learning experiences' or 'forms of knowledge.'[54] To quote an American historian, reflecting on his work with schools in the 1960s: 'Most disturbing of all was the difficulty we had in coming up with a new rationale for history in the schools that was clear and convincing even to ourselves. In the face of the teachers' hard-headed insistence on precision in defining the objectives of the social studies curriculum, we became aware that our heartfelt declamations about "historical wisdom" and "a sense of the past" didn't really convey very much.'[55] The result was that, with some individual exceptions, by the 1970s most historians were well into what Gary Nash in an American context has called their 'long walk' away from the schools.[56]

More philosophically inclined curriculum specialists were asking equally awkward questions. Pursuing Raymond Williams's observation that any curriculum was a selection from the culture of which it was a part, they asked who did the selecting, using what criteria, and for what purposes? Did the history curriculum really represent the wisdom of the ages, Matthew Arnold's best that has been thought and written, or was it merely a form of cultural imposition or ideological hegemony?[57] In a sense historians found themselves hoist with their own petard. They had made the history of education a branch of social and cultural history and viewed schooling through the lens of class, gender, race, ideology, and the like, thereby eroding its former role as an inspirational story of progress designed to boost the morale of teachers-in-training. Their researches increasingly revealed how history was often used for ideological purposes. By the 1980s the question of whose interests the teaching of history served gained extra force as postmodern influences began to appear in discussions of history education, with their Foucauldian assumption that knowledge was simply power in action and that historical objectivity was a chimera. As a result, a new question appeared on the agenda of history education: not what, but whose, history should be taught in schools?

Externally, from the 1970s onwards the main challenge to history as a free-standing subject of study came from two related sources: the social sciences and the social studies, both of which claimed to offer a more efficient and effective education for citizenship than history ever could. In one sense this was not new. In the early 1900s some American social scientists had asked why history should enjoy a favoured place in the curriculum. If the ultimate goal was citizenship, they observed, it was not self-evident that history had anything more to contribute than did economics, political science, and sociology, or that the study of the past was preferable to the study of the problems of the present.[58] Nothing much came of these early moves to implant social science in the school curriculum, though historians had to find some space in their subject for the study of government and civics. As noted earlier, in the 1930s Canadian schools replaced history with an interdisciplinary social studies in the early grades but only Alberta adopted a social studies approach throughout the curriculum. By the 1970s, however, attractive high school programs were appearing in such disciplines as anthropology, sociology, economics, political science, and sociology. In addition, some social scientists were pioneering powerful programs with an interdisciplinary social science basis, of which the best known was Jerome Bruner's *Man: A Course of Study,* which was aimed at grades 5 and 6.[59] Following Bruner's principle that anything can be taught to any one at any age in an intellectually honest way and that a curriculum should be based on the conceptual frameworks and modes of inquiry, rather than the conclusions, of the intellectual disciplines, these programs introduced students to important questions ('What is human about human beings?' for example) and concepts (power, decision-making, causation, etc.) and incorporated a pedagogy of discovery and inquiry supported by carefully designed teaching materials. Conceptually sophisticated and pedagogically adventurous, programs like these offered a powerful alternative to the pedestrian didacticism of the history classroom. Moreover, in the 1970s, psychologists, extrapolating from the work of Jean Piaget, persuaded many in history education that most adolescents had not reached a stage of intellectual development at which they could properly understand history. By the 1990s, the limitations of this research had become obvious, but in the 1970s it contributed to a rising doubt as to whether history was a suitable subject for school students.[60] In this context, the new social science programs of the 1970s proved attractive to teachers and in some provinces sociology began to supplant history as the organizing basis of secondary school curricula.[61]

This disillusionment with history, combined with a growing feeling that society was changing so rapidly that the past had nothing to teach it, also explains the growing popularity, in Canada as elsewhere, of social studies, an interdisciplinary, social science–based, subject that had been popular in the United States since the 1930s. Two influential American reports had appeared in 1916 and 1918 that urged that the amount of time devoted to history in school curricula should be scaled back to make room for the study of contemporary society using the social sciences, and by the 1930s such courses as community civics and problems of democracy had become staples of the American curriculum.[62] In Canada, although social studies was adopted in elementary schools in the 1930s, it was only in the 1970s that it began to shape the high school curriculum, notably in the form of an interdisciplinary Canadian Studies and of courses in contemporary social problems. Thus began a process that continues today in which history is either absorbed in (some would say submerged by), or sometimes displaced by, an interdisciplinary social studies. Students still are taught the core topics of the Canadian past but increasingly in the context of social studies. Even when history remains on the school curriculum as a distinct subject, it is increasingly presented to students in a quasi-interdisciplinary form, organized around themes or issues such as immigration, identity, federalism, regionalism, and the like.

In 1970 only Alberta taught social studies at the high school level. Every other province taught history, usually organized as a chronological survey of what were seen as the main events of Canada's past. Today, this kind of chronological narrative is the exception, not the rule. The boundary line between history and social studies is increasingly blurry, to the point that it is often impossible to decide whether a course should more accurately be described as one or the other. Critics see this as a sign of conceptual confusion and pedagogical incoherence; supporters see it as a welcome indication of healthy interdisciplinarity.[63] To some extent, this shift towards social studies is an understandable extension of the conventional pedagogical principle that is endorsed by many historians that we study the past better to understand the present. Once this principle is accepted, however, it is difficult to resist the argument that, if this is indeed the case, it makes a certain sense to begin with the concerns of the present and organize our study of the past accordingly. There are, in addition, some pedagogical advantages in using the here-and-now concerns that students see described in the daily news to arouse interest in the past. Moreover, the blurring of the line that once separated history from social studies in some ways reflects trends in the discipline of history itself as historians increasingly seek to integrate the findings and methods of the social sciences into their work and to seek other ways than chronological narrative on which to base the teaching and writing of history.

Educationists have long debated whether history is more or less effective than social studies as a way of teaching students about the past and preparing them for the exercise of citizenship. To date, the debate remains inconclusive, not least because so much depends upon the quality of any given course and the way in which it is taught, but also because of the difficulties of deciding where history ends and social studies begins. Perhaps the most that can be said is that social studies appeals to those who see the past as valuable to the extent that it illuminates the present; while history attracts those who value the past for its potential to shape the way we see ourselves and the world in which we live. In a sense, to argue for the study of history in terms of its contribution to the education of citizens is to weigh the odds in favour of social studies, especially if citizenship is understood as the ability to understand and cope with the demands of the present. What history offers, and social studies does not, is not so much a way of addressing current concerns in the short term, but a historically informed way of thinking that enables us to contextualize those concerns by enlarging our sense of what it means to be human.

If the social studies and the social sciences challenge history education from without, developments in the discipline of history have influenced it from within. By the 1970s the traditional dominance of political-constitutional history was being rapidly eroded by a new kind of social history. The old conception of social history as 'history with the politics left out,' which reflected itself in textbooks with stories about habitants, Loyalists, homesteaders, and other pioneers (all nation-builders in their own way), was swept aside by a new conception of social history as embracing all branches of historical study, the history of society as a whole, with the politics very much left in and much more broadly understood, with a particular emphasis on the people and institutions that traditional history had largely ignored. 'History from below' began to become fashionable and was often much more pedagogically attractive than the old nation-building narrative that it displaced. This is not the place to discuss this shift and the reasons for it, which has in any case been much discussed over the years. Suffice it to say that this new social history, to be followed in turn by a new cultural history, transformed the discipline of history and remarkably quickly made its way, albeit in simplified form, into school history curricula and textbooks.

Perhaps the most obvious change in the content of history education was the appearance in curricula and textbooks of groups previously ignored, notably women, working people, and ethnic and cultural minorities. Canadian educationists had always liked to describe Canada as a mosaic, in contrast to the American melting pot, but had usually done so in the context of a nation-building narrative of two founding peoples, French and British, with an occasional nod to the First Nations. In the 1970s, in response to the increasing political salience of human rights and to the increasing racial and cultural diversity of Canada, this traditional narrative came under question. The 1970s saw a succession of critiques of the racist, sexist, and class biases of existing textbooks and curricula, which in the words of one report were doing little more than 'teaching prejudice.'[64] The minimalist response to such critiques was to insert new sections and illustrations in existing texts, but this could easily be dismissed as tokenism, as reducing history to a feel-good story of the contribution of each and every group to the building of Canada. The maximalist response was to recast the traditional narrative in ways that called into question existing periodizations, and assessments of historical significance, while also paying attention to topics that had hitherto been ignored. To take one example, older textbooks described the period from 1890 to the First World War largely in terms of the settlement of the Prairies, English-French relations, and the growth of national autonomy. The new texts of the 1970s and beyond dealt instead with urbanization and industrialization and the resulting social tensions and attempts at social reform.

Such topics eroded the consensual assumptions that had long underlain the traditional approach to history in the schools. The 1968 report *What Culture? What Heritage?* had criticized school history for amounting to little more than a 'white, Anglo-Saxon, Protestant political and constitutional history of Canada' that presented 'a shadowy, subdued, unrealistic version of what actually happened – a bland, consensus story, told without the controversy that is an inherent part of history.'[65] In the 1970s this began to change. It was, after all, difficult to deal with the new history of women, working people, Aboriginal peoples, and minorities generally, without addressing instances of social conflict. Nation-building, it seemed, was not the cooperative, positive, experience described in older narratives, where, except for a few unfortunate episodes such as the expulsion of the Acadians, everyone was a winner, but a contentious and contested process in which the losers also had a story to tell. The new history was receptive to flexible and contested notions of nationhood, while also exposing some of the less salubrious actions of the nation-state. It showed, for example, that establishing dominion from sea unto sea included clearing Aboriginal peoples off their ancestral lands, barring the entry of African Americans, Asians, Jews, and others, interning suspects in time of war, restricting the rights of labour, and assigning women to a limited role in society.

This new attention to previously ignored aspects of Canadian history gave school history a certain multi-perspectival tone. Textbooks and curricula began to acknowledge the reality that different people experienced the past in different ways and thus saw history differently. This was particularly the case, for example, in the case of Aboriginal history, where traditional narratives of Aboriginal settlement confronted more recent, archaeologically based, explanations and where oral testimony sometimes was at odds with the archaeological record. Indirectly, this turn away from the older idea that history was an objective reconstruction of the events of the past might have been influenced by the postmodern undermining of empiricist history that had begun to appear by the 1970s, but there is no direct evidence that postmodernism had any influence on the schools. More influential was the schools' embrace of identity history consequent upon their surprisingly rapid acceptance of multiculturalism as a fundamental principle of Canadian education.

In one sense, identity history was, of course, nothing new. Ever since the 1890s, schools had taught Canadian history in order to instil in students a sense of Canadian (or in Quebec, French-Canadian or Québécois) identity. What was new in the 1970s was the schools' acceptance of the definition of Canadian identity as essentially multifaceted. The concept of 'limited identities' advanced by such historians as Ramsay Cook and Maurice Careless in the late 1960s quickly became an orthodoxy of school history. Quebec's Quiet Revolution and the resulting deliberations of the Royal Commission on Bilingualism and Biculturalism led to demands from Canadians who were neither anglophone nor francophone for greater recognition in the Canadian polity. At the same time, changing patterns of immigration made Canada increasingly multicultural and multiracial, while the increasing political salience of human rights, in Canada and elsewhere, produced greater public awareness of Canada's diversity. In this context, parliament in 1971 declared Canada to be officially bilingual and multicultural. Having long rejected the notion of so-called hyphenated Canadianism, in the 1970s schools came to embrace it as a defining feature of Canada. Minorities, in particular, saw in history a means of preserving and strengthening their particularity and, by and large, provincial ministries of education agreed with them. In Nova Scotia today, for example, grade 11 students can, if they so choose, replace Canadian history with a course in Afro-Canadian studies, Acadian studies, Gaelic studies, or Mi'kmaw studies. In northern Canada, similarly, history curricula are suffused with Aboriginal content and perspectives.

Such developments illustrate what has been perhaps the most profound, but not necessarily the most obvious, aspect of the new direction of history education since the 1970s: its recasting of the linkage between history education and the nation-state. The historiographical and pedagogical weaknesses of traditional history education were well documented by the 1970s. In an increasingly multicultural Canada, hitherto ignored minorities were making themselves heard, while new (to Canada) minorities were in the process of formation. In this context, the old master-narrative of Canada as the creation of two founding peoples came under question. Canadians of other than British and French descent insisted that it ignored their contribution to the shaping of Canada and, in some cases, their mistreatment by the Canadian state. Aboriginal peoples condemned it as a racist dismissal of their place in North America. Women noted that it contained little or no place for them. Quebec's Quiet Revolution made it clear to all but the most obdurate English-speaking Canadians that Quebec saw itself as a nation, whether inside or outside Canada.

At the same time, the explosion of historical research highlighted the differences and tensions within Canada, past and present. In Ramsay Cook's judgment, 'The old assumptions of nationalist historians that all "Canadians" shared the same interests, enjoyed the same national triumphs, and celebrated the same national heroes have been left in tatters by studies of gender inequality, ethnic prejudice, and class conflict.'[66] Others felt that the new historiography, in Canada as elsewhere, had destroyed the very possibility of a unifying national narrative: 'The new research and writing in Canadian economic and social history asked implicitly whether the old paradigm of heroic nation-building was flexible enough to produce a framework for new insights. By 1970, it was clear that it was not.'[67] Perhaps most damaging of all, the evidence indicated that nation-building history was simply not working. Most students found it boring and remembered very little of what their schools had taught them. Others found that it contained no room for their personal histories and experiences. Nor, as the continuing constitutional debates of the 1970s and 1980s revealed, did Canada seem to be especially united, even though Canadians had all studied history in school. According to one observer of Canadian history education, 'Like Humpty-Dumpty, Canada is broken and will not be put back together again.'[68]

In a 1977 survey of Canadian historiography, a noted British historian urged historians 'to write about Canadians without being constantly preoccupied with the mystery of what is Canada.'[69] Even when he wrote, his exhortation was out of date and by the 1970s historians were ahead of him. The new social historians focused on issues of social class, ethnicity, race, gender, and culture in ways that either cut across national boundaries or operated at a sub-national level. More fundamentally, the new historiography historicized the concept of the nation-state, speaking instead of 'imagined communities,' 'invented' traditions, usable pasts, and multiple histories, and drew attention to what one historian described as 'the artificiality of national categories and the coercive power of their normalizing regimes.'[70] At times it came close to equating national history with national myth, in showing how history was often used and abused in the creation of national identities. Alternatively, it separated the concepts of nation and state, seeing Canada as a multi-national state in which different national identities coexisted. To quote a Quebec historian, 'Il peut y avoir une histoire nationale des Acadiens, des Cris (des autochtones), des Québécois, et bien entendu des Canadiens ... À chacun de déterminer si telle ou telle histoire est, pour lui, son histoire nationale.'[71] In the words of Carl Berger, 'This severing of nationalism and history' was 'one of the most significant developments' of the years after 1960.[72]

This disconnection between history and nationalism sprang both from developments internal to the discipline and practice of history and from historians' reactions to changes in the wider world. Internally, the new social history, like the new cultural history that both superseded and absorbed it, focused on topics that were not directly or obviously linked to the foundation and growth of the state or of nationhood, and in some cases directly challenged them. In this regard the new histories benefited from the apparent exhaustion of the old nation-building approaches, which by the 1960s seemed to be running out of steam. There was, after all, only so much that could be done with political and economic history, especially once their major topics and themes had been thoroughly explored. Thus, conventional national history was particularly vulnerable at a time when history departments were expanding and increasing numbers of historians and their students were looking for research topics that they saw as relevant to their own experience and to wider developments in contemporary society. Moreover, many of these new historians came from ethnic and class backgrounds that were very different from those of their elders, and their experience led them to take a more equivocal view of such entities as state and nation, and indeed of national history more generally. In such circumstances, it is perhaps hardly surprising that, in their constant search for explanation, historians turned an increasingly critical eye on the concept of the nation-state.

This interrogation of the nation and its associated nation-building narrative was in turn facilitated – some would say precipitated – by developments external to the discipline of history. The Holocaust and other genocides, two world wars and a series of other conflicts, the experience of fascism and communism, and the general trajectory of the twentieth century almost inevitably raised questions about the nature of nationalism, the nation, and the nation-state. The global revolution in communications, together with increasing international travel, made the world more transparent to more people than ever before. Patterns of immigration and marriage across cultural lines led to a diasporization of consciousness as more and more people defined themselves in terms of two (or more) national or other identities. Above all, the globalization of cultural and economic life led to a diminution of national sovereignty and what one historian described as 'the waning of territoriality' in the face of both subnational and transnational pressures.[73] The result of these and other related developments led at least some historians 'to see something that was impossible before: how constructed and fragile nations are, to see that they are not self-evidently inevitable or necessary or desirable.'[74]

No doubt because they are instruments of public policy as decided by political elites, schools did not go as far as historians in separating history from nationalism. Surveys of curricula show that the traditional topics of Canadian history remain in place, and schools, especially but not only in the elementary grades, still play plenty of attention to the symbols and accoutrements of Canadian nationhood.[75] Since the 1970s schools have not so much abandoned national history as redefined it. Or, perhaps more accurately, two definitions of national history coexist, sometimes in conflict, sometimes in a state of cooperation, and sometimes in mutual ignorance of each other. The newer approach sees nation-building not as the story of larger-than-life explorers and statesmen, but as the story of so-called 'ordinary' men and women. It is also less centralist, less focused on federal politics, though it certainly does not ignore them, and more inclined to define Canada in terms of the regions and cultures that compose it. It speaks, for example, not of the Canadian people in the singular, but of the Canadian peoples in the plural. In some ways, the new approach anticipated what Habermas was to call 'constitutional patriotism,' a sense of identity defined not so much as belonging to a national collectivity in the traditional sense, but as the internalization of civic norms and political principles embedded in and emblematic of a particular statehood.

The older nation-building approach treated national identity as a more or less unitary entity which, while it experienced its share of tensions, could be defined in terms of common values and shared experiences. It treated school history as a process of assimilative socialization to a pre-existing but still emerging tradition of citizenship. The newer approach is more dialogical. It speaks not of identity, but of identities. In the words of the Alberta social studies curriculum, 'The program reflects multiple perspectives that contribute to Canada's evolving realities. It fosters the building of a society that is pluralistic, bilingual, multicultural, inclusive, and democratic.'[76] Different provinces use different words but they share this orientation. In this view, to learn history is not to be inducted into an established national tradition, but to learn to engage in a continuing debate about the meaning of the present and the direction of the future.

Pedagogically, the new conception of history education aimed to teach students the skills and habits of mind they would need if they were to join this debate as citizens. It took a more activist view of citizenship than did the older nation-building approach. The older approach in effect equated citizenship education with the transmission of official knowledge and approved values. The new approach sees it as induction into the debates that lie at the heart of any democratic polity and that, in the case of Canada, are rooted in Canadian history. This was one reason why provincial curricula in the 1970s and beyond began to present history either as themes and issues to be investigated (for example, minority rights, federalism, identity) or concepts to be understood and applied (for example, decision-making, power, continuity and change), rather than as a narrative to be internalized. Ontario's Hall-Dennis Report of 1968 spoke for all provinces when it urged that 'students be exposed to historical evidence and, through free discussion and research, be permitted to seek answers and conclusions that may be at variance with established points of view.' Such an approach, according to the Report, would develop 'not only an awareness of civic and historical issues, but also a skill in research and a habit of inquiry that will serve the student in his future role as a citizen.'[77]

These issues-based and concept-based approaches took a largely utilitarian view of history, valuing it for its ability to illuminate the concerns of the present and for its potential for preparing students to address them. At the same time, they created an environment that fostered the emergence of a different, albeit much less popular, approach that saw the purpose of history education as introducing students to the nature of history as an intellectual discipline and a way of thinking and, in particular, to the basic elements of historical method. In the 1970s and beyond, while issues and concepts were the major focus of reform efforts in history education, some teachers began to emphasize 'doing' history rather than simply memorizing it. They placed more emphasis than ever before on students undertaking genuinely original projects, for example in local or family history, not simply digesting and synthesizing information from reference books. They supplemented, and sometimes replaced, textbooks with collections of primary sources. They began, albeit cautiously, to replace direct instruction and didactic pedagogy with so-called inquiry and discovery teaching. The 1968 report *What Culture? What Heritage?* reported that the most effective history classrooms used 'dialogue methods' of teaching in which students examined a historical problem in depth through the study of selected documents and secondary readings, all under the guidance of teachers who avoided traditional didactic methods in favour of a more indirect, discussion-based pedagogy.

Though their proponents were largely unaware of it, these new developments were in fact an unwitting rediscovery of an older tradition. By the 1920s, for example, educationists and historians had identified the elements of effective history teaching, though it was only in the 1970s that circumstances were favourable to their adoption. Above all, they wanted to convert history from an 'information' or 'memory' subject into an 'educational' one. They took as their model the laboratory-based, experimental, methods of science education. They thought it better to teach a few topics in depth than many topics more superficially. They saw facts, not so much as important in themselves, but as building blocks of thinking and understanding. They believed that history was best taught in the form of problems to be investigated rather than answers to be memorized. They wanted textbooks to be supplemented, and perhaps even replaced, by source-books and other resources. They favoured the use of the primary sources in the classroom. They wanted teachers to work as guides and mentors, as orchestrators of learning, rather than as lecturers and note-givers. They saw the history classroom as a 'laboratory,' where historical problems served as experiments and sources, pictures, maps, and other materials as equipment. Above all, they described the goal of history education as the attainment of 'historical-mindedness,' or 'the historic sense,' which they defined as comprising the ability to think in terms of origins and development, rise and decline, change and continuity; the recognition that institutions change over time; the ability to distance oneself from the passions of the moment to question the conventional wisdom of one's age, and situate the present in the context of past and future; the willingness to see the world though others' eyes; and an understanding of historical method and of the elements of history as a discipline and way of thinking.[78]

History under Scrutiny: The 1990s and Beyond

Perhaps not surprisingly, the new models of history education, whether organized around issues, concepts, or the historical method, that emerged in the 1970s proved controversial, not least because they flew in the face of received notions of what history was and why it mattered. In part, the controversy was a spill-over from professional disputes among historians as to the nature and direction of history as political historians sought to turn back the advance of the new social history and as historians of many different persuasions worried aloud about what they saw as the fragmentation of their discipline. In part, it arose from differences between social and cultural conservatives and their ideological adversaries over the state of Canadian society, differences which in turn reflected the new and competing directions open to an increasingly multicultural and ideologically divided Canada. And, in part, it represented the importation into Canada of arguments occurring elsewhere, especially in the United States, which had long been a major influence on Canadian education. The result was that by the mid-1990s there was increasing public debate over what many saw as a crisis in history education.[79]

Initially, this sense of crisis stemmed from a fear, shared by commentators on all sides of the ideological divide, that history was losing its accustomed place in the school curriculum, either because it was being absorbed into an interdisciplinary social studies or because it was being displaced by more vocationally useful subjects as provincial governments moved to connect education more directly with job-training and career preparation. It was, however, a short road from worrying that history was disappearing from the curriculum to wondering just what that history could and should be and why it mattered, and it was this latter concern that came to dominate the 1990s, not least when it seemed that there was a very real chance that Canada's very existence was threatened by the dynamism of Quebec separatism and the resulting sense of confusion in English-speaking Canada, and, in the longer view, by the economic, political, and cultural imperatives of globalization. The decade opened with the post-mortem on the failed Meech Lake Agreement of 1987 and the subsequent public relations campaign for its successor, the Charlottetown Accord, both of which led to charges that Canadians either did not know their history or failed to understand it.[80] In the midst of these controversies, and their accompanying admonitions that if only Canadians knew their history all would be well, came Michael Bliss's 1991 complaint that historians had 'sundered' Canadian history and threatened to sunder Canada by abandoning the national and nation-building agenda that had preoccupied their predecessors in order to pursue the more localized and allegedly more private concerns of social history. Bliss discerned a 'parallel relationship between the disintegration of Canadian history as a unified discipline, on the one hand, and on the other the withering of a sense of community in Canada which I believe partially underlies our current constitutional and political malaise.'[81] Towards the end of the decade came the publication of Jack Granatstein's polemic, *Who Killed Canadian History?*, accusing an assortment of educationists, feminists, multiculturalists, and just about every practitioner of social history of killing Canadian history, in the schools and elsewhere, thereby threatening the very future of Canada as a sovereign state.[82] On a more positive note, the decade saw the creation of a number of organizations pledged to advance the cause of Canadian history, most notably Canada's National History Society, the Dominion Institute, and the Historica Foundation (the latter two merged in 2009). It ended with various provincial governments taking steps to strengthen the teaching of Canadian history in their schools, and with the calling of Canada's first ever truly national conference on history education, organized by Desmond Morton and McGill's Institute for the Study of Canada and inaugurating what seems to have become a regular biennial event. By the end of the 1990s the erosion of history had been halted. Manitoba cancelled a plan to make Canadian history optional in its high school program; Ontario, Nova Scotia, and New Brunswick made it compulsory in their high schools; and Quebec made history a part of its curriculum at every grade level after grade 4.

In broad terms, the critics of history education levelled five charges against the new direction in history education that had emerged since the 1970s. First, they complained that history no longer served a national purpose and might even be anti-national in its effects, as a result of the turn to social history with its attention to the local and the regional and its tendency to highlight the misdeeds of the nation-state. Second, they charged that curricula no longer told a coherent story, national or otherwise, having abandoned chronology and narrative for the analysis of themes and issues, while increasingly blending history into an interdisciplinary social studies. Third, they maintained that the history-from-below orientation of social history was turning history into 'victimology.' In their view, this 'compensatory' or 'black arm-band' history undermined students' attachment to their country by dwelling unduly on its injustices and abuses. Fourth, they feared that the schools' embrace of multiculturalism risked turning what should have been a unifying national narrative into a divisive celebration of distinct ethnic and cultural identities. Fifth, they pointed to the many surveys that showed how little history students actually knew, a state of affairs which they blamed on the undisciplined child-centred pedagogy and its dismissal of factual knowledge that they believed dominated Canadian classrooms.

Defenders of the new directions in history education rejected all five charges. First, they pointed out that surveys of provincial curricula showed that students were still taught about the standard topics of Canadian history, and that political history had not been displaced, but supplemented, by social history. Second, they acknowledged that curricula no longer told the chronological story of nation-building that they once did, but added that there was no evidence that this affected students' knowledge of history and argued that organizing curricula around themes and issues was more pedagogically effective than conventional chronological narrative. Third, they rejected the charge of 'victimology,' arguing that to tell students the truth about the past, warts and all, was a matter of honesty, not trendy propaganda, designed to ensure that the errors and misdeeds of the past would not knowingly be repeated. Fourth, they defended the schools' embrace of multiculturalism, denying that it had become divisive and suggesting that precisely the opposite might be the case as hitherto neglected groups found themselves reflected in the curriculum. Fifth, they observed that there was no evidence that history classrooms had become permissively student-centred, noting that such research as there was suggested that traditional didacticism was the rule not the exception in most classrooms. As for students' historical ignorance, they noted that this was nothing new, having been a matter of continuous complaint for the last century, and therefore could not reasonably be seen as the result of new approaches to curriculum design and pedagogy.

These charges and counter-charges were not unique to Canada. In countries such as England and the United States the design of new history curricula proved controversial. In others, such as Israel and Australia, the incorporation into curricula of new developments in historiography also provoked controversy. In newly created multi-ethnic states such as post-apartheid South Africa and the successor states to the Soviet Union, the design of new curricula stimulated debate, and sometimes conflict, about just whose history should be taught in schools. Elsewhere, as in Japan and its neighbours, demands for textbook revision created political protest. In multi-national associations such as the European Union attempts to produce new supranational history curricula drew attention to the place and purpose of history in schools.[83] In many countries, the growing salience of identity politics produced an increased awareness of how representations of the past could be used for the purposes of the present. In this climate of opinion, historical anniversaries and commemorations often generated fierce controversy, as did museum exhibitions and displays.[84]

These debates over history and history education, in Canada as elsewhere, coincided with an increasing awareness of citizenship. For many years, citizenship had been accorded the same academic status as clean underwear, desirable and good to have but too banal to be worth talking about. In the 1990s, however, it increasingly became the territory of historians, philosophers, social scientists, and political theorists. Policy-makers and theorists alike deplored the decline of social capital and the erosion of civil society. In an age of increasing immigration and expanding multiculturalism, questions arose as to just who was entitled to be a citizen and what it meant to be a citizen in the first place. Pressures of globalization raised questions as to the meaning and even relevance of national citizenship. Given the long-standing connection between citizenship and history education in schools, it was hardly surprising that this new salience of citizenship, both as a matter of policy and as an academic specialty, drew renewed attention to the place and purpose of history in the schools.[85]

In Canada most commentators missed the larger point that the debate implicitly raised. In the 1990s, as in the 1970s, few people raised the possibility that the real problem was not that one version of history education had failed and therefore needed to be replaced with another, but rather that more was being asked of it, however organized, than it could possibly deliver, especially in a country such as Canada where children and adolescents are subject to many influences, of which their history classes are far from the most powerful.[86] In and of themselves, history courses are unlikely to strengthen national unity or improve the quality of citizenship. They obviously have a contribution to make to the education of citizens but they can be only one element in that education. The most we can reasonably expect from history education is that it should arouse students' interest in the past, give them some general knowledge, teach them to think historically, and help them become more historically minded. By the 1990s, however, it had become obvious that these goals were rarely achieved. Given their choice, many high school students voted with their feet and avoided history when it was not a compulsory course. Even when they found it interesting, they did not find it particularly useful. If in the 1970s it became clear that the traditional nation-building narrative was accomplishing very little, by the 1990s it seemed that the new direction in history education was no more successful. To a large extent, the solution to this state of affairs lies in reforms in teacher education and professional development, improvements in teachers' working conditions, more innovative pedagogy, and in changes to the structures of schooling. Beyond this, however, some theorists and researchers were coming to the conclusion that what was really needed was a radical rethinking of what it meant to teach history.[87]

This rethinking is not in fact as new as its proponents appear to believe, consisting, as it does, at least in part, of a rediscovery of long-forgotten ideas that were first advanced a century and more ago, while also building on some of the innovations that appeared from the 1970s onwards. In essence, it proposes that the primary goal of history education must be to teach students to think historically, to understand history as a form of disciplined inquiry. In the United States, for example, the National History Standards speak of chronological thinking, historical comprehension, historical analysis and interpretation, historical research, and issues-analysis and decision-making. In England, the National History Curriculum speaks of knowledge and understanding, historical interpretation, and using historical sources. Peter Seixas of the University of British Columbia describes historical thinking as a composite of the ability to assess the significance of data and events; to analyse and use evidence; to understand and apply the concepts of continuity and change, and progress and decline; to employ empathy and ethical judgment; and to understand historical causation and agency.[88] Perhaps the most novel aspect of the new approach to history education is its reflexive self-awareness, as manifested in its determination, not only to teach students how history is written, but also to show them how it is used and misused to shape personal and public memory. In the words of one historian, 'If we wanted a history curriculum that taught people how to use memories, we would focus on how memories are constructed. We would help students learn how to get honest and accurate feedback for their own constructions even as they followed their natural wishes to find support for their conclusions. We would encourage them to learn how to challenge, adapt, and construct memories instead of accepting interpretations that others seek to impose on them ... We would explore the social and communal contexts in which memories are created, reshaped, and forgotten.'[89]

Broadly speaking, the new emphasis on historical thinking takes two forms: one rejects the traditional link between history education and citizenship; the other redefines it. The first is found primarily in Britain, where, to quote one recent investigation of history education, 'In Northern Ireland and throughout the United Kingdom, history educators consider the goal of instruction to be the development of historical skills – e.g. students' ability to analyze evidence or to take the perspective of people in the past – not the recounting of historical stories, whether related to national history or otherwise.'[90] In this view, history is an academic discipline with its own distinctive way of thinking and it is this that makes it educationally important. It sees no more reason for history to be made a vehicle for the teaching of citizenship than, say, trigonometry or woodwork, and holds that history deserves its place in the curriculum for educational and intellectual, not political or social, reasons. In the words of the influential British history educator Peter Lee: 'The reason for teaching history in school is not so that pupils can use it for making something else, or to change or preserve a particular form of society, or even to expand the economy. The reason for teaching history is not that it changes society, but that it changes pupils; it changes what they see in the world and how they see it.'[91] This is, no doubt, at least in part, why the British government has recently decided to introduce citizenship, separate from the study of history, as a distinct course of study throughout the British school system.[92]

In Canada, the new emphasis on historical thinking has been combined with a concern for citizenship, albeit citizenship defined in terms of critical thinking, analytical skills, tolerance for diversity, and the like. This is seen most clearly in Quebec's emerging history curriculum, where the teaching of history is explicitly tied to citizenship education, not in the old sense of instilling a nationalist myth in children or imbuing them with an essentialized national identity, but rather of teaching them to think historically. In this view, there is no contradiction between historical thinking and citizenship. Indeed, the teaching of historical thinking is seen as history's distinctive contribution to citizenship education. In the words of Quebec's Lacoursière Report, 'Because the methods and operations of historical thought are substantially the same as those used in making reasoned personal decisions and in making a contribution to collective decisions at whatever level of life in society, history is a form of civic education.'[93]

To stipulate the attainment of historical thinking as the central purpose of history education entails a particular view of knowledge. Today's proponents of historical thinking acknowledge the obvious reality that thinking cannot take place without knowledge, but in many cases they seem to see knowledge in instrumental terms, as valuable only to the extent that it fosters historical thinking. They ignore the possibility that, in any given context, some kinds of knowledge might be more important than others and should therefore be embedded in curricula that all students must follow. To date there has been little discussion of what Canadian citizens should know about the past. There is no Canadian equivalent to the national history standards in the United States or the national history curriculum in England and Wales. There are occasional calls for national standards or guidelines but, to date, they have fallen on deaf ears, and seem unlikely to become reality, though textbook writers and curriculum developers have obviously made their own de facto decisions about what students should know, the results of which reveal that, despite the alleged depredations of social historians and champions of multiculturalism, the traditional landmarks of Canadian history remain largely in place.[94]

To argue for the importance of factual knowledge does not entail seeing it as absolute and uncontested. Nor does it entail stuffing uncomprehending students full of facts in the manner described by Charles Dickens in his novel *Hard Times*, with its portrayal of the aptly named Mr M'Choakumchild of Gradgrind Academy. Rather, it means contextualizing and historicizing what counts as knowledge. The question 'How do we know what we think we know and why does it matter?' is central to history teaching. In learning history, students must learn to identify the assumptions and silences of the narratives they are studying. They must learn to ask whose stories are not being told, who is absent from the narrative under consideration, how that narrative might appear when viewed through eyes other than those of the narrator, and, not least, why and how any particular narrative comes to be regarded as 'history.' By learning to ask questions such as these, students can learn the history of Canada while simultaneously questioning and enlarging it.

This question of knowledge aside, the emphasis on historical thinking has consequences for curriculum design and pedagogy. Above all, it rejects the idea of survey courses, arguing that they reduce history to a superficial coverage of factual information that leaves neither room nor time for students to explore the past in the depth necessary to bring it to life or to become familiar with the elements of historical method. This is a long-standing debate in history education, going back to the vogue for primers in the 1890s. For the last hundred years, professional opinion has favoured depth over coverage, the in-depth examination of a few topics rather than the inevitably more superficial survey of many. The problem is, of course, that if history is to prepare students for citizenship, it must give them a broad knowledge of the past and, given the constraints of timetables and the pressures on curricula, this can be done only through survey courses. There have been useful attempts to tackle this dilemma, of which the best known is the 'post-hole' or 'patch' approach, in which a few topics are selected for in-depth treatment and connected with each other by a brief chronological outline, but to date, it has not been satisfactorily resolved.

This new emphasis on historical thinking also entails a pedagogy that requires students to 'do' history, not simply to learn the history written by others. Writing in 1910, an English educationist feared that history might be a bad school subject since 'In this subject more than in any other it seems as if the maximum of work were demanded by the teacher and the minimum from the pupil. The old relations are reversed; the teacher prepares his lessons and the pupil hears them.'[95] The 1910 solution to this difficulty was to treat history as the study of problems through the use of primary sources. Today's advocates of historical thinking follow the same route, though with greater sophistication. They favour the use of a variety of primary and secondary sources so that students learn how to locate, analyse, and synthesize historical data. They disparage reliance on a single textbook. They organize subject-matter as open-ended problems to be investigated. They want students at some point to undertake original historical research, however simplified, for themselves. They also want students to understand the fundamental distinction between the past and history and to be aware of how history can shape personal, collective, and public memory. They want students to use primary sources, for example, not so much so that they learn to construct historical accounts for themselves, but rather so that they realize that all historical accounts are of necessity inadequate and incomplete and inevitably shaped by the assumptions of those who wrote them. Moreover, recent research, unlike its Piaget-based precursor, is showing that even in the elementary grades children can do this kind of work, if they are taught appropriately. One of the strengths of recent research, in fact, is its exploration of history teaching in action, thus yielding richer data than ever before to show how history can be taught more effectively. Moreover, the results of this research are being shared with teachers and incorporated into curricula and textbooks through such organizations as the Historical Thinking Project and the History Education Network (both based at UBC).[96]

History Education Today

Today, three conceptions of history education coexist. The first is the nation-building narrative that dominated history education for much of the twentieth century. The second is best represented by the new direction that emerged in the 1970s and that approached history as issues to be investigated rather than a chronology to be mastered. The third is the result of the rethinking of history education that began in the 1990s and that sees the teaching of historical thinking as its main priority. The three embody different views of the nature of history, its purpose, curriculum design, and pedagogy, though it should be noted that none of them exists in pure, unadulterated form and the boundaries between them are relatively porous. Each of the three includes what might be called fundamentalists and eclectics who share some central assumptions but differ on others.[97]

It is too soon to tell which of these three approaches will shape history education in the future. It is more than possible that teachers will draw eclectically on all three. Teachers approach their work pragmatically rather than philosophically. Their concern is not with nation-building or the construction of collective memory or understanding the structure of history but with what works with their students. At worst, this can mean little more than looking for things that will keep students too busy to become restless. At best, it means looking for resources and approaches that will make a lesson a genuinely educational experience. It is, after all, no easy matter to keep thirty or more children or adolescents engaged with a subject such as history which they do not necessarily find interesting or useful.

If my experience is any guide, the solution comes in four parts. First, students must be shown that the history is interesting, entertaining, and instructive to read and study, not for reasons of citizenship, or career preparation, or any other ulterior purpose, but because, by showing us what people have done in the past, for both good and ill, it teaches us in concrete ways what it means to be human. Second, this is best done, not by turning the past into a classroom version of Ripley's believe it or not, embodied in John A. Macdonald's drinking habits or Mackenzie King's communing with spirits, but by showing the people of the past as flesh-and-blood human beings trying to deal with the problems they faced as best they could, on the basis of imperfect information and without knowing what the results of their decisions and actions would be. In other words, we have to teach students to look at the past, as far as this is at all possible, through the eyes of the people who lived it, looking forward to an unknown future, not backwards from the vantage point of the present with all the benefits of retrodictive hindsight. Third, to use a well-known analogy (but one that works with children and adolescents), we should teach students to approach the past as though they were detectives, trying to piece together a story or an explanation or to form a credible theory on the basis of whatever evidence is available to them. Fourth, we should explain to them that historical knowledge and thinking provides an intellectual self-defence, a protection against all those who think they know what history teaches and are only too anxious to tell us, and a way of freeing ourselves from the conventional wisdom of our times. Students need to realize that when it comes to history, what they do not know can hurt them.

To the extent that schools can do this, they will lay a foundation, not only for an increasing audience for public history, but also for an audience that approaches history with both an enriched sense of what is involved in reconstructing and interpreting the past and a heightened awareness of the ways in which history can be used and abused. Public history can and should serve to narrow the gap that exists between what non-specialists often understand history to be and history as practised by historians, not least by communicating the findings of specialist research to a larger audience. Non-specialists variously see history either as an authoritatively unproblematic description of what happened in the past; a Hollywood-style or docudrama imaginative reconstruction in which accuracy and nuance are sacrificed to the imperatives of the story-line; a History Channel recital of wars, disasters, and other exotica; or, for those of a more cynical bent, as simply a matter of opinion in which the evidence can be twisted any way the historian chooses.

These misperceptions of history are compounded by what appears to be a widespread belief that Canadian history is dull. When the CBC and Radio-Canada first aired *Canada: A People's History* in 2000, one of the commonest reactions was surprise that Canada's history was so interesting, even though the series revealed little that had not been described by historians over the years. Some commentators faulted historians for not writing for a general readership, but the problem lies deeper than this. Above all, it arises from a structural fault in Canadian institutions, at least outside Quebec. It is not so much that historians have become over-specialized but rather that there are so few vehicles, in whatever format, through which the findings of historical research can be disseminated to a non-specialist public. As a result, public discourse in

Canada is remarkably devoid of historical reference. Here, it would seem, is a void that both public history and history education in the schools can help to fill.

This does not mean that we must reinvent some kind of nation-building grand narrative. Rather, it means that we need to introduce students to the Canadian past in ways that respect the nature of history as a discipline and that treat history as an initiation into the continuing debate that lies at the heart of the Canadian experience. The greatest contribution that the study of history can make to Canadian life is to arouse students' interest in the past, for without this nothing is possible, while also showing them the enormous variety of human behaviour and institutions over time, and equipping them with the knowledge, skills, and habits of mind they need if they are to take part in the debates that constitute contemporary Canada and that are rooted in and shaped by Canada's history. History's contribution to national life lies, not in entrenching some version or other of national identity, but in its ability to open the minds and expand the horizons of children and adolescents, and citizens generally, thereby enriching their lives and enhancing their understanding of the society, and indeed the world, in which they live. In doing so, school history and public history can serve a common purpose.

NOTES

1 Cited in C.N. Cochrane and W.S. Wallace, *This Canada of Ours* (Ottawa: National Council of Education, 1926), 11.
2 G.U. Hay, *The History of Canada ... to which has been added a Sketch of the History of Prince Edward Island by H.M. Anderson* (Toronto: Copp Clark, 1905), 1.
3 Cited in A. Chaiton and N. McDonald, eds., *Canadian Schools and Canadian Identity* (Toronto: Gage Educational Press, 1977), 14–15.
4 R.S. Thornton, 'Address by the Minister of Education,' *Western School Journal* 15, 5 (May 1920): 177.
5 Examples of provincial histories specifically designed for schools that were probably still in use when Ross launched his criticisms of provincialism include D. Campbell, *History of Nova Scotia for Schools* (Montreal: Lovell, 1874); J.M. Harper, *The History of the Maritime Provinces* (Halifax: A. & W. McKinlay, 1874); F.X. Toussaint, *Abrégé de l'histoire du Canada à l'usage des jeunes étudiants de la province de Québec* (Quebec: Darveau, 1874); D. Campbell, *History of Prince Edward Island* (Charlottetown: Bremner, 1875); J.M. Harper, *The History of New Brunswick and other Maritime Provinces* (St John: J. & A. McMillan, 1876); J.B. Calkin, *A History and Geography of Nova Scotia* (Halifax: A. & W.

Mackinlay, 1878). Quebec textbooks are described in G. Laloux-Jain, *Les manuels d'histoire du Canada au Québec et en Ontario 1867–1914* (Sainte-Foy: Les Presses de l'Université Laval, 1974), 101–33.

6 A. Archer, *A Short History of the Dominion of Canada* (St John: J. & A. McMillan, 1877), iii.

7 Ibid.

8 J. Frith Jeffers, *History of Canada* (Toronto: Canada Publishing Company, 1884), 6.

9 W.H. Withrow, *An Abridged History of Canada* (Toronto: William Briggs, 1887), iv.

10 The charge was levelled against Ross in 1890 and is quoted in Laloux-Jain, *Les manuels d'histoire,* 75.

11 F-X. Toussaint, *Abrégé de l'histoire du Canada à l'usage des jeunes étudiants de la province de Québec* (Quebec: Darveau, 1882 edition), 98.

12 The references here are A. Archer, *A History of Canada for the Use of Schools* (Toronto: Nelson, 1876) and his *A Short History of the Dominion of Canada*; J. Frith Jeffers, *History of Canada for the Use of Schools* (Toronto: Campbell, 1875) and his much abbreviated *History of Canada* (Canada Publishing Company History Primers, 1884); F-X. Toussaint, A*brégé de l'histoire du Canada à l'usage des jeunes étudiants de la province de Québec*, 1874 edition. Another example is W.H. Withrow, *A History of Canada for the Use of Schools and General Readers* (Toronto: Copp Clark, 1876) and its much shorter 1887 version, *An Abridged History of Canada.* Except for Toussaint, all these authors apparently preferred a long and colourfully written narrative intended to serve a general readership and the school market simultaneously, but were forced to bow to provincial Department of Education demands for books that were cheap, short, shorn of ornament, and pedagogically easy to use. In this context, dullness was a virtue, since it provided minimal opportunities for partisan attack. The longer and more colourfully written the book, the more hostages it gave to fortune.

13 Archer, *A Short History of the Dominion,* iii.

14 Calkin, *A History and Geography of Nova Scotia,* 77.

15 Cited in Laloux-Jain, *Les manuels d'histoire,* 81. The quotation is taken from the terms of reference of the national textbook competition of the 1890s.

16 Ibid., 83.

17 Ibid.

18 For the concept of 'limited identities,' see R. Cook, 'Canadian Centennial Cerebrations,' *International Journal* 22 (1967): 659–63; and J.M.S. Careless, '"Limited Identities" in Canada,' *Canadian Historical Review* 50 (1969): 1–10. See also J.M.S. Careless, 'Limited Identities – Ten Years Later,' *Manitoba History* 1 (1980): 3–9; and P. Buckner, '"Limited Identities" and Canadian Historical

Scholarship: An Atlantic Provinces Perspective,' *Journal of Canadian Studies* 23 (1988): 177–98.

19 The winning textbook was W.H.P. Clement, *The History of the Dominion of Canada* (Toronto: William Briggs, 1898). On the textbook contest generally, see Laloux-Jain, *Les manuels d'histoire,* 80ff.

20 Hay, *The History of Canada ... to which has been added a Sketch of the History of Prince Edward Island by H.M. Anderson,* 89.

21 M. Trudel and G. Jain, *L'histoire du Canada: enquête sur les manuels (*Ottawa: Queen's Printer, 1969); K. Dewar, 'The Road to Happiness: History in Public School Textbooks,' *This Magazine Is about Schools* (Fall 1972): 102–27; K. Osborne, *'Hard-working, Temperate and Peaceable': The Portrayal of Workers in Canadian History Textbooks* (Winnipeg: University of Manitoba Education Monograph 4, 1980).

22 G. McDiarmid and D. Pratt, *Teaching Prejudice: A Content Analysis of Social Studies Textbooks Authorized for Use in Ontario: A Report to the Ontario Human Rights Commission* (Toronto: Ontario Institute for Studies in Education, 1971).

23 A.T.Q. Stewart, *The Shape of Irish History* (Oxford: Blackwell, 2001).

24 Lorne Pierce, *New History for Old: Discussions on Aims and Methods in Writing and Teaching History* (Toronto: Ryerson, 1931), 39.

25 Women's International League for Peace and Freedom, *Report of the Canadian School History Textbook Survey* (Toronto: WILPF, 1933). For a description of this report see K. Osborne, 'An Early Example of the Analysis of History Textbooks in Canada,' *Canadian Social Studies* 29 (1994): 21–5.

26 J. Katz, *The Teaching of Canadian History in Canada: A Survey Study of the Teaching of Canadian History in Junior and Senior High Schools* (Winnipeg: University of Manitoba Press, 1953), 31.

27 See, for example, L. Pierce, *New History for Old*; D.A. McArthur, 'The Teaching of Canadian History,' *Ontario Historical Society Papers and Records* 21 (1924): 206–9.

28 W.A. Deacon, *My Vision of Canada* (Toronto: Ontario Publishing Company, 1933), 9.

29 National Council of Education, *Observations on the Teaching of History and Civics in Primary and Secondary Schools of Canada* (Winnipeg: National Council of Education, 1923), 14. Perhaps the most accessible account of this report is to be found in Ken Osborne, 'Voices from the Past,' *Canadian Social Studies* 35, 4 (2001) and 36, 1 (2001), accessible on line at http://www.quasar.ualberta.ca/css/.

30 See Amy von Heyking, *Creating Citizens: History and Identity in Alberta's Schools 1905 to 1980* (Calgary: University of Calgary Press, 2006).

31 R. Samuel, *Theatres of Memory*, vol. 2: *Island Stories: Unravelling Britain* (London: Verso, 1998), 204.

32   Lucien Bouchard is quoted in J. Simpson, *Faultlines: Struggling for a Canadian Vision* (Toronto: HarperCollins, 1993), 279–81. In his memoirs, Marcel Trudel makes a similar point, noting that Quebec students before the 1960s 'didn't see what was happening elsewhere and learned nothing about the history of Ontario, the Canadian West, or the Maritimes. They only knew Quebec history really well, and what they remembered was a history of grievances, revenge, and survival.' *Memoirs of Less Travelled Road: A Historian's Life* (Montreal: Véhicule Press, 2002), 161. For a summary of the development of history education in Quebec, see S. Lévesque, 'History and Social Studies in Québec: A Historical Perspective,' in A. Sears and I. Wright, eds., *Challenges and Prospects for Canadian Social Studies* (Vancouver: Pacific Educational Press, 2004), 55–72, and S. Roy, C. Gauthier, and M. Tardif, *Evolution des programmes d'histoire de1861 à nos jours* (Université Laval: Les cahiers de recherche en administration et politiques scolaires, 1992).

33   A. Laurendeau, *Nos écoles enseignent-elles la haine de l'anglais?* (Montreal: Les éditions de l'Action Nationale, 1937). Maheux restated his argument in his *Ton histoire est une épopée* (Quebec: Charrier and Dougal, 1941), 1–25; and *Pourquoi sommes-nous divisés?* (Montreal: Radio-Canada, 1943), 147–56. This last provoked a passionate response from Lionel Groulx, who turned Maheux's question into a statement: *Pourquoi nous sommes divisés* (Montreal: Les Editions de l'Action Nationale, 1943).

34   C. Bilodeau, 'L'histoire nationale,' *Royal Commission Studies: A Selection of Essays Prepared for the Royal Commission on National Development in the Arts, Letters and Sciences* (Ottawa: King's Printer, 1951), 217–30. Recalling his 1950s Saguenay collège classique education, Lucien Bouchard observed that though students spent considerable time on the history of Quebec and Europe, the rest of Canada was 'just a blur.' See Simpson, *Faultlines*, 279. For an argument that history teaching in Quebec is similar to that in the rest of Canada, see C. Laville, 'History Taught in Québec Is Not Really That Different from the History Taught Elsewhere in Canada,' *Canadian Social Studies* 31 (1996): 22–4, 42. For a contrary view, see M. Nemni, 'Canada: The Case of the Vanishing Country,' *Cité Libre* 26, (June 1998): 61–71.

35   Bilodeau, 'L'histoire nationale,' 217.

36   For the text of the Senate debate of 1944, see Senate *Debates*, 4 May 1944 and *passim*. The debate is summarized in Osborne, 'Voices from the Past.'

37   J. Bruchési, 'L'enseignement de l'histoire du Canada,' *Report of the Annual Meeting of the Canadian Historical Association, Québec City* (1952): 3–13.

38   'Report of the Committee for the Study of Canadian History Textbooks,' *Canadian Education* 1 (October 1945): 3–35.

39 H. Neatby, 'National History,' *Royal Commission Studies: A Selection of Essays Prepared for the Royal Commission on National Development in the Arts, Letters and Sciences* (Ottawa: King's Printer, 1951), 210.

40 Historians' views of the undesirability of a national textbook are reported in A. Laurendeau, 'Pour ou contre le manuel unique d'histoire du Canada?' *L'action nationale* 35, 5 (May 1950): 337–95. For a summary see Osborne, 'Voices from the Past.'

41 Cochrane made this remark in a report he wrote for the National Council of Education in 1923. See National Council of Education, *Observations on the Teaching of History and Civics in Primary and Secondary Schools of Canada* (Ottawa: National Council of Education, 1923), 10.

42 Cited in *Report of the Annual Meeting of the Canadian Historical Association Held at Montreal, 1–2 June 1944*, 7.

43 Laurendeau, 'Pour ou contre le manuel unique d'histoire du Canada,' 345ff.

44 M.W. Keatinge, *Studies in the Teaching of History* (London: A. & C. Black, 1910), 3–4.

45 J.H. Robinson, *The New History* (New York: Macmillan, 1912), 11.

46 G.M. Wrong, C. Martin, and W.N. Sage, *The Story of Canada* (Toronto: Ryerson, 1929), vi.

47 See, for example, M.S. Barnes, *Studies in Historical Method* (Boston: Heath, 1896); F.M. Fling and H.W. Caldwell, *Studies in European and American History* (Lincoln, NE: J.H. Miller, 1897); Keatinge, *Studies in the Teaching of History*. Barnes taught history at Stanford; Fling and Caldwell were members of the history department at the University of Nebraska; and Keatinge was Reader in Education at Oxford University. For more on the 1890s enthusiasm for teaching through sources, see K. Osborne, 'Fred Morrow Fling and the Source-Method of Teaching History,' *Theory and Research in Social Education* 31 (2003): 466–501.

48 G.J. Reeve, *Canada: Its History and Progress, 1000–1925* (Toronto: Oxford University Press, 1926), iii.

49 Morton explains this in his Introduction to Katz, *The Teaching of Canadian History in Canada*.

50 A.B. Hodgetts, *What Culture? What Heritage?* (Toronto: Ontario Institute for Studies in Education, 1968).

51 Ibid., 5–6. Earlier reports include the following: National Council of Education, *Observations on the Teaching of History and Civics in Primary and Secondary Schools of Canada* (1923): W.N. Sage, 'The Teaching of History in the Elementary Schools of Canada,' in *Report of the Annual Meeting of the Canadian Historical Association Held at Montreal, May 23, 1930*, 55–63; Canada and Newfoundland Education Association, *A Report on the Text-books in Social Studies in the*

Dominion of Canada (1941); Canadian and Newfoundland Education Association, *Report of the Committee for the Study of Canadian History Textbooks* (1945); Katz, *The Teaching of Canadian History in Canada.*

52 R.M. Alway, 'The Future of Canadian History in the High School,' in E.H. Humphreys, ed., *Focus on Canadian Studies* (Toronto: Ontario Institute for Studies in Education, 1970), 50.

53 The basic references here include J.S. Bruner, *The Process of Education* (Cambridge, MA: Harvard University Press, 1960); B.G. Massialas and C.B. Cox, *Inquiry in Social Studies* (New York: McGraw Hill, 1966); E. Fenton, *The New Social Studies* (New York: Holt, Rinehart and Winston, 1967); E. Fenton, ed., *Teaching the New Social Studies in Secondary Schools* (New York: Holt, Rinehart and Winston, 1968); M.M. Krug, J.B. Poster, and W.B. Gillies, *The New Social Studies: Analysis of Theory and Materials* (Itasca, IL: Peacock, 1970); B. Beyer, *Inquiry in the Social Studies Classroom* (Columbus: Merrill, 1971); R. Ben Jones, *Practical Approaches to the New History* (London: Hutchinson, 1973); Schools Council, *History 13–16 Project: A New Look at History* (Edinburgh: Holmes & McDougall, 1976); P.J. Rogers, *The New History: Theory into Practice* (London: Historical Association, 1979). For analysis of how these developments influenced Canadian schools see G.S. Tomkins, *A Common Countenance: Stability and Change in the Canadian Curriculum* (Toronto: Prentice-Hall, 1986); K. Osborne, '"To the Schools We Must Look for Good Canadians": Developments in the Teaching of History in Canadian Schools since 1960,' *Journal of Canadian Studies* 23, 3 (1987): 104–26; G. Richardson, *The Death of the Good Canadian: Teachers, National Identities, and the Social Studies Curriculum* (New York: Peter Lang, 2003).

54 See, for example, R. Tyler, *Basic Principles of Curriculum and Instruction* (Chicago: University of Chicago Press, 1949); P.H. Hirst, *Knowledge and the Curriculum* (London: Routledge and Kegan Paul, 1974).

55 C. Sellers, 'Is History on the Way Out of the Schools and Do Historians Care?' *Social Education* 33 (1969): 510.

56 Gary B. Nash, Charlotte Crabtree, and Ross E. Dunn, *History on Trial: Culture Wars and the Teaching of the Past* (New York: Knopf, 1997), 36ff.

57 See, for example, M.F.D. Young, ed., *Knowledge and Control* (London: Collier-Macmillan, 1971); M. Apple, *Ideology and Curriculum* (London: Routledge and Kegan Paul, 1979); G. Whitty, *Sociology and School Knowledge: Curriculum Theory, Research, and Politics* (London: Methuen, 1985).

58 See, for example, American Political Science Association, *The Teaching of Government: Report to the American Political Science Association* (New York: Macmillan, 1916); 'Tentative Report of the Committee on the Teaching of Sociology in the Grade and High Schools,' *American Sociological Review* 14 (1920):

243–51; 'Report of the Committee on Economics in Secondary Schools,' *American Economic Review Supplement* 8 (1918): 308–12.

59 For a description of this program, see J.S. Bruner, *Toward a Theory of Instruction* (Cambridge, MA: Harvard University Press, 1966), 73–101.

60 For more on this, see the summary and references in S.S. Wineburg, *Historical Thinking and Other Unnatural Acts: Charting the Future of Teaching the Past* (Philadelphia: Temple University Press, 2001), 37ff; and K. Osborne, 'Some Psychological Concerns for the Teaching of History,' *The History and Social Science Teacher* 11 (1975): 15–25.

61 B. Davis, *Whatever Happened to High School History? Burying the Political Memory of Youth, Ontario, 1945–1995* (Toronto: Our Schools Ourselves/J. Lorimer, 1995).

62 For the history of social studies, see D.W. Saxe, *Social Studies in the Schools: A History of the Early Years* (Albany: State University of New York Press, 1991). Also relevant is M.B. Lybarger, 'Origins of the Modern Social Studies, 1900–1916,' *History of Education Quarterly* 23 (1983): 455–68. For the Canadian context, see P. Clark, '"Home-Grown Product" or "Made in America"? History of Social Studies in English Canada,' in I. Wright and A. Sears, eds., *Trends and Issues in Canadian Social Studies* (Vancouver: Pacific Educational Press, 1997), 68–99. See also P. Clark, 'The Historical Context of Social Studies in English Canada,' in Wright and Sears, eds., *Challenges and Prospects for Canadian Social Studies*, 17–37. For specific courses within the early social studies movement, see J.A. Reuben, 'Beyond Politics: Community Civics and the Redefinition of Citizenship in the Progressive Era,' *History of Education Quarterly* 37 (1997): 399–420; and H. Wells Singleton, 'Problems of Democracy: The Revisionist Plan for Social Studies Education,' *Theory and Research in Social Education* 80 (1980): 89–104.

63 For an attempt to assess this debate, see K. Osborne, 'History and Social Studies: Partners or Rivals?' in Sears and Wright, eds., *Challenges and Prospects for Canadian Social Studies*, 73–89.

64 McDiarmid and Pratt, *Teaching Prejudice*. Also relevant is D. Pratt, 'The Social Role of School Textbooks in Canada,' in R.M. Pike and E. Zureik, eds., *Socialization and Values in Canadian Society* (Toronto: McClelland and Stewart, 1975), 100–26.

65 Hodgetts, *What Culture? What Heritage?*, 20, 24.

66 R. Cook, 'Identities Are Not Like Hats,' *Canadian Historical Review* 81 (2000): 264.

67 J.M. Bumsted, 'Historical Writing in English,' in E. Benson and W. Toye, eds., *The Oxford Companion to English Literature* (Toronto: Oxford University Press, 1997), 539.

68 D. Francis, *National Dreams: Myth, Memory, and Canadian History* (Vancouver:

Arsenal Pulp Press, 1997), 109–10; See also I. McKay, 'After Canada: On Amnesia, and Apocalypse in the Contemporary Crisis,' *Acadiensis* 28 (1998): 76–97; and I. McKay, 'The Liberal Order Framework: A Prospectus for a Reconnaissance of Canadian History,' *Canadian Historical Review* 81, 3 (September 2000), 617–45.

69 H.J. Hanham, 'Canadian History in the 1970s,' *Canadian Historical Review* 68 (1977): 22.

70 A. Burton, 'Who Needs the Nation? Interrogating "British" History,' *Journal of Historical Sociology* 10 (1997): 237. The obvious references here are E. Hobsbawm and T. Ranger, eds., *The Invention of Tradition* (Cambridge: Cambridge University Press, 1983); and B. Anderson, *Imagined Communities: Reflections on the Origin and Spread of Nationalism* (London: Verso, 1991).

71 R. Durocher, 'Une ou des histoires nationales,' in R. Comeau and B. Dionne, eds., *À propos de l'histoire nationale* (Sillery: Septentrion, 1998), 86.

72 C. Berger, *The Writing of Canadian History: Aspects of English-Canadian Historical Writing since 1900*, 2nd edition (Toronto: University of Toronto Press, 1986), 259. Also relevant is P.M. Kennedy, 'The Decline of Nationalistic History in the West, 1900–1970,' *Journal of Contemporary History* 8 (1973): 77–100.

73 The term comes from C.S. Maier, 'Consigning the Twentieth Century to History: Alternative Narratives for the Modern Era,' *American Historical Review* 105 (2000): 829.

74 D. Thelen, 'Making History and Making the United States,' *Journal of American Studies* 32 (1998): 375. For a response to Thelen's claims see D. Hollinger, 'The Historian's Use of the United States and Vice Versa,' in T. Bender, ed., *Rethinking American History in a Global Age* (Berkeley: University of California Press, 2002), 381–95.

75 The Historica Foundation of Toronto has issued three useful reports: P. Shields and D. Ramsay, *Teaching and Learning about Canadian History across Canada* (Toronto: Historica Foundation, 2002); J.-P. Charland and S. Moisan, *L'enseignement de l'histoire dans les écoles françaises du Canada* (Toronto: Historica Foundation, 2003); K. Osborne, *Canadian History in the Schools* (Toronto: Historica Foundation, 2004). Note also this observation on the teaching of history in universities: 'Despite the complaints of certain old-school political historians about the inroads that working class history, ethnic history, gender history, and other types of social history have made into the teaching of history, political history remains firmly entrenched in history curricula at Canadian universities. The introductory survey course, most often structured around constitutional and political events, remains the backbone of the history program.' G.C. Brandt, 'Canadian National Histories: Their Evolving Content and Uses,' *History Teacher* 30 (1997): 142.

76 Alberta Learning, *Social Studies (K-12) Consultation Draft, October 2003*

(Edmonton: Alberta Learning, 2003), 1. Similar sentiments can be found in the Western Canada Protocol for Social Studies, an interprovincial curriculum for the Western Provinces and Northern Territories, and in the Atlantic Canada Education Framework, an interprovincial social studies program under development in Atlantic Canada. For recent surveys of curricular developments that confirm this point, see P. Shields and D. Ramsay, 'Social Studies in English Canada,' in Sears and Wright, eds., *Challenges and Prospects for Canadian Social Studies*, 38–54, and S. Lévesque, 'History and Social Studies in Québec: An Historical Perspective,' in ibid., 55–72.

77 Ontario Provincial Committee on Aims and Objectives in the Schools of Ontario, *Living and Learning* (Toronto: Queen's Printer, 1968), 83.

78 The term 'historical-mindedness' is taken from the American Historical Association, *The Study of History in Schools: Report to the American Historical Association by the Committee of Seven* (New York: Macmillan 1899). The term 'historic sense' appears in M.S. Barnes, *Studies in Historical Method* (Boston: Heath, 1896), 47, where she describes it as 'the sense by which we enter the life of universal man.' In her words, 'Wherever man has lived, we feel and know; our personality is widened by the personality of ages and races; until we run back for thousands of years, and out into thousands of souls; and equipped with this wider personality, this new environment of intellectual and spiritual existence, we find ourselves able more deftly and certainly to understand the present and foresee the future.' My description of teaching methods is based on my reading of the pedagogical journals of the early twentieth century, especially the Winnipeg-based *Western School Journal,* and the U.S.-based *Historical Outlook,* together with the following: Barnes, *Studies in Historical Method*; Fling and Caldwell, *Studies in European and American History*; C.A. McMurry, *Special Method in History* (New York: Macmillan, 1903); Keatinge, *Studies in the Teaching of History*; H. Johnson, *Teaching of History in Elementary and Secondary Schools* (New York: Macmillan, 1915); E.L. Hasluck, *The Teaching of History* (Cambridge: Cambridge University Press, 1920); F.C. Happold, *The Approach to History* (London: Christophers, 1928). For some recent studies see R.E. Aldrich, 'New History: An Historical Perspective,' in A.K. Dickinson, P.J. Lee, and P.J. Rogers, *Learning History* (London: Heinemann, 1984), 210–24; F.E. Monteverde, 'Considering the Source: Mary Sheldon Barnes,' in M.S. Crocco and O.L. Davis, Jr, eds., *'Bending the Future to Their Will': Civic Women, Social Education, and Democracy* (Lanham, MD: Rowman and Littlefield, 1999), 17–46;Osborne, 'Fred Morrow Fling and the Source-Method of Teaching History'; and C.H. Bohan, *Go to the Sources: Lucy Maynard Salmon and the Teaching of History* (New York: Peter Lang, 2004).

79 For more on the debates of the 1990s on the teaching of Canadian history in the schools, see K. Osborne, "'Our History Syllabus Has Us Gasping': History in

Canadian Schools – Past, Present, and Future,' *Canadian Historical Review* 81, 3 (2000): 404–35; and K. Osborne, 'Teaching History in Schools: A Canadian Debate,' *Journal of Curriculum Studies* 35 (2003): 585–626.

80 For example, reflecting on his constitutional travails promoting the unsuccessful Charlottetown Accord, Joe Clark wrote that in order to save Canada, which he described as 'a nation too good to lose,' 'we must encourage more schools to teach more facts about the history and nature of our country.' J. Clark, *A Nation Too Good to Lose: Renewing the Purpose of Canada* (Toronto: Key Porter, 1994), 198.

81 M. Bliss, 'Privatizing the Mind: The Sundering of Canadian History, the Sundering of Canada,' *Journal of Canadian Studies* 26 (Winter 1991–2): 5.

82 J.L. Granatstein, *Who Killed Canadian History?* (Toronto: HarperCollins, 1998).

83 For samples of the international debates on history education, see A.M. Schlesinger, Jr, *The Disuniting of America: Reflections on a Multicultural Society* (New York: Norton, 1991); Nash, Crabtree, and Dunn, *History on Trial*; R. Phillips, *History Teaching, Nationhood and the State: A Study in Educational Politics* (London: Cassell, 1998); C. Carpentier, ed., *Identité nationale et enseignement de l'histoire: contextes européens et africains* (Montreal: L'Harmattan, 1999); L. Hein and M. Selden, eds., *Censoring History: Citizenship and Memory in Japan, Germany, and the United States* (Armonk, NY: M.E. Sharpe, 2000); L. Symcox, *Whose History? The Struggle for National Standards in American Classrooms* (New York: Teachers College Press, 2002); S. MacIntyre and A. Clark, *The History Wars* (Melbourne: Melbourne University Press, 2003); M. Ferro, *The Use and Abuse of History* (London: Routledge, 2003).

84 See, for example, Charles S. Maier, *The Unmasterable Past: History, Holocaust, and German National Identity* (Cambridge, MA: Harvard University Press, 1988); S.L. Kaplan, *Farewell, Revolution: Disputed Legacies, France, 1789/1989* (Ithaca: Cornell University Press, 1995); M. Harwit, *An Exhibit Denied: Lobbying the History of the Enola Gay* (New York: Springer-Verlag, 1996); M. Wallace, *Mickey Mouse History and Other Essays on American Memory* (Philadelphia: Temple University Press, 1996); M. Agulhon et al., *1789: La Commémoration* (Paris: Gallimard, 1999).

85 There is a vast and growing literature on citizenship. See, in particular, D.B. Heater, *Citizenship: The Civic Ideal in World History, Politics, and Education* (London: Longman, 1990); R. Beiner, ed., *Theorizing Citizenship* (Albany: State University of New York Press, 1995); W. Kymlicka, *Multicultural Citizenship* (Oxford: Clarendon Press, 1995); A. Sears and A. Hughes. 'Citizenship Education and Current Educational Reform,' *Canadian Journal of Education*, 21 (1996): 123–42; G. Shafir, ed., *The Citizenship Debates: A Reader* (Minneapolis: University of Minnesota Press, 1998); E. Gidengil, A. Blais, N. Nevitte, and R. Nadeau,

Citizens (Vancouver: University of British Columbia Press, 2004); K. Osborne, 'Public Schooling and Citizenship Education in Canada,' *Canadian Ethnic Studies* 32 (2000): 2–30; M. Pagé, F. Dumont, and L. Cortesao, *L'éducation à la citoyenneté* (Sherbrooke: CRP, 2001); F. Ouellet, ed., *Quelle formation pour l'éducation à la citoyenneté?* (Sainte-Foy: Les Presses de l'Université Laval); A. Duhamel and F. Jutras, eds., *Enseigner et éduquer à la citoyenneté* (Sainte-Foy: Les Presses de l'Université Laval, 2005). A useful empirical study is J.P. Charland, *Les élèves, l'histoire et la citoyenneté; Enquête auprès d'élèves des régions de Montréal et Toronto* (Sainte-Foy: Les Presses de l'Université Laval, 2003).

86 An American survey asked some one thousand adults to rate seven places where they felt most connected to the past. School placed seventh out of the seven, after family, museums, celebrating holidays, reading books, and watching films or television. High school teachers placed fourth out of seven as trustworthy sources of information about the past, after family, participants, and university professors, but above books and films and television. The words most often used to describe school history were 'boring' and 'irrelevant.' See Roy Rosenzweig and David Thelen, *The Presence of the Past: Popular Uses of History in American Life* (New York: Columbia University Press, 1998), 109–14, 235–6.

87 For examples of this rethinking, see C. Portal, ed., *The History Curriculum for Teachers* (Lewes: Falmer Press, 1987); P. Gordon, A.K. Dickinson, P.J. Lee, and J. Slater, eds., *International Yearbook of History Education, Volume 1* (London: Woburn Press, 1995); C. Husbands, *What Is History Teaching? Language, Ideas and Meaning in Learning about the Past* (Milton Keynes: Open University Press, 1996); P.N. Stearns, P. Seixas, and S.S. Wineburg, eds., *Knowing, Teaching and Learning History: National and International Perspectives* (New York: New York University Press, 2000); S.S. Wineburg, *Historical Thinking and Other Unnatural Acts: Charting the Future of Teaching the Past* (Philadelphia: Temple University Press, 2001).

88 P. Seixas, 'Conceptualizing the Growth of Historical Understanding,' in D.R. Olson and N. Torrance, eds., *The Handbook of Education and Human Development* (Oxford: Blackwell, 1996), 765–93; S. Lévesque, *Thinking Historically: Educating Students for the 21st Century* (Toronto: University of Toronto Press, 2008). The pedagogical implications of Peter Seixas's work are explained on line at http://historicalthinking.ca/. See also Carla Peck and Peter Seixas, 'Benchmarks of Historical Thinking: First Steps,' *Canadian Journal of Education* 31 (2008): 1013–38. For discussion of the National History Curriculum in Britain, see Phillips, *History Teaching, Nationhood, and the State.* For the National History Standards of the United States, see Symcox, *Whose History?.*

89 D. Thelen, ed., *Memory and American History* (Bloomington: Indiana University Press, 1990), xviii–xix.

90 K. Barton, 'History Education and National Identity in Northern Ireland and the United States: Differing Priorities,' *Theory into Practice* 40 (2001): 50.

91 P. Lee, 'Historical Knowledge in the National Curriculum,' in R. Aldrich, ed., *History in the National Curriculum* (London: Kogan Page, 1991), 42.

92 For discussion of Britain's introduction of citizenship as a distinct subject of study, see T.H. McLaughlin, 'Citizenship Education in England: The Crick Report and Beyond,' *Journal of Philosophy of Education* 34 (2000): 541–70; T. Smith, 'How Citizenship Got on to the Political Agenda,' *Parliamentary Affairs* 55 (2002): 475–87; B. Crick, 'Education for Citizenship: The Citizenship Order,' *Parliamentary Affairs* 55 (2002): 488–504.

93 Quebec Ministry of Education, *Learning from the Past: Report of the Task Force on the Teaching of History* (Quebec: Ministry of Education, 1996), 4. The report was published in French with the title *Se Souvenir et Devenir.* For a persuasive argument for the centrality of historical thinking to the practice of democratic citizenship, see R. Martineau, 'L'éducation à la citoyenneté et le patrimoine culturel historien,' *Education Canada* 40 (2000): 8–14, and 'La pensée historique, une alternative réflexive précieuse pour l'éducation à la citoyenneté,' in R. Pallascio and L. Lafortune, eds., *Pour une pensée réflexive en éducation* (Sainte-Foy: Les Presses de l'université du Québec, 2000), 281–309. For a related but somewhat different argument, see K. Osborne, *In Defence of History: Teaching the Past and the Meaning of Democratic Citizenship* (Toronto: Our Schools/Our Selves, 1995), 9–48. Also relevant is a report published in 2004 by the Organization of American Historians, *History, Democracy, and Citizenship: The Debate over History's Role in Teaching Citizenship and Patriotism,* accessible on line at http://www.oah.org/reports/tradhist.html. Quebec's curriculum in history and education for citizenship has been the subject of some controversy. For the criticisms, see F. Bouvier and M. Sarra-Bournet, eds., *L'enseignement de l'histoire au début du 21e siècle au Québec* (Quebec: Septentrion, 2008); for rebuttals, see M. Dagenais and C. Laville, 'Le naufrage du projet de programme d'histoire "nationale,"' *Revue d'histoire de l'Amérique française* 60 (2007): 517–50; C. Laville, 'L'enseignement de l'histoire à travers les lunettes noires de la question identitaire,' *MENS: Revue d'histoire intellectuelle de l'Amérique française* 9 (2009): 243–83. Also useful is the special issue of the *Bulletin d'histoire politique* 15 (2007): 7–108.

94 For examples of recent surveys of Canadian history that, while blending social and political history, leave the traditional landmarks of national development largely untouched, see D. Morton, *A Short History of Canada* (Toronto: McClelland and Stewart, 2001); D. Gillmor, P. Turgeon, and A. Michaud, *Canada: A People's History,* 2 volumes (Toronto: McClelland and Stewart, 2000 and 2001); H.V. Nelles, *A Little History of Canada* (Don Mills: Oxford University Press, 2004). Relevant to the debate about the relative priorities of historical knowledge and historical

thinking in a Canadian context are the articles by Michael Bliss and Peter Seixas in *Canadian Social Studies* 36 (2000). See M. Bliss, 'Teaching Canadian National History,' and P. Seixas, 'The Purposes of Teaching Canadian History,' accessible on line at http://quasar.ualberta.ca/css/. For a summary of a related debate in the Netherlands, see A. Wilschut, 'Historical Consciousness as an Objective in Dutch History Education,' accessible on line at http://home.wxs.nl/~wilschut/ consciousness.htm. For discussion of Canadian history textbooks, see the symposium, 'New Wine or Just New Bottles?' in *Journal of Canadian Studies* 30 (1995–6): 175–201; 'Débat: à propos de deux manuels récents d'histoire du Canada,' *Revue d'histoire de l'Amérique française* 51 (1998): 549–77; and J. Guildford and M. Earle, 'On Choosing a Textbook: Recent Canadian Surveys and Readers,' *Acadiensis* 27 (1997): 133–44. For *Canada: A People's History*, see M. Starowicz, *Making History: The Remarkable Story behind* Canada: A People's History (Toronto: McClelland and Stewart, 2003), and L. Dick, 'A New History for a New Millennium: *Canada: A People's History*,' *Canadian Historical Review* 85 (2004): 85–109.

95 Keatinge, *Studies in the Teaching of History,* 4.
96 See, for example, R. Martineau, *L'histoire à l'école: matière à penser* (Montreal: L'Harmattan, 1999); B. VanSledright, *In Search of America's Past: Learning to Read History in Elementary School* (New York: Teachers College Press, 2002); and S.G. Grant, *History Lessons: Teaching, Learning, and Testing History in U.S. High School Classrooms* (Mahwah, NJ: Erlbaum, 2003); R. Martineau, *Fondements et pratiques de l'enseignement de l'histoire à l'école* (Quebec: Les Presses de l'Université du Québec, 2010); P. Clark, ed., *New Possibilities for the Past: Shaping History Education in Canada* (Vancouver: UBC Press, 2011).
97 For a different way of describing these differences, see P. Seixas, 'Schweigen! Die Kinder! or, Does Postmodern History Have a Place in the Schools?' in Stearns, Seixas, and Wineburg, eds., *Knowing, Teaching, and Learning History,* 19–37.

6 Saving the Nation through National History: The Case of *Canada: A People's History*

LYLE DICK

The advent of public history in recent decades included the expansion of historical productions into film, television, and other related electronic media, enabling authors to reach larger audiences than ever before. Varying forms have been employed, including non-fictional documentaries, historical dramas, and assorted hybrids under the rubric of docudramas, comprising an enormous shift in the ways of presenting historical information to the public. The implications of this shift are being extensively debated in the scholarly literature of communication studies, popular culture, and semiotics, although not generally within the discipline of history. If they are to have an impact on the representation of history in the new media, professional historians will need to expand their critical repertoire to include the analysis of moving images, sound tracks, and associated techniques of representing history to mass audiences. To the extent that televised historical productions continue to rely on traditional narrative conventions, scholars will also need to pay close attention to the literary forms and genres within which these productions are structured, as applied to the new media.

To explore some of the implications of presenting national history on television, this chapter examines the operative forms of representation in Mark Starowicz's *Canada: A People's History*, produced and televised by the CBC in 2000–2001. I selected this example for a number of reasons. First, the makers of the series have claimed that their production was 'definitive,'[1] asserting that this monumental work on national history is both comprehensive in its historical treatment and completely faithful to the country's past in its assorted representations. Second, the sheer scale and level of public investment in this undertaking is exceptional and commands our attention and serious scrutiny. Apparently, it was the largest production on Canadian history ever, in terms of budgets, numbers of people involved, and the size of audience. In the first five years after production, the series was repeatedly presented on CBC and other national television networks to an extensive mainstream audience, achieving levels of viewership unmatched by other recent historical productions in Canada. Beyond the sheer scope of the series' subject matter, its marketing campaign and spin-off merchandising activities were remarkable – seventeen television episodes, a glossy book on Canadian history in two volumes, VHS and DVD sets of the television production, T-shirts, mugs, books, CDs, 'Kids' Books,' VHS-PALs, coasters, playing cards, documentary videos on selected aspects of Canadian history, and a documentary on the making of the series, entitled *Making History*. The entire enterprise was memorialized in the published memoir of Mark Starowicz, the series' executive producer and head of documentary production at the CBC, which was similarly entitled *Making History: The Remarkable Story behind* Canada: A People's History. For a large number of Canadians, this series will be a major source of information and interpretation on the country's history for years to come.

In its first ten years this series was a major success for the CBC. It was broadcast and re-broadcast repeatedly on CBC Television and on other networks in Canada and in selected United States markets over the last five years. The videos of the TV series and the books were widely represented in school libraries, as well as in public and academic libraries across Canada and in the United States, and it was assigned as a resource in general courses in history or Canadian Studies at the secondary and post-secondary levels.[2] The series was widely lauded in press releases and promotional materials released by the CBC, and received generally favourable reviews in Canada's national media, including the national journals the *Globe and Mail*, the *National Post*, and *Maclean's* magazine. While it received a mixed reception in some academic assessments,[3] one scholarly reviewer hailed it as 'a crowning achievement of the 20th-century Canadian tradition of public broadcasting and documentary film.'[4]

Amid the ubiquitous airing of episodes, display and sale of books and videos, stocking of libraries, and use of these products in high school and university courses, the actual form and content of this production have received inadequate critical attention relative to its presence on the Canadian historical landscape. This chapter will not focus on the literal content of the series, as other papers have assessed issues of accuracy or balance in its treatment of topics. Rather, it seeks to identify the series' operative narrative forms, pictorial and aural representations, and their implications for understanding authorial intention and audience reception. These forms are as illustrative of the authors' intentions and goals for this series as the specific subject-matter selected for treatment. They reveal a great deal about the specific circumstances of the series' production, illuminating its specific place in Canada's society and culture of the late 1990s.

While it is difficult to find a concise statement of objectives for this series, the CBC's intentions can be gleaned from assorted remarks by its producers and executives as they relate to interpretations of their mandate under the Broadcasting Act of 1991. The clearest statement appeared on the History Home Page of the CBC's website in the section entitled '*Canada: A People's History* Merchandise.' Placed beneath sales promotions for various spin-off products, it stated: '*Canada: A People's History* chronicles the human drama that is Canada's journey from past to present. Diaries, letters and archival documents tell the stories of those who shaped this country, in their own words. Using historical re-enactments, dazzling photography and digital special effects, *Canada: A People's History* presents Canada as you've never seen it: a riveting account of our history, through the eyes of the people who lived it.'[5] The emphasis on presenting Canadian history as the story of 'those who shaped this country' confirmed the authors' preoccupation with the nation-state of 1867. This objective was consistent with the CBC's mandate, as set out in the Broadcast Act of 1969, to 'contribute to the development of national unity and provide for a continuing expression of Canadian identity.' In 1991, the updated version of the Act reiterated much the same objective in its reference to the CBC's role in building a 'shared national consciousness and identity.'[6]

Producer Mark Starowicz also referenced national unity in a memo to the CBC's executives to propose the series, which he crafted on the day following the Quebec Referendum of 1995. He wrote: 'We have not done, for this generation, the most important story of all … The nation is undergoing not only tremendous crises, but also fundamental change from Quebec sovereignty to Free Trade. There is no current material that can show our audience the exciting and dramatic evolution of our country.'[7] A focus on promoting national unity through this series was also suggested in remarks by Starowicz in an interview published in 2002. In summarizing viewers' responses to *Canada: A People's History*, he observed that in the series 'there is a profound streak of wishing to maintain Canadian sovereignty.'[8]

Canada: A People's History can also be placed within the economic and cultural contexts of the mid- to late 1990s, when the CBC was experiencing a number of pressures associated with the expansion of cable TV networks across North America, increasing penetration of Canadian television markets by American channels, and a diminishing revenue base from advertising and government appropriations. Throughout the 1990s the corporation sustained a series of cutbacks; between 1994 and 1998, its core funding was reduced by about one-third, from $1.6 billion a year to about 1.1 billion,[9] and by 1999, it was reported to have stabilized at $800 million.[10] In the same period, heightened nationalism in Quebec, culminating in the narrow referendum result in 1995, shook the confidence of Canada's national cultural institutions regarding the future of the federal state and their role within it. In an atmosphere of crisis, the documentary unit of CBC-TV discerned the potential to propose a large-scale television series on Canadian history, which was readily endorsed by the corporation's executives and televised in seventeen parts in 2000 and 2001.[11] The project also included the production of two large books summarizing the narrative line of the TV production, as well as numerous other product lines, affording opportunities to generate revenues and boost ratings, while enhancing patriotism.

Preoccupied with developing a mass audience, and evaluating the series' success according to its television ratings and book sales,[12] the producers of *Canada: A People's History* focused on developing entertaining approaches to historical representation with the potential to generate a wide audience. Much of the content of the series was driven by conventions from the literary canon and the medium of television to achieve certain reality effects, that is, to convince viewers that the series presented a true and realistic picture of Canada's past. The choice of forms flowed from decisions to present the series as a combination of television sub-genres, prompting, in turn, the adoption of specific dramatic conventions and approaches to historical representation, all significantly influencing the content as well as the form. The series relied on such literary devices as genre, plot, and theme, which, combined with selected images and a specially commissioned musical score, reinforced the main narrative line and proffered interpretation of Canadian history.

Canada: A People's History was also informed by a particular theoretical apparatus, influencing, in turn, the choice of particular structures of representation. Its historiographical approach was strongly rooted in traditional nation-building theories, especially the 'Laurentian' school of Anglo-Canadian history.[13] 'Nation-building' approaches have been present in Anglo-Canadian historiography since the early post-Confederation era, albeit more prominently in some eras than in others. In academic historiography, nation-building approaches reached their zenith in the Canadian Centenary Series, 1962–88, the largest effort in the twentieth century to write the national history of Canada. With the advent of social history after 1970, nation-building histories largely fell out of favour, although by the 1990s several practitioners such as J.L. Granatstein and Michael Bliss were calling for a return to the nation-state as the focus of research and writing.[14]

In their choice of narrative structure, temporal divisions of episodes, and highlighting of particular events, the CBC producers appeared to owe much to the prior model of the Canadian Centenary Series in particular. For example, both series featured complete segments devoted to the story of Confederation. For the Centenary Series, W.L. Morton's volume *The Critical Years*, covering the years 1857–73, was the pivotal volume of that entire series of books. For *Canada: A People's History*, the corresponding episode, entitled 'From Sea to Sea,' covering the years 1867–73, was the last segment of the first season and its culmination. For both projects, the development of the nation-state was the key and indispensable event in the great sweep of Canadian history. One significant difference between these productions was that the first volume of the Centenary Series commenced with approaches to northern North America by European explorers, while the first episode of *Canada: A People's History* was devoted to the history of Aboriginal peoples, followed by early Aboriginal-European encounters.

In the press release announcing the series in 2000, the CBC described it as an 'epic 16-part documentary,' confirming that this production incorporated characteristics of both fictional realism and historical narrative, two radically different forms of representation. According to a current definition, this combination places this series within the category of docudrama, defined as 'a mode of representation that ... combines categories usually perceived as separate: documentary and drama.'[15] For the CBC series, the producers opted for extended sequences of third-person voice-over narration, alternating with on-camera narration by actors representing historical figures and dramatized re-enactments of episodes from Canadian history. This combination of narrative and fictional techniques followed in the tradition of earlier CBC docudramas, especially *The National Dream*, a miniseries adaptation of Pierre Berton's books on the building of the Canadian Pacific Railway. This series, too, focused on the heroic role of well-known historical players and dramatizations of stories associated with its subject.

The specific character of the documentary component of the CBC's historical 'docudrama' is illuminated by the analysis of film scholar Bill Nichols, who identified four modes of representation applied in the field of documentary production: expository, observational, interactive, and reflexive. Within these modes, documentaries position themselves between two poles of representation – narrative, encompassing chronology and moral or ideological argument; and realism, or techniques of mimetic verisimilitude. Each of the identified documentary types emerged within a particular historical context, and responded to earlier modes of representation whose capacity to represent the reality of the world had become constrained or limited. The earliest mode was expository documentary, which developed in the 1920s and 1930s and has tended towards romantic and didactic filmmaking. Nichols has also noted the epistemic character of expository documentary, in its tendency to disseminate conventional wisdom. Unlike reflexive documentary, films in this mode generally do not encourage their audiences to question what is being presented. Rather, expository documentary relies on presenting an impression of objectivity and authoritative judgment, while advancing a particular version of reality for the instruction and edification of its audience.[16]

It can readily be seen that the documentary aspects of *Canada: A People's History* conformed to traditional expository form. Typical of this sub-genre, *Canada: A People's History* relied on 'voice-of-God' commentary and narration delivered in the third-person omniscient voice, combined with dramatic re-enactments to illustrate the main narrative line. Nichols has observed that such productions share formal affinities with television network news, in which an anchor person provides the central messages, supported by reporters in the field. Similarly, the storyline of *Canada: A People's History* was delivered by a principal narrator, whose words were supported and elaborated by selected quotations from a range of individuals from Canada's past. In all cases, these 'voices' were chosen to reinforce the overriding messages and were never at variance with the main narrative line. Curiously, the History home page on the CBC's website characterized the narrator as 'really the voice of the audience and the representative of the audience through the series.' According to senior producer Kelly Crichton: 'she [the narrator] will be the person leading the audience through the story and telling the story to the audience; drawing them into it; making them feel what they're seeing. It's a very important part of the whole series.'

As the audience had no part in the development of the storyline or in crafting any of the narrator's words, it is difficult to know how the narrator could have functioned as the 'voice of the audience.' In actuality, the narrator served as the voice of the authors. Voice-over narration of the authors' storyline was ubiquitous throughout the series, as actress Maggie Huculak intonated the writers' words, imbuing them with gravity or levity as demanded by the script. Through the narrator's voice, the absent authors' viewpoints were enunciated as if emanating from an Almighty authority surveying the action from on high. The narrator introduced the overall series, set the scene for each segment, provided a running account and commentary on the unfolding events, connected disparate parts of the story, drew conclusions, and provided viewers with the preferred interpretation of what they had just viewed. Independent thought by viewers was not expected or encouraged; rather, audience members were expected to absorb the wisdom imparted by the narrator, supported by selected texts and images directing them to the desired conclusions. Reinforcing the arguments of the narrator in the documentary parts of the series, the dramatic re-enactments served as mere illustrations of the interpretations that were being advanced.

In the expository documentary sections of the series, the producers placed a heavy emphasis on the diachronic or processionary approach to represent the passage of historical time. Otherwise known as 'narrative history,' this approach takes an audience chronologically through a linear sequence of events, from a selected starting point to a date or period chosen for the end point of the story. In choosing the narrative form, the producers necessarily also opted for interpretations of Canadian history rooted in narrative modes of representation, especially the 'nation-building' models referenced in this discussion. 'Narrative history' is an approach familiar to many Canadians and has been a staple of historical writing from the early national histories of the post-Confederation era to the present.[17] Elsewhere, I have argued that the choice of the narrative form carries with it a sense of implied continuity and inevitability to historical process. In linking selected historical events in linear sequence, reliance on this form suggests that its components are all part of the same process and that the chosen end point of the chain is the only possible outcome: in this case, Confederation, or the establishment of the federal state.[18]

For the CBC, the decision to take a 'narrative' approach represented a conscious rejection of a trend towards thematic or synchronic approaches represented in more recent academic scholarship of the past twenty to thirty years. In justifying this decision, the series' senior producers claimed that story-telling is integral to both the nature of history and the expectations of their audiences. In his Foreword to the series' books, Starowicz asserted a need for 'a narrative cleansing of Canadian history.' He explained: 'We have bleached the dramatic narrative out of Canadian history and reduced it to social studies units in our schools,' adding 'This is a narrative work, not an academic work.'[19] In a panel discussion on visual history, CBC producer Gene Allen, director of research for the series and the book, stated that 'most television producers are deeply attached to the narrative mode, to telling the audience what happened, and what happened next, and how it turned out.' Asserting that 'this narrative orientation is shared at an almost instinctive level by the dozens of different people I've worked with over that time,' he added: 'We talk among ourselves about maintaining the suspension of disbelief, about making the audience feel as if they're inside the story as it unfolds.'[20] For the authors of *Canada: A People's History*, verisimilitude, or the representation of 'real-life' events in narrative form, and 'maintaining the suspension of disbelief' were the keys to presenting Canadian history successfully to a general audience. In the video *Making History*, a CBC documentary on the making of the series, Starowicz explained his decision to take a narrative approach:

There are a lot of ways you could do the history of Canada. You could do it thematically, or, you know, one episode on labour, or another episode on women,
or another episode on ethnic groups. We chose to do it chronologically, which is
quite a challenge, I mean, the history of Canada begins about twenty thousand
years ago. And why, because the central unifying idea of Canadian history is, once
there was nothing here, so that's why we chose to do it as the growth of an entire
united nations of peoples, because that's the story in the end, and that's why we
decided to go back twenty thousand years and begin when there was nothing.[21]

Superficially, the narrative form seemed to hold the potential to connect with
audiences in that it echoes the way that humans organize reflections on their
own lives, through chronological sequencing and cause-and-effect explanations of their own past experiences. This widely shared sense is nevertheless at
variance with the different temporal layers operating within the consciousness
of even a single individual. The past, whether of an individual or an entire
people, is not a linear chronology or single integrated story, but a complicated
congeries of filtered memories, in some cases intersecting with and in others
diverging from whatever story is selected to organize and explain diverse occurrences according to an observer's subjective frame of reference.[22]

The authors of *Canada: A People's History* concluded that there was only
one overriding narrative in Canadian history worth telling, under which the
selected individual stories might be subsumed. Within this structure, selected
stories from a variety of observers were included as testimonials and quoted
to reinforce the main narrative line. The CBC's website stated that for the television series, Starowicz heeded advice to broadcast the same story on both
French- and English-language networks. 'So, the co-production, with one story, one executive producer, and one team was born.'[23] The focus on 'one story'
was reinforced by the series' time line on its website, presented as a single
progression from 15,000 years ago to the present, as viewed from a single perspective. This approach contrasted with the BBC's *A History of Britain*, which
presented five different time lines in parallel format. They included a British
time line and, reflecting the different histories of its constituent nationalities,
also included English, Scottish, Welsh, and Northern Irish time lines.[24]

In opting for a narrative treatment, Starowicz and his team rejected the use
of expert commentators. In the CBC's video documentary *Making History*,
devoted to the production of this series, the narrator stated: 'Although there are
dozens of historians behind the scenes, one of the surprises for viewers is the
conspicuous absence of on-screen academics.' Gordon Henderson, senior producer of *Canada: A People's History*, elaborated: 'I think one of the really cool
things about the series is that we don't have historians that come on, analysts

that come on with a tie and a tweed jacket and a bookcase behind, explaining what we just saw, giving you perspective. I mean, I'm all for perspective but I'd rather see the narrative driven. I'd rather see the story kept alive. We want to avoid history class, we want to keep telling stories.'[25]

The producers thereby attempted to chart the human history of Canada in chronological sequence from its early, pre-contact origins to the year 1990. Apart from the opening episode, the narrative segments resembled many volumes of the Canadian Centenary Series, as the CBC adopted similar turning points and time spans for its story segments. The principal difference was that the first book of the Centenary series began with early Viking approaches and concluded in the era of New France,[26] while the CBC's opening episode was devoted to both the pre-contact and early post-contact history of Aboriginal peoples.

The selected entry point for the first episode was the presumed arrival of Aboriginal peoples from Asia in northern North America around 15,000 BP, and that enormous span of history was compressed into just the first segment, concluding in the post-contact era around 1800 AD. The first episode culminated in the well-known, embellished story by John Jewitt of the alleged massacre by Mowachaht people of the crew of the ship *Boston*, ending with a dramatization of Chief Maquinna's shedding tears over the Americans' departure for the United States. This sentimental vignette served a narrative purpose as it set up a flash-forward to a report of Maquinna in his later years, 'hobbled by rheumatism,' still welcoming traders to their shores.[27] The final, resonating message of the first episode was one of Aboriginal people inviting Europeans to Canada, their histories serving as prologue to the arrival and future dominance of the Western newcomers. Much of the balance of the narrative replayed the familiar history of European trade, occupation, settlement, and constitutional and political developments, culminating in Confederation and the establishment of a transcontinental nation by the end of the first season. Following the traditional division of Canadian history into pre- and post-Confederation eras, the episodes of the second season were then devoted to the history of the Canadian nation-state, as they charted its progress to the end point of the narrative around 1990.

The CBC's decision to take a 'journalistic' approach to Canadian history influenced the producers' decision to focus on the representation of dramatic events, whether re-enactments of battles and massacres in earlier periods, or the narration of political confrontations in the modern era. In various interviews on the production, Mark Starowicz asserted his view that Canadian history was just as exciting as its American counterpart. For example, he stated: 'It is a thrill for viewers to find out that it is not the Americans alone who have the great stories such as revolution, civil war, and the taking of the west.'[28] To make history exciting for viewers, the producers sought out sensational episodes from Canada's past and dramatized them to lure viewers from competing American docudrama products being broadcast within this country. The action was advanced through the dramatization of a succession of confrontations, including pre-contact wars between Aboriginal peoples, conflicts between European and Aboriginal people following contact, wars between nations competing for North America, battles between Canada and the Métis in 1870 and 1885, the World Wars, and assorted political confrontations, culminating in the face-off between Pierre Trudeau and René Lévesque in the first sovereignty referendum of 1980 and wrangling over the patriation of the Constitution in 1982.

As with its competitors, the CBC series relied especially on the forms of melodrama, the most common type of television fictional drama.[29] The series' emphasis on historical conflict was accompanied by melodramatic situations and characters, wherein the complexities of social history were reduced to 'the tropes of victim and villain, hero and antagonist, crisis and rescue.'[30] For *Canada: A People's History*, as in American melodramas, the decision to favour particular heroes or protagonists, and to set them off by highlighting particular opponents or antagonists, made it clear which forces and values the producers were promoting, and which values they were cautioning viewers against. [31]

Within a generally melodramatic script, the authors selected protagonists from the succession of individuals and groups considered to support the proto-nation in the respective eras before Confederation, or the country of Canada after 1867. Antagonists were selected from opposing forces thought to sow seeds of disunity or discord in each period. Echoing an interpretation advanced by the conservative nationalist historians W.L. Morton and Donald Creighton, the authors presented the United States and Quebec nationalists as overarching adversaries of the federal state, hence, threats to Canadian unity and sovereignty. In the penultimate episode, 'Years of Hope and Anger,' the narrative set the stage for the appearance of its eventual hero by focusing on the presumed threats to Canada posed by the United States and Quebec in the 1960s. The narrator related that, in the 1960s, 'many students like [economist James] Laxer are awakened to nationalism.' A re-enactor then read from Laxer's reminiscences about his experience of reading George Grant's *Lament for a Nation*[32] and its impact on him: 'I was already in some sense a nationalist but this gave a coherent view that there was a constant body of ideas that distinguished Canada from the United States and made Canada a country worth saving.' The anecdote was then reinforced by the main narrator, who intoned: 'in 1965 you no longer needed a philosopher to see the difference.' This vignette was followed by a treatment of the American government's war in Viet Nam, succeeded by a section on emergent Quebec nationalism, entitled 'Maîtres Chez Nous,' focusing on the Front de libération du Québec (FLQ) Crisis ca. 1963–70.[33]

After thus commencing episode 16 with stories representing the United States and Quebec separatists as threats to Canada, the narrator introduced Pierre Trudeau, the principal hero of the overall narrative, who would reappear frequently in the last two episodes and whose words would be frequently invoked to advance the central message of pan-Canadian unity as a panacea for the imperilled nation-state. The narrative first introduced Trudeau as one of the three newcomers recruited by Prime Minister Pearson to run for Parliament in the 1965 federal general election. Following a treatment of the international exposition Expo 67, the script returned to Trudeau, who, by then minister of justice, was described as 'the political mentor of his generation.' Continuing, the narrator related: 'Trudeau introduces legislation to make divorce easier, changes the Criminal Code to allow therapeutic abortions, and he decriminalizes homosexuality.' He was then presented as laying out his vision of Canadian federalism: 'All individual citizens are to be treated equally. He is against any special status of Quebec, First Nations, or any other group. His views set him on a collision course with the Quebec government.' Revealingly, the journalists who authored the script concluded this part of the storyline with the statement: 'He's become a media star.'

The storyline followed with Trudeau's election as Liberal party leader, as the producers inserted a clip of his oft-repeated line: 'Canada must be one. Canada must be progressive, and Canada must be a just society.' This section of the narrative culminated in the story of Trudeau defying separatists at the St Jean Baptiste parade in Montreal at the end of his first federal election campaign as leader in 1968, an incident often referenced in CBC documentaries to evince his steely resolve. This sequence concluded with Trudeau's words, translated through voice-over into English as: 'There has been enough fooling around in the last few years. Now, we want to work together to build a free country, a prosperous and united country. No more fooling around.' Trudeau's words were followed by the narrator's statement: 'Soon, he will face life and death choices that will test his resolve.' Trudeau reappeared at the end of the episode, following a treatment of the Parti Québécois victory in Quebec's provincial election of 1976. A clip of the prime minister showed a steely Trudeau speaking the words: 'I am confident that Quebecers will continue to reject separatism because they still believe that their destiny is linked with an indivisible Canada.' This vignette was followed by the narrator's peroration: 'The struggle for the hearts, minds, and loyalties of Quebecers has begun. Twice, in the decades to come, the survival of Canada will be put to the test.'

The historical dramatis persona of Trudeau also dominated the last episode of the TV series, in which he was shown to appear repeatedly to save the nation from recurrent crises. Early in this episode, a scene focused on the work of his official photographer, who provided a testimonial to the prime minister's perseverance: 'He was a man who knew what he wanted and went after it. He would just relentlessly stay on something.' In this instance, the crisis was the federal-provincial wrangling over the patriation of the Constitution, wherein Trudeau was shown to rescue Canada from parochial or partisan interests. The sequence ended with the narrator's words: 'In a very few years, the Charter of Rights and Freedoms will transform Canadian society. Pierre Trudeau makes his mark on history.' Later, after leaving office, Trudeau reappeared in the treatment of the Meech Lake Accord. The narrator related: 'Trudeau dismisses the Accord as a total bungle and Brian Mulroney as a weakling. The federal government, he says, is giving away too much power to the provinces.' Trudeau's commanding role in the series was further reinforced in the packaging of the video, with his portrait presented as the featured image on the spine of the VHS version, reinforcing his dominant role in the series and its storyline. As I argued in a companion article on the books of *Canada: A People's History*, the producers selected Trudeau as a suitable saviour figure around which to rally the country to its salvation in the face of the perceived threat of Quebec separatism following the Quebec Referendum of 1995.[34]

The factor of literary genre also warrants comment, as the chosen genre also influenced the content of the series and illuminated the ideological concerns of the producers of *Canada: A People's History*. Starowicz's avowed intent was to produce an epic, a genre originating in antiquity.[35] Throughout the Western canon, the epic has been a favoured genre for national histories, usually centred on the founding or peak periods in the history of a nation or people.[36] Two current definitions of the epic are 'a long narrative poem, on a grand scale, about the deeds of warriors and heroes';[37] and 'a long narrative poem on a great and serious subject, related in an elevated style, and centred on a heroic or quasi-divine figure on whose actions depends the fate of a tribe, a nation, or the human race.'[38] Elaborating on the type, E.M.W. Tillyard identified four formal components of classical epic: high quality and high seriousness; breadth and inclusiveness of subject-matter; rigorous control and a conscious will to maintain unity of the subject; and the expression of the feelings and values of its own age.[39]

The literary theorist Mikhail Bakhtin provided a useful way of looking at this genre, as he distinguished between the epic's orientation to an 'absolute past,' characterized by remoteness from the historical past or present, and the 'zone of familiar contact,' a kind of open-endedness to the present which he associated with novels.[40] For Bakhtin, the term 'epic' signifies more than a genre. He argued that it is also an expression of a distinctive orientation to historical time and place, one in which the past is presented as whole, complete, and sealed off from revision. Bakhtin held that it was also possible for an epic work to present the past in 'familiar time,' that is, to approach the past with indeterminacy and open-endedness, avoiding the monological closure that often characterizes the genre.[41]

In Canada, a fully realized national epic was not developed until the Canadian Centenary Series, 1962–88,[42] whose narrative structure was largely replicated in the CBC series three decades later. Superficially, Starowicz's choice of the epic genre also shared affinities with the work of Ken Burns, the well-known maker of documentaries on American history and experience.[43] However, where Burns's *The Civil War* displayed several of the open-ended characteristics described by Bakhtin,[44] these qualities did not apply to *Canada: A People's History*. In emphasizing the heroism of the protagonists, the salvation of the nation, and a presumed unity and coherence of history, it displayed characteristics typical of the traditional epic. By situating the narrative within an absolute past, the CBC series also showed a remoteness from the actual contingency and possibility of history. Rather than extensively engage the actual diversity of voices and perspectives on Canadian history, the producers opted for the valorization of selected historical figures and perspectives, presented as models for advancing their goal of promoting Canadian unity in a period of uncertainty regarding the future viability and role of the nation-state.

Within this genre, the producers of *Canada: A People's History* developed a specific plot, simply defined as the events of a story, or structure of actions in a literary work.[45] Here, the action was plotted as the inexorable progress, through many challenges, of the Canadian people from their different origins to their collective realization within the nation-state of 1867. In this regard, the production's plot evoked the narrative structure of the Canadian Centenary Series, which similarly sought to weave together the separate regional strands of Canada into a unified story, 'strands of cable being wound in a rope yard,' in the words of that series' executive editor, W.L. Morton.[46]

Beyond the content of specific episodes, the authors organized the sequence of actions into a larger structure, which may be summarized. The first season's episodes were devoted to presenting a sequence of developments prefiguring the future nation-state and culminating in Confederation, while the episodes of the second season charted the fulfilment of the new country's promise in its first 123 years following the establishment of the nation-state. The Canadian Centenary Series had traced the inexorable movement of the different British North American colonies to political union, and then treated the constituted federal state as the fulfilment of the promise previously unrealized while the colonies were separate entities. The narrative of the Centenary Series was designed to culminate in 1967, the centennial of Confederation, but by the early 1960s, internal and external forces challenged Morton's vision of a unified nation-state, and so he looked back to the Confederation era and its leaders for earlier examples of unity to project on to a future fulfilment.[47] For the TV series, its producers, responding to perceived challenges to the nation-state in the 1990s, harked back to 1967, a putative peak moment of unity and patriotism selected to represent the promise of the country's future fulfilment. According to this schema, Expo 67 and Pierre Trudeau were invoked as symbols of national achievement and leadership to help shore up the nation-state in its travails following the Quebec referendum of 1995.

To advance the plot and their version of history, the makers of *Canada: A People's History* made extensive use of sound, especially music, which in non-fiction television has often been employed to impart an organic unity.[48] For such productions, musical themes have been used to create moods, evoke particular eras, and signal to an audience the continuing presence of historical developments associated with earlier applications of the same thematic material. In the Wagnerian tradition, the producers attempted to integrate narrative and music, with leitmotifs introduced to represent recurring concepts or themes in the narrative. The initial entry of melodic material linked concepts to future stories or events accompanied by the same melody, while subsequent iterations evoked earlier stories and associations represented by these leitmotifs.

As discussed on the CBC's website, the score of *Canada: A People's History* 'weaves through all 17 episodes, interpreting the action and building another layer to the story.' The principal theme, which opened all the shows, 'had to be big and powerful to signal the importance of the story.' At the same time, in the words of one of the composers, other parts of the score required a different treatment. 'When you come down to somebody who has lost their family, we might reduce that to just a single violin or a single cello and it becomes very small scale.' Generally, the score by Claude Desjardins and Eric N. Robertson eschewed the music of folk or popular culture and instead featured new popular symphonic material written specifically for this production. Driving the narrative forward was the principal theme, introduced with swelling strings at the beginning and conclusion of each episode, usually accompanying a patriotic text read by the narrator. In the prologue to each episode, the music also connoted a sense of urgency through a bass line of beating drums following a restatement of the principal theme, as the voice-over narration summarized a new chapter in the building of the nation, anticipating confrontations to be covered in the ensuing instalment. In the accompanying narration for the pre-1867 episodes, the storyline stated that these confrontations would challenge the future of existing European societies in northern North America, in other words, the nation-to-be. For episodes dealing with periods after 1867, the stentorian bass line anticipated confrontations to be presented as a threat to the constituted nation-state. During more sombre sections of the narrative, such as the treatment of hardships encountered by various immigrant groups, the music modulated to muted passages played by solo violins, while in the sections featuring military topics, drums were prominent.[49] While several complementary melodies were employed, the principal theme was ubiquitous throughout, as the massed soaring violins contributed a cosmetic coherence when the historical facts failed to unify. This homogeneously romantic score figuratively expressed the overriding importance of 'the people' over individual or vernacular expression.

In such a highly visual medium as television, the use of images also warrants comment. Between the dramatic re-enactments, Starowicz's team displayed a variety of still images from Canadian history, including paintings and photographs, as well as film footage of twentieth-century events. In their selection of both still and moving images, the producers showed a fondness for representing confrontations in history. In the episodes devoted to the periods before 1900, they staged a series of tableaux to illustrate military engagements through battle re-enactments. With the journalist's eye for compelling visuals, the CBC team also selected still images that highlighted drama, usually relating to confrontations between forces supporting the development of the nation-state and their adversaries. Just one example was the highlighting of an 1870 illustration of the execution of Thomas Scott at Red River in the segment 'A Single Act of Severity.' A propagandistic image from the *Canadian Illustrated News*, this image represented the execution as a murder, reinforcing a stereotype of the Métis participating in the North West Resistance as cold-blooded killers. Here, the image provided a backdrop to the segment title and reappeared in a sequence of still images presented to carry the story. For the series, the illustration served a dual purpose – it provided a dramatic image of the Red River Resistance and also reinforced the unifying thread of the narrative by representing the marginalization of forces perceived to be opposing the forward advance of the nation-state.[50]

The Scott image also figured prominently in the books of the series, which featured two reproductions of this tableau – a full-page rendering used as the signature image of the chapter entitled 'Confederation' and a second reproduction accompanying the text's discussion of the 'Red River Rebellion.'[51] For the chapter's title page, the image was cropped and blown up to focus more directly on the killer and victim. As with other illustrations in the book, the authors attempted no critical pictorial analysis, nor was there an acknowledgment that the CBC had artificially coloured and manipulated the image, as it was presented as a realistic treatment of the past, without explanation or context. Within the larger narrative, the Scott image served a useful function by foreshadowing the subsequent sensationalized images of implied First Nations violence, in both video and book versions, from the Oka Crisis of 1990. Presented near the end of the final volume of the book, this confrontation was illustrated by a montage of images from the standoff, featuring three photographs of masked Mohawk Warriors, with the major image representing a Warrior brandishing a rifle atop the barricade at Kanesatake.[52] Images of Scott's execution and the Oka crisis were also highlighted in the television series, where they served to dramatize stories considered to hold audience appeal, while communicating the authors' preoccupation with preserving the nation-state by highlighting confrontations with its presumed adversaries, perhaps as a cautionary tale for viewers.

The CBC series also included considerable film footage on twentieth-century events, including images of Canadian soldiers involved in the First and Second World Wars, although these shots rarely presented close-ups of violence or actual suffering. For the episodes dealing with the period after the Second World War, historical images and re-enactments were largely supplanted by television footage of historical events and personalities, including familiar material from the CBC's archives used in numerous other TV documentaries. The videotaped material included such well-known sequences as Pierre Trudeau's famous exchange with a reporter outside the Parliament Buildings during the October Crisis of 1970, which has provided stock footage for numerous CBC political documentaries on this period. The reporter asks: 'How far would you go?' to which the determined prime minister responds: 'Just watch me.' For the series, use of this clip served various functions, including reinforcement of the stature of the principal hero and also a valorization of the CBC's asserted role, not only in bringing the news to Canadians, but in actually 'making history,' the title of both the CBC's documentary video and Starowicz's own book on the making of the series.

Of equivalent importance to the plot and its actions was the thematic material of this series. As Northrop Frye has noted, the plot answers the question 'How is the story going to turn out?' while the theme is concerned with the question 'What is the point of this story?'[53] Thematically, the authors of *Canada: A People's History* placed a premium on finding and reinforcing unity in history. The series began with unity, followed by a succession of conflicts and divisions, concluding with the reassertion of a relatively unproblematic unity by the end of the narrative, as set in the present. As Starowicz summarized: 'The genius of Canada is the constant search for equilibrium, where no one ever fully gains the upper hand.' The interpretation of overriding equilibrium suggested the capacity of the nation-state to accommodate all groups and aspirations. Following its treatment of the constitutional crisis of 1980–1, the narrative included selected episodes from political confrontations that had emerged by 1990, including the Oka Crisis, the depletion of cod stocks in Atlantic Canada, and the political battle between Alberta and Ottawa over the National Energy Program.

Largely untreated were other struggles in process at the end of the story, such as the status or rights of First Peoples, racial minorities, women, people with disabilities, lesbian, gay, transgendered, and bisexual people, the homeless, the unemployed, and others. For example, despite the fact that the status of LGBT people has been part of public discourse in Canada for at least forty years, and many of the landmark judicial decisions relating to the Charter of Rights and Freedoms over the last twenty years have concerned the human rights of this minority group, the television series *Canada: A People's History* completely omitted reference to their history, apart from a single reference in the penultimate episode to the decriminalization of homosexual sex between consenting adults in Trudeau's omnibus bill of 1968. Aware of the contentiousness of same-sex rights among powerful and vocal constituencies of social and religious conservatives, the CBC took the safe route, averting possible criticism by continuing a general discourse of silence in Canadian historiography regarding these topics.[54] A few inspiring stories, including Mary Eberts's campaign to secure women's equality rights in the Charter of Rights and Freedoms, Elizabeth May's environmental crusade, and Baldej Sikh Dhillon's quest to wear a turban as part of his RCMP uniform, were cited as parables of inclusiveness.[55] Where the experience of minorities did not reinforce such a sanguine conclusion, the narrative simply omitted them from the story,[56] thereby maintaining an image of harmony and coherence for this epic representation of Canadian history.

The theme of *Canada: A People's History* was outlined by Starowicz in an interview published in 2002:

The paradigm for Canadian History is that we are all refugees and involved in a society that has little tolerance for class and a society that is insistent on the same rules for everyone. Canada is renowned internationally for its tolerance. Ninety-five per cent of us have the same story. People came here because of the tolerance of diversity and a desire to improve their lot. We are really the debris of war and famine, but I mean it in the best sense of the word. This is a unifying paradigm.[57]

Starowicz thereby discerned a unifying thread in the theme of refuge, which he asserted to be 'at the core of the Canadian identity.'[58] The series introduced this theme in the opening episode, when the narrator related a Salish creation story bearing a superficial resemblance to the hypothesized Bering Sea or Beringia migrations. By including Aboriginal people in the theme of refuge, the implication was that they were immigrants like other Canadians, effectively diminishing alternative national aspirations based on Indigenous occupation. The refuge theme was replayed in various statements throughout the series, culminating in Starowicz's peroration following the final series segment: 'Fifteen thousand years ago, the first travellers came to this continent, which became the destination for countless generations, a place where a million epic journeys ended and a million new stories began.'

This overriding message was delivered at the conclusion of the last episode of the series, in an epilogue entitled 'The Journey.' In this epilogue, the producers advanced the notion that the country's history was characterized by successive waves of refugees seeking safe haven in Canada, beginning with the Aboriginal peoples crossing the presumed Bering Land bridge that formerly linked Asia and North America. This tableau of Aboriginal peoples is quickly superseded by an image of a European settler, representing 'the landless and the dreamers who would unlock a continent and forge a New World people.' The narrative continued: 'And they kept coming, the jobless from Scotland, the landless from Ireland, the dispossessed of Europe, and they have been followed ever since by families searching for opportunity and sanctuary.' The authors elaborated this theme in the last paragraph of the two-volume book accompanying the series: 'These tensions, fundamental to many environmental issues, are reflected in Canada itself. The country arose from conflict and co-operation among people, and it was settled by those who battled the elements and the land to survive. It is defined by ongoing regional tensions and linguistic debate, by political compromise and unsettled land claims. It is a country of refugees that continually negotiates a new equilibrium.'[59]

The theme of refuge was further elaborated in Starowicz's Afterword to the second volume of the series books, which stated that 'Modern Canada was founded by two unwanted peoples.' The executive producer also referred to the 'collective experience of refuge and redemption that underlies our identity.' Conflating the terms 'immigrant' and 'refugee,' this construction suggested that all individuals who emigrated to what is now Canada had been rejected in their homelands and arrived on an equal footing. The message appeared to be that all Canadians, whether rich or poor, in the mainstream or on the margins, are metaphorically 'in the same boat.' Starowicz qualified his statement about refugees by asserting that it does not apply equally to Quebec, where the francophones' severance from the French mother country 'is at the base of

Quebec's cultural survival,' adding: 'many Québécois and Acadians consider themselves an indigenous American people.' Conversely, in the Foreword to the first volume, Starowicz included First Peoples in the theme of refuge: 'That is the single, uniting theme of Canadian history from 15,000 years ago till the last jetliner that landed yesterday.'[60] In a dramatic reversal of Canadian history, Aboriginal peoples were thereby reconfigured as 'refugees,' while francophone Euro-Canadians are construed as 'indigenous.' While this interpretation lacked empirical validity, there was a narrative logic to Starowicz's revision. The reason was that the presented story required a European 'indigenous' connection to the land in order to advance a posited Euro-Canadian covenant as the basis of Canadian history and identity.[61]

The final, resonating message of the television series was contained in a sequence of sentences and phrases in the peroration, or concluding passage of the narrated epilogue. The narrator asserted:

> Every strand is still here. This history is still in play.
> The homelands of the First Peoples.
> The future of the French and English
> The newcomers who have shaped our century
> The eternal dynamic with the United States
> Language and Culture.
> Legacy and Land.
> Political Power and Identity
> Confederation or Secession
> Our place in the emerging global constellations
> Every story you have seen is still evolving. You are creating it now. Whether you know it or not, you are all living an epic drama.[62]

Here, the authors applied devices of rhetoric to focus viewers' attention on the most important issues, from their perspective, concerning Canada's past, present, and future. To make their point, they relied specifically on the figure of polysyndeton, represented in the repetition of the word 'and' in successive clauses, before breaking the pattern in the final phrase in the sequence. Here, the terms 'Language and Culture, Legacy and Land, Political Power and Identity' were followed by 'Confederation *or* Secession,' a dramatic device intended to jolt the viewer to the posited stark choice faced by the country. This final binary opposition in *Canada: A People's History* underscored the authors' contention that national unity remained the fundamental issue confronting the country, confirming the intended application of this history of Canada as an instrument for sustaining the imperilled nation-state, whose 'history is still in play.'

Conclusions

While referencing a variety of groups in Canadian society, the plot and thematic structure of *Canada: A People's History* subordinated distinctiveness and difference to an overriding goal of valorizing unity and coherence. The series makers advanced their narrative goals through the use of various literary forms and techniques, including framing the sweep of Canada's past as a historical melodrama. In every historical era, official forces, forerunners of the elite culture to which the CBC belongs, were highlighted as protagonists, preserving society from the presumed chaos represented by their adversaries. As discussed in my article on the books of the series, in the pre-Confederation era, the protagonists were politicians and military leaders whose actions anticipated the unification of 1867, as contrasted with Aboriginal peoples, American invaders, and Quebec nationalists, who were presented as major threats to the nation-to-be.[63] In the post-Confederation era, a heroic role was accorded individuals considered to be promoting the cause of national unity in the first 123 years of the constituted nation-state, set off by adversaries, usually Quebec sovereignists or American expansionists shown to be seeking to thwart the forces of Canadian unity. Beyond story-telling components, the CBC's approach was to combine techniques of verisimilitude and authorial assertion to channel the audience to the desired conclusions.

The CBC also ambitiously sought to structure its history series within the epic genre. If, as E.M.W. Tillyard has argued, classical epics express the feelings and values of their own eras, it might be asked to what degree the CBC succeeded in achieving its objective. A clue may be found in published reports regarding their initial reception. Following the first season, the Carleton University Public History program compiled unsolicited survey data indicating that *Canada: A People's History* was particularly well received by anglophone audience members favouring patriotic representations of history,[64] although in his book *Making History*, Starowicz acknowledged that the series found a cool reception among francophone reviewers.[65] Given the pan-Canadian tenor of this series, its contrasting reception in Quebec and anglophone Canada was perhaps not surprising and tends to confirm that the CBC's epic did not resonate with all groups but connected rather more specifically to anglophone constituencies preoccupied with maintaining the traditional nation-state and its narrative. In the end, it is a conservative epic, devoted to heralding the peak periods of the nation-state's history and the role of its founding fathers, a comforting message for existing power groups desiring to buttress their lineage through valorization of the nation's heroes. As Bakhtin has observed, such epics are not primarily concerned with representing the actual past so much as the transfer of a represented world on to the past. In this case, the makers of the CBC history series advanced notions of a classless nation-state, its citizens united by their common experience as refugees, egalitarianism, and acceptance of diversity. However imaginary, this parable served the allegorical function of supporting their plea for the continuation of the traditional nation-state, and by extension, its pan-Canadian cultural institutions.[66]

The analysis of the series' storyline and images leads back to the specific historical circumstances within which *Canada: A People's History* emerged. Its production coincided with a concerted effort to buttress the federal structure in the years following one of its greatest political challenges since Confederation – the Quebec Referendum of 1995. Only a year after the referendum, the Supreme Court of Canada delivered its decision in the Delgamuukw case in 1996, which affirmed Aboriginal title to the land. Starowicz later acknowledged that the series reveals much about the political context of the mid-1990s. As with the book's narrative structure, his comments suggested an overriding concern at that time with responding to perceived challenges to the federal state.[67] Elsewhere, my review article on these books identified a particular preoccupation with stereotypical textual and visual depictions of Aboriginal peoples in the narrative.[68] For a brief moment, the series' monolithic narrative seemed to salve a longing among anglophone Canadians for greater coherence in national history and identity following the political challenges of the 1990s. Yet, this very unity and coherence was achieved by marginalizing the history of various groups considered outside the mainstream in order to advance the historical role of the traditional nation-state and its proponents.[69]

Therefore, leaving aside the problematic issues associated with the term 'definitive,' *Canada: A People's History* could not be considered a 'definitive' history of Canada. While conforming to the broad outlines of epic structure, in its form and content the series did not fully represent the diversity of Canada. Its storyline and supporting tableaux drew on quotations representing the words of selected men and women, but these voices were not expressions of difference in that they did not operate independently but rather were selected to reinforce the voices or messages of the authors. An authentic representation of diversity would be open to the inclusion of voices that sometimes challenged, rather than reinforced, the main storyline and its claims to definitiveness. A genuinely dialogical work, that is, a work respecting the diversity of the voices of humanity, would acknowledge the autonomous character of every voice as a distinctive expression of the inner speech, thoughts, and emotions of a unique individual.[70] A dialogical approach would empower historical actors to express their own necessity and aspirations, and not seek to subsume their voices under the nation-building agendas developed by others. Perhaps the notion of addressing the diversity of humanity is too daunting for many practitioners of national history. Nevertheless, by developing parallel narratives, integrating representative but autonomous voices from all social groups, breaking the discourse of silence regarding marginalized peoples, resisting stereotypes, and refraining from the impulse to choose heroes and villains, future film versions of Canada's national history might come closer than this television series to representing the plurality of identities and perspectives of the country's peoples. If *Canada: A People's History* shows by its example how much remains to be done to achieve that goal, it will have contributed significantly to the development of public history in Canada.

NOTES

1 During the period of its initial broadcasts of the history series, the CBC's website for *Canada: A People's History* stated: 'Every issue has been meticulously researched by a team of historians and provides a definitive new account of the richness of our country's past.' http://history.cbc.ca/history.

2 For example, at the University of Toronto, the series was assigned as a resource for an introductory course in Canadian Studies, Course No. UNI220Y: 'Understanding Canada Today: Re-imagining the Nation – 2005–2006.' http://individual .utoronto.ca/emilygilbert/UNI220Y/UNI220Y-syllabus.htm. At the University of Calgary, it was a featured case study in a course on historiography. Course SS 654, 'Historiography and Theories of History, Part 1.' http://hist.ucalgary.ca/courses/ F2003/HTST690L03.pdf. The Ontario Ministry of Education's course profile for Canadian and World Politics, University Preparation for Catholic schools, prescribes *Canada: A People's History* as a text for several segments, among standard textbooks included as reference works for this course. See the website of the York Catholic District School Board, at: http://www.ycdsb.edu.on.ca/; and: http://kilby .sac.on.ca/departments/HISTSOCSCI/pdf/ProfilesETC/CHI4ULongProfile.pdf.

3 'Round Table': Gene Allen, 'The Professionals and the Public: Responses to *Canada: A People's History*'; Margaret Conrad, 'My Canada Includes the Atlantic Provinces'; Patrice Groulx, 'La meilleure histoire du monde,' *Histoire sociale / Social History* 34, 68 (2001): 381–414.

4 David Frank, 'Public History and the People's History: A View from Atlantic Canada,' *Acadiensis* 32, 2 (Spring 2003): 120–33.

5 http://history.cbc.ca/history/webdriver?Mival=GENcont.html&series_id=4& episode_id =99&chapter_id=1&page_id=1&lang=E.

6 'The State of the System,' chapter 6, The National Public Broadcaster: http://www .parl.gc.ca/InfoComDoc/37/2/HERI/Studies/Reports/herirp02/07-Ch06-e.htm.

7 Mark Starowicz, *Making History: The Remarkable Story behind* Canada: A People's History (Toronto: McClelland and Stewart, 2003), 27–8.

8 Penney Clark, 'Engaging the Field: A Conversation with Mark Starowicz,' *Canadian Social Studies* 36, 2 (Winter 2002): – http://www2.education.ualberta.ca/css/css_36_2/ARengaging_the_field.htm (accessed 10 March 2010).

9 Doug Saunders, 'The CBC: Spotlight on a House Divided,' *Globe and Mail*, 16 December 1998.

10 'Remaking the CBC (2): What Defines Public Broadcasting in the 1990s?' *Globe and Mail*, 23 March 1999.

11 In his book on the making of the series, Starowicz related his rationale for using the Quebec referendum to seek support for the project. He wrote: 'The shock of the referendum was not the genesis of the Canadian History project. I had been actively talking about the idea for years, and in the documentary unit, we hoped it would be the next project for the Dawn of the Eye team. But until now, I had zero confidence I could sell it in the acrid climate in the CBC. I began to think that now might be the moment to make the formal move. The shock of the referendum, I was betting, would change the climate in the CBC, because it had given us all a brush with history' (*Making History*, 28).

12 In assessing the project, Gene Allen, senior producer and director of research for the project, stressed the extent of book sales and increased television ratings as benchmarks of success ('The Professionals and the Public,' 381).

13 Originating in the 1930s, the Laurentian Thesis asserted that metropolitan elites from the major cities of central Canada, that is, Montreal and then Toronto, exploited the geography of northern North America to forge the basis of a common identity that would become Canada. For a major early statement of this thesis, see Donald Creighton, *The Commercial Empire of the St. Lawrence* (Toronto: Ryerson Press, 1937).

14 J.L. Granatstein, *Who Killed Canadian History?* (Toronto: HarperCollins, 1998).

15 Janet Staiger, 'Docudrama,' *The Encyclopedia of Television* (Chicago: Museum of Broadcast Communications, 1997): http://www.museum.tv/archives/etv/D/htmlD/docudrama/docudrama.htm.

16 Bill Nichols, *Representing Reality: Issues and Concepts in Documentary* (Bloomington and Indianapolis: Indiana University Press, 1991), 32–3.

17 Lyle Dick, 'A Growing *Necessity* for Canada: W.L. Morton's Centenary Series and the Forms of National History, 1955–1980,' *Canadian Historical Review* 82, 2 (2001): 223–52; and Carl Berger, *The Writing of Canadian History* (Toronto: Oxford University Press 1976), 2–3.

18 See Lyle Dick, 'All's Well That Ends Well,' *Prairie Fire* 7, 1 (1986): 77–82.

19 Don Gillmor and Pierre Turgeon, *Canada: A People's History*, vol. 1 (Toronto: McClelland and Stewart, 2001), x.

20 Gene Allen, Remarks in 'Canadian History in Film: A Roundtable Discussion,' *Canadian Historical Review* 82, 2 (June 2001): 332.

21 *Making History* [video on the making of *Canada: A People's History*] (Toronto: Canadian Broadcasting Corporation, 2000).

22 See the discussion of the dialogical character of human consciousness in Michael Holquist, *Dialogism: Bakhtin and His World* (London: Routledge, 1990).

23 'Step by Step: One Story: Many Perspectives,' in 'Behind the Scenes – About the TV Series.' http://history.cbc.ca/history.

24 See the BBC History Homepage: http://www.bbc.co.uk/history/timelines/index .shtml.

25 *Making History* video.

26 Tryggvi Olsen, *Early Voyages and Northern Approaches, 1000–1632* (Toronto: McClelland and Stewart, 1962).

27 'When the World Began, 15000 BC–1850 AD,' episode 1, *Canada: A People's History* (Toronto: Canadian Broadcasting Corporation, 2000).

28 Clark, 'Engaging the Field.'

29 For an elaboration of the nature and role of melodrama in contemporary television programming, see Hal Himmelstein, 'Melodrama,' in Horace Newcomb, ed., *The Encyclopedia of Television* (Chicago: Museum of Broadcast Communications, 1997). http://www.museum.tv/archives/etv/M/htmlM/melodrama/melodrama .htm.

30 Derek Paget, *No Other Way to Tell It: Dramadoc/Documdrama on Television* (Manchester and New York: Manchester University Press, 1998), 132. In the *Harper Handbook to Literature* (New York: Harper and Row, 1985), Northrop Frye and colleagues defined melodrama as 'a play with dire ingredients – the mortgage foreclosed, the daughter tied to the railroad tracks – but with a happy ending.' Elaborating, Frye wrote: 'melodrama results from single-minded commit-ment, however admirable, conflicting with outer forces.' In *A Dictionary of Liter-ary Terms*, J.A. Cuddon added other elements in his description of melodrama as 'naively sensational entertainment in which the main characters were excessively virtuous or exceptionally evil.'

31 The term 'melodrama' has evolved to signify any scripts with exaggerated charac-terization and story climaxes, or generally a heightened appeal to sentiment. Melo-drama can be distinguished from drama in that it emphasizes plot and action rather than character, and it differs from tragedy to the extent that it can accommodate a happy ending. In its television iterations, while packaged within different sub-genres, a common denominator of melodrama is its adherence to formal conven-tions and the reinforcement of mainstream values. As the television scholar Hal Himmelstein noted in a recent article: 'Planned flow, the melodrama's highly sym-bolic heroic ideal, its formal conventions, and its reinforcement of the society's

dominant values at any given cultural moment render the genre highly significant as a centrist cultural mechanism stressing order and stasis' ('Melodrama').

32 Published in 1965, Grant's *Lament for a Nation* was one of the cardinal texts of an emerging Anglo-Canadian nationalism in the 1960s. George Grant: *Lament for a Nation: The Defeat of Canadian Nationalism* (Toronto: McClelland and Stewart, 1965).

33 'Years of Hope and Anger, 1964–1976,' episode 16, *Canada: A People's History* (Toronto: Canadian Broadcasting Corporation, 2000).

34 Lyle Dick, '"A New History for the New Millennium": *Canada: A People's History*,' CHR Forum, *Canadian Historical Review* 85, 1 (March 2004): 85–109.

35 Clark, 'Engaging the Field.'

36 Mikhail Bakhtin, 'The Epic and the Novel,' in *The Dialogic Imagination*, ed. Michael Holquist, trans. Caryl Emerson and Michael Holquist (Austin: University of Texas Press, 1981), 13.

37 Cuddon, *A Dictionary of Literary Terms*, 225.

38 M.H. Abrams, *A Glossary of Literary Terms*, 4th edition (New York: Holt, Rinehart, and Winston, 1981), 50.

39 E.M.W. Tillyard, *The English Epic and Its Background* (London: Chatto and Windus, 1954), 5–13.

40 Bakhtin, 'The Epic and the Novel,' 16–23.

41 Gary Saul Morson and Caryl Emerson, *Mikhail Bakhtin: Creation of a Prosaics* (Stanford: Stanford University Press, 1990), 419–23.

42 Dick, 'A Growing *Necessity* for Canada,' 223–52.

43 See Lyle Dick, 'National History, Epic Form and Television: Two Examples from Canada and the United States,' Heritage, History, and Historical Consciousness: A Symposium on Public Uses of the Past (Proceedings from the papers presented to the symposium) University of New Brunswick, Fredericton, New Brunswick, 22 October 2003. The Atlantic Portal E-Print Repository: http://lusankya.hil.unb.ca:8000/archive/00000030/.

44 Of his Civil War series, Burns stated: 'Film is not equipped to do what a book does, which is to attain profound levels of meaning and texture. But film has the power to reach profound levels of emotion … It can be our Homeric form, and we've tried to tell this particular *Iliad*, our Civil War, in a Homeric way, not only from the aerial perspective of the gods and kings but from the level of the spear carriers as well.' Matthew Melton, 'Ken Burns's Civil War: Epic Narrative and Public Moral Argument,' htttp://www.regent.edu/acad/schcom/rojc/ melton.html. See also Gary Edgerton, *Ken Burns's America* (New York: Palgrave, 2001); and David Harlan, 'Ken Burns and the Coming Crisis of Academic History,' *Rethinking History* 7, 2 (2003): 169–92.

45 Frye et al., *The Harper Handbook to Literature*, 352; and Abrams, *A Glossary of Literary Terms*, 137.

46 Library and Archives Canada, Donald Grant Creighton Papers, vol. 27, file 'Canadian Centenary series, 1967 Correspondence,' draft unpublished letter by W.L. Morton to the editor, *Canadian Historical Review*, 10 May 1967; cited in Dick, 'A Growing *Necessity* for Canada,' 233.

47 Dick, 'A Growing *Necessity* for Canada,' 248–52.

48 Carl Plantinga, *Rhetoric and Representation in Nonfiction Film* (Cambridge: Cambridge University Press, 1997), 165.

49 *Film Score*, The Online Magazine of Motion Picture and Television Music Appreciation. http://www.filmscoremonthly.com, Remake Scores,' Part Seven http://www.filmscoremonthly.com/articles/2003/06_May — Remake_Scores_Part_Seven.asp.

50 Lyle Dick, 'Nationalism and Visual Media in Canada: The Case of Thomas Scott's Execution,' *Manitoba History* no. 48 (Winter 2004–5): 2–18.

51 Gillmor and Turgeon, *Canada: A People's History*, 1:255 and 286.

52 Don Gillmor, Achille Michaud, and Pierre Turgeon, *Canada: A People's History*, vol. 2 (Toronto: McClelland and Stewart, 2001), 318.

53 Northrop Frye, *Anatomy of Criticism: Four Essays* (Princeton: Princeton University Press, 1957), 52.

54 On silence as a rhetorical strategy to marginalize minorities within historical discourse and more generally in the humanities and social sciences, see Michel-Rolph Trouillot, *Silencing the Past: Power and the Production of History* (Boston: Beacon Press, 1995); and Lynn Thiesmeyer, ed., *Discourse and Silencing: Representation and the Language of Displacement* (Amsterdam and Philadelphia: John Benjamins Publishing Co., 2003).

55 'In an Uncertain World,' episode 17, *Canada: A People's History* (Toronto: Canadian Broadcasting Corporation, 2001).

56 Regarding the CBC's corresponding discourse of silence in the books of the series, see Dick, '"A New History for the New Millennium,"' 100–5.

57 Clark, 'Engaging the Field.'

58 Mark Starowicz, 'Afterword,' in Gillmor, Michaud, and Turgeon, *Canada: A People's History*, 2:325.

59 Gillmor, Michaud, and Turgeon, *Canada: A People's History*, 2:322.

60 Gillmor and Turgeon, *Canada: A People's History*, 1:xi.

61 Covenantal explanations have seldom been applied to Canadian history but have a long tradition in the historiography of the United States. See David W. Noble, *Historians against History: The Frontier Thesis and the National Covenant in American Historical Writing since 1830* (Minneapolis: University of Minnesota Press, 1965); and Ernest Lee Tuveson, *Redeemer Nation: The Idea of America's Millennial Role* (Chicago and London: University of Chicago Press, 1968).

62 'In an Uncertain World,' episode 17, *Canada: A People's History* (Toronto: Canadian Broadcasting Corporation, 2001), Epilogue.

63 Dick, "'A New History for the New Millennium,'" 100–3.

64 See the website of Carleton University's graduate seminar in public history, which in 2001 and 2002 was devoted in part to analysing aspects of audience response to *Canada: A People's History*: http://www.carleton.ca/historycollaborative.ca.

65 Starowicz, *Making History*, 278–9.

66 See the discussion in Dick, 'A Growing *Necessity* for Canada,' 246–50; and Bakhtin, 'The Epic and the Novel,' 3–38.

67 In a book published by the CBC to celebrate the television corporation's first half-century, the author wrote of *Canada: A People's History*: '*History*'s executive producer Mark Starowicz accepts that his fifteen-part series says a great deal about Canada and Canadians in the mid-90's. "The world was changing so rapidly," he says. "Globalization and open borders meant that the Canada we knew seemed to be slipping away before our eyes. Railways were shutting down. Airlines failing. The Quebec referendum made us wonder if there was going to be a Canada. At the same time the millennium was approaching and there was an idea we were packing for a long, uncertain voyage."' Stephen Cole, *Here's Looking at Us: Celebrating Fifty Years of CBC-TV* (Toronto: McClelland and Stewart, 2002), 240–1.

68 Dick, "'A New History for the New Millennium,'" 85–109.

69 See the discussion in ibid., 106–9.

70 Holquist, *Dialogism*.

7 Playing with 'Nitro': The Racialization of Chinese Canadians in Public Memory

TIMOTHY J. STANLEY

In Canada today, people of colour commonly report having to justify their presence in the country in ways that people of European origins do not. People ask them, 'Where are you from?' and are not satisfied by answers such as 'Kanata' or 'Medicine Hat.' 'No, where are you really from?' the questioners persist.[1] Even First Nations, Inuit, and Métis people can have their presence on their traditional territories questioned, sometimes with devastating consequences.[2] One way of thinking about this has been identified by the Australian literary critic Vijay Mishra, who suggested that people enter into the space of national culture 'as an already-read text,'[3] as if the individual's personal history and their 'fit' within nationalized spaces, or their 'lack of fit' in the case of people of colour, were already known. People's bodies, and hence the extent to which they are alleged to belong within the imagined community of the nation, are read in relation to myriad representations that constitute the landscape of collective remembering.[4] This landscape marks racialized white Euro-Canadians as properly and naturally belonging within the spaces of the Canadian nation-state, while marking those racialized differently as 'Other,' either as newcomers whose presence needs explanation or as outsiders who can never belong.[5] In effect, depending on how people are racialized, they are pre-read as belonging or as not belonging within the imagined community of the nation-state.

In Ottawa, it is easy to find examples of cultural devices that mark belonging and exclusion. You cannot go far in the national capital without encountering one of the numerous statues to a (usually adult male) person of European origins, or a street or building named after a European, or without being aware of the local dominance of two European languages, English and French. People of European origins have colonized the space, not just physically but semiotically, having populated it with innumerable devices celebrating and marking their presence.[6] Although statues and monuments may be less frequent outside the national capital, the same processes naturalize the presence of people of European origins in other parts of Canada.[7] Taken together, the devices of public memory (monuments, museum displays, school textbooks, popular literature, and mass media) mark who belongs in the territory while their silences and omissions mark others for exclusion. Through this marking, the devices of public memory actively create the imagined community of the nation and so foster problematic readings of what kinds of bodies belong where.[8] As critics of nationalism have long noted, the existence of nation-states depends on simultaneous acts of remembering and forgetting.[9] I argue that remembering and forgetting also constitutes some racialized groups as belonging within the nation and others as not.

This play of remembering and forgetting is particularly noticeable in regard to the representation of Chinese people in Canadian popular culture. While much is known about the histories of Chinese people in Canada, especially first-generation migrants who arrived before the exclusion era, very little in the way of representation of the complex histories of self-identified Chinese people in Canada circulates in public memory.[10] The one exception to this silence is the commemoration of the participation of Cantonese workers in the building of the Canadian Pacific Railway during the 1880s. In Canada, railway-building is the subject of relatively widespread representation. It can be found in national historic sites, in museum displays, in the textbooks and curricula of government-controlled schools, in popular literature, and in mass media.[11] Prime Minister Stephen Harper even mentioned the railroad builders in his formal apology for the discriminatory head tax on Chinese immigration. According to Harper, 'over 15,000 of these Chinese pioneers became involved in the most important nation-building enterprise in Canadian history – the construction of the Canadian Pacific Railway.'[12] Thus, the event has come to assume an iconic status as 'the Chinese contribution' to the building of Canada. On numerous occasions, I have heard people claim that 'the Chinese' are Canadian, 'because after all they built the railway.'[13] The reduction of the histories of people of Chinese origins in Canada to railroad-building is all the more curious in that not only do the vast majority of Canadians who self-identify as Chinese have little or no historical connection to the railroad builders (as we shall see below),[14] but there are arguably several more important ways in which the histories of Canada and the histories of people of Chinese origins are connected. Indeed, the country would not exist today if not for its China connections. It was after all the search for the northwest passage and the route to China that first brought Europeans to the territory, the triangular sea otter trade between England, the Pacific northwest coast, and China that laid the basis for a country *A Mari usque ad Mare*, and the long struggle of Chinese Canadians for full democratic and civil rights that produced a country in which citizenship, rather than 'race,' determines democratic rights. Remembering Cantonese railway builders is even more curious, since many more thousands of European navvies also built the railroad.

In what follows, I examine one particular example of the representation of railroad-building as the so-called 'Chinese contribution' to the Canadian nation-building project: the Historica Minute (formerly the Heritage Minute) 'Nitro.'[15] 'Nitro' is interesting because of its explicitly nationalist purposes and its antiracist message, and because it is almost certainly the most widely circulated text on the history of people of Chinese origins in Canada. I argue that 'Nitro''s representation of this event only achieves its nationalizing purposes by means of a racialized reading of who and what is Canadian, at the same time as it displaces and silences the actual histories lived by racialized Chinese people in Canada.

'Races' are social and historical constructs, rather than natural or biological ones. 'Race' differences may appear natural, constant, and obvious, but they are in fact extremely dynamic and contextually specific. What is obvious in one time and place can be simply invisible in another. Yet how people are categorized racially can be a matter of life and death. To say that 'race' is not natural is thus not to say that it is unimportant. It is to say that processes of cultural representation, knowledge-making, and social organization make 'race.' Racialization is the term for these processes. Out of the myriad differences that identify individuals and groups only certain ones have historically been racialized: skin colour, culture, religion, place of origin, and language. Meanwhile specific racial categories themselves are historical inventions and as such their origins can be traced.[16] However, all racializations share certain characteristics. They are relational: one racial group is always represented, known, or organized in relation to another or others. They are absolute: racializations assign human beings to one category or another and do not allow people to live across, between, or outside of their classifications. Finally, even though over time people may adopt racialized categories as their own, racializations are always inescapable ascriptions. In the logic of racializations, the category to which someone is seen to belong, rather than the category to which they themselves may identify, is what matters. Analysing racialization draws attention to the discursive processes that promote the idea of racialized difference.[17] As we shall see, racializing discourse is fully at work in 'Nitro.'

As mentioned above, 'Nitro' is probably the most widely disseminated and influential representation of the Cantonese railway workers. As part of the original release of Heritage Minutes during the early 1990s, produced by millionaire Charles Bronfman's CRB Foundation, it was made available free of charge to schools and libraries, television stations and movie houses across Canada.[18] The minutes have since been transferred to the Historica Foundation, which was established to promote knowledge of Canadian history among young people, and have been rebranded as the Historica Minutes. Historica has also produced new minutes, including a series of radio minutes and a series on sports figures. All are available on its website.[19] These new minutes include a radio version of 'Nitro.'[20] Although it is not known how widely the minutes have been shown or whether certain minutes have been shown more commonly than others, the minutes themselves have been widely enough disseminated as to have inspired at least two television commercials, one for beer and one for tea, and an enduring controversy over their clandestine funding by the federal government in order to build support for the federalist side in the 1995 Quebec referendum.[21] Certainly much of Historica's efforts, as well as those of the CRB Foundation before it, have been devoted to popularizing the use of the minutes in the teaching of Canadian history. Thus its website also includes a series of lesson plans for teachers, including one on how to encourage students to produce their own minutes. Meanwhile the Historica Teachers' Institutes also promote the use of minutes.[22]

If we accept the idea that the minutes as a whole represent the sweep of Canadian history, 'Nitro' is quite literally the only place in which 'Chinese' people enter into the narrative of Canada as nation.[23] Given the importance of the events it represents in making space in the national imaginary (i.e., in the imagining of Canada as a nation) for people of Chinese origins, it is perhaps not surprising that Chinese community organizations also commissioned a longer version of the original minute.[24] Whether their personal and family histories connect to the event or not, for many racialized Chinese people building the railway is the one event that allows them to claim to belong in the nationalist imaginary called Canada.

'Nitro' opens with a panning shot that moves from a raging river to a tent on the shore in the foreground and some men carrying wooden planks in the background. A subtitle appears, 'The building of the CP Railway 1884.' A man approaches a group of men. He and the other men are dressed in dusty work clothes, except that he is wearing a thick belt which might possibly be holding a revolver. The man is middle-aged, rather burly, and in need of a shave. The others seem young, are short of stature and of slight build. Holding out a handful of what appear to be silver dollars, the middle-aged man offers the young men a chance to earn 'danger pay, boat fare for the wife.' He explains, 'All you have to do is go down in the tunnel with the nitro and set the charge.' A young man accepts the offer: 'And my wife you pay boat?' The first man nods and the young man continues, 'Okay, okay, I do really good, you see.'[25] He carries a jar of nitroglycerine into the railroad tunnel. Despite the first man's shouted instructions, the nitro explodes, but no one rushes in to rescue the tunnel worker. In disgust, an older bearded man who is wearing a suit jacket, and who throughout is seen to be rather indifferently smoking a cigar, says to the foreman, 'Damn it! That's the third one we lost this month! Cochrane, get another volunteer.'[26] The young man, his face blackened and clothes in tatters, then staggers out from the dust of the explosion. The scene shifts to what a subtitle identifies as 'Vancouver 50 years later,' where a seemingly prosperous old man in a tailored blue suit sits in a comfortable-looking living room and tells two young girls, also well dressed: 'I went back in again, but I lost many friends. They say that there is one dead Chinese man for every mile of that track. That's what they say.'

The narrative being told in this minute is one of Canada's progressive movement towards multicultural inclusion, but this narrative only works if the viewers of the minute read it in racialized terms, i.e., as not just about workers and bosses, but as about 'white' bosses and 'Chinese' workers in particular. Although the television version of the minute is careful to avoid stereotypes, it is filled with racializing markers of difference. The worker speaks a particular form of English commonly associated with those for whom a Chinese dialect, rather than an English one, is their first language. The stresses and grammatical constructions of the worker's English differ from those of the foreman, whose English passes for what today is a standard CBC 'Canadian' accent. The worker himself introduces the idea that he and his fellow workers are Chinese when he says that 'one Chinese man died for every mile of that track.' A series of markers – height, build, dress, beards and their lack, skin colour – establish commonalities among the workers and differences with the overseers (who even wear bigger hats). These differences are all matters of craft on the part of the makers of the minute, but they employ the types of racializing techniques long found in Hollywood movies.[27] These techniques emphasized difference between groups, while homogenizing difference within minoritized and excluded groups. In 'Nitro' their effect is to racialize the workers as a single group, 'Chinese,' while the overseas are constituted as another group, 'white.' However, while 'the Chinese' are established as a single type, the dominant group is represented as having different essences. The foreman, who seems sympathetic to the worker, speaks with the standard CBC accent, while the cigar-smoking boss is better dressed, seems indifferent, and speaks with what might pass as an American accent.

Reading the characters of the minute in racialized ways, i.e., as 'white' and 'Chinese,' also means that people are likely to interpret the actions of the overseers, particularly the one in the suit jacket, as racist. This racism is more implied than explicitly represented. The foreman's offer of 'danger pay' and 'boat fare for the wife' appears to be nothing but a few coins in his hands. He, however, seems concerned about the worker in his shouted instructions. The cigar-smoking boss by contrast seems indifferent to the fate of the worker, almost bored by the loss of 'another one.' In the last scene set in the 1930s, this racism has disappeared. The worker has survived and apparently prospered; having sent for his wife, he has had children and now grandchildren. In 1930s Vancouver, racism has become a thing of the past, something that the old man has experienced and survived but no longer has to endure.

This representation of racism as a thing of a distant past is central to the nationalizing purpose of the minute as it helps to constitute modern-day Canada as a racism-free and tolerant place, a Canadian nationalist trope almost as old as Canada itself.[28] If racism was a matter of memory in the 1930s, it is even more distant from the present of the viewers of the minute. Even the ambiguous accent of the boss plays a role here. It establishes the 'American' racialized white man as the real racist, while racialized white 'Canadians,' as represented by the foreman, are tolerant of multiculturals like the worker/old man.[29] Thus racism is explained as the result of the individual prejudices of the 'bad' American, while the 'good' Canadian gets to be antiracist. It is because of the latter's tolerance and that of those like him that the worker has not only endured but prospered. Thus the narrative is a redemptive one. The eventual success of the worker redeems the racist treatment he experienced in the past. The workers who built the CPR may have been treated abysmally. They were treated in a racist manner. Certainly, untold hundreds died, but others went on to found a multicultural Canada. Yes, Americans, like the boss in the minute, are racist, but Canadians, like the foreman, are not. Significantly, such a reading further emphasizes the redemptive form of the narrative. At the beginning of the minute, the workers are 'Chinese,' the overseers are 'white/Anglo/Canadian or American.' By the end of the minute, the 'Chinese' worker, along with the antiracist white, has become part of the 'our' of the Canadian national multicultural community. For most viewers, the connection to contemporary Canada is reinforced through the tag line at the end of the minute and by the contexts in which they are likely to see the minute. At the end of the minute, the caption 'A part of our heritage' appears, followed by a frame with the Historica logo, a large title 'Heritage Minutes,' and the logos of Canada Post Corporation, the CRB Foundation, and ACTRA across the bottom. Meanwhile, the minute is likely to be seen in the places in which CRB and Historica have distributed it, in classrooms in Canada, local television stations, and movie houses. Thus, the 'our/we/us' in 'Part of our heritage' becomes the viewers of the minute, its makers and broadcasters. Since it is 'our heritage,' the tag line calls upon viewers to see themselves as connected to the chief protagonists of the video, extending this connection from the 'our' of the viewers, the filmmakers, and the broadcasters back in time to 'The building of the CP Railway 1884.' In other words, viewers of the film are called upon to see themselves as connected to strangers both in the present and in the past, the 'our' linking individual viewers across time and space to the builders of the CPR and to a shared community of 'us' viewers in the present.[30] This is the essence of what Benedict Anderson aptly characterized as imagined community.[31] What is being told is not so much the individual story of the worker, but the story of an 'us' whose heritage this is. This is also an example of what cultural psychologist Michael Billig calls 'the deixis of nationalist representation.' Deixis are small pointing words, 'the,' 'we/our/us,' that signify enormously and that are used to present and re-present the imagined community of the modern nation-state.[32]

The minute's dramatic qualities facilitate this construction of imagined community. Viewers are drawn into the action, imagining themselves as participants in its events. When the nitroglycerine explodes, first-time viewers do not know whether the young man has survived. There is a key moment or two of suspense before they see that he has. In the logic of the narrative, the man in the sitting room at the end of the minute is the same worker, who, having survived the explosion, is now old; he is sitting in his own house, talking to his own grandchildren, having sent for 'the wife' and raised a family. Viewers are told none of this overtly, but are asked to fill in all of these details, even to assume that the old man and the young worker are the same person. His words, 'I went back in again,' suggest this link and that it was his bravery and determination that enabled his achievement of the national dream, building both the nation and his own prosperity. In effect, the minute urges viewers themselves to imagine the story that allows imagining of the nation.

Putting all of this together, the reading that emerges from the minute is that it is telling the story of male Chinese workers who endure racism and exploitation to build the CPR, and hence the country, and who succeed in resettling their families to Canada. In so doing, it presents an antiracist statement that links racialized Chinese people to one of the central tales of English-Canadian nationalism: what Pierre Berton called 'The National Dream.' This is the story of the building of the iron road that welds the country east to west created by the blood and sweat of the nameless navvies and the vision and courage of the far-seeing larger-than-life men of European origins.[33] By celebrating the workers who built much of the section from the British Columbia coast to Craigellachie, 'Nitro' is the quintessentially Canadian story that marks Canada as the land both of cultural and racial diversity and of multicultural tolerance by making room in the narrative of nation-building for people of other-than-European origins.

The problem of 'Nitro' is not that it is a work of historical fiction or that there is considerable artistic licence at work in compressing a complex history into a sixty-second commercial. After all, sixty seconds does not leave much time for context. As Patrick Watson, the director of 'Nitro' and the creative director and principal writer of the original minutes, noted, 'We're not really doing documentary here. We're making myths. That's what movies are; they're myths and this country needs a mythology of its history before it can get motivated to go and study the history as documentary history.'[34] For Watson, the dramatic ability of the minutes to draw in and interest viewers is their most important quality, and by these standards 'Nitro' seems to be one of the most successful minutes.

However, the problem is the kind of myth that the minute is making. The history to which 'Nitro' claims to be true is itself a fiction, a fiction that enables contemporary racism in Canada by making racisms seem a thing of a now distant past. Nicole Neatby has noted that the ending 'is meant to convey to the audience that Canada's racist past towards the Chinese is behind us, located in the distant 1880s. The head tax, the strict restrictions on Chinese immigration during the early twentieth century, their disenfranchisement until after the Second World War are all omitted.' According to Neatby, the minute presents 'a Whiggish interpretation of the past in which life only gets better for all past victims of racism.' Citing a comment of the historian Daniel Francis to the effect that 'the creation of unity requires some forgetting,' she further notes, 'In this case, forgetting in order to create a semblance of harmony can lead to self-satisfaction among white Canadians of European descent and intolerance for the concerns of their visible minority compatriots. Many viewers might be encouraged to think that we should not be concerned about the issue presented on the screen – after all, it is behind us.'[35]

'Nitro''s redemptive narrative of decreasing racism between 1884 and the 1930s denies that during the 1930s, people of 'Chinese race' living in Canada faced more racism than they did in 1884.[36] As such, its narrative is not about the actual past lived by racialized people so much as it is about the grand narrative of Canadian history that is primarily concerned with reinforcing contemporary nationalist myths.[37] These are the 'essential lies,' the selective remembering and forgetting upon which the nation is founded that Ernest Renan noted over a century ago in his celebrated lecture, 'Qu'est ce qu'une nation?'[38] A narrative reflective of the historic realities of anti-Chinese racism would not have allowed the minute to carry out its mythologizing purpose. Instead, such a narrative would have presented Canada as a land of white supremacy, rather than of multicultural tolerance.[39]

'Nitro' and other representations of Chinese railway workers only make room for individuals of Chinese origins in the nationalist imaginary by means of their acting as a synecdoche for the racialized group as a whole. Even if we accept that the minute has more to do with myth-making than with historical representation, we can ask how it is that this myth supposedly licenses the presence of 'the Chinese' in the country. It does so only if one accepts a racialized logic: since workers racialized as 'Chinese' made the National Dream, all similarly racialized people thus also belong. In the logic of racialization, one racialized body stands for all members of the group. In effect, memory texts like 'Nitro' are saying, 'We Canadians now include racialized Chinese as well as racialized whites.' While this is an antiracist message, it in fact underlies the ways in which Canadian nationalism is constructed on a racialized foundation that still most often equates Canadianness with whiteness at the same time that it denies the continued existence of racism in Canada.[40]

Since this is the only place within the Heritage/Historica Minutes where racialized Chinese people in Canada are represented, it is important to ask how it relates to the over one million people now living in Canada who self-identify as Chinese.[41] This grouping includes people whose family histories in the country predate the creation of Canada itself as well as those who have only recently arrived from China or elsewhere in the diaspora.[42] They include people who speak Mandarin only and others who only speak English. Their numbers include those whose popular culture is that of contemporary Hong Kong or Shanghai and those for whom it is 'American Idol' and 'Desperate Housewives.' Each self-identified Chinese has a unique personal history and differing relationships with the modern Canadian nation-state. How then can one event represent them all?

Very few, perhaps no more than a few hundred, of the over one million people who self-identified in the 2001 census as 'Chinese' are directly connected to the railway builders of 1882–5.[43] Most of those who self-identified as 'Chinese' in that census are from Hong Kong, the People's Republic of China, and Taiwan. Between 1981 and 2001, 743,000 people immigrated to Canada from these countries, with Hong Kong accounting for almost 50 per cent of this total at 366,895, followed by the PRC with 283,220 and Taiwan with 92,985. Only a quarter of the over one million who self-identified as Chinese in the 2001 census were born in Canada.[44]

Furthermore, it is unlikely that most of the Canadian-born could have descended from the railway workers. Far from being unskilled coolie workers, the CPR's railway gangs were experienced navvies who participated in similar projects elsewhere in the Pacific Rim. Very few remained in the country after the railway was completed.[45] Because of poverty, intense racism, and the immigration head tax on Chinese workers and their families first imposed in 1885, of those who did remain in Canada fewer still were able to bring their families over from China or make new ones in Canada. For over one hundred years, the Chinese communities of Canada were made up almost entirely of 'bachelor' workers,[46] who were either unmarried or whose families remained in China. These workers endured years of hardship, privation, exploitation, isolation, and legislated discrimination at the same time as they struggled to support families in China, families that they could afford to visit perhaps two or three times in a lifetime. Meanwhile racist immigration laws, including the 1923 ban on all Chinese immigration, did not allow them to bring their family members to Canada.[47] One measure of this is that according to the 1941 census, out of the 29,033 'Chinese' males in Canada, 23,556 or 81 per cent were married. As only 1177 of the 2337 'Chinese' females in Canada in 1941 were married and as interracial marriage was extremely rare, almost all of these men had their families in China.[48] Indeed, it was not until the 1980s, years after Chinese exclusion supposedly ended, that a gender balance was first achieved in Chinese-Canadian communities.[49] Thus whatever is going on 'Nitro' it does not in any way represent the actual historical experiences of the people who built the railway. In other words, even if we accept that, in some symbolic way, 'Nitro' does connect to the actual histories of the railway builders themselves, it does not connect to the actual histories of most people of Chinese origins in Canada today.

What then does 'Nitro' connect to? The answer is a nationalist mythology of Canada today as a tolerant, racism-free place. Since the minute does not actually connect to Chinese-Canadian experience either in the past or in the present, it connects to this nationalist mythology because people of Chinese origins are commonly read in racialized ways that differentiate them from equally racialized 'Canadians.' In effect, the Canadianness of 'the Chinese' needs to be explained by 'Nitro' because it is widely denied. The nationalist imaginary constitutes people racialized as Chinese as 'already-read' outsiders to the nation, so 'Nitro' and the railroad-buiding myth reconstitutes them as insiders to the nation. However, racializations always homogenize complex groups into single categories that elide people's actual differences. Thus, commemorating railway builders at the expense of silence on the complex and diverse histories of a racialized group becomes a racialized exclusion. While there are moments when other historical representations break through,[50] the dominant cultural pattern in Canada is that of the exclusion from knowledge of people's actual histories. In place of this knowledge, racialized and excluded groups become 'already-read texts.'

Such exclusions can have significant consequences. For example, in the dying days of Paul Martin's Liberal government, Heritage Minister Raymond Chan announced a 'settlement' of the redress demand for head tax payers. This settlement had been reached with the National Congress of Chinese Canadians and ten other community organizations. However, none of these groups represented the surviving head tax payers themselves.[51] Far from settling their grievances, the announcement revictimized them. Racialized logics in which one racialized person can take the place of another or the group as a whole, combined with ignorance of what people have actually lived, make victimization inevitable.

What all of this suggests is that 'Nitro' is not in fact a representation of a real historical past so much as it is a classic example of what James V. Wertsch calls 'collective memory' at work. It is a widely available text that articulates a particular entirely fictive narrative about how the present of the nation-state came to be. This narrative is uncontested, univocal, and told from the single committed perspective of a particular social group that claims the authority to speak for the whole. While for most viewers it may be simply and unproblematically the past, in fact it is very much an ongoing nationalizing project, an active effort to create imagined community.[52]

My examination of 'Nitro' suggests that the project of creating a Canadian imagined community rests on widespread patterns of racialized exclusions. These patterns rely on the exclusion from knowledge of the meanings created by racialized and excluded people themselves. Nationalisms may continually imagine communities of people who share certain characteristics, but they also inevitably position others as outsiders. As Benedict Anderson observed, all nations are imagined as limited and no nationalism claims to include all human beings.[53] In multiethnic and multiracial places such as Canada, this can prevent these others from participating in democratic life.

Canadian nationalists may well argue that the racialized understandings of Canadianness that 'Nitro' promotes are a necessary price to keep the country together. However, the historical experiences of the actual railway builders and of other racialized Chinese people in Canada show that popular nationalisms, built on racialized understandings of who belongs and who does not, inevitably become popular racism and can spawn popular violence. 'Nitro' also shows how collective memory enables racism in the present by pretending that it is merely a thing of a long-dead past. It seems to me that the only way of challenging such racism is to ensure that people's actual histories are engaged by troubling the devices of public memory that marks each of us 'as an already-read text.'

NOTES

1 'Geography Lessons: On Being an Insider/Outsider to the Canadian Nation,' in Himani Bannerji, *The Dark Side of the Nation: Essays on Multiculturalism, Nationalism and Gender* (Toronto: Canadian Scholars Press, 2000), 63–86, originally

published in Leslie G. Roman and Linda Eyre, eds., *Dangerous Territories: Struggles for Equality and Difference in Education* (New York and London: Routledge, 1997). For an anecdotal example, see Adrienne Shadd, '"Where are you really from?" Notes of an "Immigrant" from North Buxton, Ontario,' in Carl James and Adrienne Shadd, eds., *Talking about Identity: Encounters in Race, Ethnicity, and Language* (Toronto: Between the Lines, 2001), 10–16.

The paper upon which this chapter is based was produced in part with support from the Social Sciences and Humanities Research Council of Canada.

2 As the Ipperwash inquiry dramatically shows. In 1995, Dudley George was fatally shot during a peaceful occupation of Ipperwash Provincial Park in Ontario, part of the traditional territory of the Stoney Point Chippewa illegally seized by the Canadian government during the Second World War. See Ipperwash Inquiry Home Page, http://www.ipperwashinquiry.ca (accessed 23 March 2008).

3 Vijay Mishra, 'Postmodern Racism,' *Meanjin* 55, 2 (1996): 346–57. I am indebted to Cathryn McConaghy for bringing this reference to my attention. See McConaghy, *Rethinking Indigenous Education: Culturalism, Colonialism and the Politics of Knowing* (Flaxton, Australia: Post Press, 2000), 242. Mishra was commenting on the controversy in Australia over the novel by Helen Darville, *The Hand That Signed the Paper* (St Leonards, NSW: Allen and Unwin, 1995), and the issue of who has the right to speak for whom. This novel about Jewish-Ukranian relations during the Second World War was denounced as anti-Semitic even though it claimed to be told from the allegedly authentic perspective of an ethnic Ukrainian, a claim to knowledge that was itself controversial.

4 On imagined community see Benedict Anderson, *Imagined Communities: Reflections on the Origin and Spread of Nationalism* (London and New York: Verso, 1991); on landscapes of public memory including the many sites that mark belonging, see Brian S. Osborne, 'Landscapes, Memory, Monuments, and Commemoration: Putting Identity in Its Place,' *Canadian Ethnic Studies* 33, 3 (2001): 39–77; on collective remembering, see James V. Wertsch, *Voices of Collective Remembering* (Cambridge: Cambridge University Press, 2002).

5 These markings also apply to gender, sexuality, ability, social class, and nation. The importance of 'cartographies of violence' was first drawn to my attention by Cathryn McConaghy, 'On Cartographies of Anti-Homophobia in Teacher Education (and the Crisis of Witnessing Rural Student Teacher Refusals),' *Teaching Education* 15, 1 (March 2004): 63–79. On how territories are quite literally flagged in ways that make the nation, see Michael Billig, *Banal Nationalism* (London and Thousand Oaks, CA: Sage, 1995); on racialized social geography, see Ruth Frankenberg, *White Women, Race Matters: The Social Construction of Whiteness* (Minneapolis: University of Minnesota Press, 1994); and on how material technologies enter into the creation of collective memory and hence of the

collective nation itself, see the landmark study of the reconstruction of collective memory in the former Soviet Union, Wertsch, *Voices of Collective Remembering*. On the construction of whiteness in Canada, see Sherene H. Razack, ed., *Race, Space and the Law: Unmapping a White Settler Society* (Toronto: Between the Lines, 2002); see also Rebecca Raby, '"There's No Racism at My School, It's Just Joking Around": Ramifications for Anti-Racist Education,' *Race, Ethnicity and Education* 7, 4 (2004): 367–83; R. Patrick Solomon, John P. Portelli, Beverly-Jean Daniels, and Arlene Campbell, 'The Discourse of Denial: How White Teacher Candidates Construct Race, Racism and "White Privilege,"' *Race, Ethnicity and Education* 8, 2 (July 2005): 14769; and Manju Varma-Joshi, Cynthia J. Baker, and Connie Tanaka, 'Names Will Never Hurt Me,' *Harvard Educational Review* (Summer 2004): 175–208. For a recent collection of antiracist theory in Canada see Genevieve Fuji Johnson and Randy Enomoto, eds., *Race, Racialization, and Antiracism in Canada and Beyond* (Toronto: University of Toronto Press, 2007).

6 In this respect, it parallels the role of imperialism in Western culture generally. See Edward W. Said, *Culture and Imperialism* (New York: Knopf, 1993).

7 On connections between European colonialism and collective memory, see Elizabeth Furniss, *The Burden of History: Colonialism and the Frontier Myth in a Rural Canadian Community* (Vancouver: University of British Columbia Press, 1999) and Eva Mackey, *The House of Difference: Cultural Politics and National Identity in Canada* (London: Routledge, 1999).

8 Anderson, *Imagined Communities*. The active role of representations in creating meaning is noted by Stuart Hall, 'The Work of Representation,' in Hall, ed., *Representation: Cultural Representations and Signifying Practices* (London, Thousand Oaks, and New Dehli: Sage Publications, 1997), 13–74. See also Sut Jhally, dir., *Stuart Hall: Representation and the Media* (Northampton, MA: Media Education Foundation, 1997), videorecording. On the stable nature of a particular nationalist historical narrative in English Canada, see Daniel Francis, *National Dreams: Myth, Memory, and Canadian History* (Vancouver: Arsenal Pulp Press, 1997).

9 See Ernest Renan, 'Qu'est-ce qu'une nation? (1882)' in Joël Roman, ed., *Qu'est-ce qu'une nation? et autres essais politiques* (Paris: Presses Pocket, 1992).

10 Here it is important to distinguish between knowledge that is culturally available and knowledge that actually circulates in popular culture. For culturally available knowledge of the histories of people of Chinese origins in Canada, see David T.H. Lee (Lee T'ung-hai) [Li Donghai], *Jianada Huaqiao shi* [A History of the Overseas Chinese in Canada] (Taibei: Zhonghua Da Dian Bianying Hui, 1967); Edgar Wickberg, ed., *From China to Canada* (Toronto: McClelland and Stewart, 1982); see also Anthony B. Chan, *Gold Mountain: The Chinese in the New World* (Vancouver: New Star, 1983); Peter S. Li, *The Chinese in Canada* (Toronto:

Oxford University Press, 1998); and Wing Chung Ng, *The Chinese in Vancouver, 1945–80: The Pursuit of Identity and Power* (Vancouver: University of British Columbia Press, 1999). For more popular, but still limited-circulation texts highlighting the complexities of translocal links in the histories of people in Canada, see Denise Chong, *The Concubine's Children: Portrait of a Family Divided* (Toronto: Viking: Penguin Books Canada, 1994); Yuen-Fong Woon, *The Excluded Wife* (Montreal and Kingston: McGill-Queen's University Press, 1998); and Brandy Liên Worrall, ed., *Finding Memories, Tracing Routes: Chinese Canadian Family Stories* (Vancouver: Chinese Canadian Historical Society of British Columbia, 2006).

11 For example, Chinese workers on the railway has been a recurring theme of high school history textbooks. See A.C. Dorland, *Our Canada* (Toronto: Copp Clark, 1949), 334–5; Donalda Dickie, *The Great Adventure* (Toronto and Vancouver: J.M. Dent and Sons, 1950), 349; G.W. Nicholson et al., *Three Nations: Canada – Great Britain – The United States of America in the Twentieth Century* (Toronto: McClelland and Stewart, 1962), 71–2; R. Stewart and N. McLean, *Forming a Nation, Book 2* (Toronto: Gage, 1978), 84; R.C. Kirbyson et al., *Discovering Canada, Book Two* (Scarborough, ON: Prentice-Hall, 1983), 39, 110–11, 115, 117; D. Francis and S. Riddoch, *Our Canada: A Social and Political History* (Toronto: McClelland and Stewart, 1985), 305.

12 See 'Address by the Prime Minister on the Chinese Head Tax Redress, 22 June 2006, Ottawa, Ontario,' Canada, Office of the Prime Minister, http://www.pm.gc .ca/eng/media.asp?category=3&id=1220 (accessed 23 March 2008).

13 Interestingly, the role of railway-building is downplayed in the only sino-centric history of Chinese people in Canada, David T.H. Lee's *Jianada Huaqiao shi.*

14 Even the identification of the railway workers as 'Chinese' is more an ascription that speaks about the Canadian context than it is a statement of their own historical identities. See David Chuen-yan Lai, 'Home County and Clan Origins of Overseas Chinese in Canada in the Early 1880s,' *BC Studies* 27 (1975): 3–29. Despite its seeming agelessness, the category 'Chinese' is really a product of modern Chinese nationalism. See John Fincher, 'China as Race, Culture and Nation: Notes on Fang Hsiao-ju's Discussion of Dynastic Legitimacy,' in D.C. Buxbaum and F.W. Mote, eds., *Transition and Permanence: Chinese History and Culture: A Festschrift in Honour of Dr. Hsaio Kung-ch'üan* (Hong Kong: Cathay Press, 1972), 59–69. See also Rebecca E. Karl, 'Race, Colonialism and History: China at the Turn of the Twentieth Century,' in Peter Osborne and Stella Standford, eds., *Philosophies of Race and Ethnicity* (London: Continuum, 2002), 97–113; and Rey Chow, 'On Chineseness as a Theoretical Problem,' in ibid., 132–49. On the performative nature of Chinese identities, see James L. Watson, 'The Renegotiation of Chinese Cultural Identity in the Post-Mao Era: An Anthropological Perspective,' in K.G. Lieberthal,

J. Kallgren, R. MacFarquhar, and F. Wakeman, Jr, eds., *Perspectives on Modern China: Four Anniversaries* (Armonk, NY: M.E. Sharpe, 1991), 364–86; and Edgar Wickberg, 'Global Chinese Migrants and Performing Chineseness,' *Journal of Chinese Overseas* 3, 2 (2007): 177–93. The best discussion of the complexities of Chinese identities is provided by Wang Gungwu, *China and the Chinese Overseas* (Singapore: Times Academic Press, 1991). See also his 'Introduction: Migration and New National Identities,' and 'Upgrading the Migrant: Neither *Huaqiao* nor *Huaren*,' in Elizabeth Sinn, ed., *The Last Half Century of Chinese Overseas* (Hong Kong: Hong Kong University Press, 1998), 1–12 and 15–33.

15 See Historica, History by the Minute, Historica Minutes, 'Nitro,' http://www.histori.ca/minutes/minute.do?ID=10196 (accessed 7 January 2006). Compare to number 21, 'Nitro,' *The CRB Foundation Heritage Project: 60th Minute Commemorative Video* [videorecording] (Montreal: CRB Foundation, 1998).

16 On the invented nature of race, see Ivan Hannaford, *Race: The History of an Idea in the West* (Washington, DC: Woodrow Wilson Center Press; Baltimore, MD: Johns Hopkins University Press, 1996). See also Theodore Allen, *The Invention of the White Race*, 2 vols. (London and New York: Verso, 1994); and Frank M. Snowden, Jr, 'Europe's Oldest Chapter in the History of Black-White Relations,' in Benjamin P. Bowser, ed., *Racism and Anti-Racism in World Perspective* (Thousand Oaks, CA: Sage Publications, 1995),-3–26. See also the American Anthropological Association website, 'Race: Are We So Different,' http://www.understandingrace.org.

17 See Robert Miles, *Racism*, Key Ideas Series (London and New York: Routledge, 1989); Philip Cohen, '"It's racism what dunnit": Hidden Narratives in Theories of Racism,' in James Donald and Ali Rattansi, eds., *'Race', Culture, and Difference* (Newbury Park, CA: Sage Publications in association with the Open University, 1992), 62–104; Billig, *Banal Nationalism*; Amanda Lewis, 'Everyday Race-Making: Navigating Racial Boundaries in School,' *American Behavioural Scientist* 47, 3 (November 2003): 283–305; Varma-Joshi, Baker, and Tanaka, 'Names Will Never Hurt Me'; Timothy J. Stanley, 'Bringing Anti-Racist Theory into Historical Explanation: The Victoria Chinese Students' Strike of 1922–3 Revisited,' *Journal of the Canadian Historical Association* n.s. 13 (2003): 141–66. See also Robert Miles and Malcolm Brown, *Racism,* 2nd edition (London: Routledge, 2003).

18 See CRB Foundation Heritage Project, *The Heritage Minutes* [videorecording] / *Les reflets du patrimoine* (Kingston, ON: CRB Foundation, 1995).

19 See Historica, 'History by the Minute,' http://www.histori.ca/minutes/default.do?page=.index (accessed 31 January 2006).

20 See, Historica Foundation, 'History by the Minute,' Radio Minute, 'Nitro': http://www.histori.ca/minutes/minute.do?id=13574 (accessed 11 January 2006).

21 My impression is that the Heritage Minutes were more frequently shown dur-

ing the 1990s, but they continue to be shown often enough as to attract critical comments. See, for example, Jordan Bell, 'Heritage Minutes Should Celebrate Canada, Not Cast Aspersions on It,' *Kingston Whig–Standard*, 21 August 2003, 9. On the Quebec controversy, see Normand Lester, *Le livre noir du Canada anglais* (Montreal: Les Intouchables, 2001).

22 Along with my colleague Sharon Cook, I co-organized the 2000 teachers' institute during the transition from CRB to Historica. Innovative ways of teaching Canadian history, including the heritage fairs, are the major focus of these institutes. Curiously, there is a striking absence of lesson plans linked to 'Nitro' on the Historica website and in contrast to most other minutes, but in 2005 Historica launched an excellent website, co-written by Denise Chong, called 'Asia/ Canada,' which explores the histories of Asians in Canada, including experiences of discrimination. See 'Asian/Canada,' http://www.histori.ca/asia-canada/index.do (accessed 27 January 2006). This new site includes a number of lesson plans for teachers, although none are on railway-building.

23 The only other reference to Chinese people is in another radio minute on Moshe 'Two Gun' Cohen, Sun Yat-sen's bodyguard, but it does not refer to Chinese Canadians. See Historica, 'History by the Minute,' Radio Minutes, 'Two-Gun Cohen,' http://www.histori.ca/minutes/minute.do?id=14908 (accessed 27 January 2006). While it allegedly represents an incident that occurred in Canton, Mandarin is the only intelligible language other than English spoken during this minute. On Cohen's actual history, see Daniel S. Levy, *Two-Gun Cohen: A Biography* (New York: St Martin's Press, 1997).

24 Deborah Morrison, the former executive director of the CRB foundation, John Fielding, the originator of the teachers' institutes, and John Herd Thompson, the historical consultant to the minutes, have all confirmed this in personal communications with me. However, I have not been able to track down the longer version of this minute or identify the organizations that commissioned it.

25 The radio minute includes much more dialogue, including more of the stereotypical talk of the worker. Indeed, I find that the radio minute is much more stereotypical in its representation of Chinese workers than the original video minute. See Radio Minutes, 'Nitro.'

26 This part of the radio minute explicitly refers to the workers as 'Chinks,' a racist epithet for people of Chinese origins.

27 See, for example, James Snead, *White Screens, Black Images: Hollywood on the Dark Side* (New York: Routledge, 1994).

28 On 'tolerance' as a long-term marker of Canadianness, see Kenneth E. Montgomery, '"A Better Place to Live": National Mythologies, Canadian History Textbooks, and the Reproduction of White Supremacy' (unpublished PhD thesis, University of Ottawa, 2005); see also H.V. Nelles, *The Art of Nation-Building:*

Pageantry and Spectacle at Quebec's Tercentenary (Toronto: University of Toronto Press, 1999).

29 The representation of racialized white Canadians as tolerant of difference and of Americans as racist is a recurring trope of the minutes. See the minutes 'Underground Railroad,' 'Sitting Bull,' and 'Maurice Ruddick.' 'Hart and Papineau' and 'Dextraze in the Congo' further emphasizes Canadian tolerance.

30 This is of course the kind of reading the minute's producers would like to see people take away. As in all cultural production, there is no guarantee that this is the meaning that people do take away. For a very different reading of the minutes by a Québécois nationalist, see Lester, *Le livre noir du Canada anglais*. For more balanced critical assessments, see Elspeth Cameron and Janice Dickin McGinnis, 'Ambushed by Patriotism: The Wit, Wisdom and Wimps of Heritage Minutes,' *Canadian Forum* 73, 837 (1995): 12–15, retrieved 3 April 2011, from CBCA Reference and Current Events. (Document ID: 4458029); Nicole Neatby, 'The Heritage Project 60th Minute Commemorative Video,' *Canadian Historical Review* 81, 4 (December 2000): 668; Emily West, 'Selling Canada to Canadians: Collective Memory, National Identity, and Popular Culture,' *Critical Studies in Media Communication* 19, 2 (June 2002): 212–29; and Peter T. Hodgins, 'The Canadian Dream-Work: History, Myth and Nostalgia in the Heritage Minutes' (unpublished PhD thesis, Carleton University, 2003).

31 Anderson, *Imagined Communities.*

32 Billig, *Banal Nationalism.* Billig argues that nations exist only because people are continually reminded of them through such deixis.

33 Pierre Berton, *The National Dream: The Great Railway, 1871–1881* (Toronto: McClelland and Stewart, 1970) and *The Last Spike: The Great Railway 1881–1885* (Toronto: McClelland and Stewart, 1971). See also James Murray and Eric Till, dirs., *The National Dream: Building the Impossible Railway* (miniseries) (Toronto: Canadian Broadcasting Corporation, 1974).

34 See 'Minute by Minute: The Making of Canadian Mythology,' in *The CRB Foundation Heritage Project: 60th Minute Commemorative Video* (Montreal: CRB Foundation, 1998), videorecording.

35 Neatby, 'The Heritage Project 60th Minute.'

36 In the 1930s, people of 'Chinese race' in Vancouver were barred from voting federally, provincially, and municipally, were barred from bringing their relatives into the country, were barred from working for government or in provincially incorporated companies, were subject to ongoing verbal and physical harassment, were segregated geographically, socially, and politically. In addition to the histories cited in note 10 above, see Patricia E. Roy, *The Oriental Question: Consolidating a White Man's Province, 1914–41* (Vancouver: University of British Columbia Press, 2003); Kay J. Anderson, *Vancouver's Chinatown: Racial Discourse in*

Canada, 1875–1980 (Montreal and Kingston: McGill-Queen's University Press, 1991); Paul Yee, *Saltwater City: An Illustrated History of the Chinese in Vancouver* (Vancouver: Douglas and McIntyre, 2006).

37 Timothy J. Stanley, 'Whose Public? Whose Memory? Racisms, Grand Narratives and Canadian History,' in Ruth Sandwell, ed., *To the Past: History Education, Public Memory, and Citizenship in Canada* (Toronto: University of Toronto Press, 2006), 32–49.

38 See Renan, 'Qu'est-ce qu'une nation? (1882).'

39 Some readers will find this a rather strong and distasteful claim. For a larger discussion, see Timothy J. Stanley, *Contesting White Supremacy: School Segregation, Anti-Racism and the Making of Chinese Canadians* (Vancouver: University of British Columbia Press, 2011). For recent literature supporting this view, see Constance Backhouse, *Colour-Coded: A Legal History of Racism in Canada, 1900–1950* (Toronto: University of Toronto Press, 1999); Camille A. Nelson and Charmaine A. Nelson, eds., *Racism, Eh?: A Critical Inter-disciplinary Anthology of Race and Racism in Canada* (Concord, ON: Captus Press, 2004); Sherene Razack, *Dark Threats and White Knights: The Somalia Affair, Peacekeeping, and the New Imperialism* (Toronto: University of Toronto Press, 2004); Montgomery, 'A Better Place to Live.'

40 There is also a taken-for-granted gendering at work in the minute. This is a story about the activity of men, about a masculinist triumph, consistent with the normal ways in which the nation is represented. The worker, despite his physical appearance, is shown to be manly and as such a worthy participant in the nation, literally one of its builders. The only reference to woman in the film is that to the invisible 'wife.' This woman waits in the wings, apparently a passive object to be sent for. She remains invisible in the last part of the minute when viewers are left to assume that she has in fact been sent for. Even the two granddaughters who appear on screen sit in silent and rapt attention, their gaze lovingly centred on the male worker. Thus the minute articulates a masculinist narrative in which women/girls are literally decentred, passive objects of and audience for masculinist activity.

41 See Statistics Canada, Canadian Statistics, 'Population by selected ethnic origins, by provinces and territories (2001 Census),' http://www40.statcan.ca/l01/cst01/demo26a.htm (accessed 19 February 2006).

42 Won Alexander Cumyow, born in Port Douglas, BC, in 1861, ten years before that province entered confederation, was the first 'Canadian'-born Chinese. See the biographic sketch by Melanie Hardbattle, 'Won Alexander Cumyow: An inventory of his fonds in Rare Books and Special Collections, The Library of the University of British Columbia' (August 2002), http://www.library.ubc.ca/spcoll/AZ/PDF/C/Cumyow_Won_Alexander.pdf (accessed 19 February 2006).

43 There is a significant number of descendants of Yip Sang, who was the Chinese

superintendent for one of the main labour contractors of the CPR and later a successful merchant. Yip had twenty-three children. See Timothy J. Stanley, 'Yip Sang,' *Dictionary of Canadian Biography Online,* Library and Archives Canada, http://ShowBio.asp?BioId=42017&query=><http://www.biographi.ca/EN/ShowBio.asp?BioId=42017&query= (accessed 19 February 2006). However, Yip was not one of the actual construction workers.

44 On the demographics of these communities, see Li, *Chinese in Canada.* See also Tina Chui, Kelly Tran, and John Flanders, 'Chinese Canadians: Enriching the Cultural Mosaic,' *Canadian Social Trends* (Spring 2005): 24–32.

45 The best discussion of the railway workers remains Patricia E. Roy, '"A Choice between Evils": The Chinese and the Construction of the Canadian Pacific Railway in British Columbia,' in Hugh A. Dempsey, ed., *The CPR West: The Iron Road and the Making of a Nation* (Vancouver: Douglas and McIntyre, 1984), 13–34.

46 See Chan, *Gold Mountain.*

47 See Denise Chong, *The Concubine's Children* and Woon Yuen-Fong, *The Excluded Wife.* The reality of male Chinese workers in Canada is well captured in Hoe Ban Seng, *Enduring Hardship: The Chinese Laundry in Canada* (Hull: Canadian Museum of Civilization, 2003).

48 See Li, *Chinese in Canada,* 65–8.

49 See Chui, Tran, and Flanders, 'Chinese Canadians: Enriching the Cultural Mosaic.'

50 For example, the Canadian Museum of Civilization commemorates the Chinese hand laundry in its walkthrough of Canadian history. See Canadian Museum of Civilization, Canada Hall Phase 2, Chinese Hand Laundry, '5. Enduring Hardship – Chinese Hand Laundry,' http://www.civilization.ca/hist/phase2/mod5e.html (accessed 19 February 2006). Hoe Ban Seng, *Enduring Hardship,* provides the background research for this exhibit.

51 See, for example, 'Head Tax Deal Scorned as Pre-Vote "Scramble,"' *Vancouver Sun* [final edition], 25 November 2005, B8. While the Harper government has now formally apologized for the head tax, it has as yet to live up to its promise to compensate all those victimized by the tax. See Chinese Canadian National Council, 'Chinese Head Tax and Exclusion Act, CCNC and the Redress Campaign,' http://www.ccnc.ca/sectionEntry.php?entryID=10&type=Advocacy (accessed 24 March 2008).

52 See Wertsch, *Voices of Collective Remembering,* esp. the chart comparing collective memory and history (39–40). Wertsch sees history by contrast as polyvocal, contested, in flux.

53 Anderson, *Imagined Communities.* Parallel struggles for representing the past and establishing its significance in the making of contemporary Canada exist in other

communities. See, for example, Jennifer J. Nelson, *Razing Africville: A Geography of Racism* (Toronto: University of Toronto Press, 2008); Afua Cooper, *The Hanging of Angélique: The Untold Story of Canadian Slavery and the Burning of Old Montréal* (Toronto: HarperCollins, 2006); Peggy Bristow, ed., *We're Rooted Here and They Can't Pull Us Up: Essays in African Canadian Women's History* (Toronto: University of Toronto Press, 1994); Georges E. Sioui, *Pour une auto-histoire amérindienne: Essai sur les fondements d'une morale sociale* (Quebec: Presses de l'Université Laval, 1989); Daniel N. Paul, *First Nations History: We Were Not the Savages: Collision between European and Native American Civilizations*, 3rd edition (Halifax: Fernwood, 2006).

8 Democratizing the Past? Canada's History on the World Wide Web

SASHA MULLALLY

If the World Wide Web is 'the most public of media,'[1] how we represent the past on the Internet may very well be 'the most public of histories.' In their landmark publication, *Digital History,* Daniel Cohen and Roy Rosenzweig explore the profound implications of a wired world when it comes to the way historians create narrative (and other media) texts. Their study largely revolves around scholarly history, but includes a discussion about history produced for public consumption. They correctly point out how '[v]irtually every historical archive, historical museum, historical society, historic house, and historic site – even the very smallest – ha[s] its own website ... [along with] just about every reenactment group, genealogical society, and body of historical enthusiasts.'[2]

The Canadian corner of this vast public history landscape is dauntingly large in both scale and scope.[3] Many well-known public history organizations, such as the Dominion Institute and Canada's National History Society, have a well-developed online presence that helps to fulfil their mandate to 'shake the dust off' Canadian history and educate the public about Canada's past.[4] Sites such as the Canadian Mysteries Series, or Historica, the site for those well-known Heritage Minutes, provide examples of how important the Web has become for the proliferation of historical productions, and how significant Web history has become.[5] Canadian history websites are produced by a wide array of authors – a diverse mix of university-based scholars, professional historians working in the public and private sectors, and a host of interested amateurs, antiquarians, and genealogists. Some post stories, photographs, maps from Canada's past on websites just to share the information, others promulgate political positions or points of view about Canadian history. Still others, like Northern Blue Publishing and Chinook Multimedia, go online to ply historical services or sell historical products to library boards, school districts, and sometimes the post-secondary education sector.[6] The popularity of the Web for historical work, and the diversity of online historical content, invites those who are interested in public representations of the past to become more aware of Web history representations.

Online public history requires historians to think critically about how this new medium shapes messages about Canadian history. Margaret Conrad has recently linked the digital challenge to the growing importance of public history, when she encouraged Canadian history scholars to 'generate a dialogue' with the public about the past. '[T]o ignore the current knowledge revolution symbolized by the Internet,' she warned, 'is to court irrelevance.'[7] Those who create digital Web-histories are largely, and increasingly, from outside the academy. The advent of the Web will permanently change the composition of historical authorship, as well as how history is shared and presented to ever-wider readerships and audiences. Cohen and Rosenzweig argue it has the capacity to radically democratize the past.

The democratization of Web information is a key issue for historians writing about Web-based history. Cohen and Rosenzweig, for instance, have identified five 'perils' of putting history on the information superhighway. Some Web content is of dubious quality, and because the medium is ephemeral and ever-changing, it is of questionable durability. Because information seems to be at one's fingertips, the Web seems to encourage research passivity, can be a challenge to read and easily traverse, and may be difficult to for many people to access, because of uneven digital access among populations. But, in their review of digital history, the key peril for Cohen and Rosenzweig is the problem manifested by the centralization and commercialization of important storehouses of academic research.[8] Access to 'some of the best information on the Web,'[9] by which they mean scholarly publishing, is the crux of the digital revolution. Democratization of this information is, for them, the key to unlocking all the best promises of digital media: free the Web, and the world will follow. In this way, Cohen and Rosenzweig take a strong position in favour of open access, a movement to make all scholarly publishing online and accessible free of charge.[10] Supported by a host of international organizations, which have declared open access to be in the best interests of both arts and science scholarship,[11] this movement often directly engages the cultural heritage sectors, and relates closely to public history online. This debate, therefore, also figures into an assessment of the democratizing potential of the Web.

At the same time, Cohen and Rosenzweig outline seven 'promises' of digital media that have the potential to improve the dissemination of historical texts. The quantitative advantages of digital media offer unlimited information storage capacity. This capacity encompasses a diversity of Web history texts (word, image, and sound media) and diversity of Web history authorship (amateur, professional, and academic). In addition, they point towards the flexibility and manipulability of digital data, noting how these characteristics have revolutionized how we search for and organize historical material. Scholarly journal research is much easier with online access to *American History and Life* and *Historical Abstracts*. The final two beneficial characteristics are the interactive potential of digital media and its inherent hypertextuality. These offer distinct and intrinsic qualitative advantages that allow digital medial to engage larger and more diverse range of consumers than other, more traditional media.

Digital History paints a compelling picture of the future of the past, but it is incumbent upon the historical community to give some thought to the place of public history in this ever-expanding online universe. This chapter will critically assess this 'democratization.' By democratization, I refer both to the power of the Internet to make historical knowledge more accessible to the public and to its ability to multiply the number of people who create texts to narrate and represent the past.[12] This chapter will do this in two ways. First, I will explore notions of authorship and authority by assessing the role and impact of non-scholarly history producers in Canada at the turn of and during the first decade of the twenty-first century. To do this I will, via case-study, consider the diversity of online authors, read through historical discussion forums, and discuss the implications of digitization of museum and archival material emerging at this time. This leads to a reconsideration of how scholarly historians might use the power of hypertext to maintain an important role and authoritative voice as history, with most communication and knowledge, goes digital. But with the promise to democratize history, and challenge to the notion of and nature of authorship, comes a related challenge to scholarly historical authority. Using examples of Web-based Canadian history, I will then discuss the extent to which history produced for public consumption on the Web blurs and breaks down the significant barriers that traditionally demarcated the realms of academic and public history. In so doing, it will discuss the impact of hypertext – of links – on historical narrative and argument online. The linked interconnectedness of Web media enables a webpage link to take a Web-user from one site to another.[13] When Canadian histories move from static print to digital Web-based texts, this changes the ways in which history is disseminated and read. 'Hypertextuality' is the Web's salient characteristic, and it creates an environment in which the very notion of narrative cohesion and argumentation seems impossible to maintain. The chapter will then close with some thoughts on how scholars may nonetheless manage hypertextuality while at the same time serving the best interests of the public and work towards the highest goals of the open access debate.

Web Diversity and Wiki-History

The Web's capacity to democratize history is most apparent in the diversity of Web authorship. Given low barriers to media entry on the Internet, it is not surprising that, compared with book publishing and documentary-making, Web-authors are less likely to have formal academic credentials. Anyone and everyone may, in theory, publish on the Web, and this enables a wide array of institutions and individuals to participate in the creation and dissemination of historical texts and discussions. The challenge to historical authority made possible by the levelling power of Internet publishing might cause some to worry about the quality and reliability of online information. But reliability is not a concern exclusive to the Web; it is a concern with all kinds of popular history, whether these appear in print, on film, or on television.[14] The diversity of Web history authorship can be seen as a positive phenomenon in many ways. For instance, the Internet creates an environment where marginalized groups, those traditionally written out of the historical narrative, can easily discuss and talk about their pasts.

A wide array of Canadian women's history, for example, may be found on-line. The Internet seems to have enabled the creation of many forums where women's social and political achievements, as well as aspects of domestic and working life, are showcased, discussed, and often celebrated. Prominent among these are sites produced by public agencies and government organizations. *Celebrating Women's Achievements*, a site hosted by Library and Archives Canada, offers biographical tours of 'exceptional Canadian women who have made outstanding contributions to Canadian society and the world.'[15] As another example, Parks Canada's site on *Canadian Women's History* recognizes how 'there still remains much to be done to improve the representation of women in Parks Canada's programs' and engages readers to join them in the discovery and commemoration of female achievement.[16] But there are many more Canadian women's history sites created by private individuals. The *Heroines* webpage is a guide to Canadian women in history created and managed by Merna M. Forster.[17] While Forster is a public historian formerly employed by Parks Canada, her site is very much a private enterprise and her own individual creation. She designed *Heroines* to act as a repository of information and images she has collected over the years and she invites visitors to browse and share in the excitement of discovering the past in the site's free content. She also showcases new books and other media on women's history, and encourages Web users who visit her site to begin their own commemorative projects. Many students, teachers, and other history-minded individuals join her online, and together these disparate authors disseminate a digital version of Canadian women's history.[18]

Web accessibility promises to diversify historical offerings in the public sphere, but many women's history websites share important features. Most are, for instance, organized around a consciousness-raising objective, and set out with an overt mission to prove that women are 'important' enough to include in the historical narrative. As well, the majority seem to favour a biographical format to present the historical material, even when the subject-matter would otherwise fall under the category of social history. A good example of this is the website *Section 15* (whose title refers to the section on equality and affirmative action in the Canadian Charter of Rights and Freedoms), a site designed to offer 'a feminist take on the country's people, current events and culture.'[19] For the author, Nancy Jackman, and her co-creators, cultural diversification naturally involves discussions of history. The women's stories shared on *Section 15* aim to 'celebrate and expose' narratives left out of the historical canon, and their focus is on women activists, 'those who fought passionately for better treatment and more opportunities.'[20] *Section 15* builds Canadian women's history into discussion forums for feminist critique of contemporary news and politics and, like the sites referenced above, focuses on the achievements of individuals as a means to organize these debates. Online offerings from public institutions do the same. Library and Archives Canada, for instance, hosts a special webpage that gives the history of nursing in the First World War, but it does it from the diary entries and individual experiences of four women, and offers context in a relatively brief introduction.[21] Biography is a popular narrative form and its usage in public history is not surprising; it is easy for the non-specialist to identify with and learn about the past through the prism of individual experience. On the other hand, many scholars could read the focus on 'achieving women' as a gender-inverted reflection of the 'great man' theory of history. Despite some efforts, such as the *Section 15* site, to diversify historical content by race and ethnicity,[22] online iterations of Canadian women's history still tend to highlight white, European-Canadian women, their narratives, and their contributions to Canadian society. Academic historians might argue that this focus provides a dated and, in the absence of adequate contextualization, perhaps even an elitist understanding of women's history. This not only points to a disconnect between some online public history and scholarship, but also underscores how the diversity of Web history authorship does not necessarily guarantee diversity in historical content and interpretation.

Many historical characters embedded in our national narrative were selected long before the advent of the Internet, and in many ways, Web history offerings merely cement the centrality of well-known historical characters in our national narratives. The Laura Secord story, which tells how a Niagara-based farm wife undertook a dangerous journey to warn Upper Canadian British forces of a pending American attack during the War of 1812, has an important profile among Canadian public history offerings on the Web. The many Canadian history websites that feature Secord promulgate hagiographic narratives, most of these emphasizing the importance of her loyalty to the British crown. Most printed versions of her story in circulation today, the many monuments erected by local historical societies in her honour, and even the television Heritage Minute on Secord, have all chosen to emphasize her 'loyalism.' There have been many interpretations of Secord's narrative and her role in the history of Upper Canada.[23] In her review of online iterations of the Secord narrative, American scholar Marsha Tate has found that although details of her heroic journey vary among websites, the focus on Secord's loyalism remains a constant among sites, even though the Massachusetts-born Secord, from an American perspective, 'may arguably have more in common with Benedict Arnold than someone like Betsy Ross.'[24] Tate observes, 'Despite the polymorphic nature of the Laura Secord legend [online], its role in fostering Canadian nationalism appears to remain an important underlying incentive for evoking the legend even on the World Wide Web.'[25] That Secord's loyalism should remain central on the Web offers an example of how dominant public history frameworks, established before the advent of the Internet in textual, visual, and commemorative forms, might simply be transferred to the new digital forms of history on the Web. Diversity in Web authorship does not necessarily mean online histories will benefit from diverse or recent interpretive frameworks inspired by the latest historiography. One might expect that a decentralized media network such as the Internet would encourage entropy in broad historical narratives: the dispersed and diverse authorship would undermine traditional hierarchies of knowledge and bring to light multiple interpretations of past events and individuals. However, as is suggested by the Laura Secord case, historical narratives online might just as easily be characterized by content convergence.

This convergence is reinforced by the formation and proliferation of information warehouses which daily grow more prominent on the Internet. Web searches increasingly return links to these storehouses when used to find historical information. The problem of information reliability and quality is nowhere as evident as on *Wikipedia*, perhaps the most important of these warehouses. *Wikipedia* describes itself as 'a multilingual, Web-based, free content encyclopedia project ... [that] has grown rapidly into one of the largest reference Web sites.'[26] It is a well-designed information resource created around the concept of a 'wiki,' which refers to a Webpage resource that many people write and edit.[27] This collaborative project, founded in 2001, has grown exponentially into a large scale, copyright- and licence-free resource.[28] The English site on *Wikipedia* has by now surpassed a content milestone of three and a half million articles. By its very nature, *Wikipedia* is the apotheosis of Web authorship diversity, a radically democratic information resource. The site is run by a host of volunteer administrators who take care of 'housekeeping' activities and assist the growth of the increasingly important site. These volunteers perform a wide variety of tasks. They watch the articles for 'deletion debates' and carry out the consensus of the community on keeping or deleting contentious articles or contentious points made in articles. They monitor the evolution of the site and delete obvious cases of plagiarism, and 'meet user requests for help that require administrative access.'[29] None of these activities involve the vetting of information or review of submissions; the roles are facilitative rather than administrative. This stands in sharp contrast to other online sources of historical information, such as *The Canadian Encyclopedia,* whose entries are vetted by experts.[30] The evolution of information in *Wikipedia* entries defers to the expertise and knowledge of the 'collective intelligence' of its users and contributors.

The reliability of *Wikipedia*, and its viability as a quality knowledge repository, are the subject of much debate.[31] In her recent review of Canadian history entries on the site, Margaret Conrad has pointed out gaps in the quality of these entries. This important information commons overlooks much of Canada's past, and Canadian perspectives on historical events are not in the foreground. American interpretations of the War of 1812, for instance, predominate on the site. But is a gap or skewed interpretation a cause for criticism[32] or a call to action? Conrad is inspired by the potential for team research and peer review offered by the *Wikipedia* project. Recognizing it as a work in perpetual progress, Conrad refuses to merely write it off as a poor-quality site. In her assessment, 'the sheer volume of good material' is more impressive than under-representation or bias that as yet have gone uncorrected.[33] *Wikipedia* is hoping for greater participation from the academic sector. Representatives of *Wikipedia* point out the allure of 'free unlimited server space and well-designed page construction tools' for researchers who have a specialized knowledge to share and who do not have a vested financial interest in 'owning the information.' This, *Wikipedia* points out, 'matches the archetypal academic researcher.'[34] Since it is next to impossible to 'police' the Web or subject every online offering to a process of peer review and content authentication by recognized experts, the sharing of credible information and analyses by scholar-experts, either on *Wikipedia* or any other information commons, seems to be the only way to manage and offset the problem of online historical inaccuracies. In the twenty-first century, it may well become an accepted and expected part of the academic sector's public service to make research free and available online.[35] In fact, Conrad believes that professional participation in online forums, whether *Wikipedia* or other information storehouses/gateways, seems to be the only way to enable and empower the public to be discerning with their history consumption. In this way, Conrad makes the open access debate very relevant to scholarly production outside the academy; even if scholarly publishing does not evolve along open access lines, her call for scholarly participation in information commons would irrevocably, in theory, subvert attempts to commercialize knowledge online, including the important cultural knowledge encapsulated in our history.

The Costs of Digitization

When considering the wider Web as a democratic medium, it is necessary to also take into consideration whether accessibility on the Internet in a broader sense is not to a certain extent circumscribed by cost. There is no gainsaying the reality of a 'digital divide' in computer ownership and Internet use between rich and poor, central and peripheral, white and non-white communities in Canada and around the world. Over the past decade this divide has diminished somewhat in Canada, but it persists.[36] Even as more and more people acquire computers and Internet connections, they do not simultaneously acquire the skills for finding and making effective use of this new, free global resource or participating in Web publishing and digital creation.[37] Acknowledging this divide is important, because it calls into question just how 'public' public history on the Web really is.

Public historians have long sought for ways to 'share authority' with wider audiences; if the access problem can be overcome, the Web offers an ideal medium for that sharing and collaboration. Digital media make it easy to build 'knowledge communities,' by encouraging dialogue among professionals, between professionals and non-professionals, between teachers and students, and among members of the public. The ways in which we learn, read, reminisce about, and create the past are not only easier but potentially richer and more intensive with digital media.[38] Parks Canada, for instance, uses its website on women's history as a launching point, where visitors are asked to absorb material on the site, but also to submit data and launch commemorative projects of their own. They use the Web to create an online milieu where heritage is used to celebrate women's work and accomplishments, but then take the process one step further by encouraging readers to contribute to the process themselves. Members of the public are invited to interact with the past by creating their own history texts, and link to the larger project sponsored by the federal agency. Parks Canada tries to use the Web to build bridges to local sites of historical production.

But all bridges, whether virtual or real structures, take time to build and need to be maintained. This necessarily involves time and resources. Everywhere on the Internet, Web-based commercial products dominate Web-based freeware, even when it comes to history. One wonders whether amateur, professional, and academic historians will be able to compete with well-funded commercial operators for Internet attention. Many private individuals engaged in public history struggle to secure adequate resources to maintain their sites. The information highway, like the real variety, is currently built around the commerce of traffic flow. Merna Forster, for instance, hopes her *Heroines* website on Canadian women's history will eventually be 'supported through advertising and affiliate arrangements.'[39] How many sites can sustain themselves without spending the time and money to regularly reinvent and update their form and content?

If widespread digital literacy is achieved, digital networks, if disseminated more equitably across Canada and worldwide, will allow history and historians to do the work needed to reach the multiple audiences for history. In Canada, public funding for these activities for museum and archives sectors has allowed these sectors to race ahead of academic historians to 'go digital.' A consideration of these open access activities might help historians map the future of a distributed digital world of information.

Virtually all museums and publicly funded archives are putting key documents and holdings online. In many ways, this is made possible by the availability of government funds. Heritage Canada has adopted a relatively recent mandate to connect Canadians to their heritage through 'the digitization and accessibility of key collections from Canada's federal, cultural heritage institutions.'[40] Digitizing archival material will make it easier to 'do' history without the cost of research travel, and it allows individuals who never would have dreamed of doing research to experience the thrill of exploration, without the cost of a flight to Library and Archives Canada, or other public repositories. In a country the size of Canada, where transportation is expensive, the accessibility of historical documents made possible by digitization is potentially a great boon.

A number of years ago, the Nova Scotia Archives, for instance, launched a new site built around the history of the Black Loyalists in that province.[41] The site features a digital copy of a rare document, the Book of Negroes. The book provides a list of black passengers who left New York for British North America in 1783. The book gives names, physical descriptions, and ages of the passengers, documenting their status as slave or free. In the case of slaves, the owner and place of residence are also listed. Before digitization, this document was difficult to access. The only other two copies extant are at the Public

Records Office in Kew, England, and at the United States National Archives in Washington, DC. Now, however, this book is online and freely searchable, with annotations to guide the reader through various information and data. The site also provides links to other related artefacts and research. One link connects to a late eighteenth-century surveyor's map, which shows the location and size of land grants in the Black Loyalist settlement of Birchtown in Shelburne County, Nova Scotia.[42] Another link connects to a page featuring information and photos of an archaeological dig where dwellings of Black Loyalist settlers and artefacts from Birchtown settlement have been and are still being uncovered.[43] This kind of immediate access to primary and secondary sources on the Web both allows researchers to obtain invaluable data and encourages them to place this data in its historical contexts. Now, they may read the document, view the map, and then virtually experience the dig.

Website design often reveals pre-conceived expectations, on the part of the author/creator, of how the public should consume the historical information featured on these online texts. The Book of Negroes, for example, embeds the artefact in a narrative that discusses and situates it in a broader African-Canadian history. It reinforces this contextualization by linking the Book of Negroes not only to maps and digs but to other sources pertaining to Black Loyalist history and ongoing research on community's settlement. Website creators take on an authoritative voice through explanatory frameworks of both presentation (annotation and narrative contextualization) and placement (linking the document to maps and archaeological projects).

Carefully considered links are a component of all quality history websites. An increasingly popular source for twentieth-century Canadian history is the online archives of the Canadian Broadcasting Corporation (CBC).[44] The CBC archives was created through a collaborative effort with Heritage Canada in order to 'inform, enlighten and educate' the public.[45] The archives online allows visitors to access coverage of many important topics in twentieth-century Canadian history: news coverage ranging from First World War conscription debates, to the FLQ Crisis, to Terry Fox's Marathon of Hope. As with the Book of Negroes, the video footage and audio clips are accompanied by text-based outlines, and one can situate any given television and radio broadcast in a 'subject timeline' that runs at the top of the interface. The timeline includes hypermedia icons that invite site visitors to connect to other media that cover the same thematic subject-matter. 'The goal is not just to present these clips and TV and radio accounts by themselves,' says the online archives project director François Boulet, 'but to add value to this content by explaining what happened and placing these events in context.'[46] Yet, in the process of 'adding value' and 'placing these events in context,' CBC archivists must place the content in a thematic discussion, visually place the events on a timeline, and connect them to other related clips. These activities allow CBC archivists to play an important, authoritative role. Narrative contextualization in a history essay, article, or book is a subject with which all scholars are familiar, but hypertext contextualization – linking historical media among different pages and sites – is something new. On the one hand, linking empowers Web authors by allowing them to place an artefact image, a radio clip, or a text narrative within a thematic context on an individual site. But the Web author's power to control the thematic context diminishes when an external link is supplied. At that moment, the author's production becomes just another node on a vast network of information.

Qualifying Authority in the Digital World

The links on a site and between sites, and the hypertext environment where Web history resides, pose a challenge to our notions of authorship and authority. Who can predict how readers will navigate a site, choose to follow one link over another, or fit information gleaned at any URL into their personal framework of understanding history? The Web has helped foster communications among individuals who share a particular historical interest, and so observations of these online discussions, those that are open to public view, can shed light on the use of authoritative texts in the practice of public history.

A relatively recent discussion of a seventeenth-century artefact among a group of Atlantic Canada–based history enthusiasts offers some insight into how an online knowledge community, actively engaged in the sharing and creating of public history, used and interpreted 'expert opinion' in their historical consumption and production. These discussions are easily accessible on the Web; a random search for maps from early Canada takes Internet browsers to the cartography displayed on a site called *Exploring Nova Scotia.* The site is linked to a Yahoo discussion group, where just over three hundred people gather online to discuss aspects and significance of early Nova Scotian history. Members of *Exploring Nova Scotia* 'trade gps [global positioning system] waypoints, tracks and photographs, review hikes and trails, and discuss Nova Scotia history, prehistory and geography.'[47] In over eight thousand posts since the group was founded in 2002, topics for discussion range from the architectural history of particular counties and regions of Nova Scotia, to reviews of what archaeological sites one might encounter along less well known hiking trails in the province.

In one discussion thread, a member posted 'a remarkable 1610 map of New England and New France, that was discovered in the Spanish Archives at Simancas in 1885,' which featured what is now New Brunswick, Prince Edward Island, and Nova Scotia, as well as parts of New England.[48] From the moment the map was posted on the discussion group in the fall of 2004, it animated group discussion on a wide range of topics. Some opined that markings and place names on the map provided evidence that fishermen from the Pointeau region in France fished off of the North American coast in the early seventeenth century,[49] while others looked to the map and saw evidence that islands used to exist off of George's Bank.[50] The map, ostensibly made for James I of England, is actually well known to historical cartographers as the 'Velasco map.' It is named after Don Alonzo Velasco, the Spanish ambassador to England, who secretly sent a copy of this early example of English cartography of the New World to King Phillip III of Spain. The detailed cartographical information represented in the Velasco map strongly suggests that early seventeenth-century English explorers had knowledge of the New World as good as, if not better than, the French and Dutch. As the story goes, the pirated copy was received by the Spanish court and deposited in the Simancas library, until it was rediscovered in 1885.[51]

However, according to a recent publication by David Allen, librarian emeritus at Stony Brook University in New York, the map is likely a fake produced in the nineteenth century by a skilled forger. Allen's thesis is based on comparisons to other early seventeenth-century maps, an analysis of the tight social world of Jacobean cartography, and a technical analysis of the map's geodetic framework (orientation, scale, and location of different topographical features).[52] His assessment was published in February 2006 in an online journal for historical geography, *Coordinates*. Probably because the journal is available online, a URL linking the discussions on *Exploring Nova Scotia* to Allen's 'interesting article' was posted just a few weeks after publication.[53] Allen's authoritative critique failed to dampen the enthusiasm of members of *Exploring Nova Scotia*, who continued to compare the map to other early charts of North America.[54] The group's initial discovery of the map itself prompted excited discussion of several topics in 2004, but there is virtually no discussion among members of the group when Allen discredited the source two years later. Linking to each other in a discussion thread, this group placed its discussion within a context of their own making, allowing them to define authority in their own way. In this example, the World Wide Web encouraged historical analysis among an interested and well-informed group of non-scholars, a group who shared both digitized source material and analyses among members of their group and with similar online communities in the United States.[55] Mere access to the academic Allen critique was not sufficient to have an impact on these otherwise robust discussion threads. The Web allows for parallel modes of authentication and parallel communities of authority to exist simultaneously, with each community of knowledge able to accept or reject 'outside' authority according to its own particular use of historical information.

This apparent lack of interest in formal scholarly authentication is explained, at least in part, by the orientation of this public history discourse. The discussions about the Velasco map on *Exploring Nova Scotia* focus on using the map to uncover geographic history about Atlantic Canada and the northeastern United States. In their discussions, members demonstrate an impressive grasp of the technical development of European cartography. The analysis of the map by one member of the group, for instance, demonstrated a detailed understanding of historical French mapmaking techniques. After providing a summary of secondary source opinion, for instance, he concluded that the 1610 map was likely based on pre-Champlain cartographic sources. This assessment was confirmed by consultation with secondary literature, also posted to the site.[56] Allen's scholarly analysis, however, was based on a broad and deep contextual knowledge of seventeenth-century European social history, how cartographers from different nations shared information and built communities of knowledge. Despite their store of technical understanding and understanding of local history, the members of *Exploring Nova Scotia* could not incorporate Allen's larger picture of social history into their search for evidence of 'ancient inscription sites' on the Velasco map.

Issues determining 'authenticity,' defining context, and acknowledging authority in history at times worry scholars, but they pre-date the advent of the World Wide Web. With the advent of the Internet, however, any historical fraud can be perpetrated on a greater number of people with greater ease. Notwithstanding the tools for verification and material to aid research contextualization that are available online,[57] often as digitized scholarly research, it ultimately remains up to individuals and groups to seek out and use these resources. If Internet access, and the easy return of *Wikipedia* hits on a search engine query, accelerate a trend towards passive consumption of easy and narrow analyses, where do these new democratic communications media leave the contemporary voice of authority, trained to provide detailed analysis and breadth of knowledge? A voice crying in an immense, digital wilderness? How may we attract traffic to otherwise removed stretches of the information highway?

Digital Abundance and Hypertextuality

The frontiers of the new media universe, the frontiers of the Internet 'wilderness,' are expanding exponentially. New media's incredible capacity for compressing data promises to increase archival capacity for historical materials to the extent that storing information may become unmanageable. There is the potential to save copies of virtually all cultural productions, once they are in digital format. The Wayback Machine, for instance, is a massive archive dedicated to preserving 'a unique global snapshot of the Web' by saving a copy of most online material posted between 1996 and the present.[58] This at first seems like a boon to future historians, but it presents a new challenge, the challenge of source abundance.[59] The activities of archives like the Wayback Machine now present historians with the prospect of a digital future that has the capacity to preserve all information, and provide future generations of researchers with a complete historical record. This new abundance has implications for the future of archiving in our country, and the burden of abundance will undoubtedly prompt new and difficult preservation decisions. Will this digital abundance provide an excuse to destroy more 'hard' copy documents? And when digital copies of materials and text are all that exist, does that change our understanding of texts? The solidity of a 'real' document offers a certain comfort of its 'artefactory presence.' Digitizing a source like the Book of Negroes makes it not only more accessible, but also less vulnerable to the ravages of time and research use, if not the problem of technology obsolescence.

Digitization adds a new flexibility to information previously stored in linear narrative formats. Using digital media tools, we can more easily preserve, study, and present the past, and combine media and meanings into seemingly infinite new historical experiences and 'ways of seeing' history. The process of digitization has transformed the Book of Negroes, like all public history on the Web. It was, at one time in its existence as an artefact, a ledger, with a beginning and an end. Now, it exists online as a series of pages captured in portable document format (pdf), with an annotated guide, embedded in a site that enables virtually instantaneous searches through the entries. One wonders whether the transformation of the Book of Negroes, from a form where its status as an artefact was highlighted to one where its function as a database is foregrounded, will change its use in the creation of history. What about the material culture history represented by the sources and methods of binding, or the sources of its paper and ink?

If the digitization of an artefact may change its historical use, or highlight one use at the expense of others, the hypertextual environment, the power of links explicated in the previous section, certainly challenges the forms of linear thought and argument used in the typical work of history. Hypertext is perhaps the most important qualitative element of Web-based history, and is the most significant difference between 'hard copy' print publishing and online publishing. Any digital text that provides a link is making use of hypertext, but there are levels of hypertextual sophistication that allow Web surfers to manipulate text, sound, and image in a myriad of interactive ways. Unlike books with information contained within two covers, or a television program that guides the reader or viewer along a linear narrative prescribed from the outset, the Web is an information exchange on a network of possible transactions. On the Web, 'every point of consumption can also be a point of production.'[60]

Both prophets and critics of digital history unanimously agree that, in a truly hypertextual environment, 'reading' as we know it often ceases to exist. Many refer to an 'evolution in human communication' engendered by Web texts that can be linked up in unusual ways thanks to hypertext. Traversing hypertext makes considerable demands on both author and reader as it disrupts the way we traditionally process information. In a linear textual narrative, one's gaze and attention travel along the sentences of a printed page, and the reader is 'led' through a story, into the details of an argument or down an intellectual path created by the author. Information on the Web is presented in a 'non-linear' form. Instead of expecting readers to follow a text from beginning to end, a website with its hypertext links invites surfers to build their own narrative, encouraged as they are to make their own path through, between, and among websites.

Mainly through its digitization outreach efforts, the museum sector embraces the potential of hypertextuality. In 2007, the Virtual Museum of Canada, for instance, showcased 145 museum sites dedicated to the theme of History and Society. One of the newer offerings was an introduction to the history of Canadian science and medicine at a site called *Athena's Heirs*.[61] Still current and online, *Athena's Heirs* is built around an exploration of important medical technologies developed in Canada, such as developments in heart pacemaker and haemodialysis technologies. The online exhibition, created by the Canadian Heritage Information Network in association with Queen's University, uses artefacts to explain how societies 'learn science,' 'do science,' and 'apply science.' The site is open and free to the public, a fully democratized and open source of historical information, presented by experts in the field.

Web readers have many options in using this site. They can look for specific information on a particular technology, they can read about the development of science in Canada more generally, and they can virtually examine scientific artefacts. At *Athena's Heirs*, the text and analysis are basic, but this belies the potential complexity of the interface. Themes that revolve around 'learning, doing and applying' scientific knowledge provide the site with the thematic pathways through which the various artefacts and scientific technologies are discussed. The site's combination of image and text is complemented by a constant running 'sidebar' frame to the left that lends a tight organization schema to the material. If readers choose, they may explore a biographical note or artefactory explanation in very great detail. Or, by making a different set of choices, one can have a completely different experience at the site by following a thematic pathway. The 'learning science' pathway, for instance, takes one through an afternoon's worth of reading about empirical investigation in the history of the physical and biological sciences. This pathway would give the user a very European-centric view of science. On the other hand, much more Canadian content is present when the site documents 'doing' science and 'applying' scientific principles. A good deal of the science 'done' in Canada relates to cartography, managing the sheer size of the nation. One particular trajectory down this pathway offers a detailed explanation of the development of useful navigational charts and tools in the mid-eighteenth century. A random link took me from cartography to a page delineating the history of timekeeping, and how Canadian scientists created an atomic clock to determine and keep standard time in the mid-twentieth century. The design overlap among the learning, doing, and applying science pathways adds to the number of potential narratives a user might create. Perhaps museum-based public history sites such as *Athena's Heirs* lend themselves to the creation of virtual historical 'spaces' and digital texts to a greater degree than traditional scholarship because the transition to hypertextuality is less of a leap for historians in this sector than for those in academe. How one interfaces with a museum site online is similar to how one interfaces with a museum in real life. History in museums is not presented by narrative alone, but typically incorporates objects, texts, images, and sound. But to say that website history production emulates 'curatorial approaches' does not tell the whole story. While an exhibit is bounded by the museum space, any given site at the Virtual Museum of Canada can offer linkages to the innumerable and varied resources of the World Wide Web.

Web hypertextuality and interactivity make it a quintessentially postmodern communications medium. Espen Aarseth, an originator of cybertext[62] theory, coined the term 'ergodic' to describe this unique characteristic of digital text. An ergodic text is one that requires the reader to continually make choices that will shape a narrative as the text is 'traversed.'[63] Aarseth notes how every interactive website that is linked to another site via hypertext may be seen as an example of ergodic literature. Hypertextuality enables each reader (or user) to create a unique narrative flow. This hypertextual interactivity, especially when it involves images and sound in addition to, or even in lieu of, mere words, makes it difficult to find an authoritative voice within a digital document, or situate the content within a single, static interpretive framework. This poses a challenge to the traditional linear narrative form and has the potential to challenge traditional scholarship.

An increasing number of academic historians are taking on the challenge, however. A decade ago, American Historical Association president Robert

Darnton took a strong stand in favour of moving more scholarship, and more scholars, online. 'Standing here on the threshold of the year 2000,' he remarked, 'it appears that the road to the new millennium leads through Silicon Valley.'[64] More recently, David Staley called for historians to discard the inherent limitations of prose narrative and make better use of the new visual language emergent from the digital media and newly networked world.[65] Several American scholars, including Darnton, have over the past decade written articles with creatively interjected digital media components. These were published and are still maintained online by the electronic *American Historical Review* (*eAHR*). These articles link to digital sources and have multimedia elements to complement, and sometimes dominate, the textual narrative.[66]

Although William Thomas has shown how some Canadian historians are 'blazing trails' towards digital history,[67] and several newer online multimedia collaborations—on topics like enrivonmental history, oral history, and labour history – are moving scholarship into this new realm. For instance, the University of Western Ontario's Place-Based Computing Initiative stands as one of the first efforts to move scholars in this direction. Graduate history students under the direction of William Turkel,[68] a collaborator on this project, developed content for a historical walking tour of London Ontario's Old East Side, using handheld computers with global positioning system (GPS) receivers. The tour, which accompanied a Museum London exhibit and website,[69] uses computer technology to superimpose pictures of historical architecture onto scaled contemporary streetscapes,[70] and tags places with historical persons and activities.[71] Users can walk in the Old East Side, and aided with GPS-linked notebook computers, can have a spatial-historical experience on their walking tour of the neighbourhood.[72] These innovative projects, which illustrate the positive convergence of public history with digital history scholarship, remain relatively exceptional enterprises. However, several recent initiatives, often with the assistance of targeted Social Science and Humanities Research Council awards, are quickly changing this online landscape. Concordia University's Centre for Oral History and Digital Storytelling (COHDS), for instance, promises to foster 'new nonlinear ways to access, analyse and communicate life stories.' The various projects emerging from COHDS engage in the collection, analysis, and dissemination of oral histories of refugee communities, historical memory of life in the city of Montreal, and the place-based personal histories of work and workers in Canada. Through the efforts of the Centre's director, Stephen High, the COHDS uses Web-based tools and forums to do this kind of qualitative research in new ways, and also utilizes communications technologies to build and maintain dialogues between academics and the public, as well as to disseminate research results.[73]

For most scholarly researchers, however, the integration of new media technologies in teaching may represents the 'thin edge of the wedge' of the digital revolution. Digital media often now accompany textbooks. One of the earliest of these teaching tools is Chinook Multimedia's CD-ROM/website *Canadian History: Confederation to Present*.[74] The result of a collaboration with 140 scholars and professional historians, this resource narrates the past using multiple media that may be arranged into text, images, sounds, and moving pictures. *Canadian History* presents post-Confederation Canada through five interpretive narratives, or 'pathways.' Essays written by experts in the field introduce these pathways, which include Natives, Society/Culture, Women, Politics/Economy, and Regional Dynamics. These essays lead to the multimedia on the CD-ROM, as well as a fully integrated website. Despite having the benefit of introductory essays, the sheer volume of useful material therein has been described in otherwise positive academic reviews as 'overwhelming.'[75] But use of the CD-ROM is widespread in university curricula across the country, and so it might be said in the future that academic historians increasingly engage in digital history at the behest of the specific 'public' they principally serve on a day-to-day basis: students.

Organizing a course around a teaching tool rather than a series of lectures repositions the authority of the professor in the classroom in ways similar to how academic historical authority may be repositioned in the digital environment toward learning models that are more enquiry-based. It is difficult to conceptualize the role of a scholarly author in the production of 'ergodic' literature. Some historians have experimented with relinquishing this role. In his exploration of the problems of historical knowledge, American urban historian Philip Ethington presents a non-linear, multimedia-intensive exercise which literally and figuratively 'maps' historical and contemporary Los Angeles. Throughout this multimedia study, Ethington positions himself, not as an author, but as a '*Valet de place*, a specially commissioned guide.'[76] He creates, manipulates, and links discrete textual elements, but also maps and photos, to introduce readers to historical ways of experiencing the city. As historian-valet, Ethington grounds these visual representations in a theoretical argument. His sidebar essays describe the history of media forms he is manipulating, and provide methodological notes on his processes of collection and manipulation. But any 'reader' of Ethington's digital text will find that the focus is, ultimately, on the images and links made between them. Ethington calls this sort of 'mapping' 'a concrete tool for affirming the *presence* of the historical in the condition of the *present*, for mediating between the infinitely local and the infinitely global, and for building knowledge communities.'[77] Like the Place-Based Computing Initiative, Ethington is concerned with the representations of space and time.

His article makes the case that scholarship requires a new form of representation to address the challenges faced by urban historians in how they may relate to space and time, and to discuss these relationships in new ways.

Conclusion

Whether the 'ergodic' challenge of the Web is really a revolutionary challenge to historical knowledge, or just another stop along an evolutionary path in human communications, is, at this time, anyone's guess. The ability to take public texts and produce various meanings and interpretations is not unique to the Web environment. However, the interactive hypertextuality of the Web is something new and the implications for public consumption of history in this new medium are worthy of scholarly attention.

This discussion and analysis of Canadian public history on the Web allows us to make several observations. First, like much history online, Canadian public history on the Web exhibits diversity in authorship and content, with some excellent examples of historical creativity, and some good portal resources and impressive digital archives. But much public history online mirrors or recapitulates narratives available in non-electronic venues. Canadian public history on the Web is often characterized by content convergence. Canadian scholarly historians are not participating in shaping this public content online, and this absence might well explain this absence of historical debate online. With a few exceptions, Canadians in general lag in harnessing the power and potential of Web-based media to discover, debate, and disseminate our history whether in scholarly or public history forms. *Immigrant Voices*, created with funding from Industry Canada's Digital Collections Initiative, is as of this writing the sole remnant of a larger Canadian history portal project of the Canadian Historical Association.[78] This portal initiative promised to realize the dream of building an academically vetted and annotated portal to all Canadian history on the World Wide Web.[79] Although this may change, at this moment, *Immigrant Voices* is the only section open and online, and visitors seeking updates and further information are directed to the Canadian Historical Association's website. The portal's ambitious mandate to catalogue and annotate all Canadian history has lacked the ability to maintain itself as a long-term project.[80]

This leads to a second observation, that leadership in putting Canadian history on the Web resides in the museum sector, the archival community, and some of the individual initiatives of Web enthusiasts within the history fold. This may have to do with the fact that traditional forms of academic discourse are difficult to replicate in the hypertext environment, which subverts linear narrative and argumentation. It remains that, for their own research and writing, most Canadian academic historians overall still prefer the traditional, didactic narrative forms associated with print media although there are some signs this is changing quickly. A final observation regards the overabundance of information on the Internet, including historical information, as a situation that makes it easy for scholarly expertise to be drowned out. Source access and abundance, and the easy availability of information on sites like *Wikipedia*, also encourage individuals to become their own historians, as they create their own narrative understandings of the past. Whether they will use quality information vetted by expert historians will depend on the decisions the historical academy makes about the value of public history on the Web, and what role scholars should play in the maintenance of the information commons.

The online environment's promise to 'democratize history' is real, but at present a digital divide between scholars and public historians seems to be widening a gulf between how 'the academy' and 'the public' see, experience, and understand Canada's past. Certainly, even if open access prevails and scholarly content is free and available, this does not guarantee that non-scholars will see value in and use this research. Moreover, the more digital history embraces interactivity and hypertextuality, the greater the power and agency that will be assigned to the Web reader/browser at the expense of the author/creator. But to make these points is not to discourage the participation of scholarship in the creation of online history, nor are they made to argue against the open access movement. Rather, the fact of distributed authority online should underscore the importance of linkages in the production of historical knowledge on the Web. This discussion of digital history should encourage academic authors, when we do engage in online productions, to take as much care in the fostering of linked environments online as we do the quality of our content.

Because of the good job the archives and museum sectors are doing in the race to go digital, public interest in and consumption of history appear to be on the increase. The American Institute of Museum and Library Services (IMLS) recently released the results of an extensive survey that delves into the use of libraries, museums, and the Internet. These results show that the use of the Internet and related technologies actually increased museum and library use in the United States.[81] The survey also found that historical material posted online by libraries and museums is trusted by users above other sources of information, and the connection between museums and public libraries enhanced the online reputation and usefulness of both sectors to the public. Moreover, the study found that the 'explosion of available information' on the Internet did not overwhelm users. Instead, the IMLS researchers found that online accessibility 'inspire[d] the search for more information' among members of the public, and whetted their appetite for more historical knowledge.[82] This encouraging research bodes well for the online education of the Canadian public about our national past. And it is encouraging for proponents of public history to learn that the many online museums produced by the Virtual Museum of Canada project were designed for eventual cross-domain searching to the holdings of Library and Archives Canada. Its developers within the federal government had hoped by now to have an interoperable national museum, library, and archival online network of sites.[83] While this connectivity has yet to be realized in the Canadian museum, library, and archival sectors, the lag behind our American counterparts presents an opportunity for Canadian scholarship to become a part of this trusted network of historical knowledge on line. Such linkages would make optimal use of the potential inherent in digital media, and provide a linked set of sites where scholarly participation would be beneficial to the ongoing democratization of historical knowledge. The participation of scholars and professional historians is not required for any new emerging information democracy to exist – this is happening anyway – but inclusion of academic knowledge and expertise would certainly make the democracy a much richer and more rigorous place to create and consume history.

NOTES

1 Margaret Conrad, 'Public History and Its Discontents or History in the Age of Wikipedia,' Canadian Historical Association Presidential Address, University of Saskatchewan, 29 May 2007.

2 Daniel Cohen and Roy Rosenzweig, *Digital History: A Guide to Gathering, Preserving and Presenting the Past on the Web* (Philadelphia: University of Pennsylvania Press, 2006, http://chnm.gmu.edu/digitalhistory/ (accessed 29 May 2007).

3 A Google search for 'Canadian history' returns 716,000 webpages (even when limited by enabling the 'pages from Canada' filter).

4 The Dominion Institute, http://www.dominion.ca (accessed 31 May 2007); Canada's National History Society, http://www.historysociety.ca (accessed 31 May 2007).

5 'Great Unsolved Mysteries in Canadian History' http://www.canadianmysteries.ca (accessed 31 May 2007); 'Historica: Your Place in History' http://www.histori.ca (accessed 31 May 2007).

6 See, for instance, the list of products and resources for sale at 'Northern Blue Publishing's e-Learning Portal' http://www.northernblue.ca (accessed 17 March 2008). These include a Canadawiki and Encycloportal on Canadian History, but their main product is Canada History Online http:www.canadachannel.ca (accessed 20 March 2008).

7 Conrad, 'Pubic History and Its Discontents.'

8 These exclusive, fee-for-use archives, such as Proquest and Elsevier, ultimately make the best of digital history – as with much quality information and research – less accessible. Cohen and Rosenzweig, *Digital History.*

9 Ibid.

10 'Open Source' http://www.opensource.org/ (accessed 15 June 2007).

11 The open access movement has seen the strong support of European, American, and Canadian signatories from arts and science academies and organizations on both sides of the Atlantic with the Declaration of the Budapest Open Access Initiative (available at http://www.soros.org/openacess/read.shtml), the Berlin Declaration of Open Access to Knowledge in the Sciences and Humanities (available at http://www.zim.mpg.de/openaccess-berlin/berlin_declaration.pdf), the European Cultural Heritage Online (ECHO) Charter (available at http://echo.mpiwg-berlin. mpg.de/policy), and the Bethesda Statement on Open Access Publishing (available at http://www.earlham.edu/~peters/fos/bethesda.htm). These declarations and position statements emerged in the early years of the present decade, and represent a critical mass of scholarly support for the open access position.

12 I am not specifically referring to the 'open access' movement here, a movement that aims to make all scholarly publishing free and available online, but this plays a part in the democratization of public history. Readers interested in current snapshots and debates of the open access movement might consult the following: Frances Groen et al., *Open Access in International Perspective: A Review of Open-Access Policies in Selected Countries* (Ottawa: Social Science and Humanities Research Council of Canada, 2007); John Willinsky, 'The Unacknowledged Convergence of Open Source, Open Access and Open Science,' *First Monday: Peer-reviewed Journal of the Internet* (available at http://www.firstmonday.dk/ issues/issue 10_8/willinsky/index.html); Jean Claude Guedon, 'The Green and Gold Roads to Open Access: The Case for Mixing and Matching' (http://eprints .rclis.org/archive/00003039/01/science.pdf (accessed 16 March 2008).

13 The term 'hypertext' was coined by Theodor Nelson in the 1960s to refer to how information on a computer database can be combined and recombined for a variety of purposes. See Theodor Holm Nelson (Theodor Holm Nelson, 2007) http:// hyperland.com/ (accessed 9 August 2007). In the past few decades, many theorists have contributed to the critical theory of electronic or digital texts, especially as enabled by the Internet and presented on the Web. Linking the idea of hypertext to poststructuralist intellectual genealogy was, for instance, the subject of George Landow's influential book, *Hypertext: The Convergence of Contemporary Literary Theory and Technology* (Baltimore: Johns Hopkins University Press, 1992). See also George Landow, *Hypertext 3.0: Critical Theory and New Media in an Era of Globalization* (Baltimore: Johns Hopkins University Press, 2003). For very

succinct and useful (if somewhat dated) history of the word and the notion of hypertextuality, see Susan Delagrange, 'Evolving Sites for the Teaching of Writing: Notes on Hypertextuality' (Ohio State University, 1997), http://people.cohums .ohio-state.edu/ulman1/courses/E883C/E883C_SP97/Research/delagrange/ hypertxt.htm (accessed 9 August 2007).

14 In recent Canadian media history, two examples are the inaccuracies in the portrayal of Gardiner in the television miniseries *Prairie Giant*, the biographical treatment of Tommy Douglas in 2006, and the outcry from Second World War veterans over the depiction of their service in the CBC documentary *The Valour and the Horror*. See 'Prairie Giant' treads on toes in Saskatchewan' (CBC, 21 March 2006), http://www.cbc.ca/arts/story/2006/03/21/tommy-fallout.html (accessed 9 August 2007), and, for a recap and update on the impact of the veterans' protest and $500-million lawsuit on Terrence and Brian McKenna's careers after making *The Valour and the Horror*, especially the impact on how they approached historical documentaries, see (the ironically titled) 'Birth of a Nation' (CBC, 5 April 2007) http://www.cbc.ca/arts/tv/birthofanation.html (accessed 9 August 2007).

15 'Celebrating Women's Achievements,' http://www.collectionscanada.ca/women/ index-e.html (accessed 25 May 2007).

16 'Canadian Women's History: Be Proud of It, Be Part of It!' http://www.pc.gc.ca/ progs/lhn-nhs/femmes-women/index_E.asp (accessed 25 May 2007).

17 Merna M. Forster, 'Heroines.ca: A Guide to Women's History,' http://www .heroines.ca/ (accessed 30 May 2007).

18 See, for example, 'Cool Women: Women of Canada Making History,' http://www .coolwomen.ca (accessed 17 March 2008); 'Herstory: An Exhibition,' http:// library2.usask.ca/herstory.html (accessed 15 March 2008).

19 'Section 15: Rebels without a Clause,' http://www.section15.ca (accessed 17 March 2008). Section 15.ca grew out of the CoolWomen site, referenced above (note 18). The CoolWomen site was launched in 1996 and, according to the author, quickly became Canada's largest women's history website, featuring the inspirational stories of many women in Canadian history.

20 'About Section15.ca,' http://www.coolwomen.ca (accessed 17 March 2008).

21 'The Call to Duty: Canada's Nursing Sisters,' http://www.collectionscanada.ca/ nursing-sisters/index-e.html (accessed 8 August 2007).

22 Parks Canada has self-consciously adopted the mission of diversifying their historical productions to include more women, ethnicities, races, and First Nations in representations and narratives. This element can therefore be expected to grow. There is also subsection on their labour history site ('Canadian Workers in History, an Interpretation 1600–1975') where they briefly narrate a history of women workers in Canada to 1975. 'Women Workers until 1975' (Parks Canada, 2006), http://www.pc.gc.ca/culture/proj/tch-cwh/page5_e.asp (accessed 8 August 2007).

Merna Forster has a small but growing aspect of the site she calls 'group histories.' To date, however, they only feature the Dionne Quintuplets and Canada's War Brides. See 'Group Histories,' http://www.heroines.ca/people/grhistories.html (accessed 8 August 2007).

23 The work of Colin Coates and Cecilia Morgan, however, has revealed how Secord's narrative has been subject to varied and multiple interpretations since 1812, and that representations of the Niagara farm wife have changed over time depending on the objectives of the storytellers involved, whether they were early tourist promoters in the Niagara region or centennial-era nationalist educators. See Colin Coates and Cecilia Morgan, *Heroines and History: Representations of Madeleine de Verchères and Laura Secord* (Toronto: University of Toronto Press, 2002). The tourism uses of the Secord narrative are analysed in chapter 9, 'Laura Secord, the Niagara Region, and Historical Tourism' (233–55) while the changing depictions in children's textbooks is the subject of chapter 7, 'Children's Texts and Readers' (164–94).

24 Marsha Ann Tate, 'Looking for Laura Secord on the Web: Using a Famous Figure from the War of 1812 as a Model for Evaluating Historical Web Sites,' *History Teacher* 38, 2 (February 2005), http://www.historycooperative.org/journals/ht/38.2/tate.html (accessed 24 July 2007).

25 Ibid.

26 'Wikipedia,' http://en.wikipedia.org/wiki/Main_Page (accessed 3 June 2007).

27 For a more detailed description, see Margaret Conrad, 'Public History and Its Discontents.' The name 'Wiki' was inspired by the Hawaiian word 'wiki' or 'wiki-wiki,' which means 'quick.' It was coined in 1995 by programmer Ward Cunningham. An accessible breakdown of the 'wiki' concept is available at Marshall Brain, 'How Wikis Work,' http://computer.howstuffworks.com/wiki.htm (accessed 8 August 2007).

28 A short history of Wikipedia project is at Marshall Poe, 'The Hive,' *Atlantic Monthly* 298, 2 (September 2006). Available online at http://www.theatlantic.com/doc/200609/wikipedia (accessed 8 August 2007).

29 'Wikipedia: Administrators,' http://en.wikipedia.org/wiki/Wikipedia:Administrators (accessed 8 August 2007)

30 'The Canadian Encyclopedia' http://thecanadianencyclopedia.com/index.cfm?PgNm=TCESubjects&Params=A1 (accessed 8 August 2007). The *Canadian Encyclopedia* went online in 2001, the same year as Wikipedia.

31 Roy Rosenzweig wonders whether history can ever be done well in an 'open source' environment, and after comparing the quality of several Wikipedia entries against other more established encyclopedic sources, and discussing the history of its organizational development, feels that the organization of professional scholarship does not recognize the kinds of contributions and work that make Wikipedia

possible, and the ways scholarly historians traditionally work stands in opposition to the commons ideal. Wikipedia does, however, stand as a potent alternative
model for organizing knowledge, which may have an impact on scholarship. Roy
Rosenzweig, 'Can History Be Open Source? Wikipedia and the Future of the Past,'
Journal of American History 93, 1 (June 2006): 117–46. Available online at http://
chnm.gmu.edu/resources/essays/d/42 (accessed 9 August 2007).

32 For an insightful review of many scholarly objections to Wikipedia, a review also
accompanied by a robust commentary, see Scott Jaschik, 'A Stand against Wikipedia,' http://www.insidehighered.com/news/2007/01/26/wiki (accessed 10 August
2007). See also Brock Read, 'Can Wikipedia Ever Make the Grade?' (Chronicle of
Higher Education, 2006) http://chronicle.com/temp/reprint.php?%20id=z6xht2rj6
0kqmsl8tlq5ltqcshc5y93y (accessed 8 August 2007).

33 Margaret Conrad, 'Public History and Its Discontents.' In 2005, *Nature* published
a content analysis comparing Wikipedia with the *Encyclopedia Britannica*. The
magazine found that while Wikipedia contained errors, the accuracy of its science
entries (based on a sample) was comparable to that of *Britannica*, long considered
the gold standard source of information. See Jim Giles, 'Internet Encyclopedias
Go Head to Head,' http://www.nature.com/news/2005/051212/full/438900a.html
(accessed 8 August 2007). The *Encyclopedia Britannica* disputed the results in
2006, but *Nature* dismissed their objections in a lengthy counter-rebuttal, noting
that 'of the 123 purported errors in question [in *Britannica*], the company takes
issue with less than half, and … Britannica has subsequently corrected many of
the errors that our reviewers identified.' See 'Nature's Responses to Encyclopaedia
Britannica,' http://www.nature.com/nature/britannica/index.html (accessed
8 August 2007).

34 Their description of academic work might be seen as somewhat idealistic. In the
next sentence, they draw another parallel between the aims of academic work and
the aims of Wikipedia by saying 'Academics generally get their jobs because they
like learning and/or teaching others. We do both here.' It is important to point out
that a major objective in Wikipedia is to encourage more academic authors and
administrators to volunteer. 'Wikipedia: replies to common objections – motives
of intellectuals,' http://en.wikipedia.org/wiki/Wikipedia: Replies_to_common_
objections#Shortage_of_intellectuals (accessed 10 August 2007).

35 It is recognized that this will dramatically change the economics of academic
publishing. The many sides of this issue are outlined in Margaret Conrad, 'Going
Down the Digital Highway,' *CHA Bulletin* 32, 2 (2006): 4–6.

36 Those in the information studies field recognize this disparity and its implications,
especially in the large provinces with large rural geographical expanses. The province of British Columbia, for instance, claimed to be the most connected province
in Canada in 2002, but the digital divide between urban and rural areas was still

profound. That same year, the province discovered that over 60 per cent of those in urban areas had home Internet access, while only 45 per cent of those living in rural locations enjoyed the same. This rural-urban divide is particularly strongly felt among rural First Nations communities. Five years ago, a study commissioned by the Premier's Technology Council found that 'The Internet can provide First Nations reserves with the ability for access to more information on government and health matters, and well as the increased ability to communicate with other communities. However, some problems with the [digital] divide include the lack of public access to the Internet on reserves, no training or skills in information technologies, and a lack of socially relevant content.' See Jeffrey Voon/'Digital Divide in Canada,' http://www.slais.ubc.ca/courses/libr500/02–03-wt2/www/J_ Voon/index.htm (accessed 8 August 2007).

37 Cohen and Rosenzweig, *Digital History.*

38 Ibid.

39 Forster, 'Heroines.'

40 See, for instance, the sources of funding listed through Canadian Culture Online (CCO). 'Canadian Culture Online,' (Library and Archives Canada, 2005), http://www.collectionscanada.ca/notices/016–300-e.html (accessed 8 August 2007).

41 'Book of Negroes, c. 1783,' *Remembering Black Loyalists: Black Communities in Nova Scotia,* http://museum.gov.ns.ca/blackloyalists/17751800/objects1775/ booknegroes_lg.htm (accessed 15 June 2007).

42 'Survey of Birchtown,' *Remembering Black Loyalists: Black Communities in Nova Scotia,* http://museum.gov.ns.ca/blackloyalists/17751800/objects1775/survey.htm (accessed 15 June 2007).

43 'Excavation at the Acker Site, 1998,' *Remembering Black Loyalists: Black Communities in Nova Scotia,* http://museum.gov.ns.ca/blackloyalists/19002000/ Events1900/acker_lg.htm (accessed 15 June 2007).

44 'CBC Archives: Relive Our History through CBC Radio and Television,' http:// cbc.ca/archives (accessed 30 April 2007).

45 The site explains, 'During the summer of 2001, the Department of Canadian Heritage approved a joint proposal from the CBC and its French counterpart, Radio-Canada, to create a Web site which would highlight selections from its radio and television archives. Using the latest technology, digital copies of selected programs would be made available online … Though the primary audience is educational, the site was designed and built with every Canadian in mind. Everyone who visits will enjoy its unique perspective on Canada's history.' CBC Digital Archives, 'A Vision for the Archives Online,' http://archives.cbc.ca/info/ apropos_en2.shtml (accessed 23 June 2007).

46 Ibid.

47 The use of the term 'prehistory' is problematic here, reflecting only the slow adop-

tion of language (preferably, in this case, the term 'pre-contact') that recognizes the historical presence of First Nations as a part of history. The http://www .nsexplore.ca site redirects you to http://groups.yahoo.com/group/NSExplore/.

48 'Simancas or Velasco Map of New England and New France (1610),' http://www .nsexplore.ca/simancas/ (accessed 31 May 2007). The original post was: Terry J. Deveau, comment on 'Simancas Map of 1610,' NS Explore – Exploring Nova Scotia, comment posted on August 6, 2004, http://groups.yahoo.com/group/ NSExplore/message/4249 (accessed June 21, 2007).

49 Terry J. Deveau, comment 'Re: Simancas Map of 1610,' NS Explore – Exploring Nova Scotia, comment posted on September 9, 2004, http://groups.yahoo .com/group/NSExplore/message/4371 (accessed June 21, 2007); see also Terry J. Deveau, comment 'Re: Lost Acadia?' NS Explore – Exploring Nova Scotia, comment posted on November 24, 2004, http://groups.yahoo.com/group/NSExplore/ message/4618 (accessed 21 June 2007).

50 Port Cove, comment 'Re: Simancas Map of 1610' NS Explore – Exploring Nova Scotia, comment posted on September 14, 2004, http://groups.yahoo.com/group/ NSExplore/message/4377 (accessed 21 June 2007).

51 The first discussion of the map, and a discussion of who could be the author, is in Isaac Stokes, *The Iconography of Manhattan Island, 1498–1909, vol. II.* Stokes writes that a contemporary of Henry Hudson, an explorer 'whose identity is at present unknown,' but who had the knowledge gathered by Hudson, was sent by James I to find another inland-reaching river that might possibly lead to 'the Western Sea.' Stokes identified 'a man in England at that date, a cartographer, by name John Daniel' (57). See 'Map of Atlantic Coast of North America, 1610 (also known as the 'Velasco Map')' (She-philosopher, 2006), http://www.she-philosopher.com/gallery/1610map.html (accessed 5 June 2007).

52 David Y. Allen, 'The So-Called "Velasco Map": A Case of Forgery?' *Coordinates: The Online Journal of the Map and Geography Round Table of the American Library Association*, series A, no. 5, http://www.sunysb.edu/libmap/coordinates/ seriesa/no5/a5.pdf (accessed 8 June 2007).

53 Terry J. Deveau, comment 'Historical Maps Online' NS Explore – Exploring Nova Scotia, comment posted on February 27, 2006, http://groups.yahoo.com/group/ NSExplore/message/6619 (accessed 21 June 2007).

54 Terry J. Deveau, comment 'Re: Simancas/Velasco Map of 1610,' NS Explore – Exploring Nova Scotia, comment posted November 6, 2006, http://groups.yahoo .com/group/NSExplore/message/7607 (accessed 21 June 2007).

55 Deveau, the first person to post about the Velasco map, went to Maine to give two talks to a group in New England dedicated to exploring the history and significance of what they call ancient stone or 'lithic' sites of the northeast. See 'The New England Antiquities Research Association (NEARA),' http://www.neara.org/

(accessed 20 June 2007). While travelling, he made copies and distributed the map to his American colleagues. Terry J. Deveau, comment on 'NEARA meeting & Ancient Inscription Sites in Nova Scotia,' NS Explore – Exploring Nova Scotia, comment posted November 4, 2004, http://groups.yahoo.com/group/NSExplore/message/4568 (accessed 21 June 2007)

56 Terry J. Deveau, comment 'Re: Simancas Map of 1610,' NS Explore – Exploring Nova Scotia comment posted November 15, 2004, http://groups.yahoo.com/group/NSExplore/message/4588 (accessed 21 June 2007).

57 'Detecting the Truth: Fakes, Forgery and Trickery,' http://www.collectionscanada.ca/forgery (accessed 5 June 2007).

58 'The Wayback Machine,' http://www.archive.org/web/web.php (accessed 15 June 2007).

59 Roy Rosenzweig, 'Scarcity or Abundance? Preserving the Past in a Digital Era,' *American Historical Review* 108, 3 (June 2003): 735–62.

60 Cohen and Rosenzweig, *Digital History*.

61 'Athena's Heirs: Exploring Four Centuries of Canadian Science and Medicine,' http://www.virtualmuseum.ca/Exhibitions/Heirs/index.html (accessed 4 June 2007).

62 Cybertext can be read as roughly the equivalent of hypertext, especially for the purposes of this chapter, which seeks to use hypertextuality to describe non-linear texts. It is a term apparently used more by continental Europeans (Aarseth, below, is Norwegian), whereas hypertext is the dominant word in Anglo-American usage.

63 Espen J. Aarseth, *Cybertext: Perspectives on Ergodic Literature* (Baltimore: Johns Hopkins University Press, 1997).

64 Robert Darnton, 'An Early Information Society: News and Media in Eighteenth Century Paris,' *AHR* (February 2000), available online at http://www.historycooperative.org/journals/ahr/105.1/ah000001.html (accessed 31 May 2007).

65 David J. Staley, *Computers, Visualization, and History: How New Technology Will Transform Our Understanding of the Past* (Armonk, NY: M.E. Sharpe, 2002).

66 As of this writing, these offerings are Jack Censer and Lynn Hunt, 'Imaging the French Revolution: Depictions of the French Revolutionary Crowd,' *electronic – American Historical Review [e-AHR]* (February 2005), http://chnm.gmu.edu/revolution/imaging/home.html (accessed 31 May 2007); William G. Thomas III and Edward L. Ayers, 'An Overview: The Differences Slavery Made: A Close Analysis of Two American Communities,' *e-AHR* (December 2003), http://www.vcdh.virginia.edu/AHR/ (accessed 31 May 2007); Roy Rosenzweig, 'Scarcity or Abundance? Preserving the Past in a Digital Era,' *e-AHR* (June 2003), http://www.historycooperative.org/journals/ahr/108.3/rosenzweig.html (accessed 31 May 2007); Ted Steinberg, 'Down to Earth: Nature, Agency and Power in History,' *e-AHR* (June 2002), http://www.historycooperative.org/journals/ahr/107.3/

ah0302000798.html (accessed 31 May 2007); Darnton, 'An Early Information Society'; Phil Ethington, 'Los Angeles and the Problem of Urban Historical Knowledge,' *e-AHR* (December 2000).

67 William G. Thomas III, 'Blazing Trails toward Digital History Scholarship,' *Histoire Sociale/Social History* 34, 68 (November 2001): 415–26.

68 Turkel is a professor of history, and the creator of Digital History Hacks, an award-winning (Best New Blog, Cliopatria 2006) research weblog wherein he discusses 'the kinds of techniques that are appropriate for an archive that has near-zero transaction costs, is constantly changing and effectively infinite.' William J. Turkel, *Digital History Hacks: Methodology for the Infinite Archive* [Weblog], http://digitalhistoryhacks.blogspot.com/ (accessed 23 July 2007).

69 See 'Public History MA Project (2005–2006)' (Digital History, 2006), http:// digitalhistory.uwo.ca/ma0506/ (accessed 23 July 2007).

70 The term used for this is superposition, which is defined as 'putting more than one thing at a time in the same place or the same space.' William J. Turkel, 'Photogrammerty and Superposition' (Digital History, 2006), http://digitalhistory.uwo.ca/ pbc/index.php/photogrammetry-and-superposition/ (accessed 23 July 2007).

71 William J. Turkel, 'Tagging Places' (Digital History, 2006), http://digitalhistory .uwo.ca/pbc/index.php/tagging-places/ (accessed 23 July 2007).

72 'Public History MA Project (2005–2006)' (Digital History, 2006), http:// digitalhistory.uwo.ca/ma0506/ (accessed 23 July 2007).

73 See also the innovative Oral Historian's Digital Toolbox, http://storytelling. concordia.ca/oralhistorianstoolbox/ (accessed 4 April 2011). These Concordia projects were funded through the Oral History and New Media Knowledge Synthesis Project awarded to Stephen High and Stacey Zembrzycki, although Stephen High's interest in oral history and digital storytelling goes back to 2006 with the founding of CODS and the Montreal Life Stories Project. See Oral History: Concordia University, http://storytelling.concordia.ca/oralhistory/index.html (accessed 11 April 2011). For more examples, see also Joy Parr's site for interactively exploring Megaprojects New Media, http://megaprojects.uwo.ca/ (accessed 11 April 2011), or the site for the major CURA-funded project on Labour History in New Brunswick, http://www.lhtnb.ca/00/en_welcome.cfm (accessed 11 April 2011).

74 Bob Hesketh and Chris Hackett, *Canada, Confederation to the Present* [CD-ROM], Chinook Multimedia Inc., 2003 [first issued 2001].

75 Magda Fahrni, 'Review – *Canada: Confederation to Present* [CD-ROM],' *Canadian Historical Review* 85, 3 (September 2004): 535–7.

76 Ethington, 'Los Angeles and the Problem of Urban Historical Knowledge.'

77 Ibid.

78 'Immigrant Voices' (Chinook Multimedia, 2000), http://www.canadianhistory.ca/ iv/ (accessed 30 May 2007).

79 Chinook Multimedia brought us the first widely distributed new media courseware
    for Canadian history, the CD-ROM *Canada: Confederation to Present.* Hesketh
    and Hackett, *Canada, Confederation to the Present.*.

80 The Association received a $381,418 grant from the Millennium Bureau of
    Canada plus $37,000 from the Department of Canadian Heritage. Conrad, 'Public
    History and Its Discontents.' Among the portals which do exist on the Web, the
    Atlantic Canada Portal, created by Margaret Conrad and maintained at the Uni-
    versity of New Brunwsick, offers a model for how thematic pathways to online
    history and digital documents can storehouse these items along with course syllabi
    and links to other sites. 'Atlantic Canada Portal/Portail du Canada Atlantique,'
    http://atlanticportal.hil.unb.ca/ (accessed 31 May 2007). But for Canadian content,
    one must often rely on the federal government. See Heritage Canada's cultural
    gateway, 'Culture Online: Made in Canada' (Department of Canadian Heritage, no
    date) http://www.culture.ca/english.jsp (accessed 31 July 2007).

81 Interconnections Survey Results, http://interconnectionsreport.org (accessed
    17 March 2008).

82 'Interconnections: The IMLS National Study on the Use of Libraries, Museums
    and the Internet: Conclusions Summary,' http://interconnectionsreport.org/
    presentations/IMLSConclusionsOverview022708.ppt (accessed 17 March 2008).

83 Heather Dunn, 'Collection Level Description – The Museum Perspective,'
    D-Lib Magazine 6, 9 (September, 2000), http://www.dlib.org/dlib/september00/
    dunn/09dunn.html (accessed 4 June 2007).

PART THREE

Visualizing and Revising the Past

9 The Art of Nation-Building: Canadian History Painting, 1880–1914

H.V. NELLES

This chapter is about something that didn't happen, but I hope it will help us see more clearly something that did. I also propose to take my title literally, laying stress upon the first noun, Art. In what follows I will look at a brief and largely overlooked moment in Canadian art history when artists – painters mainly – attempted to act as conscious nation-builders by creating a visual vocabulary of the past for an emerging nation. I invite you to suspend disbelief momentarily and entertain with me the possibility that among other things a nation might be made out of paint.

To those familiar with the recent multidisciplinary literature on nationalism this is not as outlandish a proposition as it once might have seemed. The influential phrase 'imagined communities' places as much emphasis upon the cultural history of imagining together as it does upon the social history of community formation. Political scientists may disagree whether the nation is primordial or essentially modern, whether nations come with navels or without, whether the nation is a necessary or contingent form of political organization, and whether nationalism is a destructive false consciousness whose time is mercifully passing or a constructive, practical force within the global political order. However, they would all agree, in the words of one of the hardest primordialists: 'Nationalism can survive only through an exercise of the imagination, both collective and personal.'[1] Imagining together is the central process of state formation. Beyond Benedict Anderson's famous triumvirate of 'Maps, Museums and Census,' the historical analysis of nation-building turns to the activities of those cultural producers who have shaped imaginations: architects, poets, novelists, musicians, social scientists, historians, school teachers and let us not forget those most hypnotic nation-makers, politicians. Nor is the audience passive; it produces as well as consumes, and even in this latter respect it makes choices. Traumatic mass experiences – wars, depressions – and more quotidian experience, sports, landscape, diet, currency, a conceptualized national economy, and a secular calendar all play their roles in this process. I know of no compendium of nationalizing factors, nor of any choreography showing how they work together. In that context the notion of painters as 'imagineers' of nation is not so unusual.[2]

Nations differ as to kind. It is not simply that they differ in the particular cultural content of their myths; structurally they are also quite different. Theorists have categorized the several kinds of nationalisms: ethnic nationalism or nationalism of the blood, to describe those states (mainly in Eastern Europe) where the boundaries of the nation-state are supposedly coincident with the boundaries of the social nation; civic nationalism captures the experience of those states (Britain, France, and the United States are the usual examples) wherein a variety of different peoples have been melded into one (E pluribus unum). To this pairing Anthony Smith has added a third large category, plural nationalism, a more loosely associated form of unity, where the parts brought together within the nation retain much of their distinctive identities. This is a very large class of states in which Canada figures prominently as a case-study. Compared with the strong civic nationalism of the United States, Smith argues:

> In Canada similar federal arrangements, but without the concomitant unifying myths of origin and foundation, have ensured that within an overarching national legal and political framework, the ethnic communities enjoy wide powers in the economic, political and cultural spheres. Recently, after Quebec's silent revolution, there has been a growing commitment to multiculturalism and the ideal of a plural, polyethnic nation, so much so that, together with the effects of Quebecois secessionist tendencies, the very fabric of any historical identity sustaining the Canadian federation has, many would claim, been jeopardized. In the Canadian case, the dual cultural origins of the state and society, and its liberal immigration policies, have created a unique situation at the very limit of sustainable national identity.[3]

Be that as it may, it is important not to treat the past as prologue, to anticipate change and look backward for origins, influences as causes. Canada developed a distinctive national form during the late nineteenth and twentieth centuries; whatever the future might hold, that historical fact deserves attention on its own terms. The centre was weak, the marches volatile, and to be sure French, British, Indigenous, Male and Female, Immigrant and Region had differential access to power in the shaping of the nation. Nevertheless, that Canada deserves study, to provide a corrective to a literature heavily influenced by the strong ethnic and civic nationalist cases, to provide opportunities for comparative study with the vastly larger number of countries that resemble Canada in their pluralist nature, and to better understand Canada's distinctive past. In that project argument should focus not so much upon explaining why the Canadian case differed from the other models, or why in relative terms nationalism failed, as upon why things were the way they were, why the Canadian experience fitted, why a nationalism of a particular kind emerged in this place, and what that process has to say about other comparable places. To that end I think the experience of Canadian painters, who consciously set out to recreate metropolitan styles locally, offers some insight into the particular character of the Canadian nation-making. Their contribution to the nation-making project was to try to paint its past. They aspired to be the makers of graven images. As we will see, their work was not well received. What does this say about them and their Canada?

History Painting – the word doesn't exist in either of our official languages. Or at least the genre does not appear in any of the major surveys of Canadian art history. This is in a sense a surprising omission when you think about it, for history painting was for several centuries the highest form of art in most Western countries. Moreover, history painters produced the images central in the imaginative construction of several nations. Is this silence or absence an indication that there was no history painting in Canada? Or rather, that there was, but for some reason it did not resonate the way it did in other cultures? Doing the research for my book on the Quebec Tercentenary I stumbled across what appeared to me to be a diverse movement among a small group of Canadian artists, working in several cities, and without much communication between them, aimed at the creation of an indigenous painted history for what might be called civic or nationalist purposes. Together they produced, as I hope to show, a significant body of work. It seemed to me on reflection that this movement might have appeared between chapters 7, 'The French Period in Canadian Art,' and 8, 'Watson and Leduc,' in Dennis Reid's *Concise History of Canadian Art*.[4] Or surely there was room for it among 'French Academic Influences,' 'Contrasts in Quebec,' and 'Painting as an Aesthetic Experience,' before 'Nationalism and Internationalism after 1910,' in J. Russell Harper's canonical *Painting in Canada*.[5] Monographically this episode might have been the unwritten book that would fit on the shelves chronologically between Dennis Reid's *Our Own Country*, about the nationalist impulses of the landscape artists of the 1870s and 1880s, and Maria Tippett's *Canada's War Art* and Charles Hill's *Group of Seven*.[6] Before the First World War, before the Group of Seven, simultaneous with the Royal Academy Period in the organization of Canadian artists, it is possible to detect the stirring of an artistic impulse to paint Canadian history so that art might inspire the nation.

I am certainly not the first person to touch on this matter. In the 1970s Dennis Duffy and Robert Stacey explored the historical output of one of these artists.[7] At about the same time Robert Derome and Jean-René Ostiguy documented the work of the artist who decorated the Quebec Legislative Assembly.[8] More recently Rosalind Peppall and Marylin McKay have written incisively about the civic murals phase of this movement.[9] No one, however, has attempted to put the scattered pictures together and try to see the evanescent movement as a whole.

I didn't know it at the time but my growing curiosity about the Canadian history painters coincided with a renewed interest in this heretofore unfashionable genre of painting among art historians in England, and particularly in the United States.[10] In Great Britain, of course, where history painting may be said to have experienced an earth-shaking revival in the late eighteenth century, the work of Benjamin West, his school, and his rivals has been the subject of lively reinterpretation in recent years. And in France the history painters of the nineteenth century – David, Delacroix, Delaroche, Guericault – have begun to come out of the critical penumbra cast by the later impressionists and modernists.

I do not need the legitimacy of this external intellectual scaffolding to approach my subject, but this scholarship has certainly helped me understand the inspiration for, some of the common features of, and those things that were distinctive about the historical moment in Canadian art. Canadian painters, when they set to work at the end of the nineteenth and beginning of the twentieth century, had these conscious models in their heads. In this chapter I will be talking about Napoleon Bourassa, Robert Harris, George Reid, Marc-Aurèle de Foy Suzor-Coté, Henri Julien, Charles Huot, and Charles W. Jefferys – another Canadian Group of Seven. Travelling and painting abroad, these artists had seen many of the classic historical paintings, and discovered the importance of art in shaping the national pantheon and the corresponding prestige of the artists who had executed these images. For themselves, for the country, and for the future of their people they believed it important to paint their past.

I

From the Renaissance onward History Painting was deemed in theory at least to be the highest form of art. In the standard definition, 'history painting portrayed incidents of actual or fictive history involving significant identifiable personages; it tended to be large in scale, lofty in tone, noble in expression, and didactic in intention.' The ascendency of the genre has been traced to Leon Battista Alberti's fifteenth-century treatise *On Painting*, which instructed artists to look for proper subjects in the works of tragic and comic poets, images of which were certain to move the soul of the beholder. The French, codifying this advice in the seventeenth century, tended to find inspiration in sacred or ancient history. By the beginning of the eighteenth century in Europe a well-understood hierarchy had been established in the art world, with history painting at the top, portraiture next in importance, followed by landscape and at the lowest level still life. In England, Sir Joshua Reynolds reaffirmed this hierarchy, insisting that the proper subject-matter for an artist 'ought to be either some eminent instance of heroic action, or heroic suffering.'[11] The hierarchy in genres created in turn a pecking order among artists. Part of the pleasure of reading John Brewer's immensely rich *Pleasures of the Imagination* comes from observing promoters like Reynolds attempting to improve their reputation from mere tradesmen to the more elevated social status of what today would be called cultural producers. By the end of the eighteenth century, in England and in France history painting commanded at least notional respect as the highest and noblest form of art. Don't take my word for it; go either left or right at the top of the stairs in the National Gallery of Great Britain at the year 1600 divide and you will see the relative truth of this assertion. Though the paintings themselves commanded only a small portion of the total market in pictures – 10 per cent is the current estimate – they were accorded the greatest prestige, a sentiment carried to North America in the early nineteenth century by knowledgeable artists and critics. In the salon these massive 'grandes machines' were hung higher up on the walls, dominating the upper reaches of the galleries. One literally looked up to history painting.[12]

Benjamin West's *The Death of General Wolfe*, shown first in 1770, revolutionized the genre by putting a modern face on historical art. The frostiness of the reception of his innovation of heroes in contemporary dress by the king and the critics, and the enormous popular success of the work, are the stuff of legend. West's justification as quoted to the novelist and biographer John Galt, equally well known, is worth repeating in this context. Defending himself against the charge that he had failed to drape his figures in the classic costumes of antiquity suitable to their inherent greatness, he replied:

... the event intended to be commemorated took place on the 13th of September, 1759 in a region of the world unknown to the Greeks and Romans, and at a period of time when no such nations, nor heroes in their costumes, any longer existed. The subject I have to represent is the conquest of a great province of America by British troops ... If, instead of the facts of the transcription, I represent classical fictions, how shall I be understood by posterity! ... I want to mark the date, the place and the parties engaged in the event; and if I am not able to dispose of the circumstances in a picturesque manner, no academic distribution of Greek or Roman costume will enable me to do justice to the subject.[13]

'Picturesque manner' is hardly the phrase to describe his second achievement. His flight from the absurd and pursuit of the literal truth are not nearly so important as something else he did to history painting. West assembled his figures in a form that gave a literal rendering a deeper, symbolic meaning. Oddly enough for a profoundly Protestant connoisseurship, the deep structure is a *pietà*, a death of Christ. In such a transfiguration the death is not a loss. To make the obvious point, despite the ebbing of a brilliant life and the grief evident among the survivors, this is not a painting of a British defeat. Victory not only creeps in from the edges (the French banner borne by the runner, the clouds giving way to sunshine), but in the cruciform main grouping, a victory more enduring than life shouts out its name to anyone familiar with Christian iconography. West's revolution in history painting consisted in infusing the genre with visual attention to historical accuracy[14] and giving the event 'epic intent,' which, by superimposing archetypes on events, was slightly at odds with the first goal. Thirdly, West set out to convey moral intent through the representation, to inspire viewers with the values on display. His painting is infused with moral and national purpose, which is why it is on the cover of Anthony Smith's book *Nationalism and Modernism*.[15] Taken together these three achievements in West's painting constitute the 'modern' in the revival of history painting in the late eighteenth century. It was West's genius as a symbolist, combined with his realism and patriotic purpose, which gave history painting new life.[16]

To make a petty point, this modernism was an American infusion in two respects: the artist was American, from Philadelphia, and the subject was Canadian, the Battle of the Plains of Abraham, a novel theatre for heroic art. It is fitting, therefore, that this first modern history painting, and for a century or more to come the reigning inspiration for all inspiring history painters, should now be situated in the National Gallery of Canada. That is where you can see the original painting, the one initially rejected by George III and damned with faint praise by Reynolds. It was purchased by Lord Grosvenor, whose descendants generously donated it to Lord Beaverbrook's Canadian War Art Memorials committee in gratitude for Canada's contribution to the First World War. Meanwhile George III had a change of heart as a result of the enormous public acclaim. So, West painted another version for him. Not stopping there, he and his students painted at least four more copies for other patrons and some of Wolfe's officers.[17]

West's success launched him on a lucrative career. If anyone rose through art to the highest reaches of society, professional recognition, and critical acclaim – a lifetime of commissions, a princely income, a Royal appointment, and eventually the presidency of the Royal Academy – it was he. He spawned a host of imitators. As artists searched to repeat his magic formula, the walls of salons were covered in a plague of dying figures, mainly military: *The Death of Major Pierson, The Death of Major Warren, The Death of the Earl of Chatham, The Death of Colonel Moorehouse, The Death of General Montgomery, The Death of Lord Nelson*, and so on.[18]

Nor was the revolution in history painting confined to Britain. Some of the most memorable and lasting images of nineteenth-century French art flow from this revivified genre: David's *Death of Marat*, Delacroix's *Liberty Leading the People* – these pictures distilled the spirit of the Revolution, becoming in time familiar icons of French nationality.[19] Peasants were made into Frenchmen in part by pictures like these and the symbols embedded in them or derived from them – such as Marianne. Delaroche's *Execution of Lady Jane Gray* and Guericault's *Raft* are more purely moments of pathos. French painters sought to render a moment in a narrative flow when the final outcome remained suspended in doubt. The viewer both shared in the momentary exhilaration of other possibilities and brought closure and release of the tension by knowing how it all would end.[20] It is this tension between apprehension and anticipation in the mind of a knowing viewer that painting of this sort depended upon for its effect.

West also attracted three generations of students, most of them American, who created a wonderfully rich body of work, and here, after this excursion, we begin to circle back towards the main theme. John Singleton Copley, another expatriate American, echoed West's triumph with a much more animated scene of British military heroism, *The Death of General Pierson*. The work of another student, John Trumbull, re-exported this artistic revolution back across the Atlantic to the United States. Trumbull consciously chose similar moments in U.S. history which, painted in this manner, would tell the story of America in a moving and memorable way. His *Death of General Warren*, painted in Benjamin West's studio, rested upon the same emotion of a personal triumph that would transcend defeat and death. This is a picture of an American defeat, but of course it is not. Rather, the virtue that shines through in the symbolism, the bravery, dedication, and democratic comradeship, notwithstanding the social tensions and status anxieties also embedded in the picture, would, as the viewer well knew, eventually triumph. Trumbull brought history painting to America where it took root.[21]

Throughout the first half of the nineteenth century, U.S. painters, feeding the desire for patriotic images, and responding to the aesthetic imperative of history painting, created a body of work that amounted to a painted pantheon for the nation. The government of the United States acted as a hesitant patron of this movement, purchasing paintings to be applied to the walls of the Rotunda, including Trumbull's *Declaration of Independence*, John Vanderlyn's *Death of Jane McCrea* and *The Landing of Columbus*, John Chapman's *Baptism of Pocahontas*, Robert Weir's *Embarkation of the Pilgrims at Delft*, and William Powell's *Discovery of the Mississippi* and *Westward the Course of Empire Takes*.[22] Emanuel Leutze's *Washington Crosses the Delaware*, painted in 1851, represented the apotheosis of history painting in the United States. With this the history painters found an image that fused realism, idealism, and patriotism into one iconographic statement. It too is a suspended moment – a crossing contested by nature and the enemy, the figures in their separate but complementary ways bending into the common cause and melting into a single mass projecting form led by the figure of George Washington. Leutze's career, with its roots in Dusseldorf, reminds us of currents other than British, French, and Italian flowing through this genre.[23]

The art history of the United States in the first half of the nineteenth century afforded even closer stimulation for the nascent Canadian artistic imagination. There was a large body of well-known work, critically acclaimed, highly popular, imbued with nationalistic purpose, right next door. Here was a model for the grand manner of heroic history painting applied successfully in a North American setting. Most of the Canadian painters would have seen the European models as well in their tours and years of study in London and Paris. What would happen in Canada would be wholly derivative in a theoretical and a practical way from this previous history.

To conclude this part of the chapter with a few propositions upon which the rest will depend: History painting played a significant role in the making of nations and of artists. Some of the most memorable and moving images of all time were inspired by this genre. Aspiring colonial artists had this achievement in the back of their minds. History painting offered both a purpose for art and a route to security and respectability for the artists. With West's *Death of General Wolfe* burning in their imaginations and three generations of European and U.S. images as further inspiration, Canadian artists also responded to the implicit challenge of history painting. What then did they accomplish?

II

Before I launch into an analysis of the Canadian history painting oeuvre it might be useful to answer a few questions. Who precisely are the artists I am talking about? When and where did they work? And what, if anything, did they have to do with each other?

The active careers of the seven artists who might be called the Canadian History Painters, Napoleon Bourassa (1827–1916), Robert Harris (1849–1919), George Reid (1860–1947), Marc-Aurèle de Foy Suzor-Coté (1869–1937), Henri Julien (1800–1908), Charles Huot (1855–1930), and C.W. Jefferys (1869–1951), covered more than a century, but history painting proper was confined primarily to the two decades before the First World War. These men – and they were all men – were not of the same generation, but for a brief moment they were all doing similar things at about the same time. They lived in different cities; they did not for the most part communicate with one another (except perhaps occasionally at Royal Academy meetings if they were members); they most certainly did not constitute a self-conscious group. Notwithstanding their differences and their distance from one another, they all sought to paint a history for the country for quite similar reasons. An idea and an agenda bound them together.[24]

For a group of not particularly well known artists you might reasonably expect at this point a brief digression into biography. But in a short paper this is not possible. The most salient point about them with respect to the argument I wish to make is that, with the exception of Henri Julien and C.W. Jefferys, all of these artists had been formally trained abroad, and had spent considerable time living and working in Europe. Napoleon Bourassa left Theophile Hamel's Montreal studio, where he did his apprenticeship, for two years of study and travel in Italy and France in the early 1850s. Robert Harris, who had been trained in Boston, Liverpool, and London, had attended the Slade School and haunted the National Gallery and spent two years in Paris in the late 1870s studying at the Atelier Bonnat. He returned again, continuing to Florence and Rome in 1881. A few years later George Reid had installed himself in Paris for two years of study, having received his initial training in Philadelphia with Thomas Eakins. Indeed there were enough Canadian artists in Paris in the last decades of the nineteenth century for the National Gallery of Canada to mount a very creditable touring exhibition of their work. Suzor-Coté and Charles Huot, arriving in Paris just after the turn of the century, represented the third generation of Canadians to be trained in Paris and in the process exposed to the major works in Western art history. The point is that these men may have been provincials in the sense that they came from the provinces, but they acquired metropolitan sensibilities through their instruction and exposure to the art in Florence, Rome, Paris, London, New York, and Philadelphia. They were familiar with the hierarchies in the world of art. They knew of the status, power, and career possibilities associated with history painting in England, France, Italy, and the United States. And they had seen with their own eyes many of the major works in the genre.[25]

When they returned to Canada they naturally tried to replicate the process in their own country. I do not wish to overdetermine this tendency, nor in hindsight make it a coherent and coordinated campaign. It was not. Rather, a group of quite disparate artists, from different generations, working in different styles, with little or no contact with one another, tried individually over a long period of time to accomplish similar ends. This was a movement without a leader and without a consciousness of itself. Their effort might be styled more of a collective inclination than a school. It came from their training and experience rather than a joint manifesto. There is no *Refus Global* or Studio Building to integrate their work. Indeed their association exists only within the logic of this chapter. Individually and over a long period of time each artist attempted whenever possible to paint history. It had not happened before, and it has not occurred much since. It is this fragile, fleeting, will-o'-the-wisp moment in the history of essentially central Canadian art that interests me.

Bourassa returned from Europe sceptical about the possibility of creating a great Canadian art in part because of the inadequacies of Canadian history. All of the great myths were geographically situated in other regions, the biblical Middle East, classical Greece and Rome, Renaissance and early modern Western Europe. In his career as an artist, critic, and church architect, he nevertheless tried to find ways of linking North America with European iconography. Within the Catholic religious tradition, of course, he was able to directly transfer imagery, churches echoing metropolitan models, murals and decorations influenced by great religious frescos and paintings. It was in the secular realm that he experienced much greater difficulty. As early as 1869 he completed a sketch for a large work entitled the *Apothéose de Christophe Colomb*. For the rest of his life he toiled away at this massive painting, which in symbolic terms attempted to represent the curvilinear descent of North American genius from its European and classical roots. He reported to the Quebec government on the importance of art education and in 1883 advised on the decoration of the proposed new Legislative Building. Here was an opportunity, he argued, to open up a dignified showcase for artists and for 'l'art national' which in a memorable and indelible way would preserve 'la mémoire des hommes et des faits glorieux de notre histoire.'[26] Neither his plan for the legislature nor his own picture was achieved in his lifetime. History painting, in Bourassa's case, became a magnificent obsession never to be fully consummated.[27]

For Robert Harris, on the other hand, history painting came to him more or less unbidden. Returning from Europe, Harris had established himself in Montreal and then in Toronto as Canada's leading portrait painter. During the 1880s, the age of integration overtook many of the participants of the Confederation movement, and the Parliament of Canada found itself in a momentary mood of moderate satisfaction. It was in this auspicious moment that the Royal

Academy of Arts suggested that the government commission a formal painting to commemorate Confederation and even proposed that Robert Harris should do it. Wilfrid Laurier, speaking for the Liberal opposition, commended the idea to the government as well as the selection of Robert Harris, a Canadian artist much celebrated in Europe, to do the job. Such a painting would both promote Canadian art and commemorate an important event. These words coming from the opposition and from someone who had been among the opponents of Confederation at the time carried some weight. In what surely must have been one of the few occasions in which art was discussed on the floor of the House of Commons in the nineteenth century, John A. Macdonald, discussing a painting in which he himself would necessarily be the central figure, handed the commission to Harris with gracious and amusing self-deprecation:

> As regards this particular painting he could have no personal objection to have another artist try his hand upon himself. There was another Canadian artist who had drawn him with great power and graphic skill, and he thought, under the principle of wholesome competition, he might hope that Mr. Harris, whose paintings he had not yet seen, might, by slow degrees, rise to the artist's skill and perfect accuracy in portraying his countenance that his friend Bengough possessed (Laughter). He believed from the kindly manner in which this proposal had been spoken of, that the general sense of the House was in favour of it, and the Government would take care that a sum was placed in the estimates for carrying out the will of the House (Applause).

And thus began a commission that started off as a painting of the Charlottetown Conference to gradually become *The Meeting of the Delegates of British North America to Settle Terms of Confederation, October, 1864*, more popularly known ever since as *The Fathers of Confederation*.[28]

By the 1890s the Toronto artist George Reid had established himself as the leading genre painter in the country. In a manner Christine Boyanski has aptly styled 'sympathetic realism,' Reid achieved great success capturing individuals or groups in suspended instants of intense emotion, perhaps even melodrama. Teaching in the art school, painting prolifically with his wife Mary Heister Reid, and enjoying life in an upper New York State artists' colony, Reid was at the peak of his powers and reputation at the turn of the century, yet he yearned for something more for himself as an artist, for the fledgling community of artists around him – many of them his students – and for the wider community. He would too have known the relative status of genre art in his profession. As a result of his French experience he had begun to conceive of art as having a civic purpose, a powerful means of inculcating beliefs, stating what the community valued in a way readily grasped by a wide audience, thereby transmitting those virtues to succeeding generations.[29]

In 1897 he launched a campaign for what today we would call ' public art' that would continue for the rest of his long life. Reid, as spokesman for a group of these 'mural decorators,' had to defend his public crusade before a suspicious, turf-protecting Ontario Society of Artists. He had been inspired in 1889, during his stay in Paris, by the extensive program of decoration of the newly constructed public buildings of the Third Republic.[30] On his return to Toronto he had gathered a few like-minded artists together to promote mural decoration for the newest public space, Union Station. But the railways had no money for art. Reid's group then turned to the City of Toronto, whose new city hall was taking shape on Queen Street. Artists knew they didn't have much standing with politicians; they hoped bourgeois respectability would. Under the banner of the Toronto Civic Guild of Art on 18 March a small delegation of civic-minded businessmen, led by the respected banker and art patron Edmund Byron Walker, descended upon the Board of Control, urging the municipal government to seize the opportunity to embellish the spacious hall of the new building with ennobling art. The four walls need not be covered all at once, reducing the expense. Paintings completed over a longer period of time would also demonstrate, as Walker tactfully explained, the progressive development of Canadian art: 'The work thus progressing, step by step, would show the progress of home art during a long period, and the designs, representing the history of the municipality, and the ideals and virtues of its citizens, would be of historic interest and artistic value.' The four artists behind the scheme, George Reid, Wylie Grier, William Cruickshank, and Frank Challener, had conceived of an overall design for the four panels including one hundred figures: 'At the south end of the Chamber three panels illustrating the city's motto, Industry, Integrity and Intelligence. And on the centre of the west wall Government having on either side panels representing Peace and Prosperity. The whole is a representation (simplified according to the requirements of decoration) of the pioneer days of Toronto. Art and Science are the subjects of the two entrance panels, and these are treated classically on account of the nature of the theme.' The murals would cost in total $4000 or, for the practical-minded, real estate–addled alderman, $4.50 a square foot.[31] To suggest something of what might be accomplished and to further prepare the way, the Toronto Civic Art Guild also organized an exhibition of prints by the American history painter Thomas Copley. At the opening Walker spoke not only of the civic utility of art, but also of its simultaneous representation of progress in the material realm and demonstration of the higher cultural achievements of the society. The Copley prints showed what had already been done in the Library of Congress in Washington and the Public Library in Boston. The quality of public art, he implied, measured the degree of advancement of civilization. Toronto therefore needed more civic art to confirm its progressive standing.[32] Nevertheless, the parsimonious city council demurred. Reid famously went ahead and painted one of these murals by himself, *Hail to the Pioneers*, donating it to the city as a demonstration project, in the hope of jump-starting the larger enterprise. To no avail. The city fathers remained unmoved both by his generosity, and, apparently, by the finished product. The other three spaces remain bare to this day.[33]

Undaunted, Reid's forces regrouped. Early in the new century, with prominent businessmen once again providing protective cover, they campaigned for public patronage at the provincial and federal levels. Both governments occupied large public buildings, brand new in the case of Ontario, entirely devoid of patriotic decoration. In Ontario the Toronto Guild of Civic Art shifted its attention northward from the new City Hall to the new legislative building in Queen's Park. When their preliminary report on a possible scheme of decoration received some encouragement, the artists worked up a comprehensive program of historical pictures for the main entrance, corridors, grand staircase, and foyer leading into the Legislative Chamber. Walking through the vestibule into the entrance hall, visitors would be surrounded first by images of Indian Life, and then a succession of canvases depicting exploits of the explorers and episodes of founding: Cabot discovering Cape Breton in 1497, Cartier at Quebec, Maisonneuve laying out Montreal, Franklin on the Arctic Ocean, Champlain building Port-Royal, LaVerendraye in the Saskatchewan Valley, Mackenzie at the Pacific, Hennepin at Niagara Falls, the Founding of Fort Frontenac, Lasalle at the launch of the *Griffin*, and Champlain on Lake Huron. On the walls of the east and west corridors on the main floors would be represented the North West Company post at Fort William, a 'Grand Council of Whites and Indians' on Manitoulin in 1837. The upper corridor would be given over to settlement, Highlanders in Glengarry, French settlers on the Detroit River. The grand staircase leading up to the library and then the legislature was clearly a place of honour. On these walls the Guild of Artists proposed to paint images of Joseph Brant, Galt and the Founding of Guelph, Fort Rouillé, Penetanguishine, side by side the Death of Brock and the Death of Tecumseh, opposite the Battle of Chrysler's Farm and Laura Secord's brave journey. Flanking the entrance to the legislature on the upper floor were scenes of United Empire Loyalists landing at Johnstown, immigrants arriving at Toronto, Governor Simcoe landing at Toronto, and the opening of the First Parliament of Upper Canada. Painting these scenes would require a 'strong grasp of the dramatic aspect of the subject,' accuracy of historical detail, and technical excellence, but the result would be a gallery representing 'the best work of our most distinguished painters.' It was, to be sure, an ambitious program that filled virtually all of the blank wall-space of the legislature with history paintings, but the program could be broken up into smaller packages to be accomplished over an extended period. Once again newspapers offered muted support and the politicians mewed encouragement, but found various excuses for not being able to afford the luxury of $20,000 worth of decoration when building costs exceeded earlier estimates. According to Reid, a fire that required extensive rebuilding of parts of the legislature finally doomed the project.[34]

Reid was not easily discouraged. At about the same time, as president of the Royal Canadian Academy, he pressed upon the Government of Canada a similar program of art for the bare walls of the Parliament Buildings. The governor-general, Earl Grey, who understood the role of symbols in the building of nations, was extremely enthusiastic. Sir Wilfrid Laurier pronounced a more cautious blessing. Reid and his colleagues in the Academy, who included William Brymner, Montreal, Frank Challener, Toronto, E. Dyonnet, Montreal, William Cruikshank, Toronto, Franklin Brownell, Ottawa, and Gustav Hahn, Toronto, met several times, devised an overall theme, divided labour on it, and even arranged some studio space to work up a plan and some preliminary drawings for presentation to a committee headed by the deputy minister of public works. Whereas the plan for the Ontario Legislature consisted of documentary tableaux, for the national parliament the artists proposed a three-part design: an entrance hall of allegorical themes, historical subjects for the Senate and Commons chambers, and an encircling frieze and decorated dome in the library depicting 'great men of literature.' To begin, the Royal Academy committee focused its attention on the first part of the grand plan, the entrance hall. No particular artists had been suggested for the Toronto commission, whereas in Ottawa named artists from the Academy were assigned wall-space upon which they were to work out a theme within the framework of the overall design. Collectively they believed that 'a symbolic subject in processional form' depicting 'Canada Receiving the Homage of Her Faithful Sons,' to be painted by Reid himself, ought to command the central location of honour on the north-facing wall. In this painting, 'The various sections of the Dominion could be appropriately represented with their various occupations, and to make a picturesque effect the typical products could be borne in various ways, allowing the introduction of animals and vehicles; these, with figures of men, women and children, would combine in a Pageant of brilliant colour with a centre where a figure symbolic of Canada, supported by figures representing the Provinces, and pages bearing the coats of arms, receives with acclaim the homage of her children.' Flanking and facing Reid's mural, *Ave Canada*, which he worked up in sketch form, were to be complementary murals by the other members of the committee depicting 'western and eastern development reaching toward the centre in the foreground [see figure 9.1]. The figures representing the early beginnings of Canada to be in the centre and semi-circular part of the south wall, the panels on the right and left of the same wall, and those of the east and west walls to show the gradual steps of development to the present time; the west side to represent the west, the east to represent the east.' A statue by Gustave Hahn would occupy the centre of the court.[35]

The plan was received with considerable enthusiasm by the politicians, and the deputy minister of public works was authorized to include a significant sum in the next year's estimates to begin the work. At this point something derailed the project. Perhaps the glitch occurred when the artists raised the estimated price from $15,000 to $25,000. It could have been shelved in a fit of fiscal prudence; or perhaps other artists objected; perhaps, too, some people thought the whole scheme a little too ambitious given the state of the arts in Canada. Laurier, who had given the artists a good deal of rhetorical support, next proposed the creation of an Art Advisory Council, chaired by Sir George Drummond of Montreal, with Walker of Toronto and an MP from Montreal as members, to evaluate the whole question of government support for art, including art for the parliament buildings. Notwithstanding Walker's eagerness to get on with the Academy's mural project, the other members of the committee were considerably less enthusiastic. It was in this advisory committee that the Parliamentary mural project died in 1907. Much later Reid claimed that Drummond did not believe Canadian artists were capable of carrying off a major commission of this sort.

But all was not lost. From 1904 when the idea had first been broached, and annually thereafter as the Royal Academy used its Ottawa exhibitions to lobby for more government support of the arts in Canada, the artists had gradually moved themselves from a specific project of parliamentary decoration to the promotion of another institutional vehicle for Canadian art. Not only did the government increase the grant to the Academy, but also as a result of the Art Advisory Council the National Gallery was rejuvenated, rehoused, given a proper budget and a director, and began to purchase the work of Canadian artists. The Academicians had failed in their efforts to turn the Parliament Buildings into a showcase for Canadian art and to assume their role as creators of a visual vocabulary of nation-building; nevertheless they did succeed in creating a National Gallery to which they were able to sell their pictures. History had not disappeared from the agenda; it was expressed, however, in a different form. Nor had it been entirely banished from Parliament Hill. The Council also busied itself running a competition for a Baldwin-Lafontaine memorial statue. The Art Advisory Council minutes reveal that it acted in effect as the

9.1 George A. Reid, *Ave Canada*, 1907, altered 1918, oil on canvas. National Gallery of Canada, Accession 30049.

purchasing committee for the new National Gallery. History painting would therefore acquire display space, but it would be on the walls of a National Gallery rather than Parliament.[36] In hindsight, given that the Parliament Buildings were destined to burn down, destroying Harris's *Fathers of Confederation* in the process, this is perhaps not a bad outcome.

Reid's imagination was obviously fired by the historical pageants and re-enactments at the Quebec Tercentenary in July 1908. He was there on the Plains of Abraham, along with most of the other artists in this group, sketching rapidly with pastels. He dashed off six gossamer representations of pageants on the spot, including a large triptych of the spectacular Francis I Fontainbleau scene. Champlain obviously fascinated him; in one drawing he captures in blues and greys the melancholy of the adventurer at the margin of the known, looking back. In his studio afterwards Reid worked up one of these sketches into a glowing oil of Champlain's arrival at Quebec in the ship *Don de Dieu*. Significantly this canvas, executed in 1908 from drawings made during the Quebec Tercentenary re-enactments, became one of the earliest acquisitions of the newly revived National Gallery.[37]

During this period the prime minister found himself under pressure from another source, closer to home, a young artist named Marc-Aurèle de Foy Suzor-Coté, a Laurier protégé from his home constituency of Arthabaska. In 1900 Suzor-Coté prevailed upon the prime minister for letters of introduction and recommendation. The prime minister obviously liked his young friend, and went to considerable lengths to promote his career, obtaining railroad passes for him and wherever possible intervening gently on his behalf. Suzor-Coté hoped to launch his career with the sale of large historical paintings. On his return from Paris in 1902 he had hoped to sell his *La Mort de Montcalm* to the government of Quebec; it was still available. A second sojourn in Paris produced another large canvas, *Cartier rencontre les Indiens*.[38] Laurier's publicly expressed interest in encouraging the arts and the noisy campaign by largely anglophone artists of the Royal Academy for the decoration of the Parliament Buildings quickened Suzor-Coté's interest, and in 1907 he approached the prime minister directly about selling his *Cartier* to the government. It would fit nicely on the walls of the Senate as part of the larger scheme of historical works. Laurier agreed. But by this time the decision was no longer Laurier's alone, if it ever had been. The Arts Advisory Committee had been established; it would have to be persuaded. Accordingly Laurier did what he could, writing each member of the Council, urging them to visit Suzor-Coté's studio in Montreal to look at this historical canvas with a view to purchasing it. Suzor-Coté gathered letters of recommendation from his Parisian teachers, thinking this might impress the committee. Laurier knew better.[39]

Once again this committee became the burial ground for the ambitions of historical painting. The adverse judgment of the Arts Advisory Council is unambiguously recorded in the minutes of 1 February 1908: 'The Council wish to state that they are opposed to the placing of Coté picture of the Landing of Jacques Cartier or any other style of picture in the Senate.' Connoisseurship, emphasizing the value of authenticity, conflicted with an artistic sensibility of heightening the contrast between civilization and 'savagery.'

Suzor-Coté did carve out a niche for himself in the art world as a sculptor of habitant 'folk figures,' and a painter of impressionist-inspired winter landscapes and of genre scenes. He had already painted two large historical works, but he could not sell them. Both his *Montcalm* and his *Cartier* were much on display during the 1908 Quebec Tercentenary, but still there was no interest in them. Though his career as an artist prospered, he never lost his desire to paint and sell large scale-history paintings. Perhaps encouraged finally by his sale of his *Cartier* to the new Musée de Québec in 1913, he tried a large-scale historical work once again, this time depicting Champlain's landing at Quebec, probably inspired by the re-enactments of the Tercentenary (see figure 9.2). Only a fragment of this painting survives because, as his biographer asserts, after struggling in vain to get any Canadian museum or patron to purchase it, he tore it to pieces in a rage. This frustrated fury of slashing and ripping provides a suitable emotional climax to the unconsummated relationship between the artists and their audience during this historical turn in Canadian painting.

Suzor-Coté's friend Charles Huot had somewhat greater success with the genre. Having passed an extended apprenticeship in France and Belgium, Huot returned to Quebec permanently in 1907 following the death of his wife. In France he had concentrated on painting figures, landscapes, and historical costumes. At some point around the turn of the century he had worked up a study in oils of *La Bataille des Plaines d'Abraham*. Upon his homecoming for the Tercentenary he received a lucrative commission to design the costumes for the historical pageants. About 130 small watercolours from this project still survive in the archives of the National Battlefields Commission. The spectacle of the Tercentenary perhaps played a role in reviving enthusiasm among Quebec legislators to complete the much delayed interior decoration of their ornate Legislature, already generously adorned outside with statuary. Huot's location in Quebec City, and his reputation as a popular painter of village scenes and Quebec life, stood him in good stead when the government commissioned a large historical work for the Assembly. From 1910 until his death in 1930, Charles Huot was engaged more or less full time in the execution of a succession of three large works for the Legislature: *Le débat sur les langues* (1910–13) for a wall of the Legislative Assembly; an allegorical work, *Je Me*

9.2 Marc-Aurèle de Foy Suzor-Coté, Étude pour *L'Arrivée de Samuel de Champlain à Québec*, 1908–9, pastel on paper. Musée national des beaux-arts du Québec, 34.32.

Souviens (1916–20), modelled on Bourassa's *Apothéose*, for the ceiling; and a large painting entitled *Le Conseil Souverain* for the Legislative Council chamber (1926–31), the latter completed by assistants when his health failed. Huot then, under the patronage of the Government of Quebec, was able to realize several large-scale historical paintings.[40]

Henri Julien and Charles Jefferys, on the other hand, came from entirely different artistic backgrounds. They were newspaper artists, magazine and book illustrators, masters of the quick sketch from life, and in Julien's case the political cartoon. Jefferys had received formal instruction in Toronto with George Reid. Julien was essentially self-taught. Despite their immersion in current events, both men developed an interest in historical representation. In the 1880s Julien had produced more than a hundred sketches of the Rebellions of 1837–8. In the 1890s Jefferys and a group of his friends, who made their living as commercial artists, had some success with a calendar depicting scenes from Canadian history. Julien developed a profitable sideline drawing habitant figures and painting scenes from French-Canadian 'folk tales,' the most famous being *La Chasse Galerie*. His most fully realized history painting, however, was done for the Tercentenary of Quebec, a large fold-out lithograph of the Historical Procession, done in a style vaguely reminiscent of the Bayeux Tapestry, which was included as a supplement to the rotogravure weekly Montreal *Standard* in July, 1908. Julien died prematurely soon afterwards, his heart supposedly fatally strained by the effort to complete this grandiose work.[41] Jefferys too did some striking work for the Tercentenary, a golden lithograph of Champlain assuming possession of the vast Kingdom of Canada from the Native people. Thereafter historical illustration became the mainstay of his career. His lithographs illustrated the Makers of Canada Series and numerous other historical works. Alienated somewhat from contemporary modern trends in art, Jefferys threw himself ever deeper into historical research in order to render more accurately the visual dimensions of the past. Indeed it could be said that gradually he became more of a historian and less of an artist. He must be the only artist who has published an article in the *Canadian Historical Review*. Active in the Ontario Historical Association for most of his life, he became its president in the 1940s. He was consulted by the Historic Sites and Monuments Board during the reconstruction of Port-Royal, and he led historical tours. In time he became sufficiently well known to publish multivolume illustrated histories on his own, which ran into several printings.[42] There is no telling where history painting might have taken Julien had he lived; but for Jefferys a highly specialized form of the genre became his livelihood. His spare line drawings of political and domestic life became indelibly imprinted upon several generations of Canadian schoolchildren from their history textbooks as the way the past looked.

The historical turn in Canadian painting ran from the 1880s through to the first war, though Jefferys continued to earn his living from his historical drawings into the 1950s. Huot continued to paint away at the walls and ceilings of the Quebec Legislature until 1930. As we have seen, Suzor-Coté momentarily resumed his career as a history painter in the mid-1920s, only to abandon it in disgust. George Reid also returned to history painting about the same time, designing a magnificent cabinet with painted historical panels of 'The Discoverers' for Sigmund Samuel, and a series of murals about the exploration of Canada for Jarvis Collegiate Institute in Toronto. But the centre of gravity in Canadian art had shifted decidedly away from this kind of representation by the outbreak of the First World War, and most certainly afterwards. The artists, as we have seen, wanted to paint more of the past than their audiences and patrons seemed prepared to support. Only a small portion of what they wanted to paint even reached the study stage, much less the fully realized large-scale oil. But if you look carefully there is a small body of work there where the tide of Western history painting belatedly washed up on the Canadian shore.

III

So much for the politics and ambition of Canadian history painting. What of the work itself? What if anything can be said about this oeuvre? First of all I do not wish to 'rehabilitate' these paintings, or make exaggerated claims for them as works of 'art.' Nor can I attempt a comprehensive survey of the complete works from this distance in a short chapter. Instead what I would like to do is look closely at several examples of Canadian history painting, try to see what there is to be seen within the frame, and then attempt to understand their limitations in this context as iconographic representations. The painters wanted to assume their rightful role as nation builders. As cultural producers they offered – for a price – to provide a visual vocabulary of historical identity. To be blunt about it, the patrons and the politicians said in effect, no thanks. Why was the connection, forged successfully in other countries, so incompletely made in Canada? Why did the audience resist?

Bourassa's towering monochromatic images were too cerebral, idealist, and cold for his time; in any event his major work was never displayed. Henri Julien and C.W. Jefferys, though prolific and influential on the popular imagination, never worked up their drawings into a grand machine. For the purposes of this discussion I will zero in on Harris's *Fathers of Confederation*, Suzor-Coté's *Death of Montcalm* and *Arrival of Cartier*, Huot's *Battle of the Plains of Abraham* and *The Language Debate*, and Reid's *Champlain*, six major attempts at iconographic statement in the grand style.

Let's begin with Robert Harris's *Fathers of Confederation*, perhaps the best known of these works. The first thing to be said about this image is, of course, that it no longer exists. The painting was destroyed by fire in 1916. The artist was asked to repaint the lost picture three decades after he had first painted it. We know it now only by a graphite study done by the artist for the larger work, a few black-and-white photographs of the original, and an unauthorized copy made by Frank Challener for the Hotel Macdonald in Edmonton (see figure 9.3). Our understanding of the image is necessarily degraded by the several degrees of copying involved in its transmission. The most accessible version of the picture is Challener's copy of his copy commissioned by the Government of Ontario in 1919, which since the 1950s has been hanging in the grand stairway at the Ontario Legislature.[43]

The Fathers of Confederation is a picture devoid of drama and in large measure colour. The artist sent a questionnaire to the participants asking about the clothing worn on the occasion; the answers came back almost uniformly black. Most of the classic elements are there, balance, geometry, a flattened perspective, but it is not an inspiring picture. The scene is much brightened, and a future for the country symbolically opened up, by the large windows imported into the Quebec scene from the Toronto Normal School. But there is no action here caught in suspension; no outcome held in doubt, no archetype that flashes into mind. It is rather more in the nature of a team photograph, a posed arrangement, staged for the purposes of observation. It might just as readily mark a real estate transaction or the closing of a business deal. The *Fathers* owes much to photography; indeed it greatly resembles in my mind those composite photographs of legislatures and city councils assembled from individual portraits in the late nineteenth century. There is no action in the picture; no signing, coming together in agreement. Rather the delegates are scattered about the central actors in little provinces; structurally the painting is a federation rather than an organic union. On reflection it is astonishing how the room dominates the scene. The men do not fill the frame. To get everyone in on the lateral axis, the vertical had to be adjusted proportionately. As a result there is a great deal of empty space within this picture, a sign perhaps of the creative deficiencies of the artist. There is a heavily varnished warmth in the Challener reproduction that too quickly becomes a muddy dullness. In the process of reproduction the image has also been revised in the interests of historical accuracy to include three people Harris accidentally omitted. Harris's *Fathers of Confederation* is an image then that vaguely resembles in its history the country; conceived as an afterthought, mortally wounded by war, rising phoenix-like from the ashes in a way that transformed shame into pride, and continually being tinkered with to satisfy the regions.

9.3 Frank Challener, *Fathers of Confederation*. Ontario Legislature.

The most appropriate comparison with Harris's *Fathers* is Charles Huot's *Language Debate*, painted about twenty-five years later (see figure 9.4). In this picture there is motion and emotion, but you have to look closely to see it and possess information not contained in the picture itself and not easily found elsewhere. In the centre someone is declaiming; to the left a chair has been overturned as the main body of participants crowds anxiously into the vortex of the painting. Something is happening, but what? The painting captures a moment in Canadian history, 13 January 1793. In the process of equipping the newly created jurisdiction of Lower Canada with a body of operating regulations, a committee of the legislature has just brought in a resolution recognizing both English and French as official languages of government. Two anglophone members have in response moved an amendment effectively calling for English to be declared the only official language. C. de Lotbinière commands the centre stage arguing the case for the contras; the members of the assembly are grouped around the central figure in the manner in which they will eventually vote down the amendment 29 to 11 (against to the right and left, for in the centre); there is a scattering of voting and non-voting members in the background, and far off in the left background three French-speaking members who voted for the English amendment. Huot too has a problem of empty space, but he uses the top of his picture more effectively than Harris.

Huot chose the moment in consultation with a friend, the historian Thomas Chapais, who was also, coincidentally, a member of the committee adjudicating the competition. It must be said that this debate on an amendment is scarcely mentioned in the standard histories of the period, perhaps because of its ambiguous outcome. The incident was so unfamiliar to the general public that after the unveiling the artist had to provide an explanation and a diagrammatic key to the painting. Nevertheless, for those in the know, Chapais, in his history, had raised this debate to a moment of national self-assertion, the beginning of a continuous struggle to re-establish and maintain French-Canadian cultural survival under the English regime. Whether it was, or was not, is beside the point; the painting reified Chapais's moderate nationalist interpretation. But visually the difference between the two sides in the debate is indiscernible. It is virtually impossible to tell, without the program, what all of this shouting, arm-waving, and clustering means, who is for, who is against.

As is usually the case in these things, the painting acquired some of its symbolic power at the expense of authenticity and stylistic incongruity. Huot was much praised for getting the windows and architectural details of the chapel right, but he took the liberty of relocating the building into the Lower Town and reorienting it so that the Chateau Saint-Louis, which had survived the bombardment of 1759, and the Citadel are visible through the windows on this

9.4 Charles Huot, *The Language Debate*. National Assembly of Quebec.

bright January day. More than the usual amount of artistic licence is involved in this instance to invoke the symbolism of French-Canadian survival under British rule, as the Citadel was not there in 1793. Potentially more controversial, though it seems to have passed without comment at the time, is that Huot took as his model for this French-Canadian nationalist icon in an ultramontane age an image depicting the French Revolution. Although the painting owes something to Trumbull's *Declaration of Independence*, structurally *The Language Debate* relies upon a plaster relief of Mirabeau responding to the king's attempt to dismiss the Estates General on 23 June 1789. Huot had been in Paris in 1883 when this plaster cast had been unveiled and subsequently popularized in a widely distributed print. The original relief commemorated a moment at the very beginning of the Revolution when, challenged by the representative of the Crown to disperse, the tribune of the Assembly proclaimed that its legitimacy rested upon a higher sovereignty than that of a king, the will of the people. The democratic, anticlerical, and ultimately republican paternity of the image would not have gone down well with French-Canadian nationalist sensibilities at the time. Curiously, the painting did pass muster with the art critic of Tardivel's ultra-vigilant *La Vérité*: 'On y voit peinte de la manière la plus heureuse tout un jeune peuple représenté par ses députés, et luttant courageusement pour conserver ce qu'il a de plus noble, de plus beau et de plus précieux: sa propre vie nationale.'[44] The ultimate irony, though, is the incongruity that comes with time. An act of proud defiance in one generation can be somewhat embarrassing to descendants. Huot's picture captures a moment when the principle of bilingualism is being defended; it hangs now in a room where Bill 101 reigns. It represents a somewhat ambiguous legacy.

Huot's somewhat earlier *Battle of the Plains of Abraham* presents a more difficult problem of interpretation (see figure 9.5). First of all, this is little more than a study for a painting, only a small canvas 16 by 22 inches. As a sketch it also offers simply an impression, necessarily ambiguous, of a range of possibilities of what the final work might contain. But it comes down to us as a painting, as something in its own right. (Apparently a larger version exists in a private collection, but I have not seen it.) It would appear that the painting captures a moment early in the morning of 13 October 1759, when the British troops have established themselves en masse on the Plains of Abraham. After some initial skirmishing, General Montcalm has ridden out to lead his troops into the main engagement of the battle. The outcome is foretold in the shadow across the French lines; the uncertain future is registered in the cloud, honour maintained by the French banners held aloft. The English are ordered, arrayed in ranks. The French seem disorganized, the leaders somewhat uncertain. It is the eve of defeat, but the dawn of an enduring moral victory. As a colour field

9.5 Charles Huot, *La Bataille des Plaines d'Abraham*, oil. Private collection.

the painting is essentially four horizontal bands, white vigorously brushed into grey across the top; a blood-red slash across the heart of the image; autumnal earth tones below on which the French muster; and the darker shades of the grave slanting across the bottom quarter. It is, to be sure, a bold and arresting colour field. Its model may well have been the numerous Napoleonic battle scenes. The pathos of the image arises from the vastly outnumbered French defenders; the forces were more evenly matched than this suggests. While Huot would have certainly constructed his image with Benjamin West in mind, his painting even in sketch form lacks the deep symbolic structure that animates *The Death of Wolfe*. This is primarily a battle scene in which the action, notwithstanding the clouds of gunpowder wreathing the central group, is yet to come. *The Battle of the Plains of Abraham* stands as a modest triumph of Canadian impressionism. Huot is attempting to push history painting perhaps in new directions, away from detail and authenticity and even symbolism towards the capturing of a mood or impression through the application of vigorously brushed colours and more abstract, vaguely suggested representations.[45]

9.6 Marc-Aurèle de Foy Suzor-Coté, *La Mort de Montcalm*, 1902, oil on canvas. Musée national des beaux-arts du Québec, 43.176.

A reading of Suzor-Coté's *Death of Montcalm*, painted at about the same time, follows logically from Huot's image (see figure 9.6). Here clearly the artist is engaged in a direct dialogue with West, historically, formally, stylistically, and symbolically. Even though this too is a small painting, it is an image of considerable power. Its debt to the French academic tradition is softened, literally, by a brush with impressionism. This is not a sharply focused or crisply rendered moment, but rather an ethereal, timeless event. The soft, dark, richly coloured palette conveys a vaguely religious sense, heightened by the candles, the prelate, and the nun. This might be the death of a king but it is more likely the passing of a pope. West has cloaked his proto-Jesus in a conqueror's uniform; Suzor-Coté drapes his Montcalm entirely in white, a different kind of Jesus from West's, perhaps metaphorically the one to rise from the dead. He is at once head of both his people and his church. The painting reeks of incense and ultramontane piety.[46] It joins the debate at the level of religious symbolism, but it is not a sufficiently powerful or skilfully realized construction to do battle with West on anything like equal terms. It is more of a catcall than

9.7 Marc-Aurèle de Foy Suzor-Coté, *Jacques Cartier rencontre les Indiens à Stadaconné*, 1535, oil on canvas. Musée national des beaux-arts du Québec, 34.12.

a rebuttal. Suzor-Coté painted this *Montcalm* in 1902 as his entry to a competition sponsored by the Quebec government to decorate the chamber of the Legislative Assembly. The legislators, who could not imagine themselves being inspired sitting under the influence of its sepulchral gloom, chose a brighter but more undistinguished rendering of Champlain aboard ship by Henri Beau instead.[47]

With Suzor-Coté's painting *Cartier's Encounter with the Indians at Stadacona*, we come face to face with a fully realized history painting, a genuine grand machine (see figure 9.7). Curiously, this was the work that was rejected by the connoisseurs, according the prime minister's report, because Cartier was represented as being too pretty. A saddened prime minister informed an even more disappointed painter that even though Sir William Van Horne wanted to buy his *Cartier* for the Senate, 'Sir George Drummond et monsieur Boyer sont un peu moins enthousiastes. Leur principale critique, ou plutôt leur seule critique, est que ton Jacques Cartier est décidément trop beau. Entre nous ça toujours été aussi mon impression; je crois pas que Cartier, en descendant de son navire, ait porté d'aussi beaux habits que ceux dont tu le revêts.' The correspondence ends with the prime minister giving a young painter some editorial encouragement: 'Je suis disposé à croire qu'on va te demander de le retoucher.'[48] Cartier was not retouched in a dressed-down mode and the picture remained unsold for many years.

A seeming lack of authenticity condemned the picture as history. There is, I think, another possibility, that it captured an unbidden truth. Suzor-Coté had painted an invasion, not a peaceful cohabitation. The Native people to the left blend into the foliage; they seem to emerge from the earth. One is dazzled by the light, another crouches like a cat, a third grips a club. Suzor-Coté has dressed the French like Spanish conquistadores. Cartier has his sword sheathed, he has outstretched arms of greeting, but his colleague has his sword at the ready. Pikes and axes bristle behind the flag. Metal helmets and armour set the tone. A crowd of armed men rush up the hill behind. This is, to be sure, an ambiguous, suspended moment of encounter. Native people are at home, one with the earth; the French are invaders from a geometrical place, a violent wedge of Western civilization, welcoming their new subjects, about to knife into the land and take possession of it. The tangled forest on the left, with the naked Indigenous people knotted up in it, gives way to a military pyramid in the central focal point with an expansive cleared space in its van. This fraught encounter did not sit well with the Canadian grand bourgeoisie. It did not comport well either with the grand narratives of Canadian history. And so for more than twenty years Suzor-Coté tried in vain to find a buyer for it. *Cartier's Encounter with the Indians at Stadacona* speaks perhaps a little too brutally of the violation of contact.

George Reid's *The Arrival of Champlain*, on the other hand, was snapped up with alacrity soon after it had been painted by the purchasing committee of the National Gallery of Canada (see figure 9.8). In this painting European power is represented in code, softened and made more 'natural' in the process. In this picture technology, the alchemical engine, has turned everything to gold. The bowsprit wand is about to transform a sleeping continent. The *Don de Dieu*, glowing with gilded confidence, towers over the swarming canoes of Native people. A small caravel has, in the painter's hand, been turned into a massive Spanish galleon. In this painting the Native people are numerous, potentially hostile, but clearly subordinate. The Natives have been drawn by their awe to the flanks of the ship. A chief, standing off in the foreground, waves a paddle: a greeting, or defiance. It is an ambiguous gesture. In this case the thoroughly incongruous Plains Indian war bonnets worn by the Indians did not seem to have offended the purchasing committee's sense of authenticity. This is the acceptable face of contact circa 1910.

9.8 George A. Reid, *The Arrival of Champlain at Quebec*, 1909, oil on burlap. National Gallery of Canada, Accession 115.

Several more examples of the history painting genre could be added to the list, but would not materially change the picture. Canadian artists did not get as many opportunities to paint the nation as they wanted, but when they did what they wanted to do they did not vividly capture the public imagination. These are not great or memorable paintings. Nor did they engender much enthusiasm or inspire more patronage. Perhaps because of their deficiencies as works of art, they did not strike a chord of recognition. But that is surely not the case. After all, revered second-rate works of art fill the walls of national galleries around the world. To say simply that history painting in Canada was not popular begs the question why? There must be other reasons why history painting didn't 'catch on' in Canada. To conclude, I would like to suggest a few.

IV

Attempting to explain why something did not happen is a risky business. Better spend scarce energy on the things that did happen. But in this case I think the incomplete connection between history painting and nationalism in Canada is worth a few more paragraphs of reflection, because the character of this historical turn in art reflects on some of the characteristics of the nation being constructed. Painting and nationalism would make connections in Canada, but not in this genre. Confederation would reverberate through landscape rather than representations of the past.

First and most obviously, painting the Canadian past laid emphasis upon divisions within the society. *The Battle of the Plains of Abraham*, for example, does not pit 'us' against 'them' as West's *Death of Wolfe* does. Instead it shows two of the main cultural forces in Canada locked in combat. We, in these pictures, are plural and often at odds. History in a Canadian context more often divides than unites.

There is, of course, a further ambiguity about these paintings. Which nation is being constructed? This point is perhaps more acutely felt now than it was at the time. The heroic period of French Canada was then thought to be more integrally connected to the historical development of the country. The history of New France was also the history of Canada. Similarly, French-Canadian artists could feed French-Canadian nationalist sensibilities without the conscious intent of separation. They could build a consciousness of *ethnie* and paint a certain kind of Canada, one in which survival and self-determination often meant struggle, not with some external force, but rather with neighbours. *La survivance* focused upon division within.

History painters experienced great difficulty bridging cultural divisions; they were only slightly more successful in representing them. That is perhaps why the Advisory Art Committee was more enthusiastic about commissioning a Baldwin-Lafontaine statue than history paintings for the Parliament Buildings. While the main fault line lay between English and French, a much deeper chasm was openly represented between both and Native Canadians. These paintings will work only for an audience prepared to accept an identity or identities defined against Native presence. They will not work at all in the construction of a civic nation in which Native people might form a distinct part of the collectivity. While the question 'What nation is being made in these pictures?' has salience with respect to English and French, Native peoples as 'other' are represented inside the frame but are not assumed to be numbered among the viewers.

So why did Canada reject history painting as a nation-building instrument? The answer is only in part the intractable nature of Canadian history and cultural differences within. Many countries have experienced deep internal divisions, yet still boast some of the greatest history paintings. Recall that Delacroix's

Liberty Leading the People spent much of the nineteenth century going into and coming out of storage as regimes changed. Up until the introduction of the Euro, both the painter and his painting adorned the 100-franc note. There are I think four reasons for the Canadian situation: changes in art theory, the form of state patronage, the failure of Canadian artists to find a symbolic language to animate these paintings, and the fact that the Great War killed many things, among them a belief in a heroic past upon which history painting depended.

In art historical terms the critical moment for history painting had decisively passed by 1900 and everyone knew that, including these artists themselves. Most of them made a living doing something else, portraits, landscapes, drawings, sculptures. History painting exercised only a brief reign in the countries of Western Europe and America, essentially from the late eighteenth to the mid-nineteenth century. Its power and influence can be easily exaggerated. By the time Canadian artists became seized of the possibilities of history painting, as a genre it had already been superseded in its metropolitan spaces. Even in the United States the era of history painting could be said to have ended at mid-century. It was most decisively terminated by the Civil War, which, not surprisingly, generated no great history paintings but much memorable photography.[49] For authenticity the camera took the wind out of history painting's sails. In the art world the creative centre of gravity had shifted topically and stylistically from history to the impressionistic representation of landscape, and theoretically from a conception of art as noble, civic inspiration to art for art's sake, an interior aesthetic. Coming late to the party, the Canadian artists suffered this disadvantage of having the theoretical ground cut from under their feet. That did not make their task impossible, just more difficult. Knowledgeable private patrons passed over this outdated work, choosing instead more recent fashions.

That meant that the primary patron of this sort of art was the state. It must be said that this was largely true during the high-water years of history painting earlier in the century in Europe and the United States. Government sustained historical painting. In Canada the federal government seemed a reluctant patron. When the prime minister of Canada is acting as your agent and you can't sell a history painting to the government, the state is not playing its role of 'bureaucratic incorporation' in the manner predicted by theory.[50] Or perhaps it was performing it in another way. And further, there were other governments also at work in the identity formation business. The federal government commissioned one history painting, *The Fathers of Confederation*, then lost heart. Even though the prime minister wanted to cover the walls of Parliament with ennobling scenes from Canadian history, he could not do so. Painters were certainly willing, perhaps too willing. They were also perhaps too greedy.

Beset by artists with designs on the walls of Parliament, the federal government did what it did in other realms: it created a rational bureaucratic process for adjudicating rival claims, a separate institution, with a dedicated budget, a professional director, and an external board of selection. In the regulation of art for the nation the government acted in much the same way it did in regulating transportation. This 'progressive' response created a further bias against history painting as it placed the burden of acquisition upon connoisseurship, and professional judgment. The new National Gallery was more inclined towards new trends in art, and especially to 'nativist' trends, though it would be stretching things too much to say that it had a modernist bias. Canadian art and nationalism would be fused in large measure through the instrumentality of the Gallery, but not through the genre of history painting. Canada's icons would be lakes, rocks, and trees, not heroes.[51]

It is interesting to note the relative assertiveness of the provinces in the field of history painting. Quebec, with its legislative decorations, stands out. The exterior of the legislature is a garden of heroic sculpture; after the turn of the century the Quebec government turned to interior decoration, focusing upon history painting and keeping Huot more or less fully employed for twenty years. But Ontario too must be included in the picture. If anything, the province of Ontario had been even more aggressive in the promotion of art through its program of acquisitions, and its continuing support of the Ontario Society of Artists. It would resist an expensive program of history painting for its new legislature, but it did continue to commission portraits of Ontario notables for its walls and statuary for its grounds. Indeed, it is to Ontario that we are indebted for a reworked *Fathers of Confederation*.[52] The comparatively stronger role of the provinces can perhaps be attributed to their more direct responsibilities in the field of public education. Once again federalism reminds us that in Canada the state is divided; that the process of identity formation ('bureaucratic incorporation' in the political science jargon) goes on at several levels when the polity is divided.

At the level of achievement, however, the performance of the artists did not live up to their own elevated expectations for the genre. Their work did not inspire much enthusiasm, much less patriotism and emulation. I think the main reason for this is that they failed to find a symbolic vocabulary suitable to the Canadian situation. Biblical and classical motifs had served to animate European and American history painting. The Canadian artists could not find a suitable model for their work that moved the observers, not by its attention to accuracy and detail, but rather by its deeper representation of meaning. Self-conscious attempts by the artists to avoid this difficulty led in two directions: documentary art on the one hand and allegorical treatments on the other. Huot, on the wall and ceiling of the Legislative Assembly, represented both tendencies. So did Reid with his *Ave Canada* mural proposal for the Parliament Buildings, and his stocky earth-hued *Hail to the Pioneers* in Toronto City Hall. Jefferys represents perhaps the most extreme case of documentary representation. He gave up high art for illustration, acquiring in the process the antiquarian's fanaticism over matters of authenticity and detail. Jefferys disappeared into the genre to emerge out the other side as a historian who happened to draw. He would make a living as a prolific historical illustrator. The allegorical treatments stirred neither blood nor enthusiasm among potential sponsors. Reid's sketch of his proposed mural brings to mind a comment from a Minnesota politician giving instructions to architects regarding the decoration of the state legislature: 'Care must be taken not to fill the building with Greek gods and goddesses.'[53]

Ultimately it could be argued Canadian history painting was a further casualty of the Great War, even though the war occasioned a tremendous expansion of the role of the state as art patron. Canadian painters would be set to work capturing history, but not the distant past, rather current history. But at the same time, ironically, this war destroyed the notion of a past filled with heroes. It also badly damaged the notion of history as a story of progress. This kind of war was a form of madness, a tremendous destroyer of men, materiel, landscape, and dreams. Its misery could not sustain myths; artists struggled in new ways to tell unpleasant truths. The fractured and tormented brushstrokes of modern idioms of painting were more suited to expressing the incomprehensibility of war.[54] War thus created a new field for modernism, and it is this kind of painting that adorns the walls of the Senate, not to inspire legislators with fables of a golden age, but to remind them never again.

Nation-building often requires more forgetting than remembering. Canadians had a brief brush with history painting, and the artists certainly wanted to do more, but on the whole Canadian private patrons and governments showed more interest in other things. In time both would embrace with considerable enthusiasm a supposedly indigenous Canadian way of seeing and painting the northern landscape that would completely overshadow this brief brush with historical didacticism. Though this is not much commented upon, but can be readily seen in contrast with these history paintings, the new nationalist genre was one in which conflict between Canadians did not appear. Indeed, the glaciers that had scraped the ancient shield of its earth also removed almost all evidence of humanity from the Group of Seven canvases. Iconographic Canadian art would not have people or history in it.[55] It was art for a country with a bad memory, in which symbols of power were softened and made invisible by being buried in snow. Where power was contested and history divisive, Canadians preferred it that way.

NOTES

1 The quotation is from Adrian Hastings, *The Construction of Nationhood: Ethnicity, Religion and Nationalism* (Cambridge: Cambridge University Press, 1997), 27. The quotation continues: 'and imagined things can prove very impermanent. Yet some of them can be toughly enduring as well. The history of the way we see ourselves, the interaction of social understanding and the world around us, is never predictable and in the experience of nationhood, as of ethnicity too, the level of unpredictability seems particularly high.' The target of Hastings's primordialist critique is the modern social constructivist literature flowing in part from E.J. Hobsbawm and T. Ranger's influential collection *The Invention of Tradition* (Cambridge: Cambridge University Press, 1983), from Hobsbawm's collection of lectures, *Nations and Nationalism since 1780: Programme, Myth, Reality* (Cambridge: Cambridge University Press, 1990), and from Benedict Anderson's *Imagined Communities: Reflections on the Origin and Spread of Nationalism* (London: Verso, 1983, revised 1991). Ernest Gellner in various works, for example in *Nationalism* (London: Weidenfeld and Nicolson, 1997), shares Hobsbawm's modernism, but rejects the hostility towards nationalism Hobsbawm shares with Elie Kedourie's fiercely critical earlier work, *Nationalism* (London: Hutchinson, 1960). Anthony Smith, author of the influential *The Ethnic Origins of Nations* (Oxford: Blackwell, 1986) and the leading 'soft primordialist,' restates his antimodernist position, more positively inclined towards nationalism on historical, functional, and theoretical grounds, in *Nations and Nationalism in a Global Era* (Cambridge: Polity Press, 1995). He updates his earlier work on theories of nationalism and surveys writing in the field in *Nationalism and Modernism* (London: Routledge, 1998); his essays have been collected in *Myths and Memories of the Nation* (Oxford: Oxford University Press, 1999). These debates can be surveyed most conveniently in John A. Hall's collection of essays using Gellner's writings as a point of departure, *The State of the Nation* (Cambridge: Cambridge University Press, 1998); see particularly the overview by Brendan O'Leary.

2 See, for example, Geoffrey Cubitt, ed., *Imagining Nations* (Manchester: Manchester University Press, 1998); the reader edited by Geoff Eley and Ronald G. Suny, *Becoming National: A Reader* (Oxford: Oxford University Press, 1996); M. Teich and Roy Porter, *The National Question in European Historical Context* (Cambridge: Cambridge University Press, 1993); and for an interesting comparative study Lyn Spillman, *Nation and Commemoration: Creating National Identities in the United States and Australia* (Cambridge: Cambridge University Press, 1997). For an extended treatment of the importance of the 'collective imaginary' in nation-making, see Gérard Bouchard, *The Making of Nations and Cultures of the New World* (Montreal and Kingston: McGill-Queen's University Press, 2008). As I was writing this chapter I discovered that Anthony Smith has written a paper

on artists as nation-builders I have not been able to locate, 'Art and Nationalism in Europe,' in J.C.H. Blom et al., eds., *De onmacht van het grote: Cultur in Europa* (Amsterdam: Amsterdam University Press, 1993), 201–20.

3 Smith, *Nations and Nationalism in a Global Era*, 108.

4 Dennis Reid, *A Concise History of Canadian Art* (Toronto: Oxford University Press, 1988).

5 J. Russell Harper, *Painting in Canada* (Toronto: University of Toronto Press, 1977).

6 Dennis Reid, *'Our Own Country Canada': Being an Account of the National Aspirations of the Principal Landscape Artists in Montreal and Toronto, 1860–1890* (Ottawa: National Gallery of Canada, 1979); Maria Tippett, *Art in the Service of War* (Toronto: University of Toronto Press, 1984); and Charles Hill, *The Group of Seven: Art for a Nation* (Toronto: McClelland and Stewart, 1995).

7 Dennis Duffy, 'Art History: Charles William Jefferys as Canada's Curator,' *Journal of Canadian Studies* 11(1976): 3–18; Robert Stacey, '"Salvage for Us These Fragments": C.W. Jefferys and Ontario's Historic Architecture,' *Ontario History* 70 (1978): 147–70, and *Charles W. Jefferys* (Ottawa: National Gallery of Canada, 1985).

8 Robert Derome, 'Charles Huot et la peinture d'histoire au Palais législatif de Québec (1883–1930),' *National Gallery of Canada Bulletin* no. 27 (1976), and Jean-René Ostiguy, *Charles Huot* (Ottawa: National Gallery of Canada, 1979).

9 Rosalind Peppall, 'The Murals in the Toronto Municipal Buildings: George Reid's Debt to Puvis de Chavannes,' *Canadian Journal of Art History* 9 (1986): 142–61; Marylin McKay, 'Canadian Historical Murals, 1895–1939: Material Progress, Morality and the "Disappearance" of Native People,' *Canadian Journal of Art History* 15 (1992): 63–83, and her monograph *A National Soul: Canadian Mural Painting, 1860's-1930's* (Montreal and Kingston: McGill Queen's University Press, 2002). Brian Osborne, a cultural geographer, in a suggestive synoptic essay, 'The Iconography of Nationhood in Canadian Art,' skips over this phase to focus on landscape imagery before and afterwards, in Dennis Cosgrove and Stephen Daniels, eds., *The Iconography of Landscape* (Cambridge: Cambridge University Press, 1989), 162–77, with the sentence: 'Remarkably, a more didactic style of patriotic art did not develop' (167). I agree with him but at greater length.

10 Inter alia, William H. Gerdts and Mark Thistlethwaite, *Grand Illusions: History Painting in America* (Fort Worth: Amon Carter Museum, 1988); Peter Cannon-Brookes, ed., *The Painted Word: British History Painting: 1750–1830* (Woodbridge: Heim Gallery and Boydell Press, 1991); Michael Kammen, *Meadows of Memory* (Austin: University of Texas Press, 1992); William Ayres, ed., *Picturing History: American Painting 1770–1930* (New York: Rizzoli, 1993); Patricia M. Burnham and Lucretia Hoover Giese, eds., *Redefining American History Painting* (New York: Cambridge University Press, 1995). In addition there have been

several monographs on individual artists, for example Nancy Rush, *The Painting and Politics of George Caleb Bingham* (New Haven: Yale University Press, 1991).

11 Patricia Burnham and Lucretia Geise, 'History Painting: How It Works,' in Burnham and Geise, eds., *Redefining American History Painting*, 1–2; Mark Thistlethwaite, 'The Most Important Themes: History Painting and Its Place in American Art,' in Gerdts and Thistlethwaite, *Grand Illusions*, 7–8.

12 Martin Butlin, Introduction to Cannon-Brookes, ed., *The Painted Word*, 7–8.

13 Quoted in Ann Uhry Abrams, *The Valiant Hero: Benjamin West and the Grand-Style History Painting* (Washington: Smithsonian Institution, 1985), 14.

14 Colonel Stacey, in a puckish, revisionist mood, went to considerable effort to deflate West's claims of historical accuracy by pointing out mistakes in the uniforms and the presence in the picture of figures who were far from the battle at the time. C.P. Stacey, 'Benjamin West and "The Death of Wolfe,"' *National Gallery of Canada Bulletin* no. 4 (1966).

15 Smith, *Nationalism and Modernism*, cover and commentary in the preface, x–xiv.

16 I am following here Burnham and Giese, 'History Painting: How It Works,' 1–14; Abrams, *The Valiant Hero*, 161–209. The story of West's artistic revolution has been told many times, most authoritatively in the works cited above and in neo-narrative style by Simon Schama in *Dead Certainties: Unwarranted Speculations* (New York: Knopf, 1991).

17 See Helmut von Erffa and Allen Staley, *The Paintings of Benjamin West* (New Haven: Yale University Press, 1986), chapter 4 for an account of the painting of the picture, and pp. 211–16 for a brief history of the production and changing ownership of the six known examples, three of which remain in Britain – one in the Queen's Picture Collection, another at the Duke of Bath's gallery at Ickworth House, and a third smaller study still owned by the Moncton family. There are two versions in Canada, at the National Gallery and at the Royal Ontario Museum (a purchase by Sigmund Samuel of one of the later versions done for one of the officers), and a final copy in the Samuel Clemens Library at the University of Michigan. There are only minor variations between them, mainly on the two edges and in the footwear.

18 On the diffusion of this kind of image see Peter Cannon-Brookes, 'From the Death of Wolfe to the Death of Lord Nelson: Benjamin West and Epic Representation' (*The Painted Word*, 15–22), and two essays in the same volume by David Alexander, 'Print Makers and Print Sellers in England, 1770–1830,' and 'Patriotism and Contemporary History' (23–36).

19 See Hélène Toussaint, *La 'Liberté Guidant le peuple' de Delacroix* (Paris: Musée du Louvre, 1982), for a brief account of this famous painting, its composition, reception, and incorporation into national memory.

20 I am indebted here to Stephen Bann, *Paul Delaroche: History Painted* (London: Reaktion, 1997); Peter Brooks, *History Painting and Narrative: Delacroix's Moments* (Oxford: European Humanities Reseasrch Centre, 1998); and Julian Barnes's reading of the Guericault painting in *The History of the World in 10 ½ Chapters*.

21 Dorinda Evans, *Benjamin West and His American Students* (Washington: Smithsonian Institution, 1980); Patricia Burnham, 'John Trumbull, Historian: The Case of the Battle of Bunker's Hill' (*Redefining American History Painting*, 37–58), and Mark Thisthethwaite, 'The Most Important Themes: History Painting and Its Place in American Art' (*Grand Illusions*, 7–58).

22 See the essays by Barbara Mitnick, 'The History of History Painting,' Wendy Greenhouse, 'The Landing of the Fathers: Representing the National Past, 1770–1860,' and Ann Uhry Abrams, 'National Painting and the American Character: History Murals in the Capitol Rotunda,' in Ayres, ed., *Picturing History*, 29–80.

23 Thistlethwaite, 'The Most Important Themes,' 10–12, and William H. Gerdts, 'On Elevated Heights: American History Painting and Its Critics,' and 'The Dusseldorf School,' in *Grand Illusions*, 61–124.

24 The list could possibly be extended with the addition of Frances Hopkins in the 1860s, Eugène Hamel, Henri Beau, Charles Alexander Smith, and Frank Challener, each of whom painted at least one historical picture, though in Challener's case surreptitiously. Clarence Gagnon and Thoreau Macdonald might be included as historical illustrators.

25 Harper, 'French Academic Influences,' *Painting in Canada*, 217–34; Reid, 'The "French" Period in Canadian Art,' *A Concise History of Canadian Art*, 91–105; 'Canadians in Paris and the French Influences,' an exhibition organized by the Glenbow Museum in Calgary, October, 1999.

26 Quoted in Derome, 'Charles Huot et la peinture d'histoire au Palais législatif de Québec,' 3.

27 Raymond Vezina, 'Napoléon Bourassa,' *DCB*, 14:113–15.

28 Moncreif Williamson, *Robert Harris, 1849–1919: An Unconventional Biography* (Toronto: McClelland and Stewart, 1970), 42–110. The 1883 Sir John A. Macdonald quotation is on p. 99. In the discussion Macdonald agreed with Laurier that Canadian artists must regrettably but necessarily find distinction in 'the centres of art and civilization, like London and Paris.' The full discussion can be followed in Canada, *House of Commons Debates*, 14 May 1883, 1170–4.

29 Muriel Miller Miner, *G.A. Reid: Canadian Artist* (Toronto: Ryerson Press, 1946), 23–108; Christine Boyanski, *Sympathetic Realism* (Toronto: Art Gallery of Ontario, 1988).

30 For a much more detailed identification of the precise French influences at work here see Peppall, 'The Murals in the Toronto Municipal Buildings.' See also Marylin McKay, *A National Soul*, especially chapter 2, 'Civic Mural Paintings,' 24–59.

31   Ontario Archives, Ontario Society of Artists Papers, Minute Books, 19 March 1897; 8 February 1898; and interleaved newspaper clippings, Toronto *News*, 19 March 1897; Toronto *Mail*, 23, 24 March 1897 (for letters from Marmeduke Mathews, president of the OSA); *Mail*, 8 February 1898. The leadership of the Ontario Society of Artists at first sensed the presence of a rival in the Toronto Civic Guild of Art, but gradually backed down. See also Miner, *G.A. Reid*, 102–8.

32   University of Toronto, Fisher Rare Book Room, Walker Papers, box 27A, Guild of Civic Art File, clipping, *Mail*, 20 March 1897, Walker before the Board of Control; clipping, *Mail*, 13 April 1898, Walker speech on opening of the Copley Prints.

33   Art Gallery of Ontario, E.P. Taylor Library, George Reid Scrapbook, for sketches of the design medallions of the Toronto Guild of Civic Art; sketches of the panels Industry, Intelligence, Integrity, Art, Science (not completed); a drawing of the Council Chamber as it would appear fully decorated; clippings regarding Reid's 'Christmas Gift to the Citizens,' photographs, studies for, and sketches of *Hail to the Pioneers*; invitations to the opening (16 May 1899), clipping of Walker's address at the opening, newspaper description of the celebration, and as a footnote, a newspaper account of Reid's 'retouching' of the civic murals after thirty years in 1929.

34   George Reid Scrapbook, Toronto Guild of Civic Art, November 1905, Programme; Bulletin no. 1 of the Toronto Guild of Civic Art, which contains a drawing of the proposed entrance; typescript Report of the Committee of the Toronto Guild of Civic Art for the initial phase of the project; two newspaper clippings from 1905 in which the emphasis falls on the encouragement of native art and the elevation of public taste. Much later in 1917, in a memorandum prepared by Reid to advocate a program of war art, he recounted his twenty-three years of disappointing experience with 'civic art.' Notwithstanding the many setbacks, he remained optimistic and firmly convinced of the value of history painting, 'Note on Mural Painting in Canada prepared for the information of the Council of the Royal Canadian Academy for use at its meetings called for the consideration of the work now in progress in England and France to commemorate the operations of the Canadian forces in the war by means of paintings,' December 1917. See also the Walker Papers, box 27A for the first approach to the provincial government in 1897, clipping from the *Globe*, 20 March 1897, 'Artists to the Front, The Committee of the Guild of Civic Art Respectfully Desires To Present the Following Report Regarding the Initial Part of the Proposed Scheme of Decoration for the Legislative Building,' and another copy of the 1905 Guild program. See also Fern Bayer, *The Ontario Collection* (Toronto: Fitzhenry and Whiteside, 1984), 92.

35   George Reid Scrapbook, G.A. Reid, Report prepared 12 June 1905, Tammersville, NY, Specifications for Proposed Decorations for the Main Entrance Hall of the Parliament Buildings, Ottawa, handwritten; Sketch of Ave Canada, Memorial

from the Royal Academy of Art, 1907; clippings from various newspapers on the response of the government to the Academy brief calling for the support of 'native talent.' See also the Walker Papers, Vol. 27A, Royal Canadian Academy File, Petition, April 1904 to Sir Wilfrid Laurier; G.A. Reid, Report prepared 12 June 1905.

36 Walker Papers, box 27B, Advisory Art Council, Appointed 19 April 1907, Sir George Drummond, Mr Byron E. Walker, Hon. Arthur Boyer, Montreal Memorandum for Meeting – for Walker, 18 July 1907. The Council authorized the purchase of Reid's *Arrival of Champlain* for $2500 on 9 February 1910. For the elite-led campaign for a program of art education in Canada, a parallel campaign for a revitalized National Gallery, and the creation of the Advisory Art Council, see Maria Tippett, *Making Culture: English-Canadian Institutions and the Arts before the Massey Commission* (Toronto: University of Toronto Press, 1990), 35–46, 81–2.

37 For Reid at the Tercentenary see H.V. Nelles, *The Art of Nation-Building: Pageantry and Spectacle at Quebec's Tercentenary* (Toronto: University of Toronto Press, 1999), 280–2; these Tercentenary pastels are now in the Library and Archives Canada Picture Collection; sketches for them and studies taken from them can be seen in the Art Gallery of Ontario, E.P. Taylor Library, George Reid Scrapbook. When Reid returned to these themes in the 1920s and 1930s he built upon these visual memories, as his scrapbook clearly reveals. For the purchase of Reid's *Arrival of Champlain at Quebec* in 1909 for $2500 see Walker Papers, box 27B, Art Advisory Council, Minutes, 9 February 1910.

38 Hughes de Jouvancourt, *Suzor-Coté* (Montreal: Stanké, 1978), 87–95; LAC, Laurier Papers, Microfilm, Suzor-Coté to Laurier, 19 May 1900 (45733–6); Laurier to Suzor-Coté, 18 June 1900 (45737); Suzor-Coté to Laurier, 11 September 1903 (76948–51); Laurier to Suzor-Coté, 24 September 1907 (129615); Suzor-Coté to Laurier, 1 October 1907 (129931–36); Laurier to Suzor-Coté, 2 Octobrer 1907 (129937). Suzor-Coté addressed Laurier as 'Cher monsieur Laurier'; Laurier in return tu-toied his young friend, 'Mon cher Aurèle.'

39 Laurier Papers, Microfilm, Laurier to Sir George Drummond, 2 October 1907: 'Please see if you would favour its acquisition to hang on the walls of the Senate. My idea is that we should cover the walls of our Upper Chamber with works illustrating the history of Canada' (129938); Laurier to L'honourable Arthur Boyer, 2 October 1907 (1299939); Suzor-Coté to Laurier, 7 October 1907 (130172–5); Letter of recommendation from Mr Bonnat, 28 October 1907 (130176); Laurier to Suzor-Coté, 11 November 1907: 'Je crois, cependant, qu'il vaudrait mieux n'en rien faire; ni Sir George Drummond ni monsieur Boyer ne sera influencé par ces lettres' (130179).

40 Ostiguy, *Charles Huot*; Derome, 'Charles Huot et le peinture d'histoire au Palais législatif de Québec.'

41 Paul Gladu, *Henri Julien* (Montreal: Lidec, 1970); Marius Barbeau, *Henri Julien* (Toronto: Ryerson Press, 1941); Harper, *Painting in Canada*, 223–4. Julien's *His-*

torical Procession is reproduced in colour in my book *The Art of Nation-Building* between pp. 262 and 263.

42 Robert Stacey's monograph, *C.W. Jefferys*, concentrates primarily upon Jefferys's career as a painter and watercolourist; see also William Colgate, 'C.W.J. A Victorian Portait,' in *The Educational Record of the Province of Quebec* 69 (July-September 1954): 142–50 and the list of publications containing his illustrations, Art Gallery of Ontario, E.P. Taylor Reference Library, C.W. Jefferys Papers, boxes 16 and 18. Jefferys's visual legacy is the subject of Dennis Duffy's essay 'Art History.' Jefferys's article, 'The Visual Reconstruction of History,' appeared in the *Canadian Historical Review* 14 (1936): 249–65, and argued that historians should regard images from the past with the same professional scepticism as written documents, that artistic conventions introduced inaccuracies into representation, and that the artist's necessary concern with the artefacts of history could both encourage a popular historical consciousness and lead the professionals towards a better understanding of social history.

43 For a succinct account see Bayer, *The Ontario Collection*, 125–6.

44 I am greatly indebted to Robert Derome's well-researched monograph, 'Charles Huot et la peinture d'histoire au Palais législatif de Québec, 1883–1930,' for assistance in reading this image; the quotation is from p. 17.

45 My interpretation of the picture is my own; Ostiguy, *Charles Huot*, does not pay much attention to the picture; though it figures prominently as a colour plate in Harper, *Painting in Canada*, 240, it is not discussed; Reid, *A Concise History of Canadian Painting*, reproduces a halftone and calls the painting 'an exhilarating virtuoso performance' and leaves it at that. The lack of critical commentary may have something to do with the fact that the painting is still in a private collection.

46 Again this is essentially my own interpretation of the picture. The standard texts skip over this phase of Suzor-Coté's career. I am indebted, however, to Hughes de Jouvancourt's monograph *Suzor-Coté* for some illuminating comments. I am also grateful to Charles Hill of the National Gallery, who provided me with a copy of his memorandum on another Suzor-Coté from this historical period, *Le coureur de bois*, in which he comments on the artist's career and style.

47 Eventually they tired of it, and opened a further competition in 1910, which Huot won with his design. For the details see Derome, 'Charles Huot.'

48 Laurier Papers, Microfilm, Laurier to Suzor-Coté, 22 November 1907 (13598); Walker Papers, Vol. 27B, Minutes, Advisory Art Council, 1 February 1908.

49 Burnham and Geise, 'History Painting: How It Works.'

50 Smith, *Nations and Nationalism in a Global Era*, 89–90.

51 Hill, *The Group of Seven*.

52 See for the full story see Bayer, *The Ontario Collection*.

53 Quoted in Emily Fourmy Cutrer, 'Negotiating Nationalism, Representing Region:

Art, History, and Ideology at the Minnesota and Texas Capitols,' in Burnham and Geise, eds., *Redefining American History Painting*, 277–93.

54 Tippett, *Art in the Service of War*.

55 Hill, *The Group of Seven*; Eric Kaufman and Oliver Zimmer, 'In Search of the Authentic Nation: Landscape and National Identity in Canada and Switzerland,' *Nations and Nationalism* 4 (1998):483–510, and Osborne, 'The Iconography of Nationhood in Canadian Art,' 169–72. This argument about the empty landscape has been developed with more fervour and moral indignation in two books published since this chapter was written: *Beyond Wilderness: The Group of Seven, Canadian Identity, and Contemporary Art* (Montreal and Kingston: McGill-Queen's University Press, 2007), an anthology of images and text edited by John O'Brien and Peter White; and from a West Coast perspective, Leslie Dawn, *National Visions, National Blindness: Canadian Art and Identities in the 1920s* (Vancouver: University of British Columbia Press, 2006).

10 Tricky Myths: Settler Pasts and Landscapes of Innocence[1]

EVA MACKEY

[M]emory ... must serve as an instrument of information to enable us to judge and analyze the present.[2]

Getting its history wrong is crucial for the creation of a nation.[3]

Memory, History, and Landscapes of Nationalism

'What does it mean at the end of the twentieth century to speak ... of a Native land?'[4] James Clifford's question seems even more important today, as conflicts about land and forms of identity dominate the world stage. However, the problem of the link between national identity, history, and specific topographic spaces has been with settler nations for a long time. Ex-colonial British settler nations such as Canada, Australia, New Zealand, and the United States were created as a result of earlier transnational flows of capital and populations, and usually involved destruction of Native peoples[5] and the appropriation of *their* native lands. This chapter examines the cultural politics of the processes through which Canada attempts to make the geographical space of the nation a 'Native Land.' It examines 'authoritative' or 'official' representations of Canadian nationhood that are produced within state institutions as part of their pedagogical programs to create or reflect national identity. Specifically how do state institutions choose to officially remember the colonial and national past in order to build collective national identity?

During recent decades in Canada, members of minority groups have challenged official national cultural institutions, and demanded both their inclusion in representations of the nation and control over representations of their own cultural groups. These challenges include the controversies over 'The Spirit

Sings' exhibition at the Glenbow Museum[6] as well as the 'Into the Heart of Africa' exhibit at the Royal Ontario Museum.[7] In response to this changing social and cultural context, some of the designers of official national public culture have begun to mobilize imagery of, or cultural productions created by, historically marginalized groups such as Aboriginal people and 'ethnic minorities,' in their representations of official 'multicultural' national culture. The result is representations of nationhood that highlight the hybrid and diasporic nature of its population. What are the cultural politics of these apparently inclusive processes?

In the late twentieth and early twenty-first centuries, national identities are formed through mass media, spectacles of nationhood, and social institutions. These sites of identity production – national art and literature, national museums and art galleries, television and radio programs, advertising, nationalist festivals, and education programs – create what Stuart Hall calls 'narratives of nationhood.'[8] These narratives construct a body of stories and myths with which people identify and which 'stand for, or *represent* the shared experiences, sorrows, and triumphs and disasters which give meaning to the nation. As members of such an "imagined community," we see ourselves in our mind's eye, sharing in this narrative.'[9]

Particular constructions of history are central to such narratives. Brian Osborne suggests that nation-state building has always been 'ardently historical' because of its emphasis on 'reconstructing and preserving the past, to encourage the present, to build and secure the future – and this has often required the use and misuse of history and heritage' (citing Lowenthal).[10] Nationalist narratives do not, of course, represent the actual lived and multiple sentiments of the entire heterogeneous and diverse population of nations such as Canada, which are cross-cut by region, language, race, gender, class, and culture.[11] Official versions of national history may be different from, in fact deeply contradictory to, individual and collective people's acts of remembering specific events and processes.

Memory has become a popular focus in the humanities and social sciences. In anthropology, according to David Berliner, there has been some 'danger of overextension' of the term memory that perhaps results from lack of clarity. Anthropologists have tended to focus on how history and memory is lived and negotiated by actual people, exploring the malleability of the past and the 'bricolage' dimension of how we create it and relate to it.[12] Yet there has been terminological confusion about whether we are discussing 'memory as recollection' or 'memory as cultural reproduction.'[13] This is why I distinguish between 'vernacular' (lived, contested) and 'official' forms of memory.[14] Official nationalist memory focuses on nurturing a sense of common history shared by people who probably have never met, the construction of collective awareness promoted through a narrative of shared historical experience – what I call 'official nationalist narratives.' 'Narratives of nationhood' are 'discursive devices' that represent difference as unity, and which try to 'stitch up' differences into one identity, an identity that represents everyone as belonging to the 'same great national family.'[15] Osborne suggests that what we are really talking about is 'the choreographing of the power of imagination by locating it in an invented history, and grounding it in an imagined geography. The orchestration of such collective remembering, and if necessary, collective amnesia, constituted the crucial underpinning of national-state identities.'[16] I therefore use the term 'official nationalist narratives' to describe and analyse such orchestrations of national history and to distinguish between them and vernacular histories and memories.

Official nationalist narratives also consistently mobilize images of land – be it homeland, motherland, or fatherland – to do the work of constructing a sense of 'oneness' from diverse populations which may never meet face-to-face. From images of England's green and rolling hills, to representations of Australia's outback,[17] to the vast expanses of 'The West' in America – the land itself becomes a 'repository of historic memories and associations.'[18] There is, however, no '*inherent* identity to places' or land: meanings are constructed by humans, and geographers use the term 'landscape' to refer to such culturally loaded geographies.[19] Nationalist representations of space and place have been called 'patriotic landscapes,'[20] and 'landscapes of sovereignty.'[21] Since the formation of the Dominion of Canada in 1867, images of nature, the wilderness, and the north have defined Canadian national identity, often in racialized terms as white settler identity.[22] In late twentieth- and twenty-first-century Canada, a settler nation with an official policy of multiculturalism, such natural and wilderness images are still ubiquitous, although now they are coupled with images of cultural pluralism which highlight Canada's Native peoples. This chapter examines three contemporary land- and nature-based[23] official nationalist narratives, and explores how cultural difference and national culture are formulated in them. Specifically, I explore how First Nations peoples' relationships with settlers are represented in official memories of the past. These present-day pluralist official nationalist narratives emerge at the end of the twentieth century and yet represent the problematic past of Canada. Do they represent a radical break from previous more exclusionary versions of national identity?

Cultural Difference: Homogeneity, Hybridity, Inclusion, Exclusion

Globalization, identity, space, and place have recently become important foci of social inquiry.[24] A key assumption in much of this literature is that there has been a profound shift in how people conceptualize the local and how they negotiate the link between identities and specific topographical spaces as a result of globalization. Some theorists celebrate the radical potential of the mobility, marginality, and 'cultural hybridity' that they see emerging with globalization.[25]

Many analysts celebrate globalization and transnationalism because they argue it allows for formulations of identity that disrupt the oppressive features of modernity. Modern identities such as national identity are said to function through the erasure of difference and the construction of a singular, unified, homogeneous subject.[26] As Homi Bhabha contends, dominant power and political supremacy seek to *'obliterate'* difference.[27] It is argued that modern identities are based on binary oppositions of self and other and the notion of fixed homogeneous cultures. On the other hand, identities emerging with globalization and transnationalism – defined as fractured, fragmented, mobile, diasporic, and hybrid – are seen to create spaces in which identities can be enunciated outside of, or rather *in between*, modern forms of identity such as national identity. According to Bhabha, this 'Third Space' is one that 'makes it possible to begin envisaging national, anti-nationalist histories of the "people."'[28] These cultural forms are thus seen as essentially radical, because they disrupt the homogeneity of modern identities and allow for the enunciation rather than the erasure of difference.

This chapter suggests that the above dualism between repressive homogeneity and radical hybridity does not hold, especially in the Canadian context. I contend it is important to account for the ways in which some nation-states such as Canada have taken up issues of pluralism in official forms of national public culture, and that it is necessary to do so before celebrating the radical potential of the simple enunciation of difference. This chapter analyses several official nationalist narratives, including the design of the Canadian Museum of Civilization, the plot of a nationalist play performed as part of the 125th anniversary celebrations, and an exhibit at the National Gallery curated by Aboriginal people. Based on this analysis, I question the uncritical celebration of hybrid cultural forms, pluralism, and cultural difference that characterizes some recent theory. The chapter demonstrates that inclusive and celebratory images of diversity, grounded on specific and partial versions of history and representations of the nation's relationship to land, subtly reproduce particular forms of white settler national identity and also key Western concepts such as progress. It argues that such historical narratives are very tricky myths: they do not *erase* cultural difference, rather they *include* and highlight Native people and Aboriginal imagery, and yet at the same time they draw on 'buried epistemologies'[29] that reinforce the very Western views of nature and human/nature relations that justified the destruction of Native people. These narratives reshape problematic historical cultural, political, and economic differences into a celebratory narrative, and then use that mythological celebration of difference to create a unified (although hybrid) narrative of national progress. Thus, representations of Indigenous peoples and their cultural heritage are mobilized to bolster settler nationalist mythology. Ultimately, such tricky mythologies, I suggest, use Native peoples' perceived link to the land not only to reinforce narratives of national progress, but also to create settler innocence in both the past and the present. Further, representations of Aboriginal people are appropriated to help the settler nation find and articulate a 'natural' link to the land – to help settlers become 'indigenous.'

Narrating the Natural Nation: Official Pedagogies of Patriotism

Designed as a sculpture to evoke the 'eroded land forms and streambeds of post-glacial Canada,'[30] the Canadian Museum of Civilization perches on the edge of the Ottawa River. The structure's features are 'drawn directly from the landscape and the forces of nature which shaped the landscape.'[31] Douglas Cardinal, the Native Canadian architect of the museum, came up with the design, which prioritizes natural and Native imagery. It resulted specifically from the 'ritual inspiration' and 'ancestral help' that he found during a sweat lodge ceremony.[32] The museum is intended to play a pedagogical role in the creation of national identity. According to the director of the museum, George MacDonald, it is part of a 'cultural master-plan' to create a 'cultural pilgrimage centre' in Ottawa, the nation's capital.[33] He writes:

> A national museum ... helps define cultural identity and the country itself. It stimulates pride amongst Canadians in their own culture. It announces to the world that Canada is a nation with special and unique characteristics. It reflects the ways in which various peoples, bringing their own cultures, have met the challenge of the land, by shaping it and shaping themselves to it. CMC offers to Canadians and non-Canadians an initiation into the national identity ... As a temple of culture CMC is very much a ritual space.[34]

As a 'ritual space,' a 'treasure-house,' or a stop on a pilgrimage to discover national identity, the message and symbolism of the Canadian Museum of Civilization (CMC) is an overt attempt to create a national narrative in which the land and Native people have a central role.

The nationalist play *Spirit of a Nation*, organized by the Canadian Heritage Arts Society as part of Canada's 125th anniversary celebrations in 1992, also combines the themes of nature and pluralism to fulfil its pedagogical goal. The play, funded by the federal government for the 125th anniversary of Canada's confederation, was performed by 125 students of diverse cultural backgrounds in 125 performances over the summer of 1992, as well as at televised Canada Day celebrations. It was explicitly designed as a pedagogical endeavour, and sold to the federal government with the promise to contribute to the task of educating and instilling 'pride of nationhood'[35] to communities all over the country.[36] Its narrative, similar to that of the Canadian Museum of Civilization, in an official narrative of nationhood which combines a celebration of cultural diversity, a glorification of Canadian achievement and shaping of the environment, and a message of harmony with the land.

Land, Unity and Diversity

The director of the Canadian Museum of Civilization argues that the national museum 'reflects the ways in which various peoples, bringing their own cultures, have met the challenge of the land, by shaping it and shaping themselves to it.'[37] A key theme therefore, in the Canadian Museum of Civilization, is the notion of a nation being moulded by 'the challenge' of the land. [38] Douglas Cardinal shared this perspective when he described his vision of the museum in his design statement, made public shortly after he was chosen as architect.

His proposal takes chronological narrative form, beginning with the emergence of the land from the sea and the development of 'a culture ... entwined with the forces of nature': Canada's Aboriginal peoples. Later, people came from 'across the oceans,' from 'diverse cultures all over the world, drawn to the beauty and *bounty of this land.*' Although at first 'they visited and *took from the land* to reinforce their empires,' they later stayed, writes Cardinal, and '*gave to the land* their sweat and hardships' (my emphasis).[39] The story continues with the development and building of the nation, described as if it were a gift to the land. 'Today,' he argues:

> Canadians, with their roots in several different cultures, now are evolving a new culture. Their cultures are merging and a greater understanding and appreciation are becoming part of Canada's national character. Our challenge should be to express the goals and aspirations of our society in our structure so that they will be physical manifestations of the best of our multicultural society.[40]

He finishes his narrative of the peaceful evolution of Canada from a state of pure nature to multicultural nation by suggesting that modern technology will now allow Canadians to move from being land creatures to star creatures. Our only limit is our own imagination.

For both MacDonald and Cardinal, the land plays a central role in unifying various cultures and peoples, from the First Canadians, to the settlers, to later immigrants. Cardinal's national narrative does not erase cultural diversity, but rather highlights it. The image of the land is also key, because it is through meeting the 'the challenge of the land' and 'by shaping it and shaping themselves to it' that Native people, British and French colonizers, and newer immigrants all *become* Canadian and progress together into the future.

A similar story is told in *Spirit of a Nation*, the nationalist play sponsored by Canada 125 Corporation. While the stage fills with the sounds of Aboriginal drumming, rushing wind, and water, the narrator tells the audience that the 'People of every nation are nourished by the land. Their spirit and their strength have their roots in the land, and the air, and the sea.' Several female dancers enter the stage and, dressed in natural earth-coloured costumes, move to express harmony between humans and nature. Then two storytellers, dressed in Native attire of buckskin and feathers, tell stories about their harmony with and their love of the land. Suddenly they appear to know instinctively that their time of living in peace with the land is over. They disappear, while actors dressed as early settlers slowly enter the stage. Then sounds of hammering, sawing, work, and 'progress' (as defined by settlers) increases to a cacophony as the cast transform the stage into a bustling modern scene: lawyers, doctors, pilots, nurses, and builders energetically performing urban modern life. They sing 'We have built a nation,' which focuses on the industry and energy of Canadian nation-building.

The next stage of development is multiculturalism. The land is brought into the story again when immigrants and refugees are invited (by the white narrator) into 'the land' which is a 'garden,' if they promise to 'give to the land.' Yet, conflict breaks out when people from different cultures arrive in the land. The conflict results in environmental degradation. However, conforming to the pattern of nationalist narratives intended to build unity, conflict is resolved when all the diverse people of Canada decide to 'give to the land' – to take care of the natural beauty which has been bestowed upon them. The Aboriginal people – who had previously disappeared from the story of the development of the nation – reappear to help create harmony with the land. The narrative ends with the entire cast, dressed in similar modern suits of differing colours, energetically singing 'The Future Begins with You.' Caring for the land is the key to uniting different cultures, to creating a narrative that links past, present, and future.

Such official narratives of nationhood cannot be faulted for their erasure of Aboriginal people. These are not stories of the conquered land as *terra nullius*: Aboriginal people are not erased from history. In fact their link to the topographic space of Canada is absolutely necessary for the narrative line of these stories. It is not their erasure, but precisely *'how they are made present,'*[41] that reveals a complex cultural politics.

Frontier Narratives and Canada's 'Tolerance'

Official nationalist narratives of the late twentieth and early twenty-first centuries draw on particular versions of earlier nationalist mythology. As I have argued in detail elsewhere, official Canadian nationalist narratives have often been explicitly exclusionary, assimilationist, and racialized, but they have often also included Aboriginal people and highlighted Canada's specific forms of 'tolerance' of Aboriginal people, although in different ways through time.[42] Bruce G. Trigger suggests that in Anglo-Canadian historical writing leading up to and immediately after Confederation, patriotic versions of history painted a portrait of the colonizers of Canada as more generous than those of the United States: while the Americans violently and brutally conquered their 'Indians,' the Native people of Canada, according to mythology, never suffered these horrors of conquest.[43] Trigger argues that these interpretations 'required great self-deception, or hypocrisy, on the part of writers whose governments were treating their former allies with much the same mixture of repression and economic neglect as American governments were treating defeated enemies.'[44] Such self-deception and hypocrisy can also be seen in Canadian frontier myths, particularly around the activities of the Royal Canadian Mounted Police, and as epitomized in a postcard I purchased in 1992.[45]

On the postcard, the red-coated Mountie smiles calmly and reaches out to shake hands with Chief Sitting Eagle, who is dressed in a multicoloured headdress, buckskins, and beads. The caption reads: these 'are the symbols of Canada's glorious past. A Mountie, resplendent in his famed scarlet greets Chief Sitting Eagle, one of Canada's most colourful Indians.' Such an image of reconciliation and equality, presented so picturesquely, recalls a longer mythology of Canadian identity that I call the 'Mountie Myth,' a myth based on the story of the Western expansion of the nation at the end of the nineteenth century. The Royal Canadian Mounted Police, representatives of British North American justice, went out west to promote assimilation and subdue Native resistance. Yet in the mythological representations of that project they are often constructed as heroically managing the inevitable and glorious expansion of the nation (and the subjugation of Native peoples) with much less bloodshed and more benevolence and tolerance than the violent U.S. expansion to the south. Haydon, in his 1912 history of the RCMP, wrote that

In the space of a few years ... the northwest had witnessed a revolution taking place within its borders, a bloodless revolution of the most remarkable kind. Over thirty thousand Indians, at war with one another and hostile to the white invasion, had been transformed into a peaceful community showing every disposition to remain contented and law-abiding.[46]

In popular literature and histories, a typical scene of confrontation between the Mounted Police and 'Indians' shows the latter, like children, easily cowed by a display of authority. Often this confrontation is between an unarmed officer and a gang of 'angry braves.' The Mountie, apparently not noticing the rifles aimed at his head, would coolly dismount and walk up to the leader of the gang. In the story the Native people, 'completely disarmed by this mixture of reckless courage and self-confidence,' did meekly as they were told.[47] What actually happened, according to some historians, was that westward expansion did not initially require use of force, because the capitulation of Native land rights was brought about by disease (smallpox) and loss of subsistence (buffalo).[48]

The representation of Canada's Native peoples as childlike, trusting, and friendly to their Canadian government invaders was important in the construction of myths about Canadian identity because it was based on the idea that Canada had superior forms of British justice,[49] a legal framework seen as important to the development of an emerging national identity intent on differentiating Canada from the United States. Canadians still like to believe they are tolerant and benevolent people, and certainly *more* tolerant than Americans.[50] The inclusion of Native peoples in the Canadian Museum of Civilization and *Spirit of the Nation* is a late twentieth-century reshaping of this older 'Mountie myth.' Certainly there are differences between the attitudes and structures of the past and of the present. Native people are not overtly constructed as 'savages,' nor is their relationship to the land seen as wasteful, as it was in earlier colonial times. Yet, these later representations reaffirm a central aspect of how the *mythology* of the Mountie confirms Canadian benevolence. By including Native people in specific (yet limited) ways, they reaffirm the notion of Canada's benevolence and inclusion of Aboriginal people. These official narratives at the same time erase Canada's complex, brutal, and difficult history of dispossession, erasure, and cultural genocide.

Native People and Nature

Both narratives discussed so far equate Aboriginal people with the land and with nature. In the museum narrative they become 'a culture ... entwined with the forces of nature,' and in the *Spirit of a Nation* performance they dance and tell stories of their harmony with the land. They represent harmony between humans and nature, and the untouched and virgin natural land that comes to represent Canada's beginnings.

Aboriginal peoples and nature have long been equated in colonial, nationalist, and tourist discourses.[51] From early representations of Aboriginal people as noble savages, to the great exhibitions in the nineteenth century which showed Aboriginal people in their natural environments,[52] Aboriginal people have been seen as closer to nature, a representation which helped to affirm the superiority of Western civilization. Without 'the Rest (or its own internal "others"),' Hall argues, 'The West would not have been able to recognise and represent itself as the summit of human history.'[53] It was only in comparison with the so-called 'uncivilized,' 'savage,' and 'backward' peoples of the New World (seen eventually as an earlier stage of evolution) that the 'the West' could define and measure its own 'progress' and 'development,' eventually defining that *distance from* a natural state as the universal criterion for ranking all forms of society.[54] The ways in which 'others' were represented in Western discourse changed over time, and were a matter of serious contest and debate through time.[55] Aboriginal people could also be idealized and romanticized as 'Noble Savages' who were closer to nature. In Canada and in the United States at the end of the nineteenth and the beginning of the twentieth century as the frontier closed and racism became codified,[56] people began to deify nature and Native peoples. This reverence towards 'the natural' occurred just as the destruction of the natural environment intensified. Renato Rosaldo calls this process of yearning for what one has destroyed 'imperialist nostalgia': a process in which people destroy their environment or the cultures of other peoples, and then turn around to worship what they have destroyed. Rosaldo argues that imperialist nostalgia uses a pose of 'innocent yearning,' which conceals complicity in brutal domination and produces a sense of innocence.[57]

It is significant that, simultaneous with the 'march of progress' and 'civilization'[58] in Canada, the very phenomena that were being destroyed were now called upon to represent the nation. The Group of Seven, a group of Canadian painters whose work represents and embodies the origin of Canadian modern art, began to use the wilderness to represent the essence of Canada. The Group of Seven's wilderness paintings have a revered place in the symbolic construction of nationhood today. Indeed, it was the work of these artists which 'contributed most to the development of a national identification with a distinctive sense of place.'[59] Their work as a whole, characterized by its focus on northern landscapes as unpeopled wilderness, used the rugged and rocky terrain of the Canadian pre-Cambrian shield and the northern woods as its central imagery.[60]

At the same time, Native artefacts became national treasures, 'a visible link with the country's first peoples and a part of its heritage which had to be preserved,'[61] and Native artefacts were sold as Canadian tourist souvenirs, markers of authentic Canadian identity. Native people and Nature also began to be integrated into official national iconography as Canada's 'heritage'; they even appeared carved into the walls of the Parliament Buildings in Ottawa.

'Indians' in the Parliament

The Parliament Buildings, similar to the Canadian Museum of Civilization, are seen as a reflection and symbol of Canadian identity.[62] A pamphlet by the Public Information Office of the House of Commons says the Parliament Buildings, 'like a mirror ... reflect our diversity and uniqueness yet, at the same time, they are an enduring symbol of our unity.' Constructed originally between 1859 and 1866, the buildings burned to the ground in 1916 (except for the library). Rebuilt in Gothic Revival style and completed in 1922, the buildings integrated many sections of blank stone, to be carved and sculpted later. Over the decades, carvings have been added, including imagery that highlights Canada's Native peoples. In 1932, the Dominion Memorial Sculpture, designed by Dr R. Tait McKenzie, was placed in the Hall of Honour. The official Guide Manual of the Parliament Buildings describes its first panel: 'In the foreground are four figures. On the left, is Canada enthroned; her right hand on a shield emblazoned with the current Arms of Canada. Her left hand is outstretched to receive the offerings of her children. A youthful figure, Canada wears a headdress of a Caribou mask with antlers, a short chiton and moccasins.'[63]

In the sculpture, Canada begins as a childlike Native: Aboriginal imagery here represents the early foundations of Canada, its youth, its past. As the narrative progresses, the settlers reshape, categorize, map, and civilize nature itself. As the story moves from left to right, the sculpture has engineers and cartographers mapping the Canadian wilderness. Lumberjacks and fishermen build and harvest the land and sea. To the side of one panel is a white family, who the Guidebook says represent Canada's pioneers. They are 'watched' by an 'Iroquois Indian.'[64]

In this 1932 sculptural representation of Canada's development, Native people have already been appropriated to represent Canada's heritage and past, and they are idealized as nature itself. Idealization, it has been argued, is one characteristic of a colonizing and orientalist aesthetic.[65] Further, pure untouched nature can be constructed as the raw material for the civilizing work of settlement; it allows the settlers to construct themselves as the agents who transform raw nature into developed civilization. Indeed, in this image, the early natural/Native roots of Canada are then integrated into a narrative of settlement and progress. Native peoples here provide a link between the settlers and the land – they help to negotiate the rocky terrain of creating Canada as 'Native land' to settlers, when the nation is made up mostly of colonizers and immigrants. Further, although Native people are present in this image of hard work and settlement, this presence is limited: either as Canada's youthful and natural beginnings or as the passive unnamed Iroquois *watching* the pioneers.

The Canadian Museum of Civilization similarly locates Native peoples as Canada's heritage and Canada's past. The Grand Hall is designed to be one of the first spaces a visitor enters and is organized hierarchically – designed to draw people and control movements in specific ways.[66] A breathtaking space of huge proportions, filled with totem poles and artefacts of Canada's West Coast peoples, it curves around the central courtyard of the museum and looks out across the river to Canada's Parliament Buildings. The director of the museum argues that the Grand Hall is made central to the design of the museum so that it will 'emphasize the contribution of Native peoples to the heritage of the nation and the world.'[67]

Heritage is understood to be property which may be inherited and which devolves by right of inheritance, specifically 'something handed down from one's ancestor or the past, as a characteristic, a culture, tradition, etc.'[68] If Aboriginal culture within the museum emphasizes the contribution of Aboriginal peoples to the 'heritage of the nation and the world,' as MacDonald and Alsford stress, then Native culture becomes a form of *cultural property* that is transformed into the inheritance of the nation.[69] Through the national museum the world also has access to this heritage, and the museum becomes a place of global significance, a 'world class' heritage site. The process of transforming Aboriginal culture into 'heritage' enables the culture of the colonized to be put into the service of building national and international identity.

Further, if Aboriginal culture becomes national 'heritage,' the long history of conflict over the contested space of the land is minimized and transformed. The Oxford English Dictionary also suggests that 'heritage' means 'land and similar property which devolves by law upon the heir,' as '*distinguished from conquest*: land inherited and not purchased.'[70] Heritage functions, as John Corner and Sylvia Harvey suggest, to 'promote the dissolution, or at least the temporary forgetting, of radical differences and inequalities and to do so in the interests of celebrated unity.'[71] The celebration of Canadian national 'heritage,' made possible by appropriating Aboriginal culture, entails no less than the erasure of the history of *conquest*. Aboriginal people become the ancestors of the nation who pass on an inheritance, not the survivors of conquest and colonization.

Further, to claim Native culture and peoples as Canada's heritage provides a longer continuum and tradition of culture for particular versions of the nationalist cause. Native people and their culture and artefacts have the unique quality of being entirely from this specific geographical space that is now called Canada. Native people are perceived to be actually linked to this piece of land, and, as we have seen, the land is a primary symbol of the nation. This construction of Native peoples as 'heritage' also means they become caught in the past. If one visits the museum in the summer, several tepees occupy the central courtyard of the museum. Placed as if embraced by the landscape form of the museum and facing the Parliament Buildings across the river, the tepees send the signal that Canada recognizes its Native peoples: a contemporary version, we might say, of the Mountie myth. However, although Native people are highlighted as Canada's heritage, they are at the same time frozen in the glorious past of tepees and headdresses. Most Native people in Canada do not live in tepees. As citizens of the twenty-first century with a long history of colonization, many live in poverty in small, unromantic homes on reserves, in apartments and houses in urban centres, or on the streets. Official nationalist narratives allow no authoritative space for the living and breathing twenty-first century descendants of the Native people who first encountered the colonizers. Their presence would raise problematic questions about justice, history, and the present.

Nature and Progress?

Central to theories of evolution and race emerging in the late eighteenth and early nineteenth century was the idea of progress; societies progress through stages to reach the ultimate pinnacle of evolution – European 'civilization' – a concept that emerged with its new meaning in the eighteenth century. The official nationalist narratives I discuss in this chapter are all *linear* narratives that pivot on the idea of Canada's progress from a wild and virginal land to a developed, forward-looking, tolerant nation that cares for its environment. Aboriginal peoples represent nature and the past: they are contained in the place of *origin*. Progress, in Western thought, has often entailed the subduing, mastering, and transforming of nature – of making wilderness into civilization.[72] The binary opposition in Western thinking between natural and human life worlds – and the idea that progress entails *mastering* nature – have been seen to bear some responsibility for the destruction of nature in modern society, and the destruction of Aboriginal peoples.

These narratives of Canadian nationhood present the Western narrative of progress as if it is natural and inevitable. The designer of the museum, Cardinal, says that the museum should be a celebration of 'man's evolution and achievement,'[73] and that it should send people away 'optimistic that we are progressing as human individuals and as a nation.'[74] He describes the museum as 'a symbolic form' which 'will show the way in which man first learned to *cope with the environment, then mastered it and shaped it to the needs of his own goals and aspirations.*'[75] Although this progress is described as in 'harmony' with nature, it also entails 'mastering' and 'shaping' nature.

These are, perhaps not surprisingly, not only Western narratives of progress, but stories with a particular nationalist twist. They narrate the progress of a specific settler nation, one that has developed a national identity revolving in part around the idea of its tolerance. The linear narrative – beginning with Native peoples in harmony with the land and ending with Canadians of all cultures in harmony with the land – functions by appropriating Native people, and by incorporating cultural pluralism and environmentalism into a Western linear narrative of national progress. This is facilitated through the construction of Native peoples as guardians of the land and as helpmates in the project of progressive nation-building.

Guardians of the Land/Helpmates in Progress

A key issue in the narratives is the way in which the moment of contact between Native people and the colonizers is represented by the colonizers. In Cardinal's museum narrative, for example, Native people are presented first as the guardians of the land, living in perfect harmony. When the story moves on to the meeting between 'old- and new-world' peoples, the colonizers first 'visited and *took from the land* to reinforce their empires.' Later, however, they 'stayed and *gave to the land* their sweat and hardships' (my emphasis).[76] This move constructs the colonizers as people who *share* in the Native people's defined task of 'giving to the land' and living in harmony with it. In doing so it erases the myriad negative effects colonialism had and has on Native peoples and cultures (and the environment). Moreover, the European settlers, history tells us, did not have the well-being of the land and harmony with nature as their goal. Yet presenting the story in this way allows the profound differences and deeply asymmetrical relations between Native people and settler cultures to be transformed into a mythic narrative of natural, peaceful, and tolerant progress. 'Giving to the land' is integral to a process of reconciliation between Native people and colonizers – a process of reconciliation in which Aboriginal people forgive the settlers.[77] This official nationalist narrative transforms the past. It tells a story that, through its silences, allows some white Canadians to construct a sanitized collective memory which leaves them with a comforting sense of national settler innocence about the negative effects of colonization. Native people and the land, and the link between them, therefore, play a central role in negotiating the rocky terrain of developing, within official settler nationalism, a narrative of progress that links colonizers to the specific topographical space, at the same time producing national innocence regarding the colonial encounter.

In these narratives the process of 'giving to the land' through colonial progress is presented as if it were on a continuum with what *Native people wanted*: as if settlers and Native peoples were really, after all, involved in the same sort of transformative, yet ecologically sound, endeavour. This has interesting results for the ways in which land and forms of cultural identity are constructed. If the settler project of transforming nature into civilization is framed as 'giving to the land,' it recasts settlers as actually quite similar to Native peoples. They, too, can see themselves as living in harmony with the land. Native people also become more like settlers: they appear to believe in and work for the shared progressive project of 'caring for the land' through nation-building. They are thus transformed into picturesque helpmates of the settler project of progress.

Finally, in both of these narratives, the land appears to be populated by Canadians of all races and cultures who are desperately 'giving' to it. If the land can be 'given to' in this way, it is seen to have a certain amount of agency, even desire. Hence, the conflict-ridden and often devastating realities of colonization and urbanization are presented as if the *land itself* naturally desired to be 'given to.' It is presented as if *nature wanted* its inevitable and glorious transformation into progressive civilization. As Bruce Willems-Braun points out, 'nature' is not an a priori thing, but a construction 'invested with, and embedded in, social histories.' Further, '*how* nature is constructed matters.'[78] This version of nature constructs it as desiring its own transformation into a 'resource landscape' for the nation to develop.[79] This construction naturalizes progress itself, and appropriates Aboriginal people and an ideological version of nature into the story of a unified and progressive nationhood.

The segment of *Spirit of a Nation* in which conflict breaks out also utilizes the land as a focus to create unity and quell conflict. The section begins with a group of war-torn, grey, and tired-looking refugees entering the stage, while sounds of war and strife fill the background. They come from 'distant lands where barely a dream of a better life dares to survive.' An Asian refugee woman leads them, singing of her dreams for a brighter future. The tall white male narrator of the play invites them into Canada, the land which 'is a garden,' if they promise to 'give to the land.' The white narrator invites the refugees to join a celebration of Canada, and the scene miraculously changes to a joyous multicultural festival in which people from different ethnic groups dance and sing in traditional and colourful clothes. Yet, conflict soon erupts. Near the end of this celebration, two rap singers dressed in urban black and white street clothes enter. They sing a rap song that is a critique of the way people want to separate and fight, even though the land gives them so much. As the urban rappers continue their critique of environmental degradation, the harmonious pluralism of the multicultural festival begins to dissolve. Everyone on stage begins to argue and fight – until the very set is destroyed.

The Asian refugee woman, who had led the refugees in the previous scene, remains forlorn and alone on the stage full of smoke and silence. She cries out that she does not want her dream of a better life destroyed by the divisions and anger she sees around her. She raises her head and begins to sing about her dream of a safe place, a safe land. Finally the white male Canadian narrator and the two First Nations storytellers join her, and, epitomizing multiracial harmony, they sing in unison of their shared love of the land.

> There is a land, I believe
> Where one can dream, and see their dreams come true,
> And to this land, I want to give
> I want to be in Canada

Suddenly the stage transforms, as dozens of young Canadians of all races and cultures (yet dressed in similar modern suits of differing colours), dance and sing 'The Future Begins with You.' The hopeful lyrics suggest that if people work side by side they can make their dreams come true.

> We come from many distant countries
> We bring a promise to this land
> That we will honour and protect her
> All her people working hand in hand

The themes of cultural pluralism and respect for the land are still present, although the ethnic costumes and Native imagery have now disappeared. This is a story of the chaos of diversity resolved, ordered, and unified, through the shared project of caring for the land. The Asian refugee (who shares the Canadian dream of progress), the Native people (who want to care for the land), and the white narrator save the dream of the nation, and do so through their love of the land. In this ordered nation, all the people are dressed in similar modern outfits, but marked by their different colours. The colours (signifying cultures) may be different, but the goal of working together for the future of the nation makes them unified, and creates order from chaos. Paradoxically, *giving to the land* signifies this environmentally sound and now naturalized and multicultural (multicoloured?) process of progress.

This view of national identity mobilizes and highlights the idea of 'hybrid' identities. All of these individual ethnic identities, which are ambiguous and unstable on their own – so unstable that they create chaos and destruction – are presented as needing the project of nation-building (caring for the land) to give them an anchor and a goal, which then creates the heterogeneous (hybrid), yet unified, nation. This is the nation reshaped for the late twentieth and early twenty-first centuries, not in the old model of a culturally homogeneous collective, but as collective hybridity engaged in a shared and progress-oriented project. This, however, is not the supposedly liberatory hybridity that is mobilized to create 'anti-nationalist histories of the people' of the kind Bhabha envisages.[80] Rather, it constructs the nation itself as a 'Third Space' of hybridity, a hybrid space that nevertheless reshapes central and well-worn nationalist ideologies in which Aboriginal people are representatives of nature and helpmates to settlers. Further, in this space, the modern project of progress is still the key to nation-building.

Hybridity and Aboriginal Self-Representation

The narratives of nationhood discussed above all construct Native people as guardians of the land, as allies in progress, and as representatives of Canada's heritage. However, in 1992 – in part because of the contests over the five hundredth anniversary of Columbus's arrival in the Americas – newer and more critical forms of representing Native peoples also had legitimate cultural and political space. The most significant difference between the two was that Native peoples themselves produced these representations. The National Gallery of Canada in Ottawa presented 'Land, Spirit, Power: First Nations at the National Gallery of Canada,' an exhibition of art by contemporary Aboriginal artists and co-curated by Native curators. Below I discuss this exhibit in order to examine how this officially sanctioned self-representation by Native people might operate in the Canadian national imaginary.

In the 'Land, Spirit, Power' catalogue, co-curator Diana Nemiroff suggests that the exhibition is part of 'new discourses in First Nations art.'[81] She argues that in the 1980s, spurred by Native activism on the one hand and the move from modernism to postmodernism on the other, there was a marked shift in how First Nations art was represented. A new emphasis on identity and difference 'weakened the ethnocentrism of the art establishment.'[82] In the 1990s, as a result, more often Native people themselves controlled the exhibits. This situation, she argues, resulted in a less totalizing and generalizing approach to Aboriginal artwork.

Most important to Nemiroff is the question of Native self-representation and self-definition. She suggests that the presence of articulate individuals posing and responding to the question 'who shall speak for me?' is an 'essential step in addressing what Cornel West, writing of African American cultural identity, has termed the "problematic of invisibility and namelessness," and what has for native peoples, until recently, been their *mythic presence but real absence* in contemporary consciousness. Now ... a discourse is emerging in which First Nations individuals are telling it their way.'[83]

But does 'telling it their way' and asking 'who shall speak for me?' challenge deeply felt hegemonic assumptions and paradigms? In considering just this point, Gayatry Chakravorty Spivak said:

> For me, the question 'Who should speak?' is less crucial than 'Who will listen?' 'I will speak for myself as a Third World person' is an important position for political mobilisation today. But the real demand is that when I speak from that position I should be listened to seriously; not with that benevolent kind of imperialism, really, which simply says that because I happen to be an Indian or whatever ... A hundred years ago it was impossible for me to speak, for the precise reason that makes it only too possible for me to speak in certain circles now.[84]

These are crucial questions. What role does this 'speaking' or 'telling it their way' play in this exhibition? If one is to reach an understanding of how identities work in Canada today, one must explore what role Aboriginal self-representation plays, not for the artists, but rather for the consumers and audiences of the exhibition, and in the Canadian nationalist imaginary more generally. Who is listening? And how? Is this exhibit an example, as Nemiroff proposes, of a *new* and a *better* discourse about Native peoples? Does it challenge official nationalist narratives?

Certainly this exhibit was an improvement on discourses about Aboriginal people and Aboriginal art. It did not locate Native people in the space of 'origins,' as many of the representations I have discussed in this chapter do, thereby reinforcing the view of Native people as stuck in a primordial past. It was not 'salvage' collecting of Aboriginal artefacts to use for nationalism, or white Canadian artists mining Native art forms. 'Land, Spirit, Power' highlighted the artwork of vibrant, dynamic, critical Aboriginal artists in 1992 – five hundred years after Columbus's so-called 'discovery' of the 'New World.' Clearly Native people did more than just survive. 'Land, Spirit, Power' can be seen as a celebration of that survival and resistance.

Nemiroff suggests that in 'Land, Spirit, Power' the artists present their identities as political. While their identities are fixed, bounded, and historical, they are also fluid, constructed, and dynamic. They are embedded in the land and

Aboriginality, but also resolutely conjunctural, postmodern, ambiguous, and paradoxical.[85] One might say these are indeed 'hybrid' identities. Spivak argues that if an Indian woman or an immigrant (or by extension an Aboriginal person) 'speaks as' a representative of a particular group, she ends up being a token of what is perceived as a homogeneous group.[86] In this exhibit, however, Aboriginal artists are not presented as a homogeneous group with a fixed identity – they are presented as artists with hybrid, complex, and fluid identities.

If one were to follow Bhabha's reasoning about the radical nature of hybridity, one would think that speaking as they do from a position of hybridity – of *non*-homogeneity and cultural *un*boundedness – should challenge the problems of 'speaking as' and being listened to. However, a closer examination of the reception and presentation of the exhibit suggests that even the discourse of ambiguous, conjunctural, and hybrid Native identities can be appropriated and transformed by their location within dominant nationalist imaginings. Hybrid identities can reaffirm *national* history and identity, as well as reaffirm stereotypes. This is evident in a discussion of 'Land, Spirit, Power' by Shirley Thomson (the director of the National Gallery of Canada), in the foreword of the catalogue:

> The organization and presentation of Land, Spirit, Power at the National Gallery of Canada as Canada celebrates its 125th birthday is a particularly welcome occasion. As the first major international exhibition of contemporary art by artists of native ancestry to be held at the National Gallery, *it serves to recognize the contributions* of a remarkable group of artists and marks an important step towards the *openness of spirit* that we hope will characterize the next 125 years. (Emphasis mine)[87]

Despite Nemiroff's claim that this exhibit represents a 'new stage' in discourses about Native people, Thomson's discourse sounds surprisingly similar to the older patterns of representations of Native peoples I have discussed in this chapter. Native people are once again mobilized to reaffirm *national* identity. Similarly to the discourse of 'official multiculturalism,' a discourse in which minority groups are valued for their *contributions* to the Canadian nation,[88] Thomson recognizes Native people in this exhibit for their '*contribution*' either to art or to the nation. The existence and value of the nation as the primary site of importance is not questioned. She does not ask what Canadian national culture has contributed to Native communities because the value of nation and its progress is normative. She also mentions 'openness of spirit,' implicitly referring to Canadian tolerance, a nationalist mythology with a long history. She continues her discussion by affirming the link between Native people and land:

> In particular, *as nations search for new and compelling visions to hold them together*, and the earth is endangered by our carelessness towards the environment, Land, Spirit, Power may remind us in a very contemporary way of one of the oldest sources of *unity and sustenance – the land* in all its aspects. (Emphasis mine)[89]

Here Native people (hybrid or not) are once again appropriated into national identity to do the work of providing a natural link to the land – a link that gives Canada a 'new and compelling vision,' providing 'unity and sustenance' for the Canadian *nation*. Once again, Aboriginal people have been invited into official Canadian identity to do the job of negotiating that rocky terrain of legitimating settler ownership and occupation of the land. They fill the space of heritage where settler occupation might be contested.

While perhaps not what the artists and curators of the show had hoped for, Thomson's discussion is an example of one form of 'listening' that occurred with 'Land, Spirit, Power.' The exhibit was appropriated into nationalist imaginings in apparently contradictory ways, yet in ways that follow a particular version of nationalist logic. This logic, while on one hand embedded in past patterns of identity construction, also emerges as a new, improvisational and flexible response to an ambiguous situation. It is an example of the constitution, recognition, and institutionalization of a new kind of difference – and in recognizing this difference, the nation is recreated as unified, progressive, and tolerant.

The way these exhibits include images of Native peoples constitutes a rewriting of the old Mountie myth in a new and refurbished form. By the Mountie myth I mean the idea that Canadian justice – the Canadian way of dealing with difference and conflict – is more peaceful and friendly than that of the United States. The myth is re-enacted here through the notion of Native self-representation. For Nemiroff, Native people have, '*until recently*,' had to struggle with their '*mythic presence* but *real absence* in contemporary consciousness,'[90] a statement that assumes the problem is in the past. She presents the contemporary situation of Native peoples as if *self*-representation has solved all problems of representation for Native peoples. Yet does such self-representation in 'Land, Spirit, Power' fundamentally challenge the historical construction and institutionalization of difference? Further, how does self-representation function if it encounters powerful counter-discourses of unifying nationalism that draw on earlier representations of Aboriginal-white relations?

Some of these difficulties are exemplified in Lisa Balfour Bowen's review of 'Land, Spirit, Power.' She suggests that the exhibit is timely because it takes place in the year of the five hundredth anniversary of America's discovery by Columbus,[91] and that it 'represents a high-profile moment in the constitutional evolution of our country's aboriginal people.' She describes the artwork glowingly and writes admiringly of Native people's links to the land. Near the end of the article, she quotes James Luna, a U.S. Native artist who provides just the right tone of closure. He says that 'We are held back by the Native art in the US, most of which is clichéd and commercial.' He adds that '*in comparison to Canadian Natives* who are very *visible,*' U.S. Natives are still at the bottom of the social and political heap. Certainly, he argues, 'there hasn't been anything like this show – anything of this scope – in the US, so it *helps confirm the view* that *your Natives* are *much further ahead*' (emphasis mine).[92] The assumption is that visibility and self-representation, in themselves, answer the problems of power and history. Further, the tone of this article suggests that the oppression is over: 'we' let 'them' into Parliament and into the National Gallery; 'we' are good to 'our' Natives; and most importantly, we treat them *better than* they do in the United States.

Aboriginal people's essential link to the land, *and* their 'hybrid' and politicized presence, is here transformed into the mythic tale of Canadian tolerance. Suddenly, by allowing Native people into mainstream institutions, as living and vibrant people – not simply as two-dimensional stereotypes located in a fixed place on a historical continuum, but rather whole, conflicted, 'hybrid' human beings – Canadians may think that it is time to celebrate the end of the past and the beginning of the future. Canadian nationalism can appropriate Native hybridity and self-representation into its continuing redemption of its sins. In this redemption, crimes against Native people become conveniently located in the *past*. However, it is too soon to suggest that the past is over and the myth-making done. Such celebrations of Canadian tolerance – focusing on how far *Canada has come* by celebrating how far Canada has *let them come* – elide the difficult question of how far the nation still needs to go in order to have genuine justice and equality for Aboriginal people.

Canada's perceived tolerance and inclusion of Native peoples not only fills in the blanks of the settlers' original occupation of this land; more importantly, it *legitimates* in a contemporary way the nation's continued possession of it. The logic suggests that even if Canadians were intolerant or mistaken in the past, the nation is now making up for it. Canadians are perceived to be good and honest and rational, not like those horrible people to the south. Native self-representation can produce a conception of 'white Canadian' that perceives itself innocent of racism. Hybridity, radical critique of dominant culture, and

Native self-representation can also be appropriated into a dominant discourse, even if only temporarily.

Integrating Hybridity/Reconstituting National Identity

This chapter has examined several official nationalist narratives in Canada and has argued that these narratives, intended to be inclusive and to highlight cultural difference in the name of national unity, also reproduce particular forms of white settler national identity and key Western concepts such as progress. They therefore reinforce the 'buried epistemologies'[93] of Western views of nature and relations between humans and the natural world that justified the destruction of Native people. In these narratives, cultural difference has been reconfigured and appropriated to strengthen national identity – to create a unified (although hybrid) narrative of national progress. Yet the very inclusion of these cultural differences allows for the construction of white settlement as innocent in both the past and the present.

This chapter has questioned the often uncritical celebration of hybrid cultural forms, pluralism, and cultural difference in recent cultural theory. I therefore join recent analysts who have begun to critique the 'hybridity discourse normative to postcolonial analysis' and who argue for detailed and situated analyses that 'stress enduring asymmetries of domination.'[94] An important aspect of situated analyses, I argue, is an awareness of how, despite the mobility and 'ontological homelessness'[95] celebrated in the focus on '*post*national social formations,'[96] the nation-state is still, as Sanjay Srivastava argues, an important site for social inquiry.[97] This is precisely because nation-states, as this chapter demonstrates, are still in the business of constructing and reinforcing identities tied to specific (national) spaces, and because in the global world system national identity is a form of located identity which still has 'the widest appeal, the longest staying power, the most political clout, and the heaviest armaments in its support.'[98] Rather than focusing solely on celebrating 'postnational' social formations, I suggest we must also explore in more detail how national and other modern forms of identity are being reconfigured and reconstituted in the age of globalization, and how they can integrate and assimilate hybrid social forms along the way. New or old, in colonial history or in the present-day 'new world order' of globalization, power does not manifest itself in one easily readable and homogeneous form. For this reason it has been useful to examine the trickiness – the flexibility and ambiguity – of nationalist myth-making projects, rather than to secure epistemic security in the dialectical opposition between what is seen as radical hybridity (the celebration of difference) and its supposed opposite, repressive homogeneity (the erasure of difference).

What is particularly striking in the narratives I have discussed in this chapter is how history, landscape, and nature are mobilized in this task. Canada's national anthem begins with the phrase 'O Canada, our Home and Native land.' This chapter has raised some questions about how official narratives of nationhood have appropriated Aboriginality and cultural difference to make 'Native land' into what settler Canadians like myself can uncritically think of as 'our home.'

NOTES

1 This is a substantially revised version of work previously published in Eva Mackey, 'Becoming Indigenous: Land, Belonging, and the Appropriation of Aboriginality in Canadian Nationalist Narratives,' *Social Analysis* 42, 2 (1998): 149–78, and in Eva Mackey, *The House of Difference: Cultural Politics and National Identity in Canada* (London: Routledge, 1999; Toronto: University of Toronto Press, 2002). Thank you to Beth Finnis, Brian Street, Mary Millen, Susan Wright, Julie Marcus, and many others. Research funding was provided by the Commonwealth Scholarship Commission, the Royal Anthropological Institute, the Wenner-Gren Foundation, the Social Sciences and Humanities Research Council of Canada, and Charles Sturt University.

2 Tzvetan Todorov, *Facing the Extreme: Moral Life in the Concentration Camps* (New York: Metropolitan Books, 1996), 264.

3 J.E. Renan, 'What Is a Nation?' in Homi Bhabha, ed., *Nation and Narration* (1882; London: Routledge, 1990).

4 James Clifford, *The Predicament of Culture* (Cambridge, MA: Harvard University Press, 1988).

5 A note on terminology: In Canada the terms to describe Indigenous people have changed over the years, and now terms such as 'Native people,' 'Aboriginal people,' or 'First Nations communities' are used, often by request of people in these communities. I therefore use these terms interchangeably in this chapter. I use the term 'Indian' only in quotation marks.

6 Cf. Julia Harrison, '"The Spirit Sings" and the Future of Anthropology,' *Anthropology Today* 4, 6 (1988): 6–9; Bruce G. Trigger, 'Reply by Bruce Trigger' to Harrison's '"The Spirit Sings" and the Future of Anthropology,' *Anthropology Today* 4, 6 (1988): 9–10.

7 Cf . Hazel Da Breo, 'Royal Spoils: The Museum Confronts Its Colonial Past,' *Fuse* (Winter 1989–90): 27–37; Enid Schildkrout, 'Ambiguous Messages and Ironic Twists: Into the Heart of Africa and the Other Museum,' *Museum Anthropology* 15, 2 (1991): 16–23; Marlene Nourbese Philip, *Frontiers: Essays and*

Writings on Racism and Culture (Stratford: Mercury Press, 1992); Eva Mackey, 'Postmodernism and Cultural Politics in a Multicultural Nation: Contests over Truth in the "Into the Heart of Africa" Controversy,' *Public Culture* 7, 2 (1995): 403–32; Linda Hutcheon, 'The Post Always Rings Twice: The Postmodern and the Postcolonial,' *Textual Practice* 8, 2 (1994): 205–38.

8 Stuart Hall, 'The Question of Cultural Identity,' in Stuart Hall, David Held, and Tony McGrew, eds., *Modernity and Its Futures* (Cambridge: Polity Press in Association with Open University, 1992), 293.

9 Ibid.

10 Brian S. Osborne, *Landscapes, Memory, Monuments, and Commemoration: Putting Identity in Its Place*, Department of Canadian Heritage (for the Ethnocultural, Racial, Religious, and Linguistic Diversity and Identity Seminar), DRAFT Paper (Halifax: Department of Canadian Heritage, 2001), http://canada.metropolis.net/events/ethnocultural/publications/putinden.pdf.

11 The foundation or base of official Canadian identity, past and present, has often been deeply contested, and crisis-ridden, and these official versions of identity have changed over time as the nation-building project has changed and transformed. To simplify a complex process, analysed in more detail elsewhere (Mackey, *The House of Difference*), official versions of pre–Second World War identity celebrated British, French, and European roots. After much contest and debate, multiculturalism emerged as official national policy and identity in 1971. Neither of these official versions actually represents the diverse sentiments of all Canadians. Most recently, the rise of a new right in Canada, and the emergence of a 'white backlash' to the gains made by minorities, means that some Canadians might now prefer to downplay the role of Aboriginal people and multiculturalism as the basis of Canadian identity. These voices, although strengthening in recent years, are still marginal to official state-sanctioned representations such as those I discuss in this chapter; representations which seek to construct a unified yet diverse 'multicultural' national identity. For a more in-depth discussion of these issues, and the relationship between official multiculturalism and the white backlash, see Mackey, 'The Cultural Politics of Populism: Celebrating Canadian National Identity,' in Cris Shore and Susan Wright, eds., *Anthropology of Policy* (London: Routledge, 1997); Mackey, *The House of Difference*; and Mackey, '"Universal" Rights in National and Local Conflicts: "Backlash" and "Benevolent Resistance" to Indigenous Land Rights,' *Anthropology Today* 21, 2 (2005): 14–20.

12 David C. Berliner, 'The Abuses of Memory: Reflections on the Memory Boom in Anthropology,' *Anthropological Quarterly* 78, 1 (2005): 197–211.

13 Ibid., 206.

14 John Bodnar, *Remaking America: Public Memory, Commemoration and Patriotism in the Twentieth Century* (Princeton: Princeton University Press, 1992); John

Bodnar, 'Public Memory in an American City: Commemoration in Cleveland,' in J. Gillis, ed., *Commemoration: The Politics of National Identity* (Princeton: Princeton University Press, 1994), 75.

15 See Hall, 'The Question of Cultural Identity,' 297–9.

16 See Osborne, *Landscapes, Memory, Monuments, and Commemoration.*

17 Julie Marcus, 'The Journey Out to the Centre: The Cultural Appropriation of Ayers Rock,' in Gillian Cowlishaw and Barry Morris, eds., *Race Matters: Indigenous Australians and 'Our' Society* (Canberra: Aboriginal Studies Press, 1997), 29–51.

18 Anthony D. Smith, *National Identity* (London: Penguin, 1991), 9.

19 See Osborne, *Landscapes, Memory, Monuments, and Commemoration.*

20 Stephen Daniels, *Fields of Vision: Landscape Imagery and National Identity in England and the United States* (Princeton: Princeton University Press, 1993).

21 Garret A. Sullivan, *The Drama of Landscape: Land, Property and Social Relations on the Early American Stage* (Stanford: Stanford University Press, 1998).

22 Mackey, 'Becoming Indigenous'; Mackey, '"Death by Landscape": Race, Nature and Gender in Canadian Nationalist Mythology,' *Canadian Women's Studies* 20, 2 (2000): 125–30; Mackey, *The House of Difference.*

23 'Nature,' 'landscape,' and 'the environment' are not unproblematic and self-explanatory categories. Rather, recent analyses see them as social constructs that help to create identities. W.J.T. Mitchell suggests that we should examine nature, landscape, and environments not in terms of what they 'are' – as self-explanatory material entities. Nor should we attempt to discover what their essential 'meanings' are by reading them as 'texts.' Rather one seeks to explore what these concepts do, how they work and are instrumental in human cultural practice. See W.J.T. Mitchell, ed., *Landscape and Power* (Chicago: University of Chicago Press, 1994). This approach to environment and nature draws on similar frameworks developing within anthropology and sociology – approaches, which also see culture as a verb. See Brian Street, 'Culture Is a Verb: Anthropological Aspects of Language as Cultural Process,' in David Graddol, Linda Thompson, and Mike Byram, eds., *Language and Culture* (Clevedon, Philadelphia, and Adelaide: B.A.A.L. in association with Multilingual Matters, 1993). Alexander Wilson, for example, argues that 'landscape is a cultural activity.' See *The Culture of Nature: North American Landscape from Disney to the Exxon Valdez* (Toronto: Between the Lines, 1991), 13. See also William Cronon, *Uncommon Ground: Toward Reinventing Nature* (New York: W.W. Norton, 1995); Dennis Cosgrove and Stephen Daniels, eds., *The Iconography of Landscape* (Cambridge: Cambridge University Press, 1989); Daniels, *Fields of Vision*; Carolyn Merchant, ed., *Ecology: Key Concepts in Critical Theory* (Atlantic Highlands, NJ: Humanities Press International, 1994); Merchant, *Earthcare: Women and the Environment* (New York: Routledge, 1995); Max Oelschlaeger, ed., *The Wilderness Condition: Essays on Environment*

and Civilization (Washington, DC: Island Press, 1992); Val Plumwood, *Feminism and the Mastery of Nature* (London: Routledge, 1993); Simon Schama, *Landscape and Memory* (New York: Knopf; Toronto: Random House, 1995); Frederick Turner, *Beyond Geography: The Western Spirit against the Wilderness* (New York: Viking Press, 1980); and Bruce Willems-Braun, 'Buried Epistemologies: The Politics of Nature in (Post)colonial British Columbia,' *Annals of the Association of American Geographers* 87, 1 (1997): 3–31.

24 Arjun Appadurai, 'Global Ethnoscapes: Notes and Queries for a Transnational Anthropology,' in Richard Fox, ed., *Recapturing Anthropology: Working in the Present* (Santa Fe: School of American Research Press, 1991), 191–210; Appadurai, 'Patriotism and Its Futures,' *Public Culture* 5, 3 (1993): 411–30; Homi K. Bhabha, *The Location of Culture* (London: Routledge, 1994); Clifford, *The Predicament of Culture*; Clifford, 'Travelling Cultures,' in Lawrence Grossberg, Cary Nelson, and Paula Treichler, eds., *Cultural Studies* (New York: Routledge, 1992), 96–111; Paul Gilroy, *There Ain't No Black in the Union Jack* (London: Hutchinson, 1987); Akhil Gupta, 'Beyond "Culture": Space, Identity, and the Politics of Difference,' *Cultural Anthropology* 7, 1 (1992): 6–23; Akhil Gupta, 'The Song of the Nonaligned World: Transnational Identities and the Reinscription of Space in Late Capitalism,' *Cultural Anthropology* 7, 1 (1992): 63–79; Stuart Hall, 'The Local and the Global: Globalisation and Ethnicity,' in Anthony D. King, ed., *Culture, Globalisation and the World System* (London: Macmillan, 1991), 19–39; Hall, 'The Question of Cultural Identity'; Rob Wilson and Wimal Dissanayake, eds., *Global/Local: Cultural Production and the Transnational Imaginary* (Durham, NC: Duke University Press, 1996).

25 Hall, 'The Local and the Global,' 36–9; Hall, 'The Question of Cultural Identity,' 310; Gilroy, *There Ain't No Black in the Union Jack*; Bhabha, *The Location of Culture*.

26 Analysts such as Bhabha (*The Location of Culture*), Gilroy (*There Ain't No Black in the Union Jack*), and Hall ('The Local and the Global' and 'The West and the Rest: Discourse and Power,' in Hall and Bram Gieben, eds., *Formations of Modernity* [Cambridge: Polity Press in Association with Open University, 1992], 275–332) celebrate the 'diasporic' and 'hybrid' forms these identities take. Critics include Anne McClintock, *Imperial Leather: Race, Gender and Sexuality in the Colonial Contest* (New York: Routledge, 1995); Talal Asad, *Genealogies of Religion: Discipline and Reasons of Power in Christianity and Islam* (Baltimore: Johns Hopkins University Press, 1993); Nicholas Thomas, *Colonialism's Culture: Anthropology, Travel and Government* (Cambridge: Polity Press, 1994); Wilson and Dissanayake, eds., *Global/Local*; and Sanjay Srivastava, 'Postcoloniality, National Identity, Globalisation and the Simulacra of the Real,' *Australian Journal of Anthropology* 7, 2 (1996): 166–90.

27 Homi Bhabha, cited in Asad, *Genealogies of Religion*, 262.

28 Bhabha, *The Location of Culture*, 38–9.

29 Willems-Braun, 'Buried Epistemologies.'

30 George F. MacDonald and Stephen Alsford, *Museum for the Global Village* (Hull: Canadian Museum of Civilization, 1989), 1.

31 Ibid.

32 Trevor Boddy, 'Cardinal of Hull,' *Canadian Forum*, October 1989, 15–19; MacDonald and Alsford, *Museum for the Global Village*.

33 Ibid., 3.

34 Ibid.

35 Canadian Heritage Arts Society, *Experience Canada: Project Report (and Script of 'Spirit of the Nation')* (Victoria: Canadian Heritage Arts Society, 1992).

36 In the final report of the project to Canada 125 Corporation, the organizers say that a nation's culture is 'the adhesive which bonds its people. Canada does have a proud heritage and a positive outlook for the future. Canadians need to be allowed to share and celebrate their pride. They need to be encouraged to project that pride and confidence to the rest of the world. Therefore projects like EXPERIENCE CANADA must be funded and made readily accessible to the public. EXPERIENCE CANADA must continue to lead Canadians toward common goals and strengthened bonding as we continue to progress as one nation, proud and strong and free' (ibid., 3).

37 See MacDonald and Alsford, *Museum for the Global Village*, 3.

38 For interesting perspectives on Aboriginal people in Australian nationalism see Andrew Lattas, 'Aborigines and Contemporary Australian Nationalism: Primordiality and the Cultural Politics of Otherness,' *Social Analysis* 27 (1990): 50–69; on the appropriation of Ayer's Rock see Marcus, 'The Journey Out to the Centre'; and on liberal images of 'Indians' in the Hollywood film *Dances with Wolves* see Thomas, *Colonialism's Culture*, chapter 6.

39 Douglas Cardinal, 'Museum of Man Proposal, 1983: From Earth Creatures to Star Creatures,' *Canadian Forum*, October 1989, 17.

40 Ibid.

41 See Willems-Braun, 'Buried Epistemologies,' 21.

42 Mackey, *The House of Difference*.

43 Bruce G. Trigger, 'The Historian's Indian: Native Americans in Canadian Historical Writing from Charlevoix to the Present,' *Canadian Historical Review* 67, 3 (1986): 321.

44 Ibid.

45 I could not locate the origins or original date of production of the postcard, although I did find the previous owner of copyright. However, a PhD student in my department recently wrote me to say that some people from the Stoney Band she

is working with in British Columbia saw the postcard image in a previous publication of mine and recognized the Aboriginal man in the postcard. He is John Hunter (Sitting Eagle), the grandfather of contemporary elders in the community. He was a favourite subject for many of the photographers of the time, and, according to one of his grandsons, spent the week after Banff Indian Days posing for artists and photographers at the Banff Centre for the Arts.

46 Cited in Daniel Francis, *The Imaginary Indian: The Image of the Indian in Canadian Culture* (Vancouver: Arsenal Pulp Press, 1992), 64.

47 Ibid., 66.

48 J.L. Finley and D.N. Sprague, *The Structure of Canadian History* (Scarborough: Prentice-Hall of Canada, 1979).

49 See Francis, *The Imaginary Indian*, 69.

50 Mackey, *The House of Difference*; Mackey, '"Universal" Rights in National and Local Conflicts.'

51 Jonathan Bordo, 'Jack Pine – Wilderness Sublime, or the Erasure of the Aboriginal Presence from the Landscape,' *Journal of Canadian Studies* 27, 4 (1992): 98–128; Hall, 'The West and the Rest'; Kenneth Little, 'On Safari: The Visual Politics of a Tourist Representation,' in David Howes, ed., *The Varieties of Sensory Experience* (Toronto: University of Toronto Press, 1991); Renato Rosaldo, 'Imperialist Nostalgia,' in Renato Rosaldo, ed., *Culture and Truth* (Boston: Beacon Press, 1989); Willems-Braun, 'Buried Epistemologies.'

52 Curtis Hinsley, 'The World as Marketplace: Commodification of the Exotic at the World's Columbian Exhibition, Chicago, 1893,' in Ivan Karp and Steven Lavine, eds., *Exhibiting Cultures* (Washington: Smithsonian Institution Press, 1991), 344–65; Brian Street, 'British Popular Anthropology: Exhibiting and Photographing the Other,' in Elizabeth Edwards, ed., *Anthropology and Photography* (London: Yale University Press in Association with the Royal Anthropological Institute, 1992), 122–31.

53 Hall, 'The West and the Rest,' 314.

54 See also Michael Banton, *Racial Theories* (Cambridge: Cambridge University Press, 1987), 7; George W. Stocking, Jr, *Race, Culture, and Evolution: Essays in the History of Anthropology* (New York: Free Press, 1968); Stocking, *Victorian Anthropology* (New York: Free Press, 1987).

55 Cf. Banton, *Racial Theories*.

56 The increase in settlement in Canada in the late eighteenth and early nineteenth century meant that, by the end of the War of 1812, few Native people lived in southern Ontario and Quebec, the most populated areas of Canada, and the ones who did were increasingly isolated on reserves (Trigger, 'The Historian's Indian,' 318). While territorial boundaries began to take a more institutionalized form, cultural and racial boundaries began to harden, both in Canada and on a global scale.

See Sylvia Van Kirk, *'Many Tender Ties': Women in Fur-Trade Society in Western Canada, 1670–1870* (Winnipeg: Watson and Dwyer Publishers, 1980); Ann Laura Stoler, 'Rethinking Colonial Categories: European Communities and the Boundaries of Rule,' *Society for the Comparative Study of Society and History* 31 (1989): 134–61; and H. and Alan C. Cairns, *Prelude to Imperialism: British Reactions to Central African Society 1840–1890* (London: Routledge and Kegan Paul, 1965), 246.

57 Rosaldo, 'Imperialist Nostalgia,' 70.

58 In the half-century between Confederation and 1919 – the end of the First World War – Canada had transformed from a frontier nation to a Western industrial nation. J.M. Bumsted suggests that 'All Canadians were aware of the most apparent changes: the rapid growth of cities, the eventual decline of the rural population, the appearance of factories.' *The Peoples of Canada: A Post-Confederation History* (Toronto: Oxford University Press, 1992), 210.

59 Brian S. Osborne, 'The Iconography of Nationhood in Canadian Art,' in Cosgrove and Daniels, eds., *The Iconography of Landscape*, 169.

60 In my memory, most significant is the way in which they painted the lone and rugged pine trees. When I was in Northern Ontario during fieldwork, I found myself calling the trees 'Group of Seven' trees, and feeling that because of them I was now really in the '*true* Canada,' the '*true* north.' Nature itself was calling up nationalist texts.

61 Francis, *The Imaginary Indian*, 184–5.

62 I thank Stephen Delray, curator, House of Commons, for a fascinating interview, as well as Claudette Fleury Morena and Pierrette Pelletier, for providing me with much of the information about the Parliament Buildings.

63 Public Information Office, House of Commons, *Parliament Buildings Guide Manual* (Ottawa, 1994) (Active Document – in state of continual update).

64 Ibid., 201–2.

65 Hall, 'The West and the Rest.'

66 MacDonald and Alsford offer a detailed description of the architectural design grids, axes, and circulation routes that make up the hierarchy of space and control the movements of visitors (*Museum for the Global Village*, 24–7).

67 See ibid., 25.

68 *Webster's* English Dictionary, 1988 edition, 631.

69 See MacDonald and Alsford, *Museum for the Global Village.*

70 *Oxford English Dictionary*, 1989 edition.

71 John Corner and Sylvia Harvey, 'Mediating Tradition and Modernity,' in Corner and Harvey, eds., *Enterprise and Heritage: Crosscurrents of National Culture* (London: Routledge, 1991), 50.

72 Merchant, ed., *Ecology*, 2; Merchant, *Earthcare*.

73 Cited in MacDonald and Alsford, *Museum for the Global Village*, 15–16.

74 See Cardinal, 'Museum of Man Proposal, 1983,' 17.

75 Cited in MacDonald and Alsford, *Museum for the Global Village*, 15–16.

76 See Cardinal, 'Museum of Man Proposal, 1983.'

77 Also see Julie Marcus, 'The Erotics of the Museum,' paper given at the University of Sussex, March 1996. Manuscript in author's possession.

78 See Willems-Braun, 'Buried Epistemologies,' 24.

79 See ibid., 12.

80 Bhabha, *The Location of Culture*, 38–9.

81 Diana Nemiroff, Robert Houle, and Charlotte Townsend-Gault, eds., *Land, Spirit, Power: First Nations at the National Gallery of Canada* (Ottawa: National Gallery of Canada, 1992), 16–41.

82 Ibid., 36.

83 Ibid., 37.

84 Gayatry Chakravorty Spivak, *The Post-Colonial Critic* (London: Routledge, 1990), 59–60.

85 See Nemiroff, Houle, and Townsend-Gault, eds., *Land, Spirit, Power*, 37–41.

86 See Spivak, *The Post-Colonial Critic*, 59–60.

87 See Nemiroff, Houle, and Townsend-Gault, eds., *Land, Spirit, Power*, 7.

88 See Mackey, *The House of Difference*.

89 See Nemiroff, Houle, and Townsend-Gault, eds., *Land, Spirit, Power*, 7.

90 See ibid., 37.

91 There are no quotation marks on the word 'discovery,' and therefore no irony is intended, indicating that she missed the point of the exhibit: it is not possible to 'discover' a land already occupied. Based on my research, the discourses of anti-Columbus quincentennial activists during 1992 sought to reinterpret the 'discovery' of America as the 'invasion' of America (or Turtle Island).

92 Lisa Balfour Bowen, 'Native Spirit,' *Sunday Sun,* 18 October 1992.

93 See Willems-Braun, 'Buried Epistemologies.'

94 Wilson and Dissanayake, eds., *Global/Local*, 8; see also Asad, *Genealogies of Religion*.

95 Clifford, 'Travelling Cultures.'

96 Appadurai, 'Patriotism and Its Futures,' 420.

97 Srivastava, 'Postcoloniality, National Identity, Globalisation and the Simulacra of the Real,' 168.

98 Wallerstein, cited in Ien Ang and John Stratton, 'Asianing Australia: Notes toward a Critical Transnationalism in Cultural Studies,' *Cultural Studies* 10, 1 (1996): 26.

11 Settler Monuments, Indigenous Memory: Dis-Membering and Re-Membering Canadian Art History

RUTH B. PHILLIPS

A monument is a deposit of the historical possession of power.[1] Although it exhibits the traces of the particular historical 'will to memory' that caused its creation, the monument cannot maintain that memory in a stable form. Physical monuments, such as buildings or statues, are always subject to processes of destruction, erosion, and accretion, while the significance attributed to an individual work of art – its 'monumentalization' in a figurative sense – alters over time as narratives of history and art history change. The processes of monument making and unmaking and the orchestration of memory and forgetting are most visible in the aftermath of major shifts in regimes of power. During the past century global processes of decolonization have produced many such shifts. In their wake the monuments left behind by four centuries of European mercantile expansion and colonialism have often served as sites for resistance and historical revision expressed through processes of destruction, defacement, removal, or other alteration.

In Canada, as in other settler societies, such as Australia, New Zealand, and South Africa, monumental works of art and architecture have become focal points for indigenous peoples' contestations of settler narratives of history.[2] In this chapter I will examine several artistic projects undertaken during the 1990s by two First Nations artists,[3] the Saulteaux-Anishinaabe painter Robert Houle, and the Onondaga-Onkwehonwe (Iroquois) photographer Jeffrey Thomas. At the centre of the discussion will be Houle's *Kanata* (1992) (figure 11.4), a re-painting of Benjamin West's *The Death of General Wolfe* (1771) in the National Gallery of Canada (figure 11.3), and Thomas's photographic meditations on the monument to Samuel de Champlain, sculpted by Hamilton MacCarthy for Nepean Point in Ottawa, adjacent to Parliament Hill (1915–23) (figure 11.2). I will argue that both are pivotal works of postcolonial critique that intervene in settler constructions of monument and memory on two levels. On the one hand, they seek to revise specific Canadian historical discourses that have silenced Indigenous memory. On the other, they counter a more general art historical discourse of Primitive Art that, by definition, excluded Indigenous artists from participation in artistic modernism.

Settler and Aboriginal Vectors of Decolonization

Before discussing Houle's and Thomas's revisionist work in more detail, it will be useful to review briefly the political dynamics that characterize decolonization in settler societies in contrast to those of external colonies. Two kinds of anticolonial movements occur in settler societies, one advanced by settler populations desiring independence from imperial 'mother' countries, and the other by internally colonized Indigenous peoples who oppose the colonial regimes of both settlers and imperial powers. The process of decolonization can be further complicated when the conquest of one settler population by another during the colonial era has left unresolved issues of sovereignty, as is the case for Canada and Quebec. These multiple vectors of decolonization are projected and activated on a symbolic level through textual, visual, performative, and other forms of expressive culture.

A key strategy for the settler nation's establishment of an identity distinct from that of the imperial homeland has been the establishment of its own national museums, archives, and arts funding councils. Such institutions are charged with making the nation's history and distinctive identity visible to itself. Museums and archives fulfil this mandate in part by selecting and presenting certain visual and material objects as icons and landmarks that transmit the nation's origin story. Endowed with seminal or summary significance, they become shared reference points in the collective consciousness of the nation – and also key targets for Indigenous contestation.[4] Museums not only monumentalize the significance of specific images, and objects, but also function as architectural monuments in themselves.[5] As Carol Duncan has observed, 'like the traditional ceremonial monuments that museum buildings frequently emulate … the museum is a complex experience involving architecture, programmed displays of art objects, and highly rationalized installation practices.'[6]

A further complexity that marks cultural politics in the settler nation is its tendency to appropriate the images and art forms of the Indigenous population in order to differentiate its identity from that of the European mother country – a syndrome that anthropologist Nelson Graburn has termed 'borrowed identity.'[7] This syndrome is evident in the exhibitions and collecting practices of Canada's national museums during most of the twentieth century, but it was processed through three dominant aspects of modernist ideology. One of these was the belief that human cultures, like the animal and plant worlds, have evolved over time from simpler to more complex forms. Indigenous peoples were regarded as still living in a more 'primitive' state in comparison to more 'highly evolved' Western European peoples. A related belief in progress was also widespread. The emergence of the Western nation-states, as a complex form of political organization, demonstrated the superiority of Western modernity. Notions of progress and evolution were, however, contradicted to a certain extent by a third, widely held, belief that the industrialization and urbanization associated with 'progress' had a negative side, alienating the individual from nature, community, and spirituality.[8] This 'antimodernist' sensibility produced nostalgia and admiration for the 'simpler' and more 'primitive' ways of life that modernity was rendering obsolete. In the early twentieth century, groups of modern artists in Europe announced a break with the classical tradition of European art and began to draw inspiration from the Primitive Art of Africa, Oceania, and North America which had previously been regarded as inferior to the art of the West.[9] The modernists' admiration for Primitive Art was, however, restricted to types of art they deemed authentic, which were those created before their makers had become corrupted by contact with Western civilization. Since the directed assimilation policies established to 'civilize' the Indigenous peoples of Canada and the United States had been designed to eradicate the last traces of these traditional life styles, this notion of authenticity excluded the contemporary arts of Aboriginal peoples.

In accordance with these beliefs, Canada's national museums, like museums elsewhere in the West, positioned Aboriginal cultures and arts as prior to the sequence of Euro-Canadian history. When the National Gallery displayed examples of historical Aboriginal art in occasional temporary exhibitions, it presented them as a prelude to and a source of inspiration for settler artistic development and modernity.[10] Similarly, the anthropological displays of the National Museum of Canada presented Aboriginal artefacts in what Johannes Fabian has termed the 'ethnographic present' – an ideal past time imagined to have existed before change had forever altered the authenticity of Indigenous life. During the 1920s, for example, the National Gallery of Canada worked to foreground the post-impressionist landscape painting of the Group of Seven (a movement which was both modern in relation to the preceding academic tradition, and antimodernist in its focus on a pristine world of nature) and, after 1927, Emily Carr as a distinctive national school. Encouraged by Marius Barbeau, ethnologist at the National Museum of Canada, artists belonging to the Group memorialized images of largely unpeopled Aboriginal villages and totem poles that appropriated Indigenous cultures for a national Canadian iconography while at the same time inscribing the trope of the Vanishing Indian.[11]

During these years, too, the national museums and archives were actively assembling collections that would document and memorialize these disappearing cultures – a practice which, as Thomas Richards has argued, was also an 'archiving' strategy for controlling subject populations.[12]

In the years after the Second World War, a number of developments, such as the return of Aboriginal veterans, the Civil Rights movement in the United States, the granting of independence to many external colonies that had belonged to European empires, and other national liberation movements, combined to strengthen the anticolonial resistance of Canadian Indigenous peoples. Alan Cairns has charted the progress of this resistance, which has included such achievements as the entrenchment of Aboriginal sovereignty in the 1982 constitution and the 2009 Statement of Apology for Indian Residential Schools.[13] The situation of internal colonization, however, prevents the kinds of definitive acts of political liberation possible for external colonies. The lack of formal closure to the colonial era has, I would argue, endowed the arts – and especially the visual arts – with special prominence as a tool of Canadian Indigenous anticolonial activism. A key strategy of Canada's still effective Indian Act, which was designed in the late nineteenth century to engineer the assimilation of Aboriginal people into Euro-Canadian society, was the erasure of Indigenous languages, cultural traditions, and memory.[14] The need to recover and restore Indigenous accounts of the past to the national history is, therefore, at the heart of postcolonial politics. The national museums have been a particular target of this activism. Because of their prestige and power in forming the national self-image, Aboriginal cultural activists have, since the 1980s and earlier, campaigned to force them to be more inclusive, to display contemporary Aboriginal art, and to work with Indigenous curators.[15] As integral components of campaigns of political activism, the successes of Indigenous curators and artists in rewriting the settler histories displayed in the public spaces of museums, parks, and buildings have helped to prepare the ground for subsequent changes in government policy and law.

Contesting the Allegorical Indian

The critical nexus of political activism, the national capital as monumental site, and postcolonial artistic intervention can be illustrated anecdotally in relation to the artists considered here. Robert Houle first saw *The Death of General Wolfe* in 1969 when, as a rising member of a highly politicized generation of Aboriginal artists, he went to Ottawa to join a landmark protest against the Trudeau government's 1969 White Paper on Indian policy, a document that, among other things, proposed to repeal the Indian Act. (Aboriginal opposition to its repeal resulted from the guarantees that this legislation provides, despite its oppressive legal features, for recognition of the distinct legal status of Aboriginal people, their rights to reserve lands, and government funding for essential services.)[16] Jeffrey Thomas first saw the Champlain monument when he went to Ottawa to see the National Gallery's first exhibition of contemporary Aboriginal North American art, 'Land, Spirit, Power: First Nations at the National Gallery,' which was co-curated by Robert Houle.[17]

That these encounters proved to be defining moments in the artistic biographies of both Houle and Thomas is a function of the prior historical processes through which the West painting and the Champlain statue had been constructed as monuments. Both works celebrate major heroic figures of European settler history, and both were installed in the course of the key, early twentieth-century phase of Canadian settler nationalism and self-fashioning. The Champlain monument (see figure 11.1) was created as a permanent marker of the Champlain Tercentenary, launched at Quebec City in 1908 with the most elaborate pageantry that had ever been organized by the Canadian government. As H.V. Nelles has shown, the celebrations repositioned a French colonial hero as a contributor to a triumphal history of British imperialism.[18] Over the years, however, the monument has also become a site for contestations of both Anglo-Canadian and settler empowerment. It has served as a rallying point for the patriotic St Jean Baptiste Society at its annual celebration of the patron saint of Quebec, Ottawa's major public display of French-Canadian nationalist and separatist sentiment. In the 1990s the monument became the target of demonstrations organized by the Assembly of First Nations, Canada's largest Aboriginal political organization, to protest the subservient portrayal of the Indian scout, positioned on a plinth beneath Champlain's feet and rendered in reduced hieratic scale. In 1999 the National Capital Commission bowed to this pressure and removed the figure of the Indian scout from the monument to Major's Hill Park across the road.

The Champlain monument and its vicissitudes were a central reference point of Jeffrey Thomas's photographic practice during the 1990s. He photographed it from many angles, interrogating the monument in relation to the late twentieth-century social realities of urban Indians like himself. In many of the images he draws out its contemporary resonances through the carefully calculated incorporation of reworked popular culture icons of Indians. In a 1996 photograph, for example, Thomas's teen-aged son Bear sits in front of the bronze Indian, his head tilted back towards the scout at an interrogative angle (see figure 11.2). He is clothed in the fashions typical of contemporary Western youth culture, a baseball cap placed backwards on his head, sunglasses, and a sweatshirt printed with an image of a nineteenth-century Plains Indian.

11.1 Hamilton MacCarthy, *Monument to Samuel de Champlain*, 1915–23, Nepean Point, Ottawa. Courtesy National Capital Commission.

The image has been doctored by the clothing designer; the Indian warrior also wears shades and is framed by the initials 'F.B.I.' and the words 'Full Blooded Indian.' In another image, made after the removal of the scout, Thomas photographed Greg Hill, a fellow Onkwehonwe artist, squatting in the scout's pose on top of the vacated plinth. Hill wears the camouflage pants and garments of any twenty-something Canadian man together with a traditional Onkwehonwe *gustoweh* headdress made of cardboard cereal boxes. In both images the arte-facts of fashion display the punning, ironic, pop sensibility of late twentieth-century visual culture. They convey Thomas's commentary on the cumulative impact of a still-current tradition of romanticized imagery recycled through

11.2 Jeffrey Thomas, *Bear Thomas Posed at the Samuel de Champlain Monument*,
1997, gelatin silver print, 18 × 14 in. Collection of the artist.

processes of mechanical reproduction into post-industrial consumer culture. Both portraits speak to the ways that non-Aboriginal people are conditioned to see Aboriginal people and the crisis of identity many young Aboriginal people experience as a result. Both resonate with tricksterish resistance to this commodification and employ ironic juxtaposition as a strategy for interrogating stereotypes.[19]

Thomas has also used an image of the Champlain monument as the focal point of one of his most overtly political works, a five-part photographic installation entitled *Cold City Frieze* (1999–2001). In this piece the monument is aligned with four other Indian figures from architectural sculpture and monuments. Each is constructed as an icon of a city that now occupies former Onkwehonwe lands. Each is also made to stand as a 'wampum icon' representing one of the five original nations in the Onkewehonwe Confederacy, and the five images are placed in the same narrative order as are the symbols that represent the five nations in the historic Hiawatha wampum belt, a key document of the Confederacy.[20] On a third, autobiographical level each of the Indian figures is invested with meaning as a 'personal icon,' through associations made in the exhibit labels to people important to Thomas's own life. *Cold City Frieze* pulls Champlain's scout back into the Indigenous structure of political power that preceded contact and colonialism *and* into a remembered history of twentieth-century Aboriginal life. Thomas announces this strategy in the artist's statement that accompanies the installation. 'While living in the city of Toronto I came across an architectural frieze depicting a time-line of Canadian technological history. The first part of the frieze showed Indians riding on horseback and standing by tipis, images hardly relevant to the [Onkwehonwe] experience. The rest of the frieze simply ignored the continued presence of the First Nations people in Canadian History. I designed *Cold City Frieze* to represent my urban [Onkwehonwe].'[21]

Benjamin West's *The Death of General Wolfe*, which depicts the death in battle of the English general whose victory over the French in 1759 secured Canada for the British empire, was one of five works given to the nation by the British government in 1921 as part of the Canadian War Memorials (see figure 11.3).[22] The gift was a gesture of Britain's gratitude for Canada's disproportionately great sacrifices during the First World War. The transfer from England to Canada of important paintings related to its settler history can be read as an official recognition of Canada's 'coming of age' as a nation. The painting, much reproduced in Canadian history text books, quickly became a centrepiece of the National Gallery's collection and an icon of settler Canadian art history. It continues to be regularly reproduced in texts on Canadian history. Like Thomas's images of the Champlain monument, Robert Houle's repainting

11.3 Benjamin West, *The Death of General Wolfe*, 1771, oil on canvas, 152.6 × 214.5 cm. The National Gallery of Canada 8007. Reproduced by permission of the National Gallery of Canada, Ottawa.

of West's masterwork also focuses on the marginalized figure of an Indian, the warrior who sits on the ground in the lower left-hand corner. Like the Indians in official provincial and state seals, or like the picturesque figures in the foreground of paintings by eighteenth-century topographical artists, this is an invented figure for whose presence at the scene of Wolfe's death there is no historical basis. It serves, rather, to frame the main scene of settler action and to locate it in North America. On another level, as Vivien Fryd has argued, the figure – which she suggests is based on Albrecht Durer's famous 1514 figure of *Melancholia* – is an initial and highly influential example of the topos of the Vanishing American in the iconography of Western painting.[23]

From his first encounter with the West painting, the warrior became for Houle the focus of crucial questions about identity and the position of Aboriginal people in Canada: 'Who are we? We're marginal, we're largely invisible, and ninety-nine percent of the time we're fictional.'[24] In *Kanata* he renders the West painting as a preparatory sketch or 'cartoon' in conte crayon on raw canvas, interpolating other Aboriginal figures into the background. Most importantly, Houle paints only the Indian in colour (see figure 11.4). By this gesture he shifts the focus of the painting away from the pathos of the dying English general in the compositional centre to the impending tragedy of Aboriginal disenfranchisement and dislocation. 'I created *Kanata* because of a desire to invoke another history,' he has written, 'one based on underlining the historical marginalization of [Aboriginal] people by heightening the allegorical reading of the Romantic "noble savage" in the West painting. Nonetheless, it is a history based on an experience in the New World before there was a margin, the notion that "our" lifeline here goes as far back as creation according to cultural memory.'[25]

The settler origin story of Canada has defined the country's central historical drama as the struggle between the French and the English, the 'two founding nations.' Against this notion Canada's Indigenous peoples have termed themselves the 'First Nations.' The strategies of Houle and Thomas are analogous. They complicate Canada's preoccupation with French and English historical perspectives, moving the European settler history of the country off centre by manipulating the angles from which viewers can look at the canonical works of Euro-Canadian art history. By placing Houle's and Thomas's projects within the broader development of their work it will become possible to see how memory, history, and monument have been working on each other to inscribe new, postcolonial topographies in the commemorative landscape of Canada.

Robert Houle: Recovering Memory, Recuperating Barnett Newman

Robert Houle was born in 1947, grew up on the Sandy Bay reserve in Manitoba, and spent ten years of his childhood in a Catholic residential school. Only in his fifties did he reveal the abuse that he, like so many other Aboriginal children, suffered there.[26] The highlight of his summers at home with his traditionalist family was attendance at the annual Sun Dance, but such duality carried a cost. Houle has recalled that he would attend a Sun Dance one day and have to confess his 'paganism' in church on the next, and that it took years to rid himself of the imposed sense of guilt.[27] He went on to earn degrees from the University of Manitoba and McGill, falling under the sway of important abstract painters such as Guido Molinari, who taught him at McGill, the pioneering Dutch master Piet Mondrian,[28] and the American Barnett Newman. Newman was a member of the New York School of abstract expressionist painters, a diverse group who shared a belief in art's capacity to express emotion through

11.4 Robert Houle, *Kanata*, 1992, acrylic and conte crayon on canvas, 228.7 × 732 cm overall. The National Gallery of Canada 37479.1-4. Copyright Robert Houle. Reproduced by permission of Robert Houle and the National Gallery of Canada, Ottawa.

the spontaneous application of paint in abstract or semi-representational forms. Houle was particularly drawn to Newman's use of 'colour fields' – flat expanses of pure colour, applied with close attention to the texture and quality of the surface. He recognized the capacity of these artistic styles to express mystical experiences associated with mythic belief, ritual, and spirituality and the way in which this artistic style could be used to explore his own dual heritage of Christian and Saulteaux-Ojibwa religious traditions. At crucial moments of his career Houle has used specific Newman works as points of departure for major projects of his own. His 1983 series *Parfleches for the Last Supper* was inspired by Newman's *Stations of the Cross* of 1958–66, and *Kanata* contains a direct quotation from a late Newman painting, the 1967 *Voice of Fire*.[29]

Kanata was painted in 1992 and purchased by the National Gallery of Canada in the same year. It was a painting that, like many other works created by Aboriginal North American artists to mark the five hundredth anniversary of Columbus's first voyage to the Americas, directly confronted the history of Aboriginal people since contact.[30] Houle's painting leaches the life and colour out of the European figures and vivifies the Indian, reversing the power relations of Canadian history. It is a revisionist 're-painting' that attempts to change not the factual narrative of the past, but rather the way we view it. In a 1992 interview Houle spoke of his hope that viewers would be drawn to his work, in the first instance 'because of its beauty, because of its physicality and materiality,' and that he could then 'somehow … teach them something, too.'[31] This something has to do with how one sees the land and its history from an Aboriginal point of view. Quoting the remembered words of his grandfather he went on:

> And he would say *mii-aansh*. And that's just a narrative style of saying … 'it has happened' or 'used to happen' or 'this is the way it was' – like fairytales from a long time ago. And then he'd say *ko aagiikidad*, 'if something is going to happen,' *anishnabec*, 'native people will be there' and he would say *anishnabec*, 'remember when this country was named, native people were present and native people signed treaties.' And the reason for that he'd say is because we believe this is an integral part of our lifetime. We were given this land. We've always been here. So we firmly believe that we have this invisible contract with North America. That's my sense of history. And that's how I see myself even though I'm very open to the Canadian culture.[32]

Houle thrusts his image of a re-empowered Aboriginal presence in between two large colour fields of red and blue. In *Kanata* the red and the blue panels become emblematic of Canada's deadlocked French and English dualities. As noted, a key demand of Aboriginal political leaders over the past two decades has been that the First Nations be recognized alongside the French and English as 'founding nations' of Canada and that they be admitted to constitutional negotiations. The fact that the Newman painting was first shown in the American pavilion at the Montreal World's Fair, Expo 67, held to celebrate the one-hundredth anniversary of Canadian confederation, was one such resonance. Many viewers would also have understood the further reference made by *Kanata*'s blue and red fields to Newman's *Voice of Fire*, whose purchase by the National Gallery in 1990 raised an unprecedented nation-wide storm of controversy that included the raising of questions in Parliament. The debate was sparked by the expenditure of a large sum of public money on a painting by an American artist, but also revealed the general public's lack of understanding of abstract art.[33] (The controversy, however, helped the *Voice of Fire* to replace *The Death of General Wolfe*, for a time, as the Gallery's most visited work.)

Of more serious, and more recent, import was the implicit reference to the Oka crisis, which had taken place in the summer of 1990 when members of two Mohawk reserves in Quebec stood off the Quebec police and the Canadian army in a confrontation sparked by an unresolved claim to a sacred burial ground. The painting thus plays on the layered, multiple anticolonialisms that shaped twentieth-century Canadian cultural politics – Canadian-British, Canadian-American, Anglo-French, and Aboriginal-Canadian. The 'painterly' qualities of the large fields of colour, celebrated for their aesthetic qualities by critics of abstract expressionism, became secondary. In *Kanata*, Houle appropriates Newman's colour fields primarily for their political references. Although the discipline of abstract expressionism continues to lend to this painting and to a series of related prints a formal rigour and elegance that serves Houle's goal of attraction and persuasion, he seeks the affective response they evoke in the viewer in order to draw attention to the continuing vitality of the Indigenous presence within the modern world.

The visual quotation from Newman's *Voice of Fire*, I would argue, also enables Houle to invert the abstract expressionists' own celebration of 'Primitive Art' – and Aboriginal North American art, specifically – which distinguished their more general engagement with the mythic, the spiritual, and the mystical. Newman and his associates had made their interest in Northwest Coast totem poles, Navajo dry paintings, and ancient Woodlands mound builder sites clear in numerous statements and writings. As Jackson Rushing has pointed out, 'these artists did not perceive themselves in a colonial situation vis-à-vis the use of Indian art, which, after all, was considered national cultural property. Moreover, modernism's self-defined universality seemed to justify its appetite for the cultural forms of Native American and other Others.'[34] However, as noted earlier, by focusing on early, 'pure' periods of Aboriginal art and denying the authenticity of Aboriginal people and their arts within modernity, modernist-primitivism implicitly denied to contemporary Aboriginal artists the possibility that they might themselves adopt modernism as a means of re-engaging with their own historical traditions. Houle's self-imposed task was, then, dual. It was an act of recovery of the original intentions of abstract expressionists whose intended references to spirit, emotion, and history had been silenced by the dominant school of criticism of the 1960s and 1970s, led by New York critic Clement Greenburg,[35] and it also sought to endow the artistic language of abstract expressionism with even more specifically political and postcolonial references. Houle's *Kanata*, then, both recuperates and reappropriates in order to reverse the history of the exclusion of Aboriginal artists from the spaces of modernist art practice.

In 1993 Houle created an installation built around *Kanata* entitled *Contact/Context/Content* for the Carleton University Art Gallery in Ottawa within which he was able to play out the full range of his concerns.[36] One of the most important was the complementary task of 'rehabilitating' historic Aboriginal objects from anthropology museums, a commitment he had made to himself during a brief stint as curator of contemporary Indian art at the National Museum of Man in the late 1970s.[37] Curiously, in the version of *The Death of General Wolfe* owned by the National Gallery, West had omitted the Indian warrior's moccasins. By a striking coincidence, as Houle was planning his installation, the National Gallery put on view a small loan exhibition from the British Museum of recently discovered historical Aboriginal objects that West had used as props – displayed, needless to say, in glass cases. In his installation Houle parodied this treatment by 'lending' his own moccasins – placed in an adjacent plexiglass box – to the painted warrior. At the same time he 'freed' the ethnographic artefact by placing an offering of tobacco next to his parfleche (a painted rawhide container traditionally used to store sacred medicines, food, and other items) inside a circle inscribed on the floor. The circle demarcated a sacred space, open to the air, in which the parfleche could 'breathe' and live.

Another component of *Contact/Context/Content* was sound and language; as viewers looked at photographs of the National Gallery's installation of Benjamin West's Indian curiosities they heard Houle's voice, recounting Anishinaabe history in both Ojibwa and English.[38] The transcription of his spoken text, overprinted on reproductions of the contact sheets of the National Gallery's installations of West's artefact collection, activated the meanings of the diverse elements in the installation. It read:

The historical relationship between the First Nations and Canada since CONTACT spans an empire and a post-colonial era. Today, the politics of multiplicity and the ideological grounding in listening to *other* voices has given me the opportunity to challenge authority – the CONTEXT upon which my work can have maximum empowerment for the viewer. Tomorrow, the politics of representation and the spiritual integrity of the past will govern the CONTENT to be found in my art.

On some of these prints Houle lettered the names of extinct North American Indigenous peoples in mirror writing over reproductions of *The Death of General Wolfe*. This textual/conceptual element connects *Contact/Context/Content* to several other roughly contemporary projects in which Houle addressed even more specifically issues of memory, commemoration, and monument. In particular this element links *Contact/Context/Content* to an installation comissioned by the Art Gallery of Ontario in which Houle responded to German conceptual artist Lothar Baumgarten's site-specific work *Monument for the Native People of Ontario*, which had originally been commissioned in 1985 for a temporary exhibition at the AGO and was subsequently purchased for the permanent collection.[39] The work consists of a series of trompe l'oeil inscriptions of the names of 'extinct' Aboriginal 'peoples' written in a classical font above the arches of the Gallery's neoclassical Walker Court, the AGO's first purpose-built space.[40]

Like the 1969 encounter with West's *Death of General Wolfe*, Houle's encounter with Baumgarten's installation had been a pivotal moment. He had been arrested and disturbed by the white, German artist's appropriation of the right to mourn; by his confusion of the names of Indigenous nations with those of language groups and regions; and by his identification of a number of living First Nations, including Houle's own group, the Ojibwa, as 'extinct.' In *Anishnabe Walker Court* (1993) Houle reappropriated the Aboriginal names by placing them in quotation marks and reinscribing them in lower case on the outer wall of the court, surrounding Baumgarten's installation (see figure 11.5). He also included a photographic documentation of the alterations that had been made to the Walker Court over the years that was in itself a meditation on the ways that, over time, change, memory, and forgetting alter even the monumental architectures of museums. The commissioning of Houle's intervention by the Art Gallery of Ontario, like the National Gallery of Canada's periodic hanging of his *Kanata* adjacent to West's *Death of General Wolfe*, typifies the postmodern, reflexive culture of settler institutions during the 1990s. The gallery handout that accompanied Houle's piece stated, for example, that the AGO had commissioned his installation, 'being willing as an institution to exacerbate the contradictions Baumgarten's work asserts.' At the same time it stressed that both Baumgarten's work and Houle's critique were framed within contemporary art discourse: 'Houle, incidentally, admires the installation as

11.5 In the foreground is part of Robert Houle's *Anishnabe Walker Court*, 1993, and in the background, Lothar Baumgarten's *Monument for the Native People of Ontario,* 1985 (Typeface Perpetua [Eric Gill], tempera on painted concrete). Copyright Robert Houle. Reproduced by permission of Robert Houle and the Art Gallery of Ontario.

an "eloquent European work which addresses our people" ... In the process, Houle has also taken as a subject the responsibility of an institution to site-specific works.'

Anishnabe Walker Court and *Contact/Context/Content* are, then, linked by a common strategy; both retrieve from the limbo of the past images and icons of Aboriginal people who have been symbolically killed by premature acts of memorialization. Like *Kanata, Anishnabe Walker Court* worked to alter the viewer's reading of a work of art that had become monumentalized within a museum by the operation of art discourses, and to insist on the vitality and agency of Indian subjects represented as passive victims of history. This example illustrates the role that museums can play in contemporary liberal democracies as 'shock absorbers' that provide a safe forum for the debate of explosive issues before they are resolved politically or legally. At the same time, it suggests how such installations can act on the public to change their perspectives and advance campaigns of political change.

Jeffrey Thomas: The Quest for Identity and the Legacy of Curtis

Jeffrey Thomas also uses his camera as a tool for the discovery of lost histories. He regards the re-membering of the pasts of Aboriginal people – pasts that have been overlaid with romantic and popular-culture stereotypes – as an essential defence against the many threats to contemporary Indigenous identity. As I argued earlier, a key strategy of his interrogation of the Champlain monument is the juxtaposition of images that contrast the specificity and immediacy of living people and popular culture with the generality and romanticization of historic monuments. While the sculpted Indian scout gazes into the distance, Thomas's son Bear returns the viewer's gaze and his friend Greg Hill looks beyond her, their expressions at once confident, quizzical, and cheerful. The highly individualized faces of these contemporary First Nations people, rather than the generic faces sculpted into the monuments, provide the focal points of Thomas's photographs.

The portrait is one of two key photographic genres to which Thomas has been drawn in his quest for historicized understandings of Aboriginal identity. The other is what he calls the 'environment,' the real, unromanticized, often gritty world that Indians have inhabited since contact, and particularly since the wave of economically motivated early twentieth-century dislocations in which his own family was caught up – the world, that is, of urban modernity. The use of the camera as an investigative tool connects to the circumstances of Thomas's life. Jeffrey Thomas is a self-taught photographer born in Buffalo in 1956 to a family from the Six Nations (Onkwehonwe) reserve in southern Ontario. Although he visited his relatives on the reserve regularly throughout his childhood, the fundamental condition of his life has been displacement. As an adult he has lived in cities – Toronto, Winnipeg, Ottawa – built on land that had been occupied for millennia by Aboriginal people. In its largest sense, the task he set for himself was to find and document with his camera the traces of this occupation, historical and contemporary.

Thomas began taking photographs in the early 1980s as a founding member of NIPA, the Native Indian Photographers' Association, an organization committed to countering the stereotypical representation of Indians through a new project of self-representation through photography. His earliest photographs constituted a search for the traces of his family's history in the inner-city neighbourhoods of Buffalo in which he had grown up. He wanted, above all, to be able to visualize the world of his grandparents and great-grandparents, those who had first experienced out-migration from the reserves and faced the need to reformulate and defend their identities. He found no answers to his most basic questions – how it had been for the first Indians who moved to the cities, what their world had looked like, how they had felt about becoming the objects of the non-Aboriginal gaze. What his quest revealed were paradoxical conditions of *in*visibility and *hyper*visibility. As he walked the city streets his camera caught the fugitive traces of lives of alienation and displacement that lay outside of official histories. He found, on the one hand, a host of garish, highly visible, stereotyped images of Indians in advertising, on tee shirts and the covers of pulp novels, and, on the other hand, the more decorous, but equally stereotypical images of the public monuments.

Both the absence and the excess produce the condition of non-recognizability. Thomas has recalled the problems his initial inquiry posed. 'I was curious ... about the way Native people were depicted in pop culture. I found it very frustrating to see these depictions – on the Saturday afternoon westerns, for example. I wanted to investigate the history behind the stereotypes.' He began to look for answers through historical research, and specifically in the visual archive of historical photography. Since the 1970s a large number of the images of Indians that circulate in popular culture have been derived from the early twentieth-century photographs of Edward Curtis, who had set out to document the last traces of the vanishing American Indian. In an essay accompanying an exhibition of historical photographs he curated for the National Archives of Canada, Thomas quoted Curtis's own description of his monumental, twenty-volume photographic project: 'Above all, none of these pictures would admit anything which betokened civilization, whether in an article of dress or landscapes or objects on the ground. These pictures were to be transcriptions for future generations that they might behold the Indian as nearly lifelike as possible as he moved about before he ever saw a paleface or knew there was anything human or in nature other than what he himself had.'[41]

As he viewed these early photographic images, however, Thomas was troubled by a sense of his own voyeurism. 'There was a very limited amount of information that I could get from these photographs, and I felt guilty about staring at them ... I felt that I was on a field trip, staring at Indians.'[42] He located his discomfort in the early photographers' erasure from the background of their subjects' actual historical existences. 'The structure of the photographs produced this response in me,' Thomas has said, 'these people were living in poverty – they had no control over what was going on, over how the images were constructed. The results were very stylized images, tourist snapshots. On the other hand, there was a lack of environment revealed in the photographs, and this created a claustrophobic feeling for me because I was searching for information about that environment and these people.'[43] Curtis shared both his generation's conviction that authentic Aboriginal ways of life were doomed by the forces of modernity and its romantic nostalgia for these same life styles. Curtis and others produced images of the almost vanished world of American Indians to be consumed by non-Aboriginal people yearning for an authenticity thought to have been lost through industrialization and urbanization. Because work informed by antimodernist nostalgia (which also informs Baumgarten's *Monument for the Native Peoples of Ontario*) denies to its subjects a place in modern societies, the retrieval of that denied modernity is a fundamental strategy for self-legitimation in Thomas's work, as it is in Houle's.

Thomas was blocked in his search for historical environments by the very conditions that had produced Curtis's photographs. He worked the problem out, as always, through photography itself, and specifically in his pow wow photographs, one of his major series of the early and mid-1990s. These images document contemporary pow wow dancers, the modern-day descendants of the romantic warriors Curtis had sought to record. For Thomas the pow wow photographs provide both a corrective to the artificial excisions of Curtis's work and an alternative body of imagery to his own depictions of urban Indians. In pow wow dancers he finds 'a practice of that history [that] gives you that sense, that bearing in the world, that pride, that attitude'[44] that he had not been able to find in the city. These photographs satisfied his need to explore the excess and messiness of actual environments, and the ways that individuals negotiate divided subjectivities and complex modern identities. He photographed each dancer dressed in everyday clothing and in dance regalia, his competition number clearly visible on his chest. He characteristically frames and displays the photographs in diptychs and triptychs to convey the complexity of modern Indian identities. In his 1996 exhibition 'Portraits from the Dancing Grounds,' Thomas borrowed original Curtis photographs from the National Archives of Canada and incorporated them into his photographic groupings of modern pow wow dancers, finally returning these images back to Curtis.

Like Houle's use of Newman's colour fields, this inclusion was more recuperative than deconstructive. In his continuing search for the traces of the past, Thomas had come to regard Curtis's portraits as indispensable traces, or 'indices' (in the terminology of French semiotician Roland Barthes), of the ancestral lives he himself sought to understand. Curtis had written that his pictures 'should be made according the best of modern methods and of a size that the face might be studied as the Indian's own flesh.'[45] Like Curtis himself, Thomas was drawn inexorably to the faces. He has said:

The historic photographs, by Curtis and others like him, seemed to be an extension of that stripping away because they didn't provide a sense of place, time or history. If you are trying to take away someone's identity and impose a new one, of course you take the history away, the sense of place ... I also remember thinking, what if we had no record at all from the past? Although the images were lacking in many ways, they were nevertheless a record: the faces couldn't be changed. It occurred to me that there is no way that I can add a history to those early photographs. I can't make more than there already is, so, what can you do? For me, you become a photographer, and you become responsible for the time in which you are living.[46]

To find the faces of his own ancestors, then, Thomas has had to recuperate Curtis's work – at least in part – from the condemnation to which it has been subjected by postcolonial and poststructuralist writers on ethnographic and aesthetic primitivism. As Roland Barthes has written in his influential theorization, *Camera Lucida*, 'photography transformed subject into object, and even, one might say, into a museum object.'[47] But, as he also writes, that same transformation is grounded in the photograph's fundamental 'contingency,' because of which 'it immediately yields up those "details" which constitute the very raw material of ethnological knowledge.'[48] Curtis's portraits were intended to be commemorations of and monuments to the disappearing American Indian.[49] Thomas's work reaches back through this initial historical framing, through the re-romanticized images of the calendars and the postcards, and through the reworked, ironic, postcolonial images, to reassert their essential evidentiary status. Ultimately, for Thomas this value is absolute and undeniable. For him, as for Barthes, 'every photograph is a certificate of presence.'[50]

Thomas regards his research as a form of archaeology, a 'digging through the archives for the images of the past.'[51] He has also pursued his quest as a curator of exhibits of historical photographs in which he has worked with an eclectic body of work taken by amateur, commercial, and ethnographic photographers. The resulting exhibitions are, increasingly, framed as the visual history he originally set out to find in city streets. His 2000 exhibit 'Emergence from the Shadows' for the Canadian Museum of Civilization investigated what is perhaps the ultimate modernist project, the ethnographic photography of anthropologists working for the National Museum of Canada during the early twentieth century. In his exhibition, Thomas retrieved these photographs from the museum's archives and displayed them, enlarged and reframed, not only as ancestral images, but also as evidence of the historic agency exerted by the subjects – for the archives also contained correspondence showing that many of the sitters had carefully controlled their own self-presentations.

Thomas's research has, finally, begun to answer the questions with which he began, linking back to some of his most treasured memories of childhood visits to his great-aunt Emily General. 'When I was a child,' he has said, 'I stayed on the family farm at the Six Nations reserve in southern Ontario. At night or when people were visiting, I would sit in the kitchen and listen to the stories being told about people in the community ... There were no photographs of those I heard about, and none were needed because the stories created such a strong visual impression in my mind. During my research at the National Archives, I came across several photographs of people from my reserve. These photographs brought back memories of the vivid images I had as a child.'[52] Thomas's photographic practice is intimately bound up with his archival project. Both are necessary to his goal of recovering identity through the restoration of Indigenous memory to the historical record. 'I don't look at the historical photograph in a negative sense, but I think there's a place where my work as a photographer and the historical photograph come together ... and they begin to expand upon the historical limitation and the pop cultural limitations, and you begin to find this ground that's very unique to who you are today.'[53]

Bringing into History and Breaking History's Shackles

Thomas's and Houle's artistic projects are linked not by formal or generic qualities, but by common critical and political purposes – purposes that are typical of their generation of Indigenous North American artists. Both introduce into official spaces of display what Raphael Samuel has called 'unofficial knowledge.'[54] Both draw on a combination of individual, familial, and communal memory and forgotten textual and visual documentation to alter the viewer's angle of vision on official settler monuments. Pierre Nora's central argument that history's absorption of memory is transformative has useful explanatory force in suggesting that these negotiations will construct new and equally rigid orthodoxies through the selective incorporation of orally preserved histories. Such incorporations both arrest the organic processes by which Aboriginal oral traditions are repeated and transmitted and bring into the public, freely accessible domain stories which have traditionally been regarded as private property. However, close readings of Houle's and Thomas's work also complicate Nora's formulation. By its very title, for example, Nora's essay 'Between Memory and History' denominates a binary, which, like other similar binaries such as tradition/modernity or sacred/secular, colonizes discourse, limiting the terms in which the pasts of many non-Western peoples can be discussed.[55]

In his essay 'History's Forgotten Doubles,' Ashis Nandy has brought forward specific issues that arise around postcolonial history and memory. He argues that the global extension of modern Western traditions of historical representation has had the effect of devaluing other modes of representing the past:

> The historians' history of the ahistorical – when grounded in a 'proper' historical consciousness, as defined by the European Enlightenment – is usually a history of the prehistorical, the primitive, and the pre-scientific. By way of transformative politics or cultural intervention, that history basically keeps open only one option – that of bringing the ahistoricals into history.[56]

He argues further that post-Enlightenment historical consciousness, once achieved, is totalizing, 'for both the moderns and those aspiring to their exalted status; once you own history, it also begins to own you.' He leaves open, however, a second possibility, presented as unstable and fugitive but nevertheless potent, for rupturing the hegemonic power of historical consciousness:

> You can, if you are an artist or a mystic, occasionally break the shackles of history in your creative or meditative moments (though even then you might be all too aware of the history of your own art, if you happen to be that kind of an artist, or the history of mysticism, if you happen to be that kind of a practitioner of mysticism). The best you can hope to do, by way of exercising your autonomy, is to live outside history for short spans of time.[57]

This possibility art offers for 'breaking the shackles of history' is, I suggest, the second reason why the arena of visual art has been so important a sphere for postcolonial negotiation in settler societies (the first, as I mentioned earlier, being the lack of a formal political closure to colonialism).

Both Robert Houle's and Jeffrey Thomas's interventionist works 'bring into history,' in Nandy's terms. But both also 'break the shackles of history' to recover, experientially, alternate modalities that have existed historically and that survive today in fragmentary forms within the modern world. The work of recovery addresses itself not just to factual accounts forgotten in the archives or preserved in memory but never written down. It is, equally, a project whose goal is to recover that which has been lost through imaginative acts of projection and recreation. Such acts collapse time. Houle and Thomas engage Benjamin West, Barnett Newman, Hamilton MacCarthy, and Edward Curtis in dialogues that are impossible in historical time, but that are enabled through the trans-temporal physicality of the monument and the limitless potential for recontextualization present in the spaces that monuments create around themselves.

Ironically, modernity's own archival and nostalgic impulses – its intertwined projects of collecting, memorialization, and antimodernist romanticization – have guaranteed the survival of the ethnographic artefacts and the 'Primitive Art,' the documentary photographs, the literature of anthropology, and the ethnographic archive that continue to enable the production of these alternative views. There is a danger in too glibly equating the kinds of interventions artists have been making into these deposits of colonial power relations with political change itself. Interventions similar to those discussed in this essay have steadily increased in major Canadian institutions of art and culture since the 1960s, but they have not yet destabilized the fundamental narratives in which settler monuments are embedded. The anthropologist Nicholas Thomas has raised this point in relation to parallel artistic interventions made by Maori artists in New Zealand and the willingness of museums in that country to present their work. 'Can indigenous art as a whole be seen to be placed in an enabling situation,' he asks, or do their works '[exhibit] an incompatibility between cultures and institutions, and [attest] to the awkwardness of combination rather than the prospects of partnership?'[58]

Houle and Thomas, like their contemporaries in other settler nations, do not resolve the problem of postcolonial memory by telling us new and unfamiliar facts or stories. Rather, they place quotation marks around the monuments of settler historical memory in order to denaturalize them. Their works problematize and undermine the certainties of the past. They create the ambivalence and the 'awkwardness' of which Thomas speaks. Yet these multiplying moments of interrogation and opening out are important, and for those who experience them the monuments they call into question will never be the same. Perhaps Houle's and Thomas's ultimate, tricksterish, perspectival shift, however, is that their acts of self-positioning within the history of artistic and anthropological modernism reopen possibilities within the modernist tradition not only for Aboriginal, but also for non-Aboriginal subjects.

NOTES

1 This is a revised version of an essay published in Robert S. Nelson and Margaret Olin, eds., *Monuments and Memory, Made and Unmade* (Chicago: University of Chicago Press, 2003), 281–304. That collection addressed art history's role in the making and unmaking of monuments through its discursive practices. The original essay was written for an international audience primarily made up

of art historians. With the help of the editors of this volume I have attempted, I hope successfully, to adapt it for a primarily Canadian and interdisciplinary audience.

2 Nicholas Thomas's *Possessions: Indigenous Art/Colonial Culture* (New York: Thames and Hudson, 1999), which focuses on New Zealand and Australia, provides essential context for the particular problem of monuments in settler societies, particularly Canada. See also Annie Coombes, 'Translating the Past: Apartheid Monuments in Post-Apartheid South Africa,' in Avtar Brah and Annie E. Coombes, eds., *Hybridity and Its Discontents: Politics, Science, Culture* (New York, Routledge, 2000); and Paul Tapsell, Te Arawa, '*Taonga, marae, whenua* – negotiating Custodianship: A Maori Tribal Response to the Museum of New Zealand,' in Darryl McIntyre and Kirsten Wehner, eds., *National Museums: Negotiating Histories Conference Proceedings* (Canberra: National Museum of Australia, 2001),112–21.

3 The term 'First Nations' is preferred in Canada to the term 'Native American.' It is used interchangeably with 'Native,' 'Aboriginal,' 'Indigenous,' and – by many members of these communities – 'Indian.'

4 I understand the monument as a symbolic form in Victor Turner's sense, which is possessed of a multivalency that makes it possible for a broad range of meanings to be attributed to it. See *The Forest of Symbols: Aspects of Ndembu Ritual* (Ithaca: Cornell University Press, 1967).

5 The National Museum of Canada was founded by a 1907 Act of Parliament that provided for the construction of the Victoria Memorial Museum, which opened in 1911. Its neo-Gothic architecture closely resembles that of the Parliament Buildings. Along with the physical construction of buildings went an energetic project of assembling national collections. See Victoria Dickenson, 'A History of the National Museums from Their Founding to the Present Day,' *Muse* 10, 2/3 (1992): 56–63; and Edward Sapir, 'An Anthropological Survey of Canada, *Science*, 8 December 1911, 789–93.

6 Carol Duncan, 'Art Museums and the Ritual of Citizenship,' in Ivan Karp and Steven D. Lavine, eds., *Exhibiting Cultures: The Poetics and Politics of Museum Display* (Washington, DC: Smithsonian Institution Press, 1991), 90.

7 Nelson Graburn, 'Introduction,' in Graburn, ed., *Ethnic and Tourist Arts: Cultural Expressions from the Fourth World* (Berkeley: University of California Press, 1976), 19, 36–7.

8 On antimodernity see T.J. Jackson Lears, *No Place of Grace: Antimodernism and the Transformation of American Culture, 1880–1920* (New York : Pantheon Books, 1981).

9 Following Shelley Errington, I capitalize Primitive Art to refer to the specific aesthetic and intellectual movement associated with twentieth-century artistic mod-

ernism. See her *The Death of Authentic Primitive Art and Other Tales of Progress* (Berkeley: University of California Press, 1998).

10 See Diana Nemiroff 'Modernism, Nationalism and Beyond: A Critical History of Exhibitions of First Nations Art.' in Diana Nemiroff, Robert Houle, and Charlotte Townsend-Gault, eds., *Land, Spirit, Power: First Nations at the Natonal Gallery* (Ottawa: National Gallery of Art, 1992). See also Leslie Dawn, *National Visions, National Blindness: Canadian Art and Identities in the 1920s* (Vancouver: University of British Columbia Press, 2006); and Jessica Hines, 'Art of This Land and the History of Exhibiting Aboriginal Art at the National Gallery of Canada,' MA thesis, School for Studies in Art and Culture: Art History, Carleton University, 2005.

11 On the involvement with the National Gallery and National Museum of Canada with the Group of Seven see Charles Hill, *The Group of Seven: Art for a Nation* (Toronto: McClelland and Stewart, 1995); Lynda Jessup, 'Bushwackers in the Gallery: Antimodernism and the Group of Seven,' in Jessup, ed., *Antimodernism and Artistic Experience: Policing the Boundaries of Modernity* (Toronto: University of Toronto Press, 2001); Leslie Dawn, 'How Canada Stole the Idea of Native Art: The Group of Seven and Images of the Indian in the 1920s,' PhD dissertation, Department of Art History, Visual Art and Theory, University of British Columbia, 2001; and Sandra Dyck, 'These Things Are Our Totems: Marius Barbeau and the Indigenization of Canadian Art and Culture in the 1920s,' MA thesis, School for Studies in Art and Culture, Carleton University, 1995. On the constructs of authenticity and Primitive Art see Errington, *The Death of Authentic Primitive Art and Other Tales of Progress.*

12 Richards argues that the imperial archives established in Europe were as (or more) important in reifying imperial control over the colonies than actual military force. See Thomas Richards, *The Imperial Archive: Knowledge and the Fantasy of Empire* (New York: Verso, 1993).

13 See Alan Cairns, *Citizens Plus: Aboriginal Peoples and the Canadian State* (Vancouver: University of British Columbia Press, 2000).

14 The Indian Act has been amended many times. One of its most oppressive features, the proscription of Indigenous spiritual and ceremonial practices such as the Northwest Coast potlatch and the Plains Sundance, was not dropped from the Act until 1951. The franchise was granted to status Indians in Canada 1960.

15 The highly active late twentieth-century phase of postcolonial Indigenous political activism was, as I have argued elsewhere, symbolically enacted by a series of contestations of important world's fairs and exhibitions. See my essay 'Commemoration/(De)Celebration: Super-Shows and the Decolonization of Canadian Museums, 1967–1992,' in Barbara Gabriel and Suzan Ilcan, eds., *Postmodernism and the Ethical Subject* (Montreal and Kingston: McGill-Queen's University Press, 2004). It is also represented by the successes of the Society of Canadian

Artists of Native Ancestry (SCANA) during the 1980s in lobbying major Canadian museums and galleries to acquire and commission contemporary Aboriginal art.

16 The White Paper is properly known as *Canada, Statement of the Government of Canada on Indian Policy presented to the First Session of the Twenty-eighth Parliament by the Honourable Jean Chrétien, Minister of Indian Affairs and Northern Development* (Ottawa: Department of Indian Affairs and Northern Development, 1969). See Cairns, *Citizens Plus,* 51–3 and 65–70.

17 The other curators were Diana Nemiroff and Charlotte Townsend-Gault. See *Land, Spirit, Power*.

18 Over a two-week period, thousands of citizens wearing period costumes enacted scenes representing not only Champlain's initial landing, but also other major events leading up to the British conquest of the French on the Plains of Abraham in 1759. H.V. Nelles writes: 'There seemed to be some confusion as to who was being commemorated; was it Champlain, or Montcalm and Wolfe? Was it 1608 or 1759? Or was 1908 itself the object of celebration? Somehow a civic festival had taken on martial and imperial overtones. By a curious logic, the founding of a city in the seventeenth century had become connected in some way to its conquest in the eighteenth century and further linked to a celebration of imperial nationalism in the early twentieth century. Judging from these jumbled images and inscriptions, the festival seemed to be "about" many things.' *The Art of Nation-Building: Pageantry and Spectacle at Quebec's Tercentenary* (Toronto: University of Toronto Press, 1999), 12.

19 For discussions of irony, humour, and trickster strategies in contemporary Native American Art see Lucy Lippard's chapter on 'Turning,' in her *Mixed Blessings: New Art in a Multicultural America* (New York: Pantheon, 1990); and Alan Ryan, *The Trickster Shift* (Vancouver: University of British Columbia Press, 2000). Hill wore the headdress to impersonate the Revolutionary War era Mohawk leader Joseph Brant in his performance piece, *Poco-haunt(s)us*, created with Sue Ellen Gerritsen, which has had several incarnations since 1997. He addressed the Champlain monument in a video installation piece, 'Joe Scouting/ for Store Lasagne,' as part of 'In Control, Luminous Gravity,' Ottawa, June 2001. (See also http: homepage.mac.com/gahill/.)

20 For a discussion of wampum from an Iroquois perspective see *Council Fire: A Resource Guide* (Brantford, ON: Woodlands Indian Cultural Centre, 1989).

21 The work was commissioned for the travelling exhibition 'Across Borders: Beadwork in Iroquois Art.' I quote from the revised artist's statement displayed at the Canadian Museum of Civilization venue, Ottawa, summer 2001. On Jeffrey Thomas's work, see Anna Hudson, ed., *Drive By: A Road Trip with Jeff Thomas* (Toronto: University of Toronto Art Centre, 2008).

22 West painted three copies of the painting. The National Gallery of Canada ver-

sion is the original. The other paintings transferred as part of the War Memorials were portraits of Mohawk chief and British ally Joseph Brant, explorers Sir John Franklin and Alexander Mackenzie, and British general Sir Geoffrey Amherst, by Romney, Phillips, Lawrence, and Reynolds.

23 Vivien Fryd, 'Rereading the Indian in Benjamin West's *Death of General Wolfe*,' *American Art* 9 (Spring 1995): 81. The figure has also been described as a 'repoussoir' figure, which replaces the temporally distanced trope of nobility identified with ancient Greek and Roman figures with an exotic, spatially distanced noble savage. See Edgar Wind, 'The Revolution of History Painting,' *Journal of the Warburg and Courtauld Institutes* 2 (1938–9): 116–27; Charles Mitchell, 'Benjamin West's "Death of General Wolfe" and the Popular History Piece,' *Journal of the Warburg and Courtauld Institutes* 7 (1944): 20–33; and Alan McNairn, *Behold the Hero: General Wolfe and the Arts in the Eighteenth Century* (Montreal and Kingston: McGill Queen's University Press, 1997).

24 Talk by the artist, Carleton University Art Gallery, Ottawa during the showing of *Contact/Content/Context*, 1 April 1993.

25 Artist's statement in Stedelijk Museum, *Notion of Conflict: A Selection of Contemporary Canadian Art* (Amsterdam: Stedelijk Museum, 1995), 24.

26 Sarah Hampson, 'Looking for Robert Houle,' *Globe and Mail*, 27 July 2000, R3.

27 Talk by the artist, Carleton University Art Gallery, 1 April 1993.

28 Houle made a trip to Europe in 1980 in order to study Mondrian, but was already, at that time, also interested in Newman. Talk, National Gallery of Canada, 5 October 1995.

29 There is no attempt to bury the debt. Houle speaks of his own works as 'homages' to Newman's art (ibid.).

30 Two major exhibitions were held in Canada which dealt in different ways with this subject, 'Indigena' at the Canadian Museum of Civilization, and 'Land, Spirit, Power' at the National Gallery of Canada (see note 10). Among the U.S. exhibitions were 'First Encounters,' organized by the Florida Museum of Natural History, and 'Submoloc Wohs,' organized by Atlatl, a Native-run artists' organization. See W. Jackson Rushing III, 'Contrary Iconography: The Submoloc Show,' *New Art Examiner* 21 (Summer 1994): 33–4.

31 Michael Bell, *Kanata: Robert Houle's Histories* (Ottawa: Carleton University Art Gallery, 1993), 18.

32 Ibid., 19.

33 The controversy arose around two issues: first, an uninformed but noisy questioning of the merits of abstract expressionism, and, second, the expenditure of sizeable public funds on a painting by an American artist. See Bruce Parker, Serge Guilbaut, and John O'Brian, *Voices of Fire: Art, Rage, Power and the State* (Toronto: University of Toronto Press, 1996).

34 W. Jackson Rushing III, *Native American Art and the New York Avant Garde: A History of Cultural Primitivism* (Austin: University of Texas Press, 1995), 168.

35 See Michael Auping, *Abstract Expressionism: The Critical Developments* (Buffalo: Albright Knox Gallery, 1987); and Rushing, *Native American Art.*

36 The publication for the exhibition is Bell, *Kanata.*

37 See Robert Houle with Clara Hargittay, 'The Struggle against Cultural Apartheid,' *Muse* 6, 3 (1988): 58–63.

38 It also incorporated the voice of Simon Schama being interviewed by the Canadian Broadcasting Corporation about his book on *The Death of General Wolfe, Dead Certainties: Unwarranted Speculations* (New York: Knopf, 1991).

39 For example, Houle's series *Everything You Ever Wanted to Know about Indians from A to Z,* and *The Only Good Indians I Ever Saw Were Dead.* See Winnipeg Art Gallery, *Robert Houle: Indians from A to Z* (Winnipeg: Winnipeg Art Gallery, 1990).

40 See the exhibit catalogue, Germano Celant, *The European Iceberg: Creativity in Germany and Italy Today* (Toronto: Art Gallery of Ontario, 1985).

41 Quoted in Jeffrey Thomas, 'From the Collections, The Portfolio: Luminance – Aboriginal Photographic Portraits,' *The Archivist, Magazine of the National Archives of Canada* 112 (1996): 9.

42 Quoted in Carol Podedworny, 'New World Landscape: Urban First Nations Photography, Interview with Jeffrey Thomas,' *Fuse* 19, 2 (1996): 35.

43 Ibid.

44 Interview with Greg Hill, 13 December 1995, Ottawa. MS, 2, Artists File for 'Jeffrey Thomas,' Library, National Gallery of Canada, Ottawa.

45 Quoted in Thomas, 'From the Collections,' 9.

46 Podedworny, 'New World Landscape,' 39. The beginning of the quotation reads: 'I thought that in looking at historical photographs I could understand how the people pictured there had lived, what their experiences were – like when they went to the cities, how they felt about being stared at by non-Native people, the hardships they endured when they moved into an urban environment. In viewing these photographs I might understand my own world. There isn't any information like that around – dealing with issues of identity and survival – it has been stripped away.'

47 Roland Barthes, *Camera Lucida: Reflections on Photography,* trans. Richard Howard (New York: Hill and Wang, 1981), 13.

48 Ibid., 28.

49 Curtis's monumental compendium of photographs and information on language, oral history, art, and ethnographic information, *The North American Indian,* was published between 1907 and 1930. See Christopher M. Lyman, *The Vanishing Race and Other Illusions: Photographs of Indians by Edward S. Curtis* (New York: Pantheon, 1982).

50 Barthes, *Camera Lucida*, 87.

51 Podedworny, 'New World Landscape,' 38.

52 Thomas, 'From the Collections,' 7.

53 Transcript of an interview with Greg Hill, 13 December 1995, Ottawa.

54 Raphael Samuel, *Theatres of Memory, Volume 1: Past and Present in Contemporary Culture* (London: Verso, 1994).

55 Pierre Nora, ed., *Les lieux de mémoire* (Paris: Gallimard, 1984). 'Between Memory and History' was published in *Representations* 26, 9, special issue 'Memory and Counter-Memory' (Spring 1989).

56 Ashis Nandy, 'History's Forgotten Doubles,' *History and Theory: World Historians and Their Critics* 34 (1995): 44.

57 Ibid., 45–6.

58 Thomas, *Possessions*, 247.

12 Ethnic Minorities and Wartime Injustices: Redress Campaigns and Historical Narratives in Late Twentieth-Century Canada

IAN RADFORTH

On 22 September 1988, Prime Minister Brian Mulroney rose in the House of Commons at Ottawa and declared: 'Nearly half a century ago, in the crisis of wartime, the Government of Canada wrongfully incarcerated, seized the property, and disenfranchised thousands of citizens of Japanese ancestry. We cannot change the past. But we must, as a nation, have the courage to face up to these historical facts.' With these words, the prime minister began his prepared speech that answered the main demands of the Japanese-Canadian redress movement. He would go on to say that while no amount of money can right the wrong, undo the harm, and heal the wounds, it was nevertheless the determination of his government to address this issue, not only in the moral sense, but also in a tangible way – a reference to the financial settlement that had been negotiated with the National Association of Japanese Canadians. Mulroney presented the measure as one that both affirmed modern Canada as an inclusive nation and distanced late twentieth-century Canada from the racism of the past. Elderly Japanese Canadians sitting in the gallery of the Commons watched with pride and tears, as did activists who had worked long and hard to persuade the public and officials of the need for redress. Crucial to their campaign had been the construction of a public memory, the articulation and popularization of a historical narrative to the point where the historical facts of which Mulroney spoke were widely known and accepted.

The Japanese-Canadian redress campaign was both symptomatic of and a catalyst for an unusually vibrant period in public history in Canada. From the mid-1980s to the early 1990s, activists from various ethnic groups, some of them inspired by the example of Japanese Canadians, sought to instruct the Canadian public and Ottawa politicians about injustices suffered by their minority communities and to win redress from the government of Canada for past sufferings.[1] They were part of a wider, international phenomenon that placed human rights firmly on the public agenda and that resulted in the period's being aptly labelled 'The Age of Apology.'[2] On the wider scene, the politics of apology played out differently from country to country, although nearly everywhere successful groups made their claims not through the courts but rather through political activism. In Canada, various groups seeking redress of human rights abuses were influenced both by this international movement with its record of political breakthroughs and by the growing popular and governmental commitment in Canada to multiculturalism. During the 1980s, leaders of ethnic communities gained the space to assert themselves in the media and the hope that their voices would not only be heard but also heeded by Ottawa.[3] In 1988, the year of Mulroney's settlement with the Japanese Canadians, Canada got its first Multiculturalism Act and the Multiculturalism Directorate was raised in status to a ministry, partly symbolic measures aimed at further entrenching multiculturalism as a core value of the Canadian nation. It is difficult to imagine that these nation-affirming measures, like the Japanese-Canadian redress settlement, were not introduced by Mulroney's government partly to counterbalance fallout from the hottest political issue of 1988 – the successful negotiation of free trade with the United States, a development that many Canadians saw as a threat to national survival.[4]

Two campaigns in particular provide revealing parallels to the case of the Japanese Canadians because all three groups focused their redress movements on the abrogation of individual rights during wartime. Following the lead of the Japanese Canadians, in 1988 Italian Canadians demanded redress for the injustices done during the early years of the Second World War when Italians in Canada faced public suspicion and some were interned by the Canadian government because of widespread fears concerning their ties to the enemy. Yet the Italians were not the first ethnic group that the government of Canada had targeted for internment. During the First World War, Ukrainians in Canada suffered a similar fate, when authorities interned about five thousand of them as 'enemy aliens' because of their Austrian citizenship. These internments of 1914–15 became the focus of a redress campaign launched by Ukrainian Canadians in the late 1980s.[5]

This chapter examines these three redress campaigns – the Japanese-Canadian, the Italian-Canadian, and the Ukrainian-Canadian – as exercises in public history. It looks at how the communities launched their redress movements, the historical narratives that the redress campaigners constructed in making their cases to Ottawa, and the reception of these narratives by Canadian authorities, the media, and members of their own ethnic groups. For each campaign I let the redress activists themselves make their group's case, and then I present the critical debate that followed as it played out. I have intentionally avoided beginning with my own 'accurate' version of past events, followed by a commentary on distortions in the narratives told by the redress activists or their critics. Because I am an outsider to all three ethnic communities, I cannot speak for any of the groups. Nor am I an authority on the past events that concern the activists. What I do here is document what has been said in connection with each of the redress movements, make comparisons between the three experiences, and highlight the role of historians in the campaigns.

The activists who led these redress campaigns hoped that revisiting past injustices would help to unify their communities, but the results in fact varied considerably for each of the three groups. Nevertheless, in all three cases tensions developed as a result of differences within the groups over the meaning of the past. Constructing an effective redress narrative involved forging a social memory – an often contested process within the group – and then having it inscribed in the national narrative. Here too results differed among the campaigns. In each case, however, historians played a significant role in the campaign both by helping (whether intentionally or otherwise) to shape the authorized community narratives and by publicly finding fault with them.

Because the Japanese-Canadian redress campaign and its success with Ottawa inspired the two other groups to mount campaigns, let us begin with the Japanese-Canadian movement.

The Japanese-Canadian Redress Campaign

Although some Japanese Canadians had raised the idea of redress in the late 1940s,[6] it was not until 1977 that the community again launched a redress campaign. Interest was sparked by a moment in public history: the community's centennial celebrations marking the arrival in Canada of the first Japanese settler.[7] A photo exhibit, which was organized by some Japanese Canadians from Vancouver, vividly documented the Canadian government's forced removal of Japanese Canadians from coastal British Columbia during the Second World War. The display prompted the central organization of Japanese Canadians to establish a reparations committee, which held some low-key meetings.[8] Interest in the matter widened in 1980, when the United States Congress appointed the Commission on Wartime Relocation and Internment of Civilians to investigate the treatment of Japanese Americans during the 1940s.[9] Journalists in Canada began asking about Canada's wartime treatment of people of Japanese descent. These developments prompted more Japanese Canadians to become involved in a nation-wide movement for redress, and so they replaced their central organization with a new one, the National Association of Japanese Canadians (NAJC), and set up a high-profile redress committee.[10]

The NAJC redress committee was chaired by George Imai, a Toronto school teacher who for several years had been acting as an ethnic liaison (or 'power broker') with Multiculturalism officials and the Liberal government in Ottawa. Imai pursued redress in a way typical of ethnic politics at the time. After only limited consultation within his community, and some behind-the-scenes meetings with Liberal politicians, he was ready to strike an agreement with Ottawa that would have involved government acknowledgment of past injustice and group compensation to the Japanese-Canadian community in the form of a community trust foundation. He argued that it was important to move quickly. Many of the survivors of the events of the 1940s were old and had little time left to see justice done. Moreover, the Liberal government of the day was receptive to a settlement in so far as the matter was relevant to its commitment to multiculturalism and in tune with the Liberals' strategy of courting ethnic leaders.

Various Japanese Canadians, including the NAJC president Art Miki of Winnipeg, expressed alarm that things were moving too quickly and before the wider community had had an opportunity for adequate discussion of the issues. Especially in Toronto and Vancouver, where the Japanese-Canadian populations were comparatively large, groups of activists emerged to organize public meetings and other educational efforts aimed at opening up the political process to many more people and broadening the issues.[11] Critics of Imai objected to a settlement that did not also include a commitment from Ottawa that no future government would abrogate citizens' rights in the legal but objectionable way made possible under the War Measures Act in 1942.[12] Moreover, they insisted on individual compensation for those whose individual rights had been trampled.

The redress activists included Japanese Canadians of diverse backgrounds and experiences, including both those who had long been deeply troubled by memories and stories of the internment and those whose awareness came largely from the public educational campaign of the 1980s. Imai gathered around him elderly survivors who had themselves suffered the deprivations and humiliations in the 1940s and whose testimony and appearances at public meetings poignantly made the case for immediate redress. Imai's critics, though they included survivors, were mostly younger people in their thirties and forties. Some, such as Art Miki himself, had been youngsters during the removal, but most had no personal memories of the events of the 1940s. Indeed, most of the Japanese-Canadian supporters of the redress movement learned about the wartime events second-hand. For some of them, knowledge came from family discussions, when over the years, indignant survivors told and retold stories around the kitchen table about the internment. In other Japanese-

Canadian families, the trauma of the wartime events and a determination to move forward meant that painful past experiences were never referred to, and so the children of the survivors grew up learning little or nothing at home about the removal. Their knowledge of the history came from public accounts.[13]

As the critics of Imai's redress committee grew more numerous and determined, the community became sharply divided. Imai's critics accused him of selling out the interests of the community to his Liberal pals in Ottawa, while his supporters called their critics 'dissidents' who were stirring up trouble and out of touch with the older generation that had actually borne the brunt of wartime hostilities. For many Japanese Canadians who had always been hesitant to air differences in public, the redress campaign was an embarrassment and a campaign best abandoned.[14]

Unity among Japanese Canadians and a firm commitment to redress were much needed if the Liberal government of Pierre Trudeau were to be persuaded to negotiate a generous settlement. Trudeau himself opposed in principle the notion of a current government's apologizing – that is, accepting responsibility – for what a past government had done. 'I do not see how I can apologize for some historical event to which we or these people in this House were not a party,' he told the Commons. It would set a precedent and open the door for lobbyists from many quarters. Furthermore, Trudeau likened redress to attempts to rewrite or correct the past. While we may regret past injustices, we cannot undo them, he reasoned.[15] In response to pressure from Japanese Canadians, the most that the Trudeau government was willing to offer was a statement of regret coupled with a $5 million fund to establish a 'Canadian Foundation for Racial Justice.' While Imai and his redress committee signalled their readiness to accept the offer in 1984, Art Miki, speaking for the executive of the NAJC, firmly rejected it. The NAJC then appointed a new redress committee, which prompted Imai in turn to set up an opposition organization known as the National Redress Committee of Survivors.[16]

These developments were soon overtaken by a national election that brought the Conservatives to power under Brian Mulroney. When in opposition, Mulroney had criticized Trudeau's unwillingness to offer Japanese Canadians redress and a formal acknowledgment of government injustice, and Mulroney had said that if he were prime minister he would compensate the Japanese Canadians.[17] On 21 November 1984, a hopeful Miki presented to the Mulroney government the NAJC's brief, entitled *Democracy Betrayed*, which outlined the history of injustice and made the case for redress. The campaign's key text, it sets out the historical narrative as constructed by the redress leadership.[18]

Democracy Betrayed gets immediately to the point. 'In February 1942,' it begins, 'the Government of Canada ordered the expulsion of all Canadians of

Japanese ethnic origin from the West Coast of British Columbia. By its action, the government perpetrated the view that ethnicity and not individual merit was the basis of citizenship.'[19] Twenty-one thousand people were directly affected, over seventeen thousand of whom were Canadian citizens. The brief explains how the RCMP, armed with the powers of the War Measures Act, entered homes without warrant and gave people only hours to move. Men were sent to road camps far away, and those who refused to be separated from their families or who made other protests were interned in prisoner-of-war camps in Ontario. Initially women and children were housed in animal pens in Hastings Park, Vancouver, and then they were removed to various isolated sites in the interior of British Columbia. Only gradually were most of these families reunited. Other families were permitted to stay together from the start if they agreed to work on the sugar beet farms of Alberta and Manitoba, where labour shortages were acute. Still other Japanese Canadians who found sponsors in the east moved to places in Ontario and Quebec. Having been branded 'enemy aliens' by the government, wherever they went the 'Japanese Canadians were met with suspicion and distrust in their forced migrations.'[20]

The Custodian of Enemy Property, a federal agency, took possession in trust of the homes, farms, businesses, fishing boats, and other property of the Japanese Canadians on the west coast. It then proceeded, notes the brief, to sell off the property without the consent of the owners and often at fire-sale prices. The funds thus raised by the custodian were used in large part to pay for interning the Japanese Canadians – a practice outlawed by the Geneva Convention in the case of actual prisoners of war and enemy nationals.

The second uprooting began in 1945, when Ottawa made plans to prevent the resettlement of Japanese Canadians in coastal British Columbia following the war. Throughout the detention camps of the BC interior, officials conducted a 'loyalty survey.' Those unwilling to move east were deemed disloyal and preparations were made to banish them to Japan at war's end. The government planned to send ten thousand people to Japan, but a public outcry stopped the euphemistically named 'repatriation movement' after about four thousand had been sent away. One-half of these people were Canadian-born. It was not until 1 April 1949 that full citizen rights were restored to Japanese Canadians and they were free to reside along the coast.

Part 2 of *Democracy Betrayed* counters myths used by (unnamed) apologists for the wartime government of William Lyon Mackenzie King that undertook the uprooting and confiscations. The brief argues that, counter to the 'security myth,' top officials of the RCMP and the Canadian army advised the government that the Japanese Canadians posed no threat to the security of the west coast. There was no wartime evidence of any willingness to assist the enemy in the event of an attack by Japan. A second myth used to justify the King government's policies – 'the protective custody myth' – is also undermined, according to *Democracy Betrayed*, by the government's own historical files. Documents show that the removal was not motivated by a desire to protect the Japanese Canadians from their hostile British Columbian neighbours whose long-standing racism was exacerbated in the context of the war against Japan. Instead, certain BC politicians manipulated popular fears for their own political ends. The brief asks, if the government wanted to protect Japanese Canadians, why did it confine women and children to Hastings Park, 'where they presented a ready target for any one who wanted to attack them'?[21] The confiscation of property and the expulsion to Japan similarly could have had nothing to do with protection or any other benign policy.

The NAJC concludes by emphasizing that the government's policies had 'no basis in military necessity,' but were instead motivated 'by political considerations based upon racist traditions accepted and encouraged by politicians within the government of the day.' The government of Canada betrayed the principles of democracy. It had racialized a group of Canadian citizens, turning them into potentially dangerous 'Japanese,' and stripped them of their citizenship rights. The NAJC in consequence demanded that in future the fundamental human rights and freedoms set forth in the Charter of Rights and Freedoms 'be considered sacrosanct, non-negotiable and beyond the reach of any arbitrary authority.' It called for the government to acknowledge its responsibility to compensate Japanese Canadians for injustices suffered and to begin negotiation towards 'a just and honourable settlement of this claim.'[22]

Democracy Betrayed presents the community's history and case for redress succinctly and forcefully. Footnotes refer readers to many documents in government files held by the National Archives, as well as to various historical studies, most notably Ann Gomer Sunahara's *The Politics of Racism*.[23] The brief itself had been carefully prepared by a committee of NAJC members from Ottawa, Toronto, and Vancouver, who paid close attention to drafting a document in a language that would be persuasive not only to politicians and the general public, but to ordinary Japanese Canadians whose support the campaign still needed to cultivate. The strategy, recalls Roy Miki, who served on the committee, was to avoid presenting the Japanese Canadians as victims seeking compensation from the government. 'Such a narrative,' he writes, 'would have set up a "we/they" dichotomy that could result in a dangerous polarization between "mainstream Canadians" (as represented by the government) and "Japanese Canadians" (the beleaguered minority).' The writers identified Japanese Canadians as citizens of the nation who were wronged when the democratic system was betrayed. Similarly, the demand was for an acknowledgment not an apology, because the latter would 'simply reproduce the "victim" position of Japanese Canadians.'[24] Moreover, the brief's charge of racism, which *Democracy Betrayed* had accurately used to account for the wartime government's actions, had a particular power in the mid-1980s. At that time, antiracist activists in Canada had succeeded in placing the problem of racism – which was largely defined in terms of colour – squarely before the Canadian public.[25]

The brief's silence on the matter of the amount of compensation owed to individuals and the community was another strategic decision reached by the committee. Within the NAJC consideration had already been given to dollar amounts that might be demanded as reparations, but eventually it was agreed that these dollar figures would not be included in the brief. On this point the NAJC committee benefited from the advice of Don Rosenbloom, a Vancouver lawyer who had long been interested in the Japanese-Canadian removal and who, significantly, had much experience in the field of Native land claims. As Roy Miki explains, Rosenbloom reasoned that if the NAJC mentioned some large and arbitrary figure, the government and the media 'might jump on the figure itself and represent Japanese Canadians as more concerned with "money" than "justice."'[26] Thus, money matters were taken up in a separate and detailed document prepared later for the NAJC by the respected accounting firm Price Waterhouse.

During the four years following the presentation of its brief, the NAJC lobbied Ottawa persistently, but the Mulroney government stalled on negotiating with the NAJC and held back from making a generous settlement in fear of a backlash from the public or objections coming within the Conservative caucus and cabinet.

Various criticisms of a settlement were voiced in public debates that spilled far beyond Ottawa. Some critics, echoing Trudeau, objected to an apology on the ground that the responsibility of the government in office does not extend to actions taken by past governments, and dismissed redress as a misguided attempt to rewrite history. Other commentators worried variously that a settlement amounted to dwelling on the past rather than looking to the future, that it threatened to open the door to other groups seeking costly compensation packages for past injustices, and that Canada's war veterans might campaign against the NAJC. Canadian veterans, who made up a well-organized lobby in their own right, had the potential to intervene powerfully in the public debate because of their well-earned credentials as defenders of the nation. As it turned out, only the Ontario Command of the Royal Canadian Legion came out publicly (in May 1985) against reparations for the Japanese Canadians. The Ontario Command compared the internment of the Japanese in Canada to the imprisonment of Canadian soldiers in Japan. Among some veterans, the memory of Imperial Japan's brutal treatment of Canadians had dimmed not at all, nor had their wartime propensity lessened for racializing Canadian citizens of Japanese background.[27]

Prominent Canadian historian Jack Granatstein raised implicit criticisms of the redress campaign in a different way. In an article in *Saturday Night* magazine, Granatstein used historical evidence and conjecture to account for and defend some of the actions taken by the Mackenzie King government in connection with the Japanese presence on the west coast in 1941–2. He reasoned that 'the evacuation' had been a prudent step taken by a government that lacked reliable intelligence about security matters on the coast but had some grounds for suspecting fifth-column activity among Japanese Canadians, though there was no concrete proof of any such activity.[28] The publication of this article, whose arguments were criticized from a number of directions, led Japanese-Canadian redress activists concerned about damage control to seek the help of another prominent Canadian historian, Ramsay Cook. He wrote to the then minister of multiculturalism, David Crombie, stating: 'The account of events of those years given in Professor Granatstein's article is unfounded and the conclusions drawn in the final paragraph of the article are misleading.' Cook noted that Granatstein failed to provide concrete evidence of traitorous activity and that he had misleadingly suggested that fifth-column activity directed by the Japanese consul in Vancouver continued after the war had begun – which was clearly impossible because with the outbreak of war 'the Consulate was closed and the consul sent packing.'[29] Whether the *Saturday Night* article had negative effects on the campaign is difficult to judge.

The Mulroney government's strategy was to avoid recognizing the NAJC as the legitimate or sole mouthpiece of Japanese Canadians and to consult with other Japanese Canadians as well as NAJC representatives, to refuse to negotiate and instead to make periodic public offers that included an acknowledgment and community compensation, and to reject individual compensation outright. On its part, the NAJC insisted on entering into negotiations and coming to a settlement on individual compensation. In cynical moments, activists believed that the government had adopted a strategy of delay, delay, delay in the knowledge that eventually the survivors from the events of the 1940s would all pass away and there would be no one alive to compensate.

Although the NAJC leadership experienced frustration at its inability to get the government to the bargaining table, the delays gave the association time to organize many educational meetings, produce literature, strengthen the movement, and enhance the NAJC's legitimacy as *the* voice of Japanese Canadians. Particularly important was the Price Waterhouse report, released in 1986, which put a dollar value (of $443,139,000 in 1986 dollars) on the losses suffered by Japanese Canadians because of wartime government measures.[30] Moreover, as scholar and redress activist Audrey Kobayashi explains, it took time for many Japanese Canadians to re-examine their own attitudes – their shame about the past, their apprehensions about stirring up trouble – and to 'recognize their power to resist,' their need 'to become politicized.'[31]

Indeed, a key concern of redress activists was to find ways to encourage Japanese-Canadian survivors of the uprooting to come to terms with their experiences in ways that would build support for the campaign. Like other survivors of trauma, many Japanese Canadians had suppressed historical memories and been reluctant during the postwar decades to connect with co-survivors and develop a social or collective memory of the events.[32] Roy Miki explains that he and other redress activists, who understood the need for consciousness-raising, came up with specific devices for accomplishing this goal. For instance, he and Cassandra Kobayashi worked together on producing a 'how-to' kit for what were called 'house meetings.' Recognizing that many Japanese-Canadian survivors were reluctant to attend public meetings and to speak publicly, the kit encouraged individuals to invite a circle of friends to their homes, where memories would be shared. Advice was provided on how to help survivors and their families see beyond the personal and recognize common experiences and to use the language of 'rights violated' to understand and to talk about the experiences. In retrospect, argues Miki, these techniques worked. Whether through house meetings or otherwise, the redress issues prompted many individuals to pour out their hearts, come to terms with their private pasts, and develop a new collective identity: 'a redress identity.' Private pain thus became transformed into a willingness to take up a national issue, one expressed in the liberal-democratic language of citizenship and human rights.[33] Personal experience and family knowledge became incorporated into the social memory of the group. Private moments of the past – many of them traumatic – became part of public history.

Delays in getting the government to the negotiating table also gave the wider Canadian public time to learn about mass removal. Many Canadians read Joy Kogawa's moving novel *Obasan*,[34] and others learned about the wartime injustices from American news coverage of the testimony and findings of the Congressional committee investigating the wartime events that traumatized Japanese Americans. Public opinion was shifting so that by March 1986 an Environics poll showed that 63 per cent of Canadians favoured redress for Japanese Canadians and, of those, 71 per cent supported individual compensation. By this time, too, the NAJC had succeeded in becoming the sole voice of Japanese Canadians on redress, and Imai's group had slipped from public view. As momentum grew, the NAJC stepped up its campaign to broaden public backing by building a national coalition of individuals and groups from beyond the community and by holding a series of rallies that culminated in a giant one held on Parliament Hill on 14 April 1988. With its wide array of supporters, the demonstration publicly proved the NAJC's main message: redress was not so much a matter of concern to one ethnic minority group as a human rights issue of concern to all Canadians.[35]

Soon after the Parliament Hill rally, and immediately following President Ronald Reagan's signing of the bill compensating Japanese Americans, the Mulroney government secretly agreed to negotiate with the NAJC. The negotiations began in Montreal on 25 August 1988 when Gerry Weiner, minister of multiculturalism, and various officials sat down with members of the NAJC strategy committee. Just two days later they had an agreement that Mulroney and Art Miki would sign at a widely publicized ceremony held on 22 September. That agreement gave each victim still living $21,000 tax-free, while, among other provisions, the community got $12 million for educational, social, or cultural activities. (The total costs would run to about $400 million.) The government acknowledged in Parliament that the forced removal, internment, and expulsion had been unjust, and that the government policies of disenfranchisement, detention, confiscation, and sale of property had been 'influenced by discriminatory attitudes.' Official endorsement of the NAJC's rendering of the historical events confirmed its salience over other narratives and assisted in inscribing the arguments of *Democracy Betrayed* into the Canadian national narrative.

When the deal was struck, members of the NAJC executive and its strategy committee were euphoric about the success of their hard-fought campaign.[36] A *tanka* (a traditional form of Japanese poetry with a particular structure) by Takeo Juo Nkano, translated into English by Leatrice Nakano Willson, commemorates that moment:

Our dark cloud of half a century dissipated,
   The fairest day
In Japanese-Canadian history
   Dawns.
Our joy is unsurpassable.[37]

The Canadian public generally welcomed the settlement, but there were some dissonant voices, most of them raising the fear that a precedent had been set that would compel the Canadian government to compensate an endless queue of redress seekers. 'Pierre Trudeau was right,' declared the Ottawa *Sun*, 'when he said today's society can't be held accountable or responsible for past (mis)deeds. Else there is no end to atoning for man's injustice to man.' According to the Winnipeg *Free Press*, the Japanese-Canadian settlement showed that the minister responsible for multiculturalism was in 'an accommodating mood,' which would only bring forward similar demands from other aggrieved groups. It added cynically: 'Once every Canadian has paid every other Canadian $21,000 and apologized, we will all feel better.' In the same newspaper, Christopher Dafoe observed that his ancestors were Loyalists who had arrived in Canada in 1785 and joked that they were 'looked down upon by the snobs who had arrived in 1784. Compensation is long overdue. Personally, I am willing to settle for a cool million.' More thoughtfully, Jeffrey Simpson of the Toronto *Globe and Mail* worried that the government had set a precedent with the Japanese Canadians that would compel negotiations and settlements with other groups. 'There comes a point at which, in a linguistically and ethnically divided country, the search for restitutions for past wrongs not only creates precedents that lead we know not where, but also risks piling up more divisions in a country already divided.'[38]

The Japanese-Canadian redress movement and settlement were most thoroughly assessed by Japanese-Canadian activists themselves, who celebrated their achievements in publications that fill library shelves and reinforce the NACJ narrative. In 1991 the NAJC published a handsomely illustrated, commemorative history of the redress campaign entitled *Justice in Our Time*.[39] Other volumes by activists have followed, notably *Bittersweet Passage* by Maryka Omatsu[40] and *Redress: Inside the Japanese Canadian Call for Justice* by Roy Miki.[41]

In *Bittersweet Passage*, Omatsu attempts to explain the success of the NAJC campaign, asking why the Conservative government had raised its 'last and final offer' from $12 million to $400 million. She notes that Mulroney, who had a reputation for paying close heed to public opinion polls, must have taken note of the deepening support for the NAJC case. Moreover, political analysts at the time maintained that the ethnic minorities in Canada were growing restless and that Mulroney wanted to shore up his popularity with them. Mulroney's admiration for President Reagan was also well known, and it makes sense that he followed suit once Reagan signed the $1.25 billion Civil Liberties Act compensating Japanese Americans. Doing so also eliminated invidious comparisons between the U.S. government's generosity and his own government's stinginess. Omatsu tries to probe deeper by asking why it was that in the decade of the 1980s, when human rights victories were so few, the Japanese Americans and Japanese Canadians made such headway with their redress campaigns. She speculates that Japan's economic power in the 1980s might well have helped to bring about the result.[42]

Near the end of *Bittersweet Passage* Omatsu expresses her frustration when she sees 'respected Canadian historian Jack Granatstein continue to argue that a possible Japanese Canadian fifth-column activity was a justification for the government's internment of an entire community.' Rather than retreating from the position he had taken in his *Saturday Night* article, Granatstein made similar arguments in 'his book *Mutual Hostages*, published in 1990, two years after the Canadian government publicly acknowledged wrongdoing.'[43]

It is certainly the case that for historians, a political move by the Mulroney government in 1988 did not resolve the historical interpretive challenges once and for all. *Mutual Hostages: Canadians and Japanese during the Second World War*, which is actually written by a team of historians (Patricia Roy, J.L. Granatstein, Masako Iino, Hiroko Takamura), all from outside the Japanese-Canadian community,[44] avoids any direct critique of the redress campaign or its depiction of the historical events. But the authors do take aim at Ann Sunahara, author of *The Politics of Racism*, an authority upon which the redress campaign relied heavily, for tending 'to see issues in black and white and to ignore the shades of grey that often cloud history.'[45] Certainly *Mutual Hostages* marshals much evidence and elaborate reasoning to tell a complex story, one that differs significantly from the NAJC's narrative.

The authors of *Mutual Hostages* are at complete odds with key points made by the redress campaign – the 'security myth' and the 'protective custody myth.' Roy and her co-authors argue that Ottawa's intelligence information about activities among the Japanese population on the west coast was so poor that government policy had to be based on guess-work and suppositions. Individuals in positions of authority differed sharply in their assessments of what might occur in the event of an attack from Japan. (The redress activists had cited only those officials who said that there would be no trouble from the Japanese in British Columbia.) In the final analysis, say the authors, 'the simple truth is that espionage and sabotage were genuine possibilities.'[46] The King government worked from that position, and ended up undertaking the 'evacuation.' (The authors choose to use the language of the government of the time, rather than referring to the 'forced removal,' the phrase preferred by redress supporters.) Roy and the others further maintain that the evacuation came about in part because of the King government's desire to protect the coastal Japanese from possible attacks made by hostile British Columbians and that, by so doing, the government sought to protect Canadian nationals living in Japan from reprisals that most likely would have been undertaken by the Imperial Japanese government in response to such attacks. While on these key matters *Mutual Hostages* argues that there were compelling reasons for the government's actions, the authors find fault with other policies, most notably the government efforts at so-called 'repatriation,' which they say 'smack of vengeance unworthy of a democratic government.'[47] In the end, the authors conclude: 'The Canadian government, whatever the contemporary and sometimes compelling justifications for its actions against the Japanese Canadians, nonetheless behaved in ways that seemed to belie its claim to be fighting on behalf of freedom and democracy.'[48]

Although different versions of the events of the 1940s are available to serious researchers, it is evident that the Japanese-Canadian redress campaign succeeded in inscribing its collective memory onto the public record. In Ontario, for instance, beginning in the 1980s those Canadian history textbooks authorized for use in the province's schools almost invariably relate the story of Japanese-Canadian internment and usually in a way consistent with the redress movement's telling of it.[49] In the wake of the settlement, moreover, many Canadians took pride in the negotiated settlement. In the context of public understandings about the Canadian nation and multiculturalism in the late 1980s, it was satisfying to think that justice had been done. Canadians were distancing themselves from the racism of the past and through public history demonstrating their present commitment to human rights. As we will see below, activists within other ethnic communities looked enviously at these achievements made by Japanese Canadians and sought to reproduce similar results for their own communities.

The Italian-Canadian Redress Campaign

The Italian-Canadian redress campaign emerged in the context of growing public support for the Japanese-Canadian redress movement. Ethnic leaders within the much larger Italian-Canadian community[50] showed a readiness to take advantage of both the Mulroney government's greater openness to the redress principle and the Conservatives' interest in undermining the Liberal party's long-standing success with Italian-Canadian voters.

The campaign began unofficially in 1988. Prime Minister Mulroney was approached by the Canadian Italian Business and Professional Men's Association (CIBPA), whose president at the time was a former wartime internee, Antonio Capobianco of Montreal. Access to the prime minister was made possible by Italian-Canadian politicians close to Mulroney. At the meeting, no definite headway was made, but the CIBPA came away both encouraged and committed to building support for their lobbying effort. Almost simultaneously, and apparently autonomously, the national executive in Toronto of the National Congress of Italian Canadians (NCIC) developed an interest in seeking redress from Ottawa.[51] The NCIC, formed in 1974 on the initiative of activists from

Toronto's large Italian-Canadian population, was committed to encouraging mutual understanding and goodwill between Canadians of Italian descent and Canadians of other backgrounds, encouraging Italian-Canadian involvement in public affairs, and mediating between the Italian-Canadian community and governments in Canada. It brought together in a loose federation people from a vast array of organizations whose members had roots in either or both of the waves of mass immigration from Italy to Canada: the period 1900–30 and the post–Second World War period that brought many more arrivals.

In 1988 NCIC leaders in Toronto had their roots in the postwar migration to Canada, which meant that they had no first-hand or direct family connections with the Italians who had been interned in Canada during the Second World War. The driving force behind the redress campaign was Annamarie Castrilli, the president of the NCIC, a lawyer, member of the University of Toronto's board of governors, and a Liberal. She was only just discovering the history of Italian-Canadian internments that had so affected an earlier generation.[52] Castrilli heard historian Luigi Pennacchio deliver a lecture that dealt in part with the topic of internment. Astonished by what she learned about the events of 1940, she arranged for Pennacchio to present his paper in April 1989 to the NCIC executive, which agreed that the matter deserved investigation. A committee gathered further information, and the Congress soon was committed to pursuing the issue.[53]

Seeking redress for the Canadian government's wartime internment of Italians appealed to supporters of the campaign for various reasons. Redress would symbolically affirm both the equality of Italian Canadians and their national organization's right to a place at the political table in Ottawa. It would serve, as historian Franc Sturino has remarked, 'as a ritual of incorporation.' The social memory of the Italian-Canadian community continued even in the 1980s to be strongly shaped by a lingering sense of injustice that derived from the intolerance that the host society had shown Italian-Canadian newcomers in earlier decades and persistent stereotypes that linked Italians to organized crime.[54] Painful memories – of being called 'foreigners,' 'Wops,' and 'Dagos,' of being paid paltry wages for doing tough, dirty jobs – were widely shared among Italian Canadians in the 1980s. Although redress focused on a specific injustice perpetrated by the host society, the issue stood for much more. Even the many Italian Canadians who had no personal links to those interned in Canada during the Second World War might well see the issue as *their* issue. It was possible to imagine that a campaign of public memory would arouse the large and amorphous Italian-Canadian population and unite Italian Canadians behind the NCIC leadership. Yet, because so few Canadians of any background – including Italian – knew about the wartime internments of Italians, building a meaningful redress movement would require both persuading Ottawa to act and nurturing a social memory among Italian Canadians themselves.

In deciding on a strategy for seeking redress, Italian-Canadian ethnic leaders looked to the experience of the Japanese-Canadian redress activists. NCIC leaders had shown a public interest in the Japanese-Canadian cause back in 1985, when the NCIC became one of the first organizations in Canada to support the cause of Japanese-Canadian redress.[55] Aware that the internal divisions within the organized Japanese-Canadian community had hampered its lobbying efforts, leaders of the CIBPA and the NCIC agreed to work together on a national campaign. Because they knew that the Japanese Canadians had been much divided over the matter of compensation and that winning it had been a long, drawn-out process, the Italian-Canadian organizations chose to focus first on getting a formal acknowledgment from the government that an injustice had been done and to leave the matter of compensation for later consideration. It is possible too that for most of the few people involved in making the decisions, individual compensation appeared secondary because they themselves had no personal connections to the internments. This was in sharp contrast to the many Japanese-Canadian redress activists whose families had suffered the trauma of uprooting.[56]

Under Castrilli's direction the NCIC soon prepared a brief, which it presented to the government in Ottawa in January 1990. *A National Shame – The Internment of Italian Canadians* sets down a historical narrative about the relevant wartime events, offers an assessment of the harm done to Italian Canadians, and makes the case for redress.[57] It would become the NCIC-authorized version of the internment and a means for shaping social memory in the present.

As the brief explains, under the authority of the Defence of Canada regulations issued in 1939, a class of 'enemy aliens' was created that included not only foreign nationals but also Canadians. Such individuals could have their civil liberties suspended and property confiscated. A federal order-in-council required the registration of residents of Canada who were from Italy and who either had not been naturalized or who had been naturalized in the period since 1 September 1929. Canadian authorities declared 82,500 people to be 'enemy aliens,' of whom 31,000 were of Italian descent. Posters and newspaper articles made everyone aware of the regulations. 'A hard-working, largely invisible segment of the Canadian population suddenly found itself the target of racial prejudice from neighbours and of close surveillance by government.' Police photographed, fingerprinted, and interrogated the people as they came forward to register. In an atmosphere of 'hysteria and overreaction,' many of the 'enemy aliens' lost their jobs, and owners of small businesses became victims of verbal abuse, window-smashing, and boycotts. Both the Ontario and the Quebec government made unemployed enemy aliens ineligible for government assistance.

In addition to registering these people, authorities identified many individuals for special questioning and possible internment. Although the order-in-council required 'reasonable grounds' for internment, in fact, asserts the brief, men were rounded up on the basis of 'suspicious reports by paid informers of dubious credibility,' or for 'membership in associations with Italian names and involvement with organizations roughly equivalent to the heritage language classes of today.' The brief thus dismisses the charge made by Canada's wartime government that those interned had been active supporters in Canada of Mussolini and his Fascist regime. The brief then continues, noting that after the initial investigations, some men were released, while others were interned, most of them at Camp Petawawa near Ottawa. Figures vary as to how many Italian Canadians the government of Canada interned, but one official source reported 632 internees of Italian origin.[58] Internees were held for periods ranging up to three years, with the average length of incarceration being 15.8 months. All internees were men between sixteen and seventy years of age, and 87 per cent of them were Canadian citizens. They came from all walks of life: 'lawyers, doctors, candy-makers, carpenters, cigar manufacturers, bakers, blacksmith, pressers, wine makers, cab drivers, priests, contractors, postmen, shoe shiners and bricklayers.'

'The actions taken by the government,' declares the brief, 'were outrageous, arbitrary and lacked factual proof of any subversion or danger to the State.' The charge, sometimes made in the period leading up to June 1940, that Italian Canadians had shown an interest in Fascism was, according to the brief, without foundation. This had been demonstrated in the works of two historians, which are cited.[59]

The brief then describes the dreadful experiences of the internees and their families, beginning with the fears engendered by the police raids and the sudden removal, without explanation, of family members. In the camps at Petawawa, Ontario, and Fredericton, New Brunswick, a 'prison atmosphere was impressed upon these previously law-abiding and productive residents of Canada.' Correspondence was strictly limited and censored. The internees were all put to work building roads, clearing forests, and doing other manual labour tasks required at the camp. They suffered from 'depression caused by the total lack of family interaction and the frustration at being unable to provide for their families in men whose foundation was the family.' Wrenched from their families, made to feel like prisoners, unable to provide for their wives and children, 'who had to survive without the salary of the main breadwinner,' the men lost their sense of purpose. 'They had no idea of what they had done to deserve their fate and when they would be released.'

Families and family businesses suffered during the period of the men's incarceration. When the federal government froze the bank accounts of those detained, 'women who could not rely on their husbands' income could now also not use their accumulated savings.' Their properties were administered by the federally appointed Custodian of Enemy Alien Property, and families 'were forced to subsist on $12.00 per month given to them by way of government assistance.' Valued assets had to be sold, often at below-market values, so as to clothe and feed families. Many of the properties that were retained by the Custodian 'were somehow not available for redistribution to their legal owners at the end of the war.'

As for redress, the brief said that 'to that extent that individual claims can be quantified, they should be compensated.' But the brief's main demand was for the government of Canada 'to express its regrets at the treatment of Italian Canadians during the Second World War.' An acknowledgment similar to that given the Japanese Canadians on 22 September 1988 (and quoted at length) 'would go a long way towards resolving a difficult chapter in the history of Canada, a chapter which all of us must deplore.' The NCIC further urged the government and all Canadians to ensure that in future no other Canadians, regardless of cultural origins, would be subjected to gross violations of civil rights. The brief concluded by insisting that it was time 'to rectify the errors of the past and to restore the positive image of Italian Canadians as significant contributors to this country of ours in this century.'

The Italian-Canadian redress campaign gained a significant victory in remarkably short order – in less than eleven months after the brief was submitted to the Mulroney government. On 4 November 1990, Prime Minister Mulroney issued an acknowledgment of the wrongs done to 'our Canadians of Italian origin during World War Two.' He did so at a luncheon in the Toronto suburb of Concord before five hundred NCIC members and guests. In making his acknowledgment, Mulroney reiterated the main case outlined in the NCIC brief, that the Italian Canadians had been stripped of their civil liberties and detained because of their racial-ethnic origin. 'Sending civilians to internment camps without trial,' said the prime minister, 'simply because of their ethnic origin was not then, and is not now, and never will be, accepted in a civilized nation that purports to respect the rule of law.'[60]

Why such rapid success? When interviewed by historian Robert Ventresca a few years later, Castrilli explained the victory by referring to several factors: a favourable political climate, the example of the Japanese Canadians' success, strong support from the media, and 'a "really good team" of Italian-Canadian parliamentarians and professionals with "an understanding of the political machinery" and a willingness to use it.'[61] In their scholarly assessment of the redress campaign, Franca Iacovetta and Robert Ventresca observe that in 1990 Mulroney was busy mending fences with ethnic leaders following criticisms that, during the constitutional negotiations that ended in the impasse at Meech Lake, he had failed to bring ethnic minorities and their leaders into the process of reform. Here was an opportunity for Mulroney to concede to the demands of the leaders of a prominent ethnic group and show them and their group national respect. Italian Canadians formed crucial voting blocks in a number of urban ridings, and Mulroney was interested in gaining their votes for the Conservative party.[62] Moreover, a stumbling block to a quick settlement in the case of the Japanese Canadians had been their national organization's holding out for individual compensation – an expensive demand but for them an important principle. The NCIC, by contrast, had made it clear that it was willing to accept, at least as a first step, an acknowledgment alone. Because there was no cost to taxpayers, Mulroney could make his move sooner rather than later.

Mulroney's acknowledgment captured media attention with images of former internees who had been in attendance at the Concord banquet hall shedding tears of joy, but it was not the end of the redress campaign. The very next day the NCIC demanded financial restitution: individual compensation of $13,000 for internees and group compensation for all Italian Canadians placed on enemy alien lists. To broaden the campaign, in following months a newly appointed Redress Committee of the NCIC organized public hearings in Halifax, Montreal, Toronto, and Vancouver where former internees and family members gave heartfelt testimony about their experiences and discussed compensation. It was during this time that awareness of the internment grew within the Italian-Canadian population and particularly among artists and filmmakers, whose subsequent work drew yet more attention to the hardships related to the internment. Notable in this connection was a documentary co-produced by the National Film Board and the Canadian Broadcasting Corporation, *Barbed Wire and Mandolins*, which aired on national television in 1997. The film includes interviews with its historical consultants, Kenneth Bagnell and Antonio Mazza, and moving testimony from various former internees and their family members.[63] In the period following Mulroney's acknowledgment, then, progress was made in crafting and popularizing a social memory of internment, one that followed the line set down by the NCIC.

No progress was made, however, in getting Ottawa to provide financial compensation, notwithstanding the NCIC's attempt to broaden its campaign. The NCIC joined forces with other redress groups, including from the Chinese-Canadian, Japanese-Canadian, and Ukrainian-Canadian communities, to form the National Redress Alliance. Although the Alliance made clear its objection to a single settlement for all groups, that is what the government proposed. Two and a half years after Mulroney's Concord speech, Ottawa made an offer that made no mention of financial restitution but included marking the internment camps with commemorative plaques, removing from legal records the names of internees, and creating a 'Nation-Builders Hall of Records' in the National Archives. The NCIC formally rejected this offer, declaring that the internees deserved 'much more than the[se] platitudes and empty gestures.' Castrilli mused to reporters, saying: 'It makes me wonder, why disparate treatment between us and the Japanese community? We too suffered the same injustices, so why deny us the compensation afforded the Japanese?' Lobbying continued, but to no avail. In November 1994 the NCIC passed a resolution abandoning the campaign for financial restitution, a position that came under sharp fire from members of the Redress Committee and the Toronto district of the Congress. The campaign was resumed, but in a low-key manner.[64]

In contrast to the Japanese-Canadian redress campaign, the Italian-Canadian lobby got little public attention. In the mainstream press, reports covered Mulroney's 'apology'[65] and the hearings organized by the NCIC when it resumed the campaign, but they did not spark a wider debate. There was a little grumbling from the odd columnist who, saying 'I told you so,' observed that Mulroney had indeed conceded to another ethic group now that the door had been opened by the Japanese Canadians. Only the Italian-Canadian press showed anything approaching sustained interest in the campaign. Editorials in Toronto's *Corriere Canadese* endorsed the campaign and kept calling for the Canadian government to pay financial compensation. One, for instance, urged Jean Chrétien to pay up so as 'to give clear direction for the future' and render 'serious' Canada's 'talk of equality among all its citizens.'[66] Moreover, in contrast to the Japanese-Canadian case where differences regarding tactics were debated fiercely in the community press, the Italian-Canadian redress campaign sparked scarcely any debate at all in the community's newspapers. A search of *Corriere Canadese* found only a single voice that criticized the NCIC redress narrative or campaign. In a letter to the editor, one Paola Ludovici Mac-Quarrie of Hull, Quebec, called for more historical perspective on the events of 1940. She takes exception to the film *Barbed Wire and Mandolins* because the filmmakers had not interviewed even 'one internee who had worn a blackshirt or the fascio fez.' It was important, she insists, to remember the real horrors of Fascism: 'it signified the abolition of parliamentary democracy, political assassinations, repression of opponents, collaboration with the Nazis, expulsion of Jews to Auschwitz.'[67]

If the NCIC redress campaign triggered little controversy in the general population, it raised deep concerns among professional historians who are Italian-Canadian specialists. First aired at a conference held in Toronto in 1995, these critiques were brought to a wider audience in a scholarly collection of essays, entitled *Enemies Within: Italian and Other Internees in Canada and Abroad.*

It presents the findings of several historians of Italian background who were alarmed by the campaign and developments in the media, including the airing of *Barbed Wire and Mandolins*, that oversimplified and exaggerated certain past events. The volume's editors find 'downright offensive' some of the overblown rhetoric, such as when those inspired by the campaign equated the experience of Italian-Canadian internees with Holocaust victims. And equating the Italian-Canadian case with that of the Japanese-Canadian one, they reason, was both inaccurate and self-serving. In their essay on the redress campaign, Iacovetta and Ventresca concede that the redress movement greatly increased the awareness of Italian Canadians about the internments and 'encouraged film-makers, writers, students, and the elderly to participate in a collective retrieval of the past.' They object, however, to community leaders' tarring 'every present-day Italian Canadian with the stigma of internment,' and asking 'the Canadian state to help "us," as a community, overcome a legacy of shame and assist our ascent into full citizenship.'[68]

Moreover, contributors to *Enemies Within* are troubled by the way the NCIC version of the history – one written to persuade the government by driving home an uncluttered message – became *the* collective, community-based memory of the events. That history simplified and sanitized the past, charge Iacovetta and Roberto Perin in the book's introduction, by 'drawing on selective evidence, ignoring contrary views, and glossing over the fascist history of the Italian immigrant communities.'[69] Whereas *A National Shame* represented the internees as innocents, men lacking in political sophistication who simply took pride in their country of origin, contributors to *Enemies Within* show that the internees were a more diverse lot. In addition to the wrongfully interned were the community leaders and activists who had remained firmly and in some cases fiercely committed to Fascism even when the risks were obvious in Canada during the late 1930s. In effect, people in Canada who stubbornly supported Fascist Italy after Mussolini's imperialist adventures in Ethiopia in 1935 and the Fascists' adoption of anti-Semitic policies in 1938 were asking for trouble as the war clouds gathered. These were the community's leaders, the *notabili*, who had been flattered by the prestige they gained when Mussolini's consular officers in Canada targeted them for collaboration during the Fascists' successful campaign to take control of community organizations in Canada. Backed by the vice-consuls, some of these Italian-Canadian Fascists had not hesitated 'on occasion to resort to acts of violence against co-national anti-fascists.'[70] For at least a few of them, the commitment to Fascism did not wane even behind barbed wire. In *Enemies Within*, Gabriele Scardellato discusses some telling photographs taken by internees in camps that show them wearing the Fascist fez (complete with logo) and holding a banner emblazoned with the defiant slogan 'Me ne frego' ('I don't give a damn'), a motto used by Fascist squads in Italy while on their intimidating and often violent marches.[71]

As for the charge that Canadian authorities had acted arbitrarily, *Enemies Within* presents evidence that casts police round-ups in a different light. The RCMP had been gathering good intelligence on Fascist activists since 1935, when Fascist Italy had first been recognized as a potential threat to Canada. According to historian Luigi Bruti Liberati, authorities identified 3500 Italian-Canadian Fascists, but the RCMP considered less than 15 per cent of them truly a risk. By the time Canada and Italy were at war, the RCMP had a list of about 100 names of individuals deemed to be a security risk. With the outbreak of hostilities, argues Bruti Liberati, it was entirely to be expected that authorities would detain these men, using the powers of the War Measures Act. According to the logic of that statute, internment was a preventative measure to protect the state, and so charges or evidence of criminal activity were unnecessary. The fact that evidence of sabotage was never found – a point underlined in the orthodox community account which stresses innocence – can just as easily be seen as the result of timely preventative action taken by the government. This is evidence of the liberal state at war and not of a 'police state' as some redress supporters and one historian have claimed.[72]

Contributors to *Enemies Within* acknowledge that the state interned many more men than the situation warranted and, indeed, several hundred more than even the RCMP thought advisable. Pushed by the fifth-column scare, which swept Canada in spring 1940 and cried out for a massive sweep of security threats, Ottawa officials chose to act aggressively. Still, they interned just 0.44 per cent of the total Italian-Canadian population – a far cry from the situation in Great Britain, where the fifth-column scare led the government to arrest 4200 men, a far larger proportion of the total Italian population.[73] Moreover, not all the blame for the overreaction in Canada can be placed on officials. Case studies in *Enemies Within* document the destructive role played by people *within* the Italian-Canadian community who informed on their neighbours. As a result, the atmosphere in Italian neighbourhoods was poisoned by internecine disputes and fears for many years.[74] Iacovetta and Ventresca criticize redress advocates for largely sidestepping this difficult issue, one that they say 'needs public airing; the healing must come also from within the community.'[75]

The glossed-over version of internment relied on a particular stream of historical consciousness within the Italian-Canadian community, one nurtured since the 1940s by some people interested in suppressing a past more conveniently forgotten in the postwar years. As Perin has demonstrated, the earliest and most articulate of those who spun this tale of internment was Mario Duliani, author of the 1945 novel *La ville sans femmes*, a fictionalized narrative of the internment inspired in large part by the author's own experiences when he was interned for forty months in the Petawawa and Fredericton camps. In his book Duliani tells a story about men, unsophisticated in politics and swept up by world events beyond their control, who make the best of things in an unnatural camp setting where they lack contact with women or families.[76] Yet Duliani himself was far from politically naive. Before coming to Canada he supplemented his income as a journalist in Paris by working for Mussolini's secret police. In 1936 he arrived in Montreal, where he became a political journalist, theatre director, and Fascist activist. Perin argues that Duliani was 'the linchpin in a well-orchestrated campaign already begun in 1934 by the Italian consulate in Montreal that sought to intensify the disunity existing between French and English Canadians over the country's pro-British attitudes in international affairs.' At the time of his internment, Duliani was the international affairs expert writing for a right-wing publication in Montreal on which he worked with Adrien Arcand, the French-Canadian Fascist leader. After his release, Duliani felt the need to revamp his own image, and in *La ville sans femmes*, argues Perin, the author drew 'the veil of innocence that covered most Italian Canadians over himself.' Years later, when lobbying for redress, the NCIC cited Duliani's narrative in its brief to Ottawa as hard evidence in support of its case regarding the innocence and suffering of the internees. Redress supporters subsequently have sought to revive interest in and respect for Duliani's artistic achievements, including this book; in 1994 the first English translation was published under the title *The City without Women*.[77]

Among those Italian Canadians who have publicly shown an interest in the internments, then, there is no consensus on how to understand what happened in the 1940s or what should be done today about this past. The historians of Italian background who criticized the rhetoric of the redress campaign conceded that a historical document designed for use by political lobbyists must be strategic and make a bold case, but they argued that the NCIC had gone too far and hidden or distorted too much of the history. These critics from within the ethnic group were willing to go public with their research findings, which discredited aspects of the ethnic leaders' version of history and its redress campaign. Nevertheless, the critics of the redress campaign have gained little attention. The publication of *Enemies Within* created barely a ripple in the media, not even in the Italian-Canadian media, and historians more sympathetic to the NCIC-authorized version of history have not responded in print to their critics. Notwithstanding the barrage of criticisms, redress activists remain committed to their cause and their narrative. Among the general public, however, the issue has not had anything like the impact of the Japanese-Canadian redress campaign.

The Italian-Canadian redress campaign burst onto the national scene again in 2005. During the final weeks of the Paul Martin government, when defeat in the Commons was certain and an election loomed near, the prime minister announced his government's decision to acknowledge the injustice done to Italian-Canadian internees in the 1940s along with a multimillion-dollar fund for commemorative exhibits, plaques, and other historical material in connection with the internments. The deal was part of his government's Acknowledgment, Commemoration and Education Program, designed to provide funds for several ethnic groups to commemorate past injustices suffered at the hands of Canadian authorities. The Liberals' strategy was to win kudos from ethnic organizations on the eve of an election, while avoiding more costly settlements involving individual compensation on the Japanese-Canadian model. To many observers, the fund looked too much like a Liberal pork barrel, given the announcement's pre-election timing.[78] A *Globe and Mail* editorial, moreover, denounced the government's fund as a case of 'using the money, group by group, to fan the flames of grievance – the antithesis of forward-looking public policy. It is spending unwisely.'[79] Not all of the surviving Italian-Canadian internees were pleased with the scheme. Antonio Capobianco of Montreal, for instance, was quoted on the front page of the *Globe and Mail*, saying: 'I'm not happy. We're the ones who should receive indemnification. They indemnified the Japanese, but we're not receiving indemnities.'[80]

The Italian-Canadian redress lobby was not, as we shall see, the only redress lobby that was inspired by the Japanese-Canadian success, that constructed a narrative of injustice contested by historians from within the ethnic group, and that various governments in Ottawa had difficulty satisfying.

The Ukrainian-Canadian Redress Campaign

In 1980 historians alerted Canada's large Ukrainian community[81] to the harsh treatment that the Canadian government had meted out to Ukrainian Canadians during the First World War, but the matter was not immediately taken up. This was the year that the Canadian Institute for Ukrainian Studies (CIUS) held a conference on the subject of Canada's Ukrainians during the First World War, and a subsequent volume of conference papers, *Loyalties in Conflict*, stimulated interest in the matter among Canadians historians.[82] According to historian Frances Swyripa, community interest in a sixty-year-old war was minimal; the topic 'lacked the popular appeal of other CIUS conferences held in those years, dealing with contemporary issues.'[83] However, the success of the Japanese-Canadian redress campaign in gaining public attention in the mid-1980s gave Ukrainian Canadians an opportunity to do the same for what was presented as a parallel injustice. "'When Japanese raise this question and [the] Canadian government is prepared to express this kind of apology,'" Michael Marunchak, a Ukrainian-Canadian historian from Winnipeg, was quoted as saying in a May 1985 article in the Winnipeg *Free Press*, "'absolutely the events should be mentioned of the first war when Ukrainians suffered very much the same.'"[84]

The Ukrainian-Canadian redress campaign was launched in 1985 by an existing organization, the Civil Liberties Commission (CLC). The CLC, based in Toronto, had been formed early in 1985 with a mandate from the umbrella organization, the Ukrainian Canadian Congress (UCC), to deal with sensitive and pressing political developments in Canada relating to war criminals. The media had reported on allegations that a great many Ukrainian and East European war criminals who had collaborated with the Nazis during the Second World War were hiding in Canada. The CLC raised $1 million and launched legal and educational campaigns to counter such allegations and to lobby Ottawa regarding the handling of alleged war criminals, an issue then being investigated by the Commission of Inquiry on War Criminals, headed by Justice Jules Deschênes. In addition to its key mandate, the CLC assumed a broader role by helping individuals facing civil liberties issues and by subsidizing research and publications on the internments of the First World War. Lubomyr Luciuk, a historical geographer at Queen's University and the CLC's research director, claims credit for turning the attention of the CLC to the internment issue, one that he felt passionately about and that he had been researching for a number of years. It was less an instance of the UCC choosing a historian to mount the charge than one where a historian identified an injustice, seized the opportunity to make a difference, and gained the organized community's backing to pursue it.[85]

The CLC's resources, put in place because of the Deschênes Commission crisis, provided the means for launching the redress campaign. In the view of Swyripa, a critic of the campaign, the Deschênes Commission also provided the main incentive for those Ukrainian Canadians who took up the internment issue that Luciuk identified. The campaign's 'underlying message,' she writes, 'was that before Canada accused a broad section of its Ukrainian citizens of war crimes committed outside its borders, it should examine its own actions carried out in the name of freedom and democracy.'[86]

In December 1987 the CLC submitted a brief on the Ukrainian case for redress to the House of Commons Standing Committee on Multiculturalism.[87] But it was the September 1988 settlement reached between the Mulroney government and the Japanese Canadians that spurred the Ukrainian-Canadian redress campaign. In October, the CLC presented 'The Ukrainian Canadian

Case of Acknowledgement and Redress' to Gerry Weiner, minister of state for multiculturalism and citizenship. The demands of the CLC were explained to the public in an article (written by Luciuk and another Ukrainian-Canadian scholar, Bohdan S. Kordan) that appeared in the *Globe and Mail* in October 1988. First, Ukrainian Canadians wanted not an apology but an acknowledgment that 'a wrong' was done to citizens of Ukrainian and other East European origins. The community urged that historical markers be raised at various internment sites. They wanted as well changes to the Emergencies Act, which replaced the War Measures Act, the legislation that had made legal the internment of Ukrainians in the First World War and Japanese Canadians in the Second World War, so as to provide 'protection against history repeating itself.' And finally, 'as in the Japanese-Canadian redress package, Ukrainian Canadians ... called for individual compensation for the few survivors of the internment and for "symbolic redress" to the entire community in the form of a trust fund.'[88]

The public case for redress was succinctly made in a publication entitled *A Time for Atonement: Canada's First National Internment Operations and the Ukrainian Canadians, 1914–1920*, which was written by Luciuk.[89] The pamphlet begins by explaining how Ukrainians in Canada became internees and subject to other repressive measures. In 1917 about 171,000 Ukrainians were living in Canada, most of them in the prairie west. As *A Time for Atonement* explains, generally they had come to Canada from the Austrian crown lands of Galicia and Bukovynia. They were or had been Austrians in terms of citizenship, but were Ukrainian in nationality. When Britain entered the First World War in August 1914, the government of Canada passed an order-in-council that required the registration and in certain cases the internment of aliens of 'enemy nationality.' The authorities treated approximately 80,000 Ukrainians who had come to Canada from Austrian territories as 'enemy aliens,' requiring them to register with police, report regularly, and carry identification papers. Under the authority of the War Measures Act, the Canadian government interned some 5441 civilians, the vast majority of whom (perhaps 5000 or so) were of Ukrainian origin. These people, among them women and children, were 'subject to imprisonment in one of 26 receiving stations and "concentration camps" established across Canada.' Most of the camps were in the hinterland, where the internees were required to work at road-building, land-clearing, logging, and railway construction. The internments, then, 'not only uprooted families but also allowed for exploitation of many of the internees' labour.'

Authorities seized whatever valuables individual detainees had with them. 'Some of this confiscated money was stolen,' reports Luciuk, who corroborates his claim with a quotation from the officer in charge of the internment operations, Major-General Sir William D. Otter. Moreover, says the pamphlet, 'the human costs of the internment operations are, of course incalculable.'

A Time for Atonement describes the hardships of living in the camps. Internees were denied access to newspapers and were restricted in their correspondence, which was also censored. General Otter is cited to show that guards sometimes mistreated the inmates. The tough conditions, hard work, and confinement took their toll: 107 internees died, 69 of them so-called 'Austrians.' Observers at the time noted also the psychological damage done during interment. Internees manifested their objections to their treatment by various means, from passive resistance to full-scale riot.

As the war proceeded and labour shortages developed in Canadian industries, many Ukrainian internees were released on parole to work for wages. Pay was fixed at the rate paid to soldiers (25 cents per day), which was less than would have been paid in the open market. Other Ukrainians remained interned in the camps for the duration of the war and beyond. The last of the camps was not closed until late February 1920.

Throughout the period of the internments, notes Luciuk, Canadian authorities were repeatedly told that they were interning Ukrainians who had no sympathy with the war aims of the Austro-Hungarian Empire. Ukrainian-Canadian newspaper editors, organizations, and individuals informed the government of its error: Ukrainian Canadians were loyal to Canada and the British Empire. Moreover, while the internment operations continued, the loyalty of Ukrainian Canadians to Canada was shown by their joining the Canadian army in record numbers, even if they had to conceal their background or change their names to do so. Still, the Canadian government passed the Wartime Elections Act (1917), which disenfranchised most Ukrainian Canadians, and in 1918 it banned several Ukrainian-language newspapers and organizations. During the 'Red Scare' that followed immediately after the war, Canadian authorities suspected many Ukrainian Canadians of being dangerous Bolsheviki and deported several hundred of them.

According to Luciuk's brief, the damage done in the years 1914–20 haunted Ukrainian Canadians ever after. Having suffered in the past, Ukrainian Canadians in 1988 were appealing to the government of Canada to acknowledge the wrongs done to the Ukrainian-Canadian community and to compensate Ukrainian Canadians for their losses. 'Although what happened can never be undone,' concludes Luciuk, 'a time for atonement has surely come.'

When the CLC made its case to Multiculturalism Minister Gerry Weiner in late 1988, on the eve of a federal election, he promised that the issue would be dealt with 'expeditiously.' In fact, the Mulroney government, while continuing to make noises that held out hope to the lobbyists, avoided dealing decisively with the case. In early 1990, Weiner said that the matter was 'complex' and needed 'further study.' About the time of Prime Minister Mulroney's acknowledgment of the Italian-Canadian case in the fall of 1990, he met with UCC leaders in Edmonton and discussed the internments and an acknowledgment, but none came. In the meantime, the redress campaigners were disappointed to learn in 1991 that the Historic Sites and Monuments Board of Canada had recommended against raising a historical marker at Castle Mountain, the site of a large internment camp located in Banff National Park.[90] Mulroney was gone from office before any announcement of policy on Ukrainian-Canadian redress was ever made. In 1994 a new Liberal government firmly rejected giving financial compensation to ethnic groups for past discrimination, echoing the earlier concerns raised by Trudeau about the wrong-headedness of attempting to rewrite the past. The redress campaign continued, but for several years success appeared unlikely.

Even during this discouraging period, the campaign's advocates worked long and energetically to keep the matter before the public and the federal government. Luciuk wrote a number of op-ed pieces that appeared in newspapers across the country, and he got various journalists interested in the campaign and acted as the community authority they quoted. In 1990 the CLC broadened the base of its campaign by doing a mass mailing and providing supporters with postcards that they were asked to send to Ottawa politicians and their MPs urging that the government deal expeditiously and fairly with the Ukrainian case. At Christmastime that year the campaign gained newspaper attention by holding a commemorative ceremony at Old Fort Henry, one of the sites of internment, where clergy and politicians solemnly recalled the suffering of the internees. In 1991 the MP for Kingston and the Islands succeeded in getting a private member's bill through the House of Commons that expressed support for the campaign and urged action on the matter. International involvement came in May 1993, when two political leaders in Ukraine wrote letters to Mulroney asking him to do what was 'right and honourable.' Luciuk wrote about and helped bring into the campaign the last known survivor of the First World War internments. Mary Manko Haskett, who had been a six-year-old when her family went into a camp, wrote an open letter to the prime minister reflecting on her experience and urging redress, and she and redress activists visited Ottawa in a (failed) effort to meet with government leaders.[91] Her survivor's voice provided what this campaign had hitherto lacked: oral testimony derived from personal memory, a powerful form of support that had been important in both the Japanese-Canadian and the Italian-Canadian campaigns, which had the advantage of dealing with a more recent decade and a greater number of living subjects.

To some extent the redress campaign succeeded in one of its goals: bringing Ukrainian Canadians closer together on common ground. The deep chasm between Ukrainian-Canadian leftists and Ukrainian nationalists in Canada was bridged if only for a moment at the start of the campaign when both groups agreed that the Canadian state had perpetrated an injustice in the years 1914–20.[92] For leftists, the campaign threw a spotlight on a theme central to their social memory: the victimization of immigrant workers during the Red Scare. For Ukrainian nationalists, redress similarly reinforced their distinctive memory by bringing attention to the victimization of Ukrainians, a people whose national destiny had long been thwarted in Europe, not least during the long years of Soviet domination. By politicizing the internment history, observes Swyripa, the campaign turned individual pain and personal memory into a group concern and social memory. Yet reactions among Ukrainian Canadians varied widely, she maintains. For some people with roots in the early immigration that settled the prairie west and suffered wartime discrimination, the campaign awakened them to a history of discriminatory treatment that had been suppressed, downplayed, or even forgotten in family lore. Some found closure at last because the issues had been aired. On the other hand, Swyripa says that for her own family, whose ancestors were from that same background, the campaign 'meant little' because it focused on internment. Like the descendants of the vast majority of Ukrainian homesteaders, Swyripa's family had no private memories of the internment because they were not directly affected. The internments had been directed not at prairie homesteaders but at others – unemployed industrial workers.[93]

Divisions within the Ukrainian-Canadian population led to public disputes about the redress campaign. While leftists supported the demand for an apology, they objected both to their nationalist rivals' appropriation of the cause and to the demand that the government compensate the community by paying money that would in effect be in the control of the UCC, an organization that they believed had shunned them.[94] Even within the UCC itself, divisiveness had direct results on the redress campaign. Differences mainly over other issues led the UCC to disband the Civil Liberties Commission, whose members (including Luciuk) carried on the campaign by launching a new organization, the Ukrainian Canadian Civil Liberties Association.[95] The UCC, in turn, established a redress committee. As a result, the public grew confused about who spoke for Ukrainians, and Ottawa politicians who wished to stall redress could play one group off against the other.[96]

Certain historians from within Ukrainian-Canadian circles voiced criticisms of the redress campaign. In the fall of 1988, just as things were heating up, Stella Hryniuk, a historian of Ukraine at the University of Manitoba, objected in the pages of the Winnipeg *Free Press* to the campaign's equating the Ukrainian case to 'the enormity of the injustice done from 1941 onwards to Canadians of Japanese origins – men, women and children.' The campaign glossed over significant differences. While Japanese Canadians were victimized on the basis of their ethnicity, this had not been the case, she argued, for the Ukrainians who were interned. They were detained because of the enemy citizenship. Most of the 'Austrians' interned in the camps were Ukrainians who had not been naturalized. (The internees tended to be industrial labourers who had come to Canada on work sojourns and were caught here by the unemployment crisis and the outbreak of the war.) Furthermore, she adds, only 'a small number of women and children were permitted (not required) to accompany them.' She ends by making 'a call for common sense and attention to historical fact.'[97]

Historian Orest Martynowych, then at the Canadian Institute of Ukrainian Studies, University of Alberta, raised several points in a much longer critique of the redress campaign. He insisted, for instance, on the need to be clear about whom the Canadian government targeted for internment. Only 'a handful' of Ukrainian Canadians were ever interned; the vast majority of the internees were Austrian nationals who had never been naturalized in Canada. Neither were many of the internees farmers snatched from their homesteads. Instead, 'the overwhelming majority of Ukrainian internees were young, single, propertyless, unemployed, unnaturalized migrant laborers. They were interned while trying to cross the American border or because municipal councils, which were unable or unwilling to provide relief for them, insisted that they represented a threat to civil order.' At the beginning of the war, Canadian Prime Minister Robert Borden was willing to let unemployed Ukrainians with Austrian papers cross into the United States, but the British government insisted they be interned because of fears that many of these men, especially the military reservists, would drift back to Europe via the neutral United States and end up in enemy forces.[98]

Martynowych raised other points, too. As for the internees' health problems, he says that most of the deaths were either the result of tuberculosis contracted in the old country or of the influenza pandemic of 1918–19. And as for economic losses, it is quite possible, argues Martynowych, that a handful of interned Ukrainian urban dwellers lost out when authorities confiscated valuables, real estate, etc. However, nothing was confiscated from the great majority of the Ukrainian internees because they were penniless, unemployed labourers who had sent whatever money they had saved back home to the old country. The low daily pay-rate of 25 cents mentioned in *A Time for Atonement* applied only to workers performing jobs while interned, but once paroled, as nearly all 'Austrians' were by 1917, they were paid the going rates wherever they worked. Even on the matter of disloyalty to Canada, Martynowych says, there were at least some grounds for the Canadian government's suspicions. He mentions two Ukrainian-language newspapers, one Canadian and one American, that circulated in Canada and that published, during the first eighteen months of the war, 'blatantly Austrophile and Germanophile editorials and articles on a number of occasions.'[99]

Both Hryniuk and Martynowych question whether the redress campaign, by focusing on the internments, actually addressed the most important of the discriminatory measures affecting Ukrainians in Canada during the era of the First World War. The federal government's cynical manipulation of the franchise for the purposes of the 1917 election infringed on the civil rights of far more Ukrainian Canadians, and these were people who were naturalized and were in every sense Canadians.[100]

Several years later, historian Frances Swyripa wrote a scholarly essay where she reflects on the politics of redress within her community, recounting these disputes and adding some of her own criticisms of the redress version of history. She objects, for instance, to the way that, even after Martynowych's critique, the CLC continued to portray 'its picture of wrongs perpetrated against peaceful Canadian farmers and families.' Swyripa casts doubt on just how wounded the community remains decades after the events of 1914–20, and she insists on the need to appreciate the varied reactions and assessments of those events among Ukrainian Canadians. The exaggerated rhetoric associated with the campaign also troubles her; for instance, the way that the mainstream press used terms such as 'Canadian gulag' and 'slave labour.' Particularly problematic, she finds, is the campaign's use of 'concentration camp,' a term admittedly used during the period of the First World War to refer to the Canadian internment camps, but one that has taken on, as a result of the Holocaust, much more sinister and emotional meanings in the period since then. In her conclusion Swyripa writes:

> the redress campaign brought Ukrainian internment into the public consciousness and created a popular image of concentration camps incarcerating innocent Canadian men, women, and children who were snatched from their homesteads, stripped of their property, and exploited as slave labour. While acknowledging the exceptions, a historian such as I would prefer a picture, using more temperate language, of unnaturalized single men from enemy countries rounded up because they were unemployed and destitute, forced to work for paltry pay, and sometimes mistreated.

She goes on to express her belief that this second, more accurate and better balanced version of events would have been at least as effective in teaching Canadians and their governments 'something about themselves.'[101]

Notwithstanding its difficulties during the 1990s, the redress movement succeeded in bringing about various commemorative measures. Several books and pamphlets aimed at a wide readership provided informative histories of particular aspects of the internment.[102] A film documentary, *Freedom Had a Price: Canada's First Internment Operation* (1994) by Yurij Luhovy, played on CBC television and at community-organized screenings across Canada. A historical exhibit, 'The Barbed Wire Solution,' organized by the Ukrainian Canadian Research and Documentation Centre, opened in 1995 in civic space in Toronto, and a year later in Banff, Alberta, artist Sophia Isajiw deployed images of the internment in an art show entitled 'History's Exiles.' Between 1994 and 2002, the Ukrainian-Canadian Civil Liberties Association, with help from community partners, raised funds and erected historical plaques, monuments, and/or interpretive panels on the sites of at least nineteen internment sites from Amherst, Nova Scotia to Sicamous, British Columbia. These reinforced public awareness of the UCCLA-authorized history of internment. Sometimes things did not go smoothly. Parks Canada held up the erection of interpretive panels at Castle Mountain in Banff National Park, objecting to the word 'unjust' in connection with government actions, and there were conflicts with the CBC over its airing of *Freedom Had a Price*. Nevertheless, all these acts of commemoration must have had some impact on the historical understanding of some Canadians, particularly those of Ukrainian background who were most likely to take note.[103]

Regarding its main goal, however, the Ukrainian-Canadian redress campaign failed to win a victory during the 1980s and 1990s. Whereas the Italian Canadians at least got an acknowledgment from Mulroney when he spoke in Concord, the Ukrainian Canadians got nothing from either the Liberal or the Conservative governments. 'The difference,' observed Swyripa in 2000, 'no doubt reflects how the two groups – Italians living mostly around Toronto and Montreal, Ukrainians spread across the country – were assessed in terms of their voting strength.'[104] While this is most likely the case, other factors may have been significant. Because the events of 1914–20 are further in the past and thus further removed from the consciousness of Canadians today, it is harder to stir interest and concern. Survivors' testimony is sparse. Furthermore, the Japanese-Canadian case fits neatly with popular notions of racism in late twentieth-century Canada, when perceived colour differences between perpetrators and victims are considered of primary significance. Luciuk on occasion explained that racism had also been a factor in the Ukrainian case because in early twentieth-century Canada the dominant Anglo-Saxon race perceived

Ukrainians as an inferior race.[105] While scholars will readily concede the point, it was harder to persuade the Canadian public when popular understandings of race and colour had shifted so much from those of nearly a century earlier. Possibly, too, difficulties of the Ukrainian-Canadian campaign had something to do with the debates within the community, including the critical remarks of historians about the accuracy and interpretation of the redress narrative. When Weiner said that the issue was 'complex' and in need of 'further study,' he may have known that the narrative was contested or suspected that the public had not been sufficiently moved.

The Ukrainian-Canadian redress campaign revived at the turn of the twenty-first century. In 1999 the UCC commissioned a position paper on redress, which was expanded into a book, written by Bohdan Kordan and Craig Mahovsky and published under the title *A Bare and Impolitic Right*. Philosophical in approach and highlighting ethical issues, it raises new objections to the Canadian government's actions during the First World War. For instance, the authors make much of the fact that Canada broke with the international conventions of war by using civilian internee labour. Furthermore, they concede that not all of the criticism made by historians concerning the way history had been used by the Ukrainian-Canadian redress movement was 'unfounded, uninformed, or off the point.' The book's main purpose, however, is to make a case for 'symbolic redress as a necessary and useful instrument in advancing the cause of justice.'[106] Meantime, Luciuk and his Ukrainian Canadian Civil Liberties Association, once again working closely with the UCC, continued to publicize the issue and to meet periodically with prominent politicians to press the case.[107]

Progress came at last in 2005 as the minority government of Paul Martin contemplated an election. In August at a ceremony held in Regina with leaders from various organizations of Ukrainian Canadians, Prime Minister Martin announced an agreement in principle reached by his government and the Ukrainian-Canadian community on redress. In a carefully worded speech that avoided controversial points, Martin referred to the important role played by Ukrainian immigrants in settling the Canadian west and to how the federal government during the First World War had sent five thousand Ukrainian Canadians to internment camps and placed other restrictions on basic freedoms. Moreover, he explained that the agreement, part of his government's Acknowledgement, Commemoration and Education Program, committed the government to spending $2.5 million dollars to commemorate the internments through historical markers, educational materials, and the like.[108] Luciuk and other leaders welcomed the agreement, calling it 'a first step' that put the community 'on the path to securing an acknowledgement of historic injustice.'[109] A *Globe and*

Mail editorial strongly criticized the policy, saying: 'it goes beyond memory, beyond historical awareness, and feeds a culture of victimhood. It risks feeding the feeling that past grievances must be kept burning ... Harping too much on past injustices can colour the spirit in which people move forward.'[110] By contrast, in his speech at Regina, Martin had insisted that it was essential to learn from the past in order to move forward. Commemoration and redress would help Canadians 'continue to promote our values of respect, tolerance, fairness and inclusion.'

In 2005, progress was also made in Parliament, where Inky Mark, a Conservative MP from Manitoba, pursued the community's cause. Earlier he had introduced several private member's bills that provided for a settlement, but these did not gain adequate support.[111] In March 2005, however, one of Mark's private member's bills, Bill C-331, passed the crucial second reading in the Commons. The bill had the backing of all the opposition parties and some Liberals even though the minority Liberal government itself did not endorse it. The rhetoric of MPs who spoke in favour of the bill during second reading testifies to the success of Luciuk and his supporters in inscribing their social memory in the public record of the nation. If anything, the members embellished the story. According to Borys Wrzesnewskyj, MP, the victims of the internment 'were pioneers who were encouraged to leave their homeland to help build Canada.' The internees, 'which in many cases included women and children, were not only disenfranchised, but their homes and homesteads were taken away from them.' No mention is made of unemployed industrial workers. Neither was it pointed out that the great majority of the internees were aliens. In fact, Conservative leader Stephen Harper informed the House: 'Nearly 9000 Canadians were interned, the vast majority of Ukrainian origin.' 'Many of those interned,' he continued, 'were not just naturalized British subjects. They were truly Canadians. They were born in Canada.'[112] Entirely missing from the Commons' debate were the revisions to the story that various historians had insisted were needed for the sake of historical accuracy. For politicians, it was impossible to resist the compelling image of Canadian homesteaders snatched from their nation-building role and sent to internment camps. Such a narrative gave national politicians the rhetorical means to justify a generous settlement. At the same time, it publicly reinforced the original redress narrative of *A Time for Atonement*. The bill gained royal assent and became law (the Internment of Persons of Ukrainian Origin Recognition Act) on 25 November, just three days before the Liberal government called a general election.

The Conservative government of Stephen Harper, which came to power following the Liberal defeat at the polls in January 2006, has sought to put its own stamp on ethnic redress matters, notably in connection with the Chinese-Canadian and Indo-Canadian communities.[113] Moreover, in June 2006 the Harper government announced the creation of the Community Historical Recognition Program (CHRP) with a $25 million budget to fund eligible community-based commemorative and educational projects relating to issues of concern to Canada's ethno-cultural communities. (It replaced the Martin government's Acknowledgement, Commemoration and Educational Program.) In announcing the new program, officials noted that it would enable the government to honour specific funding commitments made in connection with agreements such as the one the previous government had signed with the Italian- and Ukrainian-Canadian communities.[114] The Ukrainian-Canadian community, however, objected to being told to apply for grants to 'bureaucrats.' Lubomyr Luciuk declared it was 'unconscionably paternalistic' to expect Ukrainian Canadians 'to go cap in hand to ask Ottawa to give back some of the money they took from the internees, under duress.' The community argued that, at the time their agreement was signed with the Martin government in August 2005, the understanding had been that the government would pay the community a lump sum, which it would control. In a press release dated 14 June 2007, the Ukrainian Canadian Congress declared that it had 'rejected' the Community Historical Recognition Program and it called upon the prime minister 'to immediately intervene to ensure a timely and honourable settlement as mandated by the Internment of Persons of Ukrainian Origin Recognition Act, to which he gave his support in the House of Commons in March 2005, and which received Royal Assent in November 2005.' A community leader was quoted as saying that Harper's prompt intervention was needed 'so that we might together craft a reconciliation settlement while the last surviving internee, Mary Manko, is still alive. We believe that will reflect well upon this government's record, as did Prime Minister Mulroney's much-lauded Japanese Canadian Redress Settlement.'[115] That was not to be, however: on 14 July Mary Manko died peacefully in Mississauga, Ontario.[116] Eventually a deal was struck that established a $10 million endowment fund to support projects specifically related to the internment during the First World War. This funding was to be managed by the Ukrainian Canadian Foundation of Taras Shevchenko, whereas funds for other projects were to be handled by the Integration Program Management Branch at Citizenship and Immigration Canada.[117]

The three redress campaigns, then, all of them involving Canadian ethnic groups, raised important issues relating to civil rights and freedoms arising from measures taken by the government of Canada in wartime. In the 1980s talented and articulate individuals within each of the groups leaped at a political opportunity to raise public awareness about the past through a campaign of public history. Through their organizations, they mounted lobbying efforts that relied on historical narratives crafted to mobilize public opinion and persuade officials to redress egregious past policies of the Canadian government.

In crafting their historical narratives of injustice, redress activists made strategic decisions about what to say and how to say it. With a keen eye on their audience, they selected their materials from a mass of historical facts, private memories, and scholarly interpretations, shaping them so as to get results in the current context. They tailored their redress narratives to fit the Canadian scene of the late twentieth century, when the Canadian nation was being reimagined in the context of free trade, multiculturalism, and antiracism. Ethnic groups, and most especially the Japanese Canadians as a 'visible minority,' commanded media and government attention at the time. Yet redress activists from all three groups studied here reasoned that the violation of individual human rights served as the most effective framework for making a case against past injustice.

The construction of compelling social memories depended not only on persuading the public or the government, but also on mobilizing members of one's own ethnic group whose memories needed prompting. In some cases, events had been forgotten. Many victims of trauma prefer to forget and, if they can, to get on with life, while protecting their descendants from the pain they suffered. Such was the case in some Japanese-Canadian families. Forgetting can also be about distancing oneself from events that are humiliating or embarrassing. Internment, a signifier of powerlessness, has seldom been remembered with pride. And some Italian-Canadian supporters of Fascism preferred to misremember, to deny their past political commitments and insist that they were innocents like all the rest. In the case of the Ukrainian internment of the First World War, the events are so far back in the past that memories have largely been lost. Moreover, the populations of Italians and Ukrainians in Canada have been greatly affected by waves of immigrants who have arrived in Canada after the events at hand and who therefore have no family memories of internment in Canada. Redress narratives were meant to bring a diversity of experience within each of the groups into a coherent and compelling narrative.

In each of the cases studied, critics voiced concerns about these public history campaigns. Within the Japanese-Canadian community, the critiques focused mainly on redress demands and tactics. The historical narrative authorized by the NAJC was publicly challenged only by historians from outside the group. In the case of the Italian-Canadian and the Ukrainian-Canadian groups, however, the authorized historical narratives themselves came under fire from historians from within the groups who found fault with history as rendered by redress activists. Critics worried that imprecision and half-truths contained in the authorized narratives amounted to a wilful abuse of history. It is less clear that these critiques hampered the campaigns. While the conflicts within the Japanese-Canadian community delayed a settlement, the delay allowed for a better resolution in every sense: the public airing of highly charged emotional issues; the emergence of both a powerful grass-roots campaign among Japanese Canadians and a broad movement of public support; and a negotiated settlement that was generous enough to bring satisfaction to the survivors and the campaigners. The Italian-Canadian lobby won its partial victory so quickly that it gained none of these benefits, even as it escaped the wrath of historians whose critiques came after the fact. The Ukrainian-Canadian campaign took a long time to move Ottawa, and the historians who publicly criticized the redress narrative might have had some part in the delays.

Entering into the redress debate was a risky business for historians, who experienced some of the same difficulties faced by other historians who have struggled for narrative control of the national past in other public debates in Canada.[118] Scholars who shaped the community redress narratives risked having their professional standing injured both by journalists, politicians, and activists who played fast and loose with their arguments and by colleagues who presented alternative evidence and readings of events. Similarly, historians who criticized the redress narratives invited the wrath of community leaders firmly committed to defending those narratives and anxious to keep the message clear and straightforward.

The redress campaigns sought to forge a social memory for the group and then to have it inscribed into the national narrative. Of the three groups studied here, the Japanese Canadians made more headway more quickly than the other two in this regard. While Canadian history textbooks authorized for use in publicly supported schools during the 1990s generally included the topic of Japanese-Canadian internment and often discussed redress sympathetically, the same cannot be said about the other two groups.[119] Only in the Japanese-Canadian case did redress bring state sanction of the group narrative, public validation, and incorporation of the particular social memory into the national memory.

Forging a politically powerful redress narrative unfortunately comes at a price: competing and alternative memories are put aside as the group and public mobilize around a single story. A successful campaign builds consensus around bold statements and an easy-to-follow story, and in the process the messiness of the past, with its welter of personal experiences, gets tidied up and made easily understandable. Historical sociologist Pamela Sugiman has recently brought attention to how the Japanese-Canadian redress movement, for all its achievements, has conflated the rich and varied experiences of survivors whose lives were shaped in diverse ways by age, generation, gender, and social class. 'Notwithstanding the political utility and empirical value of the official public history,' she writes, 'I would caution ... against the colonization of our thinking about Japanese Canadians and their communities by one (perhaps) dominant story.'[120]

NOTES

1 In 2005 the Canadian Race Relations Foundation counted thirteen ethnic and religious groups in Canada that have made claims for redress. See www.crr.ca. This does not include the many redress measures initiated by First Nations, including the one that led in 2008 to Prime Minister Stephen Harper's apology in Parliament for Canada's role in the operation of the residential schools and the appointment of the Truth and Reconciliation Commission of Canada. See www.trc.ca.

2 Roy L. Brooks, 'The Age of Apology,' in Brooks, ed., *When Sorry Isn't Enough: The Controversy over Apologies and Reparations for Human Injustice* (New York: New York University Press, 1999), 3–11.

3 On multiculturalism in Canada, see Augie Fleras and Jean Elliot, *Unequal Relations: An Introduction to Race, Ethnic, and Aboriginal Dynamics in Canada*, 2nd edition (Scarborough: Prentice Hall, 1996); Will Kymlicka, *Finding Our Way: Rethinking Ethnocultural Relations in Canada* (Toronto: Oxford University Press, 1998).

4 On nationalist rhetoric and free trade in Canada, see Raymond Blake, 'The Canadian 1988 Election: The Nationalist Posture of Prime Minister Brian Mulroney and the Progressive Conservatives,' *Canadian Review of Studies in Nationalism* 30 (2003): 65–82.

5 For works focusing on wartime issues relating to civil liberties in Canada, see Ramsay Cook, 'Canadian Freedom in Wartime,' in W.H. Heick and Roger Graham, eds., *His Own Man: Essays in Honour of A.R.M. Lower* (Montreal: McGill-Queen's University Press 1974), 37–54; Daniel Robinson, 'Planning for the "Most Serious Contingency": Alien Internment, Arbitrary Detention, and the Canadian State, 1938–1939,' *Journal of Canadian Studies* 28 (1993): 5–20; Larry Hannant, *The Infernal Machine: Investigating the Loyalty of Canada's Citizens* (Toronto: University of Toronto Press, 1995); Gregory S. Kealey, 'State Repression of Labour and the Left in Canada, 1914–1920: The Impact of the First World War,' *Canadian Historical Review* 77 (1992): 281–315; Reg Whitaker, 'Official Repression of Communism during World War II,' *Labour/Le Travail* 17 (1986): 135–66; J.R. Carruthers, 'The Great War and Canada's Enemy Alien Policy,' *Queen's Law Journal* 4 (1978): 43–111.

6 In 1947 the newly formed National Japanese Canadian Citizens' Association lobbied Ottawa for the franchise and for compensation for property losses suffered during the removal. In 1947 a federal royal commission, headed by Justice Henry Bird of British Columbia, was charged with inquiring into financial losses; after his report of 1950, $1.2 million was paid to individuals who submitted claims. Japanese Canadians were highly critical both of the narrow terms of reference of the Bird Commission (which could not take into account damages such as loss of income, disruption of education, emotional trauma, etc.) and of the compensation arrangements actually made. See Patricia E. Roy, *The Triumph of Citizenship: The Japanese and Chinese in Canada, 1941–67* (Vancouver: University of British Columbia Press, 2007), 242–7; Stephanie Bangarth, *Voices Raised in Protest: Defending Citizens of Japanese Ancestry in North America, 1942–49* (Vancouver: University of British Columbia Press, 2008); Roy Miki and Cassandra Kobayashi, *Justice in Our Time: The Japanese Canadian Redress Settlement* (Vancouver and Winnipeg: Talonbooks and the National Association of Japanese Canadians, 1991), 56–9; and Roy Miki, *Redress: Inside the Japanese Canadian Call for Justice* (Vancouver: Raincoast Books, 2004), 111–32.

7 For a survey history of Japanese Canadians, see Midge Michiko Ayukawa and Patricia E. Roy, 'Japanese,' in Paul Robert Magosci, ed., *Encyclopaedia of Canada's Peoples* (Toronto: Multicultural History Society of Ontario/University of Toronto Press, 1999), 1281–1311.

8 Japanese Canadian Centennial Project, *A Dream of Riches: The Japanese Canadians, 1877–1977* (Vancouver: Japanese Canadian Centennial Project, 1978).

9 On Japanese Americans and internment, see Roger Daniels and Sandra C. Taylor, *Japanese Americans: From Relocation to Redress*, revised edition (Seattle: University of Washington Press, 1991); Leslie T. Hatamiya, *Righting a Wrong: Japanese Americans and the Passage of the Civil Liberties Act of 1988* (Stanford: Stanford University Press, 1993).

10 Miki and Kobayashi, *Justice in Our Time*, 60–2.

11 The group called itself 'Sodan-Kai,' translated variously as 'study group' and 'group to reach consensus.' See Miki and Kobyashi, *Justice in Our Time*, 66; Maryka Omatsu, *Bittersweet Passage: Redress and the Japanese Canadian Experience* (Toronto: Between the Lines, 1992), 102–3.

12 Miki and Kobayashi, *Justice in Our Time*, 100–11; Omatsu, *Bittersweet Passage*, 94–108; Momoye Sugiman, ed., *Japanese Canadian Redress: The Toronto Story* (Toronto: Ad Hoc Committee for *Japanese Canadian Redress: The Toronto Story*, 2000), passim.

13 Historical reflections at this juncture were informed by books such as Ken Adachi, *The Enemy That Never Was: A History of the Japanese Canadians* (Toronto: McClelland and Stewart, 1976) and W. Peter Ward, *White Canada Forever: Popular*

Attitudes and Public Policy toward Orientals in British Columbia (Montreal and Kingston: McGill-Queen's University Press, 1978).

14 Miki and Kobayashi, *Justice in Our Time*, 74–7.

15 Trudeau summarized his views emphatically on his last day in Parliament, when goaded by Opposition leader Mulroney in reference to the Japanese-Canadian case. Canada, House of Commons *Debates*, 2nd Session, 32nd Parliament, vol. 4 (1984), 5306–7.

16 Ibid.

17 Ibid., 73; Omatsu, *Bittersweet Passage*, 128.

18 National Association of Japanese Canadians, *Democracy Betrayed: The Case for Redress* (Winnipeg: National Association of Japanese Canadians, 1984).

19 Ibid., 4.

20 Ibid.

21 Ibid., 16

22 Ibid., 24

23 Footnote 1 of the brief reads: 'For a comprehensive analysis of this period of history, see Ann Gomer Sunahara, *The Politics of Racism: The Uprooting of Japanese Canadians during the Second World War* (Toronto: James Lorimer, 1981).' As Sunahara notes at p. 3, hers was the first study of the removal that was based on hitherto closed records in Ottawa.

24 Miki, *Redress*, 234. Government legal advisors have sometimes maintained that an apology (as opposed to an acknowledgment) opens the government up to suits for damages.

25 Margaret Cannon, *The Invisible Empire: Racism in Canada* (Toronto: Random House, 1995); Frances Henry and Carol Tator, *The Colour of Democracy: Racism in Canadian Society* (Toronto: Nelson, 2005).

26 Miki, *Redress*, 232.

27 Omatsu, *Bittersweet Passage*, 147.

28 Jack Granatstein, *Saturday Night*, November 1986, 32–4, 49–50.

29 Cook's letter as cited by Omatsu, *Bittersweet Passage*, 167–8. Omatsu reports that Cook's letter to David Crombie was published in the Japanese-Canadian publication the *New Canadian*, Spring 1987.

30 Price Waterhouse, 'Economic Losses of Japanese Canadians after 1941,' cited in Miki and Kobayashi, *Justice in Our Time*, 92–3.

31 Audrey Kobayashi, 'The Japanese-Canadian Redress Implications for "Race Relations,"' *Canadian Ethnic Studies* 24 (1992): 3–4.

32 On trauma and historical memory, see especially Cathy Caruth, ed., *Trauma: Explorations in Memory* (Baltimore: Johns Hopkins University Press, 1995); Paul Antze and Michael Lambek, eds., *Tense Past: Cultural Essays in Trauma and Memory* (London: Routledge, 1996). For the Japanese-Canadian case, see Mona

Oikawa, *Cartographies of Violence: Japanese Canadian Women, Memory, and the Subjects of Internment* (Toronto: University of Toronto Press, 2011).

33 Miki, *Redress*, 251–67.

34 Joy Kogawa, *Obasan* (Markham, ON: Penguin, 1983).

35 Miki and Kobayashi, *Justice in Our Time*, 87–132.

36 Ibid., 7, 138–9.

37 Ibid., 145.

38 Ottawa *Sun*, 10 November 1988; Winnipeg *Free Press*, 17 and 22 October 1988; Toronto *Globe and Mail*, 27 September 1988 and 14 June 1990.

39 Miki, 'Preface,' in Miki and Kobayashi, *Justice in Our Time*, 12.

40 Omatsu, *Bittersweet Passage*, 9.

41 For a counterview that highlights the limited involvement of third-generation Japanese Canadians in the redress campaign, see Tomoko Makabe, *The Canadian Sansei* (Toronto: University of Toronto Press, 1998), chapter 6.

42 Omatsu, *Bittersweet Passage*, 159–72.

43 Ibid., 167–8.

44 Roy and Granatstein are Canadians, but not of Japanese descent; Iino and Takamura are Japanese.

45 Patricia Roy, J.L. Granatstein, Masako Iino, and Hiroko Takamura, *Mutual Hostages: Canadians and Japanese during the Second World War* (Toronto: University of Toronto Press, 1990), xi.

46 Ibid., 54. See also J.L. Granatstein and Gregory A. Johnson, 'The Evacuation of the Japanese Canadians, 1942: A Realist Critique of the Received Version,' in Norman Hillmer, Bohdan Kordan, and Lubomyr Luciuk, eds., *On Guard for Thee: War, Ethnicity, and the Canadian State, 1939–1945* (Ottawa: Canadian Committee for the History of the Second World War, 1988), 101–30

47 Roy, Granatstein, Iino, and Takamura, *Mutual Hostages*, 217. Patricia Roy argues in a more recent publication that the main reason for the government's 'evacuation of *all* Japanese' was to prevent 'hysterical attacks on Japanese residents of coastal British Columbia.' Roy, *The Triumph of Citizenship*, 17.

48 Roy, Granatstein, Iino, and Takamura, *Mutual Hostages*, 214. Some reviewers, notably those coming from within the Japanese-Canadian community, reacted to aspects of the book with controlled outrage. See, for instance, Audrey Kobayashi, review of *Mutual Hostages*, in *BC Studies* 96 (1992–3): 118–20.

49 In examining the Ontario-authorized textbooks in the collection of the Ontario Institute for Studies in Education Library, I found that Japanese-Canadian removal was never mentioned in the Canadian history textbooks published before 1980, but it was covered in eleven of twelve textbooks published between 1980 and 2000. The redress campaign or settlement was mentioned in seven of the books. The textbook that offers a counter-narrative on internment is J.L. Granatstein et al.,

Nation: Canada since Confederation, 3rd edition (Toronto: McGraw-Hill Ryerson, 1990).

50 According to the 1991 census of Canada, 65,680 people identified their ethnic group as Japanese and 1,147,775 people said they were of Italian background (Magosci, ed., *Encyclopaedia of Canada's Peoples*, statistical appendix,1335).

51 In 1990 the NCIC described itself as an organization that represented 'the over one million Canadians of Italian background living across Canada,' and its mandate as promoting mutual understanding between Italian and other Canadians, and mediating between the Italian-Canadian community and the Canadian government. (See the appendix to the NCIC brief, *A National Shame*.)

52 For a survey history of Italian Canadians, see Franc Sturino, 'Italians,' in Magosci, ed., *Encyclopaedia of Canada's Peoples*, 787–832.

53 Franca Iacovetta and Robert Ventresca, 'Redress, Collective Memory, and the Politics of History,' in Franca Iacovetta, Roberto Perin, and Angelo Principe, eds., *Enemies Within: Italian and Other Internees in Canada and Abroad* (Toronto: University of Toronto Press, 2000), 384–5. Though a catalyst for the campaign, Pennacchio soon distanced himself from the NCIC redress lobby.

54 Sturino, 'Italians,' in Magosci, ed., *Encyclopaedia of Canada's Peoples*, 804–5.

55 Omatsu, *Bittersweet Passage*, 149.

56 Ibid.

57 National Congress of Italian Canadian Archives (Toronto), National Congress of Italian Canadians, *A National Shame: The Internment of Italian Canadians*, brief presented to the government of Canada, January 1990. The authors of the brief, Annamarie Castrilli and Alfred Folco, relied mainly on secondary sources: Bruno Ramirez, 'Ethnicity on Trial: The Italians of Montreal and the Second World War,' in *On Guard for Thee*, 71–84; Joseph Anthony Ciccocelli, 'The Innocuous Enemy Alien: Italians in Canada during World War Two,' MA thesis, University of Western Ontario, 1977; Kenneth Bagnell, *Canadese: A Portrait of the Italian Canadians* (Toronto: Macmillan, 1989).

58 This total is somewhat inflated, in fact, as ninety-nine of those interned were Italian seamen who happened to be in Canadian ports when the war began. They were not in any sense Italian Canadians. The most careful study has put the number of Italian Canadians detained at 'about 500.' See Luigi Bruti Liberati, 'The Internment of Italian Canadians,' in *Enemies Within*, 89.

59 Ramirez, 'Ethnicity on Trial,' and Ciccocelli, 'Innocuous Enemy Alien.'

60 Toronto *Globe and Mail*, 5 November 1990.

61 Iacovetta and Ventresca, 'Redress, Collective Memory,' 382.

62 Ibid., 383.

63 Written by Sam Grana and Nicola Zavaglia, *Barbed Wires and Mandolins* was first shown on 4 March 1997 on the CBC-TV show *Witness*. In 2005 Ciné Télé Action

International released a dramatic TV mini-series about the internments entitled *Il Duce Canadese*.

64 Iacovetta and Ventresca, 'Redress, Collective Memory,' 386–7.

65 In popular discourse no distinction was made between an acknowledgment and an apology, but in formal moments redress activists from all three groups said they wanted an acknowledgment rather than an apology.

66 *Corriere Canadese*, editorial by Angelo Persichilli, 5 March 1997, trans. and cited by Iacovetta and Ventresca, 'Redress, Collective Memory,' 396.

67 Iacovetta and Ventresca, 'Redress, Collective Memory,' 397–8. The letter to the editor appeared in *Corriere Canadese*, 7 March 1997.

68 Iacovetta and Ventresca, 'Redress, Collective Memory,' 405, 381.

69 Franca Iacovetta and Roberto Perin, 'Italians and Wartime Internment: Comparative Perspectives on Public Policy, Historical Memory, and Daily Life,' in *Enemies Within*, 6.

70 Bruti Liberati, 'Internment of Italian Canadians,' 94; see also Angelo Principe, 'A Tangled Knot: Prelude to 10 June 1940,' 17–51, both in *Enemies Within*.

71 Gabriele Scardellato, 'Images of Internment,' in *Enemies Within*, 349–50.

72 Bruti Liberati, 'Internment of Italian Canadians,' 91–5. See also his *Il Canada, l'Italia e il fascismo 1919–1945* (Rome: Bonacci editore, 1984); Reg Whitaker and Gregory S. Kealey, 'A War on Ethnicity? The RCMP and Internment,' in *Enemies Within*, 128–47.

73 In 1940, 11,000 men were registered with UK authorities as Italians with less than twenty years' residency in the country. The 4200 arrested were selected from this group. See Lucio Sponza, 'The Internment of Italians in Britain,' in *Enemies Within*, 259. In the United States, only a tiny proportion of the Italian population was arrested or sent to military camps, but 10,000 Italians (and some U.S.-born Italian Americans) underwent forced removal from the west coast. See Rose D. Scherini, 'When Italian Americans Were "Enemy Aliens,"' in *Enemies Within*, 280.

74 Enrico Carlson Cumbo, '"Uneasy Neighbours": Internment and Hamilton's Italians,' in *Enemies Within*, 99–120; Luigi G. Pennacchio, 'Exporting Fascism to Canada: Toronto's Little Italy,' in *Enemies Within*, 52–75; Roberto Perin, 'Making Good Fascists and Good Canadians: Consular Propaganda and the Italian Community in Montreal in the 1930s,' in Gerald Gold, ed., *Minority and Mother Country Imagery* (St John's: Institute of Social and Economic Research, Memorial University, 1984), 136–58; Ramirez, 'Ethnicity on Trial,' 81.

75 Iacovetta and Ventresca, 'Redress, Collective Memory,' 402.

76 Mario Duliani, *La ville sans femmes* (Montreal: les Éditions Pascal, 1945); *The City without Women: A Chronicle of Internment Life in Canada during the Second World War*, trans. and with an introduction by Antonino Mazza (Oakville: Mosaic

Press, 1994). There is also an Italian translation, *Città senza donne* (Montreal: Gustavo D'Errico editore, 1946).

77 Roberto Perin, 'Actor or Victim? Mario Duliani and His Internment Narrative,' in *Enemies Within*; the quotations are from pp. 322 and 329.

78 A subsequent announcement of a pre-election payout to the National Congress of Chinese Canadians in connection with the Canadian government's pre-1923 Head Tax on Chinese immigrants particularly raised criticisms because of that organization's close Liberal ties. The Chinese Canadian National Council, which had been lobbying on the matter since 1984, was highly critical of the deal. See Jan Wong, '"Give the Money to Us,"' *Globe and Mail*, 26 November 2005.

79 *Globe and Mail*, 12 November 2005.

80 Ibid. Funding for community-sponsored educational and commemorative projects relating to the internments of the Second World War was eventually provided under the Community Historical Recognition Program launched in 2006 by the Conservative government of Stephen Harper. See www.cic.gc.ca/english/multi-culturalism/programs/community.asp. In 2009 another bid for a formal apology and restitution was attempted when Massimo Pacetti, a Liberal MP from Quebec, introduced a private member's bill (C-302) in the House of Commons. Although the bill was not supported by the minority Conservative government, it passed all three readings in the Commons and was being dealt with by a Senate committee when the general election was called in March 2011. See www2.parl.gc.ca/Sites/LOP/LEGISINFO.

81 According to the 1991 census of Canada, the Ukrainian-Canadian population, which was reported to number 1,054,295, rivalled in size that of the Italian-Canadian population at 1,147,775. Magosci, ed., *Encyclopaedia of Canada's Peoples*, statistical appendix, 1335. For a survey history of Ukrainian Canadians, see Frances Swyripa, 'Ukrainians,' in Magosci, ed., *Encyclopaedia of Canada's Peoples*, 1281–1311.

82 Frances Swyripa and John Herd Thompson, eds., *Loyalties in Conflict: Ukrainians in Canada during the Great War* (Edmonton: Canadian Institute of Ukrainian Studies, University of Alberta, 1983). Earlier historical works on Canadian internment during the First World War include Desmond Morton, 'Sir William Otter and Internment Operations in Canada during the First World War,' *Canadian Historical Review* 55 (1974): 32–58; Joseph A. Boudreau, 'Western Canada's Enemy Aliens in World War I,' *Alberta History* 12 (1964): 1–9.

83 Frances Swyripa, 'The Politics of Redress: The Contemporary Ukrainian-Canadian Campaign,' in *Enemies Within*, 361

84 Toronto *Globe and Mail* 22 December 1984, reprinted in Lubomyr Y. Luciuk and the Ukrainian Canadian Civil Liberties Association, *Righting an Injustice: The Debate over Redress for Canada's First National Internment Operations* (Toronto: Justinian Press, 1994), 4.

85 Lubomyr Luciuk to the editor of the *Ukrainian Weekly*, 29 March and 27 December 1992, reprinted in *Righting an Injustice*, 104, 110. See also Lubomyr Luciuk, *Searching for Place: Ukrainian Displaced Persons, Canada, and the Migration of Memory* (Toronto: University of Toronto Press, 2000), especially 347–50; Harold Troper and Morton Weinfeld, *Old Wounds: Jews, Ukrainians and the Hunt for Nazi War Criminals in Canada* (Markham, ON: Penguin Books, 1989).

86 Swyripa, 'Politics of Redress,' 362.

87 In making his presentation to the standing committee, Luciuk observed that the committee in its report, *Multiculturalism: Building the Canadian Mosaic* (June 1987), had commented on the Japanese-Canadian redress case and added the 'rather ambiguous remark' that 'there should also be "redress for other communities that suffered historical injustices."' Minutes of Proceedings and Evidence of the Standing Committee on Multiculturalism, 7–8 December 1987, reprinted in *Righting an Injustice*, 171.

88 Lubomyr Y. Luciuk and Bohdan S. Kordan, 'And Who Says Time Heals All?,' Toronto *Globe and Mail*, 28 October 1988, reprinted in *Righting an Injustice*, 42–3. The brief presented to Weiner also included demands that the internment camp at Castle Mountain in Banff National Park be reconstructed and that the community be provided with $500,000 for archival research.

89 Lubomyr Y. Luciuk, *A Time for Atonement: Canada's First National Internment Operations and the Ukrainian Canadians, 1914–1920* (Kingston: Limestone Press, 1988). Sources cited in the pamphlet include W.D. Otter, *Internment Operations, 1914–1920* (Ottawa: Department of National Defence, 1921); Vladimir J. Kaye and John B. Gregorovich, eds., *Ukrainian Canadians in Canada's Wars: Materials for Ukrainian Canadian History* (Toronto: Ukrainian Canadian Research Foundation, 1983); Swyripa and Thompson, *Loyalties in Conflict*; Lubomyr Luciuk, *Internment Operations: The Role of Old Fort Henry in World War I* (Kingston: Delta Educational Consultants, 1980); Harry Piniuta, *Land of Pain, Land of Promise: First Person Accounts by Ukrainian Pioneers, 1891–1914* (Saskatoon: Western Producer Prairie Books, 1978); Joseph Amédée Boudreau, 'The Enemy Alien Problem in Canada, 1914–1921,' PhD thesis, University of California, Los Angeles, 1965; Watson Kirkconnell, 'Kapuskasing – An Historical Sketch,' *Queen's Quarterly* 28 (1921).

90 Lubomyr Luciuk, 'A Modest Price for Justice,' *Toronto Star*, 4 November 1992, and Luciuk to the editor of the *Ukrainian Weekly*, 27 December 1992, reprinted in *Righting an Injustice*, 108–10.

91 Luciuk's work is well documented in *Righting an Injustice*.

92 Wilfred Szczesny, 'What Form of Redress?,' *Ukrainian Canadian*, December 1988, reprinted in *Righting an Injustice*, 57; Swyripa, 'Politics of Redress,' 362.

93 Ibid., 363

94 Szczesny, 'What Form,' 57.

95 Luciuk explains the split in a letter to the *Ukrainian Weekly*, 7 February 1993, reprinted in *Righting an Injustice*, 115–17.

96 Swyripa, 'Politics of Redress,' 362–3.

97 Winnipeg *Free Press*, 6 November 1988; Stella Hryniuk to the editor, Winnipeg *Free Press*, 29 November 1988, reprinted in *Righting an Injustice*, 49, 54.

98 Orest Martynowych, 'Re: Internment of Ukrainian Canadians,' *Ukrainian Weekly*, 9 April 1988 [*sic* for 1989], reprinted in *Righting an Injustice*, 65–8.

99 Ibid. See also Orest Martynowych, *Ukrainians in Canada: The Formative Years, 1891–1924* (Edmonton: Canadian Institute of Ukrainian Studies, 1991). Details can be checked against the works of other scholars, such as Donald H. Avery, *'Dangerous Foreigners': European Immigrant Workers and Labour Radicalism in Canada, 1896–1932* (Toronto: McClelland and Stewart, 1979); and Bill Waiser, *Park Prisoners: The Untold Story of Western Canada's National Parks, 1914–1946* (Saskatoon: Fifth House Publishers, 1995).

100 On disenfranchisement, see especially John Herd Thompson, 'The Enemy Alien and the Canadian General Election of 1917,' in Swyripa and Thompson, *Loyalties in Conflict*, 25–46.

101 Swyripa, 'Politics of Redress'; quotations are from pp. 365–6, 372.

102 John B. Gregorovich, ed., *Commemorating an Injustice: Fort Henry and Ukrainian Canadians as 'Enemy Aliens' during the First World War* (Kingston: Kashtan Press for the Ukrainian Canadian Civil Liberties Association, 1994); Lubomyr Luciuk and Boris Sydoruk, eds., *'In My Charge': The Canadian Internment Camp Photographs of Sergeant William Buck* (Kingston: Kashtan Press, 1997); Lubomyr Luciuk, comp., *Roll Call: Lest We Forget* (Kingston: Kashtan Press for the Ukrainian Civil Liberties Association and the Ukrainian Canadian Congress, 1999)

103 Swyripa, 'Politics of Redress,' 368.

104 Ibid., 367.

105 See Luciuk's testimony before the Senate Committee on Social Affairs, Science and Technology, 22 January 1991, in *Righting an Injustice*, 197–200.

106 Bohdan S. Kordan and Craig Mahovsky, *A Bare and Impolitic Right: Internment and Ukrainian-Canadian Redress* (Montreal and Kingston: McGill-Queen's University Press, 2004), 25, 4, 7. See also Bohdan S. Kordan, *Enemy Aliens, Prisoners of War: Internment in Canada during the Great War* (Montreal and Kingston: McGill Queen's University Press, 2002).

107 Some activities are noted in Luciuk, *Searching for Place*, 299 and on the website, www.infoukes.com/history/internment/.

108 The speech is reproduced on the UCC website: www.ucc.ca.

109 Luciuk's speech is present on the UCCLA website: www.uccla.ca.

110 Toronto *Globe and Mail*, 26 August 2005.

111 See www.infoukes.com/history/internment. See also www.uccla.ca.

112 Canada, House of Commons, *Debates*, 24 March 2005, 1645, 1634.

113 On 22 June 2006 in Parliament the government of Canada recognized 'the stigma and hardship experienced by the Chinese as a result of past legislation related to the imposition of the Chinese Head Tax.' In addition, the government offered an '*ex-gratia* symbolic payment of $20,000 to living Chinese Head Tax payers and persons who were in a conjugal relationship with a Head Tax payer ... now deceased.' See the government of Canada's Multiculturalism website, www.pch .gc.ca/progs/multi/redressement/faq_e.cfm. On 6 August 2006 Prime Minister Harper made a speech in Surrey, British Columbia, where he stated that the government of Canada acknowledged the *Komagata Maru* incident and announced a commitment to undertaking consultations with the Indo-Canadian community on how best to recognize this 'sad moment in Canada's history.' See Report of Meetings with Representatives of the Indo-Canadian Community by James Abbot ... www.pch.gc/progs/multi/pubs/ichr/Indo-Canadian-Rep-e.cfm.

114 See www.pch.gc.ca/progs/multi/redressement/faq_e.cfm.

115 See www.ucc.ca/media_releases/2007–0614–2/index.htm. See also 'The Ukrainian Canadian Community's Position on Recognition, Restitution and Reconciliation,' www.ucc.ca/media_releases/2007–03–13/index.htm.

116 'In Memoriam: Mary Manko Haskett, 1908–2007,' www.calgaryucc.org/.

117 See www.cic.gc.ca/english/multiculturalism/programs/community.asp, and www.internmentcanada.ca.

118 Graham Carr, 'Rules of Engagement: Public History and the Drama of Legitimation,' *Canadian Historical Review* 86, 2 (2005): 317–54.

119 Recent curricular changes have begun to take into account the redress issues of various groups. If any allusion is made to the topics at all in Ontario-approved high school history texts published before 2004, then there is at most brief mention of the internment of 'Austrians and Germans' during the First World War. See, for example, Ian Hundey, *Canada: Builders of the Nation*, 2nd edition (Toronto: Gage Educational Publishing, 1991), and J. Bradley Cruxton and W. Douglas Wilson, *Spotlight on Canada*, 3rd edition (Toronto: Oxford University Press, 1996), 113.

120 Pamela Sugiman, 'Passing Time, Moving Memories: Interpreting Wartime Narratives of Japanese Canadian Women,' *Histoire sociale/Social History* 37 (2004): 56.

PART FOUR

Cashing In on the Past

13 'The Normandy of the New World': Canada Steamship Lines, Antimodernism, and the Selling of Old Quebec[1]

JAMES MURTON

Imagine yourself at home – you're in Westmount in Montreal and the year is 1936. You're planning a trip and you're intrigued by the promise of the 'Normandy of the New World,' made by Montreal's Canada Steamship Lines. CSL will show you Quebec – a land, you can see from the illustrations, of peasant women and weaving, a folk society where the spirits of the past, French explorers and gentlewomen, clerics and Indian chiefs, hover in the air over the grandeur of the Saguenay River's famous Cape Trinity. Here is an opportunity to see not the Quebec you know but the real Quebec, the French-Canadian folk, the authentic core of the province. You will see all this from the deck of a modern steamer, and will perhaps stop for a stay at the Manoir Richelieu resort hotel. You hold an example of a particularly lavish CSL brochure, but one that is typical in its use of simple peasants and the spirits of the past, and in its message: that the old can be safely and comfortably experienced from the new.[2]

In the 1930s Canada Steamship Lines, in order to sell its cruise ships and luxury hotels, developed and sold an image of Quebec as a simple, premodern folk society. This image was created through a series of seemingly strange alliances: Anglo-Quebec steamship moguls, Québécois scholars, French-Canadian nationalists, and the Government of Quebec were all brought together through the cultural dynamics of the tourist market. What united them was an antimodern belief that there existed an authentic, true, and typical Quebecker, the essential core of the nation: the rural habitant. These disparate actors all met (metaphorically) on the grounds of the Manoir Richelieu, the larger and grander of CSL's two grand resorts.

In order to understand their interaction, we will need to first look at some history of CSL and consider some key cultural background. A reading of Canada Steamship Lines' promotional pamphlets will show us CSL's creation of the image. Working with CSL was the Québécois folklore scholar Marius Barbeau;

Quebec's Ministry of Agriculture and CSL worked together in the handicrafts revival. From the comfortable rooms and grounds of the Manoir, it is clear that tourism popularized the idea that the habitant was the authentic Quebecker, while ensuring that the shape of this idea would be affected by anglophone and international tastes and by the needs and methods of contemporary capitalism.

As we make this journey, we will see how antimodernism, nationalism, and the idea of the folk united these three actors. The explosion of interest during the 1990s in Canadian antimodernism was largely an English-Canadian affair. One exception, Donald Wright, discusses the idea of an antimodern habitant image of Quebec, but considers it primarily in terms of its development and use by interwar English-Canadian nationalists.[3] But antimodernism was also embraced by French-Canadian nationalists at this time; for example, Lionel Groulx, who, as Ronald Rudin has argued, was as interested in contemporary intellectual currents as anyone.[4] This suggests that antimodernism's impact was broader, longer lasting, and more central to Canadian political struggles than is suggested by the best-known work in this area, Ian McKay's studies of Nova Scotia. Particularly given the tensions generated by anglophone dominance of economic life in Quebec, antimodernism played out quite differently than it did in Nova Scotia, with lasting implications for Quebec and Canada as a whole.[5]

Canada Steamship Lines came out of the merger of the Richelieu and Ontario Navigation Company and other, smaller enterprises in 1913.[6] The result was a huge company with a near monopoly of shipping on the Great Lakes and St Lawrence River. A company brochure from 1921 boasted of a freight fleet of fifty ships, most of them on the lakes but some travelling as far as Liverpool. The twenty-two ships of the passenger fleet ranged from the excursion boat *Cayuga*, sailing between Toronto and Niagara, to ships connecting Montreal, Charlottetown, and St John's, to luxury cruise ships such as the SS *Cape Eternity* on three different cruises to the Saguenay region.[7] In 1928, the passenger fleet carried 1.25 million passengers.[8] The company also operated two shipyards and seven coalyards. It ran the Manoir Richelieu, located at Murray Bay, eighty miles below Quebec on the St Lawrence River. As well, it owned the smaller Tadoussac Hotel, located at the confluence of the Saguenay and St Lawrence Rivers.

However, CSL started life in a shaky financial condition. Many of the company's ships were old; the fleet, made up from the fleets of the various merged companies, badly needed restructuring. A series of losses finally drove company president James Norcross to the New York investment house of Kissel, Kennicott and Company for emergency help. Kissel, Kennicott insisted, as their price for bailing out CSL, on the appointment of a New York management expert as head of the company. In this way William H. Coverdale became president of CSL in 1922. Coverdale was a Canadian, a graduate of Queen's University and a native of Kingston who had made a name for himself in New York. Under him, CSL became profitable. Unfortunately, it did so just as the Great Depression started. In 1932 Coverdale announced to the annual general meeting that gross revenue had fallen by 46 per cent, or 8 million dollars, since 1928. CSL struggled for the rest of the Depression, until Second World War contracts for shipping and shipbuilding finally rescued its profitability.

By the end of the war CSL had become, primarily, a freight shipper, and as the war came to an end it was the opinion of many in the company that this was the company's future. They were, as it turned out, correct. Prosperity – allowing for more exotic cruises – and the automobile would kill the Great Lakes cruise business in the postwar period. Yet in 1944 Coverdale insisted that primary attention must be paid to rebuilding the passenger fleet. His announcement dismayed the board, and was probably more the result of Coverdale's personal convictions than any sort of hard-headed pragmatism. Coverdale had always been fascinated with the tourist business and the opportunity it presented to take part in the cultural life of Quebec. When the old Manoir Richelieu, built for the Richelieu and Ontario Navigation Company in 1899, burned down, Coverdale jumped at the opportunity to personally direct the design of a new structure. It was to be rebuilt in the French Château style, with 'towers and turrets, a steep, copper mansard roof, and such features as massive fireplaces, broad stairways, exposed beams and period woodwork.'[9] It was to be a grand addition to the neighbouring villages of La Malbaie and Pointe-au-Pic, where it was located, and to the tourist business that had been a part of the region since the mid-nineteenth century.[10]

This far below Quebec City, the St Lawrence River, at the base of the new Manoir's broad lawn, looked and smelled like the sea. The company historian echoes the tone of interwar tourist pamphlets in describing the air as 'not soft, but bracing, salty and balsam-scented. The mood, restful but not drowsy, restored the energies and made the guests eager to be active.'[11] Guests could wander in the forests and rocky hills behind the hotel or into the adjoining villages. They could play golf, swim in the heated salt-water pool, or relax on the front patio in front of wrought-iron fixings, in the shade of striped awnings. Inside hung the Coverdale Collection of Canadiana, William Coverdale's personal collection of historic or historic-themed maps, drawings, and paintings.[12] These paintings hung everywhere, lined up along the walls in the grand columned space that formed, to your right as you entered, the main lobby. They decorated the area to the left, the fireplace lounge, where the crest of Cardinal Richelieu hung over the fireplace. They marched along the walls into the dining room, which occupied the remainder of the main wing and continued into the south wing, set off at an angle from the main building. In the dining room they accompanied 'fine old open-shelved mirrors stacked with shining pewter [and] wrought iron candelabra.' They covered the walls of the Rose Room, and those of the Murray Room with its exposed ceiling beams and stuffed leather chairs and couches.[13]

But these luxuries were not the only attraction of the hotel. CSL constructed an image of Quebec as a romantic place of history inhabited by a charming people who still preserved much of the Old World. This was a past designed to appeal to tourists, whose numbers were exploding in the interwar period. Organized tourism arose with the appearance of a larger and more affluent middle class in the nineteenth century, and romanticism and tourism have been friends since at least the mid-1800s.[14] But there were significant shifts in the practice and meaning of tourism in the early part of the twentieth century. The industry boomed in the 1920s, a decade in which tourist spending in Canada tripled and the state at all levels became involved in the industry.[15] Further, tourism became bound up with far-reaching cultural changes at the turn of the century. Specifically, it came to rest heavily on antimodernism.[16]

Antimodernism is best thought of as a complex of social and cultural movements, united by a sense of 'protest against the processes of modernity and modernization.'[17] In his *No Place of Grace: Antimodernism and the Transformation of American Culture*, Jackson Lears demonstrated the unity in the activities of a diverse group of 'journalists, academics, ministers and literati' who, from about 1880, began to articulate their dissatisfaction with the Victorian era's easy belief in rationality and the inevitability of progress. Arguing that nineteenth-century society 'had become stifling and "unreal,"' they sought 'more intense forms of physical and spiritual experience.' They argued that these more intense experiences could be found in rugged landscapes or among simpler, less civilized, primitive peoples. They worshipped the traditional, the authentic, the irrational, and the natural. Weary of rapid change, they sought people and experiences stable and unchanged. Where we have an appeal to authenticity or typicality; where we find the desire for intense experience and the belief that it will cure; where we find a sense that the more simple or primitive is the more real; here we have antimodernism.

Yet, as Lears argues, by the 1920s antimodern ideas had largely lost a sense of challenging the established order. Most practitioners of antimodern protest had come to preach the virtues of intense experience and contact with the real and the authentic, but had forgotten or given up on attaching such things to actual attempts to remake liberal capitalism. They had concentrated on the health of the individual and forgotten about the community; antimodernists in the Arts and Crafts movement had stressed aesthetic concerns and the usefulness of crafts in restoring 'tired businessmen' and forgotten about attempts to reform the work process itself. Rather than becoming the basis of real reform, Lears argues, antimodernism came to preach therapy for those worn out by the difficulties of the modern order. In this way it actually bolstered the new corporate capitalism, making it liveable and giving it new products and experiences to sell.[18]

So by the 1930s antimodernism had become generally diffused in the culture while losing much of whatever reformist edge it had once had. It survived in a variety of forms, most broadly in the practice of leisure, which in this period had begun to oppose itself to the world of work and its concerns with rational business practices and the ordering of society.[19] Antimodernism encouraged the creation of new leisure activities such as camping, where contact with primitive nature allowed for an experience more real and more vital than the daily rounds of work in the city.[20] This naturally led to changes in the tourist industry. Lodges and organized guides arose to take people into the backwoods, while national, provincial, and state parks emerged to serve the same purpose.[21] At the same time antimodernism's interest in seemingly pre-modern folk peoples began to be catered to.

The concepts of folk and folklore date back to the early nineteenth century and the Romantic movement. In the late nineteenth century, antimodernism fuelled a renewed interest in these ideas. The concept of the folk, as employed at this time, held that on the margins of modern liberal society lived pre-industrial folk peoples. In out-of-the-way places such as southern Appalachia or rural Quebec, they lived a simpler life based on traditional lifeways, expressed in customary dances, songs, handicrafts, and patterns and types of work. They preserved an organic, pre-modern society, free of competition and class conflict. In their position on the outskirts of modernity, the folk were understood to have preserved the essential culture of the race or the nation. In the end, only the culture of the habitant was the true culture of Quebec, for all else had been tainted by contact with modernity. The folk held the nation's tales and tunes in trust, and by learning them people could learn about themselves. However, the folk were constantly imperilled, as the encroachment of modern culture undermined their traditional ways. They were in danger of changing from what they were and should be – a simple people, protected from modernity, preserving what was essential about the nation.[22] Looking back, we might be tempted to see these people as nothing more grand than struggling farmers and fishers. But to Edwardian intellectuals steeped in the concepts of folklore, and to a culture yearning for a reassuring contrast to the hectic pace of their everyday lives, these people were the folk.

In the late Victorian period, folklore studies began to assert itself as a legitimate form of practice and study, particularly in Britain and America. In 1888 the American Folklore Society was founded, at the same time as such seminal collections of folklore as James Frazer's *The Golden Bough* (1890) appeared. In Quebec, Marius Barbeau began in 1914 to collect French-Canadian folklore. By the 1920s, Anglo-American scholarship dominated the field.[23] All this activity was encouraged by the universal need, arising after the First World War, to create new nations and new nationalisms. Benedict Anderson argues that this need was a result of the emergence of the international system of nation-states left behind by the Great War. In order to emulate the original nation-states, new nations attempted to create for themselves such essentials as a flag and an anthem. More problematically, nationalists tried for a suitable national past, and a culture that was both distinct to the nation-state and common across its territory and peoples (what Anderson calls a 'universally grounded particularity and originality').[24] In Quebec, nationalists found it easy to appreciate the antimodern idea that the traditions of Quebec's rural population constituted the obvious basis for a nation. In an attempt to resist Anglo imperialism, the rural Quebecker had long been held up as the heart of French Canada by such intellectuals as Francois-Xavier Garneau.[25] The new Québécois traditionalist nationalist movement, starting around 1900, drew on this idea. Antimodern nationalists such as Groulx stressed the importance of the family and the Catholic Church. In the words of Fernande Roy, 'Si la famille occupe une place centrale dans la doctrine nationale que Groulx distille dans *L'Action française*, c'est la religion catholique qui en constitue le coeur.' Groulx also stressed the importance of the past as a source of national identity, pride, and continuity, as encapsulated in the slogan *Notre maître, le passé.*[26]

The Depression bolstered the antimodernism in Quebec nationalism and the popularity of the nationalist movement. The central tenets – according to Paul-André Linteau, 'the primacy of religion, language and agriculture, mistrust of the modern world, the importance of order and authority' – remained. But Groulx's Quebec-centred nationalism became more popular. Nationalism also developed a critique of the liberal economic and political order that had so obviously failed. The *Programme de restauration sociale* argued that the major cause of the Depression was people's movement away from traditional morals and ways of life. The *Programme* also proposed measures to encourage a return to the virtues of French-Canadian rural life. These included curtailing immigration, the return of women to the domestic sphere, support for agriculture and encouragement of back-to-the land movements, and support for small business, cooperatives, and the development of craft industries. At the same time, the necessity of modern scientific knowledge and industrialization was largely accepted. [27] Thus nationalism in Quebec, in a very antimodern way, married reverence for a simple and traditional life with accommodation to liberal capitalism. The idea was more to preserve tradition within the modern system than to reform the system. This interest in the development of a traditional, folk culture meshed neatly with the appeal of folk peoples to CSL's customers, who wanted to spend their leisure engaging in, or at least observing, the real, the genuine, and the authentic.

By the late 1920s and early 1930s, then, various influences in the wider culture – antimodernism, the study of folk peoples, and nationalism – had come together so that the folk theme made sense in Quebec. At the same time, with the growth of tourism as an industry, CSL's promotions shifted from an enumeration of diverse sights to a more sophisticated and unified interpretation of Quebec, based on the themes of antimodernism and the folk. CSL was moving towards creating what John Urry has called a 'tourist gaze.' Urry's term stresses the way in which the sightseeing of the tourist is directed, and the sights constructed, by professionals in the state and the tourist industry. But more important is the way that such construction responds to what the tourist expects to see. The construction of the gaze is a circular process whereby key sites are identified, this identification taking into account such practical concerns as ease of access and previous fame. The tourist then travels to her destination with the intention of visiting these sights and, in essence, viewing the scenes portrayed in the photographs of the promotional literature. The gaze of the tourist becomes a powerful force for reshaping places and peoples into a visual form that the tourist will appreciate and understand.

What the tourist wanted and understood was not structured, however, by the gaze itself, which was and is ideologically neutral. Though Urry and others talk of the tourist's search for 'authenticity,' 'typicality,' or 'difference,' as if these were inevitable parts of the tourist gaze, in reality such themes stem from the way in which leisure had come to be seen through antimodernism in the interwar period. [28] Thus by the 1930s the antimodern tourist's search for authenticity led him to see rural Quebeckers as the folk, the essential people of this land of history.

The shift to the new theme was signalled by the superseding of the company's venerable 'Niagara to the Sea' slogan. Advertising organized around this theme had two notable features compared to later examples. First, it presented many more static sights than it did people. The people of Quebec were not a major attraction before the late 1920s – pamphlets featured photos of historic buildings and natural sights. Second, the pamphlets contained more detailed information and read more as a series of attractions. The concentration on a particular theme or understanding of what the tourist would be seeing is less noticeable. To modern eyes, it appears as if promoters hadn't yet settled on the one theme that would sell Quebec to the tourist, or even the idea that this was the thing to do. A newspaper ad from 1927 invokes the image of a 'dusky Huron warrior' shooting the rapids of the St Lawrence and 'The Thrill of Adventure's Golden Days,' which could now be experienced from a modern steamer. This is just 'one of the many features of that trip of trips – Niagara-to-the-Sea. You cruise through the 1000 Islands – Venice of America; then the St. Lawrence Rapids: visit cosmopolitan Montreal and historic Quebec. The cruise reaches a climax with the awe-inspiring Capes of the Saguenay Canyon.'[29]

In the late 1920s, the folk begin to appear, though at first as just one of many attractions. 'Niagara to the Sea: Toronto, Thousand Islands, Montréal, Québec, Saguenay River,' from 1928, anticipates the later focus on the folk. At the Manoir Richelieu the tourist can see 'Murray Bay Homespuns ... [being] ... made in the near-by Habitant French Villages.' The major themes of the folk are present. The habitants live in 'another land, in the centre of an age long past ... Life in these villages is much the same as it was in France centuries ago.' Handicrafts – homespun clothes, Murray Bay blankets – are part of their everyday life. But in the booklet as a whole, the folk must compete for space with dense pages of text, tables of rates and sailing schedules, and a series of photos of historic buildings, scenes of recreation at the hotels, the rugged cliffs on the Saguenay River, and CSL ships. Very few people are seen in these photos.[30]

By the 1930s, though, CSL tourist literature had been transformed into much more focused, illustrated, and peopled productions designed around the interpretation of the tourist experience in terms of key antimodern themes. The antimodern image of Quebec, as built up in CSL's tourist literature, presented the canyons of the Saguenay River as rugged, evoked the legacy of New France as a backdrop to Quebec as a land of history, and spoke of Quebec as a piece of Europe in America (Quebec City was frequently the 'Gibraltar of North America'). Peopling this antimodern cultural landscape was the folk. Presenting the folk in tandem with the appeals to the grand history of New France left a clear message: the people of Quebec were the remnants of the old regime and the Old World, unchanged by the ravages of recent, modern history.

The 1934 'Normandy of the New World' brochure, with which we began, is a good example. The opening images, done in lovely pastels, bring you into Quebec. On the cover, the spirits of the past hovering over the Saguenay River are connected to the CSL steamer on the river by a thin, wispy line of smoke from the stacks. Inside, on a two-page spread, a French explorer salutes 'The Trail of the Pioneers,' the Great Lakes and the St Lawrence and Saguenay Rivers. Next we see a representative of the people of the province: a young,

13.1 The folk of Quebec. 'The Normandy of the New World,' 1934. Special Collections, Stauffer Library, Queen's University, N5230.C2M2.

attractive habitant woman in simple clothes and bright colours, holding a basket of multicoloured balls of yarn in her lap and sitting by geese and a small village (see figure 13.1). Next is the brochure's title page. At the bottom of this page is another bright image, of an older woman working by a spinning wheel while a goose looks on curiously. We are told that this is to be 'A Description of an Inland Voyage through a Northern Land where Yesterday Lingers on the Threshold of Tomorrow.'[31]

Here the folk, featured in the introduction to the pamphlet, have assumed a central role. They embody the yesterday that the people of tomorrow – the tourists – came to see. This is further underlined when the cruise reaches the shrine of Ste Anne de Beaupré:

> By the side of the road you see crosses and shrines. Perhaps a habitant is kneeling there in devotion, telling his beads. An ox-cart passes you, going its leisured way. In a village, perhaps it will be loaded with a huge barrel – the local waterworks.
>
> You will see the mother rocking her wooden cradle at the door of her gaily-painted cottage and crooning an age-old Norman folksong. You will see 'la bonne femme' cooking bread in outdoor ovens of stone, or running a spinning wheel on her front porch. And you will see 'butterfly' boats spreading their wings on the Lower St. Lawrence. The angelus rings as the blue Laurentians stretch out long fingers of shadow over the darkening fields …
>
> Poetry is in Québec, the poetry of folksong and tradition. Somehow, the ocean liners that pass you on the river and the automobiles on the road seem out of place, intruders on this peace. While the habitant goes his ancient ways upon the banks of the river, the vanguard of progress plies upon its waters.[32]

Quebec, it would seem, is full of enticingly odd people with strange customs. They are something extraordinary for the tourist to experience. But the idea that the ocean liner is somehow out of place, coupled with the portrayal of a lack of running water as quaint, illustrates the potential of antimodernist discourse to justify the processes of uneven capitalist development. The text ends with a cogent summation of its view of Quebec, and a good example of the therapeutic language of tourism: 'And so, refreshed alike in body and mind, you return from the mellowed yesterdays of Old Québec into the bright Todays of all the rest of North America.'[33] Quebec is a backward, slow-moving kind of place, cut off from the modern world, obeying its age-old traditions. This is to be expected of a folk society. It is thus an ideal place to recover from the stresses of modernity with a dose of the antimodern.

Traditional Quebec, however, coexists with a modern English North America. It does so peacefully, as one pamphlet shows us, neatly erasing a century and a half of French-English conflict:

> in the cities, they speak English also, for now they are loyal British subjects and have been since Wolfe captured Québec … the Province of Québec is biracial and bilingual, French and British living side by side in harmony.[34]

The cruises

show you much of Europe … Britain, France. But it is a changed Britain … a race grown younger … whose pioneers and Northwest Mounties have written a new, romantic saga of the Empire. And it is a vastly different France, though ancient in its language and customs … a France of 'voyageurs' and 'habitants' that could have been bred only by the primeval forests, the placid lakes and valleys, the stern mountains of Canada.

A mutual struggle with the land unites English and French, but while the French have retained their ancient ways in this new context, the struggles of the English have established them as the young vanguard of a vast contemporary Empire. They now 'live in the romantic glamorous present … there is a good time for all under the guidance of experienced cruise conductors.' The text then goes on to describe the attractions of sports, games, dancing, the 'social brilliance' at the resort hotels, rugged sights, and motor tours.[35]

The tourists were thus triply reassured. They would be seeing something extraordinary, something outside of their everyday experience. These extraordinary French folk people, though, were friendly. And they could be seen from the comfort of a modern ship or hotel. The contrast between ancient and modern further stressed what was extraordinary about what the tourists would be seeing. This juxtaposition of the comforts of the present and the fascinations of the romantic past is accomplished visually in a pamphlet for the Manoir Richelieu. A tableau of simple, folksy two-colour drawings, reminiscent of Cornelius Krieghoff, creates a pleasing mosaic out of a variety of discrete yet subtly interacting scenes. Habitants gaily dance in front of a small cottage to the music of a fiddle player in a floppy habitant hat; next to them two people in working clothes pray before a cross adorned with the symbols of the Passion of Christ; under them a man and woman play polo. An artist at an easel appears to paint a large woman in a peaked bonnet, full dress, and apron, riding in an ox-cart; above her a man in hip-waders pulls a fish from a pond, while above him a woman cooks over a fire next to a canoe under a woman outside a cabin working at a spinning wheel. In this imagined scene, the old and the new, the simple and the sophisticated, the rich and the poor remain separate and yet fit together.[36]

Thus was the tourist gaze constructed. These brochures were designed to focus the seeing of travellers and let them know what it was that they saw. Partly this was accomplished through photographs, but equally important was the text. Much of it was written in the second person, so 'you' moved through the landscape. Places and people were imbued with meaning, so that the traveller would understand that the Saguenay was grand and awe-inspiring, Quebec was a land of history and tradition, and a village farmer was a simple habitant. This is not to suggest that all of this was fiction. The folk image drew a number of its stock images, such as the calèche and women spinning or weaving, from nineteenth-century history. But the selection and promotion of these particular images was ultimately determined by antimodern desires to see such things as the folk.

An explicit demonstration of the wider reach of CSL's image of folk Quebec comes through the figure of folklorist Marius Barbeau. Barbeau was trained at Oxford in anthropology, ethnology, and archaeology, and was for much of his life associated with what is now the Museum of Civilization in Ottawa. His scholarly interests in French-Canadian folklore and traditions led to a concern with preserving these traditions, which he saw as the heart of French-Canadian society. This concern, along with a sharp eye for career advancement opportunities, led him into the promotion of folk festivals, most notably at the Château Frontenac, and the writing of popular works on folklore and handicrafts. He was instrumental in spreading the idea of the folk in Quebec and Canada beyond academic circles. In these popular activities Barbeau was more than willing to cooperate with the likes of the Canadian Pacific Railway and Canada Steamship Lines.[37]

In 1932 Barbeau and Hugh Eayrs, president of Macmillan of Canada, approached CSL with an idea for a book on the folklore of the Saguenay and Lower St Lawrence area, to be sponsored by the company. T.R. Enderby, general manager of Canada Steamship Lines, liked the idea.[38] This was not surprising, for this was not CSL's first venture of this sort. In the 1920s the company had published a book by McGill architecture professor William Corless on the homespun industry in rural Quebec, which it sold on its ships.[39] It had also published a book on the Saguenay River, and a book on the Great Lakes, the latter of which had inspired Eayrs with the idea for the Barbeau book.[40] Barbeau's book was to be explicitly aimed at tourists, as he made clear in a letter: 'Les touristes de la Malbaie et de Tadoussac que le Manoir Richelieu seraeit [sic] des clients pour ce volume.'[41] Barbeau also agreed to write the book so as to stress the places most relevant to CSL's tourist business, such as Murray Bay, to the point of tailoring some of the folk stories to fit. Barbeau assured Enderby that, for the purposes of publicity, 'I may localize most of the legends at various points of ... Charlevoix and Chicoutimi [Counties]. The stories lend themselves to arbitrary localization. For instance in the Witch-canoe story, I could make the lumberjacks start from a camp on the Saguenay and travel along the coast in Charlevoix. That would at the same time give an idea of the location around there.'[42]

Barbeau here shows his understanding of the requirements of the tourist gaze. The reader of Barbeau's book, published as *The Kingdom of Saguenay* in 1936, would thus be prepared to associate certain tales with areas they might see from the deck of their steamer. The quotation also reminds us of the nature of folklore and its relationship to the market. Barbeau's great dedication to and respect for the folklore of Quebec should not be doubted. That he apparently had no qualms about moving the locations of stories to suit CSL's needs, however, indicates that the stories had become detached from specific circumstances and deemed to be characteristic of the organic entity of Old Quebec as a whole. That their location could be legitimately altered had to do with the ideology of folklore. That Barbeau ended up doing so was due to the needs of the tourist market.

The Kingdom of Saguenay's final form was influenced by CSL in other ways. Barbeau sent chapters to Enderby and dropped by CSL's offices in Montreal to encourage Enderby's interest and support.[43] The book featured original artwork by major artists such as A.Y. Jackson and Arthur Lismer. The artists were all paid by CSL, who retained the original paintings with the intention of hanging them at the Manoir Richelieu.[44] This relationship resulted in a book that exhibits all the attributes of the antimodern perspective. It starts with a chapter of stories on Cartier and other French explorers and their search for the fabulous kingdom they believed lay somewhere up the Saguenay. It goes on to recount the stories of the first 'seigniors' [*sic*] of Murray Bay, two Scots soldiers named John Nairne and Malcolm Fraser, who were granted the land by the British in the 1760s. Other chapters deal with folksingers, handicrafts, wood carvers, tales and legends of missionaries, treasure hunting, and storytellers. The numerous illustrations tend to show generic scenes such as 'A Folk Singer,' or 'Wayside Shrine,' suggesting to the reader that these scenes are typical of Old Quebec in general.

Throughout, Barbeau develops the picture of the folk. He tells of the nearly lost wood-carving tradition of French Canada and the people of Isle-aux-Coudres, defined by their handicrafts. He describes people whose lives revolved around their churches and feast days. Travelling through Charlevoix county, Barbeau hears talk of Louis l'Aveugle (Louis the Blind), a wandering storyteller:

The night of his arrival, the folk gathered around him, wherever he stayed, for a 'veillée.' There he brought fresh news; he was an ambulant newspaper. And he knew everybody a hundred miles around. A child was born here, an old man had been buried there ... he had lived on so many years that death had almost forgotten him. And so went the news. He lavished upon all gossip and entertainment. His wits and utter candour were disarming, and the storehouse of his yarns, his tales and his songs was inexhaustible.[45]

Barbeau tries to pay Louis to tell him his stories, but, typically for a folk figure, 'money went nowhere with him.' Louis tells him to wait until next week, so Barbeau spends time wandering around St Irénée, where

> the people ... were leisurely and old-fashioned. They greeted me as I went by. If I liked I could walk in and look at the homespuns, the bedspreads and *portières boutonnées* with lovely coloured designs ... Country chairs of maple retained their rich natural colour, but were mellowed with age; or they were painted lacquer red or sky blue – two tuneful colours that are the preference of rural Québec.[46]

Enchanted by this pastoral scene, Barbeau decides to travel into the hills to find the villages where 'the total absence of strangers' meant that the old ways were preserved. He finds a 'fairyland,' where 'the diet was poor and the beds made of straw.' He discovers that 'These rustic folk were not rich; yet they lacked nothing essential, and they were certainly happier than town people.' Some disquieting history slips in, but is explained away. 'It is true that many of them, years ago, migrated to the United States, but it was because of their inborn taste for adventure.' An unnamed local explains that "'Some of the emigrants have returned, no richer than before, but sadly wiser.'"[47]

The book's audience never lurks too far beneath the surface. The book's characters find their way to Murray Bay or Tadoussac with an alarming fre-quency, and before travelling into the hills Barbeau himself considers stay-ing at the 'grand Manoir Richelieu.' The chapter on wood-carving and church architecture considers the church at Baie St Paul, located near Murray Bay. Barbeau sometimes refers to the 'land of Maria Chapdelaine.'[48]

Scholarship and tourism were able to offer something to each other. To scholars such as Barbeau, tourism created a wide audience for the types of books they could write. Tourists were interested in the extraordinary, and in the 1930s this often meant people seemingly rustic, primitive, or natural. Bar-beau could supply. To Canada Steamship Lines he offered legitimation. His work could reassure tourists that the folk really did exist, that tourists would see or had seen them, and that the trip was educational and worthwhile. This exchange between scholar and tourism promoter left its mark on the book. First of all, the presence of the tourist market granted to CSL the ability to affect what books were written, and to shape the contents of those books. Murray Bay and Tadoussac were constructed as areas central to the folk, and thus to the people of Quebec as a whole, because they were places where CSL owned hotels. And the book was a more powerful means of cultural construction than the promotional pamphlets, possessing greater authority and greater staying power. We can imagine a traveller reading it years later, or consulting it on the customs of traditional Quebec. It could also increase its impact through other cultural forms. In 1933, Barbeau published a version of what would become chapter 5 as 'In the Heart of the Laurentians' in *Canadian Geographical Journal*.[49] Finally, the book demonstrates the reach of the antimodern and the folk, tying together folklorists, tourist promoters, publishing houses, and antimodern artists in a common effort.

The handicrafts revival brought together an even wider range of diverse social groups, including the state, rural Quebec women, European handicraft specialists, and capitalist tourist promoters. CSL tourist literature in the 1930s understood crafts within an antimodern discourse of authenticity and traditional (as opposed to industrial) production. Craft production, as the output of the folk, seemed to be a tangible link to the more authentic world that the tourist had come looking for. Crafts were held to be the inheritance of an uninterrupted tradition going back to France. In a photo in 'The Normandy of the New World' pamphlet, a grizzled-looking old woman sits behind a spinning wheel, 'Spinning the woolen yarn for Murray Bay blankets the same way her ancestors span in Old Normandy.'[50] Another pamphlet from the 1930s shows two women, one young and one old, working at a loom in a rustic cabin. The caption explains that this is a photo of 'Habitant Women Weaving ... For generations the habitants have spun their wool and woven colourful blankets – now in high demand.' Another illustration shows 'Spinning and Making Hooked Rugs. Every female member of the family learns to work in wool. Varied and quaint are the designs and colours in these curious rugs.'[51] (See figure 13.2.)

Primed by the North America–wide Arts and Crafts movement, tourists in the twentieth century increasingly arrived looking for handicrafts. In the late 1920s and 1930s an alliance of the state, big business, and the urban bourgeoisie created a network of handicraft schools and craft shows to make sure that tourists got what they were looking for. The images shown here ignore this sort of active effort by the representatives of modern urban society. They also hide the relatively recent origins of home production of textiles in Quebec. New France was founded as a commercial colony, and its population of traders, soldiers, and craftsmen preferred and were able to afford imported textiles over the difficulties of making their own. Even as the economy began to decline in the early eighteenth century and colonists could no longer afford goods from France as readily, solutions other than home production were found. Illegal trade with New England increased. Weaving began to be practised in the colony, but it was a craft occupation performed professionally by men, in the

SPINNING AND MAKING HOOKED RUGS. *Every female member of the family learns to work in wool. Varied and quaint are the designs and colours in these curious rugs. This habitant house is axe hewn—note the great rafters in the ceiling.*

13.2 This photograph, from a CSL promotional pamphlet, is intended to demonstrate commitment to the folk traditions, and furthers this agenda by showing its folk artisans in a rough, hand-made cabin (the caption points out that the timbers are 'axe-hewn'). However, it also clearly shows how the idea of the folk – in this case, the interpretation of the rough cabin as evidence of folk tradition – hides evidence of underdevelopment. Second, notice that the younger woman is clearly more a product of the modern era and the city than she is a member of the folk – she wears a modern hair style and patent leather shoes. *Up the Saguenay, Canada's Historic Waterway*, s.d., Stauffer Library, Special Collections, Queen's University, 1930s.

same way that textiles had been produced in Europe since the eleventh century. It was not until the 1820s, as commercial agriculture declined and was replaced by a rural subsistence economy, that the type of home production that was thought of as traditional in the time of the handicraft revival became common. It was now necessary to produce such items as clothing and blankets in the home, and women began weaving.[52] Thus the women spinning yarn in the CSL pamphlets were not an exemplar of an age-old, unchanged practice, but of continuously evolving historical developments.

Weaving in nineteenth-century rural Quebec was mostly done on a basic two-shaft loom that allowed for only simple patterns. The counties of Charlevoix, Kamouraska, and Rimouski in the Lower St Lawrence, where CSL cruises were run, were where this type of production was most common. Home production was also extensive in Île d'Orleans and Île-aux-Coudres. The *ceinture fléchée* sash was an exception in that it was made north of Montreal for commercial purposes.[53] But in general, although production of the more decorative hooked rugs also went on, women wove mostly practical household items. These included the *catalogne*, a bed cover made of linen and strips of rag. Variations on standard weaving techniques were used to produce *à la planche* and *boutonné* patterning in order to create a more complex bed cover. Hooked rugs, where pile was created by pushing material through a loosely woven material such as burlap, developed in mid-century. But by 1900, increasing industrialization was creating cheaper consumer products and a decline in the rural population, both of which led to a decline in home production.

In 1906, a group of wealthy Anglo women associated with the Montreal Women's Art Association tried to halt the decline by forming the Montreal Handicrafts Guild, and in 1907 held a show at the Art Gallery. The revival picked up speed in the 1920s when a growing demand among tourists for home-made products brought both Quebec corporations and the Quebec state into the picture. The first actions of the state came through the *Cercles des fermières* (farm women circles), which had been founded in 1915 with the encouragement of the Department of Agriculture.[54] By 1926 there were 109 with a total membership of 7000. They attempted to save rural Quebec by aiding women in gardening, the raising of bees, chickens, sheep, and children, and, increasingly, the making of home textiles. The products these women made were to bring in extra income to rural families, allowing them to stay on, or even go back to, the land.[55] By the mid-1920s the Department of Agriculture was sponsoring exhibitions of handicrafts where contests were held, prizes were awarded, techniques were demonstrated, and products were classified, judged, and sold. In July 1930 a Handicrafts School (*École des Arts Domestiques*) was opened under the auspices of the Department of Agriculture.

Thus the old woman behind the spinning wheel was a doubly mythological image. Not only was she not a direct connection to her Norman roots, but her work was likely influenced by the actions of the state, particularly the Handicrafts School. The school was intended to improve craft technique and design so as to turn out products that would be appealing to tourists and other potential consumers of handicrafts. It was founded, according to its director, Oscar A. Beriau, 'in connection with the back-to-the-land movement,' or in other words as part of the attempt to keep Quebeckers on the land.[56] The minister of agriculture's annual report on the school noted that 'Revenues from the sale of home-made articles add to the family budget, thus inducing young people to stay at home because they can thus enjoy a certain financial independence.'[57] Thus nationalist ideology combined with the needs of the tourist market to encourage a new industry. Yet, perhaps paradoxically, the needs of the market determined that little attention would be paid to the techniques and designs that had actually been used by rural women. Beriau explained that 'a proven method of weaving' was needed. Existing technique 'lagged so far behind modern progress that it could not be considered as a basis for an industry whose development depends upon its earning capacity ... In old methods of weaving still found in villages, we discarded whatever was unprogressive, to combine sound theory with modern technique.' This was done in order to improve upon the *catalognes*, 'coarse rag carpets,' and *fléchée* sashes.[58]

The practical crafts of the rural household were seen as simply inappropriate for commercial purposes and as being inadequate in comparison to products from other countries. 'Instructresses' were brought in from Sweden, England, and New York, along with Marguerite Lemieux of Montreal, an expert in the *ceintures fléchée*.[59] Faculty went into the countryside to lecture to parish groups and Cercles des fermières, as well as giving more advanced courses at the school. Prominent at these advanced courses were the nuns who taught at the Écoles ménagères (household science schools run by the Department of Agriculture), and in 1931–2 a summer school was set specially for these women. From July 1932 to June 1933 instructors gave 215 lecture series to 11,926 people, and enrolled 145 people in courses at the school, including 54 nuns. Students undertook 'preliminary studies on weaving preparation; reels, winders, warp beams, shuttle filling, warp setting, thread mounting. Study of loom and accessories ... Studies on the fundamental chains and their derivatives; practical demonstrations on appliques and goffering; preliminary studies on tapestry, mounting high warp loom; forming chain and design in tapestry, *ceinture fléchée*.'[60] The school also distributed plans for looms that could be made on the farm.

The purpose of all this training was not just to improve technique. The modern training of the school would also be applied to the problem of design, and here again the wishes of tourists and international standards would dictate. Beriau explained that training in decorating was necessary in order to compete with foreign products. 'Quality of material, harmony of patterns, fine colouring will add charm and precision to our manual and artistic work,' he noted. 'A better choice of colouring matter at village exhibitions is already noticeable.'[61] In 1932, two designers were on staff. This, and the cooperation of the Montreal and Quebec Fine Art Schools with the Handicrafts School, indicate that the school hoped to encourage the production of work that would meet standards of artistry. Artists supplied models of desirable carpet designs, which were copied by women rug-makers, with the result that 'good taste and a sense of proportion are fostered among our women farmers.'[62] The results were apparently satisfactory, the report of 1936 commenting that 'Crocheté ou noué, le tapis s'améliore constamment; couleurs moins criardes, dessins plus étudiés.'[63]

Despite its bureaucratic set-up and training methods, the school was concerned that the crafts produced be authentic. Having foregone the authenticity that could have come from traditional designs and methods, the school encouraged instead an antimodernist sense of connection with nature. Just as the Group of Seven had found the essence of Canada embedded in the Canadian Shield, students at the Handicraft School were to draw their designs from nature: 'To preserve the characteristics of our art, purely Canadian scenery, flora and fauna form the subjects of ingenious decoration.'[64] This seems to have led to a fondness for snow scenes on hooked rugs, as can be seen in photos in the Quebec government Sessional Papers.[65] Also, the school encouraged the use of local materials, experimenting with the growing of wool and flax and with the use of local clay and especially local dyes. In the production of appropriate materials the school worked with the Cercles des fermières, thus expanding the contribution of handicrafts to the back-to-the-land movement. Crafts were to be rooted in Quebec through an antimodernist attempt to draw inspiration from the land itself. Quebec would, in fact, through the use of native materials, be physically part of the crafts themselves. This was a strategy with a number of contradictions. It made sense in terms of antimodernism and the idea of the folk, which stressed that the folk were more organic, closer to nature. However, these folk seemed to require artists to mediate between them and nature, to show them the way to properly represent what was around them.[66]

The other major activity of the handicraft school was in arranging exhibitions for the display and sale of products (see figure 13.3). Every year, shows were held in Quebec in such places as Baie St Paul and La Malbaie, and in Quebec City, Montreal, and Trois Rivières, and outside Quebec in Toronto, Ottawa, and Regina. Photos of these shows reveal large professional displays. A great variety of rugs, blankets, and furniture was displayed with spinning wheels and dioramas of looms.[67] At folk festivals held at the Château Frontenac in 1927, women demonstrated spinning and weaving.[68]

It is with these exhibitions that major corporations, and particularly Canada Steamship Lines, enter the picture as the other major institutional force behind

1.—Les institutrices de l'École Provinciale des Arts Domestiques.

2.—Portières avec dessins au crochet, et tapis crochetés avec guenilles.

3.—Exhibit de tapis, etc., à l'exposition de la Malbaie.

13.3 Taken from the annual report of the Handicrafts School to the Quebec legislature, this set of photographs is intended primarily to reassure the government of the progress of the program. We see a set of modern, serious, competent-looking instructors, as well as some of the handicrafts themselves, showing the images of nature and village life encouraged at the school. *Rapport du ministre de l'Agriculture pour l'année se terminant en 1929*, 1930.

the revival, providing the foreign tourists whose tastes had led to all of the work on improving technique and design. At least one contemporary, Alice MacKay in *Canadian Geographical Journal*, saw CSL as a central player. '[N] oting the popularity of homespuns among Manoir Richelieu guests and travellers on the river ships,' she explained, CSL 'undertook to enlarge the market for the material and at the same time to raise the standard of quality. For this work, the hearty co-operation of the Department of Agriculture of the province was secured, and today these two agencies are working hand in hand to secure the most superior types of work and the most favourable market for these home products.'[69] It does not seem likely that CSL was the major force behind the revival and the handicrafts school. I have come across no other references to their central role in the process, and Beriau, in an article on 'The Handicraft Renaissance in Québec,' describes the government as acting alone, although he does credit CSL and a number of other organizations with helping maintain the old traditions.[70] However, MacKay's article speaks to CSL's interest in publicizing handicrafts, as it appears the company may have been involved in some way in its publication. The fact that MacKay quotes extensively from Professor W. Careless of McGill on weaving (most likely the William Corless commissioned by the CSL to write a 1920s company brochure), and that her article features photos that appear in a CSL promotional booklet, all point to a likely collaboration.[71] Although we should doubt the idea that CSL was *the* player in the handicrafts revival, we should not doubt their interest in promoting handicrafts, and promoting their involvement with them.

Along with sponsoring magazine articles, scholarly writings, and exhibitions, CSL associated itself with the handicrafts revival in other ways. The company used homemade rugs, bed covers, curtains, and upholstery to decorate its ships and hotels. Tourists looking for an authentic piece of Quebec to take home with them could purchase such items as blankets and hooked rugs in the gift shops onboard ship or at the hotels.[72] CSL also sponsored handicraft exhibitions at the Manoir Richelieu. The official corporate history states that they did this every year in cooperation with the provincial government and the Handicrafts Guild of Montreal, but no source is given to support this. However, the reports of the Handicraft School mention shows in May of 1929, and the company had a display at a show in 1930–1 that was arranged for it by the Handicrafts School.[73] In September of 1929, CSL and the Ministry of Agriculture jointly organized a show in the ballroom of the new Manoir Richelieu, featuring the work of thirty-four Cercles des fermières displaying between 2800 and 3000 exhibits. A variety of prizes were handed out and folk singer Mlle Glen 'a régalé les visiteurs de l'après-midi de quelques une des plus jolies chansons de son répertoire ancien.'[74] From 27 July to 1 August 1931, another show was held at the Manoir Richelieu, and was described by Beriau as a 'still more brilliant exhibition.'[75]

A series of photographs, which internal evidence suggests are from 1941, shows us some of the exhibitors at a craft and flower show at the Manoir Richelieu. Evidence indicates that these are candid snapshots of people from the local villages, likely taken by an official photographer and intended for sale to the guests.[76] Several women wear a similar apron with large white checks and sport fabric flowers on their foreheads. Wagon wheels and baskets full of crafts and flowers adorn the various scenes. But though clothed in peasant-like apparel, these people also show evidence of being dressed up for the occasion. On one woman a straw hat, a plain ankle-length skirt, and a checked apron clash with loafers and a wristwatch, and several others feature similar combinations. The fact that four women wear the same apron suggests that it was something that was handed out to exhibitors.

Peasant clothing, it would seem, was used to please tourists by reassuring them of the authenticity of the items they purchased. It reinforced the traditional gender ideals of folk ideology, showing women in modest skirts and aprons involved with crafts and small plants. Guests were encouraged by the exhibitors' clothing to see something of Old Quebec in these people. Their wristwatches might preclude guests from thinking of them as pure folk figures. But the guests could be forgiven for seeing people not caught up in the rush of modern life, people with a direct connection to the country in which they lived, selling products that reflected this connection. They might even think that they were purchasing products that were a piece of the core of French-Canadian society, produced without patterns by a happy woman singing French-Canadian songs in her kitchen.

Yet the people of La Malbaie and Pointe-au-Pic were aware of the larger world. They knew that they lived in a capitalist society and understood that tourism meant at least the potential for employment and that handicrafts were meant to revive their rural economy. In April 1929 the pro-development local paper *Le Courrier du Nord* declared that tourism was 'notre devoir à tous.' Of the still incomplete Manoir, they declared:

Nous admirions déjà les superbes hôtels de Pointe au Pic, de Malbaie, St-Irénée, Les Eboulements, Cap à l'Aigle, mais voici que vient de surgir comme par enchantement une des plus magnifiques hôtels d'été du continent, le nouveau 'Manoir Richelieu.'

Tourism, they argued, was everyone's business: 'Sachons tous coopérer, pour augmenter encore chez nous les revenus de l'Industrie du Tourisme.'[77] CSL's files, however, indicate some tensions. In 1938, the expectation that the Manoir would employ local people led to political controversy. On 4 April, town council in Pointe-au-Pic complained to CSL about the use of workmen from outside the village in the building of the Manoir's new Golf Club House. The village had previously forgiven taxes on the understanding that the hotel would only employ locals. CSL replied that only three workmen were not from Pointe-au-Pic and that these were in fact from the neighbouring town of La Malbaie, where the Golf Club was actually located.[78] Nevertheless the issue dragged on. In August, aldermanic candidates Ulysse Harvey, Johnny Aubin, and Philippe Villeneuve asked Pointe-au-Pic voters whom they preferred that CSL employ: 'Voulez-vous que nos contribuables travaillent de préférence aux étrangers lorsque la Compagnie Manoir Richelieu Hotel exécute des travaux?' The candidates also brought up issues such as the employment and treatment of their children on the golf course, and noted the need to be firm with the Manoir Richelieu Company.[79] Unlike Barbeau's Louis L'Aveugle, then, money did go somewhere with the residents of Pointe-au-Pic. They understood the centrality of the Manoir to the local economy, understood that tax breaks could be used to encourage CSL to favour their workers, and were willing to protest when it seemed that the bargain they had made was not being honoured.

The *Courrier du Nord* also supported the handicraft revival. It argued in 1929 for the sort of home industry encouraged by the Cercles des fermières, advocating the growing of flax, which could be made into linen and sold 'aux marchands de La Malbaie, à la Canada Steamship Lines Ltd., aux maisons Dupuis & Frere Ltée et T. Eaton Ltée, de Montréal … un grand nombre de firmes américaines, etc., etc.' If a product of quality was produced, the paper assured its readers, revenues greater than the $80,000 of homespuns sold in Pointe-au-Pic in 1927 would be possible.[80] A year before the opening of the Handicrafts School in 1930, *Le Courrier* commented on the 1929 handicrafts show. It hoped that such activities could lead to more money for agriculturists and implored residents to understand its promise.[81] At least in the local paper, then, tourism was seen as a source of revenue and handicrafts as a potentially lucrative small industry.

Like the publications of Marius Barbeau, handicraft promotion was an example of the intersection of CSL's tourist business with attempts by French-Canadian elites to develop and protect a certain idea of Quebec. French-Canadian efforts to revive rural Quebec were partly driven by economic concerns: the effort to move the unemployed back onto the land was a common strategy employed across Canada for coping with the Depression. But government support for rural Quebec had begun before 1929. It was based on an old idea that had gained force in the twentieth century under the influence of antimodernist thinkers, namely, that the heart of Quebec was in the countryside and in the farmer. The revival was also powered by the tourist market and its antimodernistic desires for authentic products that could supposedly speak to what was essential about Quebec. The needs of this market meant that handicrafts were revived via a modern system of hierarchical bureaucratic training. Antimodern authenticity was preserved through the appeal to nature. Handicrafts were to be authentic because their designs would be inspired by the natural surroundings of the makers, even if this meant that these artisans had to be taught by urban artists to properly see the nature around them. What was important, though, was that tourists thought the crafts authentic, so that they could gaze upon themselves partaking of the essential core of Old Quebec.

Ironically, in a development that reveals the contradictions of the entire multifaceted process of constructing this tourist gaze, by 1948 Barbeau himself was unhappy with the effects that the handicraft revival was having on the folk traditions of rural Quebeckers:

> In the last two decades, a well-meant but misleading educational effort has heavily contributed to demoralize handicrafts. Under its tutelage, talent among the weavers has been snuffed out; ancient patterns, in constantly renewing forms in weaving and hooking of rugs, have fallen into discredit; invention and self-reliance among the folk-workers have been branded as futile. In their place were substituted 'cartons,' patterns and instructions printed in various periodicals. And, as if to introduce a new system, there followed the sale of standard spinning wheels, looms, yarns, tools, manuals on dyes to the rural workers. A centralized control, through the agency of rural clubs, has proved efficient but deadly, in the twenty years of its activities.[82]

Barbeau thus pointed out one of the major contradictions which resulted from the use of tourism in this period to sustain older ways of life: the dictates of the market would almost inevitably lead away from pre-industrial methods towards a process of standardization, central control, and mass production. But the central problem lies in the concept of the folk itself, for Barbeau's difficulty really arises from the fact that the folk had never really existed. In the ideology of the folk, the people of Quebec were lifted out of history and turned into a series of icons and images held to represent the timeless core of Quebec. Being timeless, these images could survive the era in which they were first created. In a series of CSL menus from the 1960s we can see an even more refined version of folk ideology. [83] Each menu illustrates a standard theme of the folk. A series of eight scenes show 'The Bake Oven,' 'Mending Net,' 'The Caller,' 'Weaving,' 'The Hooked Rug,' 'The Calèche,' 'The Wood Carver,' and 'Alouette!,' with accompanying text in English and French. Drawn with artistry in full colour in a folk-art style, the drawings evoke the appeal of the simple and the rustic with their relatively unadorned backgrounds and lack of perspective and realistic human figuration. They show happy people in simple surroundings engaged in satisfying work. The texts, short and simple compared to the texts of the 1930s pamphlets, stress the themes of the folk. Thus, 'the appeal of Old Québec lies in the charm of a quaint and simple people who, resisting this era of change, continue to follow the ways and customs of life and living established centuries ago by their forefathers.'[84]

These folk practise a communal art, one that 'comes naturally to the French Canadian habitant' and is an appropriate 'medium of expression for people who live quiet, secluded lives and who are not disturbed by the rush and confusion of our modern world.'[85] Further: the folk are at the heart of every Quebecker, as in the evocation of the French-Canadian love of 'Alouette!':

'Alouette, gentille alouette ... alouette, je t'y [*sic*] plumerai!' So great is their love of music and their devotion to their old folk songs that when a group of French Canadians get together, it is not long before somebody starts 'Alouette.' Perhaps the best known of French Canadian chansons, it is noted for its swing and tunefulness and in a typical gathering the leader, dressed in his best homespuns, leads the chanson à répondre [footnote: 'Roundelay']. With gestures, he singles out the features of alouette, that traditional French Canadian lark, carrying his audience through the various choruses with a 'joie de vivre' [footnote: 'Joy of Living'] so typical of the people of Québec.[86]

In this passage, complete with French words for authenticity and footnotes to increase scholarly authority, Quebec is the folk. Disconnected from historical reality, the image of the folk had become timeless. Even as the Quiet Revolution began, Quebeckers were still represented as being in essence a folk people of simple, timeless traditions. Yet Barbeau's folk had always been linked into a wider society. They had, for example, left for jobs in the United States not out of a spirit of adventure but because they needed a job in order to survive, and couldn't find one in Quebec.[87] They had never existed entirely out of the market economy, and had never existed at all outside of a process of historical change, had never been immune to the historical forces that affected everyone else.

What was the effect of CSL's activities on the idea of Quebec in North American society generally? The direct impact of their mythologizing of the Québécois folk is difficult to assess. A CSL report on the geographical origins of guests at the Manoir Richelieu, available for 1936, 1937, and 1938, indicates that many of them were Americans. The United States accounted for 76.5 per cent of guests in 1936, 74.9 per cent in 1937, and 71.2 per cent in 1938. The majority of these (59 per cent in 1936, 60 per cent in 1937, and 61 per cent in 1938) were from New York and New England. Of Canadians, the majority of guests were from Quebec: 68 per cent in 1936, 73 per cent in 1937, and 68 per cent in 1938.[88] Assuming that most if not all of the Quebeckers would be English speakers, we can say that CSL's biggest direct impact in Canada was among Anglo-Quebeckers.

However, we cannot quantitatively assess the number of people who came into contact with CSL promotional imagery in magazines, newspapers, or at travel agencies or trade shows, or were affected less directly by the currents set in motion by CSL's tourism-derived dollars. As I have argued, CSL's promotions took place within a larger cultural context, and built upon this context. CSL was able to work with a variety of other people who held similar ideas about the essential nature of Quebec, and also had interests in selling images of Quebec to tourists. Thus Marius Barbeau, who did more than anyone to spread interest in and knowledge of Québécois folk traditions and crafts, found in the tourist market a way to further spread knowledge of these matters, and, not unimportantly, a way to make a living. Those interested in the revival of rural Quebec, for reasons having to do with nationalist ideology and questions of economic development, also found the tourist market useful in providing a potential basis for a new industry. They hoped to preserve the rural character of Quebec society through the use of the modern market. This was a process not without its contradictions, for it involved the selection of those aspects of Québécois rural society that were essential to its character. Handicraft promoters wanted rural Quebeckers to rejuvenate the arts and crafts of their ancestors, but were willing to sacrifice customary techniques and designs to meet the demands of the capitalist tourist market.

The belief in the essential folk Quebec was, as I have shown, a widespread phenomenon. It was adhered to by respected scholars such as Barbeau. It paralleled other projects to find folk peoples in places such as Nova Scotia. It was part of a larger effort by a variety of cultural producers to construct a new myth-symbol complex for the Canadian nation as a whole.[89] But as with these other folk cultures, it cut rural Québécois off from their history, from the idea that they, too, changed over time and that they had been affected by the larger social changes that had influenced everyone else. Further, in imagining a people defined by a series of icons and images – the hooked rug, the bake oven, the 'habitant type' pictured in one CSL ad – antimodernism made it easy for Quebeckers to be symbolically cut up into pieces, packaged, and sold.[90] They became, through the workings of the tourist market, both a source of revenue and a 'therapy for tired businessmen.'[91] The lives and history of rural Quebeckers became a source of income for others. Although they could also be a source of income for rural people themselves, the distribution could only be uneven.

The use of antimodern ideas by nationalists and those interested in preserving the society and culture of French Quebec was, then, problematic. Folk festivals and handicraft revivals could foster local pride and interest in Quebec culture. The problem, however, is that Quebec was never just a mellow yesterday; the Québécois never just a quaint and simple people.

NOTES

1 Originally published as James Murton, 'La "Normandie du Nouveau Monde": la société Canada Steamship Lines, l'antimodernisme et la promotion du Québec ancien,' *Revue d'histoire de l'Amérique française* 55, 1 (Summer 2001): 3–44. Reprinted by permission. This paper would not have been possible without the knowledgeable assistance of Maurice Smith and Earl Moorehead at the Marine Museum of the Great Lakes at Kingston, repository for the Canada Steamship Lines papers. For many helpful suggestions on the manuscript, I would also like to thank Ian McKay, David Regeczi, Mike Dawson, and the two anonymous reviewers from the *Revue d'histoire de l'Amérique française*. Many thanks as well to Nicole Neatby and Peter Hodgins for their careful editing and for initiating this volume.

2 Canada Steamship Lines, 'The Normandy of the New World,' 1934, F5012.1934 C362, W.D. Jordan Special Collections & Music Library, Queen's University, Kingston, Ontario.

3 Donald Wright, 'W.D. Lighthall and David Ross McCord: Antimodernism and English-Canadian Imperialism, 1880s-1918,' *Journal of Canadian Studies* 32, 2 (Summer 1997): 137–9. The major Canadian study is Ian McKay, *The Quest of the Folk: Antimodernism and Cultural Selection in Twentieth Century Nova Scotia* (Montreal and Kingston: McGill-Queen's University Press, 1994). See also Michael Dawson, '"That Nice Red Coat Goes to My Head Like Champagne": Gender, Antimodernism, and the Mountie Image, 1880–1960,' *Journal of Canadian Studies* 32, 3 (1997): 119–39; and Ross Douglas Cameron, '"Our Ideal of an Artist": Tom Thomson, the Ideal of Manhood and the Creation of a National Icon,' MA thesis, Queen's University, 1998.

4 For Ronald Rudin's argument that Lionel Groulx worked to make himself into a modern, professional historian, see Rudin, *Making History in Twentieth Century Québec* (Toronto: University of Toronto Press, 1997), chapters 1 and 2, 13–92.

5 For McKay's work see *Quest*; also 'Among the Fisherfolk: J.F.B. Livesay and the Invention of Peggy's Cove,' *Journal of Canadian Studies* 23, 1/2 (Spring/Summer

1988): 23–45; 'Tartanism Triumphant: The Construction of Scottishness in Nova Scotia, 1933–54,' *Acadiensis* 21, 2 (Spring 1992): 5–47; McKay and Robin Bates, *In the Province of History: The Making of the Public Past in Twentieth-Century Nova Scotia* (Montreal and Kingston: McGill-Queen's University Press, 2010); and, for comments on the legacy of antimodernism, 'Handicrafts and the Logic of "Commercial Antimodernism": The Nova Scotia Case,' in Lynda Jessup, ed., *Antimodernism and Artistic Experience: Policing the Boundaries of Modernity* (Toronto: University of Toronto Press, 2001), 117–29 (comments 117–18).

6 In this section I am drawing, except where otherwise noted, on the official company history, Edgar Andrew Collard, *Passage to the Sea: The Story of Canada Steamship Lines* (Toronto: Doubleday, 1991), 130–83.

7 The brochure appears in ibid., 98.

8 'The Growth of a Giant,' *Canadian Shipping and Marine Engineering News*, [n.d.], 14, included in finding aid, Canada Steamship Lines Ltd. Subsidiaries and Predecessors Records, 1004, Canada Steamship Lines (CSL) Fonds, Marine Museum of the Great Lakes at Kingston, Kingston, Ontario.

9 Collard, *Passage to the Sea*, 165.

10 On tourism in this area see Philippe Dubé, *Charlevoix: Two Centuries at Murray Bay*, trans. Tony Martin-Sperry (Montreal and Kingston: McGill-Queen's University Press, 1990); Lise Lapointe et al., *Charlevoix et le Manoir Richelieu* (Cap-à-l'Aigle, QC: Exploracom, 1996). Murray Bay was used either as an English version of La Malbaie or, more often, to refer to the area in general. I have used it in the latter sense.

11 Collard, *Passage to the Sea*, 168.

12 The collection included commissioned works by members of the Group of Seven as well as older pieces, including a copy of Benjamin West's *The Death of General Wolfe*. Most of the pieces are now held by Library and Archives Canada.

13 Description of the Manoir Richelieu from Collard, *Passage to the Sea*, 166–8, 180–1; Peter Selnar, 'The Construction and Planning of the Manoir Richelieu,' Technical Paper, School of Architecture, Faculty of Engineering, McGill University, 1967, 1995.22.33, Public Relations and Advertising Series O, CSL Fonds; 'Winter Sports at the Manoir Richelieu ... ,' 1995.22.37, Archival Series O, CSL Fonds; 'Murray Room' (photo), Manoir Richelieu, Kenwick Pavilion and CSL passenger steamers [106], 1995.22.33, Public Relations Series, CSL Fonds; and 'The Manoir Richelieu at Murray Bay, Québec, Canada,' 1938 Manoir Richelieu, correspondence, brochure, 993.2.6, Secretary Subseries II 23A15, CSL Fonds.

14 Patricia Jasen, *Wild Things: Nature, Culture and Tourism in Ontario* (Toronto: University of Toronto Press, 1995), 7–13, 20–2; Ian Ousby, *The Englishman's England: Taste, Travel and the Rise of Tourism* (New York: Cambridge University Press, 1990), 9–22; Piers Brendon, *Thomas Cook: 150 Years of Popular Tourism*

(London: Secker and Warburg, 1991); John R. Gold and Margaret M. Gold, *Imagining Scotland: Tradition, Representation and Promotion in Scottish Tourism since 1750* (Aldershot, UK: Scolar Press, 1995), 195–6, 62.

15 Karen Dubinsky, *The Second Greatest Disappointment: Honeymooning and Tourism at Niagara Falls* (Toronto: Between the Lines, 1999), 138.

16 Various articles by Ian McKay discuss antimodernism and tourism, but in particular see 'Among the Fisherfolk'; Michael Dawson, review of Jasen, *Wild Things*, H-Net Reviews, 1997 (accessed May 2001), http://www.h-net.msu.edu/reviews/showrev.cgi?path=12175862319888; James Overton, *Making a World of Difference: Essays on Tourism, Culture and Development in Newfoundland* (St John's: Institute of Social and Economic Research, 1996), 13.

17 Fred R. Myers, 'Introduction – Around and about Modernity: Some Comments on Themes of Primitivism and Modernism,' in Jessup, ed., *Antimodernism and Artistic Experience*, 14.

18 T.J. Jackson Lears, *No Place of Grace: Antimodernism and the Transformation of American Culture, 1880–1920* (Chicago: University of Chicago Press, 1994), xi–xvii, 300–6, and passim; quotations xvi, xii, and xv. See also George Cotkin, *Reluctant Modernism: American Thought and Culture, 1880–1900* (Toronto: Maxwell Macmillan Canada, 1992).

19 Another significant area was in artistic interest in simpler peoples, for example in the work of Hungarian composer Béla Bartók, who collected Hungarian folk tunes and used them to create orchestral works with a Hungarian flavour. Another example is J.R.R. Tolkein's evocation of a mythical land of magicians and noble warriors, with its Hobbit heroes inhabiting an idealized English countryside – 'the Shire.'

20 On Edwardian anxiety over the city and the resulting Canadian back-to-nature movement, see George Altmeyer, 'Three Ideas of Nature in Canada, 1893–1914,' *Journal of Canadian Studies* 11 (August 1996): 22–7; reprinted in Chad Gaffield and Pam Gaffield, eds., *Consuming Canada: Readings in Environmental History* (Toronto: Copp Clark, 1995), 98–105. For a stimulating and important critique of one of the results of this development, see William Cronon, 'The Trouble with Wilderness; or, Getting Back to the Wrong Nature,' in William Cronon, ed., *Uncommon Ground* (New York: W.W. Norton, 1996), 69–90.

21 For example, on Canadian parks, see Alan MacEachern, *Natural Selections: National Parks in Atlantic Canada, 1935–1970* (Montreal and Kingston: McGill-Queen's University Press, 2001).

22 See McKay, *Quest*, 8–22; David Whisnant, *All That Is Native and Fine: The Politics of Culture in an American Region* (Chapel Hill: University of North Carolina Press, 1983), passim; Richard Handler, *Nationalism and the Politics of Culture in Québec* (Madison: University of Wisconsin Press, 1988), 63–4; Handler, 'In

Search of the Folk Society: Nationalism and Folklore Studies in Québec,' *Culture* 3, 1 (1983): 105.

23 See Regina Bendix, *In Search of Authenticity: The Formation of Folklore Studies* (Madison: University of Wisconsin Press, 1997), 119–31; Lears, *No Place of Grace*, 168–70; McKay, *Quest*, 17–25.

24 Benedict Anderson, 'Introduction – Staging Antimodernism in the Age of High Capitalist Nationalism,' in Jessup, ed., *Antimodernism and Artistic Experience*, 97–9, quotation 98.

25 Handler, *Nationalism*, 70–1.

26 On Groulx, I am drawing on Fernande Roy, *Histoire des idéologies au Québec aux XIXe et XXe siècles* (Montreal: Boréal, 1993), 80–1; on Quebec nationalism in general, see 79–88.

27 Paul-André Linteau et al., *Québec since 1930*, trans. Robert Chodos and Ellen Garmaise (Toronto: Lorimer, 1991), 76–82. On Groulx as a historian, see note 4, above. The idea that the long-standing practice of colonization (which became part of a general Canadian back-to-the-land effort during the Depression) was motivated by cultural concerns has been challenged by more socially oriented historians. See Normand Séguin, *Agriculture et colonisation au Québec: aspects historiques* (Montreal: Boréal Express, 1980), 30–6. However, Seguin's stress on economic motivations does not preclude the idea that the habitant ideal was, at least, also important, as it certainly must have been for the larger rural revival effort. See Christian Morissonneau, *La terre promise: le mythe du Nord québécois* (Montreal: Hurtubise HMH, 1978). In any case, it is not clear what these conclusions tell us about the interwar period and about areas, such as Charlevoix, that have been longer settled than the areas colonized in the nineteenth century.

28 See John Urry, *The Tourist Gaze: Leisure and Travel in Contemporary Societies* (London: Sage, 1990), 1–13, 83–95; see also Jonathan Culler, 'The Semiotics of Tourism,' in *Framing the Sign: Criticism and Its Institutions* (Oxford: Basil Blackwell, 1988), 155–7. The literature on tourism and its meaning is large. Dean MacCannell, *The Tourist* (New York: Schocken, 1976), 8–14, 145–7, argues that tourists look for authenticity but mostly find fake attractions. Culler counters with the argument that we should not concentrate on whether reality is being fairly represented but instead accept the constructedness of experience and look at how the ideas of authenticity and the typical structure touristic discourse. See also Jasen, *Wild Things*, 5–7. John F. Sears sees nineteenth-century American tourism as a form of religious pilgrimage, accommodated to secular bourgeois culture and the need for national identity, in *Sacred Places: American Tourist Attractions in the Nineteenth Century* (New York: Oxford University Press, 1989), 3–11. Most commentators condemn the contrast drawn by both Paul Fussell and Daniel Boorstin

between 'real' travel and the tendency of tourists to indulge in inauthentic spectacle: Paul Fussell, *Abroad: British Literary Traveling between the Wars* (Oxford: Oxford University Press, 1980), 42; and Daniel Boorstin, *The Image: A Guide to Pseudo-Events in America* (New York: Atheneum, 1972), 77–117.

29 'The Rapids of the St Lawrence … ,' 6 August 1927. Clippings of ads from newspapers and magazines, 993.2.185, Public Relations Series, CSL Fonds.

30 'Niagara to the Sea: Toronto, Thousand Islands, Montréal, Quebec, Saguenay River,' 1928, Canada Pamphlet 1928 no. 002, Jordan Special Collections.

31 CSL, 'Normandy.'

32 Ibid., 12.

33 Ibid., 24.

34 Ibid., 5–6.

35 CSL, 'All Expense Tours … ,' 1936, 1995.22.37, Archival Series, CSL Fonds. In the first quotation, the ellipses are in the original.

36 CSL, 'The Manoir Richelieu Pleasure Map,' n.d., 1995.22.37, Archival Series, CSL Fonds. Internal evidence suggests that this pamphlet is from the late 1930s or early 1940s – photos used are used in other pamphlets from this era, and a photo shows a musician who was at the hotel in 1939 and who died in the 1940s.

37 Handler, *Nationalism*, 71–5; Andrew Nurse, 'Publishing *The Kingdom of Saguenay*: Marius Barbeau, Hugh Eayrs and the Dynamics of Folklore Publishing in the 1930s,' unpublished paper, 2–7; Nurse, 'Tradition and Modernity: The Cultural Work of Marius Barbeau,' PhD thesis, Queen's University, 1997, 5–56; Janet Elizabeth McNaughton, 'A Study of the CPR-Sponsored Québec Folk Song and Handicraft Festivals, 1927–1930,' MA thesis, Memorial University of Newfoundland, 1982, 19–21 and passim. Also on Barbeau see the essays collected in Lynda Jessup, Andrew Nurse, and Gordon E. Smith, eds., *Around and about Marius Barbeau: Modelling Twentieth-Century Culture* (Gatineau, QC: Canadian Museum of Civilization, 2008).

38 Nurse, 'Publishing,' 12–13.

39 Mentioned in CSL, 'Niagara to the Sea' (1928).

40 The first is Blodwen Davies, *Saguenay, 'Saginawa,' the River of Deep Waters* (Montreal: Canada Steamship Lines, c. 1930), featuring illustrations by well-known maritime artist G.A. Cuthbertson; the latter is mentioned but not named by Nurse, 'Publishing,' 12.

41 Ibid., 13. Barbeau to E. Desrochers, 5 February 1936 (copy), file 4, box 72 Macmillan fonds, William Ready Division of Archives and Research Collections, McMaster University, as qtd in Nurse, 'Publishing,' 13.

42 Barbeau to Enderby, 16 March 1932 (copy), Barbeau fonds, T.R. Enderby file, temporary box 6, Macmillan fonds, as qtd in Nurse, 'Publishing,' 13.

43 Nurse, 'Publishing,' 14.
44 Ibid., 15. Payment for the artists was discussed, according to Nurse, in [Eayrs?] to George Pepper, 8 June 1936 (copy), box 71, folder 12, Macmillan fonds. The plans for the paintings were discussed in Barbeau to W.H. Coverdale, 24 August 1940 (copy), box 71, folder 12, Macmillan fonds.
45 Marius Barbeau, *The Kingdom of Saguenay* (Toronto: Macmillan Company of Canada, 1936), 92–3.
46 Ibid., 95.
47 Ibid., 97–8.
48 Maria Chapdelaine is the eponymous heroine of a popular novel, first published, in Quebec, in 1916, that dramatized the life of rural French Canadians as revolving around the farm, the seasons, and the overriding importance of family. In the climax of the novel Maria chooses to marry the simple boy from her village rather than a different, glamorous suitor from away. In the world of the novel she is traditional French-Canadian values incarnate.
49 Marius Barbeau, 'In the Heart of the Laurentians,' *Canadian Geographical Journal* (July 1933): 3–12.
50 CSL, 'Normandy.'
51 CSL, 'Up the Saguenay Canada's Historic Waterway,' (193?), F5012.193 .C212, Jordan Special Collections.
52 McNaughton, 'A Study,' 198–201.
53 The *ceinture fléchée* was a long (six- to fifteen-foot) scarf with a characteristic arrow pattern, worn around the middle of the body. The sashes were originally produced for North West Company (and later Hudson's Bay Company) fur traders. In the later years of the century, the sashes were produced under an outwork system by women in the villages of St-Jacques de L'Achigan, Ste-Marie Salomé, and St-Alexis in L'Assomption County, and sold in Montreal. Most worked for Joseph Dugas, a local merchant. Eventually the women grew tired of the low wages Dugas paid and his tendency to pay in kind, and refused to continue without improved conditions. Dugas refused to change, and production of the sashes in L'Assomption stopped in 1899. See McNaughton, 'A Study,' 201–9.
54 Ibid., 211 and 216.
55 Ibid., 211; Roy, *Histoire des idéologies*, 88.
56 Oscar A. Beriau, 'Home Weaving in Canada,' *Canadian Geographical Journal* 27 (1943): 22.
57 Report of the Minister of Agriculture for the year ending 30 June 1930, Sessional Papers II, Fourth Session of the 17th Legislature of Quebec, Session of 1931, 92. Quebec Sessional papers appeared in translation in this period, and I have consulted the English version.
58 O.A. Beriau, 'Provincial School of Handicrafts – Mr. O.A. Beriau,' Report of the

Minister of Agriculture for the year ending 30 June 1931, Sessional Papers II, First Session of the 18th Legislature of Quebec, Session of 1931–32, 100–1.

59 Report, 1930, Sessional Papers, 1931, 92.

60 'Handicrafts Section,' Report of the Minister of Agriculture for the year ending 30 June 1933, Sessional Papers I, Third Session of the 18th Legislature of Quebec, Session of 1934, 29.

61 Beriau, Report, 1931, Sessional Papers, 1932, 102.

62 Report, 1933, Sessional Papers, 1934, 31.

63 Rapport du ministre d'agriculture 1935–6, gouvernement du Québec, 1936, 14.

64 Beriau, Report, 1931, Sessional Papers, 1932, 102.

65 See 1932, 1934, and 1935.

66 On these points, I am drawing on McKay, *Quest*, 188–90 and 196.

67 See plates accompanying reports in the Sessional Papers, 1930–5, as well as Beriau, 'The Handicraft Renaissance in Québec,' *Canadian Geographical Journal* 4, 3 (September 1933): 144–7.

68 McNaughton, 'A Study,' 217–22.

69 Alice MacKay, 'French Canadian Handicrafts,' *Canadian Geographical Journal* 4 (1933): 28, qtd. in McNaughton, 'A Study,' 216–17.

70 Beriau, 'Handicraft Renaissance,' 146–7. The other organizations credited are 'the Canadian Handicrafts Guild, the Canadian Pacific Railway, the Cercles des Fermières, [and] the Ecoles Ménagères.'

71 MacKay, 'French Canadian Handicrafts,' 28–30. The booklet referred to is CSL, 'Up the Saguenay,' (193-?).

72 Collard, *Passage to the Sea*, 182; these items are shown in a photograph of a gift shop on a steamer, file: steamer – 'gift shop,' 995.22.33, Public Relations Series, CSL Fonds.

73 Collard, *Passage to the Sea*, 182; Report, 1931, Sessional Papers 1932, 103; Report 1930, Sessional Papers 1931, 91.

74 'L'Industrie Domestique,' and 'Beau Succès d'une Exposition,' *Le Courrier du Nord: Organe des Comtés Charlevoix-Montmorency & Saguenay*, 14 September 1929 and 21 September 1929; quotation 21 September.

75 Report, 1931, Sessional Papers 1932, 102; 'Exposition des Arts Domestiques,' *Courrier*, 31 July 1931.

76 Although there is no date on these photographs, one of them shows a ribbon with the date '1941' on it. They are included in a file of PR material and are listed as candids in the finding aid. File: Manoir Richelieu candid portraits, 995.22.33, Public Relations Series, CSL Fonds.

77 *Courrier*, 27 April 1929.

78 Henri-Pilote, secretary-treasurer, Corporation Municipale de Pointe au Pic to Mr Enderby, Gerant General, Canada Steamship Lines, Montreal, 3 May 1938;

and Secretary, CSL to Mr Henri Pilote, 27 April 1938; in CSL Fonds, Secretary Subseries II 23A15—993.2.6, 1938 hotel Manoir Richelieu, correspondence, brochure.

79 'Electeurs de Pointe-au-Pic ...' [election flyer], 1938 Hotel Manoir Richelieu, correspondence, brochure, 993.2.6, Secretary Subseries II 23A15, CSL Fonds.

80 *Courrier*, 5 January 1929.

81 *Courrier*, 14 September 1929 and 21 September 1929.

82 Marius Barbeau, 'Are the Real Folk Arts and Crafts Dying Out?' *Canadian Art* 5 (1948): 132–3; as qtd. in McKay, *Quest*, 158–9.

83 Menu 'Bake Oven,' 1996.0041.0001, 'Alouette!' 1996.0041.0003, 'Weaving,' 1996.0041.0004, 'The Wood Carver,' 1996.0041.0005, 'The Caller,' 1996.0041.0006, 'The Hooked Rug,' 1996.0041.0007, 'Mending Net,' 1996.0041.0008, 'The Calèche,' 1996.0041.0010, 1962, Graphic Records Subgroup, CSL Fonds. These are 11- × 17-inch sheets folded once, so the image is on the cover and the text on the back, leaving space inside to fill in the menu information. These particular items were used on the passenger steamer SS *Richelieu*. However, since they started blank inside (blank versions are in 1995.22.37, Archival Series, CSL Fonds), the menus may have been used elsewhere.

84 'The Bake Oven.'

85 'The Wood Carver.'

86 'Alouette!'

87 Bruno Ramirez, *On the Move: French-Canadian and Italian Migrants in the North Atlantic Economy, 1860–1914* (Toronto: McClelland and Stewart, 1991), 47, 114–48.

88 'Manoir Richelieu Company Limited: Comparative Report on Origins of Guests,' file: 1939 hotel Manoir Richelieu, 993.2.9, Secretary Series, CSL Fonds.

89 Particular examples of this diffuse and loosely directed project ranged from the mythologizing of Tom Thomson and the Group of Seven to a large variety of folk and handicraft festivals held across the country, to attempts to build the Scottish identity of Nova Scotia through the creation of festivals, tartans, and the Gaelic College of Cape Breton. Much of this intersected with tourism. The CPR sponsored folk festivals at such hotels as the Château Laurier, itself built, like the Manoir, in the supposedly Canadian 'château style.' See McNaughton, 'A Study'; Gary Bret Kines, '"Chief Man-of-Many-Sides": John Murray Gibbon and His Contributions to the Development of Tourism and the Arts in Canada,' MA thesis, Carleton University, 1988; Cameron, 'Our Ideal'; Christopher Thomas, '"Canadian Castles"? The Question of National Styles in Architecture Revisited,' *Journal of Canadian Studies* 32, 1 (Spring 1997): 5–27; Daniel Francis, *National Dreams: Myth, Memory and Canadian History* (Vancouver: Arsenal Pulp Press, 1997). On Nova Scotia Scottishness, see McKay, 'Tartanism.'

90 CSL, advertisement in *Canadian Magazine Advertiser*, n.d., 993.2.185, Public Relations Series, CSL Fonds.

91 Lears, *No Place of Grace*, xiii.

14 Cashing In on Antiquity: Tourism and the Uses of History in Nova Scotia, 1890–1960[1]

IAN McKAY

Nova Scotia from 1890 to 1960 provides a rich site of inquiry for scholars interested in the complicated dialectical relationship between tourism and history – tourism/history for short. Tourism/history entails the production and circulation of texts, images, and practices calculated both to boost state and business revenues and to displace critiques of the existing social and political order. This chapter argues that during this period in Nova Scotia, various forms of tourism/history emerged, but that a major shift occurred in the interwar period that intensified the scope, intensity, and significance of the phenomenon.

The significance of tourism/history in the twenty-first-century province is obvious. Over the two decades, for example, hundreds of *Titanic* tourists visited Halifax to take in guided tours of disaster-related museums, churches, and cemeteries (with the gravesite of one obscure sailor, Mr J. Dawson, repeatedly decorated with flowers, testimonials, and even articles of intimate apparel – devotional practices arguably directly related to the career of one L. DiCaprio, who played Dawson in the movie). Meanwhile, to the south, *Scarlet Letter* enthusiasts could flock to Shelburne, to experience the sad tale of Hester Prynne – or, rather, they could experience the New England–style *stage-sets* from the 1995 film. To the north, would-be warriors could lay siege, once again, to the expensively reconstructed Fortress Louisbourg. And, generally throughout the province, weekend Scots of various descriptions could thrill, almost incessantly it seemed, to the summertime sights and sounds of kilts and bagpipes. In present-day Nova Scotia, scarcely a summer passes without a mega-spectacle, or a weekend without its festivals. And hardly one of these pseudo-events transpires without constructing some version of 'history.'

For empirical historians, such elements of tourism/history are obviously not based upon verifiable dates, checkable footnotes, well-documented hypotheses, or empirically grounded lessons based upon the records of the past. Tourism/history is not even necessarily about things that ever actually happened. It is about constructing, marketing, and enjoying a generic 'pastness.' The state and business, aided in large measure by the academy, have since the 1930s created a vast lavishly funded matrix of words and things, a formidable *mnemonic apparatus*, for generating a sense of history-ness. At times the apparatus urges us to remember events that never actually took place, and at other times to forget or downplay others that did. It operates so as to simplify the processes of history and to minimize the conflicts and contradictions of the past.

Nova Scotia is hardly unique in experiencing these patterns. The mnemonic apparatus we find in the province bears a close resemblance to those developed in Britain and New England – unsurprisingly, given that Nova Scotia was (from 1713 to 1867) the colony of the former and (from the 1600s to the 1900s) the neighbour, trading partner, and sometimes military target of the latter. The designers of Nova Scotia's tourism/history matrix borrowed from both metropoles, yet arguably they went beyond either in naturalizing a new form of public history. 'Let's cash in on antiquity,' one prominent politician and tourism planner had urged in 1946 – and by *cashing in* he meant linking historical attractions in Nova Scotia to the Canadian and international tourist marketplace.[2] His prescription in essence outlined a new applied philosophy of historical practice, in which events become, not useful data or meaningful exemplars, but so many interchangeable units within a fully money-driven symbolic economy. Within this framework, the 'legacies of the past' were to be valued as dollar-generating capital units. And with this came a new ontology and epistemology of history, which reserved 'truly existing' history for that which might make a profit, and consigned the unmarketable and the purely sentimental to obscurity, and at times to oblivion. In this paradigm, *Titanic* (at best marginally related to the history of the province) trumps the country's first industrial trade unions, the age-old traditions of the Aboriginal peoples, or the eighteenth-century tragedies of religious-ethnic cleansing (to name but three 'excluded others').

Public history, many scholars have reminded us, means a politics of the past. It often means inventing traditions, incorporating history within nationalist myth-symbol complexes, and creating a vivid if implausible sense of seamlessly continuous traditions.[3] International studies of tourism in the 1970s and 1980s frequently outlined the ways in which tourists subverted local cultures.[4] More recent work has wondered whether some of these earlier critiques of global tourism did not err on the side of oversimplification, elitism, and defeatism: 'while tourism and vacations were increasingly enmeshed within cultures of consumption, mechanically produced images, and various political and economic agendas, tourism and vacations have enabled a persistent quest for experiences of the self and its pleasures, and for education and knowledge.'[5] Over the past two decades, Canadianists have joined an international army of scholars pursuing both tourism[6] and history-making.[7] Much of this work exhibits a tension between emphases on 'manipulation from above' and 'entrepreneurship and activism from below.'

Much of contemporary tourism/history in Nova Scotia has been shaped according to global consumer tastes. Constructing this mnemonic apparatus was a mission undertaken largely by a local elite, responding to a grave social and economic crisis. In this 'contact zone,' to use Mary Louise Pratt's useful term – that is, a 'space of colonial encounters, the space in which peoples geographically and historically separated come into contact with each other and establish ongoing relations, usually involving conditions of coercion, radical inequality, and intractable conflict'[8] – the relationships between tourists and locals were decisively mediated by a small group of cultural entrepreneurs, operating both within and outside the state, who precociously evolved new ways of profiting from supposedly age-old traditions and forms. Rather than seeing Nova Scotians as the passive 'victims' of the 'golden hordes' of tourism, this approach focuses on the ability of a small state and a local elite to respond energetically to the emergent tourism economy, yet in ways which mystified the past and marginalized alternative interpretations.

1. Early Versions

From the eighteenth century to the early twentieth century, Halifax, a British naval station and Nova Scotia's capital, was often included in the grand tour of North American cities undertaken by elite British or American travellers. The province was also toured by visiting British soldiers attached to the garrison, by French and French-Canadian searchers after the dispersed race of Acadie,[9] by potential investors in mines and other enterprises, by would-be aristocratic 'sports,' and by prominent Nova Scotians themselves, who can be overheard lamenting, in the early nineteenth century, that the local scenery lacked the historical associations necessary to truly attain the status of the picturesque.[10]

Summer visitors only began arriving in any numbers in the early 1870s, attracted by the new rail connection which made it possible to travel from New York to Halifax in a scant thirty-six hours.[11] The would-be aristocratic 'sports' of the British garrisons provide indications of a heightened tourism traffic by their complaints that outsiders – typified by 'the town loafer and the cock-tail sportsman' – were interfering with their pleasures.[12] The many books typified by the well-regarded *The Fishing Tourist* by Charles Hallock, editor of the New

York magazine *Forest and Stream*, were blamed by some for drawing such *déclassé* interlopers to the province.[13]

Yet neither mass tourism nor organized heritage entrepreneurship was really in evidence for most nineteenth-century Nova Scotians. The province clearly lagged far behind the major New England sites.[14] As late as 1922, according to the first statistics compiled by the provincial government, a total of 49,000 tourists came to the province in the season (generally defined as 1 June to 30 September) – i.e., less than a third the level recorded by less populous New Hampshire twenty-three years earlier. Given a Nova Scotia population of about 523,000, this represented an approximate resident/tourist ratio of 10.7:1. The number of tourists rose, to a pre-war height of 322,723 in 1938. Tourists arriving in automobiles, who made up 56 per cent of the 165,906 summer visitors in 1928, constituted 63 per cent of the 168,844 who arrived in 1933. Of these automobile tourists, about 47,000 were from the United States.[15] Down to the mid-1930s, there were no sites of 'historic tourism' in the province that could compare with Nantucket, Massachusetts, Litchfield, Connecticut, or Deerfield, Massachusetts, as sites of tourism/history.[16] 'By 1900, the tourist industry had penetrated almost every corner of New England, from the coast of Maine to the hill towns of Connecticut,' writes Dona Brown.[17] 'By 1900,' the Nova Scotia historian might say in response, 'the tourist industry had penetrated almost no corners of Nova Scotia, except a few stops along the Dominion Atlantic Railway from Yarmouth to Kentville, the city of Halifax (although only to a minor extent) and two resort towns, Chester on the South Shore and Baddeck in Cape Breton – and even these last two, elite resorts of long-term American summer people rather than tourists strictly speaking, were examples more of vacationing than of mass tourism.'

Yet the architects of the new tourism/history paradigm of the 1930s and 1940s did inherit many institutions and approaches from the past. If it was true, as the Halifax *Chronicle* observed in 1938, that the tourist fame of Nova Scotia was 'depression-born,'[18] it was a much-anticipated birth, presided over by a wide range of institutional actors. As Jay White has insightfully suggested, many innovations can be attributed to the newly formed Yarmouth Steamship Company in the 1880s, which provided steamship service from Boston to Yarmouth in seventeen hours. From 1892 to 1901, he notes, the steamship company launched a series of elegant booklets on *Beautiful Nova Scotia*, which made a special appeal to those longing for release from life in the industrial American seaboard.[19] From the 1890s, the Dominion Atlantic Railway promoted the Annapolis Valley as the 'Land of Evangeline' and later, in conjunction with the Boston and Yarmouth Steamship Company, offered package tours to American tourists.[20]

By the 1920s, these private business efforts were supplemented by the province-wide Nova Scotia Tourist Association – renamed the Nova Scotia Publicity Bureau in 1924, for the suggestive reason that the word 'tourist' was thought to repel 'the most desirable class of summer visitors,' for whom it suggested 'an organization for the exploitation rather than the assistance of the stranger.'[21] This body started collecting statistics (using somewhat inconsistent criteria down to the 1960s) and promoting the province.[22] The advent of automobility meant a significant shift in both the scale and the character of tourism. By 1923, the Nova Scotia Motor League had organized a variety of 'trail markings,' to guide the motoring public. The province itself embarked on a program of highway construction, 'with the result,' the Halifax *Herald* noted proudly in 1930, that Nova Scotia could boast 6500 miles of improved roads.[23] Two major Canadian railways, Canadian Pacific and the Canadian National, erected five major hotels and resorts in the province from 1927 to 1930.

Prior to the 1920s, the notion of generally using the province's history as a lure for tourists would not have commanded much assent. One can draw upon a host of nineteenth-century writers who frankly doubted whether the province actually *had* any such applicable history. Herbert Crosskill, in his emigrant tract *Nova Scotia: Its Climate, Resources and Advantages*, boldly declared in 1872: 'Emigrants from Europe care but little whether this Province possesses a history the most remarkable and extraordinary of any country in the world, or, comparatively, no history at all.'[24] Three decades later, historian R.R. McLeod suggested that 'For a certain class of tourists, Nova Scotia has no attractions. It is destitute of such human antiquities as may be found in most other portions of the globe. Here are no buried cities, nor feudal castles, and blood-stained battlefields. Professional globe-trotters will find here but little to tickle their jaded appetite for wonderful things.'[25] The construction of a profitable mnemonic apparatus – a mechanism whereby one could really 'cash in on antiquity' – was pointless, on this reading, because there really were no interesting 'antiquities' to cash in.

The nineteenth and early twentieth centuries featured a number of revealing debates between outsiders and insiders as to how Nova Scotia properly should be characterized. Richard Dashwood's 1872 sportsman's guide to the province, *Chiploquorgan*, portrayed a wild land inhabited by wild people, many of whom were 'very ignorant and rather lawless' – which was more than enough to mark him as a fool and a knave in the eyes of local writer and politician Herbert Crosskill. Dashwood's descriptions, wrote Crosskill indignantly, were 'perfect nonsense, and calculated to give to the intending emigrant an erroneous impression of the country.'[26] The copy of Dashwood's book in the Public Archives contains more hostile reviews in the form of marginal notes: 'false,' 'rot,' 'bosh,' and 'again bosh,' culminating (when Dashwood goes so far as to suggest that local girls were rather 'fast' at skating rinks) with the marginal exclamation, 'What sort of company he must have kept!'[27] Beckles Willson's 1913 opus *Nova Scotia: The Province That Has Been Passed By* prompted a debate in the House of Assembly, driven by the Halifax *Herald*'s outrage that Willson had included descriptions of the city's prostitutes and had indulged in a 'vile slander' of the local architecture.[28]

Down to the 1930s, most Nova Scotians accredited to pronounce on such questions believed themselves to be living in a modern industrializing province, integrated into a great dominion within the world's largest and most successful Empire. In essence, Nova Scotia was an example of British civilization across the sea, as forward-looking as the mother country and more civilized than the United States.[29] Nova Scotia's 'meaning' resided in its role in advancing Responsible Government and the British Empire. Such was the predominant theme of most public history, which, when it was loosely and episodically tied to tourism, was heavily didactic and imperial in tone. The early twentieth-century Halifax Memorial Tower, built to commemorate the coming of representative government, was, from its Italianate 'monarch-of-all-I-survey' heights down to the Trafalgar-Square lions guarding its portals, a stunning monument to this imperial vision.[30] The American tourist who behaved appropriately went away from the province impressed by the splendid imperial red-coats in Halifax, the LaHave River (inevitably dubbed, as were so many other rivers on the continent, 'the Rhine' of North America), and the urbanity and new electric light system in Liverpool, not to mention that progressive town's 'tramway, fine churches, school house buildings, social life, each of which would interest the visitor as his tastes dictate.'[31] The wife of the governor-general was introduced in the 1870s to the wonders of the lunatic asylum in Halifax, as well as a 'very interesting reformatory for boys.' In the 1890s, the renowned Canadian poet Charles G.D. Roberts, who had mastered the genre of Victorian travel writing, earnestly advised all visitors to experience first-hand the 'great grim pile of Mount Hope Lunatic Asylum.'[32] Travel guides down to the 1920s urged visitors to take in steel mills, coal mines, and quarries. A.L. Hardy in his idyllic celebration of *The Evangeline Land* rather more eccentrically instructed every visitor to the province to take in the splendid views provided by the Mountain Cemetery in Yarmouth. For its part, the Halifax and South Western Railway showcased 'A Unique Yarmouth Feature – the Freshest, most Splendid Evergreen Hedges in the World.'[33] Rave reviews for pastoral scenery reminiscent of Britain's Home Counties seemingly contradicted equally enthusiastic endorsements of provincial industry: yet both could be easily taken as signs of peace, order, and good government within a British province of liberal opportunity.

Critics who followed in Dashwood's footsteps – and they were numerous – operated within the same discursive universe. Halifax was repeatedly condemned as a drab, dismal disappointment – 'a mere huddle of narrow gloomy streets and cheap buildings,' wrote travel writer Margaret Morley in 1912.[34] But not many in the nineteenth century, to my knowledge, found the city to be colourful, quaint, and excitingly 'primitive.' Halifax was found to be deficient on the same North Atlantic scales of improvement and civilization that had registered other sites as desirable. 'In coming to Nova Scotia,' Herbert Crosskill lectured potential visitors, 'emigrants do not leave a civilized country to reside among savages, or in a wilderness. They must bear in mind that they are coming amongst a people who are quite as far advanced in the arts of civilization as they are themselves, and who, owing chiefly to our system of free schools, are better educated than are, on an average, the people of England. The inhabitants of this country are mostly descended from British settlers, are governed by the same laws, animated by the same feelings and sentiments, and speak the same language as their British ancestors; and in point of intelligence, in morality and religion they are second to no people in the world.'[35] Fifty years later, the Nova Scotia Tourist Association advised Nova Scotians that 'one of the main incentives to the encouragement of tourist travel lies in the justifiable expectations of interesting moneyed visitors in industrial projects,' as a justification for dropping the tainted word 'tourist' from its title.[36] The most appropriate tourist was one who might plant either some crops as a farmer or some industries as an investor.[37] The British-imperial progressive motif persisted well into the twentieth century. It was hardly an accident that one of the two great hotels opened in Halifax in the 1920s, named after Lord Nelson, was ambitiously decorated to evoke both the feats of Empire and the pastoral landscapes of Europe.

If Nova Scotia as the progressive outpost of Empire was the dominant theme in historical representations down to the 1920s, one could also construct the province as New England's therapeutic antimodern frontier. As Naomi Griffiths and Barbara Le Blanc have shown, Henry Wadsworth Longfellow's 1847 poem *Evangeline: A Tale of Acadie*, a romance of the Acadian Deportation of 1755 that drew in turn from T.C. Haliburton's 1829 *An Historical and Statistical Account of Nova Scotia*, not only secured the United States a place in world literature, but also set off two unpredictable consequences in Nova Scotia. One, surprisingly enough (given that Longfellow's poem betrayed a profound ignorance of Nova Scotia's geography and Acadian traditions), was to provide downtrodden Acadians themselves with a founding myth, which from the 1860s to the 1950s established Evangeline and her lover Gabriel as the virtual Adam and Eve of the Acadian nation.[38] The other was to prompt wave after wave of American tourists in search of the 'Land of Evangeline':

as Le Blanc notes, 'Avid readers who decided to visit Nova Scotia to see the "Land of Evangeline" became the first cultural tourists in the province.'[39] Added to a flood of Evangeline books from the 1860s to the 1940s (in as many as 130 languages and 300 editions) were films (including a Canadian production opening in 1914, and major Hollywood films in 1922 and 1929), historic sites (especially the Grand-Pré park, developed by one patriotic Acadian from 1907 to 1917 and then sold to the Dominion Atlantic Railway, which developed a memorial church and surrounding park), and organized pilgrimages (with the trips of 1924 and 1927 organized by the Montreal nationalist newspaper *Le Devoir* having a special significance).

Was the 'Land of Evangeline' the first major eruption of literary tourism on the North American continent? It seems possible. Certainly the North American literature to date on the history of literary tourism in the nineteenth century has produced little to compare it with.[40] After the Land of Evangeline was thoroughly organized by the Dominion Atlantic Railway, which gained a monopoly on the Boston-Yarmouth steamship connection after 1901, the promotion would entail a 'tourist gaze' of precocious totality. Prepared for what they would 'see' by first consulting the romantically illustrated guidebooks, the U.S. tourists would then board steamships, sometimes carrying magically royal names – the *Prince Arthur*, the *Prince George*, or the *Prince Albert*. Once in Nova Scotia, they would board trains drawn by locomotives named after the heroes of French colonization – Engine No. 42 was named after De Monts, No. 520 after Champlain – and gaze, through the frame of their Pullman car window, upon Longfellow-land. One could see, and have brought vividly back to 'memory,' things which never had existed outside of Longfellow's historical imagination – Evangeline's Well, the Forge of Basil, and a host of other images. A relatively average-looking farming valley, not really the 'forest primeval' demanded by Longfellow's poem, could nonetheless be actively transformed by the eye of romance. As the poet and local publicist Charles G.D. Roberts explained, Longfellow, 'one of the most tender and human of poets,' had cast over the Acadian landscape 'the consecration and the purple light of his imaginings. It is through such a transfiguring glow that our hills, our streams, our fields, appear to him who views us from a distance.' And it was all thanks to the Dominion Atlantic Railway: 'This is a road which may fairly claim the sympathy and service of poet, artist, and romancer, for it is surely the least commonplace of railroads, the one most concerned with matters beyond mere freights and fares. To the tourist it seems to have its *raison d'être* in a poem ... The atmosphere of Longfellow pervades it; its great red-and-black engines bear such names as Gabriel, St. Eulalie, Basil, Minnehaha; and the staunch little steamer that traverses the historic waters of Minas is called "Evangeline."'[41] 'It is one of the wonders of literature,' a British travel writer would later exclaim, 'certainly without parallel on this side of the Atlantic, how Longfellow's hexameters have fenced in this Acadian Valley, and even peopled it with poetic ghosts. Thither in their thousands come the living twentieth-century flesh-and-blood to pay their tributes to the genius loci. I came across them lingering by Evangeline's Well and gazing sentimentally upon the spot where stood the forge of Basil.'[42]

Were American tourists truly taken in by this startlingly early draft of the late twentieth-century theme park? Or were they, no less precociously, engaged in a certain wilful irony? Certainly there are many jocular descriptions of them arriving in 'the Longfellow spirit,' and being persuaded, to the vast amusement of the locals, that the most implausible landscape features had some connection with Evangeline.[43] These were *active* tourists, seeking out the magic landscape of the poem, peopling it (so they fervently hoped) with simple Acadian peasants, and – perhaps – with memories of the childhoods in which they had first read the wondrous words of Longfellow. Some were probably drawn to the tale because it confirmed them in their U.S. nationalism. Raised on tales of the American Revolution, New Englanders were perhaps disposed to believe the worst of the British colonists.[44] And some of their descriptions raise the suspicion of a delighted enjoyment with romanticism almost for its own sake – a coy 'playing with the past' that almost anticipates high camp. Here is Elizabeth B. Chase in *Over the Border* (1884), describing a place she had yet to see: 'The Basin of Minas! What a flood of thoughts rise at the name. Fancy paints dreamy and fascinating pictures of the fruitful and verdant meadow land, the hills, the woods, the simple-hearted, childlike peasants; upright, faithful, devout, leading blameless lives of placid serenity: "At peace with God and the world."'[45] If we reimagine this Edenic landscape with her, we enter a discursive construct *five times removed* from the 'extra-linguistic' realm formerly fondly known as material reality.[46] But – a contemporary tourism/history partisan would surely ask – so what? The past – or rather, a five-times-removed poetic representation of it – was there to be played with. Chase's fellow-traveller and Evangelinizer Betty D. Thornley seemingly agreed, when she playfully conceded the ambiguous epistemological status of Longfellow's fictional heroine with the phrase 'To be sure, she never lived, in the mere concreteness of seventeenhood,' which deftly subverted her own highly romanticized descriptions of the 'Land of Evangeline.'[47] Playing with history entailed no sense of ethical or epistemological responsibility for its patterns or its consequences.

Yet, for all its extraordinary power over the Acadians and its uncanny anticipation of later twentieth-century 'total tourism,' the Land of Evangeline was nonetheless a narrowly limited phenomenon. The hegemony of the *first* imagined 'Nova Scotia,' rooted as it was in obvious economic development (much of it fuelled by British capital) and everyday experience, was never put in doubt by the second. Moreover, few middle-class anglophone urban Nova Scotians would have felt personally implicated in the story of the Land of Evangeline, which applied to a different ethnic group, helpfully 'fossilized' in a romanticized feudal past.[48] Second, although one might have expected some fierce resistance from Acadians themselves to what was obviously an outsider's romanticization of their history, Longfellow's poem did cast them in a noble and tragic light, and thus played into their own emergent nationalism. After all, the Expulsion was an actual historical event. And, thanks to the geography of their relocation and the protective strategy of their church, most of the Acadians supposedly at the centre of the story were actually distant from the tourist gaze.[49] Finally, both the Imperial and the Land of Evangeline 'frameworks' of tourism/history emerged within and were applied to a small tourist *trade*, not to a fully fledged tourism *industry*. In a province with profitable manufacturing, farming, and mining sectors, exporting its products across Canada, the arrival of a few New Englanders reciting Longfellow hardly unsettled any notions of Nova Scotian identity. No fundamental cultural issues were posed by tourism, no matter how antimodern and romantic its forms, within a prospering province securely located within the most powerful Empire in the world.[50]

2. The Essences of Innocence

In the 1920s and 1930s, the imperial and Evangeline frameworks were complemented, and ultimately supplanted, by a third approach. In building on the precocious mnemonic apparatuses of the past, it also transformed them beyond recognition. In this much more expansive and integrated construct of 'Nova Scotia,' still in operation today, the major representations dwelled upon Nova Scotian *essences* – of the rockbound coast, of the Folk, of essential Scottishness, of a vanished Golden Age, and of the white male pioneers of a true Canadian nationhood. All five 'essentialisms' can be referred to collectively as *Innocence* – an intricate web of words and things testifying to Nova Scotia's essentially pre-modern insularity from the stresses and strains of a modern twentieth-century world.

Three general contexts – regional economic crisis, the new North American popularity of automobile tourism, and the rise of a new Canadian nationalism in the context of British decline and U.S. globalism – were the general preconditions of this mnemonic renovation. First, both the 1920s and 1930s delivered blows to Nova Scotia's industrial economy. The coal and steel industries in particular, once taken to epitomize the province's capitalist modernity, were plunged into a series of wage-cuts, strikes, and financial collapses.[51] Rather like the distressed inhabitants of post-whaling Nantucket in the 1870s,[52] un-willingly post-industrial Nova Scotians saw tourism, notoriously the 'industry of last resort,' as an alternative to economic oblivion. Second, if economic calamity 'pushed' the province, Nova Scotia was also 'pulled' by the new prospect of a travelling public in North America which, to an unprecedented extent, enjoyed paid vacations and ownership of motor vehicles.[53] Automobility changed the landscape of tourism. Many more tourists could access many more sites. And finally, the changing geopolitical situation – decline of the British Empire, growing power of the United States, and Canada's own rise to self-governing status – meant an attrition (albeit gradual and partial) of the tropes of British imperialism.

Perhaps the clearest indication of the transformation was the abrupt rise of new symbolic landscapes. In the nineteenth and early twentieth centuries, within both the major frameworks of tourism, industrial and pastoral landscapes were singled out for particular praise. Conversely, most promoters and commentators averted their eyes from the rockbound coast of the South Shore, seen as a desolate, even deformed region – one perversely removed from either the imperial progressive emphasis on productive cities and farmland, or the Edenic pastoral scenery demanded by the Arcadian Acadia of the Land of Evangeline. All this changed rapidly in the 1920s. Automobiles and mass tourism (and, by the early 1930s, Halifax-bound cruise ships and elite tourists) brought more and more of the province within the tourist gaze. The railways lost their monopoly in providing set pieces for the travelling public. Across North America, the general economic crisis prompted middle-class interest in back-to-the-land movements, primitivist aesthetics, and a heightened appreciation of pre-capitalist traditions and values. In the Nova Scotia case, the rocky coastline and its fishing villages, earlier neglected or condemned as unsightly, uncivilized, and dangerous, were suddenly re-evaluated. Peggy's Cove, the little fishing village on St Margaret's Bay, absent from almost all imagined Nova Scotias before 1920, became central within most of them after about 1928. Photographers and painters celebrated its rocks and wharves, and travel writers praised the homespun simplicity of its fisherfolk.[54] From the 1920s to the 1960s, while the intricate network of park-like scenery and fictionalized history of the Land of Evangeline waxed and then slowly waned in popularity, that of the rockbound coast and imagined history of the fisherfolk skyrocketed. Within novels and subsequently within tourism promotion, not only Nova Scotia's supposed social isolation from the storms of modernity, but also its peninsular quasi-insularity, were highlighted. In the nineteenth century many cultural producers had laboured to construct local landscapes as civilized and 'European.' Their twentieth-century counterparts imagined an essential Nova

Scotia that was Western civilization's polar opposite – raw, vital, stripped of its pretensions, reduced to bedrock. Both fictional and touristic representations came to focus not only on rocky coastlines, but the many islands lying off Nova Scotia's coast, which became, in a sense, the truest harbours of provincial essence. There one could cash in, not just on history, but on the eternal verities of race, rocks, and the roaring sea – in a sense, a cosmic, natural antiquity.

This was closely related to a second great transition in the language of Nova Scotia tourism: the rise of the Folk. As was the case throughout much of the Western world, the construction of the rural Folk was mainly a project of upper-middle-class city-dwellers. In the Nova Scotia case, it meant not so much an appreciation of local cultural expression as a reverence for ancient British ballads. Helped by institutions ranging from the Canadian Pacific Railway to the Carnegie Foundation, folklorist Helen Creighton succeeded in placing the songs and legends of the supposed Folk at the very heart of the mnemonic apparatus. In the case of handicrafts, which in so industrial a province had predictably languished since the mid-nineteenth century, it meant a state-sponsored effort to reinvent rural 'crafts' and to teach Acadians, who would stubbornly insist on using vivid hues in their rugs and tapestries, to tone down their colour schemes for the New England market.[55]

The new dispensation also had a racial and ethnic dimension. If a romanticized Land of Evangeline had coexisted easily with progressive tourism before the interwar period, its interwar incarnations often suggested the revival of an *ethnie*. In part inspired by, and to an extent working against, such doctrines of Acadian national identity, interwar promoters of Scottishness developed a complex provincial myth-symbol complex within which Nova Scotia itself was *inherently* and *essentially* Scottish. Overcoming the awkward facts that persons of Scottish descent numbered less than a third of the population as calculated by the 1931 federal Census, and that in the province's early history of European settlement New Englanders, Acadians, and 'Foreign Protestants' from continental Europe had all preceded the 'Scottish' moment of settlement, which itself had included many non-Scots, these active promoters of Tartanism made the 'Highland Heart of Nova Scotia' a doctrine only the querulous, disloyal, or perpetually sceptical would question. Building on the happenstance of the province's Scottish name, and on the visible presence of some Gaelic-speakers in Cape Breton, these energetic promoters engaged in what amounted to an audacious exercise in ethnic branding. By the late 1950s, tourists might be lured to the province by such Scottish-themed events as gatherings of the clans. They would be welcomed at the border by a piper. They might attend a tourism-oriented Gaelic College in Cape Breton. They could motor through the Cape Breton landscape via the new Cabot Trail, through the newly named 'Highlands,' and see sites that were designed to prove the Scottish essence of the province. They could see the Lone Shieling, a recently constructed but seemingly ancient building steeped in the culture of the romantic Hebrides. They could play at golf courses where each hole had a Scottish name – 'Cuddy's Lugs,' 'Dowie Den,' 'Muckle Mouth Meg.'[56] When they lifted their eyes unto the hills, they would drink in the sight of Highland cattle, recently imported, who added their own bovine tribute to the 'Highland Heart of Nova Scotia.' And why not supplement what was explicitly called the 'Celtic motif' by having appropriately Highlandized waitresses at the state-operated 'Keltic Lodge' carry small cards identifying their particular tartan for the convenience of diners who might want to purchase tartan gifts after their meal?[57] And they would do all these things in a province that would, in a world-historic departure from Scottish tradition, boast its own tartan and that cherished the memory of that professional Scot, Premier Angus L. Macdonald, under whose Liberal regime much of this curious 'ethnic revival' took shape.

There were similarities and differences between the Land of Evangeline and Tartanism. The similarities lay in the willingness to help history along – to embroider more than a little on what was actually the case, in order to frame the sights and sounds of the actual Nova Scotia in ways that would bring out their supposed exotic essence. The differences lay in the pervasiveness, multidimensionality, and political centrality of the later project. Humans and animals, buildings and place-names, even provincial symbols and markers were much more aggressively shaped in the second history/tourism framework. That Nova Scotia was, in a profound and unalterable way, *Scottish* (rather than English, Welsh, Irish, Black, Amerindian, or Acadian, to name a few other plausible ethnic contenders) came to seem a simple matter of common sense. To the magic of the age-old name was added the physical reality of the new provincial flag, with (of course) its St Andrew's cross providing persuasive evidence of the province's *true* ethnic identity. American travel writer Albert Deane found the motif so completely convincing that he gave his article on the 'steadfast, industrious ... friendly, God-loving' Nova Scotians the arresting title 'How to See Scotland without Crossing the Atlantic.' As he explained,

The lady of our party had come to Nova Scotia for one impelling reason. Her ancestors were Scottish and she had long hoped to get to Scotland – the old, the original Scotland. But fate hadn't co-operated, so she had settled for Nova Scotia on a hunch – and the hunch paid off. Its rocky coast *was* Scotland; its rugged hills *were* Scotland; its clear, tumbling streams sang of Scotland ...[58]

Like the Evangeline promotion, tartanism meant framing a particular landscape so that its supposedly 'historical' resources could be more efficiently viewed and purchased. Unlike the earlier exercise in branding, it also could be extended to the province as a whole. The new brand name was not limited to a geographically and ethnically defined zone of antimodernism, but, aided by the happenstance of the province's name, was extended to all of Nova Scotia.[59]

This turn to Scottishness was also enabled and justified by a new Canadian nationalism, which became a new and potent force in the new forms of tourism/history. In many respects, middle-class Maritimers generally and Nova Scotians particularly were vanguard militants in the struggle for new strategies for Canadian tourism in the 1930s, as evidenced by the 1934 Senate Report, out of which would emerge the Canadian Government Travel Bureau.[60] Tourism, not radicalism or (over the long haul) regionalism, was the province's triumphant *ism* of the 1930s and 1940s. Yet, at the same time, the emergent myth-symbol complex of Anglo-Canadian nationalism made virtually no room for the myths and symbols long cherished by many Nova Scotians – less room, in fact, than British imperialism, within which such cities as Halifax could glory in being the 'Warden of the Honour of the North.' Such constructions as the 'Empire of the St Lawrence' and 'Frontier Democracy,' important to many Canadian nationalists, did not make much room for Nova Scotia, except perhaps as that effete coastal place hardy Canadian pioneers had left behind in their westward, democracy-building adventures. And in a continent increasingly dominated by an American economic and cultural giant, Nova Scotians as 'Atlantic Canadians' – a new phrase of the mid-twentieth century – would often be represented as the doubly marginalized poor relations of the poor relations, defined not so much by what they had accomplished as by what consumer goods they lacked.[61]

Canadianization thus presented real symbolic challenges. From the 1930s to the 1950s, Canadian tourists travelling to Nova Scotia in automobiles were at least as numerous as Americans. Nova Scotia officially became 'Canada's Ocean Playground' in 1935 (an earlier version was the less appealing if more revealing 'The Playground with a History'). Canadian tourists excitedly filled their newspapers back home with accounts of this newly accessible vacationland, travel to which could be rationalized as a form of economic nationalism. This Canadian wave influenced the landscapes privileged within the tourism plant (which increasingly reflected the rugged terrains of the sort favoured by the iconic Group of Seven), the teleological reimagining of the history of colonial Nova Scotia as a series of anticipations of what would later come in liberal Canada, an aggressive campaign to 'Canadianize' local histories through historic plaques and monuments, now centrally coordinated by a central federal Board, and the positioning of such themes as Scottishness so that they also somehow confirmed a Canadian nationalism.[62]

Another theme woven into the fabric of Innocence was that of maritimicity – the claim that, in Nova Scotia, a seafaring population carried on the proud traditions of the romantic Golden Age of Sail. As with all the historical themes articulated within tourist discourse, this one was pushed beyond an empirical observation applicable to *some* Nova Scotians to make a statement about the *essence* of them *all*. The schooners of the Grand Banks fishery became carriers of identity; one in particular, the *Bluenose*, is today featured on every provincial licence-plate, in honour of its victories over American competitors in the International Fishermen's Races of the 1920s and 1930s. (A vessel very much like it is also featured on the Canadian dime.) This was a schooner bearing a freight far weightier than mere codfish. One might say that the racing exploits of the *Bluenose* transformed the 'poor relations of the poor relations' into a proud people with a noble past, who could boast of virile adventurers of the high seas – not to mention of a proven track record of beating the dastardly Americans. The province could thus be redescribed, not as the mouldy place to which one sang 'Farewell to Nova Scotia' (itself rediscovered in this period), but a frontier in its own right, a *maritime* frontier where manly individuals did manly, rugged, enterprising sorts of things. Within the new landscape of tourism, the *Bluenose* phenomenon drew attention to the newly sanctified South Shore. Within the new Folk economy, the schooner's victories stood for those of simple traditional people against decadent big-city yachting enthusiasts. Within Canadian nationalism, *Bluenose* could stand for a victory against Americans. Yet it also stood for the pivotal figure in liberalism, the white male individual who was symbolically master of his fate and captain of his soul, precisely at a time when many male workers had good reason to believe they were at the mercy of impersonal economic forces and sweeping changes in gender relations. Thus, if initially the *Bluenose* phenomenon of the 1920s seems easily enough explained by the economic and cultural motivations of its Halifax newspaper promoters and the longings of its mass consumer audience for spectacle and adventure, its persistence as the ultimate signifier of 'Nova Scotianness' requires a subtler, more complicated account of the diversity of roles it could assume within tourism/history.

Innocence, the dominant identity-shaping state-sanctioned provincial variant of antimodernism, thus worked within the tourism/history complex in pervasive, subtle, and shifting ways – in patterns that dwarfed its anticipations in earlier frameworks of tourism/history. Older tunes could indeed be preserved and sung to new effect – always provided that they harmonized with the swelling chorus that sang of older, simpler, and better ways. For example, what remained of the Land of Evangeline apparatus (whose popularity crested in the 1950s) could easily be accommodated, in the new dispensation, provided it focused more on a generic 'romance of the past' rather than on an increasingly forgotten, and perhaps intrinsically divisive, poem.[63] The traditional 'imperial motif' could be incorporated within Tartanism, via an emphasis on the kilted regiments who had fought for the Empire in the Great War, the unveiling of a plaque at Edinburgh Castle, and the visiting of somewhat bemused Scottish dignitaries to a new Gaelic College whose head, alas, could not really speak Gaelic. Discourses that seem analytically distinct and to imply different tourism strategies could be blurred together in a vast, Turneresque, antimodern romantic vista. Betty D. Thornley, writing as early as the 1920s, captured the new spirit of tourism/history with uncanny precision: 'The visitor to-day can get the soul-taste of all these phases of history, mingled with the brine of the sea and hazed with that faint dimness that adds the final touch of haunting beauty to the thoughts of yesterday.'[64]

3. The Emergence of a State Tourism/History Complex

The critical factor which allowed these diverse antimodern frameworks to be coordinated and made a hegemonic 'common sense' was the emergence of the provincial state as a pivotal cultural force. The small and vestigial state organs of the 1920s were replaced by a much more vigorous bureaucracy in the 1930s. (That a cabinet minister was answerable for tourism development was a significant breakthrough of this interwar period.) Rhetorically committed to a New Deal–like 'new liberalism' but, in practice, fiscally cautious, the Liberal regimes dominating political life from the mid-1930s to the late-1950s were drawn to tourism as a highly visible, and seemingly low-cost, investment in the province's economy. Road-paving, the promotion of new national parks, the organization of a handicrafts bureau (in part inspired by New Hampshire), the employment of a New York advertising agency to coordinate the mass distribution of images: all of these suggested a province determined to master modern systems of transportation and communication. Nova Scotia sought the most modern means of marketing its inherent pre-modernity, the most wily ways of broadcasting its guileless Innocence. What had been somewhat *ad hoc* acts of official commemoration before 1935 became a consistent policy at both levels of the state of developing what were now termed the province's 'historical resources' in the interests of promoting tourism. At the provincial level, so intense and enthusiastic was the embrace of mass media that it seems possible to speak of a 'promotional state,' one that, over two decades, ventured into film production, a startlingly early use of television, mass newspaper campaigns, the organization of such sporting pseudo-events as the International Tuna Tournament, the hiring of publicity agents – anything and everything to keep the brand name 'Nova Scotia' before the eyes of the North America buying public.

The impact of this new 'promotional state' on tourism/history was soon apparent. In 1935, for example, the province embraced the 'Order of the Good Time,' a new version of the tourists' enthusiasm for the age of French colonization (minus the disconcerting topic – at least for many English-speaking Nova Scotians – of the Expulsion). The Order historicized the tourist's experience by associating the province with 'L'ordre du bon temps' of seventeenth-century Port-Royal – an order, tourists were solemnly advised in *High Lights of Nova Scotia History*, which was 'North America's first service club.' Initiated by Champlain a full three centuries before Rotary, the Order nonetheless 'strangely' anticipated 'many of its characteristics.'[65] Reserved for visitors who stayed at least ten days in the province, membership in this twentieth-century re-enactment of Champlain's group was supposedly designed to encourage 'the maintenance of good fellowship amongst our summer visitors.' In return for filling out a registration card, a tourist received a handsome certificate. If stopped by the police, the visiting motorist could avoid paying a fine by flourishing proof of his or her special 'historic' status. 'The new members definitely do not look upon this as a 'gag,' we read in the 1949 Tourism *Report*. 'They appear to be appreciative of the opportunity to be associated with the oldest social club in America, and the certificates they carry home and display provide a good form of advertising for Nova Scotia.' Close to two hundred thousand 'members' of a semi-fictional historical 'Order' which never convened and existed only on paper could be found on six continents by 1956.[66] An 'antiquity' had paid a handsome promotional dividend.

The 'Order' was colour-coordinated tastefully with the restoration of the Port Royal Habitation, the first large-scale historical reconstruction undertaken by the federal Canadian state, based on Champlain's plans and some American archaeological work (although, as historian C.J. Taylor dryly observes, subsequent investigations 'failed to confirm that the ['restored'] habitation was in fact on the original site').[67] 'The tourist industry offers history its greatest market and its greatest opportunity,' wrote Ella K. Cork on behalf of the Canadian Tourism Association in 1950. 'If the tourist can be encouraged to tarry, he will spend money for goods and services which will penetrate to every economic level in the community.' In her view, history would ultimately provide an excellent 'return upon the investment.'[68]

However interesting and important the earlier developments in tourism/history had been, the state's new involvement meant that the mid-1930s marked a decisive moment in history's commodification. The most graphic case of the new zeal for cashing in on antiquity was that of Yarmouth's 'Runic Stone,' a rock weighing about four hundred pounds and bearing enigmatic marks. Discovered about 1820, the stone had attained a certain fame by 1880, when Henry J. Philips, Jr, the corresponding secretary of the Numismatic and Antiquarian Society of Philadelphia, reported that after intensive study he had translated the stone's enigmatic marks to read: 'Harkussen Men Varu,' or 'Harko's Son Addressed the men.'[69] In 1934, the stone was reinterpreted – this time by Olaf Strandwold of Prosser, Washington – to read 'Laeifr Eruki Risr,' or 'Leif to Eric Raises [this monument],' words which, it was said, established Nova Scotia's rightful place within the Norse sagas.[70] At a stroke, Nova Scotia's portfolio of historical resources was greatly enhanced. It now moved from being Scotland-beyond-the-seas to the veritable birthplace of the 'white race' in North America.

Apart from the transparently racialized hierarchies at play in this move, what was most interesting about the Runic Promotion were the fledgling networks of tourism/history it brought to light. There were dozens of heritage entrepreneurs ready to pounce, if and when a profitable historical resource came on the market. And there was also a state that was more than anxious to help them convert historical potential into realized profits – to complete, as it were, the circuit of mnemonic capital. The stone eloquently called out for Viking ruins, and, in the form of nebulously Norse abandoned cellars, they duly materialized. The 'League of Norsemen' of Canada came forward with plans for the reconstruction of Leif's 'capital,' for annual 'Leif Erikson' days, and for a large Leif Erikson National Park, whose chief administration building was to replicate the Viking chieftain's ancient banqueting hall. For nine magic years, the Runic Stone provided 'bedrock evidence' of Nova Scotia's primary role in Viking settlement, and hence its foundational role in the real, i.e., white, history of the continent. Then Professor A.D. Fraser, of the Division of Archeology, School of Ancient Languages, University of Virginia, informed the government that the stone had plainly been worked upon by saws. It was, he argued, likely nothing more than a discarded quarry block, whose markings – not especially 'Runic' to begin with – had probably been made accidentally. Plans for the National Park were quietly shelved; and the stone's image was hastily removed from the provincial guide to *Historic Nova Scotia*.[71] In contrast to the postmodern destiny of the gravestone that marks the final resting place of the *Titanic*'s J. Dawson, the sad fate of this earlier stone was sealed by a certain stick-in-the-mud realism.

Behind many projects of 'cashing in on antiquity' lay concerned middle-class preservationists convinced that only the interest of tourists could save the legacy of the past from the indifference of the present. American soldiers visiting Halifax's Citadel Hill in 1951 were quoted by a local newspaper as remarking, 'Why doesn't somebody get a franchise to use this place? ... This is a gold mine ... Don't you value old things in Canada? Our Government grabs everything even 50 years old and polishes it up.'[72] Another heritage booster, writing on behalf of the restoration of three blockhouses, enclosed with his appeal a note on 'What Massachusetts Has Done for History.' That particular U.S. state, with its 116 Historical Societies, restored vessels, the Bourne Whaling Museum in New Bedford, and Old Sturbridge Village, was doing rather more with (and indeed *to*) history than Nova Scotia.[73] Annapolis Royal, 'birthplace of Canada,' was 'no longer historic,' complained another preservationist, who revealingly added: 'Visitors to Annapolis say they feel gypted – expected to see some old houses open to the public – like the efforts of the Antiquarian Societies or the Colonial Dames of the adjacent N. England States.'[74] Colonial Williamsburg – 'the exquisite little eighteenth-century town, clean, tidy, and tasteful' – danced before the eyes of many Nova Scotian preservationists.[75] Yet to raise up a (somewhat idealized) American model was also implicitly to suggest why, in a troubled dependent regional economy within a country largely lacking an indigenous tradition of corporate philanthropy, middle-class preservationists would so frequently find themselves appealing to the state. They often assumed that throughout civil society everyone had come to accept that the monetary arguments of tourism/history would always trump other relationships with the past that were not as easily 'cashed in.'

The rudimentary nineteenth-century tourism/history complex had operated, in a sense, by remote control. Locals had struggled valiantly to make their landscape look like, and be represented as, the Home Counties of England or Longfellow-land. In the interwar period, local agents were far more powerful within the tourism/history complex. At the heart of the new mnemonic machine were three principal organic intellectuals, each connected to the state. One was Premier Angus L. Macdonald, whose profound, detailed interest in the commercial possibilities of tourism was combined with a severe case of Scottish Romanticism. It was largely thanks to Macdonald that Nova Scotia was 'branded' Scottish, even acquiring, evidently for the first time in the world for any political jurisdiction, its own distinctive tartan. Under Macdonald, commemorative projects that focused on Scottish personages (such as Flora Macdonald, very briefly a provincial resident) enjoyed a competitive advantage over others. He even favoured such eyebrow-raising projects as the tourist-oriented Gaelic College – headed by a Cape Bretoner characterized by vision, energy, a sense of Celtic destiny, and a near-complete inability to speak the Gaelic language.[76]

The other two figures suggested a continued blurring of the lines between historical realism and historical romance.[77] Both Thomas H. Raddall and Will R. Bird were writers of historical romances set in Nova Scotia, and they amassed a very considerable degree of influence over the tourism/history complex. Although born in England in 1903, Raddall came to be identified as the archetypal Nova Scotia 'Bluenose' because of a series of widely read historical novels. Bird, born in Nova Scotia in 1891, and also a novelist, was Raddall's sole rival as popularizer of Nova Scotia history. His most influential books were his travelogues. *This Is Nova Scotia* (1950) had sold over five hundred thousand copies by 1972.

Both men, in different ways, became militants for tourism/history. Raddall set forth his views in 1943 in a brief to the provincial Commission on Post-War Development and Rehabilitation:

> The great tourist trade of the Annapolis Valley was built on Fort Anne and the legend of Evangeline. The South Shore, with its historic towns of Shelburne, Liverpool and Lunenburg, could be equally famous with some intelligent advertising and what we might call a 'sense of showmanship.' The tourist is willing to be diverted with bathing, sailing, fishing and golfing, but as the primary object of his trip he wants to 'see something historic' ... And since he demands to be 'shown' we must provide him with things to see.[78]

What did the tourist expect to find when he or she came to Nova Scotia? Raddall asked rhetorically two years later. He answered: 'There is one answer; he expects to find a country different from his own, with a story of its own, and someone who can tell him all about it.'[79] Bird wholeheartedly agreed. He worked for the new Nova Scotia Bureau of Information for three years in the 1920s, and from 1933 to 1965 was its semi-official 'Mr Nova Scotia.' In 1972, he would estimate that he had given 1552 speeches at dinners, luncheons, and graduations over the course of his career.[80] As assistant director of publicity in the Bureau of Information, Bird generated one article after another. 'Would you care for an article on Oak Island, our "buried treasure" mystery?' he asked a publisher. 'Or on our "ship railway" which was planned for 1895 ... Or a story of Peggy's Cove? Or our quaint old churches? Or our annual Gaelic Mod? Or the founding of Halifax?'[81] In 1957, he proudly told the provincial premier, his stories had been published or were about to be published in some twenty publications, ranging from the *Canadian Geographic Magazine* to the *Springfield Republican*. It would have cost the province more than $9000 to purchase as advertising the coverage he had obtained for free.[82]

Bird's travel books probably worked as powerfully as any other representations in commodifying the Nova Scotia past. Bird wrote *This Is Nova Scotia* (1950) by trying to imagine how someone completely new to the province would be seeing it. The narrator is not who he seems to be – as evident when, for instance, Bird-as-fictionalized narrator expresses his delight and surprise at discovering plaques Bird-as-actual-bureaucrat had been instrumental in putting in place. *This Is Nova Scotia* constructs an imagined nineteenth-century realm of primitive, colourful, storytelling folk, salty old souls spending a remarkable portion of their adult lives exchanging tall tales perched on rustic wharves. The Folk Nova Scotia is a remarkably homogeneous place. Bird's characters in his travel books sound very much like each other, and in turn echo many of the turns of phrase used by his fictional characters. Just as the Evangeline Promotion was about creating material evidence for a character who had never, in fact, existed, 'Birdland' was about the creation of a Folk and a province that closely paralleled the imaginary world of Bird's historical novels.

His travel books were tremendously successful. 'Mr. Bird has reproduced for a harried age the timeless beauty and colour of Canada's most storied province,' the perceptive reviewer for the Winnipeg *Tribune* exclaimed. 'The near-sacred legends, the characters and picturesque villages of Nova Scotia are adequately prepared for the arm-chair traveller.'[83] 'It is my hope that you and your cabinet will appreciate the fact that I am doing more than getting our historical assets on array in the shop window for our visitors,' Bird wrote to Premier Robert Stanfield in 1960, using a metaphor that captured precisely the transformation of 'history' into a series of distinct, visible, and purchasable goods. 'My books have a wide circulation in New England and the New York area, and play no small part in bringing tourist business to this province.'[84] There was a huge market, in a suburbanizing, stressful Canada, for Bird's 'Nova Scotia' brand.

A signature preoccupation of the new marketplace of historical significance was locating 'first things' – what Bird called 'primary occurrences.' The primary occurrence of this sustained obsession with primary occurrences can be tracked back to the Dominion Atlantic Railway, whose *High Lights of Nova Scotia History* had proclaimed that 'The first civilized settlement on the North American Continent was made in Nova Scotia.'

From this early starting point Nova Scotia has been first in many things which it is a duty to recall, and a pleasure to read … Here was milled the first wheat and planted the first apple orchards in America … Here the first fraternal society was established, the first church erected, the first parliament in any British dominion brought into being, the first public gardens planted and the first wireless installation made.[85]

In 1936, J.W. Regan, writing under the pen name John Quinpool, dramatically extended this list in *First Things in Acadia: 'The Birthplace of a Continent.'* This book contained 100 chapters and a daunting list of no fewer than 250 'primary occurrences.' Nova Scotia now claimed the honour of having had the first Mass celebrated in the air – one had been celebrated on board the dirigible *Hindenberg* as it passed over the 'Sable Island Zone.' It could claim the first government lottery in Canada. It could claim, in Leif Erikson, the honour of having the first missionary. For that matter, it could claim the first North American Swedenborgians. And so on, for 304 pages.[86] The Nova Scotia past came to be reified as a series of discrete 'first' things, unique articles, and decontextualized oddities, reminiscent, perhaps, of a massive open-air *Ripley's Believe-It-or-Not* museum. Annapolis Royal's welcoming sign for tourists would long remain: 'Annapolis Royal welcomes you to a town of First Things.'[87]

This new form of tourism/history represented both continuities and discontinuities with the progressive and Evangeline frameworks of an earlier day. It was equally about constructing a form of history accessible and attractive to the tourist public. Starting in 1937, the province acquired and in many cases refurnished stately homes, often inspired by the New England example of restoration (and at times even relying upon expensive New England antique dealers to supply the requisite 'historic' stage props). Moreover, the new model also followed the old in wearing its Eurocentrism on its sleeve. When Bird came to imagine the First Nations of Nova Scotia, he wrote not of their undoubted 'primary occurrences,' which he generally slighted, but rather of 'the red terrors that haunted the trails of those hardy pioneers, of isolated families awakened in the night by fearsome yells and the smell of burning torches.' Far from having in any way hurt the local Native peoples, the European settlers had actually rescued the Mi'kmaq (and many other Native nations east of the Mississippi) from the bloodthirsty Iroquois.[88] Raddall's *Roger Sudden* famously concluded with the hero's meditation on the superiority of the English over the French, whose *coureurs de bois* 'had mated with savage women, and spilled their seed in the wilderness' – 'ugh! Darkness! Darkness!' is our hero's response to 'mating with this wild thing [i.e., a First Nations woman], to produce hybrid things, half beast and half himself.'[89] Both authors were, we remind ourselves, writing in a province that advertised itself to the world as the 'oldest settlement by the white race north of the Gulf of Mexico.'[90] Whiteness was marketable to tourists in pursuit of their 'roots.' An age which evinced such enthusiasm for a Runic Stone tenuously associated with the white Vikings had little time for the legacy of the First Nations. Attempts to protect ancient petroglyphs – i.e., *actual* antiquities – were turned down by Bird's council on historic sites. As late as 1949, tourists were advised that they should bring a shovel along, for a 'little digging' would turn up 'crumbled pieces of pottery, barely discernible as remains of cooking utensils,' the crude remains of Native people who 'did not do much with clay beyond biscuit firing.'[91]

If in official tourism/history, the essential Nova Scotia was defined by whiteness, Afro–Nova Scotians – many of whom could trace their actual family histories back as far as many of their 'white' fellow citizens – hardly merited sustained attention. When Bird informed Premier Stanfield that Birchtown, a Black settlement dating back to the eighteenth century, and site of memorable acts of Afro–Nova Scotian resistance against oppression, had asked for recognition of its history, he lumped it in with other communities 'with very little in the way of historic importance' that wanted things done for them. 'There is simply no foundation to their stories,' he remarked to Stanfield, 'but I am being as tactful as possible with them.'[92]

Bird's strategy of 'getting our historical assets on array in the shop window for our visitors' was similar in kind to that of the Dominion Atlantic Railway's Evangeline Promotion. Yet it was far more powerful and pervasive in its impact. The first concrete step Bird took when he became head of the Historic Sites Advisory Council was to urge every Nova Scotia town government to erect large signs at its borders advertising 'any historical details of its founding, the identity of the first settlers, data regarding any interesting feature of the locality, its recreational facilities, and leading industries.'[93] He went further in urging local governments to invent historic attractions – to pretend, for example, that an old toll-gate was still operational, since this would 'rouse the curiosity of tourists and cause many pictures to be taken.'[94]

There were other stark discontinuities between the two eras of mnemonic politics. First, there were far more tourist-consumers for such historical commodities. Having declined during the war years, tourism had rebounded in 1948, when 323,219 visitors arrived. (Among the visiting Americans, the top six home states were Massachusetts, New York, New Jersey, Connecticut, Maine, and Pennsylvania.) Ten years later the total was 599,843; and ten years after that, in 1968, the number for the first time exceeded 1,000,000. From a 1922 ratio of about 10.7 residents for every tourist, Nova Scotia had moved to an approximate 1965 ratio of 1.3 tourists for every resident.[95] Second, from the mid-1930s to the 1970s, the provincial state rose to a position of primacy within the tourism/history complex. It had the ability to seal an earlier, more porous antimodernist discourse about the past. This official state public history arose at a complex time, when a progressive narrative relating the province's forward industrial march was no longer very persuasive, when growing numbers of modern tourists were clamouring for a therapeutic holiday from modernity, and when many middle-class Nova Scotians, worried about safeguarding the 'past,' were also more and more favourably disposed towards the preservationist interventions of the state. These elements combined to transform Bird's and Raddall's idiosyncratic interpretations into something like an officially ordained and reproduced story of Nova Scotia, targeted at tourists and residents alike, and distributed far more massively than anything seen in an earlier period. Third, compared to the natural, political, and cultural boundaries restricting the Evangeline promotion, the new model was simultaneously more expansive and more invasive. It could appeal not just to the scenery glimpsed from a Pullman car but the greatly enhanced range of sites and sights made possible by automobility. And it aggressively colonized form after form, creating in the end a vast panoply of signs of essentialism, from the tartaned piper officially installed at the highway border-crossing to full-blown replicas of famous ships in Lunenburg Harbour. They all functioned to naturalize and to generalize contingent and contestable concepts of history and identity.

Yet, paradoxically, the historical categories and descriptions constructed within this much more broadly applied framework were themselves much more narrow and exclusivist. Constructing this official narrative entailed making interpretive choices, one of the most important of which was determining the beginning and the end of the story. For both Raddall and Bird, the beginning of the Nova Scotia story was marked by the mid-eighteenth-century arrival of English-speaking 'white races.' The middle of the story was the period which extended from the American Revolution to the late nineteenth century. The end of the story lay in the twentieth century, by and large seen as one of decline. For both writers, the heroic narratives that most urgently needed commemoration were those associated with the triumph of English-speaking Nova Scotians over their ethnically and racially defined adversaries: the 'Indians' (First Nations), French, and (ultimately) the Americans. Raddall's archetypal Nova Scotians were New Englanders who had settled parts of the province in the 1760s; Bird, in deference to his own family roots, would add the Yorkshire settlers to the mix. Both writers were concerned to reverse any notion of the Acadians as victims of British policy. Bird in *This Is Nova Scotia* blamed the Acadian Deportation on Quebec agents and Acadian priests, and in *Done at Grand Pré* (published in 1955 to coincide with the bicentennial of the Expulsion) concluded that an impartial examination of all the evidence would lead fair-minded people to believe that the Acadians had simply been the authors of their own misfortune. They had, after all, failed to behave properly 'as British citizens' in 1747.[96] The other culprits in the tragedy of 1755 were the aggressive New Englanders, whose 'expanding ambitions … produced the situation.'[97] Here was, within the official mnemonic apparatus, an account of 'objective truth' that, in Bird's reckoning, could be sharply distinguished from the 'biased diatribes' of 'bigots' and 'extremists.'[98] When Bird's provincial historic sites council came to preside over various claims to commemoration, a disproportionate number of Acadian applications were weeded out. On three occasions communities were allowed to switch pre-authorized designations of Acadian events to British themes. Even the Grand-Pré site, where, both Longfellow's romantic heroes and the tragedy of the Expulsion had earlier been simultaneously evoked, came to be conceived also as a site celebrating the English-speaking Planters who had supplanted the Acadians.[99]

Through the 1960s, the federal government, pursuing a combined project of economic redevelopment in the wake of Cape Breton coal mine closures and a rising francophone demand for bilingualism/biculturalism, would push through a multi-million-dollar massive reconstruction of Fortress Louisbourg – once feared and despised by the Protestants of the eastern seaboard of North America as a demonstration of the might of the Catholic French monarchy, and now oddly converted into a signifier of French/English amity and Canadian tolerance and bilingualism. Evangeline, epistemologically complicated and romanticized as she undoubtedly was, could still stand as a 'memory' of conflict and the deportation.[100] But at Louisbourg, visitors were invited to experience a decontextualized, depoliticized 'moment in time.' Patrick Wright, in his unjustly neglected 1985 study of British history-making, could have been thinking of Louisbourg when he remarked: 'National heritage,' like the 'utopianism from which it draws … involves positive energies which certainly can't be written off as ideology. It engages hopes, dissatisfactions, feelings of tradition and freedom, but it tends to do so in a way that diverts these potentially disruptive energies into the separate and regulated spaces of stately display.'[101] Such stately displays of pan-Canadian nationalism – which used 'historical resources' to bolster the federal government's official ideologies of bilingualism and regional development – became ever more prominent throughout Atlantic Canada after the 1960s, in a vast panoply of sites, festivals, and advertisements – a transition to yet another, even more state-centric variant of tourism/history, this time with Ottawa playing a much greater role.

4. Conclusion

From 1890 to 1960, superficially, no one logic had driven a tourism-oriented 'cashing in on antiquity.' Many turn-of-the-century Nova Scotians had had their eye on the tourist-as-potential-investor and -settler. The largely anglophone Dominion Atlantic Railway promoters of Evangeline targeted the New Englanders who had grown up with, or were still teaching, Longfellow's poem. Interwar tourism developers looked to a panoply of interrelated essentialisms

– Scottishness, the Golden Age of Sail, the rockbound coast, the Folk, whiteness – both as expressions of local sentiment and as traits differentiating this one tourism destination from its many North American competitors. The emergence of a provincial state-coordinated tourism/history complex – complete with stately homes, massive reconstructions, historical re-enactments, and commemorative plaques and festivals – meant that some pre-existing themes were materalized and eternalized within a seemingly natural, but in fact highly political, mnemonic apparatus. It is useful to hold this official history up to the critical light of social and cultural history, and especially to note the ways in which it marginalized and silenced awkward questions, inconvenient people, and difficult moments.

At the same time, it is important not to allow the necessary critique of tourism/history to overwhelm an appreciation of its contradictions and complexities – that is, to dehistoricize the very history of tourism/history. Although persistently influenced by an antimodern rejection of much of the twentieth-century world, and clearly exercising hegemonic powers of cultural selection, actors within the state were not fully consistent in, or fully conscious of, their own activities. There was a great deal of eclecticism and *bricolage* in the public past in Nova Scotia – a blurring of history and landscape, past and present, not to speak of fact and fiction. Overly rationalistic (and in a sense overly flattering) diagnoses of a coherent elite-dominated political strategy seem misplaced in this context. We confront, not a conspiracy, but the repetition, in one sphere after another, of homologous patterns of adaptation to an underlying socio-economic situation in which the generation of tourism commodities was a routine aspect of the functioning of the state. Even publicity minister Harold Connolly's brutally candid phrase – 'Let's cash in on antiquity' – did not in itself suggest just one program for tourism/history. 'Cashing in' might imply, not just the reaping of dividends from a few 'historic stocks,' but, over the longer term, the cultivation of a highly diversified portfolio. In essence, once tourism/history – the production and circulation of texts, images, and practices calculated to boost both state and business revenues – is fully operational, it involves, at both the most abstract and most concrete levels, a heightened degree of uncertainty. Markets are notoriously unpredictable beasts, prone to bouts of 'irrational exuberance' and equally profound depressions. Bird's eloquent description of the new framework – that of getting 'our historical assets on array in the shop window' – suggests the inherent *fragility* and *instability* of a fully market-driven history. If the function of public history is to provide saleable goods, supply-side mnemonics is the order of the day. Goods left in the shop window too long may become shop-worn, and over time unmarketable. They reach their 'best-before' date. As Cornelius Castoriadis observed,

'Neither "traditionalist," nor creative and revolutionary (despite the stories it tells on this subject), the epoch lives its relation to the past in a manner which does, as such, represent a historical innovation: of the most perfect exteriority.'[102] Many of the most popular commodities of the interwar period, such as poor old traffic-ridden Peggy's Cove, have reached this point. If the strength of applied neo-liberalism lies in the extension of market homologies through the social body, its weakness lies there as well, for brand loyalties are shifting sands upon which to build a lasting edifice.

For although it is historically important that Innocence achieved such stability as an interwar matrix that appealed massively both to insiders and outsiders, a crucial point – and the vital reason why beneath the superficial plurality of patterns in tourism/history there is in fact a more profound coherence – is that state functionaries felt both entitled and obliged to 'cash in' on *something*. Some of the stocks in the provincial portfolio might be high-risk penny stocks (like the Runic Stone). Some might be blue-chip, rather boring dividend-yielders (like the aging Evangeline product, a bit too closely tied to an unfashionable Eminent Victorian). And some might be big bond issues, like the massive Louisbourg enterprise, one of de-industrializing Cape Breton's larger employers. Yet surely a vital point is that, largely through the instrumentality of the state, they are *all* conceived as commodities, whose success or failure – and, indeed, 'truth' or 'falsity' – would be tested in the capitalist marketplace.

And their ultimate and inevitable replacement in the shop-window of the province by other historical assets could, at least in theory, be a matter of open debate, one much more realistically attuned to the costs as well as benefits of tourism/history as a strategy of development and a pattern of cultural politics. Even if the state-orchestrated tourism/history apparatus obviously functions to exclude human complexity and sustain inequitable property relations, people are often resistant and unpredictable, both as producers and consumers of 'historical resources.' In-depth genealogical research, for example – a major element of present-day historical tourism, especially after the 1970s U.S. television show *Roots* – can simply be an exercise in self-infatuated ancestor worship and one more technique of possessive individualism (as an individual comes to 'own' a decontextualized, personalized past), but it can also lead to a sense of one's self as connected to wider, intergenerational networks of people, validate the dignity and complexity of subaltern histories, and strengthen claims to empowerment. Fortress Louisbourg is undoubtedly partly in the business of providing easily digested 'historical' commodities and pseudo-experiences to tourists, but it has also functioned as a major research institution that has generated a much more complex vision of the culture and politics of an absolutist state. Evangeline was a fictional character who played to Victorian gender ideals and antimodern notions of feudalism. Yet the story of ethnic injustice and resistance kept alive by the poem could nonetheless stimulate more accurate and constructive interventions on the part of an oppressed minority. Widely disseminated romantic notions of Nova Scotia and of Canada as a whole as refuges from racism are delusive. Yet not only are they politically and ethically superior to 'founding white races' ideologies, they can also lead to constructive antiracist activism. Even Innocence, the belief that Nova Scotia and the Maritimes stand apart from the harsh realities of the twentieth and twenty-first centuries, has been enlisted in social struggles. Hegemonic history can only *appear* permanently to 'seal' the discourses it generates about the past.

For the ultimate irony is that, although tourism/history can be defined as a powerful attempt to repress even the memory of contradiction and conflict in history, it itself is subject to change and contradiction. Its hegemonic reading of history cannot be decisively 'sealed' from critique, or from historical time itself. Its unintended result, as more and more people come to depend on and identify with the state's expanding mnemonic portfolio for their very sense of identity, is that historical debate itself becomes much more deeply ingrained and generally politicized. If everyone knows that the state's management of tourism/history is influenced by present-day choices and interests as much as by historical research and scholarly values, then a multitude of groups can seek to influence public patterns of historical investment. What I want to put in the shop-window of the province may not be what you think should be there. And once we realize it is a shop-window, the rules of engagement change.

Revealing the choices and implicit ideologies which have influenced past constructions is not necessarily just another way of naively expressing the old humanist ideal – never far from the surface for many of us – that some day human beings will be able to shed the fetters of ideological history for something more honest, collective, and nurturing. It can also be much more modestly conceived as a first step to reflection on the possibility of opening up the politics of tourism/history to the challenge of a dialogue with both the tourist and the toured-upon. If the conversations around present-day tourism/history are today limited to a few planners and investors, outside their circle are found a large cast of extras, keen to gate-crash their tourism/history consensus. Tourism/history can, in principle at least, be deconstructed, critiqued, and reconstructed. It only *seems* to be capable of freezing, essentializing, and neutralizing the conflicting truths and inherent contradictions of actual history. History has a habit of confounding all, even those armed with the most impressive official mnemonic technologies, who think they have brought it to an end in vacuum-sealed packages. And the proponents of history/tourism will themselves some-day confront their own contradictory historicity.

NOTES

1 This chapter is based upon research funded by the Social Sciences and Research Council of Canada, Grant #410–02–1549. For a fuller discussion, see Ian McKay and Robin Bates, *In the Province of History: The Making of the Public Past in Twentieth-Century Nova Scotia* (Montreal and Kingston: McGill-Queen's University Press, 2010).

2 Harold Connolly to Angus L. Macdonald, 4 September 1946, Angus L. Macdonald Papers, Vol. 904, f.28 f/2, Public Archives of Nova Scotia (hereinafter PANS).

3 See *inter alia* Malcolm Chase and Christopher Shaw, eds., *The Imagined Past: History and Nostalgia* (Manchester and New York: Manchester University Press, 1989); John Davis, 'The Social Relations of the Production of History,' in Elizabeth Tonkin et al., eds., *History and Ethnicity* (London: Routledge, 1989); David Gross, *The Past in Ruins: Tradition and the Critique of Modernity* (Amherst: University of Massachusetts Press, 1992); Robert Hewison, *The Heritage Industry: Britain in a Climate of Decline* (London: Methuen, 1987); Eric Hobsbawm and Terence Ranger, eds., *The Invention of Tradition* (New York and Cambridge: Cambridge University Press, 1983); D. Horne, *The Great Museum: The Re-Presentation of History* (London: Pluto Press, 1984); Michael Kammen, *Mystic Chords of Memory: The Transformation of Tradition in American Culture* (New York: Alfred A. Knopf, 1991); Michael Kammen, *In the Past Lane: Historical Perspectives on American Culture* (New York: Oxford University Press, 1997); David Lowenthal, *The Heritage Crusade and the Spoils of History* (London: Viking, 1996); Martha Norkunas, *The Politics of Public Memory: Tourism, History, and Ethnicity in Monterey, California* (Albany: SUNY Press, 1993); Richard Terdiman, *Present Past: Modernity and the Memory Crisis* (Ithaca and London: Cornell University Press, 1993); Susan Porter Benson et al., eds., *Presenting the Past: Essays on History and the Public* (Philadelphia: Temple University Press, 1986); and Patrick Wright, *On Living in an Old Country: The National Past in Contemporary Britain* (London: Verso, 1985), among many other titles.

4 See, for instance, Louis Turner and John Ash, *The Golden Hordes: International Tourism and the Pleasure Periphery* (New York: St Martin's Press, 1976).

5 Shelley Baranowski and Ellen Furlough, Introduction to Shelley Baranowski and Ellen Furlough, eds., *Being Elsewhere: Tourism, Consumer Culture, and Identity in Modern Europe and North America* (Ann Arbor: University of Michigan Press, 2001), 10. For a most impressive collection, see David M. Wrobel and Patrick T. Long, eds., *Seeing and Being Seen: Tourism in the American West* (Lawrence: University Press of Kansas, 2001).

6 See, among other titles, Alisa Apostle, 'Canada, Vacations Unlimited: The Canadian Government Tourism Industry, 1934–1959,' PhD thesis, Queen's University, 2003; Michael Boudreau, 'A "Rare and Unusual Treat of Historical Significance":

The 1923 Hector Celebration and the Political Economy of the Past,' *Journal of Canadian Studies* 28, 4 (Winter 1993–4): 28–48; Ben Bradley, 'Roving Eyes: Circulation, Visuality, and Hierarchy of Place in East-Central British Columbia, 1910–1975,' MA thesis, University of Victoria, 2003; Michael Dawson, *Selling British Columbia: Tourism and Consumer Culture, 1980–1970* (Vancouver and Toronto: University of British Columbia Press, 2004); Karen Dubinsky, *The Second Greatest Disappointment: Honeymooning and Tourism at Niagara Falls* (Toronto: Between the Lines, 1999); Patricia Jasen, *Wild Things: Nature, Culture, and Tourism in Onttario, 1790–1914* (Toronto: University of Toronto Press, 1995); Alan MacEachern, *Natural Selections: National Parks in Atlantic Canada, 1935–1970* (Montreal and Kingston: McGill-Queen's University Press, 2001); Alan MacEachern, '"No Island Is an Island": A History of Tourism on Prince Edward Island,' MA thesis, Queen's University, 1991.

7 See Caroline-Isabelle Caron, 'Se créer des ancêtres. Les écrits historiques et généalogiques des de Forest et des Forest d'Amérique du Nord, 19e et 20e siècles,' PhD thesis, McGill University, 2001; Claire Dolan, ed., *Événement, identité, histoire* (Sillery: Septentrion, 1991); Alan Gordon, *Making Public Pasts: The Contested Terrain of Montreal's Public Memories, 1891–1930* (Montreal and Kingston: McGill-Queen's University Press, 2001); Richard Kicksee, '"Scaled Down to Size": Negotiating Amerindian Participation in Canada's Centennial Celebrations, 1967,' MA thesis, Queen's University, 1995; Viv Nelles, *The Art of Nation-Building: Pageantry and Spectacle at Quebec's Tercentenary* (Toronto: University of Toronto Press, 1999); Gerald Pocius, *A Place to Belong: Community Order and Everyday Space in Calvert, Newfoundland* (Kingston and Montreal: McGill-Queen's University Press, 1991); Andrew Sackett, 'Doing History in the "Great Cyclorama of God": Tourism and the Presentation of the Past in Twentieth-Century St. Andrews, New Brunswick,' MA thesis, Queen's University, 1995; Gerald Sider and Gavin Smith, eds., *Between History and Histories: The Making of Silences and Commemorations* (Toronto: University of Toronto Press, 1997); C.J. Taylor, *Negotiating the Past: The Making of Canada's National Historic Parks and Sites* (Montreal and Kingston: McGill-Queeen's University Press, 1990); Jonathan Vance, *Death So Noble: Memory, Meaning, and the First World War* (Vancouver: University of British Columbia Press, 1997); Jay White, 'Revisiting the Land of Evangeline: Early Nova Scotia Tourist Literature, 1850–1930,' paper presented to the Open Conference for the History of the Book in Canada Project, Quebec City, May 2001.

8 Mary Louise Pratt, *Imperial Eyes: Travel Writing and Transculturation* (London and New York: Routledge, 1992), 6.

9 On these interesting travellers, see H.R. Casgrain, *Un Pèlerinage au pays d'Évangéline* (Quebec, 1887); John Arthur de Gobineau, *Voyage à Terre-Neuve, suivi de la chasse au caribou* (Paris, 1861); trans. in Michael Wilkshaw, ed., *A Gentleman*

to the Outports: Gobineau and Newfoundland (Ottawa: Carleton University Press, 1972); and most especially Barbara Le Blanc, *Postcards from Acadie: Grand-Pré, Evangeline and the Acadian Identity* (Kentville, NS: Gaspereau Press, 2003).

10 Joseph Howe, *Western and Eastern Rambles: Travel Sketches of Nova Scotia* (Halifax, 1821; ed. M.G. Parks, Toronto: University of Toronto Press 1973), 92–3. For a pathbreaking recent discussion, see Jeffrey McNairn, 'Meaning and Markets: Hunting, Economic Development and British Imperialism in Maritime Travel Narratives to 1870,' *Acadiensis* 34, 2 (Spring 2005): 3–25.

11 See James H. Morrison, 'American Tourism in Nova Scotia, 1871–1940,' *Nova Scotia Historical Review* 2, 2 (1982): 40–51.

12 Richard Lewes Dashwood, *Chiploquorgan: Or, Life By the Camp Fire in the Dominion of Canada and Newfoundland* (London, 1872), 77.

13 See White, 'Revisiting the Land of Evangeline,' 6.

14 See Dona Brown's highly suggestive *Inventing New England: Regional Tourism in the Nineteenth Century* (Washington and London: Smithsonian Institution Press, 1995), especially chapter 6.

15 Nova Scotia, *Journals of the House of Assembly* (hereafter *JHA*), Tourism Reports, 1922–39. In 1899, New Hampshire, with a population of 411,588, was recording 174,000 summer visitors. Brown, *Inventing New England*, 155.

16 An important theme a broader North American history of tourism could pursue would be that of the northward march of a 'therapeutic frontier,' pushing up from New York and southern New England first into coastal New Brunswick, Quebec, and Nova Scotia; then into the 'provincial north,' and finally – in the 1990s – extending to Ellesmere Island.

17 Brown, *Inventing New England*, 201.

18 Halifax *Chronicle*, 14 June 1938.

19 White, 'Revisiting the Land of Evangeline.'

20 See *All-Expense Vacation Trips by Ships, Trains, and Motors to Nova Scotia and Evangeline Land* (Boston, 1928).

21 Report, Nova Scotia Tourist Association, 1923, in Nova Scotia, *JHA* (1924): 15.

22 A problem local tourist historians have yet to fully overcome is that of assessing the proportions of Canadian and American tourists in the province. Until the late 1950s, the Canadian totals were inflated by the inclusion of all automobile traffic coming across the New Brunswick/Nova Scotia border, much of which would have consisted not of 'tourists' as customarily defined, but rather commuters.

23 See the Halifax *Herald*, special edition, *Nova Scotia, The Atlantic Pier of America* (Halifax, 1930).

24 Herbert Crosskill, *Nova Scotia: Its Climate, Resources and Advantages. Being a General Description of the Province, for the Information of Intending Emigrants* (Halifax, 1872), 1.

25 R.R. McLeod, *Markland or Nova Scotia. Its History, Natural Resources and Native Beauties* (Halifax, 1903), 247.

26 Crosskill, *Nova Scotia*, 2–3.

27 Marked-up copy of *Chiploquorgan* at the Public Archives of Nova Scotia, Halifax.

28 Halifax *Herald*, 21 March 1913. The Tory newspaper's outrage was not softened by the endorsement the Liberal premier had given the book, which was, despite its title, a generally admiring portrait of a progressive province.

29 For a more general discussion of progressivism in the province, see Ian McKay, 'The 1910s: The Stillborn Triumph of Progressive Reform,' in E.R. Forbes and D.A. Muise, eds., *The Atlantic Provinces in Confederation* (Toronto and Fredericton: University of Toronto Press and Acadiensis Press, 1993): 192–229.

30 See Paul B. Williams, 'A Vision of Progress and Nostalgia: The Halifax Memorial Tower,' *International Journal of Heritage Studies* 9, 3 (September 2003): 243–65.

31 G.F. Parker, *A Tripod Trip along the South Shore of Nova Scotia* (n.p., n.d. [1902?]), 21, 24.

32 Lady Aberdeen, *My Canadian Journal 1872–8* (London, 1891; Toronto: Coles Pub., 1971), 103; Charles G.D. Roberts, *The Land of Evangeline and the Gateways Thither* (Kentville: Dominion Atlantic Railway, n.d. [1890s]), 51.

33 A.L. Hardy, *The Evangeline Land* (Kentville, n.d. [c. 1902]); Halifax and South Western Railway, *The Ocean Shore*, n.d. (c. 1907), 7.

34 Margaret Warner Morley, *Down North and Up Along* (New York, 1912), 134.

35 Crosskill, *Nova Scotia*, 74–5.

36 *Report*, Nova Scotia Tourist Association, 1923: 21.

37 For a fascinating discussion of a parallel pattern in British Columbia, see Dawson, *Selling British Columbia.*

38 See Naomi Griffiths, 'Longfellow's Evangeline: The Birth and Acceptance of a Legend,' in P.A. Buckner and David Frank, eds., *The Acadiensis Reader*, 2, *Atlantic Canada after Confederation* (1985), and Le Blanc, *Postcards*, chapter 3. This was so much the case that the major Acadian newspaper would come to be called 'Évangéline.' For an excellent visual representation of the Evangéline phenomenon, see *Evangéline's Quest*, dir. Ginette Pellerin (National Film Board of Canada, 1996). In his imagination, Longfellow imagined towering forests where there were, in fact, coastal flats; misconceived the operations of the *aboiteau* technology through which the Acadians prosecuted their remarkable marshlands agriculture; and even came up with a name for his key heroine – Evangeline – unknown in eighteenth-century Acadie.

39 Le Blanc, *Postcards*, 61.

40 Later North American literary landscapes developed within tourism/history – such as Monterey, California ('Steinbeck-land') or Hannibal, Missouri ('Twain-land') – actually do not go as far as did 'The Land of Evangeline,' in that they at least memorialize places that had a factual connection with actual people. The Nova Scotia

promotion was precocious because it effaced the fact/fiction boundary, creating a mnemonic landscape based on a character who had never existed, and created by a poet who, when he wrote his epic, had never in fact visited the province. For U.S. parallels, see Norkunas, *The Politics of Public Memory*, chapter 3.

41 Roberts, *The Land of Evangline and the Gateways Thither*, 1.

42 Beckles Willson, *Nova Scotia: The Province That Has Been Passed By* (1913), 70.

43 See Parker, *A Tripod Trip*, 22.

44 The publication of J.B. Brebner's classic *New England's Outpost: Acadia before the Conquest of Canada* (New York: Coumbia University, 1927; reprinted Hamden, CT: Archon Books, 1965) complicated the narrative of British perfidy by characterizing the Expulsion, amid a vast range of geo-political factors, as the 'fatal fruition of New England's interest and policy' (222). In John Mack Faragher, *A Great and Noble Scheme: The Tragic Story of the Expulsion of the French Acadians from Their American Homeland* (New York: W.W. Norton, 2005), the Expulsion is seen as a story of 'ethnic cleansing' in 'early America.' Taken together with Longfellow's waning popularity, such historiographical changes made it increasingly difficult to incorporate the Expulsion into American nationalist narratives.

45 Elizabeth B. Chase, *Over the Border* (1884), 22.

46 That is, there is (1) the reader's reception of Chase's description; (2) Chase's *anticipatory* reception of a landscape she herself has not seen, but can imagine, based on (3) Longfellow's 'take' on a landscape he himself had not seen but could only imagine, based in turn (4) on T.C. Haliburton's second-hand account of eighteenth-century Nova Scotia, dependent on (5) the patchy and (for him) somewhat inaccessible narratives of those who actually experienced it.

47 Betty D. Thornley, *Acadia* (n.p., n.d.).

48 As Le Blanc points out, such indulgence of the romanticism of others reached its limits: 'While locals were not disturbed by tourists invading the land to revel in romance and nostalgia, they were definitely not interested in having Acadians settle in the land of Evangeline. The presence of real Acadians was not as acceptable as the dreamlike image of a romantic Evangeline haunting the Grand-Pré landscape' (*Postcards*, 85).

49 There is more work to be done on this. See for general indications Jean Daigle, *The Acadians of the Maritimes: Thematic Studies* (Moncton: University of Moncton, Centre d'études acadiennes, 1982); Dolan, ed., *Événement, identité, histoire*.

50 Nova Scotia as the United States' northern therapeutic frontier also worked in other ways less romantic and striking than the Evangeline Promotion. The American vacationers' colonization of the Atlantic seaboard had spilled over the Canadian border, in smaller resorts, at Chester and Baddeck, that appealed to those who did not want, or could not afford, places closer to Boston and New York. The Intercolonial Railway in 1908 did lure Americans to Cape Breton with the promise of

quaint Highlanders, speaking Gaelic. Nova Scotians also competed with the White Mountain resorts for the favour of Americans fleeing the subtle menace of neurasthenia and the less abstract nuisance of hay fever. For hay-fever correspondence, see Grand Hotel Papers, Dalhousie University Archives, MS-4–210, 'Correspondence 1898–1982,' John Peacock to A.W. Eakins, 10 April 1900.

51 See E.R. Forbes, *Challenging the Regional Stereotype: Essays on the 20th Century Maritimes* (Fredericton: Acadiensis Press, 1989).

52 Brown, *Inventing New England*, Epilogue. The parallels between the discovery of Cape Cod as described by Brown and that of Nova Scotia's South Shore are uncanny.

53 See Michael Berkowitz, 'A "New Deal" for Leisure: Making Mass Tourism during the Great Depression,' in Baranowski and Furlough, eds., *Being Elsewhere*, 185–212.

54 See Ian McKay, 'Among the Fisherfolk: J.F.B. Livesay and the Invention of Peggy's Cove,' *Journal of Canadian Studies* 23, 1/2 (Spring/Summer 1988): 23–45.

55 See Ian McKay, *The Quest of the Folk: Antimodernism and Cultural Selection in Twentieth-Century Nova Scotia* (Kingston and Montreal: McGill-Queen's University Press, 1994).

56 Albert Deane, 'How to See Scotland without Crossing the Atlantic – Impressions Gained While Roaming the Province of Leisurely Loveliness – Nova Scotia,' unidentified clipping [1950], Macdonald Papers, vol. 972, f.40–2.

57 I.H. Macdonald to Angus L. Macdonald, 18 August 1952, Macdonald Papers, vol. 972, f.40–2/11; Angus L. Macdonald to I.H. Macdonald, 28 August 1952, Macdonald Papers, vol. 972, f.40–2/10.

58 Deane, 'How to See Scotland without Crossing the Atlantic.'

59 For a more complete discussion, see McKay, 'Tartanism Triumphant: The Construction and Uses of Scottishness in Nova Scotia, 1934–1954,' *Acadiensis* 21, 2 (1992): 5–47. Had they pursued similar strategies, New Jersey would presumably have found and promoted its essential *Jerseyness* and New Hampshire its underlying *Englishness*.

60 For this important institution, see Apostle, 'Canada, Vacations Unlimited.'

61 Note the discussion à propos of Canadian attitudes towards Americans in Karen Dubinsky, '"Everybody Likes Canadians": Canadians, Americans, and the Post-World War II Travel Boom,' in Baranowski and Furlough, eds., *Being Elsewhere*, 320–47.

62 For example, in the 1923 festivities surrounding the anniversary of the landing of the *Hector*, the province's first large publicly funded historical extravaganza, this vessel carrying Scots to Nova Scotia was re-presented not just as a proud moment in Nova Scotia, but also in Canadian history: the governor-general himself was on hand to commemorate this Scottish-Canadian equivalent of the *Mayflower*. See

Boudreau, 'A "Rare and Unusual Treat of Historical Significance."' The kilted Canadian soldiers in the Great War of 1914–18, many of whom found their kilts to be less than ideal accoutrements for trench warfare, also tied together the themes of the Romance of the Scots and the Valour of the Canadians. For an important recent statement on the theme of antimodernism and Canadian nationalism, see Benedict Anderson, 'Staging Antimodernism in the Age of High Capitalist Nationalism,' in Lynda Jessup, ed., *Antimodernism and Artistic Experience: Policing the Boundaries of Modernity* (Toronto: University of Toronto Press, 2001), 97–103.

63 For a fascinating glimpse of the fate of the poem 'Evangeline,' see Le Blanc, *Postcards*, chapters 7 and 8.

64 Thornley, *Acadia*.

65 Dominion Atlantic Railway, *High Lights of Nova Scotia History*, entry under 'Membertou.'

66 *JHA* (1949): 68; (1956): 50.

67 Taylor, *Negotiating the Past*, 118. See also C.W. Jeffreys, 'The Reconstruction of the Port Royal Habitation of 1605–13,' *Canadian Historical Review* 20 (December 1939): 369–77.

68 Ella K. Cork, Memorandum to the Members of the Historical Committee of the Canadian Tourism Association, 21 June 1950, Historic Sites Advisory Council Papers, MG 20, vol. 933, PANS.

69 J. Murray Lawson, *Description of the Runic Stones Found Near Yarmouth, Nova Scotia* (Yarmouth, 1898), 2–3.

70 Olaf Strandwold, *The Yarmouth Stone* (n.p. [State of Washington], n.d. [1934]).

71 Ian McKay, 'History and the Tourist Gaze: The Politics of Commemoration in Nova Scotia, 1935–1964,' *Acadiensis* 22, 2 (Spring 1993): 102–38. Even the print was destroyed.

72 New Glasgow *Evening News*, 23 August 1951.

73 C.H. Wright to W.R. Bird, with enclosure, 9 March 1951, Historic Sites Advisory Council Papers, MG 20, vol. 933, PANS.

74 James D. How to W.R. Bird and members of the Historic Sites Advisory Council of Nova Scotia, n.d., Historic Sites Advisory Council Papers, MG 20, vol. 933, PANS.

75 See Michael Wallace, 'Visiting the Past: History Museums in the United States,' in Benson et al., eds., *Presenting the Past*, esp. 147–8.

76 McKay, 'Tartanism.'

77 Herein lies a theme which might well be explored across North America: the role of historical novelists in making their romances 'come alive' in tourist settings. In Prince Edward Island, the Anne of Green Gables phenomenon suggests parallels with Evangeline; in both cases it is significant that a young woman is offered up as a signifier of regional essence. An interesting parallel to pursue would be that

of New Orleans, where Frances Parkinson Keyes played a pivotal role in developing tourism/history in the French Quarter. In this case, the novelist had the private means to make her historical vision 'come true,' whereas like-minded Canadians have more commonly had to enjoy access to the state.

78 Thomas Raddall, Brief Submitted to the Royal Commission on Post-War Development and Rehabiltiation, on behalf of the Town of Liverpool, NS, 27 July 1923. Thomas Raddall Papers, Dal MS. 2–202, File Addresses, 27 July 1943, Dalhousie University Archives.

79 An Address by Thomas Raddall to the Commercial Club, Halifax, NS, on the subject 'Halifax and the Tourist Trade,' 15 November 1945, Raddall Papers, Dal MS. 2–202, File Addresses, 1945, Dalhousie University Archives.

80 W.R. Bird to Ruth Fraser, 4 February 1972, Bird Scrapbooks, Dalhousie University Archives.

81 W.R. Bird to E.A. Batchelor, 20 October 1948, Historic Sites Advisory Council Papers, MG 20, vol. 933, PANS.

82 W.R. Bird to R.L. Stanfield, 25 April 1957, Historic Sites Advisory Council Papers, MG 20, vol. 933, PANS.

83 Winnipeg *Tribune*, 10 June 1950.

84 W.R. Bird to R.L. Stanfield, 16 December 1960, Historic Sites Advisory Council Papers, MG 10, vol. 934, PANS.

85 Dominion Atlantic Railway, *High Lights of Nova Scotia History*.

86 John Quinpool [J.W. Regan], *First Things in Acadia, 'The Birthplace of a Continent'* (Halifax: First Things Publishers, 1936). Note the discussion of 'Being First' in Lowenthal, *The Heritage Crusade*, chapter 8.

87 Will R. Bird, *This Is Nova Scotia* (Toronto: Ryerson Press, 1950), 77.

88 W.R. Bird, 'The Original Nova Scotians,' Halifax *Sunday Leader*, 19, 26 July 1925.

89 Thomas Raddall, *Roger Sudden* (1944; Toronto: McClelland and Stewart, 1972), 357, 166. Of course, this is admittedly not necessarily Raddall's own voice. But his own activities within the Historic Sites Advisory Council confirm that, for him, the history of Nova Scotia principally had to do with white people.

90 *JHA*, Report of the Department of Industry and Publicity (1944): 10.

91 Untitled note on Shubenacadie [probably written by W.R. Bird], 8 August 1949, Historic Sites Advisory Council Papers, MG 20, vol. 933, PANS.

92 W.R. Bird to R.L. Stanfield, 8 February 1963, Historic Sites Advisory Council Papers, MG 20, vol. 934, PANS.

93 Report of the Historic Sites Advisory Council for the Period ending 31 March 1960. *JHA* (1961): 26.

94 W.R. Bird to R.L. Stanfield, 18 August 1959, Historic Sites Advisory Council, MG 20, vol. 934, PANS.

95 *JHA*, 'Tourism Reports,' 1951–70.

96 W.R. Bird, *This Is Nova* Scotia, 157; *Done at Grand Pré* (Toronto: Ryerson Press, 1955), vii. That one could hardly behave as a 'British citizen' in northern North America in the eighteenth century eluded him. In fact, even the category 'Canadian citizen' did not achieve legal existence until 1947.

97 Ibid., 170.

98 Ibid., 2, 172. Here Bird was popularizing, in reductionist form, Brebner's thesis.

99 Historic Sites Advisory Council, 13 September 1957, MG 20, vol. 934, PANS; Le Blanc, *Postcards*, chapter 8, documents the ongoing debates over the meaning of Grand-Pré.

100 On the interesting transformations within the Evangeline tradition, see G.J. Ashworth, *On Tragedy and Renaissance: The Role of Loyalist and Acadian Heritage Interpretations in Canadian Place Identities* (Groningen: Geo Pers, 1993); C.A. Brasseaux, *The Search for Evangeline: Birth and Evolution of the Evangeline Myth* (Shreveport, LA: Blue Heron, 1988).

101 Wright, *On Living in an Old Country*, 78.

102 Cornelius Castoriadis, 'The Crisis of Western Societies,' *Telos* no. 53 (Fall 1982): 26–7.

15 'Leaving the Past Behind': From Old Quebec to 'La Belle Province'[1]

NICOLE NEATBY

On one level, one could argue that tourist advertisers of the government of Quebec were unremarkable: like their counterparts in other regions of Canada they were in the business of promoting their province as a tourist destination, trying to lure foreigners – largely Americans – to visit Quebec.[2] Like many other Canadian governments, the Quebec state got gradually involved in the tourism business in the late 1910s, at an accelerated pace in the 1920s, and was even more fully committed to the industry with the outbreak of the Depression. Those who have studied the history of tourism both in Quebec and elsewhere point to the fact that the past was a marketing tool from the beginning. Indeed, marketers were quick to understand that travellers were not only keen to visit foreign lands but also wanted to be transported to foreign times as well. The antimodernist motivations of the city-dwelling tourists, at the end of the nineteenth century and in the first few decades of the twentieth century, have been a recurring explanation to account for the seduction of destinations that could offer sharp contrasts to urban and industrial landscapes. As several scholars have made clear, Quebec, along with other destinations on the North American continent, was well positioned to attract those sensitive to the lures of antimodernist scenery both natural and cultural.[3] But tourist promoters overall did not only take their cues from visitors' hopes and expectations. Their marketing initiatives were also influenced by developments at home. In Quebec,[4] tourism, hand in hand with a particular vision of the past, was enlisted, at times explicitly and others indirectly by government promoters and policy makers, to strengthen a particular and mutating sense of French-Canadian national identity.

The few historians[5] who have studied tourism in Quebec have focused their attention on the ideas and initiatives of members of the French-Canadian traditional nationalist elite, who, starting in the 1920s and more so in the 1930s, viewed tourism promotion as a means to a superior and pressing end. They point out that members of this elite believed that, through tourism, it would be possible to revitalize the past traditions and culture of their forefathers and so help to secure French Canadians' distinct national identity. They would use tourists' expectations to rejuvenate what they saw as the authentic Quebec – a nation they considered to be in direct opposition to a particular North American present. The hope would be that when French Canadians themselves saw this 'Old Quebec' promoted by the state, it would not simply conjure up nostalgic evocations of the 'good old days' but would also serve as an inspirational spur to regenerate what made them truly French Canadian.

Geographers,[6] who have shown the most sustained interest in Quebec tourism, have also recognized the influence of specific members of Quebec's cultural elite in the promotion of this brand of tourism. However, their attention has essentially been drawn to the initiatives and policies of the provincial government, which transformed the Quebec built landscape[7] to attract the ever-increasing number of tourists over the twentieth century. They confirm the fact that the Quebec state's gradual intervention in the field of tourism, starting in the 1920s, was geared towards 'highlighting the rural identity of the countryside for the benefit of the tourists.'[8] However, when analysing how nationalism has influenced the marketing strategies of Quebec as a tourist destination, both historians and geographers have tended to focus on the impact of *traditional* nationalism during the early decades of the twentieth century. They ignore initiatives that reflect a more multifaceted understanding of what being French Canadian meant at the time. Closely linked to this is the fact that they show less interest in analysing how the evolution of nationalist thought up to the 1960s played out on Quebec tourism promotion. In fact, for some scholars, the 'Old Quebec' marketing brand survived well up to the end of the 1960s.[9]

My research leads to a different conclusion. For the period leading up to the late 1950s, the influential government tourist promoters, imbued as many of them were with traditional nationalist values, did continue to picture the province as 'Old Quebec,' although a more thorough reading of government publicity forces us to qualify this portrayal. There is evidence to suggest that government promoters made some attempts to point to the province's industrial expansion, increasingly offering some signs of greater change to come in the way they represented the past and present. And these were to come in the 1960s, the years of the Quiet Revolution. Nationalist debates over the meaning of Quebec's national identity and its past clearly led some government tourism promoters to re-evaluate the way Quebec should be marketed to visitors. In their eyes, relying on the past no longer appeared to be the effective and appropriate marketing strategy it once had been. It becomes apparent that they wanted to repackage the product in order to more explicitly reflect the contemporary Quebec and the changing French-Canadian national identity.

Drawing Up the Invitations to Old Quebec

The Quebec government got involved in the tourism industry as the Roads Department was officially enlisted to develop it in the 1920s. In short, it had become 'tourist conscious' as it recognized that 'tourism [was] an undisputed source of economic good for all.'[10] In 1926 it housed a newly created Provincial Tourist Bureau. This administrative reconfiguration speaks volumes about the role the state considered it should play at this stage and the priority it gave to this field of activity. The Department would on the one hand act as an 'enabler' making it easier for the ever-growing number of motorized American tourists[11] to visit the province and guiding them to what it considered the most alluring sites.[12] But by way of its Tourist Bureau it would also quickly take on a more proactive role initiating ever more extensive publicity campaigns. Some of these involved producing ads and tourist brochures. Others were aimed at beautifying the countryside for the benefit of tourists. In fact, by 1922, the department had already launched an 'Embellishment campaign' specifically targeting rural Quebec. It involved distributing lime for the purpose of whitewashing buildings and ornamental trees to municipalities and farmers who owned land along the highways.[13]The department also worked to modernize the countryside hospitality infrastructure, focusing on its small hotels and restaurants. To that end, in 1926, the newly established Hotel Improvement Services invited innkeepers to follow the advice contained in its 60-page booklet entitled *L'Hôtellerie moderne*. It also published a 176-page recipe book, *La bonne cuisine canadienne*, meant to teach innkeepers and restaurant owners basic cooking skills and encourage them to offer a distinctive local cuisine.[14] To assist them in these endeavours, the bureau also offered frontline hosts the services of its 'lady lecturers' who, upon invitation, would provide them with advice on how to improve their establishments.

This newly emerging government involvement was influential in many ways. Not only did it contribute to improving accessibility and services for the growing number of incoming tourists, but by choosing which roads to build or to improve, producing the first guides, and crafting the first government advertisements, the Roads Department was in fact laying out the ground and orienting the direction of tourism promotion policies for years to come. It was also influencing what tourists would consider worth the trip, or shaping the tourist gaze.[15] More to the point, it would add its government-sanctioned image of the province to other representations of Quebec available to tourists, namely those produced by the private sector, further influencing what they would expect to see before setting off on their trip.

In the advertisements produced by the large private companies operating in Quebec in the 1920s, such as Canadian Pacific Railways, Canada Steamship Lines, and the Canadian National Railways, the province was systematically labelled as 'Old Quebec.'[16] Coming to Quebec was like walking into the past, 'a trip to yesterday,'[17] where 'History is everywhere.'[18] Although the past was more often than not of 'no fixed address,' when it was located, prospective tourists were told that the 'Old World atmosphere' that would surround them in Quebec was that of a romanticized seventeenth-century France. Promoters would occasionally circumscribe the destination of this time travel even further to Normandy. The 'beautiful religious festivals ... sturdy reverent peasantry ... ox-drawn ploughs and dog-drawn cars'[19] they would come across during their travels would bring them back to those vaguely bounded bygone days. Clearly then the past was Quebec's major selling point. The city of Montreal was not overlooked. Yet in these advertisements, it appeared essentially to provide an appealing contrast to what tourists could expect to find elsewhere. As for what the companies would offer, they promised all the modern amenities tourists could hope for, allowing them to enjoy 'A Gem of the Old World, transplanted in America'[20] with 'every comfort of Parisian service.'[21]

In many ways, the government initiatives in representing Quebec did not depart from this corporate imaging of the province. Essentially, the Tourist Bureau adopted the 'Old Quebec' trademark, making use of the past and history to lure tourists to the province. In line with this branding, visitors would learn that Quebec city was a 'city of remembrance,' 'a medieval French city' living 'in the memory ... of old France.'[22] Continuing into the 1930s, they were invited to 'the Old Historic Province of Quebec'[23] and told that Quebec's 'picturesqueness lifts you almost completely out of the Twentieth Century into the age of the French regime.'[24] One headline declared quite simply: 'Quebec! The very name is History.'[25] And the accompanying illustrations of handlooms, spinning wheels, handicrafts, calèches, oxen, and dog carts gave them a taste of the Old World decor that awaited them.

The Roads Department, however, did much more than promote the province as 'Old.' As we have seen, it 'worked on' the countryside and, by doing so, expanded the Quebec tourist landscape in such a way as to meet the expectations of those looking to travel in time as far back as the seventeenth century and as far away as France. It is no coincidence that in 1929, for the first time, motorists were given the opportunity to safely circle the Gaspé Peninsula with the construction of the 555-mile-long Perron highway. Indeed, by opening up to travellers this region where traditional fishing and agriculture were still central to the economy, the Roads Department was in effect further extending the land mass of what it was promoting as 'Old Quebec.' From then on, the Gaspé was given pride of place in Quebec government publicity, labelled as a destination where 'modern progress has not stripped it of its natural picturesqueness,' a place where tourists will come across a people who 'live the lives their forefathers ... lived in centuries gone by.'[26] In line with this attempt at extending the frontiers of traditional Quebec, the Roads Department also took some initiatives in making the Île d'Orléans more accessible by building a highway in 1927 linking its isolated rural communities. And a few years later, in 1935, reaching the Île d'Orléans itself was made that much easier when a bridge was erected, linking it to the mainland on the Côte Beaupré.

It was also at this time (1932) that the Roads Department built a highway to the Lac Saint-Jean region. As with the Gaspé, this region was one that could easily be promoted as containing the prized features of 'Old Quebec.' It was more often than not identified as 'Maria Chapdelaine Country' inspired by the Louis Hémon novel (1916) of the same name.[27] This novel presented Quebec as a rural province, devoutly faithful to its traditions and the Catholic Church. Shortly after, in 1938, the inhabitants of the community of Peribonka inaugurated a Maria Chapdelaine museum in the home of the Bédard family in which Hémon had resided and worked during his stay in the Lac Saint-Jean area. Eva Bouchard, a relative of the Bédard family,[28] worked in the museum, convinced that she had been the model for the novel's central character, and presented herself to tourists as such. Government promoters never officially endorsed her claim but nor did they contradict this self-appointed 'muse.'[29] One can only speculate that since this innocuous, albeit undocumented, young woman's speculation served to further cement the 'Old Quebec' label, officials reasoned it did not warrant censorship.

All this being said, a closer reading of the early Tourist Bureau guidebooks offered a less one-dimensional portrait of Quebec's tourist landscape. Indeed, in the very same tourist brochure in which Quebec was described as a 'city of remembrance,' a 'medieval city,' it was also characterized as the 'principal industrial and commercial city of the province after Montreal,'[30] providing evidence to confirm its status as a metropolitan centre. Tourists were informed that when travelling Quebec roads, they would note that 'most up-to-date characteristics in commerce, industry and agriculture blend with a touch of ancient days particular to French Canada.'[31] In addition to historic sites, the guidebooks also invited the motorists to take the time to visit newly emerging cities with their newly developing industries: 'If sufficient time is available, a side trip to Shawinigan and Grand'Mère will prove very instructive.' Shawinigan, they were told, 'owes its birth to water power development. A number of industries are established there,' while 'Grand'Mère, pop 8 000[,] has the same characteristics, and, owing to very up-to-date management, is a fast growing town.'[32] No information on their history was offered to entice the visitor. In other words, tourists were encouraged to visit areas where modernity and progress were the main attractions. During that time, visitors could also avail themselves of a 90-page publication entitled *Quebec, French Canadian Province: A Harmony of Beauty, History and Progress* (1927). While Beauty and History were undoubtedly given pride of place, in the very same booklet readers were informed that the habitants – the ultimate incarnation of Old Quebec – no longer existed. Indeed, they would learn that 'under modern conditions, they [the habitants] have both undergone such a rapid change that they have now almost vanished,' mostly because of the 'accessibility to the cities by automobile.' The habitant had now 'evolved into a practical farmer.' Not only that, 'the folk dances and songs are disappearing before photographs, pianos and modern dances' and 'the spinning wheel has been removed to the attic.'[33]

However, another 12-page tourist booklet entitled *The Old World at Your Door* promoted what it labelled 'The Historic Quebec.' In this instance, it chose to highlight the traditional Quebec. Here the readers would learn that, in rural Quebec, the 'population ... has most faithfully kept the traditions, language, customs and dress of the past.'[34] Prospective tourists could very well have wondered what they would encounter when they reached the countryside. Would they come across an 'Old Quebec' or one in which traditions of yesteryear were fast disappearing?

How can one account for this double imaging of the province? It definitely contravened tourism promotion best practice, which is all about clear, simple, and direct branding. There are instances when officials at the Roads Department suggested that tourists needed to be made aware of the province's impressive economic successes as it 'combines a very developed industrial and commercial activity. [It] has the largest city in Canada and a large number of less populated centers no less active.'[35] Statistics covering most areas of economic development in the province certainly bore this out. 'The value of manufacturing doubled between 1901 and 1919 and the number of workers in manufacturing increased from 101 600 to 125 400 in 1921.'[36]The province was also undergoing extraordinary urbanization. The proportion of city dwellers 'increased from 36.1 per cent in 1901 to 63.1 per cent in 1931 and Montreal quintupled between 1881 and 1931 ... which represented 28.4 per cent of the province's population.'[37] Thus could it be that tourist promoters were trying to reconcile what they knew would make Quebec popular among tourists with what they thought these tourists should also appreciate about the province's industrial development? Or was it that government tourist promoters believed that what made Quebec distinct and attractive included modernity as well? Finally, perhaps, were they concerned that inviting tourists to only visit an 'Old Quebec' would represent a form of false advertising? Further evidence suggests another factor that overshadows the others. Indeed those in charge of promoting Quebec as a tourist destination were in effect tasked with a double mandate as they could not ignore the overarching priorities of the department in which they were ensconced. These involved, among others, attracting capital investment. As a result, its publications end up addressing two distinct sets of readers: prospective tourists and businessmen. Nothing illustrates this better than the information about economic output in commercial and industrial activity presented in the Department's most comprehensive guidebook, *Along Quebec Highways, Tourist Guide* – the 900-page one published in 1930.[38] Not only was this text loaded with detailed information about the economic output of the province's various industries, complete with numerous tables and statistics, but readers were also told that Quebec's 'industrious, laboring population, absolutely impervious to the theories of socialism, is, perhaps, [its] most valuable asset from the economic and social points of view.'[39] Tourists may very well have found such information interesting from a sociological point of view, but it obviously would speak much more directly to the self-interest of business investors.

It should be noted that there is no evidence to suggest that tourists took the advice of the guides to visit newly developing industrial towns.[40] Officials regularly pointed to the fact that travellers were increasingly heading for the countryside. And the fact that the emphasis on 'Old Quebec' would continue to be reinforced in government promotional material and through other initiatives only confirms the primacy of the identification that was established right from the start between Quebec as a tourist destination and the past.

The 'Old Quebec' Product Needs a Face-Lift

In order to better understand the primacy of the 'Old Quebec' marketing brand, one must turn also to the wider social context in which tourist promoters were operating. During the 1920s and increasingly by the early 1930s, there were louder and louder voices among the Quebec traditional elite arguing that the Quebec government needed to take measures to revitalize what they perceived to be Quebec's authentic culture – a traditional culture based on a rural society with a strong Catholic Church and a dominant and vibrant French language and culture.[41] On some level, these critics subscribed to the famous and often quoted line in *Maria Chapdelaine* in which readers were told that 'in this land of Quebec naught shall die and naught shall suffer change.'[42] In their minds, this observation should be read as a wise and timely motto to guide social behaviour and orient government policies. As many historians point out, these traditionalists were not advocating a return to pre-industrial times, but they remained deeply suspicious of those who advocated and praised progress and all things modern. They clearly associated the growing industrialization and urbanization of the province and its accompanying Anglicization during the period – developments they regularly lumped together under the label of 'Americanization' – with the erosion of the foundations of the French-Canadian nation. Thus, they strongly advocated the extension of rural areas through colonization policies in northern Quebec,[43] the production of domestic arts and crafts among farming families to ensure the viability of life on the land, the increased use of the French language, and the promotion of an 'achat chez nous' campaign.[44] While traditional nationalist elites had been backing such measures in the past and the government had already taken several steps to implement them, the context of the Depression added further fuel to this traditional nationalist fervour as unprecedented economic hardship appeared to confirm the bankruptcy of what was perceived to be an essentially English-Protestant-led industrial order. An increased sense of being vulnerable to this 'Americanization' was accompanied by an equally intense belief in the urgent need to tackle this invasive threat. Jean Bruchési warned that 'we are noticing all of a sudden … that this province of Quebec, cradle of our people, the "douce province" is in the process of rapidly losing the characteristics it has of a French country.'[45]

It is in this context that the traditional elite added a distinctly new weapon to its arsenal of nationalist entreaties and arguments. It began to link the fate of the French-Canadian nation to the health of the tourism industry, arguing that those who 'want to change everything want to kill tourism.'[46] And traditional nationalists did so precisely at the time when that industry was increasingly attracting the attention of the state.[47] (It must be noted that the Depression made all governments in Canada quite receptive to those who advocated the development of the tourist industry.)[48] In the eyes of many nationalists, 'tourism is in the process of becoming one of the principal industries of the country.'[49] In fact, several among them ended up working either in collaboration with or directly for Quebec tourist promotion agencies. They also turned out to be virulent critics of the industry as they measured its success against French-Canadian decision-makers' and citizens' capacity to adequately preserve and rejuvenate their society's traditional identity.

If, in their eyes, tourism was first and foremost a means to a nationalist end,[50] they nonetheless started out by justifying their conservative agenda by invoking what they believed American tourists wanted to see when they came to Quebec. Typical of this line of argument are the comments made by Mgr Camille Roy:

> Since it is this French character, traditional, of our Quebec that makes it so popular abroad, that attracts to it so many visitors, that directs to our cities and our countryside a flow, ever replenished, of American tourists: let us preserve Quebec's French character.[51]

Readers were told again and again that American tourists looked for *difference*, and in Quebec this difference was defined by the province's French traditions and culture,[52] reflected in

> the outer shape of our buildings and farms, in the countryside ... in the furniture of our Canadian homes [foyers], in the manners and the language of our people; it appears along our roads in the names of the villages ...in the French language of the ads and signs.[53]

In other words, it was the French-Canadian past that made the province such a popular tourist destination.

Once this had been established, there followed a lament deploring the fact that, increasingly, American tourists were not finding this 'Old Quebec': 'How many are disillusioned, in spite of efforts that a few traditionalists and a few patriots are making to safeguard what is left to us of our ethnic character and our distinct [*physionomie*]!'[54] This is when traditional nationalists addressed the issue that preoccupied them the most. Scanning the Quebec landscape through the lenses of the 'tourist-in-search-of-Old-Quebec,' they identified its shortcomings, and it inevitably came up sorely wanting.

They deplored first and foremost the fact that 'there remains nothing of our beautiful ancestral face.'[55] It was being increasingly and relentlessly disfigured by the Anglicization of the province. The commercial signs used by French-Canadian restaurant, hotel, and store owners made this obvious. But more troubling for nationalists was the fact that their fellow French Canadians had adopted the dominant English North American lifestyle and culture. The exterior disfigurement was only the symptom of a more serious condition: 'the caving in [affaissement] of our French soul.'[56] As they would relentlessly point out: 'a face conveys a state of mind [état d'âme].'[57] While the facial metaphor was a recurring theme in the discourse of these nationalist tourist promoters, it was meant to convey the need for more than cosmetic change. Restoring the province's traditional French character would include preserving the architecture of buildings erected during the New France regime – the heroic period of French-Canadian history – building new ones in accordance with a 'French Canadian style,'[58] producing arts and crafts the old-fashioned way, reviving the cuisine of the ancestors, and keeping alive the religious rituals and family traditions so faithfully observed by those who came before them. This was what would ensure the survival of the authentic French Canada and, by force of circumstance, guarantee the success of its tourism industry.

Traditional nationalists would also direct their ire at provincial government decision-makers in charge of tourism promotion who, they contended, had not done enough to protect and revitalize the 'Old Quebec.' One of the first prominent French-Canadian nationalists to produce a substantive analysis which outlined both the disfigurement of French-Canadian society and its detrimental impact on the tourism industry was the renowned journalist Olivar Asselin. In 1932 he wrote an editorial in the newspaper *Le Canada* entitled *Sur une organsation du tourisme*, offering the Quebec government a road map to improve the ways in which it could promote the province in line with much of what traditional nationalists were advocating.[59] He shared their view that there was an urgent need to give the hotel industry a French face. This meant using French names, decorating establishments in a rustic style with products not made off the assembly line, and serving local cuisine. He suggested that the government use only French terminology to identify geographical sites such as rivers and seaways.[60] All this would ensure the province's originality and further lure the American tourists. He also made more practical and strategic recommendations. In his view, all the organizations both public and private involved in the tourist industry should coordinate their efforts and work under the direction of one authority.[61] This idea of having a government body solely dedicated to tourism would be a reccurring demand throughout the period.

L'Abbé Albert Tessier would pursue Asselin's campaign, building upon many of his recommendations. He was a well-known public figure, promoter of regional history in the Saint-Maurice Valley, prolific writer, energetic propagandist of the beauties and attractions of the province,[62] and pioneering documentary filmmaker dedicated to making known the traditional French-Canadian rural life and the beauties of Quebec's natural surroundings. In 1933, he declared to the Société du parlez français at Laval University that 'from the banks of the Outaouais river to the tip of the Gaspésie, one comes across scarcely ten signs that are truly French.'[63] He then went on to make a point he would reiterate again and again: that with complacency French Canadians proclaimed themselves the 'Old province of Quebec.' And while 'This refrain comes back like an obsessive leitmotif in all our patriotic speeches and brochures dedicated to the glory of the "France of America,"' regrettably the unanimous belief in its existence 'does not do justice to our sense of observation nor to our sense of reality.'[64]

These complaints would not fall upon deaf ears. Indeed, in the 1930s, several nationalist organizations and government officials embarked on a campaign of *refrancisation* aimed at resurrecting 'Old Quebec.' Members of the Société des arts et des lettres de Québec[65] officially started the ball rolling by setting their sights on the smaller countryside hotels in an attempt to convince their owners to give French names to their establishments and rebaptize the all too prevalent '"Hotel Commercial," "Hotel Central," "Petit Windsor," "American House," "Hotel Canada."'[66] The Association of Countryside Hotels offered its full co-operation and it did not take long for the French-Canadian press and most other notable nationalist associations to follow suit. Paul Gouin, an eminent lawyer, politician, and art collector, and others, were eager to give their consulting services to hotel, restaurant, and shop owners. They strongly encouraged them to seek the advice of those who, like themselves, were versed in French-Canadian architecture, literature, history, and arts and crafts. They could provide them with appropriate ideas for the names of their establishments as well as suggestions for the design of their signs, buildings, and interior decoration. As Paul Gouin argued:

> It is in our customs, in our legends, in our history, in our fauna and our flora, that we will find the most flavoursome [savoureux], the most picturesque and the most characteristic names.[67]

Over a relatively short period of time, then, tourism had become a nationalist cause – one that now inspired members of the province's elite to send recommendations to the government, make public pronouncements, and initiate a reform campaign to see more of 'Old Quebec' in Quebec.

How did tourist promoters in government respond? They proved most receptive. By the 1930s, state promoters would adopt an increasingly interventionist approach. A telling sign of this more proactive involvement is the fact that in 1936, the Quebec government placed its Tourist Bureau under the jurisdiction of the Department of Municipal Affairs, Industry and Commerce. In this way, tourism was given the imprimatur of a full-fledged industry, as it was housed in a department with more visibility and a more explicit mandate of economic development. It was baptized the Tourist Branch and the following year it changed homes yet again, moving to the new Department of the Executive Council whose director answered to the chief of staff of the premier. While tourism would be reconfigured administratively yet again several times[68] well into the early 1960s, until then it would remain under the ultimate responsibility of the premier, suggesting, at least officially, that its administrators could get the attention of the highest authority in the province. In the words of architectural historian Lucie K. Morisset, tourism became 'une affaire d'État.'[69]

On the ground, government officials accelerated their early support to various *refrancisation* efforts. In 1937, for instance, they offered financial support to the Syndicat d'Initiative de la Mauricie, which organized a French sign contest for hotels, restaurants, stores, and products of all kinds.[70] But government officials also multiplied their initiatives to help revitalize what they perceived to be the authentic 'French-Canadian' way of life. Reactivating the production of arts and crafts following the tradition of the ancestors figured prominently in this campaign. The Quebec government had early on been a strong backer of the production of arts and crafts in an attempt to encourage farm families to remain on the land. By the mid-1920s and early 1930s, however, these nationalists would increasingly invoke another argument to justify this government support: meeting the tourist demand for souvenirs that reflected the traditional way of life visitors had set out to experience on their trip to 'Old Quebec.'[71] Many, like Paul Gouin, also felt that more should be done to make available to tourists the products of French-Canadian artisans and in turn reduce the number of souvenirs 'manufactured in Japan, in Switzerland and in Germany.'[72] The themes depicted by these artisans certainly reflected this traditional way of life: old men with pipes, old women at their spinning wheels, women in front of outdoor ovens, 'habitants' with a toque and *ceinture flèchée* or the fatherly blessing. All were reproduced in various ways to the delight of those in search of 'Old Quebec.'[73]

But traditional nationalists also believed that greater efforts should be made to encourage French Canadians *themselves* to purchase these artefacts. French-Canadian hotel keepers would be an obvious target clientele. As Gouin intoned, by buying 'the products of our rustic art: furniture, paintings, materials, carpets, ornaments etc,' they 'will give to their hotels a French-Canadian cachet not only in name but in actual fact' and provide tourists that difference they are in search of. But for Gouin such purchases 'would [also] be ... an eminently salutary patriotic deed.'[74] The Quebec government was clearly convinced by such arguments, as it continued to encourage hotel keepers in the countryside through its Hotel Improvement Services to decorate their establishments with recognizable French-Canadian furniture and offer patrons 'typical' French-Canadian cuisine.

But nationalists cast a wider net, entreating the population as a whole to interpret their patriotic duty in this way: 'engraving, furniture, carpet, and book are in some sense the external affirmation of the homeland, its palpable manifestations.'[75] Thus, French Canadians 'should decorate the child's room and the home "à la canadienne," that is to say with the products of our domestic or rustic arts ... because ... they constitute a national education opportunity for which we are increasingly recognizing the value.'[76] While addressing the Société Saint-Jean-Baptiste, Paul Gouin also suggested that members should inscribe in their rules and regulations that all should 'buy at least once a year an article of "fabrication domestique" for their living room or office,' and secondly, 'give as a gift at least once a year an object of the same provenance.' A 'fine' should be imposed on members who violated these regulations.[77] For his part, Jean-Marie Gauvreau, who was appointed in 1935 by the provincial government as director of the École du Meuble, declared:

> Many friends of the cause of arts and crafts are agreed that it must not be commercialized, it must be first made to serve domestic needs. We share this point of view.[78]

In effect, the hope was that these 'palpable manifestations' of the homeland would be reintroduced into the everyday lives of the host society not simply to confirm in the minds of visitors that they had entered a land of the past or as nostalgic reminders to French Canadians of a time gone by. They should be considered as tangible legacies of the artistry and pragmatism of French Canada's ancestors – a usable past to be reactivated in the present. It was by fortunate 'coincidence' that they corresponded to many of the markers of 'Old Quebec' appreciated by visitors.

That the government made the connection is further confirmed by the fact that while the Department of Municipal Affairs, Industry and Commerce mandated Jean-Marie Gauvreau to draw up an inventory and make a study of the arts and crafts resources of the province, he was also asked to look into the tourism industry.[79] For this, he hired Abbé Albert Tessier, who produced a *Rapport sur le tourisme* (1939)[80] that was given wide publicity when it was later reprinted for the general public.[81] This government-commissioned document ended up echoing many of the points made by Olivar Asselin a few years earlier.[82] In fact, it could be read as a manifesto of the traditional nationalists' view of tourism. While pointing out that 'tourism has become the most promising industry in the province,'[83] it argued that its value was first and foremost 'NATIONAL' [*sic*].[84] It thus followed that

> all efforts to intensify our distinct qualities, to give back to our ethnic personality its full vitality, will amplify in direct proportion our tourist value.[85]

This 'personality' was clearly different. Tessier defined it in terms of the French

Canadians' faithful connection to the past. He stated with pride that Quebec was 'the oldest civilized land' in America, 'the only one on the whole continent that keeps the memory and the imprint of four centuries of French and Catholic life.' More importantly, it was only by preserving and expanding these memories that Quebec would be in a position to attract tourists.[86] Concretely, 'it is essential to take measures so that visitors attracted by our appeals find "chez nous" what our publicity promises!'[87] And this explains why he devoted such importance to history in this report, or what he called the province's 'history-capital.' According to him, it was nothing less than 'the #1 value of our tourist resources.'[88] Thus, a report destined to provide guidance to decision-makers about the best way to promote tourism was one that provided advice on how to enhance the development of traditional French-Canadian identity.

During the 1940s and 1950s, government initiatives confirmed that traditional nationalists continued to find support among decision-makers. Indeed, administrators and politicians still defined Quebec's difference in terms of a distinct culture rooted in the past and encouraged those involved in the tourism industry along with the population to do their share to revive this French Canada. Quebec's premier himself, Adélard Godbout, speaking to the first National Tourism Congress in 1943, declared that 'We in Quebec offer a "something that is different" and stress the quaintness, the romantic history of our Province as the cradle of Canada among outstanding attractions to the visitors.' Further highlighting what he understood to be Quebec's difference, he added that this '"Old Quebec" atmosphere is just as important an attraction for tourists to the Province of Quebec as the Dionne Quintuplets for our sister Province of Ontario.'[89]

Yet, by the 1940s and increasingly so by the 1950s, it is possible to identify some signs of change in marketing techniques, harbingers of more profound changes to come. Government publicity still emphasized the characteristics of 'Old Quebec.' Tourists would still read about 'the historic centuries – old towns and villages.'[90] One brochure informed them that in Quebec, 'amid the upheavals of modern times, we have been able to retain the tempo, the true atmosphere of *Old France* in *America*.'[91] The cover image of the booklet itself underscored this statement, as it foregrounded a seated elderly woman doing needlepoint, with part of a spinning wheel in front of her.

However, at the same time, the slogans and headlines in these government advertisements no longer referred to 'Old Quebec.' During the 1940s, they invited tourists to a 'French Canadian Vacation' and by the 1950s to 'La Province de Québec.' These new labels anchored Quebec in the present by emphasizing its distinctive ethnicity and language – features that were not specifically associated with an 'Old Quebec.' Tourist promoters were also more systematically and more forcefully then ever making the point that Quebec was a place of contrasts where past and present coexisted, where 'the bustle of metropolitan Montreal contrasts with the fortifications of Quebec.'[92] While tourists had been invited before to take note of the remarkable modern industrial and urban developments across the province, by the 1950s, these were more fully integrated into the general text of the tourist brochures. Thus, along with commentary pointing to the historic sites, government publicity provided more boastful descriptions, unrestrained in their praise of adjoining industrial centres. Trois-Rivières was labelled 'the pulp and paper capital of the world'[93] and the Saint-Maurice River was described as 'the highest developed power stream in the world.'[94] In the 'pristine' Laurentians, tourists were called upon to admire its 'mighty hydro-electric plants.'[95] Overall, prospective visitors were told that by coming to ' La Province de Québec' they would come across 'cities and towns as up-to-the minute as today's newspaper.'[96] When one considers that, by this time, tourist promoters had gained a certain autonomy in the government bureaucracy, and that their task was to develop the tourism industry *per se* (and not concern themselves with wider economic development), more prevalent boastful comments about Quebec's industrial performance and urban modernity point to evolving perceptions about the province and the tourist clientele. At the very least, tourist promoters of the 'La Province de Québec' product appeared to be more interested, if not proud, of showcasing the 'New' Quebec as they turned it into a more prominent marketable asset.

This growing willingness to put the modern Quebec face forward could also be a reflection of tourist promoters' recognition that the post–Second World War travelling public was by then looking for more than a trip 'back in time.' Certainly other differences in Quebec tourist promotion suggest that the Tourist Bureau was aware that additional strings needed to be pulled to lure the postwar tourist clientele – the 'consumer string.'[97] Indeed, it is at this time that the promotional literature begins to make increasing references to the alluring stores and the opportunities to purchase high-quality consumer products in Quebec cities (in addition to traditional local arts and crafts). Tourists are also being told more and more systematically that by coming to Quebec they will have the opportunity to enjoy French from France cuisine. Clearly, what tourist promoters were trying to respond to here were the demands of visitors in search of modern experiences associated with materialistic and epicurean pleasures – consumer-oriented experiences mainly available in larger urban settings. It would appear that by the 1950s, Quebec tourist promoters had come to the conclusion that travellers' motivations and expectations could not only be understood as guided by an antimodernist quest.[98]

This being said, it is important to keep in mind that promoters were not downplaying the antimodernist appeal of Quebec. The 'Old World' attractions of the province had far from been eclipsed in the full gamut of Quebec tourist advertising. The illustrations of elderly French Canadians in traditional occupations, priests and churches, and fishing villages outnumbered the pictures of ports, power plants, and modern highways by a long shot, while the expressions 'Old World' and 'Old Quebec' continued to pepper the accompanying texts in this publicity. The importance still given to 'Old Quebec' is not surprising when one considers that during the 1950s, some prominent traditional nationalists were still heavily involved in the tourist promotion of the province. Indeed, the principles and assumptions underlined by Asselin, reiterated by Tessier, would be defended with vigour in the person of Paul Gouin. He, in fact, regularly quoted Tessier throughout his tenure as technical advisor to the Executive Council of the province from 1948 to 1960. This position officially put him in charge of the preservation and development of the French-Canadian cultural and artistic heritage. But his job description also included the promotion of tourism. This mandate confirmed that decision-makers in the 1950s continued to make a direct link between the promotion of national identity *and* tourism. This national identity would also continue to be defined largely in traditional terms. Gouin himself made this association clear when he stated:

> If I am interested in tourism, it is because it constitutes the easiest way, the most logical and also, which is not to be sneered at, the most remunerative means to make our culture stand out, to revitalize our traditions and our customs, that is to say to give back to our province its French face.[99]

He went so far as to say that it was 'Providence that made it so that this heritage contains all that tourists look for.'[100] In effect, Gouin considered himself a man on a mission to promote tourism as a safeguard for the French-Canadian nation, one that he had actively contributed to define as early as the 1930s. His official position gave him a visibility and a unique opportunity to publicize these views and take appropriate initiatives. He appears to have lost few opportunities to speak out. At the beginning of his appointment, he gave close to a hundred radio talks inviting the wider public to 'refranciser la route.' Among other things, he encouraged his listeners to renovate their homes, hotels, or barns in the 'French-Canadian' style.[101]

Paul Gouin's ideas and recommendations had a familiar ring to them, pointing to a certain continuity in the attitudes of those involved in government tourist promotion since its early days. Thus, while recognizing that some progress had been made since the *refrancisation* campaign of the early 1930s –

particularly in the case of the small hotels – he kept deploring the fact that the French face of the province was still 'made up, disfigured by an Americanism of doubtful quality.'[102] To make his point more forcefully, as Albert Tessier had done so before him, he also invoked the ever-present disappointed tourist, claiming that 'more and more, the foreigner considers our "French face" as a publicity stunt.'[103] In line with other traditionalists, he continued to understand the need for *refrancisation* in its wider sense, defining this French face as 'our traditions and customs, our folklore, our way of thinking, of living, our way of humanizing our countryside, of building, of decorating and furnishing our churches and our houses.'[104] As did his predecessors, he also argued that as French Canadians we needed to 'become ourselves again, that is to say give our province its true face' because it 'constitutes our main tourist attraction.'[105] Those who actively collaborated in this ongoing project of 'rediscovery' by seeking his advice were congratulated for their 'practical patriotic act.'[106]

Yet, Gouin was not averse to the advantages of progress. As he put it in 1955, the idea was not 'to back pedal':[107]

> I have never asked ... my compatriots to wear as in the past the blue, red, or white toque, wool mittens, the *ceinture fléchée* ... I mean to say that we must preserve our cultural heritage while we adapt to it the demands of modern life.[108]

He was adamant that 'we can without worry entrust to our "master the future," that is to say progress, the care to ensure the survival of the culture, the traditions, and the customs bequeathed to us by "our master the past."'[109] He had come to the conclusion that it was not only crucial 'to transport [this folklore],' 'to revive it in the theatre, the cinema, or the public place,' but to inspire oneself from it 'to create radio sketches ... ballets, festivals, literary and artistic oeuvres.'[110] In other words, it was essential to make use of the modern means of communication to disseminate this culture rooted in the past, and vital to draw from it when further developing French-Canadian culture in the present.[111]

Thus, during the 1950s, while Gouin continued to affirm that the past is our master, his thinking had clearly evolved when it came to defining the relationship between this traditional culture and French Canadians. His attitude towards arts and crafts is telling in this respect. He remained an ardent promoter of French-Canadian arts and crafts. Much as he did in the 1930s, he still argued that 'It is thanks to [our arts and crafts] that we can reconstitute the French-Canadian atmosphere, the patriotic atmosphere of our homes.'[112] However, by the 1950s, he also clearly recognized that craftsmen had had to adapt to the demands of modern life: 'our artisans do not practice arts and crafts as they did in the past.' More specifically, they do not try to create furniture, knick knacks, clothes to furnish their own homes or to support their own family. Having become producers of knick-knack souvenirs they look for the tourist clientele.

They were also looking for a French-Canadian clientele who would use their crafts in much the same way as the tourists did – to embellish their homes. In his view, 'our domestic arts have evolved, they have become decorative arts, they have modernized.'[113] He had visibly accepted that these tangible markers of the past had become increasingly commodified, removed from their traditional usage. And he considered this a positive development, since these 'modernized' arts and crafts did not preclude them from offering an exemplary manifestation of French-Canadian culture.

In sum, the 1950s offered signs of change against a backdrop of continuity. The 'Old Quebec' slogan was replaced by the more present-minded label of 'La Province de Québec.' And while it remained true that the tourist publicity and tourist promoters continued to present Quebec's difference as essentially founded on a traditional national identity, the modern Quebec and the newly emerging consumer-oriented expectations of postwar tourists were given more attention. As developments in the 1960s make clear, change would increasingly be the order of the day.

From 'Old Quebec' to 'La Belle Province'

Debates over the significance of the Quiet Revolution as a harbinger of dramatic change, propelling Quebec society into modernity, have engaged scholars over the last thirty five years. While many historians have argued that the changes of the 1960s revealed a stark break with the past, their revisionist counterparts point to origins that predate these transformations. In the case of tourism promotion, there is no doubt that significant changes emerged in the 1960s, most notably when one considers the way in which the past and history were used to market the province.

To begin with, tourism was given greater visibility in the government bureaucracy. In fact, during the 1960 election, the Liberal Party of Jean Lesage, running under the slogan 'It's time for a change,' promised to create a Department of Tourism. This was far from being a revolutionary idea – it had been recommended by every expert in the field since the 1930s in one form or another. However, in the 1960s, it would be taken up by a politician who would become premier and one who would keep his promise. In 1963, the Department of Tourism, Hunting, and Fishing was created. In the meantime, in 1961, Robert Prévost became the director of a newly formed Province of Quebec

Tourist Bureau,[114] which gave tourism a separate administrative identity as its director answered directly to the Provincial Secretariat. Once the department was set up, Prévost would occupy the position of assistant deputy minister.

The way Quebec was promoted and the initiatives that were undertaken under Robert Prévost's tenure clearly confirm that some significant changes were underway. The 'Old Quebec' and 'La province de Québec' marketed to tourists would be replaced by 'La belle province.' More significantly, Quebec tourism itself would be divested of the role many traditional nationalists had ascribed to it to revitalize a French Canada and its heritage where 'naught shall suffer change.' In other words, tourism would no longer be held up as a means to the end of reviving the traditional 'Old Quebec.' Nevertheless, the link between tourism and nationalism would not be severed for all that. Tourism promoters such as Prévost wanted to make sure that their imaging of the province reflected the Quebec of the 1960s. As a result, they ended up validating and marketing to visitors and to Quebeckers themselves a modern face of the Quebec nation.

It must be noted that by the early 1960s, tourism had fully come into its own and was seen first and foremost as a business, since its promoters had become tourist conscious as never before. Prévost's own definition of tourism made this clear: 'Tourism constitutes first an industry; it is a source of foreign currency, a money transfusion … it multiplies jobs; it contributes to a large extent to maintaining our standard of living at a high level of pleasure. In sum, it guarantees a certain material happiness to the population.'[115] As for the visited, they were 'the shareholders of the tourism industry, [they] all draw dividends from it, without exception, even though they do not all come into contact with travellers.'[116]

Certainly the economic context can help to account for this greater emphasis placed on the financial value of the tourism industry. After the Second World War, tourism was proving to be an ever-growing source of revenue for an increasing number of nations around the globe. In Quebec, in the immediate postwar period, the number of tourists coming to the province had tripled,[117] making tourism its third largest industry. All economic indicators gave tourist promoters every reason to be optimistic that things would only improve, and these indicators served as a spur to take action.[118] However, Prévost never failed to point out that the competition for the tourist dollar would steadily increase with the growing affordability of air travel, making Europe, and France in particular, more accessible, along with other more exotic destinations such as Mexico.[119] The fact that Canada had been experiencing an increasing 'travel deficit' since the early 1950s only made such warnings more convincing.[120] In this new climate, Quebec's 'natural advantages,' such as its geographical proximity to the United States and its distinct 'personality,' would not necessarily be sufficient drawing cards for its principal American tourist market. Such concerns made it inevitable that tourism promoters in the 1960s would spend much more time than did their predecessors discussing marketing strategies *per se*, trying to come up with ever more effective and inventive ways to grab the attention of prospective tourists. In contrast to an Albert Tessier or a Paul Gouin, Robert Prévost would be much more preoccupied with monitoring the number of incoming tourists and evaluating the success of a promotional campaign based on yearly increases in budgets and tourist entries. His reports and public allocutions were meant to keep his readers and listeners informed about the work accomplished, the progress made, and the needs and challenges ahead for the Quebec tourist industry.

Reflecting some of these changes is the fact that in the early years of the decade, the Tourism Bureau undertook a series of new promotional strategies explicitly thought out to cope with the increasingly competitive climate. Prévost noted that for the year 1959/60, the Tourist Bureau 'invested close to one million dollars to invite our neighbours beyond the forty-fifth or from our sister provinces to come to Quebec.'[121] In 1960, while the bureau did not see its credits increase significantly, it did increase its advertising efforts in newspapers and magazines outside Quebec by 30 per cent, mostly 'publications of so-called "prestige" destined for the well-off classes, from which are recruited tourists with larger budgets for travel and holidays.'[122] In 1961, as well, the bureau undertook to replace and redesign all its printed publicity materials, to bring them up to date and give them 'an impeccable typographical appearance' and 'elegance' meant to better reflect the 'prestige of Quebec.'[123]

But the early 1960s were not only a time of improving on past strategies, of producing more of the same. Robert Prévost was eager to draw attention to the modern nature of some of his bureau's new projects, the extent to which they broke with past practices. He was, for instance, particularly proud of the fact that in 1961, the bureau had carried out a new initiative, producing four 'four-colour advertisements in prestigious large-circulation American magazines.'[124] That same year, he explained that the Tourist Bureau was interested in making increasing use of television to promote tourism in Quebec. Already, in 1960/61 the number of presentations on American television had multiplied by four, going from 39 in 1959/60 to 164 in 1960/61.[125] Again in 1961, Prévost was proud to announce that in Times Square, New York, prospective American tourists would be able to see a Tourist Bureau electronic billboard advertisement of four thousand light bulbs, a first of its kind in Canadian provincial tourism promotion.[126]

Quebec tourism promotion had thus become not only a competitive business but a proudly modern one as well. In fact, Quebec ended up attracting the attention of the advertising community at large for its accomplishments. For instance, in 1962, the *Marketing* journal selected the bureau's four-colour ad as one of the best ones produced that year. In Prévost's words: 'Already Quebec had taken the lead of all Canadian provinces in the field of advertising. It was now time to rise to the first rank in the field of printed material.' His concluding remarks neatly encapsulated some aspects of the changes taking place: 'We like to think that Quebec's tourism advertising has passed from the "artisanal" stage to the professional one.'[127]

Tourist promoters by the 1960s were certainly very focused on running a professional and successful business with state-of-the-art know-how and techniques. But they also had clear ideas about what they should be advertising. Comparing their views with those who marketed the province in earlier decades reveals noteworthy contrasts. To begin with, promoters such as Robert Prévost were more concerned about making sure that their ads reflected what Quebec had to offer than about making sure *Quebec itself* offered what tourism publicity promised to the incoming tourists. To put it differently, tourism promoters during the time of the Quiet Revolution were more satisfied with the Quebec product they had to market to tourists than their traditional nationalist predecessors. By the early 1960s, those who advocated a more secular nationalism, fully recognizing Quebec as an industrialized and urban society, had taken over the reins of power while those who still upheld the traditional French Canada had lost ground. It was clear that tourist promoters' main concern was to make sure that the content of the advertising effectively reflected the Quebec that *had* changed and was still changing – a Quebec that was now fully embraced by the newly emerging nationalist elites and politicians. It is in this respect that tourism promoters in the 1960s found themselves in the position of strengthening Quebec's newly emerging sense of national identity.

This evolution is made evident when one considers the issue of language. As had already become apparent in the 1950s, tourist promoters were using some French spellings and a few French words in their advertisements. By the early 1960s, tourism promoters made the use of the French language a key feature of their marketing strategy. The texts in the new advertisements were interspersed with French words or expressions as never before. Always taking care not to transform the French language into a barrier, promoters made a playful use of it, adopting words that either had their literal equivalent in English or were well-known expressions. The Provincial Tourist Bureau's 1961 ad series 'See La Province de Québec Say – Magnifique!' provides a good illustration of this new approach. Using the French language more extensively in advertisements destined to English speakers was justified as an effective marketing strategy to bring out Quebec's difference. Prévost described 'the

French face of Quebec' as 'an extremely remunerative asset and very precious for our economy.'[128]

However, this new approach proved to be motivated by more than strategic and business considerations. It was also directly linked to the social transformations taking place in Quebec at this time. Scholars of the period have stressed that French Canadians' sense of what made them different became more strongly associated with the French language, which replaced their Catholicism as the primary defining feature of their identity. Tourist promoters were thus also asserting the existence of a distinct French culture in North America in a bold unprecedented way in line with other more assertive nationalist initiatives undertaken by their compatriots at the time. In the words of Robert Prévost, the revamping of Quebec's advertisements in the early 1960s was an explicit attempt to 'ensure the omnipresence of our French face.'[129] The 1965 Annual Report of the Department of Tourism, Hunting, and Fishing was explicit on this matter as well:

> For a few years now, Quebec tourist advertising has been peppered with French words chosen in such a way that their meaning does not escape English-speakers. The objective is to constantly keep the reader aware of the French face of *la belle province*.[130]

The Tourism Bureau also decided to produce a French-English lexicon for the benefit of anglophone travellers – a compilation of practical French words and expressions they could use with their hosts. In the view of 1960s tourist promoters: 'Our English-speaking compatriots and our neighbours across the forty-fifth parallel often wish to ... address the people they meet in the street or in commercial establishments in French. This gives them the chance to practise the language of which they have sometimes acquired a few elements.'[131]

Tourist promoters in the 1960s were thus demanding a more active recognition from their visitors that Quebec was a French destination, all the while assuming that this would add to the pleasure of their visit. It must be noted that promoters also made it reassuringly clear in the more detailed tour guides[132] and when addressing prospective anglophone visitors directly that while '80 per cent of Quebec's five million citizens are French speaking ... most of them are bilingual, so there is no language barrier whatsoever for the English-speaking visitor.'[133] For his part, Robert Prévost invited visitors to come to the province to 'witn[ess] the charm that springs from our bilingual status, one of the characteristics of Quebec's appeal.'[134] He would later explain at a Société Saint-Jean-Baptiste meeting that 'of course ... when we address the anglophone clientele of the continent we do not present Québécois as essentially unilingual ... We must reassure them on this point.'[135] Clearly national affirmation would be a contained one so as not to put the tourism industry in jeopardy.

The boldest experimental initiative with regard to marketing the province as French was undertaken in 1962 and 1963. The Tourist Bureau then published an advertisement in the *New Yorker*[136] and *Time* magazines where the words were entirely in French while also easy to translate for unilingual anglophones (see figure 15.1). Prévost was well aware that this initiative was risky, but to his delight it was fully rewarded with a 42 per cent increase in the number of requests from tourists at the end of the first year. And peers in the tourism promotion business recognized its originality by discussing it at the International Union of Official Travel Organizations in Dublin, Ireland, in 1964.[137]

All this being said, tourism promoters in the 1960s did share some of the concerns of their traditional nationalist predecessors when it came to the disfigurement of the French face of the province. Thus, Robert Prévost warned an audience in the newly developing tourist area of the North Shore not to make the mistakes that were made in other popular and more established Quebec tourist destinations. Reminiscent of his forerunners, he deplored the fact that the roads in these areas appeared as 'canyons encased between two rows of signs advertising English corporate names much more representative of Ontario, Florida, or Texas than the "belle province."' He pleaded with his audience:

> For Heaven's sake, do not let the French face of the North Shore deteriorate to the point where it will eventually require painful plastic surgery ... Do not tolerate that ugliness come to mar such a magical panorama.[138]

Yet when Prévost proclaimed this familiar *refrancisation* refrain, he did not go beyond demanding that signs be *refrancisés*. Unlike Paul Gouin and other traditional nationalists, for him *refranciser* did not entail changing French-Canadian lifestyles, values, and character; much less did it mean resurrecting those of 'Old Quebec.' At the same time, he did not share the solutions put forth by many contemporary nationalists who favoured coercive measures such as state intervention to encourage business owners to make use of French signs. In his view, the 'task could not be accomplished by a series of government decrees.' Instead he suggested having 'intermediary groups' such as local chambers of commerce, syndicats d'initiatives, parish councils, and the like set up their own vigilance committees.[139] He would never tire of saying that *refrancisation* would be impossible without the massive involvement of individuals.[140]

When one reads over government tour guides published during this period one is struck by the extent to which promoters went out of their way to

Prenez des vacances à la française au Québec!

Le Québec la belle province, vous invite Si vous aimez l'atmosphère historique, la gaîté et la joie de vivre les charmes de la nature, la cuisine (ah! la bonne cuisine française!) la photographie, les sports ...vous aimerez le Québec! Et au Québec, pas de problèmes: pas d'océan à traverser, pas de passeports, pas de monnaies compliquées, et tout le confort moderne On parle français et anglais, et partout on parle le langage de l'hospitalité Pour des vacances magnifiques, visitez le Québec! Au revoir et bienvenue!

QUÉBEC

Now that you've tried your French, come visit us and give us a chance to show off our English

For more information, mail in coupon

Provincial Tourist Bureau, Parliament Buildings, Québec City, Canada.   Dept. AC-2-6

Please send me FREE your new travel folders and road map of la Province de Québec.

My main interest is

Name

Address

City   State

15.1 'Prenez des vacances à la française.' Quebec Provincial Tourist Bureau advertisement, *New Yorker*, 5 May 1962, 131.

make the point that Quebec was in fact no longer a traditional society rooted in the past. In a 1963 brochure entitled 'The Province of Quebec,' the authors proudly proclaimed that 'a prodigious industrial expansion has transformed [Quebec] at an accelerated pace.'[141] The idea was clearly to convey a sense of rapid change and modernization. While describing the continuous economic development in northern Quebec, the brochure informed tourists that 'gigantic exploitations reap rich minerals from the soil. Around the paper mills, mines, and giant hydro-electric power-plants, numerous modern cities are rising in the midst of forests.' In the early 1960s, tourism promoters also decided to include in their tourist film repertory one entitled *Le Québec Industriel*, arguing that 'the industrial expansion of the province has attracted a large external publicity and numerous are the tourists who want to see for themselves the accomplishments that have resulted from it.'[142] More specifically, promoters did not limit themselves to lauding this modernization and speaking in glowing terms of Quebec's future. In the 1963 publication, for instance, they actually projected a negative assessment of the province's past. Thus, while explaining that agriculture still 'occupied a significant place in the general economy of the province,' and that one could still find rural regions around Quebec City 'where agricultural tradition, despite its adaptation to industrial progress, stays marked by the "fragrance of Old France,"' the guide was quick to point out that 'long gone are the days when the only goal was to survive, where culture remained the exclusive purview of a small elite.' Visitors were told that today:

> Freed of its material worries, Quebec is heading for new heights. Now fully mature, culture is penetrating all levels of society, which is leading to a burgeoning of scientists, novelists, and artists who carry as far as the great capitals the prestige of French Canada.[143]

It should be noted that the fact that in 1962 Montreal was declared the host of the international exhibition of 1967 only further reinforced the sense among French Canadians that they were living in a modern society and should be recognized as such by the outside world, including tourists. Among city planners and promoters, change would become the operative word. Thus, while provincial tourist promoters were reimaging the province as a whole, those marketing Montreal were embarking on an ambitious rebranding campaign of their own. In the words of Mayor Jean Drapeau, 'within a very short time, throughout the world, Montreal must be mentioned repeatedly in all conversations, in all newspapers and on all stations and television screens.'[144]

The city had long been advertised by provincial tourist promoters as a mixture of old and new, and proudly as Canada's industrial and commercial metropole as well as the second largest French city in the world. But that was never foregrounded in its publicity. Through other means the city had developed a well-established reputation as 'sin city' – one that provincial promoters were clearly hesitant to highlight (if only euphemistically, when referring to it as the Paris of North America), but glad to bank on. By the 1960s, however, city officials felt that more needed to be done to showcase the city's modern and specifically French-Canadian personality.[145] Lucien Bergeron, who became the first director of the city's new Municipal Office of Tourism in 1962, was charged with this task. Overall it meant taking over from the Montreal Tourist and Convention Bureau, which represented Montreal's major English-Canadian business interests and had been responsible for the lion's share of the city's tourism publicity. Typically, its ads portrayed the French areas of Montreal as traditional enclaves while modernity was associated with its anglophone population. Indeed, a journalist from *La Presse* deplored that in one instance tourists were being told that 'on Jacques Cartier Place, one can encounter the habitants and the Indians selling their wares in typical costumes.' In the opinion of Bergeron, 'now ... tourists do not come to visit Old Montreal but simply want to visit a "big city," a cosmopolitan one.'[146] To start bringing the marketing more in line with reality, city officials thus took more control over Montreal's tourism promotion to present its modern French face. At the provincial level, this desire to showcase a modern and dynamic Quebec was further brought out when one considers Robert Prévost's reaction to an article written about Quebec in a 1968 issue of *Maclean's* magazine[147] sent to him by Gilles Charron, the deputy minister of industry and commerce, entitled 'The Little Town of Saintly Miracles.' It was one of five articles recommending to its readers particular tourist sites of interest across Canada. In Quebec, prospective tourists were invited to visit the village of Sainte-Anne-de-Beaupré with its famous shrine. The four photographs accompanying the text featured various religious subjects. In other words, the 'Old Quebec' familiar to traditional nationalist tourism promoters was put on display – in this case, the devoutly Catholic one. Clearly this public servant working for a department mandated to promote the economic development of the province was irked by the images of 'cows with cathedrals in the background and pictures of the eternal religious souvenir shop.' Not only did Charron feel that this 'is enough to make someone concerned about producing well-orchestrated publicity nauseous,' he concluded: 'If this is modern Quebec, let's not expect to be invaded by foreign investors in Quebec industry and commerce.'[148]

Robert Prévost could not have agreed with him more, yet he tried to reassure his colleague that government tourist promoters were on side working to promote the 'modern Quebec' he was referring to. He described the article as 'one of the rare jolts of an old prejudice.' This type of article was to be considered a thing of the past because the great majority of those written about Quebec now, often by journalists hosted by the Direction générale du tourisme, 'reflect a change in attitude towards the "quaint old Province."' Prévost attributed part of this transformation to 'the orientation that our advertisements, our brochures, and our public relations have taken already several years back.' Adopting a slightly defensive tone, he argued that 'for every article in which the author talks about a Quebec entrenched in retrograde habits, there are one hundred that do not refer to this formula long ago expired,' presenting instead 'la belle province.' He pointed out that the 'regrettable exceptions' 'don't justify the drawing of general conclusions.' However, this did not prevent him from sympathizing with the intense frustration expressed by his counterpart: 'some of these feature reports loaded with a malodorous dust of yesteryear' inspires nothing less than 'nausea.'[149] As this exchange makes clear, tourism promoters in the 1960s were consciously working to reimage the province, replacing a 'quaint Old Quebec' with 'la belle province.' The intensity and vehemence of their reactions to the *Maclean's* article also make clear that their quarrel with the traditional packaging of Quebec was not only born out of professional frustration. It was also a very personal response to what they perceived to be an affront. The *Maclean's* article and the like associated them with what was in their view a world of the past, a society whose lifestyle and values they could not identify with and indeed one that they had rejected. Robert Prévost's assurances that by the early 1960s government publicity had changed its message can certainly be documented. Many of the features of the 'Old Quebec' commonly displayed to lure tourists to the province in the past were obscured by new markers of identity more in line with Quebec's brand name of 'La belle province.' This development took place in a relatively short period, confirming yet again that this decade was a time when changes hinted at in previous decades were being consolidated in quick succession. More specifically, what had appeared to be an almost indissoluble and privileged association established by tourism promoters between Quebec and the past was being undone. This is not to say that the past and history would no longer be highlighted as tourist attractions in the province. The point is that they would become one among many of the alluring features to be enjoyed when coming to Quebec. Concretely, this meant that comparisons to seventeenth-century rural Normandy and New France with their oxen, spinning wheels, and dog carts would no longer occupy pride of place. Instead, tourist promoters chose to define Quebec in terms of the pleasures it would offer to the visitors' senses. Quebec would be marketed first and foremost as a modern-day epicurean's paradise encapsulated by the new 'la belle province' label. In other words, coming to Quebec would be less about travelling in time than taking the time to enjoy unique contemporary French-Canadian pleasures in a predominantly Anglo-Saxon North America.

This is strikingly apparent when one considers the unprecedented importance given to what tourist promoters would from then on identify as Quebec's 'mouth watering cuisine'[150] in government advertising literature of all kinds. While tourist promoters in the past had made some attempts to encourage hotel keepers and restaurant owners, particularly in the countryside, to serve up 'typical' regional French-Canadian dishes inspired by recipes handed down from past generations, going so far as to publish a recipe book for their benefit, these entreaties had been sporadic. And while Montreal had been labelled early on as the 'Paris of America' and increasingly identified as a centre of exceptional cuisine, unique on the continent, this cuisine had not been highlighted as a main attraction in the publicity about Quebec as a whole, certainly not as intrinsic to the French-Canadian lifestyle as such. By the 1960s, however, things had changed and the promise of culinary delights was being featured as nothing less than a central and distinctive drawing card of the province and part and parcel of French-Canadian culture.

In 1960, the Provincial Tourist Bureau's 'See La Province de Québec Say – Magnifique!' campaign – which featured various attributes of the province – included 'La cuisine,'[151] in which prospective visitors were told that 'Québec is famous for food.'[152] In 1961, an ad on Quebec as a whole devoted a good part of its text to lauding 'French Canada's distinctive *cuisine.*'[153] But this change also got tourist promoters involved in a debate over tradition: to what extent should this cuisine actually be *French Canadian*? In other words, how faithful to the recipes of 'Old Quebec' should they be in this regard? Certainly chefs and restaurant owners were encouraged to use local produce and adapt traditional recipes to the discerning tastes of their patrons. In 1966, the Hotel Services branch, under the Tourist Bureau, published a second edition of its compilation of 'Old Quebec recipes' that 'chefs in the hotels ... had revived in their kitchens.'[154] Yet, it was understood that the cuisine from France was the ultimate bench-mark of sophisticated culinary excellence and the type of cuisine most appreciated by American tourists. Chefs and restaurateurs needed to take this into account when producing a distinctive French-Canadian cuisine – a cuisine that Quebeckers could be proud of as well. In the words of Robert Prévost: 'A province that welcomes each year millions of tourists must of course offer an international cuisine, and, more specifically, the one that rallies the most votes from all continents: French cuisine.' And when one looks at the dishes featured at the annual *Grands Salons culinaires* and the menus of reputed restaurants in Quebec City, Montreal, and other popular tourist destinations, there is no doubt that pride of place was given to French cuisine and that culinary refinement was judged according to a chef's capacity to emulate this cuisine's reputed dishes, food presentation, and etiquette.[155] The 'La Cuisine – Magnifique!' drawing (see figure 15.2) certainly made a point of highlighting what would easily be identified as a refined French dining experience. It featured a clearly sophisticated-looking couple seated at a table with a chequered table cloth, wine glasses, and an attentive sommelier pointing to 'the delicate finesse of French cooking.' However, it also alerted tourists to the wonders of typically French-Canadian cooking. It contrasted the 'robust onion soup to [the] delicate *crêpe suzette*' and reassured its readers that both would 'flatter the gourmet's palate.' This nod to French-Canadian cuisine reflected another view expressed by Robert Prévost that 'it was important to revalorize Quebec regional dishes.' But this revalorization did not necessarily mean a full-fledged resurrection of the French-Canadian culinary traditions:

> It has often been noted that the stomach of the urban citizen of the twentieth century would not be able to assimilate with as much ease as the one of the first pioneers dishes such as tourtière, ragoût de pates, etc. Yet, when one takes into account the great ability of our chefs, there is no reason to doubt that they will be able to offer their clientele lighter versions, more digestible, of this cuisine enjoyed by our ancestors.[156]

Clearly, then, promoters felt that traditional French-Canadian cuisine could be marketed as an asset once it was presented as *one* component of French-Canadian cuisine (and not the main one) or if it acquired the more sophisticated veneer of its French-European counterpart. While this was far from an unqualified endorsement of tradition, it was an affirmation of Quebec as a land that could cater to the taste buds of the most discerning and up-to-date connoisseurs.

What is most remarkable is that by the early 1960s, the *whole* province was marketed as a land of sensual experience. Tourists were invited to 'Take your pick of Pleasures in Québec.'[157] The province in its entirety mutated into a 'state of mind,' a 'life style,' a 'heart that beats.'[158] To further reinforce this message, the Tourist Bureau decided in the mid-1960s to make use of drawings in addition to photographs in its advertisements in the belief that this more suggestive representation would 'better reflect the French face of Quebec,'[159] for Quebec's 'difference is not only visual: it is a lifestyle. Such characteristics often elude the camera lens.'[160] This 'new [Quebec] expérience' would be defined in cultural terms, as tourists would be invited to 'a land where *franche gaieté* [*sic*] is a way of life'[161] and to enjoy what was considered one of its

15.2 'La Cuisine – Magnifique!' Quebec Provincial Tourist Bureau advertisement, *Toronto Star*, 2 July 1960, 15.

typical French-Canadian personality trait, its 'joie de vivre.'[162] Clearly by the 1960s, Quebec's appeal and difference were meant to be understood as essentially rooted in a lifestyle and temperament very much in tune with modern-day pleasures. Contrary to traditionalists who, first and foremost, emphasized the need for the host society to be faithful to its 'history capital' and traditional values based on loyalty to its ancestors, to a rural way of life, and to the Church, tourist promoters in the 1960s focused on Quebec's distinct temperament and the pleasure it offered the senses. This was further illustrated by the fact that they equally made a point of highlighting French-Canadian friendliness and hospitality in their advertisements. Tourism promoters had been doing so for decades but *hospitalité* was highlighted as *the* defining French-Canadian personality trait by the 1960s, regularly included in advertising slogans. In fact, the slogan 'Hospitalité Spoken Here' would become a fixture in government ads.[163] This change in imaging strategy was yet another indication of a changing sense of French-Canadian national identity.

This is underscored when one looks at the way in which Robert Prévost and his colleagues addressed the Quebec general public. Like their predecessors, they believed that the host society had some responsibilities vis-à-vis visitors. And like their predecessors, they entreated their French-Canadian audiences to behave in line with the tourist publicity. In Prévost's words: 'one must absolutely avoid that all the people who come into contact with our visitors lead them to believe that we have invited them under false representation.' In the 1960s, this meant French Canadians would be encouraged to be welcoming, courteous, and friendly to tourists: 'it is incumbent on each one of us to do his part so that, in the minds of our visitors, the words "hospitalité" and "Québec" be synonymous.'[164] And while tourist promoters also made the point that efforts to save the French linguistic face of Quebec were of first importance, their entreaties, as we have seen, would amount to a much less ambitious reformist agenda than the one advocated by fellow promoters such as Albert Tessier and Paul Gouin. It was a question of putting French Canadians' best *contemporary* French face forward – its language of course but also its much-lauded attributes of French hospitality, joie de vivre, and sophistication. In effect, French Canadians were being asked to live up to their reputation by simply being watchful of their behaviour towards tourists. This in turn meant that contemporary French-Canadian lifestyle and values could remain intact. There were no direct attempts at pulling survivalist heartstrings or calling for loyalty to the forefathers. Such entreaties, which had been the mainstay of tourist promoters in the past, would, by the 1960s, largely fall upon deaf ears when it had been established that, in addition to language, Quebec's distinct national identity rested primarily on the distinct contemporary atmosphere of the province, the personable behaviour and sophisticated lifestyle of French Canadians – all very much rooted in the present.

This is not to say that the past and history were out of the tourist promotion picture. These continued to be considered drawing cards and tourist promoters continued to use them to market the province. But in government newspaper and magazine advertising, gone are the references to time-specific events or historical figures in the headlines and slogans. History had been distilled to an intangible 'Old World charm.'[165] History when it was mentioned was more often than not paired with Quebec City. As for tradition, it was associated to specific rural areas, more often than not the Île d'Orléans.[166] Furthermore, the past was not mentioned systematically in all advertisements as had been the case previously. This could not be made more obvious than in the 1960 series 'See La Province de Québec Say – Magnifique!' advertisement entitled 'L'atmosphère – Magnifique!'[167] This was the publicity in which tourism promoters made specific reference to Quebec's past. It was also where one could clearly appreciate the extent to which the past had now become simply one among several of Quebec's attributes. More significantly, the fact that the past had been paired with *atmosphère* reinforced the overriding message that Quebec was first and foremost something to be experienced through the senses. Interestingly enough, the ad focused specifically on arts and crafts. Tourists were told that they might '*feel* [this atmosphere] as you marvel at the talented fingers of a native wood carver or at the shuttle on a rural loom. You'll *sense* it as you watch a woman operating her spinning wheel [my emphasis].' Doing so would allow tourists to 'discover the old traditions of French Québec.'[168] But no longer were visitors informed that coming to Quebec was like travelling back in time. The province instead now simply offered tourists some opportunities to *feel* the past and encounter some traces of it.

The way tourism promoters envisaged arts and crafts in general offers further insight into this changing perception of the past as a Quebec tourist attraction and, in turn, as a marker of national identity. In previous decades, as we have seen, arts and crafts were heralded as a concrete manifestation of French-Canadian traditions, confirming the skills of the ancestors and affirming French-Canadian culture as rooted in 'Old Quebec.' By the 1950s, although much of government publicity, most notably its illustrations, represented arts and crafts as part and parcel of Quebec's traditional lifestyle, attitudes were changing as these artefacts were starting to be advertised primarily as decorative objects. In the 1960s, this view of arts and crafts came to predominate. They were publicized as products that showcased the sophisticated level of artistry of Quebec craftsmen. They had also completely lost any pretensions to utilitarian value and were no longer held up as reminders of 'the good old days.' Thus, the 1960 'L'atmosphère – Magnifique' advertisement, in addition to highlighting the talents of the craftsmen who followed the traditions of their trade, informed tourists that 'you'll know [the atmosphere] has transcended time as you view the works of Quebec's *avant-garde*.'[169] In a guidebook of the period, Charlevoix artisans were presented much as contemporary artists would be: 'The weavers, the wood carvers and the others are themselves artists in the media of wool, wood, and linen.'[170] This recasting of Quebec's arts and crafts' distinctive attributes speaks to a changing French-Canadian self-image. Tourist promoters were eager to market Quebec as a fount of highly talented artisans eager to display their distinctive creations to those seeking beautiful objects. In this way, tourists and French Canadians alike would discover what artistic innovations contemporary French Quebec artisans were capable of, befitting a dynamic and highly cultivated society. Clearly, by the 1960s, arts and crafts would no longer be considered an asset by tourist promoters simply because they were by-products of the past. Robert Prévost sums up this new perspective when he states: 'Until a quarter of a century ago, arts and crafts in the province of Quebec boiled down to hooked rugs and representational sculpture. We have in this field gone beyond a remarkable stage and the accomplishments of our artisans are often comparable to those of reputed European masters.'[171]

Comparing the way Quebec was marketed as a tourist destination by government tourist promoters before and during the 1960s confirms that this period witnessed a significant change. One could argue that what accounts for this change is the very fact that tourist promoters were, each in their own way, reacting to changes in the manner French Canadians defined their sense of national identity. In the early days, tourist promoters both set out to modernize the province's tourism infrastructure and worked to market the province as 'Old Quebec.' However, being ensconced in the Roads Department – tasked with facilitating and also promoting the province's economic development – they could not ignore the very real and expanding 'Modern Quebec.' This dual mandate could at times lead to an incoherent imaging of the province where the 'Old World' traditional habitants were advertised simultaneously as alive and well, as a part of a vanishing race, and as well-suited for business investors in search of a compliant work force. By the 1930s, those in charge of tourism promotion proved less ambivalent. Being traditional nationalists, they were reacting *against* the modernizing changes taking place around them – what they perceived to be the Americanization of Quebec society. Tourism would serve as a spur to revitalize 'Old Quebec,' what they perceived to be the true and authentic one. In the next couple of decades, however, increasing changes emerged in the way the province was marketed, reflecting a period when a growing number of French Canadians were questioning as never before what defined them as distinct. Were they to continue to present their homeland as 'Old' or as 'La province de Québec'? In the 1950s, the two labels were used in varying degrees in government publicity with the 'Old' still very much in evidence. By the 1960s, new decisions had clearly been made, with 'la belle province' becoming the label of choice. The tourist promoters along with their fellow French Canadians had embraced with open arms the changes that had transformed Quebec society over time. Just as traditional nationalists had hoped that tourism could promote an 'Old Quebec,' tourism promotion in the 1960s had become a way to market and celebrate the modern Quebec that tourists would see upon arrival. The past not only became simply one attraction among several but it was promoted first and foremost as a 'sensual magnet' rather than an opportunity for tourists (and French Canadians) to gain some historical knowledge about the province. As with the other tourist marketing slogans that preceded it, la 'belle province' mirrored how French Canadians perceived their homeland and how they wanted visitors to perceive them. By the 1960s, it reflected a new sense of national identity less reliant on the legacies of the past and more willing to welcome with enthusiasm the conditions of the present.

NOTES

1 This chapter is based upon research funded by the Social Sciences and Research Counci of Canada. I would like to thank Matthew Hayday for providing me with invaluable archival documentation during his tenure as research assistant. I am also very grateful to Peter Hodgins and Serge Jaumain for their thoughtful comments. All French-language quotations have been translated by me unless otherwise indicated.

2 During the greater part of the period, the majority of tourists coming to Quebec were Americans, largely from New York state and the New England states. If, by the 1960s, Canadians including Quebeckers would take over that first place, Americans would never be far behind. Thus Quebec would attract 39 per cent of the American tourist market, and although that figure would be down to 20 per cent in 1964, Americans remained a significant proportion of the tourist clientele. Georges Delage, 'Le tourisme, comédie ou tragédie?' *Commerce* 66 (May 1964): 87–9, 91–2.

3 James Murton analyses this phenomenon fully, focusing on the aims of the tourism promoters of private companies, in his chapter in this volume, '"The Normandy of the New World": Canada Steamship Lines, Antimodernism, and the Selling

of Old Quebec.' See also Nicole Neatby, 'Meeting of the Minds: North American Travel Writers and Government Tourist Publicity in 1920–1955,'*Histoire sociale/Social History* 36 (November 2003): 465–95. And outside Quebec, a sampling would include Ian McKay's work, including 'History and the Tourist Gaze: The Politics of Commemoration in Nova Scotia, 1935–1964,' *Acadiensis* 22, 2 (Spring 1993): 102–38; *The Quest of the Folk: Antimodernism and Cultural Selection in Twentieth-Century Nova Scotia* (Montreal and Kingston: McGill-Queen's University Press, 1994); and with Robin Bates, *In the Province of History: The Making of the Public Past in Twentieth-Century Nova Scotia* (Montreal and Kingston: McGill-Queen's University Press, 2010). For the United States, see also among many others Martha Norkumas, *The Politics of Public Memory: Tourism, History and Ethnicity in Monterey California* (Albany: SUNY Press, 1993); Dona Brown, *Inventing New England: Regional Tourism in the Nineteenth Century* (Washington: Smithsonian Institution, 1995); Jane S. Becker, *Selling Tradition: Appalachia and the Construction of an American Folk, 1930–1940* (Chapel Hill: University of North Carolina Press, 1998).

4 See Murton, '"The Normandy of the New World."' For the expectations of tourists travelling to Quebec see Nicole Neatby, 'Meeting of the Minds.'

5 See Alain Roy, 'Le vieux Québec, 1945–1963: Construction et fonctions sociales d'un lieu de mémoire nationale,' MA thesis, History, Université Laval, 1995; Nathalie Hamel, 'Coordonner l'artisanat et le tourisme, ou comment mettre en valeur le visage pittoresque du Québec, (1915–1960),' *Histoire sociale/Social History* 34, 67 (May 2001): 97–114; and James Murton, 'La "Normandie du Nouveau Monde": la société Canada Steamship Lines, l'antimodernisme et la promotion du Québec ancien,' *Revue d'histoire de l'Amérique française* 55, 1 (Summer 2001): 3–44. Others have focused on the development of the tourist industry and the activities of tourists in certain regions of the province. See, for example, Jules Bélanger, Mara Desjardins, Jean-Yves Frenette, et al., *Histoire de la Gaspésie* (Montreal: Boréal Express, IQRC, 1981); Philippe Dubé, 'Deux cents ans de villégiature dans Charlevoix ou l'histoire d'un pays visité,' PhD thesis, Université Laval, 1985. Robert Prévost, who occupied high-ranking positions as a public servant in the 1960s in the area of tourism promotion, published a broad overview of the history of Quebec tourism, *Trois siècles de tourisme au Québec* (Sillery: Septentrion, 2000).

6 Roger Brière, 'Géographie du tourisme au Québec,' PhD thesis, Université de Montréal, Faculté des lettres, 1967; Serge Gagnon, 'L'émergence de l'identité rurale et l'intervention de l'État québécois en tourisme, 1920–1940,' *Téoros* (Autumn 2001): 24–31 and *L'échiquier touristique québécois* (Sainte-Foy: Les Presses de l'Université du Québec, 2002); Normand Cazelais et al., eds., *L'espace touristique* (Sainte-Foy: Les Presses de l'Université du Québec, 1999). In this

same collection, see also Martine Geronimi, 'Permanece paysagère et consommation touristique: le cas du Vieux-Quebec' (199–212) and 'Voyage au pays de l'identité: de la définition d'un paysage touristique à la création de la spécificité culturelle canadienne-française' (213–36) by Lucie K. Morisset, who teaches in the UQAM Département d'études urbaines et touristiques. Although she is an architectural historian, she has also published numerous articles addressing these questions.

7 Morisset writes of a built landscape ('paysage construit') or of a 'mise en tourisme' in 'Voyage au pays de l'identité,' 216 and 225. For his part, the geographer Serge Gagnon uses the expression 'mise en scène,' the equivalent to 'tourist staging,' to underline the idea of construction ('L'émergence de l'identité rurale,' 28).

8 My translation of ibid., 24.

9 See Gagnon, *L'échiquier touristique québécois,* 256.

10 Karen Dubinsky, *The Second Greatest Disappointment: Honeymooning and Tourism at Niagara Falls* (Toronto: Between the Lines, 1999), 151.

11 Indeed, by 1920 there were approximately eight million cars registered in the United States. By 1930, the number had risen to almost twenty-three million. Marguerite Shaffer, *See America First: Tourism and National Identity, 1880–1940* (Washington: Smithsonian Institution Press, 2001), 137. Three-quarters of the visitors to Quebec came by car from the United States. Their number had increased from 1 500 in 1915 to close to 650,000 in 1933(Prévost, *Trois siècles de tourisme,* 90).

12 Between 1912 and 1918, the Quebec government had laid down a network of provincial highways covering a total of 350 miles. By 1928, 4972 miles of so-called first-class roads accommodated close to a half-million cars coming from across the border (Prévost, *Trois siècles de tourisme,* 66).

13 By 1929, 210,530 of these trees had been planted. Official Annual Report of the Roads Department, submitted to the Legislative Assembly of the Province of Quebec, 1929, 87.

14 See also Gagnon, *L'échiquier touristique québécois,* 230–5, and Morisset, *Voyage au pays de l'identité,* 229.

15 John Urry, *The Tourist Gaze: Leisure and Travel in Contemporary Societies* (London: Sage, 1990). For a fuller discussion of John Urry's 'tourist gaze' see James Murton's chapter in this volume.

16 See Murton's chapter in this volume.

17 'Old Quebec: Niagara to the Sea,' advertisement for Canada Steamship Lines, *New York Times,* 6 May 1926, 51.

18 'Come Up! ... Quebec Says "Bienvenue!"' *New York Times,* 23 May 1926, sect. 8, 20.

19 'Vacation in Old Quebec,' advertisement for the Château Frontenac in *New York Times*, 2 May 1926, sect. 8, 18.

20 'Jaunts through Normandy in History Quebec,' advertisement for the Château Frontenac, a Canadian Pacific Hotel, *New York Times*, 2 May 1926, sect. 8, 18.

21 'Explore ! ... North America's Normandy,' advertisement for Château Frontenac, *New York Times*, 26 June 1926, sect. 17, 16.

22 '4, 5 and 6 Days in Quebec/Canada,' Provincial Tourist Bureau, Roads Department, 2nd edition, May 1928, 30.

23 Provincial Tourist Bureau, Roads Department, in *Travel*, June 1935, 3. In 1936, the Provincial Tourist Bureau headline also highlighted the past: 'Slip back to olden times, Vacation this summer in the Old Province of Quebec,' *New York Times*, 14 June 1936, sect. 11, 16.

24 Provincial Tourist Bureau, Roads Department advertisement of 1936, *Halifax Herald*, 1 August 1936, 8.

25 'Old Quebec ... where the Spirit of the Past lives again,' Provincial Tourist Bureau, Roads Department, Quebec, *Saturday Night*, 17 July 1934.

26 The Provincial Tourist Bureau published a guide on the Gaspé region the very same year (1929): 'The Gaspé Peninsula: History, Legends, Resources, Attractions,' Quebec Department of Highways and Mines, Provincial Tourist Bureau, April 1929, 10, 11.

27 Louis Hémon, *Maria Chapdelaine: A Tale of the Lake St John Country*, trans. W.H. Blake (Toronto: Macmillan Co. of Canada, first published in 1921).

28 See Eugene Achard, *Le Royaume du Saguenay* (Montreal: Librairie générale canadienne, 1942), 199.

29 Tourists could buy postcards with pictures of Marie Bédard at the museum, leaving no doubt as to her muse-like vocation. Other members of the family could also feel a certain kinship with the characters in the novel, since a few did have the same first names as the central characters in the novel. Thus, for instance, Samuel Bédard and Samuel Chapdelaine were both fathers. As noted indirectly by Ian McKay (note 77 in his chapter), there is an interesting study yet to be written about the use of fictional characters for the purposes of tourism promotion.

30 *4, 5 and 6 Days*, 28.

31 Ibid., 6. Interestingly enough, the first two photographs in this guide on page 2 are (1) the 'Quebec Bridge, longest single span bridge in the world' and (2) 'Ox team, reminiscent of olden days.'

32 Ibid., 26.

33 *Quebec, The French Canadian Province: A Harmony of Beauty, History and Progress*, Provincial Tourist Bureau, Roads Department, Quebec, 1927, 39.

34 *The Old World at Your Door, The French Canadian Province*, Provincial Tourist Bureau, Roads Department, Quebec, 1932, 3.

35 Taken from 'Excerpts of the Official Annual Report of the Roads Department, Minister of Roads for the year 1927, submitted to the Legislative Assembly of the Province of Quebec,' published in *L'Hôtellerie*, 31 January 1928, 3.

36 John Dickinson and Brian Young, *A Short History of Quebec*, 3rd edition (Montreal and Kingston: McGill-Queen's University Press, 2003), 211.

37 Ibid., 203.

38 *Along Quebec Highways, Tourist Guide*, Provincial Tourist Bureau, Department of Highways and Mines, February 1930.

39 Ibid., 45.

40 See Neatby, 'Meeting of the Minds.'

41 See also James Murton's brief summary of this surge in French-Canadian nationalism in his chapter in this volume, 424–5.

42 Hémon, *Maria Chapdelaine*, 283.

43 From 1930 to 1937, the Quebec government spent 26 million dollars to establish settlers in northern Quebec. See Paul-André Linteau et al., *Histoire du Québec contemporain, Le Québec depuis 1930*, 2nd edition (Montreal: Boréal compact, 1989), 47

44 See Paul Gouin, 'Causerie donnée au poste CKAC, sous les auspices de la Ligue des droits de la femme, le 10 mars 1933,' in *Servir 1 – La Cause nationale* (Montreal: Les Éditons du Zodiaque, 1938), 57. See Murton, '"The Normandy of the New World"'; Hamel, 'Coordonner l'artisanat'; and Irene Durand, 'Essai d'analyse de la pratique de l'artisanat au Québec,' MA thesis, Sociology, Université du Québec à Montréal, 1981.

45 Jean Bruchési, 'L'aveu d'une faute,' *Le Terroir* 14, 12 (May 1933): 13.

46 Alphonse Désilets, 'Pour le tourisme,' *Le Terroir* 13, 1 (June 1931).

47 In Quebec, the increasing revenues gained from the tourist industry over the period certainly provided convincing evidence to support their claims: 1920–27: $4,400,000; 1928–32: $262,000,000; 1933: $35,000,000. Reported by Arthur Bergeron, assistant deputy minister of the Roads Department of Quebec in the Senate Report and Proceedings of the Special Committee on Tourist Traffic, Ottawa, J.O. Patenaude, King's Printer, 1934, 84.

48 In 1934, the Canadian government set up a Special Committee on Tourist Traffic to study the possibilities of increasing tourist traffic, evaluate the existing government policies in that regard, and make recommendations.

49 Paul Gouin, 'L'architecture et l'hôtellerie,' *Le Canada*, 4 August 1932, in Gouin, *Servir*, 19.

50 Ibid., 42.

51 Mgr Camille Roy, 'Un Témoignage,' *Le Terroir* 14, 12 (May 1933): 12.

52 Ibid. What the author calls the 'paysage spirituel.'

53 Ibid.

54 Désilets, 'Pour le tourisme,' 1.

55 Roy, 'Un témoignage,' 15.

56 Abbé Albert Tessier, 'Vieilles enseignes,' lecture given at the annual meeting of the Société du Parlez français held at Laval University, 31 January 1933, 13. Document that comes with the advertisement of a 'Concours d'enseignes artistiques du Syndicat d'Initiative de Mauricie sous le patronage de l'Office provincial du tourisme,' 1937, Fonds Paul Gouin P190 (hereafter P190), dossier 'Hôtellerie-Documentation,' 1983 03–038/72, Archives nationales du Québec à Montréal (hereafter ANQM).

57 Roy, 'Un Témoignage,' 15.

58 See Luc Noppen and Lucie K. Morisset, 'À la recherche d'une architecture pour la nation canadienne-française: entre le paysage et la patrie, de la crise à la Seconde Guerre mondiale,' *Les Cahiers d'histoire du Québec au 20ᵉ siècle* 5 (Spring 1996): 9–36.

59 Olivar Asselin, 'Sur une organization du tourisme,' *Le Canada*, 7 December 1932.

60 Ibid.

61 Ibid.

62 He estimated that between 1932 and 1941, he had given more than 2200 conferences of propaganda, meant to increase audiences 'knowledge and love of the province' in a document dated 11 January 1941, Séminaire de Trois-Rivières, 'Tessier fait de la photographie et du cinéma à ses frais. Non aux frais du Gouvernement!' E16/181 7C37 2603A, Archives nationales du Québec à Québec (hereafter ANQQ). He was appointed to the Chair of History at Laval University in 1937 and the provincial government bought several of his seventy films lauding the traditional lifestyle. See Christian Poirier, *Clergé et patrimoine cinématographique québécois: les prêtres Albert Tessier et Maurice Proulx*, Encyclopédie du patrimoine culturel de l'Amérique, 2009.

63 Tessier, 'Vieilles enseignes,' 13.

64 Ibid., 12.

65 Of Quebec City.

66 Letter to the editor written by someone from Sainte-Foy, Quebec, to *La Presse* lauding the *refrancisation* campaign. *La Presse*, 16 June 1930, 6. It was felt by tourism promoters that small hotels were more likely than their big city counterparts to be managed by French Canadians and that they would be more amenable to the campaign's objectives. They were also more numerous. Statistics from the Service d'Hôtellerie of 1930 confirm that 85 per cent of 'hospitality enterprises' were family-run and were located outside large urban centres. Henri-Paul Garceau, *Chronique de l'hospitalité hôtelière du Québec de 1880–1940: Les pionniers* (Montreal: Les Éditions du Méridien, 1990), 197.

67 Paul Gouin, 'Noms français et meubles "esperantos,"' *Le Progrès du Golfe*, 27 May 1932, in Gouin, *Servir*, 11. In line with this desire to offer expert advice on cultural matters, he recommends the creation of an 'aesthetics commission' which could, among other things, offer advice to institutions, commercial establishments, and individuals on how best to give 'to the whole province a worthy French-Canadian character,' 'whithout coercive measures.' Gouin, 'L'architecture et l'hôtellerie,' in Gouin, *Servir*, 19,18.

68 In 1946 the Provincial Publicity Office was created in charge of all government publicity and the Tourist Branch became one of its services.

69 Morisset, 'Voyage au pays de l'identité,' 228. This is certainly how politicians justified tourism's place in the structures of government. During a speech he delivered at the First National Tourist Congress in Quebec City in 1943, Premier Adélard Godbout declared: 'We in Quebec fully realize the importance of tourism and proof of this is to be found in the fact that I have kept tourism in my own Department in order that I may give it particularly careful attention and close supervision.' Speech by Adélard Godbout at the first National Tourist Congress, Château Frontenac, Quebec City, 1943, P172, file 3, ANQQ, 2.

70 The idea for this contest came from Abbé Albert Tessier. Document 'Concours d'enseignes artistiques. Le Syndicat d'Initiatives de la Mauricie,' Syndicat d'Initiative de la Mauricie, sous le patronage de l'Office provincial du tourisme, Trois-Rivières, Québec. P190, 1983–03–038/72, dossier 'Hôtellerie-Documentation,' ANQM.

71 The provincial government thus founded specialized schools to train artisans. These included the École Provinciale des Arts Domestiques in 1930, the École du Meuble de Montréal in 1935, and the Atelier de céramique at the École des Beaux Arts de Montréal, as well as a binding section at the École Technique de Montréal. See James Murton in this volume, 436–7. Natalie Hamel provides an in-depth analysis of this development, revealing the extent to which the traditional techniques were in fact invented or 'improved upon' in order to better lure the tourist dollar ('Coordonner l'artisanat et le tourisme,' esp. 99). See also Natalie Hamel, *Notre maître le passé, notre maître l'avenir: Paul Gouin et la conservation de l'héritage culturel du Québec* (Quebec: Les Presses de l'Université Laval, 2008).

72 Paul Gouin, 'Les arts domestiques,' talk given at the Congrès de la Société Saint-Jean-Baptiste de Montréal, 10 March 1938, in Gouin, *Servir*, 193.

73 See Durand, 'Essai d'analyse,' 271.

74 Gouin, 'Nom français et meubles "esperantos,"' in Gouin, *Servir*, 12, 13.

75 Paul Gouin, 'En marge du féminisme,' talk given at the Club Wilfrid Laurier, 3 December 1934, in Gouin, *Servir,* 137.

76 Ibid., 138.

77 Gouin, 'Les arts domestiques,' in Gouin, *Servir*, 198–9.

78 Jean-Marie Gauvreau, 'Artisans du Québec,' Les Éditions du Bien Public, 1940, 42.

79 Jean-Marie Gauvreau, *Rapport général sur l'artisanat*, Ministère des affaires municipales, de l'industrie et du commerce, Province de Québec, 1939.

80 Albert Tessier, *Rapport sur le tourisme*, Ministère des affaires municipales, de l'industrie et du commerce, Province de Québec, 1939.

81 Abbé Albert Tessier, *Les valeurs nationales et économiques du tourisme* (Quebec: Comité permanent de la Survivance française en Amérique, 1943).

82 In fact, the report contains many direct quotations from the Olivar Asselin report.

83 Tessier, *Rapport*, 3.

84 Ibid., 4.

85 Ibid.

86 Ibid.

87 Ibid., 1.

88 Ibid., 9.

89 Adélard Godbout's speech to the National Tourist Convention, at the Château Frontenac, Quebec, 1943, P712/1, file 3, ANQQ, 1 .

90 'Enjoy your honeymoon in Romantic Québec,' *Toronto Star*, 15 May 1950, 7.

91 Brochure entitled 'La Province de Québec, Canada,' 6th edition, Tourist Branch, Provincial Publicity Office, 1, date unknown but most likely from the early 1950s.

92 'Bienvenue à Québec!' *Saturday Night*, Tourist Branch, Provincial Publicity Office, June 1953.

93 'La Province de Québec, Canada,' 31.

94 Ibid., 38.

95 Ibid., 21.

96 Ibid., 1.

97 For a more thorough analysis of the connection between consumerism and tourism see Michael Dawson, *Selling British Columbia: Tourism and Consumer Culture, 1890–1970* (Vancouver: University of British Columbia Press, 2004).

98 The historian Serge Jaumain points out that by the late 1950s and 1960s, Belgian guidebooks increasingly highlight Brussells's modernity – a response to urban developments particular to the capital itself but also in response to a newly emerging appetite for modernity among the post–Second World War waves of tourists. Serge Jaumain, '"Une grande capitale moderne": Bruxelles dans les guides touristiques de la deuxième moitié du XXe siècle,' in Philippe Duhamel and Remy Knafou, eds., *Mondes urbains du tourisme* (Paris: Belin, 2007), 308–22. See also Jaumain, 'L'image de Bruxelles dans les guides touristiques (XIXe–XXe siècles),' in *Bruxelles, 175 ans d'une capitale* (Sprimont: Madaga, 2005), 155–66.

99 Presentation by Paul Gouin most likely dated 1952 or 1953 beginning with the words 'Mesdames, Messieurs, Au cours de mes causeries,' 1, Paul Gouin Collection, P190, 1983–03–038/63, ANQM.

100 Paul Gouin, 'Au pays de Québec rien ne doit mourir et rien ne doit changer ... ,' *Culture, Revue trimestrielle/A Quarterly Review* 12, 1 (March 1951): 45.

101 See the printed copies of his 'Causeries,' P190, 1983–0-03/1, ANQM or in E4 1960–01–483/436, ANQQ.

102 'Causerie prononcée sur le réseau français de Radio-Canada, le dimanche 5 novembre 1950, à 6 hrs p.m. par M. Paul Gouin, Conseiller Technique auprès du Conseil Exécutif de la Province de Québec,' E4 /1906–01–483/436, ANQQ, 7.

103 Paul Gouin, Texte Technique of 1951, 12, P190, ANQM.

104 Presentation given by Paul Gouin to the Saint-Jean-Baptiste Society of Ottawa on 27 February 1955, P190, 1983–03–038/72, ANQM, 3. Gouin would be active in the new *refrancisation* campaigns of the 1950s including the 3e Congrès annuel de refrancisation of 1952 organized by the Société Saint-Jean-Baptiste and the following one, in 1957, which he presided over in Quebec City under the auspices of the Quebec government and the Conseil de la vie française en Amérique. See Hamel, *Notre maître le passé, notre maître l'avenir*, for a detailed study of his involvement in these initiatives.

105 'Excerpts of the lecture given by Paul Gouin at the closing of the Congrès de refrancisation, on June 24, 1957,' P190 1983–03–038/35, ANQM, 2.

106 Letter dated 10 June 1950 from Paul Gouin to M. Léo Trépanier, cabin owner in Trois-Rivières. Gouin is responding to his inquiry by sending him a list of suggested names for his cabins and the names of craftsmen who could build the signs as well. P190 1983–03–038/61, ANQM.

107 Presentation given by Paul Gouin to the Société Saint-Jean-Baptiste of Quebec at the Palais Montcalm in Quebec, 1 April 1951, P190 1983–03–038/72, ANQM, 23.

108 Gouin, presentation of 27 February 1955, 2.

109 Gouin, 'Au pays de Québec,' 45.

110 Presentation given by Paul Gouin to the Société Saint-Jean-Baptiste of Joliette at the Seminaire de Joliette on 20 October 1953, P190 1983 03–038/72, ANQM, 7.

111 Gouin, 'Au pays de Québec,' 48, 50. For a fully fleshed out analysis of this interpretation, see Natalie Hamel's nuanced and comprehensive study *Notre maître le passé, notre maître l'avenir* on Paul Gouin's contribution to the preservervation of the province's heritage and his central involvement in the crafting of its cultural policies.

112 Lecture given by Paul Gouin in Chicoutimi for the Société Saint-Jean-Baptiste on 6 May 1954 entitled 'Patrimoine au Foyer,' P190 1983–03–038/72, ANQM, 17. During that talk he also gives the SSJB members the same advice he gave in the late 1930s encouraging them to have in their statutes rules obliging them to purchase crafts at least once a year. See note 77 above.

113 Gouin, 'Au pays de Québec,' 46. In 1946, he opened in Montreal a boutique sell-

ing arts and crafts and other art objects. He himself was also an avid art collector. See Hamel, *Notre maître le passé, notre maître l'avenir*.

114 In 1959 he had been director of the Province of Quebec Tourist and Publicity Bureau, which included the Tourist Branch; the position had been left vacant since 1956, when Georges Léveillé passed away.

115 'Mémoire à M. Arthur Labrie, d. sc., Sous-ministre du tourisme, chasse et pêche, 19 décembre 1966 de Robert Prévost,' Fonds Robert Prévost (hereafter P573) P573/S1, 20004–07–07–001, ANQM, 2.

116 Lecture given by Robert Prévost to the Rotary Club of Drummondville, 3 July 1962, P573, Conférences de Robert Prévost, ANQM, 6.

117 See Roy, 'Le vieux Québec, 1945–1963,' 45.

118 As the Statistical Year Book, Department of Industry and Commerce, Quebec, Queen's Printer, 1961 states: 'The tourism industry deserves to retain our attention all the more as it can, depending on its orientation, increase or decrease the deficit of our commercial balance' (543).

119 Indeed in 1959, statistics reveal that for the first time American tourists spent more money in Mexico than in Canada. See lecture given by Robert Prévost at the annual dinner for guides, Association des marchands de la Place de l'Hôtel-de-Ville, Québec, 16 June 1960, P573, Conférences de Robert Prévost, ANQM, 5.

120 For a full discussion of the Canadian tourist industry in relation to the Canadian economy, see Alisa Apostle, 'Canada, Vacations Unlimited: The Canadian Government Tourist Industry, 1934–1959,' PhD thesis, History Department, Queen's University, 2002, especially chapters 3 and 4.

121 Lecture given by Robert Prévost, director of the Provincial Office of Publicity, 'Conférence prononcée devant les membres du "Bureau Touristique et Economique des Laurentides" – Alpine Inn, Sainte-Marguerite, – 30 mars 1960,' Robert Prévost Collection, P573, ANQM, 2.

122 Ibid., 4. The budget devoted to advertisement amounted to $230,000 in 1959/60 and was increased to $367,468.70 in 1960/61. See Prévost, *Trois siècles de tourisme*, 211.

123 Translation of 'une toilette typographique impéccable,' in document 'Congrès annuel de la Régionale des Chambres de Commerce du Lac Saint-Jean, Roberval, 20 mai, 1962, "Résumé du travail accompli depuis la réorganisation des services touristiques,"' P573, Conférences de Robert Prévost, ANQM, 2.

124 Lecture given to the 'Club Vente: Publicité de Québec,', 24 April 1961, entitled 'Les annonces touristiques du Québec.' P573, ANQM, 5.

125 Lecture given to the Congrès de l'Association canadienne de la Radio et Télévision de la langue française, Toronto, 12 September 1961, 4.

126 In 1960, the Tourist Bureau made use of billboards. Three hundred were erected

along Ontario and Maritimes highways close to the American border for the first time. In 1961, the number increased to four hundred. See Prévost, *Trois siècles de tourisme*, 203.

127 Lecture given to the Association canadienne des éducateurs de langue française, Université de Montréal, 16 March 1963, entitled 'Techniques publicitaires modernes,' P573, Conférences de Robert Prévost, ANQM, 5.

128 Lecture given by Robert Prévost, director, Province of Quebec Tourist Bureau, to the 'Advertising and Sales Clubs of Canada, Congrès annuel,' Château Frontenac, 26 May 1962, P573, Conférences de Robert Prévost, ANQM, 9.

129 Lecture given by Robert Prévost, director, Province of Quebec Tourist Bureau, at the Olivar Asselin awards ceremony to Miss Germaine Bernier, from *Le Devoir*, Société Saint-Jean-Baptiste, Montréal, 20 February 1962, titled 'Notre Visage français, un actif rentable,' P573, Conférences de Robert Prévost, ANQM, 11.

130 Annual Report, 1965, Alphonse Couturier, minister of tourism, hunting, and fishing, Quebec, January 1966, 14.

131 Annual Report, 1966, Gabriel Loubier, minister of tourism, hunting, and fishing, Quebec, Provincial Tourist Bureau, January 1967, 19. Accompanying the brochure 'Travelling in Quebec "La Belle Province"' is a lexicon entitled 'Fun with Fonetic French.' In 1967, it is reissued under the title 'Travel Fun en Français in Québec, la belle province.' (The early 1950s Tourist Branch guide entitled 'La Province de Québec, Canada' had included two pages with roughly forty useful questions translated into three languages, including French.)

132 In the tour guide entitled 'The Province where Friendliness is a way of life. Québec: l'aimable province,' Department of Tourism, Hunting, and Fishing, I-LXIV (Lionel Bertrand, minister), tourists were told that 'the majority of its citizens, while they are of French origin are bilingual.'

133 Robert Prévost, director, Province of Quebec Tourist Bureau, speaking at the 'Travel Forum, Wilmingon (Delaware),' 17 January 1962, P573, Conférences de Robert Prévost, ANQM, 1.

134 Lecture given by Robert Prévost, 'New-York, Vermont Interstate Commission on the Lake Champlain Bassin, Stowe Vermont,' 27 September 1962, P573, Conférences de Robert Prévost, ANQM, 4.

135 Lecture given by Robert Prévost to the Société Saint-Jean-Baptiste, 26 February 1973, P573, Conférences de Robert Prévost, ANQM, 7.

136 Provincial Tourist Bureau advertisement 'Prenez des vacances à la française au Québec!' *New Yorker*, 5 May 1962. See Prévost, *Trois siècles de tourisme*, 212–13.

137 See the Annual Report, 1963/4, Gérard Cournoyer, minister of tourism, fish, and game, Quebec, January 1965, 12.

138 Lecture given by Robert Prévost at the 'Premier festival du Caplan – Sept-Île,' 31 May 1964, P573, Conférences de Robert Prévost, ANQM, 2.

139 Lecture given by Robert Prévost to the Quebec Chamber of Commerce, Journée d'études de 1964, Holiday Inn, 12 November 1964, P573, Conférences de Robert Prévost, ANQM, 7, 8.

140 Lecture given by Robert Prévost, director, Province of Quebec Tourist Bureau, 'Advertising and Sales Clubs of Canada, Congrès annuel,' Château Frontenac, 26 May 1962, P573, Conférences Robert Prévost, ANQM, 9.

141 In the Foreword of the brochure entitled 'La province de Québec,' 1963, Provincial Tourist Bureau, Department of Tourism, Fish, and Game (bilingual). The audience for this brochure must have also been businessmen, since bureaucrats from the department often asked the Provincial Tourist Bureau for copies of its brochures.

142 'Rapport préliminaire sur le tourisme' to the Honourable Lionel Bertrand, Secrétaire de la Province, from Robert Prévost, director of the Provincial Office of Publicity, July 1960, 24.

143 Taken from the Foreword of 'La province de Québec,' 1963.

144 Letter from Jean Drapeau to Mr N.R.Crump, Canadian Pacific Railway President, 2 February 1964. Montreal City Archives, Tourisme, real #106.

145 See William Weintraub, *City Unique: Montreal Days and Nights in the 1940s and 50s* (Toronto: McClelland and Stewart, 1996).

146 In addition to paraphrasing Bergeron, he reported that a few such sentences were cut from the French version of this publicity when it was submitted to the Municipal Office of Tourism for approval. 'Aux touristes: Présenter une image fidèle de Montréal.' *La Presse*, 21 March 1962.

147 'The Little Town of Saintly Miracles,' *Maclean's* 81, 5 (May 1968): 26–7.

148 Letter addressed to M. Gérald Bosse, director-general of tourism, to the attention of Robert Prévost, assistant deputy minister, Department of Tourism, Hunting, and Fishing, from Gilles Charron, deputy minister of industry and commerce, 6 June 1968, P573, ANQM.

149 Letter from Robert Prévost responding to Gilles Charron concerning the May 1968 *Maclean's* article, Fonds P573, ANQM.

150 Provincial Tourist Bureau advertisement, 'Visit Quebec First,' Montreal *Gazette*, 28 May 1960, 21.

151 Provincial Tourist Bureau advertisement, 'La Cuisine – Magnifique!' *Toronto Star*, 2 July 1960, 15. The others are sports, panorama, and atmosphere.

152 Ibid.

153 Provincial Tourist Bureau advertisement, 'Hospitalité Spoken Here,' *Maclean's*, 20 May 1961.

154 Annual Report, 1966, Gabriel Loubier, minister of tourism, hunting, and fishing, January 1967, Province of Quebec Tourist Bureau, 19. It was entitled 'Adventures in French Canadian Cuisine.'

155 Paul-Henri Garceau, *Chronique de l'hospitalité hôtelière du Québec de 1940 à 1980* (Montreal: XYZ Éditeur, 1995), 46–54.

156 Lecture given by Robert Prévost at a diner-causerie for the Association canadienne des restaurateurs, Rond Point du Québec, 4 October 1966, P573, Conférences de Robert Prévost, ANQM, 3. Garceau notes that in 1966, Prévost and Gabriel Loubier, the minister of tourism, hunting, and fishing, had invited the American Travel Writers Society organizing committee to the 9th annual Salon de dégustation, during which most of the 125 dishes/courses on display were prepared with Quebec products from its lakes and farms (Garceau, *Chronique de l'hospitalité hôtelière du Québec de 1940 à 1980*, 54).

157 Provincial Tourist Bureau advertisement, 'Hospitalité Spoken Here,' *Maclean's*, 20 May 1961.

158 See the Introduction by Lionel Bertrand, Department of Tourism, Hunting, and Fishing to the guidebook entitled 'The Province where Friendliness is a way of Life, Quebec l'aimable Province,' published by the Provincial Tourist Bureau, 1964. The expression 'state of mind' was used by Robert Prévost in a lecture he gave at the 'Club-Vente-Publicité de Québec,' 7 November 1966, entitled 'Tourisme provinciale et Expo '67,' P573, Conférences de Robert Prévost, ANQM, 7.

159 Annual Report, 1965, Alphonse Couturier, minister of tourism, hunting, and fishing, Quebec, Provincial Tourist Bureau, January 1966, 14.

160 Annual Report, 1966, Gabriel Loubier, minister of tourism, hunting, and fishing, Quebec, Provincial Tourist Bureau, January 1967, 14.

161 Advertisement of the Tourist Branch of the Department of Tourism, Hunting, and Fishing, 'Come and Enjoy Les Beautés du Québec,' *Toronto Star*, 16 April 1966, 20.

162 See Provincial Tourist Bureau advertisement, 'Les Sports-Magnifiques!' *Toronto Star*, 25 June 1960, 16; advertisement of the Tourist Branch of the Department of Tourism, Hunting, and Fishing, 'Come and Enjoy Les Beautés du Québec,', *Toronto Star*, 16 April 1966, 20.

163 See, for example, the advertisment of the Provincial Tourist Bureau, 'Hospitalité Spoken Here,' *Maclean's*, 20 May 1961; Tourist Bureau of the Department of Tourism, Hunting, and Fishing, 'Mémorable Quebec-Hospitalité Spoken Here,' *Holiday Magazine*, April 1964, 32.

164 Lecture given by Robert Prévost to the 'Club Saint-Laurent, Montreal, 8 février 1961,' as director of the Province of Quebec Tourist and Publicity Bureau, P573, Conférences de Robert Prévost, ANQM, 6.

165 Advertisement of the Provincial Tourist Bureau, 'Hospitalité Spoken Here – "You're Invited Next Door,"' *Canadian Geographic Magazine* 64, 5 (1962); advertisement of the Tourist Bureau of the Department of Tourism, Hunting, and Fishing, 'Hospitalité Spoken Here,' *Maclean's*, 1 May 1965.

166 For example, see the Provincial Tourist Bureau advertisement, 'Enjoy a Vacation in French Canada,' *Toronto Star*, 28 May 1960, 16, in which tourists are invited to visit 'Historic Québec City – Metropolitan Montreal.'

167 Provincial Tourist Bureau, 'L'atmosphère – Magnifique!', *Toronto Star*, 16 July 1960, 17.

168 Provincial Tourist Bureau, 'See Quebec Say – Magnifique! L'atmosphère – Magnifique!' *Toronto Star*, 16 July 1960, 17.

169 Provincial Tourist Bureau, 'L'atmosphère – Magnifique!' *Toronto Star*, 16 July 1960, 17.

170 Guide book 'Inviting … La Province de Québec vous accueille … ,' Provincial Tourist Bureau, Department of Tourism, Hunting, and Fishing, Ministe Lionel Bertrand, date unknown but around 1963.

171 Preliminary Report on tourism to the Honourable Lionel Bertrand, provincial secretary, from Robert Prévost, director of the Provincial Tourist Bureau, Office of Publicity, July 1960, 23. In 1961, when justifying the production of four new tourist films on Quebec arts and crafts including enamelling, ceramic, ironwork, and cabinetmaking, Prévost noted their 'vital' importance from a tourist point of view, but he measured this importance in terms of their artistic value. These films would be useful 'to reach a certain elite that, often, is more sensitive to artistic manifestations than to picturesque attractions or life in the open air.' Lecture given by Robert Prévost to the 'Comité Culturel de l'Association des Employés Civils,' Quebec, 21 November 1961, P573, Conférences de Robert Prévost, ANQM, 11.

16 Peace, Order, and Good Banking: Packaging History and Memory in Canadian Commercial Advertising[1]

IRA WAGMAN

Many scholars – including contributors to this volume – have reflected upon the relationship between mass media, popular culture, and collective memory. Barbie Zelizer has observed that while media forms from newspapers to television have 'organized information at a point contemporaneous to the event, so too have they helped organize information at a point somewhat distant from the event.'[2] For George Lipsitz, the distribution of popular culture through media 'has played an important role in creating the crisis of memory, but it has also been one of the main vehicles for the expression of loss and the projection of hopes for reconnection to the past.'[3] The emergence of virtual museums and digital archives on the Internet, along with websites ranging from Flickr to Facebook that allow people to display visual works ranging from personal photographs to images of the Mona Lisa, marks the latest electronic 'vehicles of memory' to attract attention from those interested in questions about the ways people comprehend their past, present, and future.[4]

In spite of the interest in media forms and the shaping of historical consciousness, studies of the dissemination of history through commercial advertising campaigns have been ignored. Recognizing their role as historical artefacts, Marshall McLuhan once observed, 'historians and archaeologists will one day discover that the ads of our times are the richest and most fruitful daily reflections that any society has ever made of its entire range of activities.'[5] This is based on advertising's ubiquity and its diversity. Whether we like or not, advertising messages are everywhere, selling everything, at every time of the day. When we encounter advertising messages, we experience a range of signs and symbols which are 'pitched' at a level intended to encourage people to consume. An important component of many product pitches is memory. In this chapter I explore the use of a particular kind of memory, national historical memory, as it has circulated in a range of Canadian advertising campaigns in print and broadcast media. This is intended to resituate the role of commercial advertising as a key contributor in the circulation of public memory. In short, advertising has been ignored either because analysts immediately disqualify it owing to its consumerist objectives or because the profit motives of the companies deploying these ads make them unworthy for study. Instead, scholars have focused on more 'serious' forms of advertising, such as elections,[6] public education campaigns, or times of national crisis.[7] A recent initiative to gain attention has been the CRB Foundation's 'Heritage Minutes,' a series of short films attempting to highlight and popularize aspects of Canadian history. Those interrogating the 'Minutes' have speculated upon how such efforts act to inculcate Canadian values.[8]

However, the scholarly focus on official forms of historical consciousness-raising such as the Heritage Minutes occludes the importance of unofficial forms of meaning-making such as advertising. What about the times when Canadians see fragments of the past in more vernacular domains, such as when Paul Henderson's goal against the Russians in the 1972 Summit Series is followed by a direct appeal to change long-distance providers? I suggest that elements of Canadian history are so pervasive in ad campaigns that Canadians have probably encountered their past more often through appeals to purchase beer than by attending museum exhibits or watching episodes of *Canada: A People's History*. As distributors of images on a national scale across different media platforms, it is safe to say that most commercial advertising campaigns offer an audience reach most public history initiatives could only dream of. Therefore, it is imperative to take account of how advertisements serve to distribute and inflect national memory as it circulates in the public domain.

Those that have turned their critical attention to advertising campaigns generally fall into two camps. The first, represented by a study of Canadian magazine advertising by Hildegard Hammerschmidt, seeks to explore how 'images of Canada' appear in Canadian advertising.[9] The second camp, represented by the slew of articles dealing with Molson beer advertisements, seeks to uncover the ways in which these campaigns represent *and* articulate anxieties associated with national identity.[10]

Two problems arise from these analyses. Both ignore the fact that many of the same historical images have been repeated through advertising campaigns throughout Canada's history. In other words, studies on ads in magazines during the early 1980s or the televised beer ads of the new millennium are moments in a long history of the recirculation of visual imagery and textual motifs drawing on aspects of national history in Canadian advertising campaigns. The use of particular themes is also remarkably consistent; images of the Canadian Pacific Railway that appeared in ads from 2005 were also present in ads eighty years earlier. In selecting aspects of Canadian history to promote their company or products, why do advertisers only draw from a relatively small thematic palette?

The second problem is that the overwhelming emphasis on the study of advertising *language* or visual imagery comes at the expense of an exploration of advertising *rationale*. It is one thing to speculate about the ways such ads articulate the nation, but it is quite something else to ask why historical references perform an idiomatic function in the language of advertising. The argument that such an approach is useful to sell products or to convey a company's patriotism, or to appeal to the patriotism of its customers, is only half the story. For the message to be effective, an advertisement that draws on history has to speak to a particular set of concerns related to a particular historical context and imply a certain set of consequences that may arise from failing to capture the message. The interplay between historical memory and historical context in advertising guides my subsequent analysis of advertisements drawn from Canadian print and electronic media.

Advertising campaigns typically use two different techniques when deploying historical imagery. In some cases, a campaign reshuffles the characters within the historical tableaux to make a bank or bottle of beer assume a more prevalent role in the narrative. In others, the association between product and event is more indirect. Referring to an event in Canadian history symbolizing achievement or exploration can evoke patriotism or nostalgia. These are feelings the advertiser hopes will resonate the next time consumers select a supermarket or apply for a car loan.

To appreciate how this combination of memory, seduction, and concern structures 'historical' advertisements, consider a campaign from the Royal Bank of Canada that aired on English-language television during the 2006 Winter Olympics in Turin, Italy.[11] The advertisement featured a re-enactment of the Canadian hockey team's performance during the 1947 Olympics in St Moritz, Switzerland. The ad discussed efforts of a Royal Canadian Air Force captain to assemble a team for the Olympics. However, it spent just as much time detailing the efforts of the anonymous bank official sitting in his office in Toronto, assuring the enterprising young captain that the company would make the arrangements to get the team to St Moritz. Against the backdrop of the Canadian team celebrating, the ad concluded with the narrator telling the audience that Canada 'didn't do too badly, considering we almost didn't go.' With its slogan 'Canada's First Olympic Sponsor,' the Royal Bank's advertisement appended banking to the more obvious pairing of sport and nationality, indicating that this great moment in Canadian history would not have been possible without the financial institution's national commitment. The story's focus on the team captain as spunky entrepreneur working against the odds also conveyed the message that the bank would sponsor other Olympian attempts in the future, including those that occur within the business arena.

It is easy to say that the strategy behind the advertisement was to use history in order to build brand loyalty. It is also fair to conclude that advertisements such as this one represent the commodification of history, using the Olympic spirit of community to bowdlerize the past in the interest of hawking mutual funds. However, to stop the analysis at this somewhat safe juncture would obscure as much as it would reveal. Such conclusions give little insight into questions of *how* the connection between customer and company is made in order to establish that relationship and *why* references to history are a useful technique in achieving those objectives.

To better explore the relationship between advertising, history, and public memory, I begin this chapter with a brief discussion of the role of memory in nationalist discourses and advertising practices. This will allow for an understanding of how the deployment of historical references in advertising campaigns mingles collective memory with product retention. I then provide a series of historical case-studies of advertisements drawn from Canadian magazines and television from the 1920s to the present day that incorporate what I consider to be fairly obvious allusions to fragments of Canadian history as part of the overall product pitch. I have selected time periods that reflect either key moments in Canada's history such as the Diamond Jubilee, or broader cultural movements, such the postwar reconstruction effort; and the more recent mode involving Canada's place in contemporary processes of globalization. What I am presenting here, therefore, is clearly a sample drawn from a long history of advertising in Canada. However, I believe that the selective nature of my study does not detract from the overall points that I wish to make about advertising serving as a form of communication that relocates a product or company as an integral part of a national experience.

With that in mind, my analysis of these advertisements proceeds along two fronts. First, I examine the ways these advertisements utilize historical events, messages, myths, and symbols as part of the commercial pitch. I argue that the advertisements under analysis draw upon themes of transportation, exploration, and nation-building articulated through narratives of partnership and unity. Second, I draw from David Thelen's observation that the issue at stake in memory studies is not how accurately a recollection of the past matches with reality, but 'why historical actors constructed their memories in a particular way in a particular time.'[12] In this chapter, I maintain that at the same time that historical references to partnership, unity, and progress operate in conjunction with larger cultural discourses ranging from postwar development to multiculturalism, and from separatism to globalization, they also reflect specific *commercial* anxieties, usually resulting from changing business conditions produced by these socio-cultural shifts. I conclude by suggesting that the failure to appreciate the way in which advertising perpetuates certain historical narratives has occluded the role of this particular form of communication in mediating feelings of national and industrial anxiety felt both by individual Canadians and by the companies that employ them.

Stories Worth Remembering: History and Memory in Nationalism and Advertising

In his famous lecture to students at the Sorbonne in 1882, Ernest Renan pointed to two key components that make up the 'spiritual principles' of the nation. The first 'is the possession in common of a rich legacy of memories, the other is present-day consent, the desire to live together, the will to perpetuate the value of the heritage that one has received in an undivided form.'[13] As Anthony Smith, Jacques Barzun, and many others have written, only certain aspects of national memory are deemed 'worth remembering' by would-be nation-builders, and they must be narrated in very specific ways. Stories of wars and war heroes, religious movements, mass migrations, discoveries and colonization, sporting heroes, dynasties, pieces of legislation, and the work of architects and creative artists are then replotted along heroic lines to connote authenticity, continuity, identity, and collective destiny.[14]

Many commentators have accounted for the different ways in which the individuals, objects, and narratives that constitute collective memory have been disseminated through various institutions and social practices. For Ernest Gellner, educational curricula structure the delivery of common heritage and shared value systems to a nation's youth.[15] Tony Bennett has written about the ways in which, in selecting and disseminating aspects of a country's history, the national museum plays a significant role in the citizen-making process.[16] Michael Billig has examined the role played by 'banal' aspects such as the appearance of flags on buildings (to mark national space), weather forecasts (to visualize and reinforce the physical boundaries of the nation), and national sports heroes (as champions both of and for the nation) within memory formations.[17] The shared daily ritual of newspaper reading serves as a key component in Benedict Anderson's conception of nations as 'imagined communities.'[18] These various techniques serve to 'perpetuate the value of the heritage one has received,' which Renan cited as essential to the spiritual makeup of the nation. As Smith explains, these discursive formations operate on four different levels: a normative component that helps to define the character of the community;[19] a stimulant for national feelings of regeneration; a filial component used to convey the desire for things as they once were, and as means to articulate feelings of collective destiny.[20]

Advertising historians have also noted that memory becomes an important component of advertising campaigns at the turn of the twentieth century. As Russell Johnston explains, advertising in the nineteenth century was more descriptive in nature, telling the reader what the product did and how it went about doing it.[21] By the 1920s the tone of advertising messages began to change towards connecting the objects being advertised to social desires of consumers.[22]

This transformation was brought on by a number of developments. With technological innovations facilitating standardized mass production, companies needed new ways to allow their products to stand out from the competition. If all advertisements shared the same style and tone, there was little possibility that a product could stand out. In this new pursuit for distinction, the advertising profession began incorporating statistical and psychological research into its business practices. This allowed advertisers to break up mass audiences into different communities that could be targeted by different kinds of product pitches tailor-made to match the perceived mental processes of the new consumer demographics. From this point on the successful advertiser was one 'who forged a vivid association in the minds of readers between an everyday need and its product ... so much so that all other associations would be secondary to that product.'[23]

Some of these associations took on the character of positive inducements – if you buy this room spray, your home will smell like a spring glade. Others, however, preyed on consumer anxieties by suggesting that failure to purchase the product would lead to social humiliation, ostracism, and loneliness. It became a commonplace among advertisers that a campaign's ability to create such vivid positive and negative psychological associations 'depended upon its ability to touch something deep in the consumer – "memory value."'[24] In other words, the object of advertising is to develop a system of images and words to construct messages that will produce a response with an audience both at the moment of initial contact and once the advertising message has ended. The ephemeral nature of the ad is important to understand advertising's communicative characteristics. A commercial message on the page of a magazine or in a thirty-second segment on television has a very short shelf-life. In order for an advertisement or campaign to resonate, it must not only provide a message intended to pique interest, it must also draw upon the assumed personal recollections and an established body of knowledge and concerns of its intended audience for the message to have its full effect. The viewer or reader must be able to 'fill in the blanks,' about what the benefits of using a certain product will be as well as the consequences of inaction.[25]

We can see this attempt to use the past to define the character of the community in an advertisement for Hudson's Bay liquors that appeared in *Maclean's* magazine in May 1975 (see figure 16.1).[26] The ad begins with the headline 'Canadians enjoyed the taste of Hudson's Bay when gold was in the Klondike,' followed by a photograph featuring men drinking in a saloon (it is unclear whether this is an original or a re-enactment of the event). This is followed by the line, 'They're still enjoying its taste today.'[27] This is followed by a smaller contemporary image of young adults at a bar, presumably imbibing Hudson's Bay whisky, vodka, white rum, or gin. The expository text brings together the relationship of taste to history, and aligns the company to Canada's national memory:

> When weary prospectors heard about the first big gold strike at Rabbit Creek, you can bet they started to celebrate. And Hudson's Bay has been part of Canada's big moments for over 300 years. And we've learned a lot about Canadian tastes in that time.[28]

The advertisement drew upon themes of Canadian ruggedness and appealed to the readers' sense of nostalgia, their remembrance of Canada's gold rush, and their appreciation of Hudson's Bay's long history in Canada in order to complete the advertising message. The intended result was simple: when one drinks a Hudson's Bay liquor, one digests the set of identity markers, including collective memory of Canadian-ness, with every sip. The line 'we've learned a lot about Canadian tastes in that time' works on two levels: equating experience with knowledge but also implying that other products lack this particular local expertise. Entailed is the negative consequence of forgetting: the decision to drink another kind of product – one produced by a foreign distiller – implies an act of alcoholic treason. Furthermore, the association that the ad creates between the rugged adventurers of the Klondike and contemporary male drinkers implies a second set of negative consequences: to drink anything but Hudson's Bay liquor is also an act of treason against the traditional construction of rugged Canadian masculinity.

Connecting Canada in Celebration: CPR and the Diamond Jubilee, 1927

If the Hudson's Bay ad uses the past to define the Canadian community, an advertisement for the Canadian Pacific Railway published in the March 1927 issue of the *Canadian Magazine* uses the past to, in Smith's terms, 'articu-

16.1 Hudson's Bay Company advertisement. *Maclean's*, May 1975.

late feelings of collective destiny' and affiliation. The ad was part of a series of advertisements published by CPR to celebrate Canada's Diamond Jubilee, an event characterized by great pomp and circumstance, including the first national radio network broadcast, with the sounds of the Carillon from Parliament Hill, aired across the CPR lines.[29] The Jubilee also occurred in a time of heightened feelings of national spirit and pride and amid calls from intellectuals, social elites, and members of the artistic community for increased commitments by the state to promote Canada's 'national consciousness,' and by extension, strengthen the federation from coast to coast.[30]

The advertisement in the *Canadian Magazine* spoke directly to this moment in time. The top half of the ad featured a reproduction of the Robert Harris painting of the Fathers of Confederation lying over an open book whose title, 'Pages from Canadian History,' appeared at the top of the page. Only one line from the book, 'Like the Elizabethan age in England, the era of Confederation in Canada was a time of giants,' was visible to the reader.[31] The title for this image, 'Colourful Names Throng Canada's Pages of Sixty Years Ago,' appeared in the middle of the page, with a list of the individuals captured in the Harris painting. The text of the ad celebrated their accomplishment in uniting 'the scattered communities of Victoria's subjects in British North America into one magnificent whole, and laid down the basic principles of the Empire's largest unit.'[32] The ad continued by describing the characteristics of some of the men responsible for bringing the country together:

> Presiding over the Conference which resolved on Union was Etienne Pascal Taché, a veteran of the War of 1812, who expressed the loyalty of his fellow country-men when he said 'The last gun to be fired for British supremacy in America would be fired by a French-Canadian.' John A. Macdonald was a commanding figure in the Conference, with his insight into character and his knowledge of British institutions. By his side were George Brown, of the Toronto *Globe*, a 'dyed in the wool Liberal' who forgot party in his desire for Union; T. Alexander Galt, master of finance; Thomas D'Arcy McGee, poet, historian, orator; William MacDougall, distinguished son of a loyalist; Oliver Mowat, a legal giant, who afterwards became Premier of Ontario; Charles Tupper, master debater; his political opponent Samuel Leonard Tilley, a power in the Maritime Provinces; Adams G. Archibald, great parliamentarian.[33]

The advertisement drew upon three key themes: the importance of unity over differences, the role of transportation in binding the nation, and the significance of partnership. Leaving aside the obvious significance of the unity theme expressed in George Brown's decision to eschew party affiliation 'for the sake of the Union,' the other two themes deserve further elaboration.

As Maurice Charland has argued, the railway represents the first of a series of transportation and technological revolutions which, through their ability to bind Canada's vast geographical expanse, form a key part of Canada's rhetorical tradition. It is this formulation – what Charland calls 'technological nationalism' – that forms the 'dominant discourse' within Canada.[34] Commenting on the televised rendition of Pierre Berton's book *The National Dream*, Charland explains:

> This television image of a railroad as the 'national dream' heroically spanning the wilderness to fashion a state reveals in a condensed narrative the manifold relations between technology and a Canada which can imagine. Here we are encouraged to see technology as constitutive of Canada, and as a manifestation of Canada's ethos.[35]

For Charland, the rhetoric of technological nationalism 'equates the construction of the CPR with the constitution of Canada and praises each with reference to the other.'[36] By extension, this implies that failure to complete the line would have resulted in the dissolution of the state.

If themes of unity and technological nationalism serve as the two most obvious notions present in the advertisement, the trope of partnership is also significant here. This is a sentiment expressed in the ad's concluding sentence that the men of Confederation were the ones who 'foresaw the necessity of a transcontinental railway that would link Canada, and their vision became reality with the subsequent achievement of the Canadian Pacific Railway.'[37] This is because the Canadian Pacific Railway is also symbolic of a long-standing partnership between the state and the private sector linking national development with industrial development.

As I mentioned earlier, the establishment of communications and transportation systems in Canada assisted in delineating the physical boundaries of the Canadian state. However, an important component of the establishment of those boundaries was the realization that neither of those systems could have been completed without extensive government intervention. Through his early work on the fur trade and his studies of staples economies, Harold Innis revealed that 'the heavy expenditures on transport improvements, including railways and canals, have involved government grants, subsidies, and guarantees to an exceptional degree.'[38] The weakness of private capital implicit in Canada's early development has had an impact on the relationship between the private and public sector throughout Canada's history. From direct investments to import quotas, foreign ownership restrictions, and subsidies, the Canadian state has twinned with companies employing Canadians to assist in building and maintaining the country's status. Emerging out of this arrangement is the fusion of the state's 'national interests' with the economic interests of Canadian private firms, a move that effectively marries the Canadian citizenry and private investors as shareholders in the companies' success and failure, thus complicating rigid dichotomies between the 'public' and 'private' sectors in analyses of Canadian life.

This lack of a clear boundary between the public and the private explains why the theme of partnership is so central to the CPR's Jubilee ad as well as why it emerges at a time of national celebration. The commemoration of Canada's establishment is also a celebration of the railway itself, the country's federalizing partner. Furthermore, within the context of Canada's Diamond Jubilee, these advertisements served as a key pivot between the imagined past and desired futures. More than simply reminding Canadians that the company has been an active participant in Canadian history in both the present and past, the advertisements also articulated the importance of continued partnership between railway and state as Canada continues to develop in the future.

Helping Canada Grow: The Bank of Nova Scotia and the Dunlop Rubber Company, 1954

Both the Bank of Nova Scotia and the Dunlop Rubber Company ran a series of historically themed advertisements in the pages of *Maclean's* magazine in 1954. These advertisements appear in the context of a postwar period of economic expansion and burgeoning social change. The country's heroic experience in the battle against fascism inspired feelings of national pride in the young nation, and spurred on a number of national stock-taking exercises to make sense of the country's resources. In the cultural sphere, the Royal Commission for National Development in the Arts, Sciences, and Letters, otherwise known as the Massey Commission, outlined the importance of heavy public investment in Canada's cultural and educational communities and the creation of new institutions such as the Canada Council to improve national unity and to provide a cultural line of defence against the creeping cultural influence of the United States.[39]

The advertisements were also published during one of the few downturns in Canada's postwar economic boom. The period between 1953 and 1954 saw Canada experience a mild recession. As historians John English, Ian Drummond, and Robert Bothwell point out, changes in banking policy encouraged Canadians to invest in foreign banks, to help pay for rising imports.[40] Furthermore, as part of Canada's membership in General Agreement on Tariffs and Trade (GATT), import tariffs fell on selected items, a change that 'opened the Canadian market more visibly to foreign competition, even though for many goods the tariff was still prohibitive.'[41] For Canadian banks and manufacturing organizations, these developments introduced new forms of instability that are clearly reflected in their advertising, and in the decision to turn to Canadian history as part of the pitch. What results are advertisements profiling enterprising inventors, explorers, and investors.

The Bank of Nova Scotia advertisements, entitled, 'They Helped Canada Grow,' appeared over the course of 1954. Each ad told of the exploits of a number of prominent Canadians 'and their partners,' who were responsible for Canada's national development. The ads used a comic book format to structure each narrative, a genre that emerged in the 1930s, as part of an attempt to bring advertising into the 'funny pages' section of the newspaper.[42] In the context of our discussion so far, it is also fair to conclude that, through its combination of stylistic cues, the comic book format also appealed because it helped to make stories incorporating a product or service memorable.

One ad featured the story of Sir Sandford Fleming, the contributor to the CPR, designer of the beaver stamp, and founder of standardized time, 'and his partners.'[43] Each of these achievements was presented in a separate square, complete with opportunities to eavesdrop on conversations expressed through dialogue balloons: Fleming and the postmaster-general; Fleming and the Washington conference on Standard Time ('Gentlemen, here are my suggestions for a standard time system');[44] Fleming and a telegraph operator ('For you, Sir Sandford – the first message to Canada across the Pacific Cable');[45] and a journal entry addressing the reading audience ('I have always felt that the humblest among us has it in his power to do something for his country').[46] In the summary text at the bottom of the advertisement, Fleming is presented as the beneficiary of the entrepreneurial spirit of Canada's moneylenders:

> Great through his genius, Fleming was but one of a parade of pioneers whose vision built Canada, backed by men and institutions who provided the financial means to bring their exploits to realization. The Bank of Nova Scotia is today providing the same backing to our modern pioneers. When you save with your bank you share in the partnerships which are shaping the future of your country.[47]

The final panel of each vignette featured the first and only appearance of the company name and its slogan, 'Your Partner in Helping Canada Grow.' It is in this paragraph that the connection between the bank and other historical trailblazers was articulated.

Other ads in the series incorporated other celebrities from the Canadian past. The exploits of explorer John Cabot and Henry VII, featured in a later issue of *Maclean's* from the same year, are presented in a similar fashion, with Canada's banks representing the new enlightened royalty (see figure 16.2):

16.2 Bank of Nova Scotia advertisement. *Maclean's*, 15 September 1954.

The Cabots of today have plenty of adventure ahead, as Canada's rapid development demands initiative in every field. New Cabots are venturing into both charted and unchartered areas of financial risk. Who are the Henry VII's of today? The lending institutions of Canada! ... When you deposit your savings, whenever you do business with your bank, you are contributing to Canada's growth — for your growth with Canada.[48]

In another advertisement from the series, highlighting the achievements of J.A.D. McCurdy and 'his associates' who designed the Silver Dart airplane (see figure 16.3), the narrative reminds readers that such accomplishments did not occur in a financial vacuum:

The initiative of men like J.A.D. McCurdy has made our country strong. But their work depends on all-important associates – the far sighted lending institutions of the banks of Canada ... whose funds are the invested savings of Canadians like you. When you deposit your savings or do business with your Bank, you add to the financial power helping to develop your country.[49]

As one can see, each 'episode' in the Bank of Nova Scotia series follows a similar structure. The first sentence summarizes the accomplishments of the profiled individuals. The second sentence reminds the reader that such accomplishments would have been impossible without the support of some financial assistance. The third sentence completes the connection and pivots from past to present and from historical moment to future endeavour by drawing associations between the accomplishments of the explorers and those of the institution as 'partners' in the growth of individuals, businesses, and by extension, Canada. Against an economic backdrop characterized by recession and amid concerns over increased competition, the advertisements invoke Canadian history to articulate the kind of partnership themes we have seen earlier as part of an appeal for consumer loyalty or as part of a larger strategy for future state protection.

A similar dynamic is evident in another campaign from the same year, this time from the Dunlop Rubber Products Company (see figure 16.4). One ad, 'The spike that started a nation on the move,' featured a painted rendition of the 'last spike,' linking Canada from sea to sea by rail. Here the ad explained the economic benefits of the railroad ('Now the young nation was open for business and prepared to meet and master the challenge of its own vastness'), its ushering of Canada into a 'new era of industry and a new sense of economic unity,' and the creation of new communities, new settlers, and new industries, including Dunlop. The final paragraph switched the time-frame and situated the company both in the present and future:

16.3 Bank of Nova Scotia advertisement. *Maclean's*, 15 June 1954.

16.4 Dunlop Rubber Products Company advertisement. *Maclean's*, 15 February 1954.

Today Dunlop's contribution to the task of keeping Canada on the move is evident everywhere you turn – on land and water and in the air. Dunlop products carry coal from the mine, wheat from the elevators, pipe oil into the tankers. There are a dozen Dunlop products in use on today's trains. There are Dunlop products for bicycles, passenger cars, trucks and aircraft – for the modern home too. All these products are made to provide higher standards of safety, comfort, and efficiency. And they help keep Canada, its people and its products on the move.[50]

Another Dunlop ad, which appeared in *Maclean's* four months later, returned with the image of J.A.D. McCurdy's Silver Dart as an example of an invention that 'Gave Wings to a Nation.' Here the ad attempts to link the Silver Dart and the company by pairing two different developments together as if they were part of the same moment of national significance (see figure 16.5):

A young nation 'got its wings' when John A.D. McCurdy's *Silver Dart* flew for three-quarters of a mile over the Bras d'Or lakes near Baddeck, Nova Scotia – the first powered flight in Canada, in fact, in the entire Commonwealth.

That was February 23, 1909. One year later, in its Coventry factory, Dunlop turned to producing tires and wheel rims for aircraft. Dunlop, too, was launched into the air age.[51]

The advertisement continued, merging past and future:

Today, Canada is a nation in motion … the perpetual motion of a busy, growing industrial country. To carry minerals from Canada's rich earth, to convey abundant harvests to ship or freight car – to move goods by road, rail, or air – to send happy families on vacation motor trips – here is where Dunlop products contribute strength or speed or safety or comfort. A farmer on a tractor, an engineer in a cab, a child on a bicycle, a man in a jet … all share in the use of rubber products made by Dunlop.[52]

Together, these advertisements utilize a number of key ideas which form the backbone of Canadian historical consciousness, including the role of the CPR in binding the vast nation and themes of survival against a rugged environment, and pair them with important themes associated with the country's economic consciousness: entrepreneurial initiative supported through government partnership.

While also open to increasing markets, the rationale behind the Dunlop campaign had more to do with internal commercial matters. Since this is the period

16.5 Dunlop Rubber Products Company advertisement. *Maclean's*, 15 June 1954.

that sees the construction of two major transportation projects – the St Lawrence Seaway and Trans-Canada Highway – the advertisements can be read as appeals to be included in these projects, just as they were in other space-binding initiatives on the rails and in the skies.

In both of these campaigns, the historical moments chosen drew upon familiar myths and themes of transportation, exploration, discovery, and nation-building that their audiences would have learned in childhood. Together, they appeal, following Charland, as technologies which bind the great nation, as well as act as metaphors for future endeavours of a country 'in motion,' first on the rails, then in the air. One can see how the need to remind Canadians of historical moments of development – and of the companies that played a role during those moments – serves as part of a strategy of self-defence, or at best, as a means to differentiate the companies from 'foreign' competitors by stressing the extent to which such companies serve as essential Canadian 'institutions.' As globalizing processes continued and companies increasingly found themselves competing in an international marketplace, presenting companies to national audiences as essential institutions became a wider commercial strategy. Perhaps the most compelling example occurred across Canadian media platforms in the last decade and a half – all part of an attempt to sell beer.

Standing on Guard for Beer: Molson's History of Canadian Pride, 1993–2005

As cultural texts, beer advertisements are a ripe area for analysis because of the allusive character of the product pitch. They have this character for a couple of reasons. The most obvious is the existence of legislative restrictions on alcohol advertisements in Canada. Alcohol advertisers in Canada must conform to a rigid set of standards upheld by the Canadian Radio-Television and Telecommunications Commission that prohibit both direct modes of address (including the use of imperative language, spokespeople that would influence underage drinkers, and overt images of mass consumption) and many indirect modes of address which imply social benefit from beer consumption.[53] As a result, advertisers for alcohol must engage in a delicate symbolic dance that imbues the product with certain kinds of characteristics without crossing the line towards direct associations with status, power, and pleasure. Turning towards patriotic and historical references represents a technique able to toe the line between advocacy and indiscretion.

Furthermore, from a marketing perspective, advertisers for alcohol need to dress up their product – the lubricant for various forms of social activity – in the most appealing way. A direct appeal – that alcohol consumption will make you drunk – cannot be made in the way that other product advertisements can, for obvious reasons. The traditional and most effective marketing strategy has been to connect the taste of beer with tropes of masculinity. An ad for Labatt's India Pale Ale, for example, which appeared in *Canadian Labour* magazine in 1959, claimed that the product's 'hearty strength' and 'full bodied character' were necessary for 'men who demand the zest and snap of a full-strength ale.'[54] As the number of beer products proliferated in the years that followed, beer advertisements attempted to differentiate their product by supplementing the appeal to masculinity with different associations, including sex, sports, music, and tradition.

We can see these strategies of product differentiation, indirect address, and allusion at work in the famed Molson 'I am Canadian' advertisements. These began in 1993 as an aggressive attempt to seize control of the lucrative Canadian beer marketplace from the rival Labatt brewery. The company used the fact that it was, as of 1998, a wholly owned and operated Canadian organization (versus the Belgian-owned Labatt) as a point of distinction for its advertising campaign.[55] The patriotic turn also coincided with the company's own demographic research, which found that its clientele, composed primarily of young males between eighteen and twenty-four, had a 'strong sense of national pride.' Many of the advertisements transposed the themes of youthfulness, rebellion, and difference onto the established discourses of the distinctiveness of Canadian identity, particularly vis-à-vis the United States.[56] But the company also engaged in a series of public relations exercises intended to further extend the association between itself and events of national significance, most notably during the 1 July Canada Day holiday. In 1993, the company was a principal sponsor of 'The Great Canadian Party,' and a few years later held the 'Molson Canadian Big Birthday Bash,' a series of coordinated parties across the country.[57] These efforts were complemented by the consistent deployment of symbols of Canadian enjoyment and articulations of Canadian identity, but also the celebration of what the company selected as key events or periods of Canadian history.

For a better sense of how the ad campaign used the Canadian past, consider the commercial aired on Canadian television in June 2001. The advertisement, entitled 'Anthem,' featured a collection of predominantly male voices singing in unison in a fashion similar to a beer hall ballad. Accompanying the prosaic lyrics[58] were a number of jump-cut images from Canadian history, including re-enactments of the 'last spike' (re-enacted with *faux*-sepia colouring and film scratches to mimic early film stock); images of the Second World War's V-E Day; the 1972 Summit series between Canada and the Soviet Union; and a simulation of the 1965 event where the Union Jack–bearing Canadian Red Ensign flag is replaced by the one bearing the red maple leaf. Other slices of Canadian life included scenes of Niagara Falls, log-rolling, gap-toothed hockey players, and beer halls. Taken together, the ad represented a stirring montage of images of unity, strength, teamwork, and power – what one Molson official characterized as a 'whirlwind tour of Canadian pride' – which would appeal to the company's predominantly male audience.[59] The demographic tilt of the ad is evident by the fact that there are very few women and even fewer members of Canada's numerous multicultural communities. The 'pride' expressed in the 'Anthem,' therefore, is based on a palette of imagery and historical references that appears to stop at the Trudeau era. It seems that, in the eyes of Molson, cultural developments from the 1970s onward are of little interest to the target market for Molson *Canadian.*

Elsewhere I contend that, contrary to those who argued that the 'I am [Canadian]' ads represented an assertive form of nationalist expression, the campaign actually represented a form of commercial self-defence.[60] When considering the ad in its historical context, it is clear that the company's attempt to wrap the 'Canadian' product and the company in the Canadian flag was in response to recent threats to the market dominance of Canadian brewers caused by GATT rulings against interprovincial trade barriers.[61] Like the advertisements from the Bank of Nova Scotia, these advertisements served as a kind of public service message to Canadians, to remind them of the importance of the company to Canada's culture. However, this address did not work only within a commercial or supra-national vacuum. Protests over the negative consequences of global trading agreements were taking place all around the world, from Seattle to Davos, and many Canadians were expressing concerns associated with the impact of such agreements on the future of the country. The references to the 'I am Canadian' ads in speeches by government officials, most notably by then–heritage minister Sheila Copps in a speech about the perils of globalization, represented a public relations coup for the company, and symbolized the company's successful integration into the cultural sphere.[62]

It is also fair to say that advertisements such as 'Anthem' derive meaning through their appeal to the patriotic sentiments of their audience. As Robert Seiler recently noted, the use of dramatic music such as Edward Elgar's 'Hope and Glory' or the beer-hall ballad style of the 'Anthem' alongside prominent Canadian symbolism evokes strong feelings of national pride and companionship among the ads' viewers. However, as Seiler points out, this is not a moment drawn from a time of official celebration or an official holiday for national expression. Through the 'I am Canadian' campaign, the ads celebrate both product and company itself for providing a means to express patriotic feelings.[63] In this way, the ad acts as a public service announcement suffused with product retention objectives.

That analysis took place before the company's merger with the American brewer Coors, which occurred in 2005. The company has since dropped the 'I am Canadian' campaign for its flagship brand, and, at the same time, has toned down its more overt nationalist themes and historical references. Instead, the company's advertising strategy has returned to more stereotypical cultural images of Canadian cottages, attractive males and females, and pastoral winters as part of its new campaign, 'It all starts here.' This strategy was similar to the strategies of other multinational companies advertising in Canada which present a patina of Canadian-ness in their advertising. With the company no longer exclusively Canadian, it makes no sense to draw on symbolic notions of historical partnership or national progress. Instead, advertisements for the company have reverted to the safe territory of nostalgia in which de-localized images of the friendly brewer stand in for the faceless foreign corporation.[64]

Conclusion

The historian Daniel Boorstin once wrote, 'advertising has expressed the optimism, the hyperbole, and the sense of community, the sense of reaching which has been so important a feature of our civilization.'[65] These themes have been present in corporate advertising for a diverse range of activities ranging from liquor to rubber manufacturing. In these ads, fragments of Canadian history associated with technological nationalism and events emphasizing partnership and unity have been used as one strategy to produce those diverse sentiments referred to by Boorstin. In fact, history in these ads acts as an important memory cue, encouraging the viewers or readers to make the connection between their memory of a moment and the product being advertised.

The question that emerges from this study is what impact the routine distribution of such imagery has on Canadian historical consciousness, on the way Canadians recollect and understand their past. Where other examinations of the use of history in collective memory projects have been criticized for masking their producer's true intentions, such a claim cannot be levelled in this case. We therefore cannot place these advertisements in the context of a discussion about what George Lipsitz called 'the neo-conservative critique of history,' which 'lauds history while fearing historical inquiry, because that inquiry might lead to critical appropriation of the past by aggrieved groups.'[66] Since such ads do not purport to act for any other purpose than corporate self-interest (either to sell products or project positive public relations), there is little utility in suggesting that corrective or counter-historical tales should be produced to sell products.

It is interesting to note, however, that the case studies profiled here routinely draw from a relatively small set of images and themes associated with unity, the use of technology to bind space, and ideas of national development. While there may certainly be other thematic variations than those drawn from the sample selected for this chapter, the consistency with which this package of symbolic markers appears in Canadian advertising is worth noting. This attests either to the fact that companies are not particularly creative when using history for the purposes of selling, or that they believe that the intended audience wishes to see them again and again. In either case, this reveals a certain conservatism about Canadian cultural life, one which appreciates various kinds of difference, but not without some need to reassert a past in which such differences were less prominent than they are today. These strains of Canadian cultural life appear in a more pronounced form in these ads than in more 'official' attempts to constitute public memory, such as the Heritage Minutes. The apparent distance between the Canada presented in the case-studies offered here and that perpetuated in official attempts to 'sell Canada,' discussed in many of the other chapters in this volume, is all the more reason why advertising must be considered more seriously in discussions about the constitution of public memory.

Over the long run, will viewers ultimately make the connection between an Olympic hockey success and the activities of the Royal Bank? This remains to be seen. This is not to imply that there is no effect at all on historical consciousness, and there certainly remains a risk in moving away from national histories to corporate histories. There are also important implications about the ways these campaigns serve as the medium through which people are able to express and enact either their patriotism or their national identity. However, in order to fully understand this it may be productive to move away from quizzes that reveal Canadians' historical ignorance towards an appreciation of the elements of their history that they do know. It would be fascinating to see the contribution of advertising campaigns that deploy historical imagery in this regard. Since advertising is hardly an exact science, it is likely that such a study would produce mixed results.

So what is the significance of these ads? Here I would like to offer two prescriptions. From a methodological perspective, I believe that we must accept the fact that advertising forms a vital part of Canada's audiovisual heritage and, by extension, we need to pay greater attention to what Lipsitz calls the 'remembering of history' and 'forgetting of commercialized leisure.'[67] We must also be flexible in our consideration of sites for memory studies. As Barbie

Zelizer warns, 'We cannot predict the instances in which memory takes on new transformations,' and 'memory work brings together unusual bits of the past in unpredictable ways.'[68]

This latter point is important for my second suggestion. It has been simply too easy or too convenient to lump Canada's commercial sector together as profit-seeking, swashbuckling practitioners of *laissez-faire* globalization, immune to the concerns of local or national interests. Instead, I suggest that in the advertisements presented in this chapter, historical memory is produced for the purposes of articulating a more complex message of economic nationalism. This message uses partnership motifs to remind consumers that the company was directly or indirectly part of the moment and, by extension, represents an essential aspect of the Canadian way of life in the past and could play a similar role in the future.

With that in mind, I believe that such imagery suggests that companies, like Canadians themselves, have been uneasy about the openness of Canada to these internationalizing influences for some time. The affinity for historical vignettes that draw on nationalist themes and narratives present in this survey does not suggest a pining for the past, but reflects an unease about the future for both individual Canadians and those within the corporate sector and an indirect appeal to the state to maintain or develop means to protect companies through an implicit appeal to protect culture. As many have suggested, this unease is a product of the fact that the country itself has always been at the forefront of processes of globalization: as colonial outpost, as resource exporter, as multicultural gateway, and as active participant in today's knowledge economy. Canada's historic participation in the global economy has not been without its consequences: the promise of increased access to foreign capital, commodities, ideas, and images has always been accompanied by the threat of greater foreign influence, and both processes have done much to alter the state of Canadian life and culture. To account for this historical tension in more detail, we would be well advised to think twice the next time we skip past the commercials.

NOTES

1 I am grateful to the editors for the invitation to expand upon conclusions drawn in an earlier publication, Ira Wagman, 'Wheat, Barley, Hops, Citizenship: Molson's I AM [Canadian] Campaign and the Defence of Canadian National Identity through Advertising,' *Velvet Light Trap* 50 (2002): 77–89.
2 Barbie Zelizer, 'Reading the Past against the Grain: The Shape of Memory Studies,' *Critical Studies in Mass Communication* 12, 2 (1995): 232.

3 George Lipsitz, *Time Passages: Collective Memory and American Popular Culture* (Minneapolis: University of Minnesota Press, 1990), 12.

4 I borrow the term 'vehicles of memory' from Peter Hodgins, 'Our Haunted Present: Cultural Memory in Question,' *Topia* 12 (2004): 106.

5 Marshall McLuhan, *Understanding Media* (New York: Signet, 1964), 206.

6 See Jonathan Rose, *Making 'Pictures in Our Heads': Government Advertising in Canada* (Westport, CT: Praeger, 2000), and 'Government Advertising and the Creation of National Mythologies: The Canadian Case,' *International Journal of Non-Profit and Voluntary Sector Marketing* 8, 2 (2003): 153–65.

7 For an excellent example of this, see Eva Mackey's discussion of the 'Canada 125' campaign and other forms of 'corporate nationalism' in *The House of Difference: Cultural Politics and National Indentity in Canada* (New York: Routledge, 1999), 107–40 and her chapter 10 in this volume.

8 See Peter Hodgins, 'The Canadian Dream-work: History, Myth and Nostalgia in the Heritage Minutes,' PhD thesis, Carleton University, 2003; Emily West, 'Selling Canada to Canadians: Collective Memory, National Identity and Popular Culture,' *Critical Studies in Media Communication* 19, 2 (2002): 212–29; and Tim Stanley 'Playing with "Nitro": The Racialization of Chinese Canadians in Public Memory,' chapter 7 in this volume. The ads are available for viewing online at http://www .histori.ca/minutes (accessed 15 August 2006).

9 Hildegard Hammerschmidt, 'Images of Canada in Advertising,' *Journal of Canadian Studies* 18, 4 (1984): 154–71.

10 For example, see Robert McGregor, 'I Am Canadian: National Identity in Beer Commercials,' *Journal of Popular Culture* 37, 2 (2003): 276–86; and John Wright, Gregory Millard, and Sarah Riegel, 'Here's Where We Get Canadian: English-Canadian Nationalism and Popular Culture,' *American Review of Canadian Studies* 32, 1 (2002): 11–34.

11 See http://rbc.com/sponsorship/olympics/60_years_of_support.html.

12 Thelen quoted in Zelizer, 'Reading the Past against the Grain,' 217.

13 Ernest Renan, 'What Is a Nation?' in Geoff Eley and Ronald Grigor Suny, eds., *Becoming National: A Reader* (New York: Oxford University Press, 1996), 52.

14 Anthony D. Smith, *Myths and Memories of the Nation* (Oxford: Oxford University Press, 1999), 263; Jacques Barzun, 'History as Counter-Method and Anti-Abstraction,' in Michael Murray, ed., *A Jacques Barzun Reader* (New York: HarperCollins, 2002), 19–26.

15 Ernest Gellner, *Nations and Nationalism* (London and Oxford: Blackwell, 1983); see also Ken Osborne's chapter 5 in this volume.

16 Tony Bennett, *The Birth of the Museum* (New York: Routledge, 1995).

17 Michael Billig, *Banal Nationalism* (London and Thousand Oaks, CA: Sage, 1995). Another excellent example of this is Pierre Nora's three-volume work, *Les lieux de mémoire* (Paris: Gallimard, 1984).

18 Benedict Anderson, *Imagined Communities: Reflections on the Origin and Spread of Nationalism*, revised edition (New York: Verso, 1991), 35–6.

19 Smith, *Myths and Memories of the Nation*, 263.

20 Ibid., 263–4.

21 Russell Johnston, *Selling Themselves: The Emergence of Advertising in Canada* (Toronto: University of Toronto Press, 2001), 145.

22 See Sut Jhally, 'Advertising at the Edge of the Apocalypse,' in Robin Andersen and Lance Strate, eds., *Critical Studies in Media Commercialism* (London: Oxford University Press, 2000), 31.

23 Johnston, *Selling Themselves*, 160.

24 Stewart Ewen, *All Consuming Images: The Politics of Style in Contemporary Culture* (New York: Basic Books, 1988), 246.

25 Advertisements for prescription drugs are extreme examples of this. Since advertisers cannot directly equate a drug brand name with its use, the advertisement simply uses suggestive images or language to gesture towards the drug's actual purpose and to encourage the viewer or reader to 'talk to your Doctor.'

26 *Maclean's*, May 1975, 89.

27 Ibid.

28 Ibid.

29 For a detailed discussion see Robert Cupido, 'The Medium, the Message, and the Modern: The Jubilee Broadcast of 1927,' *International Journal of Canadian Studies* 26 (2002): 101–27.

30 See Mary Vipond, 'The Nationalist Network: English-Canada's Intellectuals and Artists in the 1920s,' *Canadian Review of Studies in Nationalism* 7 (1980): 32–52.

31 *Canadian Magazine*, March 1927, 1

32 Ibid.

33 Ibid.

34 Maurice Charland, 'Technological Nationalism,' *Canadian Journal of Social and Political Theory* 10, 1–2 (1986): 197. For a fascinating discussion on the history of Canadian rhetoric see Maurice Charland and Michael Dorland, *Law, Rhetoric, and Irony in the Formation of Canadian Civic Culture* (Toronto: University of Toronto Press, 2002).

35 Charland, 'Technological Nationalism,' 196.

36 Ibid., 197.

37 *Canadian Magazine*, March 1927.

38 Innis quoted in Kevin Dowler, 'The Cultural Industries Policy Apparatus,' in Michael Dorland, ed., *The Cultural Industries in Canada* (Toronto: James Lorimer and Company, 1996), 331.

39 See Paul Litt, *The Muses, the Masses, and the Massey Commission* (Toronto: University of Toronto Press, 1991), for an excellent discussion of the historical and philosophical influences behind the commission's findings.

40 Robert Bothwell, Ian Drummond, and John English, *Canada Since 1945: Power, Politics, and Provincialism,* revised edition (Toronto: University of Toronto Press, 1989), 171–4.

41 Ibid., 174.

42 Roland Marchand, *Advertising the American Dream: Making Way for Modernity, 1920–1940* (Berkeley: University of California Press, 1985), 110–15. Marchand explains that advertisements drawing upon comic book styles were popular because they integrated the best aspects from other media, such as continuity and quick cutting from film, confession testimony from magazines, and conversational styles from radio.

43 *Maclean's,* 9 June 1954, 46.

44 Ibid.

45 Ibid.

46 Ibid.

47 Ibid.

48 *Maclean's,* 1 September 1954.

49 *Maclean's,* 15 June 1954.

50 *Maclean's,* 15 February 1954.

51 *Maclean's,* 15 June 1954.

52 Ibid.

53 For the full list, see the Code for Broadcast Advertising of Alcoholic Beverages on the CRTC's website, www.crtc.gc.ca/eng/general/codes/alcohol.htm (accessed 27 November 2005). See also William Leiss, Steven Kline, and Sut Jhally, *Social Communication in Advertising,* 2nd edition (New York: Routledge, 1997) 331–3.

54 *Canadian Labour,* January 1959, 1

55 Between 1993 and 1998, the company had been part owned by the American Miller Brewing company and the Australian Foster's Brewery.

56 Robert Hough, 'I Am, Eh?' *Financial Post,* 1 July 1998, 24.

57 For a discussion of this see Mark Duffett, 'Going Down Like a Song: National Identity, Global Commerce and the Great Canadian Party,' *Popular Music* 19, 1 (2000): 1–11.

58 The lyrics are as follows: 'I know this place is where I am, No other place is better than, No matter where I go I am. Proud to be Canadian! I am, you know I am, I am Canadian. I am, you know I am I am Canadian! I love this country where I am. This is the land where I make my stand. No other heart is *comme celui-là.* The one we call Canadian, Canadians. I am, you know I am, I am Canadian. I am, you know I am I am Canadian!'

59 This statement comes from a Molson press release entitled 'Molson Canadian Gives Proud Canadians Something to Sing about with Latest Ad,' found on the

'Investor Relations' section of the company's corporate website, www.Molson .com (accessed 2 February 2002).

60 For an example of the 'assertive nationalism' argument, see John Wright, Gregory Millard, and Sarah Riegel, 'Here's Where We Get Canadian: English-Canadian Nationalism and Popular Culture,' *American Review of Canadian Studies* 32,1 (2002): 11–34.

61 For the full discussion, see Ira Wagman, 'Wheat, Barley, Hops, Citizenship,' 82–5.

62 Copps was quoted as saying to the International Press Institute's World Congress in Boston that 'Those of us in positions of influence, in politics, and the media, need to listen to the basic feelings expounded by the "Joe Canadians" of the world so that our understanding reflects the vital importance of the views of our fellow citizens in every country or in every part of our shared globe.' See Government of Canada, 'Speaking notes for The Honourable Sheila Copps, Minister of Canadian Heritage on the occasion of the International Press Institute World Congress,' Department of Canadian Heritage, http://www.pch.gc.ca/wnqdn/boston/english.htm (accessed 2 February 2002).

63 Robert Seiler, 'Selling Patriotism/Selling Beer: The Case of the "I Am Canadian" Commercial,' *American Review of Canadian Studies* 32, 1 (2002): 45–66.

64 Ironically, the attractiveness of this strategy appears to have been recognized by the Belgian-owned Labatt. Their latest campaigns draw on the 'tradition of John Labatt.' Not surprisingly, Molson has countered, with its own campaigns drawing on their signature beer's 'Canadian heritage.'

65 Daniel Boorstin, 'The Rhetoric of Democracy,' in Daniel Boorstin and Ruth Boorstin, eds., *Hidden History* (New York: Harper and Row, 1987), 128.

66 Lipsitz, *Time Passages*, 27.

67 Ibid., 7.

68 Zelizer, 'Reading the Past against the Grain,' 221.

PART FIVE

Entertaining the Past

17 Why Must Halifax Keep Exploding?: English-Canadian Nationalism and the Search for a Usable Disaster

PETER HODGINS

Canadians, it must be said, are a funny lot. Much as they praise Canada's peaceful and orderly character, they seem to be secretly envious of members of other nation-states whose violent histories provide them with events that make for exciting myths, movies, or adventure stories. The Americans have the Revolutionary and the Civil Wars, the French have the Revolution and Napoleon, and the British have Runnymede and Nelson. The foundational events of the current configuration of the Canadian nation-state, on the other hand, typically involve rich white male lawyers and businessmen sitting around various tables and carving up the map and the riches that it represents between them.[1] This history envy is further reinforced by (and reinforces) one of the deep pathologies of English-Canadian cultural nationalism: status panic and anxiety. As Will Straw has written, envy, status panic, and anxiety are 'at the core of what it means to engage in a cultural life in a country that lies just beyond the centres of cultural power.'[2]

Like all nationalisms, English-Canadian cultural nationalism seeks to establish the boundaries of the Canadian nation by constructing and over-inflating what are often fairly insignificant differences between Canada and its Others. However, also like all other nationalisms, the efforts of Canadians nation-builders are always accompanied by an anxiety-provoking suspicion of the contingency and even the ultimate vacuity of their efforts. This awareness of the contingency of the Canadian identity is exacerbated by the presence of internal and external Others. As Kieran Keohane has argued, these Others threaten to rob the nation of its ability to enjoy the expression of its distinct cultural identity because 'the infinitude of the difference' associated with them further exposes the contingent and arbitrary character of the national identity.[3]

Given this, it has been commonplace in nation-states that when those actors who purport to speak for 'the nation' possess sufficient military, economic, institutional, and cultural resources to do so, they will enact a variety of measures to minimize the ability of external Others to 'penetrate' the nation-space and to reduce the abilities of internal Others to express difference in order to ward off the speakers' own suspicions about the fragility of their nation-building projects. In the case of Canada, however, the Canadian nation-state has never really had the power to significantly control the flow of American difference across the forty-ninth parallel, for a wide variety of reasons. As a result, for much of the career of English-Canadian nationalism, the American Other took on the form of a castrating father who prevents Canadians from developing and expressing their own cultural identity. Furthermore, unlike Oedipus, Canadian nationalists are under no illusion about their ability to kill the father. Instead, Canadian nationalists have developed a variety of cultural strategies to deal with the anxiety-provoking weakness of the Canadian nationalist project vis-à-vis the American juggernaut. For the purposes of this chapter, I will discuss only two.

The first is deeply rooted in what Nietzsche called 'ressentiment.'[4] It begins by tacitly ceding to the Americans the fact that they have more or less always (with the exception of a handful of border skirmishes fought nearly two hundred years ago) had the military, economic, and political upper hand in North America and are now the world's only 'superpower.' However, it then argues that this ostentatious display of worldly power is, at the end of the day, insignificant because it is accompanied by a whole series of moral failures: genocidal Native policies, slavery, imperialisms of all forms, unilateralism, institutionalized racism and poverty, a barbarous popular culture, a deification of crass commercialism, and many other sins. Like Nietzsche's slaves, Canadian nationalists pride themselves on the fact that while Canada might be weak in conventional terms, our alleged national genius for 'tolerance,' 'inclusion,' 'compromise,' and 'peacekeeping' makes Canada a moral 'super-power.' In other words, perhaps we can't kill the father on the military and economic front but we can do so on the moral front.

The second strategy is closely related. One of the necessary conditions for the construction of cultural identities is the possession of the economic and institutional power to repeat as often as possible to as large an audience as possible that 'you are one of us.' In Canada, the power of the nationalist apparatus to do so has historically been limited by the fact that the English-Canadian media market has been saturated by imported American cultural products. As a result, nationalists lament that much of what English Canadians know about, for example, Mounties or French-Canadian fur traders comes from American TV and movies. This evokes in them a strangely ambivalent response: at the same time that they call for more Canadian content in order to allay their fears that this American representation will cause Canadians to somehow misrecognize their own country, they also often celebrate the American success of Céline Dion or Nickelback.

This latter response is rooted in the same quasi-Oedipal complex as the strategy of ressentiment. At the same time that Canadian nationalists want to somehow eradicate American culture, they also rely upon the recognition of Americans for their self-image. As Keohane explains, Canada is stuck in a Hegelian master-slave relationship in which American recognition is necessary to reassure Canadians of their own distinct existence and global importance. As a result, much energy and money has been spent to ensure that Canadian culture somehow finds its way onto American TV screens. Furthermore, as we shall see, in many of the cultural products issuing from Canadian nationalist institutions, the ultimate *frisson* of nationalist pleasure is produced when the American Other comes to recognize and accept Canadian existence as a distinct and morally superior nation.

This perennial fear of Hollywood-induced misrecognition and the belief that Canadians need to develop new mechanisms for self-recognition has taken on a new form over the past two decades. Beginning in the late 1980s, several prominent Canadians have argued that many threats to Canadian unity could be traced back to a failure in public pedagogy. For example, Mark Starowicz, the executive producer of the CBC's documentary division, has argued that 'There is a crisis in the transmission of our society's memory. In fact, I think there is no real memory. Canadian society has had a stroke which has virtually eliminated long-term memory, leaving us with flickering short-term memory alone.'[5] This crisis, he goes on, is the product of all of the *bêtes noires* of the cultural nationalist imaginary: the Americanized mass media, its mesmerized and infantilized audience, 'the hundred particularities of regions, ages, beliefs or tastes,'[6] linguistic dualism, and economic and technological change.

However, such laments about Canadian national memory are often quickly followed by a call to arms: in order for the nation to preserve its past and secure the future, 'something must be done.' Two basic solutions are offered. The first is a massive public and private reinvestment in and expansion of the Canadian memorial infrastructure – more money should be given to museums and other memorial institutions and Canadian history should be made mandatory at all levels of public education.[7] The second, related, solution is to try to make Canadian history 'more exciting' for young Canadians. As Peter Mansbridge attested in a speech in 2004, in spite of the efforts of various popularizers of Canadian history, there exists a lingering tendency in Canada 'to dismiss Canadian history as uninteresting and use that as an excuse to ignore it.' Even more galling, this situation endures in spite of the fact that it has more recently 'become the conventional wisdom that our history is not at all dull. That it's full of rock 'em sock 'em action, noble deeds, fascinating individuals, remarkable achievements, and soaring examples of nation-building against all odds.'[8]

According to Mansbridge and others, this situation of popular indifference and ignorance persists because of the failure of Canadians to exploit the mobilizing powers of the electronic media and its associated genres, visual style, narratives, and conventions. Espousing McLuhanesque arguments about the medium being the message, they argue that the only way to reach young Canadians is through what they now believe to be their 'native language' – the codes of contemporary American commodity and media culture. As Patrick Watson, CBC veteran and the creative director of the Heritage Minutes, has argued: 'If we can use 30 second or 1 minute slots on television to persuade people that Corn Flakes or underarm deodorant or Cadillacs are interesting, could we not use the same period on television to persuade Canadians that they have an interesting past?'[9] In other words, recent attempts at popularizing Canadian history operate with a grounding assumption that in order to attract and entertain young viewers, Canadian history must be narrated using Hollywood codes, conventions, plots, and genres, and that the success of these attempts in provoking Canadian pleasure will be directly linked to how closely they approximate Hollywood standards of 'excitement' and 'significance.'

In order to demonstrate how these assumptions about audience tastes and expectations are combined with an investment in a certain version of the Canadian past infused with an almost magical power to construct and unify the nation, I will now examine two cultural nationalist texts on the Halifax Explosion – the Heritage Minute on the Halifax Explosion and the CBC's 2003 docudrama *Shattered City*. While the former is a short vignette that has been screened on Canadian TV and film screens for more than a decade, the latter is a more recent disaster narrative that sought to capitalize on the global media attention surrounding the terrorist attacks on New York and Washington on 9/11 as well as the popularity of the disaster film *Titanic*. As we shall see, in both, the undeniably tragic and destructive Halifax Explosion is reconfigured as a positive development in Canadian history.

The Heritage Minute on the Halifax Explosion is perhaps the best-known representation of the event. It begins with two telegraph operators standing outside the door of their office looking at the burning *Mont Blanc* in the Halifax Harbour. A sailor runs by and alerts them that the ship is full of explosives and that 'you gotta get outta here!' The younger of the two (identified as Vince Coleman), however, ignores his suggestion and runs instead into the street to urge others to flee the scene. Rather than heed his warning, the passers-by dismiss him as a crank and carry on with their everyday life. His attempt to save others foiled, Coleman returns to his office and begins to type out a telegraph message to an oncoming passenger train that a munitions ship is on fire in the harbour and that the train should stop. His colleague rushes in and urges him to run and save his own life. Coleman retorts, 'There are seven hundred people aboard it [the train], I've got to stop it!' He turns to the telegraph and pleads with it: 'C'mon, c'mon, acknowledge!'[10] The telegraph starts to respond and Coleman smiles and pumps his fist. Suddenly, an explosion is heard, the sky brightens, and Coleman stands up with a look of horror. His panicked countenance then fades into a scene of the aftermath of the explosion and a voice-over tells us that Coleman was one of two thousand people who died in Halifax on that day.

Like most of the Heritage Minutes, this one gains some of its dramatic impact as a result of its elision of historical facts and the addition of fictional elements in order to spice it up. For example, the scene of Coleman running out into the street (and, in a comic based on the minute, into schools) is pure fiction. Most historical accounts hold that he remained seated in his office during the moments leading up to the explosion.[11] Furthermore, evidence has recently come to light that suggests that the only person who knew the *Mont Blanc* carried munitions was its captain.[12] Therefore, the sailor could not have warned Coleman, who, in turn, could not have warned the people in the streets and the train. Furthermore, Coleman might not even have fully appreciated the suicidal nature of his decision to stay at his post and warn the train conductor.

This relatively minor fictionalization increases the exemplary power of Coleman's actions as a narrative of heroic sacrifice. In a miracle of narrative condensation, we watch as Coleman progresses through what Joseph Campbell has described as 'the hero's journey.'[13] The minute begins by situating Coleman in profane space and time – the hustle and bustle of a city street. He is then 'called to adventure' by the sailor and runs off to rescue the community/nation from imminent disaster. This call to adventure places him in the sacred space of heroism that effectively cuts him off from other members of the community who continue to muddle along in the prosaic and the profane and are thus incapable of understanding his message. In keeping with the hero cycle, he then undergoes a further series of trials – his awareness that he has a limited amount of time to send his message to the train conductor and his concern for his own safety. In the end, however, he is successful and at least part of the nation is saved through his actions.

However, what makes Coleman's actions truly heroic for many is the fact that he sacrificed his own life for the good of the nation. Sacrifice has always played an important role in forging communal and national unity and in eliminating any lingering sense that nations and communities are artificial constructs. As Richard Koenigsberg has argued in the case of modern war, 'actual human bodies are sacrificed in the name of perpetuating a magical entity, the body politic. Sacrificial acts function to affirm the reality or existence of this sacred object, the nation. Entering into battle may be characterized as a devotional act, with death in war constituting the supreme act of devotion.'[14] In other words, sacrifices like Coleman's lend the nation a sacred and transcendental character that we often lose sight of in the busyness of what Heidegger called 'average everydayness.' These heroic sacrifices are often held to possess a power to reduce the communal tensions, rivalries, and pursuit of self-interest that tend to fester when members of the community remain 'trapped' in the profane spaces of the interpersonal, the home, and the marketplace. In making the ultimate sacrifice, Coleman and other sacrificial heroes open up lines of communication between the sacred and the profane, reanimating the communal awareness that each individual is a part of a larger transcendent entity. Furthermore, in Christian and other versions of the sacrificial myth, the death of the sacrificial hero redeems the community by expiating its sins. As Henri Hubert and Marcel Mauss explain, the devotee who provides the sacrifice 'is not, at the completion of the operation, the same as he was at the beginning. He has acquired a religious character which he did not have before, or has rid himself of an unfavourable character with which he was affected; he has raised himself to a state of grace or has emerged from a state of sin.'[15]

In Western modernity, war has been the traditional site of collective rituals of sacrifice, purgation, and redemption. As Genevieve Lloyd and Susan Linville have pointed out, thinkers like Kant and Hegel argued that war was a necessary corrective to what they viewed as peaceable civil society's natural tendency towards self-interest, political and cultural fragmentation, and decadence. Kant, for example, wrote that 'a long peace generally brings about a predominant commercial spirit and, along with it, low selfishness, cowardice, and effeminacy, and debases the disposition of the people.'[16] Following Kant, Hegel argued that in order for the members of the male population to regain their vigour, their sense of being part of something greater than themselves, and, ultimately, their masculinity, the nation must periodically go to war. War, Hegel argued, provided the members of the nation with opportunities for sacrifice and spiritual rebirth because it 'shatters the isolation of individuals and calls them out of their shadowy existence within the family. War plays for ethical consciousness the same role that the possibility of death in general plays for self-consciousness: its shakes consciousness out of its attachment to mere nature into spirit.'[17] In sacrificing their lives for the greater good, Hegel argued, soldiers reunified the nation and secured it for the next generation.

However, while this celebration of the regenerative power of sacrifice and violence continues to attract audiences for Hollywood action movies, the celebration of war is a tough sell in Canada.[18] While the conscription crises of the First and Second World Wars suggest that there has always been a resistance to militarism in Quebec, since the 1960s antiwar movement, many English Canadians came to see the proper role of the military as being one of peace-keeping. Even in the case of the latter, the Somalia Affair took off much of its lustre. Furthermore, as the debate over *The Valour and the Horror* in 1992 revealed, even the attempt to commemorate a 'good war' is fraught with perils. Brian and Terrence McKenna's critical depiction of the often incompetent, duplicitous, and callous manner in which the British High Command and the subservient Canadian military leadership led to unnecessary Canadian and civilian casualties during the Second World War outraged many veterans' groups and led to inquiries by the CBC's ombudsman and the Senate Sub-Committee on Veterans' Affairs.[19] As a result, while the Halifax Explosion did occur during wartime, the fact that it occurred on Canadian shores created a situation in which the whole community was drawn into the drama. Furthermore, the fact that it was the product of human error and bad luck also provided the community with a sense of blamelessness for Coleman's sacrifice. Try as one might, it is very difficult to ascribe to Coleman anything but purely selfless motives. In other words, the Halifax Explosion provided a stage for the community to see acts of heroism unencumbered by guilt or remorse.

This underlying theme of the Halifax Explosion providing an opportunity for heroism, expiation, redemption, and reconciliation becomes fully explicit in the CBC's three-hour docudrama titled *Shattered City: The Halifax Explosion* (2003). The dramatic tension of this film is propelled by the changes wrought in the fictionalized Collins family in the aftermath of the explosion and follows closely the generic conventions of the disaster narrative. Genres and subgenres, as many have pointed out, play a central role in human attempts to make even the most seemingly ineffable or singular experiences understandable, communicable, and relevant to a larger audience. As Douglas Kellner and Michael Ryan explain, 'Genres hold the world in place, establishing and enforcing a sense of propriety, or proper boundaries which demarcate appropriate thought, feeling, behavior and which provide frames, codes, and signs for constructing a shared social reality.'[20] In so doing, however, genres tend to privilege the already-known and the expected over the new. As a result, critics often argue that genres have an implicitly conservative and even nostalgic character. As Judith Hess argues, film subgenres like the disaster film, the adventure, the historical drama, science fiction, and the western all seek to address present social and political conflicts but do so in a 'non-present' in which the social structure is greatly simplified and in which complex and seemingly intractable contemporary problems can be neatly resolved.[21]

These critical concerns about film genres in general are echoed in the literature on the disaster genre. According to writers like Kellner and Ryan and Maurice Yacowar, the disaster genre generally begins by bringing 'together a diverse group of characters whose personalities and foibles are sketched out in quick, broad strokes, relying on familiar stereotypes.'[22] The next step is to show how this microcosm of society is divided against itself and risks being torn apart by revealing the existence of growing class, gender, racial, ethnic, and generation conflicts. It is at the moment that these rising tensions threaten to boil over that the disaster generally strikes. Through its offer of purification by fire, the disaster offers the divided society a hope for redemption and renewal. In light of their common plight, the previously divided members of the society unite and rally around the typically white and male hero who is charged with the role of building a new and improved society on the ashes of the old. In spite of the tragic character of the central event, the disaster genre fits therefore within the framework of the classical definition of comedy.[23] In the disaster film, society always moves from a state of division to one of unity, and thus the film works to reaffirm our faith in the status quo by reassuring us that 'the center holds even when chaos has broken loose.'[24]

The first part of *Shattered City* closely follows the disaster narrative in using the synecdoche of the psychodrama of the Collins family to figure Halifax (and by extension Canada) as a community divided against itself. In one of the opening scenes, the family is decorating a Christmas tree, and we are introduced to its members: the stodgy father, the matronly mother, the uniformed adult son, the adult daughter, Beatrix, Courtney, the younger son, and Connie, the younger daughter. This ceremony is being held on 4 December, we learn, because Charlie, the older son, is returning to the front in a few days. Suddenly, the Christmas lights begin to explode and the uniformed adult son and main protagonist of the film, Charlie Collins, starts to have flashbacks of battle scenes and removes himself from the family ritual. This brief scene thus establishes Charlie as a victim of post-traumatic stress disorder whose visions of the horrors of war disconnect him from the everyday reality and rituals of the community.

The viewer's sense of Charlie's disconnection from the community grows in the early part of the film. Compounding the traumatic memories of death and destruction are an unshakeable sense of guilt for having followed orders to lead his troops into suicidal missions to repeatedly capture, lose, and then regain what he describes as 'a stinking patch of mud,'[25] and a tragic awareness that he cannot turn back the hands of time. As he tells Jamie, one of his former troop members who has been hospitalized after having half of his face blown off in a battle: 'I'd give my life to have that moment back again.'

Charlie's psychic torment over the unmasterable character of his memories and his seeming inability to atone, in any meaningful way, for what he sees as his sins is further exacerbated by his father's reactions. Like Charlie, his father is also a veteran and he even lost a leg in the Boer War. However, unlike Charlie, his memories of that war were profoundly shaped by the nineteenth-century masculinist/imperialist narrative of war as a heroic adventure which afforded boys the opportunity to become men. Throughout the early scenes, we watch as Charlie struggles with his desire to relate his own traumatic experience of war and his father's expectations that he will encode that experience in the narrative framework of heroic adventure.

This intergenerational conflict over war and how it should be remembered comes to a head in one of the climactic scenes of the first act of the film. After a trip to the hospital in which Charlie learns that Jamie has committed suicide, the grieving Charlie wanders the Halifax streets until he enters a building in which a War Bond rally organized by his father is taking place. Soon after Charlie enters, a speaker takes to the podium. Identified by Charlie's father as George Adam, a former MP, professor at Dalhousie University, and, as his clothing reveals, a minister, Adam immediately launches into a fiery patriotic speech that makes full use of the rhetoric of the nation as a patriarchal family in which men are given the roles of 'saving the women and children' and securing the home front. He describes the soldiers in the trenches as 'our boys' and tells a story about one soldier who told him that he was fighting the war in order to defend 'my mom in Truro.' However, he warns, in terms that were used at the time yet still contain a less than subtle allusion to the rhetoric of Ronald Reagan and George W. Bush, the Kaiser's 'evil empire' is still powerful and the ranks of Canadian soldiers must be replenished.

After he is alerted to Charlie's presence in the meeting hall by Charlie's father, Adam invites Charlie to stand up and say a few words in support of his call to arms. When Charlie politely demurs, Adam then challenges Charlie by shouting that 'you owe it to your fallen comrades and their families.' This challenge is then echoed by the crowd, which responds with a chant of 'Hear, hear!' The appeal to Charlie's responsibility to his fallen comrades galvanizes him into action. He stands up and begins to tell a story of how his British commanders would send him and his troops each day on a series of suicidal and pointless missions that would result in no gains in territory but massive casualties. Each day, he would lose a quarter to half of his men, but each morning, 'headquarters sent more men.' This pointless slaughter of young Canadian and German men, he concludes, 'is such a waste ... it's gotta stop!' As Charlie utters these final words, Adam tries to shout him down, and the crowd erupts into jeers and cries of 'German lover!' Charlie gets up to leave the building. As he leaves, however, he looks back at his father, who is bowing down his head in shame.

In this scene, the simmering intergenerational tension surrounding the narration of war is made explicit, as is Charlie's isolation from the rest of the community. Charlie's father and the jingoistic Adam represent the old Canada and Charlie represents the new Canada. In setting up the debate in this manner, *Shattered City* closely follows Hugh MacLennan's *Barometer Rising*. Like *Shattered City*, *Barometer Rising* is a story of intergenerational conflict. On the one hand, we have Patrick, a shell-shocked soldier who has secretly returned to Halifax to confront his uncle – a corrupt and incompetent careerist, the man who raised the orphaned Patrick, and Patrick's former field commander in France. During one battle, we learn, he gave Patrick contradictory battle orders that resulted in the troops under his charge being nearly wiped out. In order to avoid taking the blame for this, he then made the fraudulent claim that Patrick was openly mutinous and deserving of a court martial. As in *Shattered City*, the narrative tension builds in the first half of the novel leading up to the explosion. In a particularly egregious example of the use of the device of *deus ex machina*, the explosion resolves this tension by killing the uncle, curing Patrick of his shellshock, and bringing to light the evidence needed to avert Patrick's court martial. In *Barometer Rising*, the 'father/old Canada' versus 'son/new Canada' conflict is fully explicit. The uncle is used to represent Canadian society at its most colonial – corrupt, jingoistic, embarrassed about his status as a colonist, desperate for the recognition of the 'mother country,' and thus unquestioningly following it into imperialistic bloodbaths. The character of Patrick, on the other hand, is described as the harbinger of a new, more self-confidently American Canada that is profoundly sceptical of militaristic and imperialistic calls for blood.[26]

While MacLennan's book was written in the 1940s, contemporary English-Canadian nationalists are far less likely to embrace 'Americanism' as a strategy of cultural and political decolonization. Since the middle of the twentieth century, Canadian nationalist discourse has been increasingly more animated by fears of American economic and cultural imperialism and a profound suspicion of American military interventions in Vietnam and Iraq. As a result, *Shattered City* strongly diverges from *Barometer Rising* on the question of the proper relationship between Canada and the United States. This becomes most clear from the speech of Adam, which draws directly on the rhetoric of 'the evil empire.' However, suspicion of American military motives also structures much of Charlie's discussion of the war. As he explains to Barbara, his American love interest, he believes that the war has dragged on because the British government 'still likes the idea of another year of a war economy. See it started out as war of defence but now it's become one of aggression.' Similarly, at another point, he tells her that 'I didn't ask you to solve my problems ... I don't want your help. This is so typically American, the U.S. cavalry riding in at the eleventh hour. Sometimes things are best left the way they are and you have to accept that. You'll just make it worse.' If, as many have pointed out, the past serves as an allegory for the expression of political beliefs about the present, it's hard to find a better example than in these cases. In these scenes, George W. Bush and Tony Blair's War on Iraq and the left/centrist Canadian discourse on that war provide key intertextual resources for the construction of *Shattered City*'s narrative.

In constructing the jingoistic discourse of Adam and Charlie's father as deriving from Canada's past and present colonial overlords, *Shattered City* works to create a distinction between an 'authentically Canadian' attitude towards war and one that has been implanted in Canadian soil by arrogant and domineering 'outsiders.' This act of spatially separating these competing discourses is reinforced by an act of temporal separation. As Johannes Fabian has argued, one of the major ways in which the West established its sense of superiority over the colonized world was through what he calls the 'denial of coevalness.' Since the eighteenth century, the West has ordered the movement of time according to the linear and universal schema of evolutionary progress. In this schema, different cultural groups are held to have attained different levels of development or modernity. Such an arrangement of time, he argues, allowed those who placed themselves at the cutting edge of the movement of progress to reinforce their sense that they were more 'advanced' than the groups whom they wrote about. As he puts it, the evolutionary arrangement of time typically has 'the purpose of distancing those who are observed from the Time of the observer.'[27]

In *Shattered City*, this denial of coevalness occurs in several ways. The most obvious way in which this happens is through the representation of this discursive struggle as a struggle between generations, which the son, the symbol of national progress, is destined to win. The second is in the manner in which the two generations are figured. As we have seen, Charlie's father, Adam, and other men of their generation are constructed as flat characters who cling to what most educated members of twenty-first-century Canada would consider to be childish and regressive fantasies about masculinity and war and to traditional loyalties to a bloodthirsty British government, and who lack any awareness of the psychological effects of war. Charlie, on the other hand, is a complex and sympathetic character who embodies the post-Vietnam, post-feminist, and post-Oprah ideal of heroic masculinity.

In constructing Charlie in this manner, *Shattered City* seems to borrow heavily from the character of *Saving Private Ryan*'s Captain John Miller. Like Charlie, Miller is a white Anglo commander who has been psychologically damaged by his wartime experience – he too suffers from flashbacks and he too has lost any illusions about the heroic nature of war. In one scene, he even freezes and is incapable of leading his men to safety while under heavy enemy fire. In spite of his fear, cynicism, and psychic suffering, Susan Owen writes, he remains 'disciplined, resourceful and responsible. He is both courageous and compassionate, a warrior dedicated to his duty, and yet disdainful of romantic idealizations of war. He both sees the remarkable ineptitude of American military hierarchies and continues to doggedly affirm that social order and performs his role as a soldier.'[28] Furthermore, like Charlie, he is a '90s man' in that he is psychologically aware, unafraid to express his feelings, and able to use persuasion rather than coercion to maintain cohesion among his troops. In so doing, Owen concludes, *Saving Private Ryan* reconfigures the traditional ideal of heroic white masculinity in a manner that integrates aspects of feminism and the post-Vietnam disillusionment about war to make it more palatable to contemporary audiences and to forestall more serious challenges to the racial and gender order of things associated with that ideal.[29] In characterizing Charlie in the same manner, *Shattered City* works to persuade the audience to identify with Charlie by suggesting that, unlike his seniors, he is 'just like us.' In other words, he fits within our present sensibilities while his father and his generation are left in the past. This, in turn, implies another denial of coevalness. Since the older generation voices beliefs that we have outgrown but which are now being voiced by our past and present colonial overlords – the British and the Americans – *Shattered City* creates a hierarchy of times in which Canada is seen to be morally and epistemically superior to the latter.

In this way, the film closely follows the textual logic of ressentiment as well as what Partha Chatterjee has called 'anticolonial nationalism.'[30] In postcolonial contexts, nationalist elites cultivate a sense of national superiority by dividing the world into two realms – the material and the spiritual. Following the logic of ressentiment, it is granted that the material realm will continue to be dominated by the colonizing powers. However, the decolonizing nation has its own spiritual essence that differentiates it from its colonial overlords. In countries with long pre-colonial histories like India or Iran, this spiritual essence is typically figured in the rhetoric of roots, ancestry, origins, purity, and authenticity. In settler colonies like Australia, Brazil, and Canada, however, this appeal to the nation's roots is far more problematic. Histories of colonial domination, slavery, the near-genocide of Aboriginal peoples, and recurring intercultural conflicts make appeals to the shared past more likely to exacerbate social tensions than to unite those being interpellated by the discourse of the nation. Cut off from the rhetorical appeal to the nation's golden age, the elite of these former settler colonies turn instead to an equally powerful rhetoric for the cultivation of national identity. As Julie Skurski explains in her study of Venezuelan nationalism, instead of appealing to the nation's origins, the discourse of national progress took centre stage. In this discourse, 'the nation was conceptualized in terms of the Enlightenment promise that national unity could be achieved by eschewing the past and embracing the rule of reason and citizens rights.'[31] This is also the underlying message of *Shattered City*: for the nation to progress, the father must die and the son must take his place.

This discourse of national progress is also constructed in the relationship between the viewer and the characters on screen. Given the conventions of the historical docudrama in which the historical character of the film is typically secured through the use of a variety of markers of 'pastness' ranging from costumes to props to vaguely old streets and buildings to depictions of quaint customs and linguistic behaviours, it should come as no surprise that no matter how contemporary their attitudes may be, the characters on screen are situated in a different historical period from their target audience. At the same time, however, a much subtler form of temporal distancing also occurs in the film. While I have been concentrating on only one narrative thus far, the early part of the film as a whole is structured around a multi-stranded plot in which diverse characters are shown to be concurrently engaging in discrete actions in various parts of Halifax. This multi-stranded diegesis reinforces the sense of a city and a family divided against itself – because of the constraints of time and space, the various characters are always in the dark about what the others are doing and what they believe. The viewer, on the other hand, is constructed as being omniscient – unlike the temporally and spatially bound characters, only she has a synoptic vision of their present diverse and seemingly discontinuous activities. Furthermore, the opacity of the future is also conquered by a heavy-handed use of foreshadowing in this early part of the film. The result of this is that the viewer is situated by the film in a position of epistemic superiority in relation to the benighted characters. *Shattered City* constantly flatters the viewer by constructing her as the only one who really knows what is going on and what is going to happen. On the other hand, the characters must, like children, muddle towards a series of empirical, political, and moral truths that we, the 'advanced' viewers, already know. In this way, *Shattered City* reinforces the narrative of national progress. It seems to want to tell us that 'Yes, Charlie was pretty smart but *we* are even smarter.'

Running in parallel to this story of simmering Oedipal conflict is the story of the conflict between traditional and modern femininity. As we have seen,

Charlie's family is composed of three women – the mother, the younger sister Connie, and the older sister Beatrix. The first two fulfil two of the major roles assigned to women by patriarchal nationalist ideology: the guardian of the hearth and the Florence Nightingale figure who selflessly tends to the wounded. The mother, for her part, is figured as a highly two-dimensional character. She is generically maternal, her main concern seems to be with matching china cups to their saucers, and she is generally revealed to be a stereotypical housewife who has little or no sense of the world beyond the domestic sphere. Connie, on the other hand, is represented as a healer. She is the one who comforts Charlie when he suffers from flashbacks or questions his own bravery. She accompanies Charlie to the military hospital and happily sits and talks with the wounded soldiers.

Counterposed to these two representatives of traditional patriarchal femininity is Beatrix, a doubly threatening synthesis of the transgressive 'modern' woman and the traditional 'whore.' We learn early on that she works outside the home in a print shop, and is a central player in the drive to unionize it. She confesses her sympathy for the Bolsheviks and declares her faith 'in the new ideas of freedom for women and socialism.' In voicing such revolutionary ideas, Beatrix faces the same kind of scepticism and hostility as Charlie. At one point, her co-workers tell her that 'they'll either make you prime minister or hang you,' while her lover describes her at one point as a 'stupid cow' with 'nothing in her head but silly politics.' Even her closest friend at the print shop tells her that 'I'd rather have a husband than a union.'

However, these political transgressions are minor in comparison with her sexual transgressions. Early on in the film, Beatrix lies to her parents about going to an IODE meeting. Instead, she sneaks off to meet with her lover, Ernst. Ernst has been revealed to the viewer as a German spy who has stolen a large amount of TNT from the Canadian army and is conspiring with another spy to blow up the *Mont Blanc*. (This subplot is a complete fabrication; there was never any evidence of German spies in Halifax at the time.) He tells Beatrix that he is Dutch and uses her as a 'prop' to disguise the fact that the photos she thinks that is she is taking of him standing by the ships in the harbour are really being used to plan his attack.

Shattered City goes to great lengths to represent the full extent of her sexual treachery. In lying to her parents in order to sneak off, she violates her parents' trust and subverts their authority to control and regulate her sexuality. Furthermore, because she is literally sleeping with the enemy, Beatrix's unregulated sexual behaviour is shown to put the nation at risk. Finally, this act of treason is personalized through the device of cutting back and forth between scenes of her selfish pursuit of sexual pleasure and hospital scenes of wounded and maimed soldiers, many of whom will never again be able to enjoy the pleasures of the body. This juxtaposition of images of frivolous hedonism and suffering and sacrifice reinforces the underlying message that her selfish pursuit of illicit sexual pleasure threatens to undo all that the soldiers sacrificed themselves to defend.

This figuration of Beatrix's act of treason in familial and sexual terms has deep roots in nationalist discourse. As many have argued, nationalism figures the nation as one large extended family and individual families are represented as a microcosm of the national whole.[32] As George Mosse has pointed out, in order to ensure that the nation remains unified in its goals and actions, the nation-state assigns the role of moral regulation to the patriarchal family because the latter had the great potential to control 'the passions at their source. Clearly, the family was the policeman on the beat, an indispensable agent of sexual control as directed by physicians, educators and the nation itself. Any threat to its survival endangered the nation's future.'[33] In this complex of national and familial sexual regulation, policing the sexuality of young women is the central focus. As Cynthia Enloe explains, nationalist men see women as the nation's most valuable possessions because they are the literal bearers of the nation's future generations and, because they still do the majority of child-rearing, the main transmitters of the nation's values. However, they are also seen as being easily duped or seduced away either by 'foreign' men or their own uncontrolled sexual passions from fulfilling those roles. Unlike steadfast men, they are highly 'susceptible to assimilation and cooption by insidious outsiders'[34] and thus can easily switch from securing the nation's future to becoming, like Beatrix, 'a menace to society and the nation, threatening the established order they were intended to uphold.'[35]

Shattered City's construction of this antinomy between the dangerous and transgressive 'new woman' and the wholesome 'traditional' woman might strike many contemporary viewers as a nostalgic and even reactionary response to the changes in gender roles since the 1960s. Furthermore, it seems to contradict the narrative of progress, rebirth, and renewal that animates the Charlie storyline. As a result, a fourth main female character is introduced as a compromise that seeks to synthesize aspects of both forms of femininity and to reintegrate the new femininity back into the nationalist narrative. This character is an American doctor named Barbara who becomes Charlie's love interest. In many ways, she represents the epitome of the 'new woman.' She works in a male-dominated profession, she is unmarried and independent. At the same time, however, she is endowed with many of the attributes of traditional femininity. She is sexually chaste, morally conventional, and apolitical. Like Connie and unlike the male surgeons in the film, who treat the patients as mere objects upon which to practise their surgical techniques, she is a healer who is animated by an ethic of care both for Charlie and for her patients. While this characterization makes her a nice compromise formation that can integrate some of the aspects of feminism into a 'new and improved' version of patriarchal femininity, *Shattered City* also works to 'Canadianize' her. When we first meet the doctor, we learn that she is a plastic surgeon who has accompanied a male doctor who is presumably her mentor to study how to perform reconstructive surgery on wounded soldiers. Her mentor is portrayed in much the same way as Adam – as a callous and superficial technocrat who views the bodies of young men as mere objects to be sacrificed to his own personal interests. When Charlie's friend Jamie kills himself, for example, the only dismay that this doctor voices is that it was a 'such damn waste of good work.' Similarly, when Charlie raises the issue of shell-shock, the doctor retorts that 'We've heard of the term shell-shock but where we come from it's called cowardice.'

In the early scenes of the film, Barbara is represented as faithfully mimicking her mentor's attitudes. However, as a result of her contact with Charlie, her views begin to change. She grows to recognize the psychological effects of war, admits to Charlie that 'Dr. Sherman is wrong ... I was wrong' in attributing shell-shock to cowardice, and pleads with Charlie to get treatment for his PTSD. In other words, her contact with Charlie was one of education and enlightenment. In another interesting parallel between Charlie and Beatrix, we see how this film's faith in the Canadian genius for civilizing others – best encapsulated in the smug sound-byte offered to us by the Liberal Party during the 2006 election campaign, 'The world needs more Canada' – even extends to our presumed enemies. In spite of the fact that he was using Beatrix as a cloak for his planned attack on the *Mont Blanc*, even the German spy Ernst ends up sacrificing his own life to try to save the lives of innocent Haligonians by scuttling the ship before it had a chance to explode.

Before I pass on to the discussion of the explosion and its aftermath, one final parallel between Charlie and Beatrix must be pointed out. Both are presented as rebels against the established political order – Charlie with his public pronouncements against the war and Beatrix with her advocacy of feminist and pro-union ideals. However, while Charlie's rebellion is seen as legitimate because of its reformist character, Beatrix's is transgressive and dangerous. Their sexuality is also seen differently. While Charlie's relationship is pure, loving, and chaste and ends with the possibility of adding a virtuous Canadianized outsider into the national fold, that of Beatrix is doubly treasonous. Not only does she betray her parents' authority by sneaking off behind their backs to cavort with Ernst, she also betrays the nation by allowing her womb – the wellspring of the next generation of Canadians – to be penetrated and occupied by the enemy. While the explosion and its aftermath will reward Charlie's reformism and his addition of a new source of future nationalized babies, Beatrix will be punished for her breach of the nation's sovereignty.

These scenes of interpersonal, intercultural, and intergenerational conflict work to establish Halifax, and by extension Canada, as a society divided against itself. As Charlie's mother puts it on the morning of the explosion and the day after Charlie's confrontation with Adam, 'why are we ... why are things falling apart?' The early part of the film also sets the stage for the explosion. In a series of scenes that are interspersed with these more melodramatic tableaus, we learn that due to a combination of American rapacity and French incompetence, the *Mont Blanc* is a slow ship commanded by the ineffectual Captain Medec that has been overloaded with explosives. We are informed that the management of ship traffic in Halifax harbour has been taken over by an officious British commander named Wyatt whose initiatives to 'deregulate' traffic are seen by many Haligonians as putting the city at risk. We are also introduced to Haakon, the Norwegian captain of the *Imo* – the ship with which the *Mont Blanc* would later collide. He is a difficult man who refuses to heed speed limits within the harbour. Finally, thrown into this mix is Francis Mackey, a Cape Breton–born pilot who is given the job of safely steering the *Mont Blanc* into harbour. Unlike the dyspeptic Haakon, the cold and arrogant Medec, and the pompous Wyatt, Mackey embodies all of the usual traits of the Maritime 'fisherfolk' – good-natured, fun-loving, and guileless.[36]

While the first half of the film heavily foreshadows the gathering disaster, it takes centre stage in the middle. We watch as the *Mont Blanc* and the *Imo* steam towards each other with only Mackey making any attempt to avert the disaster. Furthermore, once the ships have crashed, Mackey is the only one aboard the ship who attempts to put out the fire created by the explosion. Medec, for his part, does not offer help. Instead, he immediately orders the crew to abandon ship, and Mackey eventually also flees the ship. The only persons besides Mackey to even attempt to avert this disaster are an Indigenous fisherman named Cobb who rows his dory to the crash site to offer help and, later, Ernst, who tries to scuttle the ship. Medec and his crew think only about their own safety.

Very soon thereafter, the *Mont Blanc* explodes, and we watch spectacular scenes of half of Halifax being reduced to rubble, killing many and leaving those who survive to walk the streets in a post-traumatic daze. Much of the final half of the film centres on a narrative of the legal proceedings set up to determine responsibility for the explosion. Three people are charged for their part in it: Wyatt (the deregulating British officer in charge of the harbour), Medec (the cowardly French captain of the *Mont Blanc*) and Francis Mackey (the 'good lad' from Cape Breton). While the viewers know that Mackey was the only one who tried to prevent the blast, we watch as Wyatt and Medec conspire together to hang the blame on his shoulders. We then learn that their respective governments have successfully used diplomatic channels to have the charges dropped against them.

This leaves Mackey as the only person to stand trial for his role in the explosion. In line with his construction as the defender of the 'authentic' Canadian nation, Charlie acts as his defence counsel. As the trial progresses, it seems more and more likely that Mackey will be unjustly convicted and that evil will prevail over good. However, he is saved in the end by the *deus ex machina* of Charlie's discovery of Cobb, the Indigenous fisherman (whose characterization as a simple, authentic, and trustworthy rustic closely parallels that of Mackey). Cobb tells Charlie that even though he was right next to the *Mont Blanc* when it exploded, he and his boat were not immediately incinerated (as one might expect) but rather the blast propelled him and his boat into the air to land safely onshore. He is called by Charlie to testify and ends up exonerating Mackey, leaving no doubt in the public's mind of the authenticity, innocence, and virtue of the Canadian Mackey and the duplicity, incompetence, and cowardice of Canada's former colonial overlords. In other words, in consonance with anticolonial nationalist discourse, the explosion and its legal aftermath become another stage for the narrative of the spiritually pure nation's blamelessness and its need to break with its corrupting and disastrous colonial past.

Furthermore, not only does it blame the French and the English for the disaster – a relic of Canada's colonial history – this part of the film is also overcoded with not-so-subtle references to what it figures as Canada's present colonial overlords: the Americans. Given the temporal proximity of the production of the film to 9/11 and its aftermath, it is not surprising that many of the descriptions of the explosion use much of the same visual imagery and language as those of 9/11. In the aftermath of the explosion, we see ash-covered survivors wandering around aimlessly in the same manner as the surviving Manhattan office workers, and in one scene, for example, Charlie mentions 'firemen rushing into their death.' Such parallels give a 'presence' to the past represented in the film which is used to editorialize about post-9/11 American foreign policy. In good Canadian nationalist fashion, Charlie repeatedly asserts Canada's moral and epistemic superiority in spite of its impotence in the face of empire. His closing arguments in Mackey's defence, for example, are a study in Canadian ressentiment. Francis Mackey, he tells the jury, 'comes before you alone not because of guilt but because of interventions of powers outside of this courtroom. Those truly guilty have been set free. Now I can do nothing about that but I can tell you that Francis Mackey is a good man ... a good man who became a pawn in the war, just like all of us. We're all pawns when we allow a government without question to wage war for vengeance or glory, for political or economic gain.'

At the same time that the Halifax Explosion seems to offer Canada the opportunity to make a break with its colonial past (and present), this narrative of purgation and renewal by fire also structures the story of the Walsh family in the last half of the film. As in *Barometer Rising*, the Halifax Explosion has a purgative and restorative power for Charlie. In its aftermath, he miraculously shakes off his PTSD and takes control of the rescue and relief operation and then defends Mackey in court. Furthermore, his act of Oedipal rebellion is rewarded – his father dies as a result of the wounds he suffered in the explosion but not before using his dying words to voice his approval of Charlie's understanding of the horrors of war. Not only is Charlie released from paternal authority by this passing of the torch, his relationship to his mother also changes. In an interesting twist on the Oedipal story, it is the mother who is blinded and thus loses her position to Charlie as the head of the household.

For Beatrix, on the other hand, it's a different story. She is punished repeatedly for her transgressions. Injured in the explosion, she awakes to find all of her friends and her lover dead and passes out from grief and guilt. She is eventually discovered and brought to a hospital, where we learn that she is pregnant with Ernst's child. However, by the end of the film, she too redeems herself. We watch as she puts aside her politics and her desire to be an independent woman and assumes a new role as a nurse to the wounded and as an expectant mother.

Finally, the film ends with not one but two acts of American recognition of Canada's existence as a morally superior and independently existing entity. The penultimate scene shows the family gathered around a Christmas tree. The house has been rebuilt and the family is reunited for a family photo, which, in very Canadian fashion, is meant to commemorate the fact that 'we survived.'[37] While the father is obviously absent, a new member has joined: Barbara the American doctor, who lovingly gazes upon Charlie, the benevolent and enlightened new family patriarch. This scene of American adoration of the emblematic Canadian is then followed up by a flash forward to the present, where we watch a now elderly Connie attend a ceremony in Boston in which Americans gather around a giant Christmas tree (i.e., a Canadian phallus) that is lit to commemorate the explosion. In this way, what would seem to be an event of senseless death, carnage, and destruction is reconfigured as a nationalist utopia: it united the nation under a new and progressive leadership and made the Americans notice, love, and respect us.

Conclusion

For the Canadian nationalist discourse that uses early twentieth-century Halifax as a means to voice anxieties about its present, recent Canadian history appears as a series of disasters: the fractious workers' movement, the rise of feminism and its attack on traditional masculinity, the emergence of a continental economy, the continued influence of its past and present colonial overlords, and the selfish pursuit of the pleasures of the flesh and the market over the sense of duty to the nation have conspired to chisel away at the very possibility of performing heroic nation-binding acts. Like Charlie at the beginning of *Shattered City*, Canadian national heroic masculinity is seen as impotent, paralysed by memories of traumas not of its making, and, like Coleman in the Heritage Minute, a frustrated male Cassandra whose warnings of the imminent national disaster go unheeded by the insouciant, ignorant, and materialistic Canadian population. However, this pent-up sense of impotence, paralysis, and frustration is expiated in the *jouissance* of the explosion of the *Mont Blanc*. In the aftermath of its climactic violence, the world is redeemed and all is put back into its rightful place. Given the way in which these texts raise and then assuage fears of national impotence through the performance of heroic and explosive national self-assertion, Cynthia Enloe's observation that 'nationalism typically has sprung from masculinized memory, masculinized humiliation and masculinized hope'[38] starts to make more than a bit of sense.

NOTES

1 Daniel Francis, *National Dreams: Myth, Memory and Canadian History* (Vancouver: Arsenal Pulp Press, 1997).

2 Will Straw, 'Dilemmas of Definition,' in Joan Nicks and Jeannette Sloniowski, eds., *Slippery Pastimes: Reading the Popular in Canadian Culture* (Waterloo, ON: Wilfrid Laurier University Press, 2002), 101.

3 Kieran Keohane, *Symptoms of Canada: An Essay on the Canadian Identity* (Toronto: University of Toronto Press, 1997).

4 Nietzsche described *ressentiment* in section 10 of the first essay in *On the Genealogy of Morals* (New York: Vintage Books, 1967). For applications of the concept of *ressentiment* to the study of Canadian culture, see Michael Dorland, 'A Thoroughly Hidden Country: *Ressentiment*, Canadian Nationalism, Canadian Culture,' *Canadian Journal of Political and Social Theory*, 12, 1–2 (1988): 130–64; and Glenn Willmot, 'Canadian *Ressentiment*,' *New Literary History* 32, 1 (2001): 133–56.

5 Mark Starowicz, 'The Crucible of History,' *Opinion Canada* 2, 15 (20 April 2000), available online at http://www.cric.ca/en_html/opinion/opv2n15.html#food.

6 Ibid.

7 Jack Granatstein, *Who Killed Canadian History?* (Toronto: HarperCollins, 1998).

8 Peter Mansbridge, 'Does the Media Reflect Canadian History?' 2004 Canada Post Lecture delivered at University Of Ottawa, 3 December 2004, available online at http://www.media.uottawa.ca/mediaroom/news_details-e.php?nid=430.

9 Patrick Watson, 'Minute by Minute: The Making of a Canadian Mythology,' in *The Heritage Project's 60th Minute Commemorative Video* (Montreal: Heritage Project, 1998).

10 'Halifax Explosion' in ibid.

11 Cf. 'Rewriting History' at http://archives.cbc.ca/IDC-1-70-971-5513/disasters_tragedies/halifax_explosion/clip9.

12 John Armstrong, *The Halifax Explosion and the Royal Canadian Navy: Inquiry and Intrigue* (Vancouver: University of British Columbia Press, 2002).

13 Carl Boggs and Tom Pollard, *A World in Chaos: Social Crisis and the Rise of Postmodern Cinema* (Lanham, MD: Rowman and Littlefield, 2003).

14 Richard Koenigsberg 'As the Soldier Dies, So Does the Nation Come Alive: The Sacrificial Meaning of Warfare,' available online at http://home.earthlink.net/~libraryofsocialscience/as_the_soldier.htm.

15 Henri Hubert and Marcel Mauss, *Sacrifice: Its Nature and Function* (Chicago: University of Chicago Press, 1964), 9–10.

16 Kant quoted in Susan Linville, *History Films, Women and Freud's Uncanny* (Austin: University of Texas Press, 2004), 24.

17 Genevieve Lloyd, 'Selfhood, War and Masculinity,' in Carole Pateman and Elizabeth Gross, eds., *Feminist Challenges: Social and Political Theory* (Boston: Northeastern University Press 1989), 73–4.

18 This essay was written when Pearsonian ideals were still hegemonic. Over the past half-decade, however, war has probably become an easier sell in Canada.

19 For an excellent overview of this controversy, see Graham Carr's 'Rules of Engagement: Public History and the Drama of Legitimation,' *CHR* 86, 2 (2005): 317–54.

20 Michael Ryan and Douglas Kellner, *Camera Politica: The Politics and Ideology of Contemporary Hollywood Film* (Bloomington: University of Indiana Press, 1988), 52.

21 Judith Hess, 'Genre Films and the Status Quo,' in Barry Grant, ed., *Film Genre: Theory and Criticism* (Metuchen, NJ: Scarecrow Press, 1977).

22 Ryan and Kellner, *Camera Politica*, 52.

23 The basic plot movement of classical comedy is: 1) it begins with the society is divided against itself – typically this division is figured as an intergenerational struggle between a morally corrupt and obstructing father figure or father figures and an enlightened young hero who seeks to reform the society; 2) the hero, with the help of various allies, fights to overcome the obstacles to change placed in his

way by the father figure; 3) it ends with the victory of the hero over the father and the unification of the community under a more just social order. For more on classical comedy, cf. Northrop Frye, *Anatomy of Criticism: Four Essays* (Princeton: Princeton University Press, 1957); Hayden White, *Metahistory* (Baltimore: Johns Hopkins University Press, 1973).

24 Maurice Yacowar, 'The Bug in the Rug: Notes on the Disaster Genre,' in Grant, ed., *Film Genre*, 228.

25 Bruce Pittman, dir., *Shattered City: The Halifax Explosion* (television show), Toronto: CBC, 2003. All future references to the film will be from this source unless otherwise indicated.

26 Hugh MacLennan, *Barometer Rising* (Toronto: McClelland and Stewart, 1991).

27 Johannes Fabian, *Time and the Other: How Anthropology Makes Its Object* (New York: Columbia University Press, 1983), 25.

28 Susan Owen, 'Memory, War and American Identity: *Saving Private Ryan* as Cinematic Jeremiad,' *Critical Studies in Media Communication* 19, 3 (2002): 266.

29 Ibid.

30 Partha Chatterjee, *Nationalist Thought and the Colonial World: A Derivative Discourse?* (Tokyo: United Nations University, 1986).

31 Julie Skurski, 'The Ambiguities of Authenticity in Latin America: Doña Bárbara and the Construction of National Identity,' in Geoff Eley and Ronald Suny, eds., *Becoming National: A Reader* (Oxford and London: Oxford University Press, 1996), 376.

32 Cf. Étienne Balibar, 'The Nation Form: History and Ideology,' in Étienne Balibar and Immanuel Wallerstein, *Race, Nation and Class* (New York: Verso, 1991).

33 George Mosse, *Nationalism and Sexuality: Respectability and Abnormal Sexuality in Modern Europe* (New York: H. Fertig, 1985), 20.

34 Cynthia Enloe, *Bananas, Beaches and Bases: Making Feminist Sense of International Politics* (Berkeley: University of California Press, 1989), 54.

35 Mosse, *Nationalism and Sexuality*, 90.

36 For more on the constructed 'authenticity' of the fisherfolk, see Ian McKay, *The Quest of the Folk: Antimodernism and Cultural Selection in Twentieth Century Nova Scotia* (Montreal and Kingston: McGill-Queen's University Press, 1994).

37 For more on 'survival' as a core English-Canadian myth, see Margaret Atwood's *Survival: A Thematic Guide to Canadian Literature* (Toronto: Anansi, 1972). For a parallel analysis that also articulates with Dorland and Willmot's observation on Canadian *ressentiment*, see also Northrop Frye's seminal conclusion to Karl Klinck et al., eds., *Literary History of Canada: Canadian Literature in English* (Toronto: University of Toronto Press, 1965).

38 Enloe, *Bananas, Beaches and Bases*, 44.

18 The Past Is an Imagined Country: Reading Canadian Historical Fiction Written in English

RENÉE HULAN

David Lowenthal's influential work on public history *The Past Is a Foreign Country* takes as its title the opening line of L.P. Hartley's 1953 novel *The Go-Between*: 'The past is a foreign country: they do things differently there.'[1] The line elegantly conveys the principal insight of Lowenthal's study by capturing in metaphor the perception of difference between past and present shaping contemporary acts of commemoration and preservation. To understand this meaning, it is not necessary to know that the line in the novel refers specifically to the fictional narrator's feelings of alienation and bewilderment as he looks back on his own life and recollects the painful loss of his youthful innocence. Indeed, it is not necessary to know very much about the novel at all. By exemplifying the tendency to quote literary works without taking into account the meaning created by form and style, Lowenthal's reference to Hartley signals but does not explore the relationship of history and literature. From the viewpoint of literary scholarship, form and style are as important as content, and the interpretation of these aspects of the literary work is of particular importance in understanding fiction that conveys a sense of historical consciousness by artistic means. For this reason, a deeper understanding of how literature contributes to ways of thinking about the past can be gained from interpreting the form and style of the work. This chapter provides a literary perspective on historical fiction written in English, first by arguing that imagining the past is a perennial concern in Canadian literature, and then by briefly comparing the changing modes and styles of historical fiction in Canadian literary history. It will suggest that the writing and reading of historical fiction has been and continues to be one of the ways Canadians collectively imagine the past and thus remember, commemorate, and re-evaluate history.

Looking Back

In the last decade of the twentieth century, the relationship of history and literature came under scrutiny as a number of prominent Canadian authors, including Margaret Atwood, Mordecai Richler, Wayne Johnston, Guy Vanderhaeghe, Douglas Glover, and Jane Urquhart among others, published historical novels to great popular and critical acclaim. The appearance of these works of historical fiction coincided, paradoxically, with a wave of intense panic about declining historical knowledge in Canada. As headlines warned readers that the nation was in peril, threatened by its citizens' diminishing general knowledge and lack of interest in their own past, Canadians were writing and reading historical fiction; in fact, readers were making novels like *Alias Grace* and *Solomon Gursky Was Here* into bestsellers. While Canadian literature seemed to have taken a sudden turn towards historical fiction, historical novels published in the late twentieth century are part of a tradition of historical fiction that can be traced back through literary history and that needs to be seen in the context of a concern with the past that reaches beyond both temporal and generic boundaries. What changes over time in this tradition is not the interest in the past but the style in which it is expressed and how it is received by the audience.

In 1996, Margaret Atwood reflected on the reasons for the apparent rise in historical fiction in a public lecture entitled 'In Search of *Alias Grace*: On Writing Canadian Historical Fiction.'[2] By taking a retrospective look at Canadian literature, this lecture, which was later the focus of a panel of the *American Historical Review*, demonstrates how writers and literary critics shape the reconstruction of the *literary* past according to the literary tastes and values of the present. Indeed, Atwood's career illustrates the many ways in which writers participate in discussions shaping perceptions of the past. The historical novel *Alias Grace* revisits an episode in Canadian history that Atwood had already explored in the 1960s by writing a play entitled 'The Servant Girl' after reading about the case of Grace Marks in Susanna Moodie's *Life in the Clearings*. The poems in *The Journals of Susanna Moodie* (1970) also explore this period in history, as does Atwood's history for young readers entitled *Days of the Rebels, 1815–1840* (1977).[3] Despite her own lifelong interest in historical subjects, particularly from the nineteenth century, Atwood's lecture attributes the popularity of historical fiction in late twentieth-century Canada to 'the age we are now,' signifying both the older demographic of individual readers and the maturity of the culture they inhabit collectively.[4] More than the 'lure of time travel' or feelings of nostalgia, she suggests, it is the aging of both the culture and a large number of its citizens that has inspired this interest in history. Canadian culture, having shed its youthful (and, as we will see, modernist) disdain of the past, is now ready to look back on itself. Seeing this as a new interest, Atwood does not present a survey of historical fiction in Canada but rather focuses on the literature written by herself and her contemporaries.[5] According to Atwood, writers of her generation who were brought up to believe that history 'either didn't exist, or it had happened elsewhere, or if ours it was boring' are now drawn to the Canadian past in part because the past holds 'the lure of the unmentionable – the mysterious, the buried, the forgotten, the discarded, the taboo.' The Canadian past seems strange, even foreign, because it is unknown, and as 'a foreign country,' the unknown past may be conquered, annexed, and possessed, and finally, to use Lowenthal's term, domesticated for the present. It is this ability to claim the past that Atwood accents in her conclusion:

> In the recent film *Il Postino*, the great poet Neruda upbraids his friend, a lowly postman, for having filched one of Neruda's poems to use in his courtship of a local girl. 'But,' replies the postman, 'poems do not belong to those who write them. Poems belong to those who need them.' And so it is with stories about the past. The past no longer belongs only to those who lived in it; the past belongs to those who claim it, and are willing to explore it, and to infuse it with meaning for those alive today. The past belongs to us, because we are the ones who need it.[6]

We need the past, according to Atwood, because 'by taking a long hard look backwards, we place ourselves'; thus imagining the past is part of imagining who 'we' are individually and collectively.

The idea that we must tell 'our' stories in order to understand who we are resonates deeply in contemporary Canadian culture, especially in Canadian literary criticism and history, which tends to emphasize the role that literature plays in creating an imagined community of the kind Benedict Anderson describes.[7] In literary studies, the search for distinctly Canadian characteristics has emphasized literature's representation of the social, political, and historical realities of life in Canada with the view that 'a documentary impulse is inherent in Canadian literature.'[8] This interest in the documentary is also apparent in visual media with *Canada: A People's History* a typical offering. In what literary critics call settler literature, that is, writing by European settlers and their descendants, the documentary tradition is apparent in the numerous works of drama, poetry, and prose that feature written documents as a central part of the narrative. First Nations and Aboriginal writers use oral as well as documentary sources to resist the historical conditions imposed by colonization.[9] Poems such as Marilyn Dumont's 'Letter to Sir John A. Macdonald' or Jeannette Armstrong's 'History Lesson' powerfully contest the history of Canada.[10]

Indeed, it is difficult to imagine a work of literature by a First Nations author that would not be historical in this sense. As novelist Joseph Boyden observes in an interview with Herb Wyile, 'history is a fluid thing. Especially with Native people, the past is always a part of the present as well as the future.'[11] Similarly, the past is ever present in literary works that explore individual and collective memory such as Joy Kogawa's *Obasan* and Anne Michaels's *Fugitive Pieces*.[12]

When literary critics use the term *historical fiction*, however, they usually apply it strictly to a specific form of creative writing about the past. As Avrom Fleishman explains, what makes a literary work an example of historical fiction is 'the active presence of a concept of history as a shaping force – acting not only upon the characters in the novel but on the author and readers outside it.'[13] Though Fleishman studies the novel specifically, the definition usefully applies to historical fiction generally. From the standpoint of literary history and criticism, historical fiction refers to fiction that is concerned with historical experience and consciousness. It is a broad category of writing comprising poetry, drama, and prose, and it includes works in which historical events and figures are peripheral as well as those in which they are central. The historical *novel* is a relatively new sub-genre of prose fiction developed in the early nineteenth century.[14] The classical form is thoroughly described in Georg Lukács's *The Historical Novel* (1962), a work which continues to influence how we think of the genre. Lukács traces the history of the form to the social and political conditions of post-Revolutionary Europe which made it possible for writers and readers to imagine human experience in historical terms. For Lukács, and the critics who would follow, the historical novel is concerned with historical truth, and its methods arise from the attempt to depict characters and events as particular to a given time period; thus he distinguishes between historical novels that represent and engage historical consciousness, and novels that merely clothe the manners and attitudes of the present in the appearance of the past. This important distinction continues to inform what literary critics think of as historical fiction.

The approach to the past taken by writers of historical fiction may seem strikingly similar to the historian's craft; indeed, the archives deposited by fiction writers reveal how important research is to the creative process. The fiction writer, like the historian, delves into the documents and artefacts that remain of the past and reconstructs a past world using the imagination. When imagining that past world, fiction writers, like historians, select evidence that supports a particular interpretation of the past. Where they differ is in the criteria guiding selection. The historians' criteria for selection are rhetorical; the fiction writers' are primarily aesthetic. As Avrom Fleishman puts it, historical fiction gives aesthetic form to historical experience. The historian seeks to present the most likely version of historical events and ignores evidence at the peril of sacrificing the plausibility of the interpretation. Fiction writers, in contrast, invent while attempting to remain faithful to historical truth.[15] Fiction writers, therefore, are less concerned with presenting specific information than they are with creating an experience for the reader. As Guy Vanderhaeghe remarks,

> Many readers look at the historical novel as being a genuine historical experience. As readers they feel that they are inhabiting that time, that place, and that they are getting a sense of how individual lives were lived in a personal fashion. To me, that is an element of historical consciousness, but it's not an element that I think many historians exploit, because the historical mind tends to be analytic, it tends to be explanatory ...[16]

The difference between what a fiction writer does and what a historian does is recognized by David Lowenthal as 'more one of purpose than of content,' though like most historians, he continues to dwell on the *stuff* of historical fiction by comparing history and fiction on an empirical basis. Such comparisons, though revealing, tend to leave aesthetic matters aside and thus to deny historical fiction its own character.[17]

In her lecture, Atwood addresses this important difference by stating that it is the writer's responsibility to respect the historical record but that he or she is free to 'fill in the gaps' left behind. Atwood's approach to the past has been described as pragmatic, suggesting that the historical record serves mainly as a source of verifiable details on which to base the fictional world. Indeed, what Atwood describes in the lecture as her interest in the 'how to store parsnips' details of history demonstrates the continued importance of verisimilitude and faith in the realist precept that the truth of small things will guarantee larger truths.[18] In a work of realism, the author strives for verisimilitude, a representation of reality that faithfully corresponds to observable phenomena. To achieve the illusion of correspondence, the writer crafts the text using realist techniques in the description, narrative perspective, and language. The story is usually told from the narrative perspective of an omniscient, and therefore authoritative, narrator, which creates the illusion of looking at things as they are. In plain and unadorned prose, the realist text describes the surface of the fictional world in minute detail. The faithfulness of the correspondence is meant to ensure the truthfulness of the work. What shapes the reconstruction presented by the fiction writer is the aesthetic coherence and integrity of the literary text being written. Through a series of artistic choices, the writer creates a work that articulates historical consciousness through its aesthetic form and features. Though it may seem that the historical fiction writer's freedom to invent is absolute, it is actually quite the contrary, for the further a work strays from actual evidence, the closer it comes to the realm of fantasy and to no longer being 'historical.'[19] Atwood's pragmatism notwithstanding, the aesthetic experience of the past through fiction writing is not, as I believe Lowenthal suggests, merely the service of the necessary creation of an 'illusion'; rather, it is the expression of historical consciousness grounded in the differentiation of past and present.

In its classic form, the historical novel creates a world which is sufficiently different to seem historical to the reader yet similar enough to make the past seem relevant in the present. It is therefore a literary form that appeals at times when there is concern about where we are, where we have been, and where we are going, times when knowledge of national history seems essential for a strong national identity. In the two periods in Canadian literary history that exhibit a particular enthusiasm for historical fiction, changing political realities created anxiety about national sovereignty. In the late nineteenth century, the threat of annexation loomed; in the late twentieth century, globalization threatened national boundaries. In the late nineteenth century, historical romance flourished, and in the late twentieth century, the postmodern novel reached its height. While these periods share a preoccupation with history, they present different interpretations of the past that are deeply influenced by the prevailing conventions in historiography in each period and by the literary forms and conventions contemporary with them, as well as ideas of what the nation could be.

Nineteenth-Century Historical Romance

In the late nineteenth century, historical fiction was as prominent as it is today, though most of the period's works are now forgotten and many are no longer in circulation. What survives from the nineteenth century reflects both the literary culture of the time and the changing ideas of literary value which have developed since. Poetry from the period continues to dominate critical discussion, not only because there was more of it written then, but also because it was considered to have the greatest literary value. In *A Purer Taste*, Carole Gerson reconstructs the reading practices of late nineteenth-century Canada by reading literary works in the context of the critical essays and editorials of the period and reveals how 'throughout the century prose fiction was held to be of less literary value than poetry or history, but novels might be acceptable if they combined instruction with entertainment, presented a moral and wholesome vision of society, and reinforced conventional norms of sexual and religious behaviour.'[20] Subjects selected from the past, especially the political and military history of the nation, could satisfy such expectations if presented in the right way and could therefore lend greater credibility to the novel as a genre. In their reading practices, nineteenth-century readers showed an appreciation for both histories and historical fiction.

The general neglect of nineteenth-century historical fiction has much to do with what Gerson describes as 'the modernist assumption that the place of the serious fictional writer is at the vanguard of social and artistic progress.'[21] In the twentieth century, the influence of modernism on ideas of literary value and the sharpening of the distinction between popular and 'literary' fiction tend to obscure the presence of historical fiction, especially in the form of the novel. As a genre, the historical novel was relegated to the category of 'popular fiction' valued for entertainment rather than literary merit. Indeed, the apparent newness of interest in historical fiction has more to do with how literary value has been determined in twentieth-century literary criticism than with an absence of work in the genre prior to the contemporary period. These developments demonstrate how aesthetics deeply influence literary history. By modern standards, the historical novel, like the romance novel or mystery novel, is believed to be escapist, formulaic, and shallow, a critical prejudice that points to the fact that the historical novel was – and often still is – written in the style of romance.

When readers think of romance today, they may think of the modern commercial genre of bodice-rippers and purple-prose love stories, rather than tales of heroism and valour. Romance is both a genre, or type of literary work, and a mode, in the sense given the term by Northrop Frye; that is, a style indicating the author's attitude to the subject matter. Novels written in the romance mode emphasize plot and event and feature highly stylized situations and characters.[22] In the Victorian period, the romance genre gradually fell from favour, yet the romance mode continued to animate historical novels as novels replaced the epic as the narrative form in which to celebrate the life of a people. Significantly, it was the successful grafting of realist convention and technique on the romance form following Walter Scott's example that critics and readers admired in the Canadian authors who emulated it.[23] Works narrating the nation's progress continued to be written in the mode of romance, casting figures in history as heroes facing the challenges of the New World.

Recent studies of reading in the nineteenth century by Heather Murray and others are expanding knowledge of this period in Canadian literary history. As Murray shows, reading was a public activity in nineteenth-century Upper Canada – and there is no reason to doubt that this was true of other British North American colonies as well. Readers formed literary societies and established lending libraries in order to obtain access to books and other printed materials. Public places such as taverns, printing shops, and military mess halls were common 'scenes of reading' for men, while men and women would encounter, and presumably read, printed handbills and proclamations in public. At home, as Murray shows, reading often took place in groups as family members shared books and the light by which to read them. Recitations and readings were popular theatrical entertainments as well as common methods of instruction in the classroom. The strict separation of public and private reading we know today had yet to take hold.[24]

In these varied settings, readers were reading a variety of printed materials, and, though poetry was appreciated as the superior literary genre, readers also appreciated other forms, including fiction. Between 1880 and 1920, 'more than 400 Canadians published over 1400 volumes of fiction,' a considerable activity given the population at the time. In their choices, readers then as now were not constrained by national boundaries, and 'Canadian literature' had yet to be created as a category by which to classify, market, and consume books. In the colonial and Confederation periods, readers' tastes were shaped in part by availability. Copyright legislation that favoured American reprints of British books made reprints readily available while Canadian publishers struggled with high costs and a small, though growing, local market.[25] By the 1880s, there was a noticeable 'demand for historical romance' which proliferated from the 1890s into the first few years of the twentieth century.[26] Though 'Histories' were a staple of reading, Murray's study of the Halifax Library catalogue reveals 174 entries categorized as 'Novels and Romances,' that is, 'almost double any other category.'[27] If these numbers can be taken as an indication of readership, then it would seem that though novels and romances did not enjoy the status of poetry, they were nevertheless being read, and readers' preferences could cross the line between history and historical fiction. The Halifax Library catalogue illustrates the extent to which the romance and the novel were treated as distinct, though related, genres.

Canadian authors of such works, Gerson suggests, were eager to deal with the immediacy of their New World surroundings by representing what was particular in their experience. This content demanded the kind of 'faithful' depiction of the place, the people, and the times which is characteristic of realism. Readers and writers who were acquainted with the writing of such historians as Francis Parkman, or sketches of pioneer life like those written by Susanna Moodie, would naturally consider realism the prose style appropriate for history imagined as both 'historical narrative' and 'fictional or dramatic narrative.'[28] At the same time, the romance offered the possibility of aggrandizing that content to create an ideal of what Canada could be. Realist techniques created a plausible vision of the ideal as the accuracy of verifiable details of Canadian history and life would authenticate the representation of the past presented, but plot structure and characterization retained some of the romance form's idealism.

If nineteenth-century historical romances seem like formulaic costume drama to readers of today, mere entertainment was not necessarily what their nineteenth-century authors had in mind. Calls for a literature that would inspire national unity and pride were commonplace, with many writers explicitly referring to the need for more writing about Canadian history. In discussions of whether or not there was such a thing as a distinct Canadian literature, writers often commented on the importance of Canadian history. In 1881, Kate Seymour MacLean advised readers: 'Let us not be compelled to reproach ourselves with the injustice of having failed to preserve the sacred memories of the great founders of our country and thus defraud posterity of a patrimony so precious.'[29] In 1888, G. Mercer Adam, publisher and co-author of the historical romance *An Algonquin Maiden: A Romance of the Early Days of Upper Canada* (1887), warned Canadians that if they did not 'learn to speak with sympathy of our historic and literary past, we shall have, and deserve to have, neither.'[30] In the late nineteenth century, as the nation was emerging, the past was a place where writers could go to explain how the nation came to be.[31]

Nineteenth-century writers treated the historical novel as a serious way of representing the nation's past, and moments such as the arrival of the Loyalists, the War of 1812, and the North West Rebellion provided the material for literature narrating the nation's birth. Agnes Maule Machar's *For King and Country: A Story of 1812* (1874), William Withrow's *Neville Trueman, The Pioneer Preacher: A Tale of the War of 1812* (1880), and Sarah Anne Curzon's *Laura Secord, a Heroine of 1812* (1887) are some examples of the tales of heroism set in the past. Indeed, fiction set during the War of 1812 was published regularly well into the twentieth century, though more topical literature appears in the early twentieth century as writers looked to more recent events for subjects. In addition to the romantic setting, the past also offered access to cultures that could be depicted as both heroic and exotic: tragic and stoic Acadians, brave Loyalists, and noble Aboriginal peoples populate the literature.

The reception of Sara Curzon's *Laura Secord* exemplifies the way changing literary tastes influence how literary history is remembered and reconstructed. A founder and pioneering figure in the early Canadian literary and historical societies and the prolific author of articles, stories, and poems, Curzon is best remembered for her role in commemorating Laura Secord, as described by Colin Coates and Cecilia Morgan in *Heroines and History*. A play written in blank verse, *Laura Secord,* like the novels devoted to the War of 1812, shows the way writers satisfied the interest in political and military subjects by imagining events from an individual's point of view, in this case a woman whose example serves the author's feminist argument. As Beverly Boutilier also shows, though Curzon 'viewed a knowledge of history as an essential ingredient of national identity,' her writing was devoted to making sure women were equal citizens of the nation. In this light, *Laura Secord* was 'a justification of Curzon's basic political contention that women and men shared a common humanity that was at once equal and complementary.'[32] Despite the historical importance of her feminist work, Curzon is sometimes relegated to the status of a playwright who 'wrote only two plays' and whose work serves to show that 'patriotic enthusiasm is no recipe for compelling drama.'[33] *Laura Secord* has also been dismissed as a play that was never performed, even though few Canadian plays, even the few that *were* performed, became part of the varied repertoire of plays entertaining theatre audiences at the time.[34] Shakespeare's plays were by far the most popular, and travelling companies of players from the United States and Britain performed material from those countries. Yet, Canadian plays were available in print. Curzon's *The Sweet Girl Graduate*, a play protesting discrimination against women at the University of Toronto, was printed in *Grip-Sack* in 1882 and reprinted in an edition of *Laura Secord* in 1887. As Ann Saddlemyer notes, Canadian plays such as *Laura Secord*, Charles Mair's *Tecumseh* (1886), and other published plays 'doubtless achieved a relatively wide readership' even if they were never performed on stage.[35] Colin Coates and Cecilia Morgan concur, stating that the play 'was one of the better-known celebrations of Secord.'[36]

In addition to describing the importance of literary and historical societies in the period, recent historical essays have shown that there was an audience for so-called 'scribbling women' like Curzon. What specific role the audience's perception of literary fashion played in shaping this literature is more difficult to determine, yet the publication of historical romances set in Acadia and New France, including *Constance of Acadia* by Rev. E.P. Tenney (1886), *The Young Gunbearer* by George Waldo Brown (1900), *The Notary of Grand Pré* by A.J. MacLeod (1901), and a series of novels by Sir Charles G.D. Roberts, including *Sister Evangeline* (1898), *The Raid from Beausejour* (1894), and *The Forge in the Forest* (1896), may have been inspired by the success of Philippe Aubert de Gaspé's *Les anciens Canadiens* (1864)[37] and William Kirby's *The Golden Dog* (1877). Micheline Cameron and Carole Gerson see the choice of setting as an attempt by English-speaking authors 'to compensate for their own perceived lack of colourful origins by identifying with the history and folklore of New France,' for as Gerson observes, in the French past writers saw 'a New World counterpart to the folklore, history, and local colour of Scott's fiction.'[38]

In a work such as Thomas Guthrie Marquis's *Marguerite de Roberval: A Romance of the Days of Jacques Cartier* (1899), French colonization allows the author to take full advantage of romantic settings in both the New and Old Worlds. Best known for writing *Stories of New France: Being Tales of Adventure and Heroism from the Early History of Canada* (Boston, 1890), which followed Agnes Maule Machar's first volume in the series, and for *Stories from Canadian History* (1893), Thomas Guthrie Marquis (1864–1936) was a prolific author of biography, sketches, and history whose other works included *Stories from Canadian History* (Toronto, 1893), *Canada's Sons on Kopje and Veldt: An Historical Account of the Canadian Contingents* (1900), *Brock: The Hero of Upper Canada* (1912), and *The Voyages of Jacques Cartier in Prose and Verse* (1934).[39] In his only book of literary criticism, *English-Canadian Literature* (1913), Marquis remarks that 'Canada is exceedingly rich in material for historical literature,' though he regrets that these materials have been 'invaded by an American historian,' namely Francis Parkman, and that 'many able novels have had as their inspiration incidents strikingly presented by Parkman.'[40] Marquis's own novel *Marguerite de Roberval* is based on the story of a young woman who was said to have been abandoned on a small, uninhabited island in the St Lawrence as punishment for a secret love affair.[41] Apart from the heroine's name and purported connection to Sieur de Roberval, little is known about the story which was told in Marguerite de Navarre's *Heptameron des nouvelles* (1559) and in André Thevet's *Cosmographie universelle* (1575).[42] In constructing the plot, Marquis includes many of the details from Thevet's version, including the lover who swims ashore to join the castaway and her servant and the account of how the three worked to shelter, feed, and clothe themselves. Marguerite's pregnancy and the subsequent deaths of her lover, their baby, and the servant are also recounted. Marquis fictionalizes the account by giving Marguerite a fictional companion named Marie – who dies romantically after falling from a cliff while picking flowers for Marguerite – and by representing a number of historical people in the tale, including Cartier's friend Claude de Pontbriand as Marguerite's lover and another historical figure, Charles de la Pommeraye, as her eventual rescuer.

In Marquis's rendering, Marguerite de Roberval is the cause of a great deal of daring, male action: several stormy voyages across the sea, galloping rides across the French countryside, and regular sword fights. Though Marquis filled his cast of characters with actual people, all of the characters are idealized types: the suitor, de Pontbriand, is known for 'the purity of his life, the generosity of his disposition, and his dauntless courage'; his friend, the swashbuckling de la Pommeraye, has the 'heart of a child, and the arm of a giant'; Marguerite's uncle de Roberval's spy, Michel Gaillon, is 'a sleek, shiftless-looking individual' with a 'sickly-green complexion.'[43] As the object of male rivalry and chivalry, Marguerite herself is a typical romantic heroine with dark flowing hair and a tall willowy figure:

> Her beauty would have been flawless but for one defect – her chin was a shade too prominent, giving her face an expression of determination, which, while destroying its symmetry, told of a strong will, and a firmness amounting almost to obstinacy. She had the lithe grace of a panther, and though her repose was perfect, a close observer might have noticed a nervous tension in her attitude and bearing that told of a hidden force and energy tightly controlled.[44]

With her features marking an innate capacity for wilful disobedience – but also for survival – Marguerite's heroism is signified through stoic suffering and self-sacrifice. After her lover dies, and she is left alone with their baby, she steels herself: 'Not for herself, but for the sake of the little life which depended on her, she must continue to live and be strong. She pressed her baby to her breast, and with amazing fortitude and heroism, set herself to face the task before her.'[45] Despite her efforts, the child dies before she is rescued by de la Pommeraye. As she prepares to leave, her desire to remain on the island where her loved ones are buried is overcome by her sense of duty: 'Silent she stood there, torn between the fearful pang of parting, and the realization that she must go.' On the return voyage, 'Night and day she saw before her eyes that lonely grave on the hillside where her heart lay buried; and at times the longing to return to it grew too strong for her.'[46] These passages representing idealized womanhood contrast the cruel actions of Sieur de Roberval and the ineffectual French men who seek to colonize the New World.

Into this romance peopled with historical figures, Marquis introduces a hint of the realism his audience would have appreciated by depicting Marguerite's uncle, the villainous Sieur de Roberval, with a degree of psychological complexity, his tyrannical bearing explained by a deep fear of losing what power and authority he has over others. Marguerite learns from her nurse that de Roberval's hatred of Claude de Pontbriand is explained by the fact that he had once been in love with Claude's mother, though she spurned him and married another.[47] Marguerite tells how de Roberval has changed from a kind, loving uncle into the sinister character we meet, and how she hopes that an 'active life' in the New World will restore his former good nature.[48] As the story unfolds, the omniscient narrator takes the reader inside de Roberval's mind as he becomes more and more cruel in order to assert control over the crew of his vessel. By the time he discovers that Marguerite and Marie have liberated Claude from his rat-infested prison below decks, the motivation for his action has been well established:

His niece and her companions must be punished. Kill them with his own hand he could not, and to put them out of the way, without making a public example of them, would be revenge without purpose; for the man, despite his mad barbarity, was convinced that he was working for great and noble ends. Now a glorious opportunity was given to him to teach a salutary lesson. He would land the women on this desolate spot, giving them provisions for a year, and before that time he could return for them and bring them to his colony. This would surely establish his authority, and be a warning to all wrong-doers for the future.[49]

The critique of absolute authority implied in the characterization of de Roberval can be extended to the *ancien régime* he represents, suggesting the moral corruption of the French colonizers and the inevitability of conquest by the British, who represent the superior values of the Enlightenment. What few references there are to Aboriginal people further serve to illustrate French failure. Early in the story, de Pontbriand contradicts Cartier's claim that he is well liked by the 'red men,' for now that their ally Donnacona has died after being taken to France, he doubts the Native people will trust them or help them to establish a colony.[50] In nineteenth-century literature, authors consistently imagine New France as rife with the problems that would lead to its demise and ultimately to British conquest and colonization, yet despite such implied criticisms of the French, the novel does not so much glorify the supplanting of French colonial authority by the British as demonstrate how de Roberval violates the Old World ideals of chivalry. The colonists return to France where chivalry triumphs in the end: Marguerite lives out the rest of her life as a chaste widow; Charles dies valiantly on the field of battle; and de Roberval's death by his own treachery is poetic justice.

The number of historical romances like Marquis's peaked in the last decade of the nineteenth century and began to decline after the turn of the century, though the genre did not disappear; for instance, *A Romance of the Halifax Disaster* by F. McElvey Bell, a novel about the Halifax Explosion, was published by 1918, just one year after the actual event. Literary styles and tastes were changing, however, with the modernist call to 'make it new' and to break with the literary forms of the past, and though some historical writing may have satisfied modernist aesthetics, most would not. Critical bias towards the modern and avant-garde literature consigned popular works to the critical dustbin even though, as Clarence Karr demonstrates in *Authors and Audiences,* popular authors were in many ways at the forefront of cultural modernity.[51] To the modernists, popular fiction, including historical novels written in the romance mode, probably seemed like quaint echoes of the Victorian age in Canada, an age they were working to bring to an end. Despite its gradual decline from favour, historical fiction continued to be published by Canadian writers throughout the 1940s and 1950s. In 1983, Alan R. Young observed that Canadian literary critics had been 'reluctant to accord historical fiction a respectable status,' thus banishing the subject of his study, the prolific historical novelist Thomas Raddall, to the critical wilderness.[52]

Twentieth-Century Historical Fiction

The critical focus on literary value in the twentieth century, including the preoccupation with innovation encouraged by the modernist movement, would recast the historical novel, especially those written in the romance mode, as a form with little literary merit.[53] The changing status of historical fiction from the early twentieth century also marks a shift in focus on the past from events in the life of the nation to the relevance of the past in individual lives. Fiction exploring the past through individual consciousness, such as Alice Munro's short stories written in the fictional memoir form, exemplifies this shift towards the past as it is understood in human time. Not much critical attention would be paid to historical novels until the appearance of Dennis Duffy's *Sounding the Iceberg* in 1986, followed by Linda Hutcheon's *The Canadian Postmodern* in 1988. The latter introduced the term 'historiographic metafiction' to describe 'fiction that is intensely, self-reflexively art, but is also grounded in historical, social, and political realities,'[54] and applied it to works such as Timothy Findley's *The Wars* with its depiction of the researcher carefully constructing the story from an archive of documents and photographs.

Literary criticism of postmodernist writing in Canada has tended to accept Hayden White's portrait of all historiography as essentially historicist and to embrace the critique of historical realism at its basis because, as I argue elsewhere, Hutcheon's analysis of historical narrative was deeply influenced by *Metahistory*.[55] Postmodern literature and criticism query historical truth by rejecting historicism and embracing literary techniques such as parody, self-reference, and multiple narrative perspectives, all meant to actively revise the 'master narratives' of history. To varying degrees, Canadian postmodern novels suggest an imaginative revision of historical narratives by continuing to display the work of art in various stages of construction, exposing the structure of the literary work in its very architecture and showing how the past is accessed through documents. In *Speculative Fictions: Contemporary Canadian Novel-*

ists and the Writing of History (2002), Herb Wyile sees this literary revisionism as 'part of a much more substantial reshaping of attitudes towards history' characterized by recent historiography that is 'questioning and reworking the very ideological, philosophical, and methodological principles of historical writing' and replacing the sort of historical discourse that acts as 'a metanarrative naturalizing unequal relations of power through its selection, interpretation, and exclusion of material – in short, through its deeming of what is "historical."'[56]

As Thomas Guthrie Marquis's romance about the legend of Marguerite de Roberval reflected aspects of nineteenth-century historiography and literary history, *Elle* (2003), the novel by Douglas Glover based on the same legend, reflects many of the characteristics of postmodern historical fiction. As winner of the Governor-General's Award for Fiction, *Elle* is within the mainstream of literary fiction, and its critical reception indicates a contemporary taste for the style and content of the book. Told almost entirely from the first-person perspective of Marguerite, *Elle* illustrates the attempt of postmodern fiction to create the illusion that there is a truer version of history told by those who have been left out. As Wyile notes, postmodern historical fiction relies on the reader's willingness to accept this premise. Glover gives a historically silent woman a voice with which to revise history as she does in this spoof of Cartier's discovery:

> On his first voyage past Newfoundland, M. Cartier met a fishing ship from La Rochelle sailing in the opposite direction. He reported, not that these sailors had discovered the New World before him, but that they were lost. Thus he became the official discoverer of Canada, behind the crowds of secretive, greedy, unofficial Breton cod fishermen, unofficial, oil-covered Basque whalers, unofficial Hibernian monks, and who knows who else. (Not to mention the inhabitants.) So much for the official version.[57]

Here, and throughout the novel, Glover engages in creative anachronism by using language more appropriate to postmodern literary criticism than to sixteenth-century reflection. As a result, Marguerite's version of events offers a very contemporary, characteristically postcolonial interpretation of her experience; for instance, she states that she is in 'a place where the old definitions, words themselves, no longer apply, a world strange beyond anything I could have imagined.'[58]

In addition to creating characters who voice postmodern ideas, Glover revises the legend by deconstructing the conventions of the romance genre used to tell it. When we meet the heroine on board ship for the New World, she is literally falling out of her bodice as she straddles her lover, in this version Richard,

Comte d'Épirgny. With her skirts hitched above her waist, her head throbbing with toothache that an ungainly mustard plaster is failing to soothe in a cabin that stinks of 'shit, vomit and cloves,' the coupling is anything but idealized.[59] In this parody of the conventional bodice-ripper, Marguerite is imagined as a lively, bawdy, spoiled girl who admits, 'I am a headstrong girl, shallow and frivolous, born to a little land in the provinces but never meant to take part in the so-called great events of my time even if I had wanted to. Instead I wanted to read books and make love, which only made me an object of lust or ridicule and bound me to the periphery, the social outlands, to Canada.'[60] These qualities contrast the chaste, virtuous, and pious Marguerite in the versions by Thevet and Marguerite de Navarre, constructions that Glover's Marguerite explicitly rejects: 'I write this memoir as a protest against all the uplifting, inspirational and exemplary texts claiming to be about my life. I am myself, not what they have written.'[61]

Similarly, the men in the novel are far from heroic, and Marguerite doubts the future of Canada if it is to be built by such 'heroes as Richard and the Sieur de Roberval, who, if combined, still might not amount to a real man.'[62] Throughout the novel, men are as ridiculous as Richard's heroic leap into the sea after Marguerite has been set adrift by Sieur de Roberval:

> Brandishing his favourite tennis racquet like a broadsword, Richard, Comte d'Épirgny himself leaps to the rail, balancing there briefly, imitating the General's great dog Léon in his zeal. My love, he shouts, I shall never abandon you. He leaps but misses the boat, lands in the water, comes up spluttering near enough to be rescued, though he loses one of his great boots and the tennis racquet. He ends up shivering next to me, looking a great deal less heroic than I daresay he intended. I do not know what to make of this afflatus of romance and courage in a tennis player. It occurs to me that he will eat a lot of salt fish, and there won't be quite so much for me.[63]

As Marguerite observes, Richard's 'range of verbal expression is limited to bromides he picked up reading popular books of chivalry and romance.'[64] In the style of postmodern fiction, the passage deflates as it parodies the amplified language and glamorous imagery associated with the romance.

In addition to revising historical narratives, postmodern historical fiction is characterized by attempts to include historically marginalized people, notably women and First Peoples. In *Elle*, Native characters are fully individuated rather than characterized as types occupying the background as they are in nineteenth-century novels; instead, the novel imagines the heroine's contact with and appropriation of Aboriginal culture and knowledge. After the deaths of her lover and her nurse, her first visitor is an Inuk named Itslk who teaches her the story of another headstrong girl, Sedna, mother of the sea animals, a comparison developed when Marguerite gives birth alone, and the baby is 'strangely deformed and sexless' with 'tiny appendages like fins.'[65] Knowing the baby, whom she calls Emmanuel, will soon die, she cradles him and tells him stories, but when he does die, 'words fail.'[66] After his death, she remains alive and has a kind of dream vision in which she becomes a bear-woman. Each version of Marguerite's legend recounts how she killed a bear threatening the camp, and Glover recalls this event in order to establish her sympathy with the Aboriginal people she meets after leaving the island via an ice bridge. Using the lexicon provided by Cartier, she learns their language, listens to their stories, attends a sweat, and watches as the people are fired upon by French ships. Like the Marguerite in Marquis's romance, Glover's character feels a connection to her new home, but as she leaves, thinking of those left behind, her language is unsentimental:

> I look toward the Isle of Demons, not far off but out of sight round a bend in the coastline. Richard, Comte d'Épirgny, lies buried there, as does my son Emmanuel and my old nurse Bastienne. My soul is hidden among the trees. Adieu.[67]

Once in France, Marguerite becomes the lover of F, a character representing François Rabelais, but no longer feels at home, and missing the New World, befriends a Native woman named Comes Winter, the last of Donnacona's people brought from Canada by Cartier. The story ends with an aged Marguerite, now living in a cemetery with a bear, taking revenge on her uncle in a dream-like scene.

The contrasting manner in which Thomas Guthrie Marquis and Douglas Glover imagine the story of Marguerite de Roberval demonstrates how historical fiction uses conventions and techniques suiting the literary tastes of the time in which it is written. While historical fiction in the late nineteenth century tended to be written in the romantic mode, contemporary historical fiction tends to use the ironic mode. Contemporary historical fiction maintains an ironic distance from both the historical record and narrative history while constructing revisions of existing narratives that present an absent or alternative point of view. The selection of particular historical narratives and themes, particularly the stories of women and Aboriginal peoples, makes the form seem innovative as contemporary historical fiction written in English envisions Canadian histories made up of the different voices and viewpoints of a complex, multicultural society. Just as popular historical fiction has been assumed to be conservative, mere entertainment that does not challenge the mind, postmodern literary fiction is often seen to be progressive, even radical or subversive.

Though most contemporary novels are postmodern in theme and tone, the metafictional elements detailed in Hutcheon's description of the postmodern, especially its overt self-consciousness in the narrative style, have been tempered. Recent historical fiction remains highly self-conscious and sceptical about the veracity of any single interpretation of history, but it also holds out the possibility of veracity in historical representation by incorporating elements of realism. Guy Vanderhaeghe's *The Englishman's Boy* (1996), which exemplifies this form of historical novel, positions the narrative perspective and descriptive detail associated with realism in ironic relation to the subject matter:

> History is calling it a day. Roman legionaries tramp the street accompanied by Joseph and Mary, while a hired nurse in cap and uniform totes the Baby Jesus. Ladies-in-waiting from the court of the Virgin Queen trail the Holy Family, tits cinched flat under Elizabethan bodices sheer as the face of a cliff. A flock of parrot-plumed Aztecs are hard on their heels. Last of all, three frostbitten veterans of Valley Forge drag flintlocks on the asphalt roadway.[68]

In this scene, the reader gets a first glimpse of Hollywood from the point of view of the narrator, Harry Vincent, the Canadian screenwriter who becomes embroiled in the making of *Besieged*, a movie version of the Cypress Hills Massacre. By presenting Hollywood history as a game of dress-up made convincing by the surface details of verisimilitude, the passage announces the 'metafictional scepticism' towards historical film and, by extension, historical representation that characterizes the novel. The chaotic and seemingly random array of historical images in the passage, what Herb Wyile cleverly calls a 'carnival of anachronism,'[69] brings to mind Walter Benjamin's 'The Angel of History' with its imagery of debris moving forward through time, and the tone, or attitude of the narrator, towards the scene is critical of the notion that the past is only a useful source of material. Even though sections of *The Englishman's Boy* are narrated using an omniscient perspective and, like the passage quoted, use techniques that create the illusion that the narrator is an eye-witness to the scene unfolding before him, the novel's scepticism suggests a rejection of the pragmatic or utilitarian approach to the past whereby writers excavate the sources for the details that will make the surface of the narrative convincing. Elements of realism are also found in Atwood's *Alias Grace*, whose long passages of detailed description evoke the prose style of the nineteenth-century novel and thus are part of the representation of that period. The truthfulness of the account, suggested by the accuracy of details, is then undermined by the unreliable perspective of the heroine as the past becomes a useful and safe setting for a contemporary novel about the nature of guilt and innocence, a topic of much discussion in the aftermath of the Bernardo and Homolka trials. In Atwood's afterword to the novel, she reveals the idea about history behind the work when she claims that both the title character and her story remain an 'enigma,' and it is this idea that shapes the novel to reflect her belief that 'truth is sometimes unknowable, at least by us.'[70]

While there is no doubt that successful novels such as *Alias Grace* have made historical fiction popular in the contemporary period, more work needs to be done to explain the influence exerted by the market on the type of literary fiction published and on the role of publishers, editors, and agents in determining literary taste and value. In *Speculative Fictions*, Herb Wyile makes the tantalizing suggestion that the 'prevailing commodity-conscious literary culture' has given rise to the new form of historical fiction that tempers postmodern scepticism with historical realism.[71] If he is right that there has been a return to realism in Canadian fiction, and I think he is, then it is a wonderful irony that the very qualities that once assigned the genre to the popular realm outside the critical gaze of literary scholars should now make it a respectable and lucrative form of literary fiction. As the study of Canadian historical fiction written in English, including how and why it is published, continues to evolve, it will further reveal the contribution writing and reading make to public historical consciousness in both the past and the present.

Rather than a new awakening of interest in the past, the flourishing of contemporary historical fiction in the late twentieth and early twenty-first century signals renewed interest in historical fiction, which is one of several literary genres used to imagine the past. By reading historical fiction with attention to form and style, not merely to the story being told or the accuracy of historical detail used to create the fictional world, we gain a deeper understanding of the sense of the past historical fiction conveys, and the country imagined in it.

NOTES

1 The ubiquity of this formulation struck me as I read the Acknowledgments to novelist, critic, and Governor-General's Award–winning poet George Elliott Clarke's *Odysseys Home* in which he thanks Desmond Morton for sharing 'the plain but profound notion that "people in the past are different from us. They think differently."' Clarke goes on to write, 'The concept has haunted my own attempts

to imagine how eighteenth- and ninteenth-century African Canadians considered – and wrote out – their identities and realities.' *Odysseys Home: Mapping African-Canadian Literature* (Toronto: University of Toronto Press, 2002), vii.

2 Atwood's Charles Bronfman lecture in Canadian Studies was delivered on 16 November 1996 at the University of Ottawa. It was published soon after as part of a panel on history and fiction in the *American Historical Review* and later appeared as a monograph. See Margaret Atwood, *In Search of* Alias Grace: *On Writing Canadian Historical Fiction*, Charles R. Bronfman Lecture in Canadian Studies Series (Ottawa: University of Ottawa Press, 1997).

3 Margaret Atwood, *The Journals of Susanna Moodie* (Toronto: Oxford University Press, 1970); *Days of the Rebels, 1815–1840* (Toronto: Natural Science of Canada, 1977).

4 Atwood, *In Search of* Alias Grace, 19.

5 Ibid, 13.

6 Ibid, 39.

7 Benedict Anderson, *Imagined Communities: Reflections on the Origin and Spread of Nationalism* (London: Verso, 1983).

8 In 'The Documentary Poem: A Canadian Genre' (1969), Canadian poet Dorothy Livesay describes the 'documentary' as an approach that displays 'a conscious attempt to create a dialectic between the objective facts and the subjective feelings of the poet.' Alan Filewod would update the concept in his work on Canadian theatre, tracing parallel traditions of historical drama and agitprop in 'a long line of plays that seek to revise Canadian history, a list that begins in the early nineteenth century and continues to the present day.' *Collective Encounters: Documentary Theatre in English Canada* (Toronto: University of Toronto Press, 1987), 3.

9 The relationship between writing and acting as a witness to the history of Native people was captured in Beth Brant's title *Writing as Witness: Essay and Talk* (Toronto: Women's Press, 1994).

10 Marilyn Dumont, 'Letter to Sir John A. Macdonald,' in *A Really Good Brown Girl* (London, ON: Brick, 1996), 52; Jeannette Armstrong, 'History Lesson,' in Daniel David Moses and Terry Goldie, eds., *An Anthology of Canadian Native Literature in English*, 3rd edition (Toronto: Oxford University Press, 2005), 228–9.

11 Joseph Boyden, 'Pushing Out the Poison,' in Herb Wyile, *Speaking in the Past Tense: Canadian Novelists on Writing Canadian Historical Fiction* (Waterloo: Wilfrid Laurier University Press, 2007), 235.

12 There is an impressive body of critical essays on collective memory, history, and identity in these novels and others as well as a growing number of books that explore memory in historical and individual experience, such as Norman Ravvin's *A House of Words: Jewish Writing, Identity, and Memory* (Montreal and Kingston: McGill-Queen's University Press, 1997). For critical discussion of cultural

memory in Canada, see the special issue of *Essays on Canadian Writing* edited by Roxanne Rimstead, 80 (2003).

13 Avrom Fleishman, *The English Historical Novel: Walter Scott to Virginia Woolf* (Baltimore: Johns Hopkins University Press, 1971), 15.

14 Since this essay was written, Jerome de Groot has published an introduction to the genre that includes a comprehensive discussion of the critical works cited here. See *The Historical Novel* (Routledge, 2010).

15 This distinction between 'false' and 'true' invention in relation to the use of the past in film is outlined by Robert A. Rosenstone in *Visions of the Past: The Challenge of Film to Our Idea of History* (Cambridge, MA: Harvard University Press, 1995).

16 Guy Vanderhaeghe, 'Making History,' in Wyile, *Speaking in the Past Tense*, 27–8.

17 David Lowenthal, *The Past Is a Foreign Country* (Cambridge: Cambridge University Press, 1985), 229.

18 See Renée Hulan, 'Margaret Atwood's Historical Lives in Context: Notes on a Postcolonial Pedagogy for Historical Fiction,' in Cynthia Sugars, ed., *Home-Work: Postcolonialism, Pedagogy, and Canadian Literature* (Ottawa: University of Ottawa Press, 2004), 441–60.

19 For example, Wayne Johnston's character Fielding, the fictitious love interest he created for Joey Smallwood in *The Colony of Unrequited Dreams*, was met by some readers with a kind of empirical rigour.

20 Carole Gerson, *A Purer Taste: The Writing and Reading of Fiction in English in Nineteenth-Century Canada* (Toronto: University of Toronto Press, 1989), 35.

21 Ibid., 153.

22 Northrop Frye, *Anatomy of Criticism: Four Essays* (Princeton: Princeton University Press, 1957), 305–6.

23 See Gerson, *A Purer Taste*, 70–9.

24 Heather Murray, 'Readers and Society,' in Patricia Lockhart Fleming, Gilles Gallichan, and Yvan Lamonde, eds., *History of the Book, Volume I Beginnings to 1840* (Toronto: University of Toronto Press, 2004), 173–4.

25 H. Pearson Gundy, 'Literary Publishing,' in Carl F. Klinck, ed., *Literary History of Canada: Canadian Literature in English* (Toronto: University of Toronto Press, 1965), 183–7.

26 Gordon Roper, Rupert Schieder, and S. Ross Behariell, 'The Kinds of Fiction 1880–1920,' in Klinck, ed., *Literary History of Canada*, 307, 284.

27 Murray, 'Readers and Society,' 177.

28 For historical studies that provide extensive illustrations of this attitude see Colin Coates and Cecilia Morgan, *Heroines and History: Representations of Madeleine de Verchères and Laura Secord* (Toronto: University of Toronto Press, 2002), 157; and Heather Murray, *'Come Bright Improvement!': The Literary Societies of Nineteenth-Century Ontario* (Toronto: University of Toronto Press, 2002).

29 K. Seymour MacLean, 'Education and National Sentiment,' *Rose-Belford's Cana-dian Monthly* 6 (February 1881): 190–4, reprinted in Carl Ballstadt, *The Search for English-Canadian Literature: An Anthology of Critical Articles from the Nineteenth and Early Twentieth Centuries* (Toronto: University of Toronto Press, 1975), 103.

30 G. Mercer Adam, 'Nationalism and the Literary Spirit,' *The Week* 5 (19 January 1888): 118–19, reprinted in Ballstadt, *The Search for English-Canadian Litera-ture*, 169.

31 For example, Coates and Morgan note that historians viewed the past as 'a linear narrative of improvement, one in which the past held the seeds of present triumphs' (*Heroines and History*, 132), and Dennis Duffy observes that literature was just as 'buoyant in its assumptions of progress and the perpetuity of a social order.' *Sounding the Iceberg: An Essay on Canadian Historical Novels* (Toronto: ECW Press, 1986), 11.

32 Beverly Boutilier, 'Women's Rights and Duties: Sarah Anne Curzon and the Poli-tics of Canadian History,' in Beverly Boutilier and Alison Prentice, eds., *Creating Historical Memory: English-Canadian Women and the Work of History* (Vancou-ver: University of British Columbia Press, 1997), 58, 62. Coates and Morgan also emphasize the contribution of the play as a 'response to the issue of gendered differences in both past and present contexts' (*Heroines and History*, 143).

33 Eugene Benson and L.W. Conolly, *English-Canadian Theatre* (Toronto: Oxford University Press, 1987), 13.

34 Robertson Davies, 'The Nineteenth Century Repertoire,' in Ann Saddlemyer, ed., *Early Stages: Theatre in Ontario, 1800–1914* (Toronto: University of Toronto Press, 1990), 90.

35 Ann Saddlemyer, Introduction, in Saddlemyer, ed., *Early Stages*, 10.

36 Coates and Morgan, *Heroines and History*, 152.

37 George L. Parker, 'The Evolution of Publishing in Canada', in Yvan Lamonde, Patricia Lockhart Fleming, and Fiona A. Black, eds., *History of the Book in Canada, Volume II 1840–1918* (Toronto: University of Toronto, 2005), 20.

38 Micheline Cameron and Carole Gerson, 'Linguistic and Cultural Dialogue,' in Lamonde, Lockhart Fleming, and Black, eds., *History of the Book in Canada, Volume II*, 132; Gerson, *A Purer Taste*, 71. In their investigation of the legend of Madeleine de Verchères, Coates and Morgan view the depiction of historical figures from New France as 'an attempt to appropriate the past of French Canada in order to provide a longer genealogy to the Canadian nation' (*Heroines and His-tory*, 44).

39 See Ken MacKinnon, 'Thomas Guthrie Marquis,' in *The Oxford Companion to Canadian Literature* (Toronto: Oxford University Press, 1997), 743–4.

40 Thomas Guthrie Marquis, *English-Canadian Literature* (Toronto: Glasgow, Brook, and Company, 1913), 496.

41 The novel can be readily accessed at www.canadiana.org.

42 See Roger Schlesinger and Arthur P. Stabler, eds. and trans., *André Thevet's North America: A Sixteenth-Century View* (Montreal and Kingston: McGill-Queen's University Press, 1986), 62–9; and Arthur P. Stabler, *The Legend of Marguerite de Roberval* (Pullman: Washington State University Press, 1972).

43 Thomas Guthrie Marquis, *Marguerite de Roberval: A Romance of the Days of Jacques Cartier* (Toronto: Copp, Clark, 1899), 7, 15, 78.

44 Ibid., 17.

45 Ibid., 205–6.

46 Ibid., 225, 229.

47 Ibid., 74.

48 Ibid., 83. Ironically, it is Marguerite herself who claims the benefits of life in the harsh but healthful environment, where she 'grew more robust,' her skin browned by life outdoors and her arms strengthened by manual labour (176).

49 Ibid., 118–19.

50 Ibid., 6.

51 The public preference for literature that would instruct and entertain had developed a market for historical romance in the late nineteenth-century era of commercialization that Clarence Karr describes in *Authors and Audiences*, and as the publishing industry continued to grow, so did the number of types of fiction it would produce. The international success of the early twentieth-century authors Karr studies – Lucy Maud Montgomery, Nellie McClung, Ralph Connor, Robert Stead, and Arthur Stringer – shows how Canadian authors and readers remained in step with the literary culture of the wider English-speaking world. Yet, popular success did not ensure lasting critical acclaim, more often the reverse. See Clarence Karr, *Authors and Audiences: Popular Canadian Fiction in the Early Twentieth Century* (Montreal and Kingston: McGill-Queen's University Press, 2000).

52 Alan R. Young, *Thomas H. Raddall* (Boston: Twayne Publishers, 1983).

53 In his study of Canadian historical fiction, Dennis Duffy concludes: 'While the historical romance remains with us today, it no longer attracts writers of significance.' Duffy analyses representative historical novels written in both English and French in each of three periods: 1832–1919, 1919–66, and 1970–83. He is interested in the way each novel relates to its historical time period, not in its impact or reception. Thus, the novels from the mid-twentieth century, with the exception of those by Raddall, are fairly obscure, and by choosing to end with an example that is not a historical novel, Duffy suggests the relative insignificance of the form in that period (*Sounding the Iceberg*, 1).

54 Linda Hutcheon, *The Canadian Postmodern: A Study of Contemporary English-Canadian Fiction* (Toronto: Oxford University Press, 1988), 13.

55 Renée Hulan, 'Historical Method in Canadian Literary Studies: Some Recent Examples,' *Acadiensis: Journal of the History of the Atlantic Region* 34, 2 (2005): 131–2.

56 Herb Wyile, *Speculative Fictions: Contemporary Canadian Novelists and the Writing of History* (Montreal and Kingston: McGill-Queen's University Press, 2002), 7–8.

57 Douglas Glover, *Elle* (Fredericton: Goose Lane Editions, 2003), 131–2.

58 Ibid., 37–8.

59 Ibid., 21.

60 Ibid., 148.

61 Ibid., 114.

62 Ibid., 43.

63 Ibid., 36.

64 Ibid., 42.

65 Ibid., 102–3.

66 Ibid., 104.

67 Ibid., 164.

68 Guy Vanderhaeghe, *The Englishman's Boy* (Toronto: McClelland and Stewart, 1996), 5.

69 Wyile, *Speculative Fictions*, 247.

70 Atwood, *In Search of* Alias Grace, 39.

71 Wyile describes this fiction as 'largely, if somewhat ambivalently rooted in historical verisimilitude and engagement with (rather than abandonment or disruption of) the historical record' (*Speculative Fictions*, 263).

Select Bibliography

Books and Chapters in Books

Agulhon, Maurice. *Marianne into Battle: Republican Imagery and Symbolism in France, 1789–1880*. Cambridge: Cambridge University Press, 1981.

Allen, Theodore. *The Invention of the White Race*, 2 vols. London and New York: Verso, 1994.

Ames, Kenneth L., et al., eds. *Ideas and Images: Developing Interpretive Historical Exhibits*. Nashville: AASLH, 1992.

Anderson, Benedict. *Imagined Communities: Reflections on the Origin and Spread of Nationalism*. London: Verso, 1983, revised 1991.

– 'Staging Antimodernism in the Age of High Capitalist Nationalism.' In Lynda Jessup, ed., *Antimodernism and Artistic Experience: Policing the Boundaries of Modernity*, 97–103. Toronto: University of Toronto Press, 2001.

Antze, Paul, and Michael Lambek, eds. *Tense Past: Cultural Essays in Trauma and Memory*. London: Routledge, 1996.

Ashworth, G.J. *On Tragedy and Renaissance: The Role of Loyalist and Acadian Heritage Interpretations in Canadian Place Identities*. Groningen: Geo Pers, 1993.

Ashworth, G.J., and B. Goodall, eds. *Marketing Tourism Places*. London: Routledge, 1990.

Ashworth, G.J., and J.E. Tunbridge. *Dissonant Heritage*. London: Bellhaven, 1993.

Atwood, Margaret. *In Search of Alias Grace: On Writing Canadian Historical Fiction*. Charles R. Bronfman Lecture in Canadian Studies Series. Ottawa: University of Ottawa Press, 1997.

– *Survival: A Thematic Guide to Canadian Literature*. Toronto: Anansi, 1972.

Bakhtin, Mikhail. *Speech Genres and Other Late Essays*, Austin: University of Texas Press, 1986.

Balibar, Étienne, and Immanuel Wallerstein. *Race, Nation and Class*. New York: Verso, 1991.

Bangarth, Stephanie. *Voices Raised in Protest: Defending Citizens of Japanese Ancestry in North America, 1942–49.* Vancouver: University of British Columbia Press, 2008.

Bann, Stephen. *The Clothing of Clio: A Study of the Representation of History in 19th-Century Britain and France.* Cambridge: Cambridge University Press, 1984.

– *Paul Delaroche: History Painted.* London: Reaktion, 1997.

Bannerji, Hamani. *The Dark Side of the Nation: Essays on Multiculturalism, Nationalism and Gender.* Toronto: Canadian Scholars Press, 2000.

Baranowski, Shelley, and Ellen Furlough, eds. *Being Elsewhere: Tourism, Consumer Culture, and Identity in Modern Europe and North America.* Ann Arbor: University of Michigan Press, 2001.

Barringer, Tim, and Tom Flynn, eds. *Colonialism and the Object: Empire, Material Culture and the Museum.* London: Routledge, 1998.

Barzun, Jacques. 'History as Counter-Method and Anti-Abstraction.' In Michael Murray, ed., *A Jacques Barzun Reader*, 19–26. New York: HarperCollins, 2002.

Baym, Nina. *American Women Writers and the Work of History.* New Brunswick, NJ: Rutgers University Press, 1995.

Beiner, Ronald, ed. *Theorizing Citizenship.* Albany: State University of New York Press, 1995.

Bell, Michael. *Kanata: Robert Houle's Histories.* Ottawa: Carleton University Art Gallery, 1993.

Bendix, Regina. *In Search of Authenticity: The Formation of Folklore Studies.* Madison: University of Wisconsin Press, 1997.

Bennett, Tony. *The Birth of the Museum.* New York: Routledge, 1995.

Benson, Susan Porter, et al., eds. *Presenting the Past: Essays on History and the Public.* Philadelphia: Temple University Press, 1986.

Bercuson, David, and S.F. Wise, eds. *The Valour and the Horror Revisited.* Montreal and Kingston: McGill-Queen's University Press, 1994.

Berenbaum, Michael, and Abraham J. Peck, eds. *The Holocaust and History: The Known, the Unknown, the Disputed, and the Reexamined.* Bloomington: Indiana University Press, 1998.

Berger, Carl. *The Writing of Canadian History: Aspects of English-Canadian Historical Writing since 1900.* Toronto: University of Toronto Press, 1986.

– *The Sense of Power: Studies in the Ideas of Canadian Imperialism 1867–1940.* Toronto: University of Toronto Press, 1970.

Bhabha, Homi K. *The Location of Culture.* London: Routledge, 1994.

Bialystok, Franklin. *Delayed Impact: The Holocaust and the Canadian Jewish Community.* Montreal and Kingston: McGill-Queen's University Press, 2000.

Billig, Michael. *Banal Nationalism.* London and Thousand Oaks, CA: Sage, 1995.

Bird, S. Elizabeth, ed. *Dressing in Feathers: The Construction of the Indian in American Popular Culture*. Boulder, CO: Westview Press, 1996.

Blatti, Jo, ed. *Essays about Historic Interpretation and Public Audience*. Washington: Smithsonian Institution Press, 1987.

Bodnar, John. 'Public Memory in an American City: Commemoration in Cleveland.' In J. Gillis, ed., *Commemoration: The Politics of National Identity*, 74–89. Princeton: Princeton University Press, 1994.

Bodnar, John. *Remaking America: Public Memory, Commemoration, and Patriotism in the Twentieth Century*. Princeton: Princeton University Press, 1992.

Boorstin, Daniel. *The Image: A Guide to Pseudo-Events in America*. New York: Atheneum, 1972.

– 'The Rhetoric of Democracy.' In Daniel and Ruth Boorstin, eds., *Hidden History*, 127–38. New York: Harper and Row, 1987.

Bouchard, Gérard. *The Making of Nations and Cultures of the New World*. Montreal and Kingston: McGill-Queen's University Press, 2008.

Boutilier, Beverly, and Alison Prentice, eds. *Creating Historical Memory: English-Canadian Women and the Work of History*. Vancouver: University of British Columbia Press, 1997.

Boyanski, Christine. *Sympathetic Realism*. Toronto: Art Gallery of Ontario, 1988.

Boyles, Georgina. *The Imagined Village: Culture, Ideology and the English Folk Revival*. Manchester: Manchester University Press, 1993.

Brah, Avtar, and Annie E. Coombes, eds. *Hybridity and Its Discontents: Politics, Science, Culture*. New York: Routledge, 2000.

Brant, Beth. *Writing as Witness: Essay and Talk*. Toronto: Women's Press, 1994.

Brasseaux, C.A. *The Search for Evangeline: Birth and Evolution of the Evangeline Myth*. Shreveport, LA: Blue Heron, 1988.

Brendon, Piers. *Thomas Cook: 150 Years of Popular Tourism*. London: Secker and Warburg, 1991.

Brooks, Peter. *History Painting and Narrative: Delacroix's Moments*. Oxford: European Humanities Research Centre, 1998.

Brooks, Roy L., ed. *When Sorry Isn't Enough: The Controversy over Apologies and Reparations for Human Injustice*. New York: New York University Press, 1999.

Brown, Dona. *Inventing New England: Regional Tourism in the Nineteenth Century*. Washington: Smithsonian Institution, 1995.

Burgoyne, R. *Film Nation: Hollywood Looks at American History*. Minneapolis: University of Minnesota Press, 1997.

Burnham, Patricia M., and Lucretia Hoover Giese, eds. *Redefining American History Painting*. New York: Cambridge University Press, 1995.

Burstein, Miriam Elizabeth. *Narrating Women's History in Britain, 1770–1902*. Aldershot, UK: Ashgate, 2004.

Butler, Shelley. *Contested Representations: Revisiting 'Into the Heart of Africa.'* Amsterdam: Gordon and Breach, 1999.

Butler, Thomas, ed. *Memory: History, Culture and the Mind*. Oxford: Basil Blackwell, 1989.

Canadian Heritage Arts Society. *Experience Canada: Project Report (and Script of 'Spirit of the Nation')*. Victoria: Canadian Heritage Arts Society, 1992).

Cannon-Brookes, Peter, ed. *The Painted Word: British History Painting: 1750–1830*. Woodbridge: Heim Gallery and The Boydell Press, 1991.

Carlson, K.T. *The Power of Place, the Problem of Time: A Study of History and Aboriginal Collective Identity*. Vancouver: University of British Columbia Press, 2003.

Carnes, Mark, ed. *Past Imperfect: History According to the Movies*. New York: Henry Holt, 1995.

Carroll, Michael Thomas. *Popular Modernity in America: Experience, Technology, Mythohistory*. Albany: SUNY Press, 2000.

Caruth, Cathy, ed. *Trauma: Explorations in Memory*. Baltimore: Johns Hopkins University Press, 1995.

Cazelais, Normand, Roger Nadeau, and Gérard Beaudet, eds. *L'espace touristique*. Sainte-Foy: Les Presses de l'Université du Québec, 1999.

Charland, Maurice, and Michael Dorland. *Law, Rhetoric and Irony in the Formation of Canadian Civil Culture*. Toronto: University of Toronto Press, 2002.

Chase, Malcolm, and Christopher Shaw, eds. *The Imagined Past: History and Nostalgia*. Manchester and New York: Manchester University Press, 1989.

Chatterjee, Partha. *Nationalist Thought and the Colonial World: A Derivative Discourse?* Tokyo: United Nations University, 1986.

Clarke, George Elliott. *Odysseys Home: Mapping African-Canadian Literature*. Toronto: University of Toronto Press, 2002.

Clifford, James. *The Predicament of Culture*. Cambridge, MA: Harvard University Press, 1988.

Clifford, James. 'Travelling Cultures.' In Lawrence Grossberg, Cary Nelson, and Paula Treichler, eds., *Cultural Studies*, 96–111. New York: Routledge, 1992.

Coates, Colin, and Cecilia Morgan. *Heroines and History: Representations of Madeleine de Verchères and Laura Secord*. Toronto: University of Toronto Press, 2002.

Cohen, Daniel, and Roy Rosensweig. *Digital History: A Guide to Gathering, Preserving and Presenting the Past on the Web*. Philadelphia: University of Pennsylvania Press, 2005.

Conn, Steven. *Museums and American Intellectual Life, 1876–1926*. Chicago: University of Chicago Press, 1998.

Connerton, Paul. *How Societies Remember*. Cambridge: Cambridge University Press, 1989.

Cook, Ramsay. *The Maple Leaf Forever: Essays on Nationalism and Politics in Canada*. Toronto: Macmillan, 1971.

Coombes, Annie E. *Reinventing Africa: Museums, Material Culture and Popular Imagination*. New Haven: Yale University Press, 1994.

Corner, John, and Sylvia Harvey. 'Mediating Tradition and Modernity.' In John Corner and Sylvia Harvey, eds., *Enterprise and Heritage: Crosscurrents of National Culture*, 45–75. London: Routledge, 1991.

Cosgrove, Dennis, and Stephen Daniels, eds. *The Iconography of Landscape*. Cambridge: Cambridge University Press, 1989.

Cronon, William, ed. *Uncommon Ground*. New York: W.W. Norton, 1996.

Cubitt, Geoffrey, ed. *Imagining Nations*. Manchester: Manchester University Press, 1998.

Daniels, Stephen. *Fields of Vision: Landscape Imagery and National Identity in England and the United States*. Princeton: Princeton University Press, 1993.

Davies, Gwendolyn, ed. *Myth and Milieu: Atlantic Literature and Culture, 1918–1939*. Fredericton: Acadiensis Press, 1993.

Davis, Bob. *Whatever Happened to High-School History?: Burying the Political Memory of Youth, 1945–1995*. Toronto: Our Schools Ourselves/Lorimer, 1995.

Davis, Fred. *Yearning for Yesterday: A Sociology of Nostalgia*. New York: Free Press, 1979.

Davis, Natalie Zemon. *Slaves on Screen: Film and Historical Vision*. Cambridge, MA: Harvard University Press, 2000.

Davision, Graeme. *The Use and Abuse of Australian History*. St Leonards, NSW: Allen and Unwin, 2000.

Dawn, Leslie. *National Visions, National Blindness: Canadian Art and Identities in the 1920s*. Vancouver: University of British Columbia Press, 2006.

Dawson, Michael. *Selling British Columbia: Tourism and Consumer Culture, 1890–1970*. Vancouver and Toronto: University of British Columbia Press, 2004.

De Groot, Jerome. *The Historical Novel*. London and New York: Routledge, 2010.

Dicks, Bella. *Heritage, Place and Community*. Cardiff: University of Wales Press, 2000.

Dolan, Claire, ed. *Événement, identité, histoire*. Sillery: Septentrion, 1991.

Dubinsky, Karen. *The Second Greatest Disappointment: Honeymooning and Tourism at Niagara Falls*. Toronto: Between the Lines, 1999.

Dubrow, Gail Lee, and Jennifer B. Goodman, eds. *Restoring Women's History through Historic Preservation*. Baltimore: Johns Hopkins University Press, 2003.

Duffy, Dennis. *Sounding the Iceberg: An Essay on Canadian Historical Novels*. Toronto: ECW Press, 1986.

Durocher, Réné. 'Une ou des histoires nationales.' In R. Comeau and B. Dionne, eds., *À propos de l'histoire nationale*, 85–9. Sillery: Septentrion, 1998.

Edgerton, Gary. *Ken Burns's America*. New York: Palgrave, 2001.

Edgerton, Gary, and Peter C. Rollins, eds. *Television Histories: Shaping Collective Memory in the Media Age*. Lexington: University Press of Kentucky, 2001.

Eley, Geoff, and Ronald G. Suny, eds. *Becoming National: A Reader*. Oxford and London: Oxford University Press, 1996.

Elkin, Frederick. *Rebels and Colleagues: Advertising and Social Change in French-Canada*. Montreal: McGill-Queen's University Press, 1973.

Errington, Shelley. *The Death of Authentic Primitive Art and Other Tales of Progress*. Berkeley: University of California Press, 1998.

Ewen, Stewart. *All Consuming Images: The Politics of Style in Contemporary Culture* New York: Basic Books, 1988.

Fabian, Johannes. *Time and the Other: How Anthropology Makes Its Object*. New York: Columbia University Press, 1983.

Falk, Pasi. *The Consuming Body*. London: Sage, 1994.

Fentress, James, and Chris Wickham. *Social Memory*. Oxford: Blackwell, 1992.

Fiske, John. *Understanding Popular Culture*. New York: Routledge, 1994.

Forbes, E.R. *Challenging the Regional Stereotype: Essays on the 20th Century Maritimes*. Fredericton: Acadiensis Press, 1989.

Francis, Daniel. *National Dreams: Myth, Memory and Canadian History*. Vancouver: Arsenal Pulp Press, 1997.

– *The Imaginary Indian: The Image of the Indian in Canadian Culture*. Vancouver: Arsenal Pulp Press, 1992.

Frankenberg, Ruth. *White Women, Race Matters: The Social Construction of Whiteness*. Minneapolis: University of Minnesota Press, 1994.

Friesen, Gerald. *Citizens and Nation*. Toronto: University of Toronto Press, 2000.

Frisch, Michael. *A Shared Authority: Essays on the Craft and Meaning of Oral and Public History*. Albany: SUNY Press, 1990.

Fuji Johnson, Genevieve, and Randy Enomoto, eds. *Race, Racialization, and Antiracism in Canada and Beyond*. Toronto: University of Toronto Press, 2007.

Furniss, Elizabeth. *The Burden of History: Colonialism and the Frontier Myth in a Rural Canadian Community*. Vancouver: University of British Columbia Press, 1999.

Fussell, Paul. *Abroad: British Literary Traveling between the Wars*. Oxford: Oxford University Press, 1980.

Gabriel, Barbara, and Suzan Ilcan, eds. *Postmodernism and the Ethical Subject*. Montreal and Kingston: McGill-Queen's University Press, 2004.

Gaffield, Chad, and Pam Gaffield, eds. *Consuming Canada: Readings in Environmental History*. Toronto: Copp Clark, 1995.

Gagnon, Serge. *L'Échiquier touristique Québécois*. Sainte-Foy: Les Presses de l'Université du Québec, 2002.

– *Le Québec et ses historiens de 1840 à 1920: La Nouvelle-France de Garneau à Groulx*. Sainte-Foy: Les presses de l'Université Laval, 1978.

Gellner, Ernest. *Nationalism*. London: Weidenfeld and Nicolson, 1997.

– *Nations and Nationalism*. London and Oxford: Blackwell, 1983.

Gerson, Carole. *A Purer Taste: The Writing and Reading of Fiction in English in Nineteenth-Century Canada*. Toronto: University of Toronto Press, 1989.

Gillis, John, ed. *Commemorations: The Politics of National Identity*. Princeton: Princeton University Press, 1994.

Gillmor, Don, and Pierre Turgeon. *Canada: A People's History*. Vol. 1. Toronto: McClelland and Stewart, 2000.

Gillmor, Don, Achille Michaud, and Pierre Turgeon. *Canada: A People's History*. Vol. 2. Toronto: McClelland and Stewart, 2001.

Gilroy, Paul. *There Ain't No Black in the Union Jack*. London: Hutchinson, 1987.

Glaser, Jane R., and Artemis A. Zenetou, eds. *Gender Perspectives: Essays on Women and Museums*. Washington: Smithsonian Institution Press, 1994.

Glassberg, David. *American Historical Pageantry: The Uses of Tradition in the Early Twentieth Century*. Chapel Hill: University of North Carolina Press, 1990.

– *Sense of History: The Place of the Past in American Life*. Amherst: University of Massachusetts Press, 2001.

Gluck, Sherna Berger, and Daphne Patai, eds. *Women's Words: The Feminist Practice of Oral History*. New York: Routledge, 1991.

Gold, Gerald, ed. *Minority and Mother Country Imagery*. St John's: Institute of Social and Economic Research, Memorial University, 1984.

Gold, John R., and Margaret M. Gold. *Imagining Scotland: Tradition, Representation and Promotion in Scottish Tourism since 1750*. Aldershot, UK: Scholar Press, 1995.

Goldie, Terry, et al., eds. *Canada: Theoretical Discourse/Discours théoriques*. Montreal: Association for Canadian Studies, 1994.

Gordon, Alan. *Making Public Pasts: The Contested Terrain of Montreal's Public Memories, 1891–1930*. Montreal and Kingston: McGill-Queen's University Press, 2001.

Grainge, Paul. *Monochrome Memories*. Westport, CT: Praeger, 2002.

Grainge, Paul, ed. *Memory and Popular Film*. Manchester: Manchester University Press, 2003.

Granatstein, J.L. *Who Killed Canadian History?* Toronto: HarperCollins, 1998.

Gregorovich, John B., ed. *Commemorating an Injustice: Fort Henry and Ukrainian Canadians as 'Enemy Aliens' during the First World War*. Kingston: Kashtan Press for the Ukrainian Canadian Civil Liberties Association, 1994.

Groen, Frances, Leslie Chan, and Jean-Claude Guédon. *Open Access in International Perspective: A Review of Open-Access Policies in Selected Countries*. Ottawa: Social Science and Humanities Research Council of Canada, 2007.

Gross, David. *The Past in Ruins: Tradition and the Critique of Modernity*. Amherst: University of Massachusetts Press, 1992.

Groulx, Patrice. *Pièges de la mémoire: Dollard des Ormeaux, les Amérindiens et nous*. Hull, QC: Vents d'Ouest, 1998.

Hahn, C. *Becoming Political: Comparative Perspectives on Citizenship Education.* New York: SUNY Press, 1998.

Halbwachs, Maurice. *The Collective Memory.* Translated by Francis J. Ditter, Jr, and Vida Yazdi Ditter. New York: Harper and Row, 1980.

– *On Collective Memory.* Translated by Lewis Coser. Chicago: University of Chicago Press, 1992.

Hall, John A. *The State of the Nation.* Cambridge: Cambridge University Press, 1998.

Hall, Stuart. 'The Local and the Global: Globalisation and Ethnicity.' In Anthony D. King, ed., *Culture, Globalisation and the World System,* 19–39. London: Macmillan, 1991.

– 'The Question of Cultural Identity.' In Stuart Hall, David Held, and Tony McGrew, eds., *Modernity and Its Futures,* 273–326. Cambridge: Polity Press in Association with Open University, 1992.

– 'The West and the Rest: Discourse and Power.' In Stuart Hall and Bram Gieben, eds., *Formations of Modernity,* 275–332. Cambridge: Polity Press in Association with Open University, 1992.

Hall, Stuart, ed. *Representation: Cultural Representations and Signifying Practices.* London, Thousand Oaks, and New Dehli: Sage Publications, 1997.

Hamel, Natalie. *Notre maître le passé, notre maître l'avenir: Paul Gouin et la conservation de l'héritage culturel du Québec.* Sainte-Foy: Les Presses de l'Université Laval, 2008.

Hamilton, Paula, and Paul Ashton, eds. *Australians and the Past.* St Lucia: University of Queensland Press, 2003.

Handler, Richard. *Nationalism and the Politics of Culture in Québec.* Madison: University of Wisconsin Press, 1988.

Hannaford, Ivan. *Race: The History of an Idea in the West.* Washington: Woodrow Wilson Center Press; Baltimore: Johns Hopkins University Press, 1996.

Harris, Cole. 'Regionalism and the Canadian Archipelago.' In L. McCann and A. McGunn, eds., *Heartland and Hinterland.* Scarborough, ON: Prentice-Hall, 1998.

Harris, Neil. *Cultural Excursions: Marketing Appetites and Cultural Tastes in Modern America.* Chicago: University of Chicago Press, 1990.

Hartman, Geoffrey H., ed. *Holocaust Remembrance: The Shapes of Memory.* Oxford: Blackwell, 1994.

Hastings, Adrian. *The Construction of Nationhood: Ethnicity, Religion and Nationalism.* Cambridge: Cambridge University Press, 1997.

Hayes, Peter, ed. *Lessons and Legacies: The Meaning of the Holocaust in a Changing World, Vol. 2.* Evanston: Northwestern University Press, 1991.

Healy, Chris. *From the Ruins of Colonialism: History as Social Memory.* Cambridge: Cambridge University Press, 1997.

Henry, Frances, and Carol Tator. *The Colour of Democracy: Racism in Canadian Society*. Toronto: Nelson, 2005.

Hewison, Robert. *The Heritage Industry: Britain in a Climate of Decline*. London: Methuen, 1987.

Hill, Charles. *The Group of Seven: Art for a Nation*. Toronto: McClelland and Stewart, 1995.

Hinsley, Curtis. 'The World as Marketplace: Commodification of the Exotic at the World's Columbian Exhibition, Chicago, 1893.' In Ivan Karp and Steven Lavine, eds., *Exhibiting Cultures*, 344–65. Washington: Smithsonian Institution Press, 1991.

Hobsbawm, E.J. *Nations and Nationalism since 1780: Programme, Myth, Reality*. Cambridge: Cambridge University Press, 1990.

Hobsbawm, Eric, and Terence Ranger, eds. *The Invention of Tradition*. Cambridge and New York: Cambridge University Press, 1983.

Hooper-Greenhill, Eilean. *Museum and the Shaping of Knowledge*. New York: Routledge, 1992.

Horne, Donald. *The Great Museum: The Re-Presentation of History*. London: Pluto Press, 1984.

Hulan, Renée. 'Margaret Atwood's Historical Lives in Context: Notes on a Postcolonial Pedagogy for Historical Fiction.' In Cynthia Sugars, ed., *Home-Work: Postcolonialism, Pedagogy, and Canadian Literature*, 441–60. Ottawa: University of Ottawa Press, 2004.

Hutcheon, Linda. *The Canadian Postmodern: A Study of Contemporary English-Canadian Fiction*. Toronto: Oxford University Press, 1988.

Iacovetta, Franca, Roberto Perin, and Angelo Principe, eds. *Enemies Within: Italian and Other Internees in Canada and Abroad*. Toronto: University of Toronto Press, 2000.

Irwin-Zarecka, Iwona. *Frames of Remembrance: The Dynamics of Collective Memory*. New Brunswick, NJ: Transaction Publishers, 1994.

James, Carl, and Adrienne Shadd, eds. *Talking about Identity: Encounters in Race, Ethnicity, and Language*. Toronto: Between the Lines, 2001.

Jasen, Patricia. *Wild Things: Nature, Culture, and Tourism in Ontario, 1790–1914*. Toronto: University of Toronto Press, 1995.

Jean, Marcel. *Le cinéma québécois*. Montreal: Éditions du Boréal, 1991.

Jessup, Lynda, ed. *Antimodernism and Artistic Experience: Policing the Boundaries of Modernity*. Toronto: University of Toronto Press, 2001.

Jessup, Lynda, Gordon Smith, and Andrew Nurse, eds. *Around and about Marius Barbeau: Modelling Twentieth Century Culture*. Ottawa: Canadian Museum of Civilization, 2008.

Jhally, Sut. 'Advertising at the Edge of the Apocalypse.' In Robin Andersen and Lance

Strate, eds., *Critical Studies in Media Commercialism*, 27–40. London: Oxford University Press, 2000.

Johnston, Russell. *Selling Themselves: The Emergence of Advertising in Canada.* Toronto: University of Toronto Press, 2001.

Kammen, Michael. *In the Past Lane: Historical Perspectives on American Culture.* New York: Oxford University Press, 1997.

– *Meadows of Memory.* Austin: University of Texas Press, 1992.

– *Mystic Chords of Memory: The Transformation of Tradition in American Culture.* New York: Alfred A. Knopf, 1991.

Karamanski, Theodore J., ed. *Ethics and Public History: An Anthology.* Malabar, FL: Robert E. Krieger Publishing Company, 1990.

Karp, Ivan, et al., eds. *Museums and Communities: The Politics of Public Culture.* Washington: Smithsonian Institution Press, 1992.

Karp, Ivan, and Steven D. Lavine, eds. *Exhibiting Cultures: The Poetics and Politics of Museum Display.* Washington: Smithsonian Institution Press, 1991.

Karr, Clarence. *Authors and Audiences: Popular Canadian Fiction in the Early Twentieth Century.* Montreal and Kingston: McGill-Queen's University Press, 2000.

Kaufman, Polly Welts, and Katherine T. Corbett, eds. *Her Past around Us: Interpreting Sites for Women's History.* Malabar, FL: Krieger Publishing Company, 2003.

Kedourie, Elie. *Nationalism.* London: Hutchinson, 1960.

Keohane, Kieran. *Symptoms of Canada: An Essay on the Canadian Identity.* Toronto: University of Toronto Press, 1997.

Kilpatrick, J. *Celluloid Indians: Native Americans and Film.* Lincoln: University of Nebraska Press, 1999.

Kitch, Carolyn. *Pages from the Past: History and Memory in American Magazines.* Chapel Hill: University of North Carolina Press, 2005.

Klein, Norman M. *The History of Forgetting: Los Angeles and the Erasure of Memory.* London: Verso, 1997.

Knowles, Norman. *Inventing the Loyalists: The Ontario Loyalist Tradition and the Creation of Usable Pasts.* Toronto: University of Toronto Press, 1997.

Kordan, Bohdan S., and Craig Mahovsky. *A Bare and Impolitic Right: Internment and Ukrainian-Canadian Redress.* Montreal and Kingston: McGill-Queen's University Press, 2004.

Kushner, Tony. *The Holocaust and the Liberal Imagination: A Social and Cultural History.* Oxford: Blackwell, 1994.

Lagerwey, Mary D. *Reading Auschwitz.* Walnut Creek, CA: Altamira Press, 1998.

Laloux-Jain, G. *Les manuels d'histoire du Canada au Québec et en Ontario 1867–1914.* Sainte-Foy: Les Presses de l'Université Laval, 1974.

Landsberg, Alison. *Prosthetic Memory: The Transformation of American Remembrance in the Age of Mass Culture.* New York: Columbia University Press, 2004.

Landow, George. *Hypertext: The Convergence of Contemporary Literary Theory and Technology*. Baltimore: Johns Hopkins University Press, 1992.

– *Hypertext 3.0: Critical Theory and New Media in an Era of Globalization*. Baltimore: Johns Hopkins University Press, 2003.

Landy, Marcia, ed. *The Historical Film: History and Memory in Media*. New Brunswick, NJ: Rutgers University Press, 2001.

Langer, Lawrence L. *Holocaust Testimonies: The Ruins of Memory*. New Haven: Yale University Press, 1991.

Le Blanc, Barbara. *Postcards from Acadie: Grand-Pré, Evangeline and the Acadian Identity*. Kentville, NS: Gaspereau Press, 2003.

Le Goff, Jacques. *History and Memory*. Translated by Steven Rendall and Elizabeth Clamon. New York: Columbia University Press, 1992.

Lears, T.J. Jackson. *No Place of Grace: Antimodernism and the Transformation of American Culture, 1880–1920*. New York: Pantheon, 1981.

Leblanc, Barbara. *Continuité: le patrimoine en perspective*. Quebec: Éditions Continuité, 1961.

Lee, Peter. 'Historical Knowledge in the National Curriculum.' In Richard Aldrich, ed., *History in the National Curriculum*, 39–65. London: Kogan Page, 1991.

Lee, Peter, et al. *The Aims of School History: The National Curriculum and Beyond*. London: Institute of Education, University of London, 1992.

Leiss, William, Steven Kline, and Sut Jhally. *Social Communication in Advertising*. 2nd edition. New York: Routledge, 1999.

Lester, Normand. *Le livre noir du Canada anglais*. Montreal: Les Intouchables, 2001.

Létourneau, Jocelyn. *A History for the Future: Rewriting Memory and Identity in Quebec*. Translated by Phyllis Aronoff and Howard Scott. Montreal and Kingston: McGill-Queen's University Press, 2004.

– *Passer à l'avenir: histoire, mémoire, identité dans le Québec d'aujourd'hui*. Montreal: Les Éditions du Boréal, 2000.

– 'Remembering Our Past: An Examination of the Historical Memory of Young Québécois.' In Ruth Sandwell, ed., *To the Past: History Education, Public Memory and Citizenship in Canada*. Toronto: University of Toronto Press, 2006.

Lévesque, Stéphane. 'History and Social Studies in Québec: A Historical Perspective.' In A. Sears and I. Wright, eds., *Challenges and Prospects for Canadian Social Studies*, 55–72. Vancouver: Pacific Educational Press, 2004.

Levinson, Samuel. *Written in Stone: Public Monuments in Changing Societies*. Durham, NC, and London: Duke University Press, 1998.

Linenthal, Edward T. *Preserving Memory: The Struggle to Create America's Holocaust Museum*. New York: Viking, 1995.

Linenthal, Edward T., and Tom Engelhardt, eds. *History Wars: The Enola Gay and*

Other Battles for the American Past. New York: Metropolitan Books, Henry Holt and Company, 1996.

Linville, Susan. *History Films, Women and Freud's Uncanny*. Austin: University of Texas Press, 2004.

Lipsitz, George. *Time Passages: Collective Memory and Popular Culture*. Minneapolis: University of Minnesota Press, 1990.

Litalien, Raymonde, and Denis Vaugeois, eds. *Champlain: The Birth of French America*. Translated by Kathe Roth. Montreal and Kingston: McGill-Queen's University Press, 2004.

Litt, Paul. *The Muses, the Masses, and the Massey Commission*. Toronto: University of Toronto Press, 1991.

Little, Kenneth. 'On Safari: The Visual Politics of a Tourist Representation.' In David Howes, ed., *The Varieties of Sensory Experience*, 149–63. Toronto: University of Toronto Press, 1991.

Loewen, James W. *Lies My Teacher Told Me: Everything Your American History Textbook Got Wrong*. New York: New Press, 1995.

Lorenz, Chris. 'Towards a Theoretical Framework for Comparing Historiographies.' In Peter Seixas, ed., *Theorizing Historical Consciousness*. Toronto: University of Toronto Press, 2004.

Lowenthal, David. *The Heritage Crusade and the Spoils of History*. London: Viking, 1996.

– *The Past Is a Foreign* Country. Cambridge: Cambridge University Press, 1985.

– *Possessed by the Past: The Heritage Crusade and the Spoils of History*. New York: Free Press, 1996

Luciuk, Lubomyr. *Searching for Place: Ukrainian Displaced Persons, Canada, and the Migration of Memory*. Toronto: University of Toronto Press, 2000.

Luciuk, Lubomyr, comp. *Roll Call: Lest We Forget*. Kingston: Kashtan Press for the Ukrainian Civil Liberties Association and the Ukrainian Canadian Congress, 1999.

Luciuk, Lubomyr, and Boris Sydoruk, eds. *'In My Charge': The Canadian Internment Camp Photographs of Sergeant William Buck*. Kingston: Kashtan Press, 1997.

Lyman, Christopher M. *The Vanishing Race and Other Illusions: Photographs of Indians by Edward S. Curtis*. New York: Pantheon, 1982.

MacCannell, Dean. *The Tourist*. New York: Schocken, 1976.

MacEachern, Alan. *Natural Selections: National Parks in Atlantic Canada, 1935–1970*. Montreal and Kingston: McGill-Queen's University Press, 2001.

Mackey, Eva. 'The Cultural Politics of Populism: Celebrating Canadian National Identity.' In Cris Shore and Susan Wright, eds., *Anthropology of Policy*, 136–64. London: Routledge, 1997.

– *The House of Difference: Cultural Politics and National Identity in Canada*. London: Routledge, 1999; Toronto: University of Toronto Press, 2002.

Maier, Charles S. *The Unmasterable Past: History, Holocaust, and German National Identity*. Cambridge, MA: Harvard University Press, 1988.

Marcus, Julie. 'The Journey Out to the Centre: The Cultural Appropriation of Ayers Rock.' In Gillian Cowlishaw and Barry Morris, eds., *Race Matters: Indigenous Australians and 'Our' Society*, 29–51. Canberra: Aboriginal Studies Press, 1997.

Marcuse, Harold. 'Memories of World War II and the Holocaust in Europe.' In Gordon Martel, ed., *A Companion to Europe, 1900–1945*, 487–503. Oxford: Blackwell, 2006.

Mathieu, Jacques, and Jacques Lacoursière. *Les mémoires québécoises*. Sainte-Foy: Les presses de l'Université Laval, 1991.

Mathieu, Jacques. *Étude de la construction identitaire des Québécois au XXe siècle*. Sainte-Foy: Cahiers du Célat, 1986.

Mathieu, Jocelyne, ed. *Femmes et traditions – Women and Tradition*. Sainte-Foy: Laval University, 1993.

McIntyre, Darryl, and Kirsten Wehner, eds. *National Museums: Negotiating Histories Conference Proceedings*. Canberra: National Museum of Australia, 2001.

McKay, Ian. 'Helen Creighton and the Politics of Antimodernism.' In Gwendolyn Davies, ed., *Myth and Milieu: Atlantic Literature and Culture, 1918–1939*, 1–16. Fredericton: Acadiensis Press, 1993.

– *The Quest of the Folk: Antimodernism and Cultural Selection in Twentieth Century Nova Scotia*. Montreal and Kingston: McGill-Queen's University Press, 1994.

– 'The Rise of Tourism.' In J.M. Bumsted, ed., *Interpreting Canada's Past*, vol. 2: *Post-Confederation*, 487–512. Toronto: Oxford University Press, 1993.

McKay, Ian, and Robin Bates. *In the Province of History: The Making of the Public Past in Twentieth-Century Nova Scotia*. Montreal and Kingston: McGill-Queen's University Press, 2010.

McKay, Marylin. *A National Soul: Canadian Mural Painting, 1860's-1930's*. Montreal and Kingston: McGill-Queen's University Press, 2002.

McClintock, Anne. *Imperial Leather: Race, Gender and Sexuality in the Colonial Contest*. New York: Routledge, 1995.

McNairn, Alan. *Behold the Hero: General Wolfe and the Arts in the Eighteenth Century*. Montreal and Kingston: McGill-Queen's University Press, 1997.

Merchant, Carolyn. *Earthcare: Women and the Environment*. New York: Routledge, 1995.

Merchant, Carolyn, ed. *Ecology: Key Concepts in Critical Theory*. Atlantic Highlands, NJ: Humanities Press, 1994.

Michalski, Sergiusz. *Public Monuments: Art in Political Bondage*. London: Reaktion Books, 1998.

Miki, Roy. *Redress: Inside the Japanese Canadian Call for Justice*. Vancouver: Raincoast Books, 2004.

Miles, Robert. *Racism*. Key Ideas Series. London and New York: Routledge, 1989.

Miles, Robert, and Malcolm Brown. *Racism*. 2nd edition. London: Routledge, 2003.

Mitchell, W.J.T., ed. *Landscape and Power*. Chicago: University of Chicago Press, 1994.

Morgan, Cecilia. *'A Happy Holiday': English-Canadians and Transatlantic Tourism, 1870–1930*. Toronto: University of Toronto Press, 2008.

Morissonneau, Christian. *La terre promise: le mythe du Nord québécois*. Montreal: Hurtubise HMH, 1978.

Mosse, George. *Nationalism and Sexuality: Respectability and Abnormal Sexuality in Modern Europe*. New York: H. Fertig, 1985.

Nash, Gary B., Charlotte Crabtree, and Ross E. Dunn. *History on Trial: Culture Wars and the Teaching of the Past*. New York: Alfred A. Knopf, 1997.

Naylor, C.T. *Negotiating the Past: The Making of Canada's National Historic Parks and Sites*. Montreal and Kingston: McGill-Queen's University Press, 1990.

Nelles, H.V. *The Art of Nation-Building: Pageantry and Spectacle at Quebec's Tercentenary*. Toronto: University of Toronto Press, 1999.

Nelson, Camille A., and Charmaine A. Nelson, eds. *Racism, Eh?: A Critical Interdisciplinary Anthology of Race and Racism in Canada*. Concord, ON: Captus Press, 2004.

Nelson, Robert S., and Margaret Olin, eds. *Monuments and Memory, Made and Unmade*. Chicago: University of Chicago Press, 2003.

Nichols, Bill. *Representing Reality: Issues and Concepts in Documentary*. Bloomington and Indianapolis: Indiana University Press, 1991.

Nicks, Joan, and Jeannette Sloniwoski, eds. *Slippery Pastimes: Reading the Popular in Canadian Culture*. Waterloo, ON: Wilfrid Laurier University Press, 2002.

Nora, Pierrre. *Les lieux de mémoire*. 3 vols. Paris: Gallimard, 1984, 1986, 1992.

Nora, Pierre, dir. *Realms of Memory: Rethinking the French Past*. Edited by Lawrence D. Kritzman, translated by Arthur Goldhammer. 3 vols. New York: Columbia University Press, 1996.

Nora, Pierre and E.-Martin Meunier, eds. *Les impasses de la mémoire: histoire, filiation, nation et religion*. Montreal: Fides, 2007.

Norkunas, Martha. *The Politics of Public Memory: Tourism, History, and Ethnicity in Monterey, California*. Albany: SUNY Press, 1993.

Nourbese Philip, Marlene. *Frontiers: Essays and Writings on Racism and Culture*. Stratford, ON: Mercury Press, 1992.

Novick, Peter. *The Holocaust in American Life*. Boston: Houghton Mifflin, 1999.

Nugent, Maria. *Botany Bay: Where Histories Meet*. Crows Nest, NSW: Allen and Unwin, 2005.

O'Brien, John, and Peter White, eds. *Beyond Wilderness: The Group of Seven, Canadian Identity and Contemporary Art*. Montreal and Kingston: McGill-Queen's University Press, 2007.

Oelschlaeger, Max, ed. *The Wilderness Condition: Essays on Environment and Civilization.* Washington: Island Press, 1992.

Oikawa, Mona. *Cartographies of Violence: Japanese Canadian Women, Memory, and the Subjects of Internment.* Toronto: University of Toronto Press, 2011.

Omatsu, Maryka. *Bittersweet Passage: Redress and the Japanese Canadian Experience.* Toronto: Between the Lines, 1992.

Opp, James, and John C. Walsh, eds. *Placing Memory and Remembering Place in Canada.* Vancouver: University of British Columbia Press, 2010.

Osborne, Brian S. 'The Iconography of Nationhood in Canadian Art.' In Dennis Cosgrove and Stephen Daniels, eds., *The Iconography of Landscape*, 162–78. Cambridge: Cambridge University Press, 1989.

– 'Interpreting a Nation's Identity: Artists as Creators of National Consciousness.' In Alan R.H. Baker and Gideon Biger, eds., *Ideology and Landscape in Historical Perspective: Essays on the Meanings of Some Places in the Past*, 230–54. Cambridge: Cambridge University Press, 1992.

Osborne, Ken. *'Hard-working, Temperate and Peaceable': The Portrayal of Workers in Canadian History Textbooks.* Winnipeg: University of Manitoba Education Monograph 4, 1980.

– *In Defence of History: Teaching the Past and the Meaning of Democratic Citizenship.* Toronto: Our Schools/Our Selves, 1995.

Overton, James. *Making a World of Difference: Essays on Tourism, Culture and Development in Newfoundland.* St John's: Institute of Social and Economic Research, 1996.

Paget, Derek. *No Other Way to Tell It: Dramadoc/Documdrama on Television.* Manchester and New York: Manchester University Press, 1998.

Parker, Bruce, Serge Guilbaut, and John O'Brian. *Voices of Fire: Art, Rage, Power and the State.* Toronto: University of Toronto Press, 1996.

Passerini, Luisa. *Fascism in Popular Memory.* Cambridge: Cambridge University Press, 1987.

Patterson, David. *Along the Edge of Annihilation: The Collapse and Recovery of Life in the Holocaust Diary.* Seattle: University of Washington Press, 1999.

Phillips, Ruth B. *Trading Identities: The Souvenir in Native North American Art from the Northeast, 1700–1900.* Seattle: University of Washington Press, 1998.

Piehler, Kurt. *Remembering War the American Way.* Washington: Smithsonian Institution Press, 1995.

Plantinga, Carl. *Rhetoric and Representation in Nonfiction Film.* Cambridge: Cambridge University Press, 1997.

Pocius, Gerald. *A Place to Belong: Community Order and Everyday Space in Calvert, Newfoundland.* Montreal and Kingston: McGill-Queen's University Press, 1991.

Pratt, Mary Louise. *Imperial Eyes: Travel Writing and Transculturation.* London and New York: Routledge, 1992.

Ravvin, Norman. *A House of Words: Jewish Writing, Identity, and Memory.* Montreal and Kingston: McGill-Queen's University Press, 1997.

Razack, Sherene. *Dark Threats and White Knights: The Somalia Affair, Peacekeeping, and the New Imperialism.* Toronto: University of Toronto Press, 2004.

Razack, Sherene H., ed. *Race, Space and the Law: Unmapping a White Settler Society.* Toronto: Between the Lines, 2002.

Reid, John. *Acadia, Maine and New Scotland: Marginal Colonies in the Seventeenth Century.* Toronto: University of Toronto Press.1981.

Renan, Ernest. 'What Is a Nation?' In Geoff Eley and Ronald Grigor Suny, eds., *Becoming National: A Reader*, 42–55. New York: Oxford University Press, 1996.

Renan, J.E. 'What Is a Nation?' In Homi Bhabha, ed., *Nation and Narration.* London: Routledge, 1990 [1882].

Richards, Thomas. *The Imperial Archive: Knowledge and the Fantasy of Empire.* New York: Verso, 1993.

Ricoeur, Paul. *Memory, History and Forgetting.* Translated by Kathleen Blamey and David Pellauer. Chicago: University of Chicago Press, 2004.

Rider, Peter E., ed. *Studies in History and Museums.* Hull: Canadian Museum of Civilization, 1994.

Rittner, Carol, and John K. Roth. *Different Voices: Women and the Holocaust.* New York: Paragon House, 1993.

Roman, Joël, ed. *Qu'est-ce qu'une nation? et autres essais politiques.* Paris: Presses Pocket, 1992.

Roman, Leslie G., and Linda Eyre, eds. *Dangerous Territories: Struggles for Equality and Difference in Education.* New York and London: Routledge, 1997.

Rosaldo, Renato. 'Imperialist Nostalgia.' In Renato Rosaldo, ed., *Culture and Truth*, 68–87. Boston: Beacon Press, 1989.

Rose, Jonathan. *Making 'Pictures in Our Heads': Government Advertising in Canada.* Westport, CT: Praeger, 2000.

Roseman, Mark. 'Surviving Memory: Truth and Inaccuracy in Holocaust Testimony.' In Robert Perks and Alistair Thompson, eds., *The Oral History Reader*, 2nd edition, 230–43. London: Routledge, 2006.

Rosenstone, Robert A. *Visions of the Past: The Challenge of Film to Our Idea of History.* Cambridge, MA: Harvard University Press, 1995.

Rosenzweig, Roy, and David Thelen. *Presence of the Past: Popular Uses of History in American Life.* New York: Columbia University Press, 1998.

Rousso, Henry. *The Vichy Syndrome: History and Memory in France since 1944.* Translated by Arthur Goldhammer. Cambridge, MA: Harvard University Press, 1991.

Roy, Fernande. *Histoire des idéologies au Québec aux XIXe et XXe siècles.* Montreal: Boréal, 1993.

Roy, Patricia E. *The Triumph of Citizenship: The Japanese and Chinese in Canada, 1941–67.* Vancouver: University of British Columbia Press, 2007.

Rudin, Ronald. *Founding Fathers: The Celebration of Champlain and Laval in the Streets of Quebec, 1878–1908.* Toronto: University of Toronto Press, 2003.

– *Making History in Twentieth Century Québec.* Toronto: University of Toronto Press, 1997.

– *Remembering and Forgetting in Acadie: A Historian's Journey through Public Memory.* Toronto: University of Toronto Press, 2009.

Rukszto, Katarzyna. 'Up for Sale: The Commodification of Canadian Culture.' In Bohdan Szuchewycz and Jeanette Sloniowski, eds., *Canadian Communications: Issues in Contemporary Media and Culture.* Scarborough: Prentice Hall and Bacon Canada, 1998.

Rüsen, Jörn. *History: Narration, Interpretation, Orientation.* New York: Berghan Books, 2005.

Rushing, W. Jackson, III. *Native American Art and the New York Avant Garde: A History of Cultural Primitivism.* Austin: University of Texas Press, 1995.

Rutherdale, Myra, and Katie Pickles, eds. *Embodied Contact.* University of British Columbia Press, 2005.

Ryan, Alan. *The Trickster Shift.* Vancouver: University of British Columbia Press, 2000.

Ryan, Michael, and Douglas Kellner. *Camera Politica: The Politics and Ideology of Contemporary Hollywood Film.* Bloomington: University of Indiana Press, 1988.

Said, Edward W. *Culture and Imperialism.* New York: Knopf, 1993.

Samuel, Raphael. *Theatres of Memory. Volume I: Past and Present in Contemporary Culture.* London: Verso, 1994.

– *Theatres of Memory. Volume II: Island Stories, Unravelling Britain.* London: Verso, 1998.

Samuel, Raphael, and Paul Thompson, eds. *The Myths We Live By.* London: Routledge, 1990.

Sandwell, Ruth, ed. *To the Past: History Education, Public Memory, and Citizenship in Canada.* Toronto: University of Toronto Press, 2006.

Savage, Kirk. *Standing Soldiers, Kneeling Slaves: Race, War, and Monument in Nineteenth-Century America.* Princeton: Princeton University Press, 1997.

Schama, Simon. *Dead Certainties: Unwarranted Speculations.* New York: Knopf, 1991.

– *Landscape and Memory.* New York: Knopf; Toronto: Random House, 1995.

Sears, John F. *Sacred Places: American Tourist Attractions in the Nineteenth Century.* New York: Oxford University Press, 1989.

Seixas, Peter, ed. *Theorizing Historical Consciousness.* Toronto: University of Toronto Press, 2004.

Shackel, Paul. *Memory in Black and White: Race, Commemoration and the Post Bellum Landscape*. Walnut Creek, CA: Altamira Press, 2003.

Shaffer, Marguerite S. *See America First: Tourism and National Identity, 1880–1940*. Washington: Smithsonian Institution Press, 2001.

Sherbert, Garry, et al., eds. *Canadian Cultural Poesis*. Waterloo, ON: Wilfrid Laurier University Press, 2006.

Sherman, David J., and Irit Rogoff, eds. *Museum Culture: Histories Discourses Spectacles*. Minneapolis: University of Minnesota Press, 1994.

Sider, Gerald, and Gavin Smith, eds. *Between History and Histories: The Making of Silences and Commemorations*. Toronto: University of Toronto Press, 1997.

Smith, Allan. *Canada. An American Nation: Essays on Continentalism, Identity, and the Canadian Frame of Mind*. Montreal and Kingston: McGill-Queen's University Press, 1994.

Smith, Anthony D. *Chosen People: Sacred Sources of National Identity*. Oxford: Oxford University Press, 2003.

– *The Ethnic Origins of Nations*. Oxford: Blackwell, 1986.

– *Myths and Memories of the Nation*. Oxford: Oxford University Press, 1999.

– *National Identity*. London: Penguin, 1991.

– *Nationalism and Modernism*. London: Routledge, 1998.

– *Nations and Nationalism in a Global Era*. Cambridge: Polity Press, 1995.

Smith, Bonnie G. *The Gender of History: Men, Women, and Historical Practice*. Cambridge, MA: Harvard University Press, 1998.

Snead, James. *White Screens, Black Images: Hollywood on the Dark Side*. New York: Routledge, 1994.

Sobchack, Vivian, ed. *The Persistence of History: Cinema, Television and the Modern Event*. London: Routledge, 1996.

Spillman, Lyn. *Nation and Commemoration: Creating National Identities in the United States and Australia*. Cambridge: Cambridge University Press, 1997.

Spivak, Gayatry Chakravorty. *The Post-Colonial Critic*. London: Routledge, 1990.

Staley, David. *Computers, Visualization and History: How New Technology Will Transform Our Understanding of the Past*. Armonk, NY: M.E. Sharpe, 2002.

Stanley, Timothy J. *Contesting White Supremacy: School Segregation, Anti-Racism and the Making of Chinese Canadians*. Vancouver: University of British Columbia Press, 2011.

Starowicz, Mark. *Making History: The Remarkable Story behind Canada: A People's History*. Toronto: McClelland and Stewart, 2003.

Stearns, Peter N., Peter Seixas, and Sam Wineburg, eds. *Knowing, Teaching and Learning History: National and International Perspectives*. New York and London: New York University Press, 2000.

Stocking, George W., Jr. *Race, Culture, and Evolution: Essays in the History of Anthropology*. New York: Free Press, 1968.

- *Victorian Anthropology*. New York: Free Press, 1987.

Street, Brian. 'British Popular Anthropology: Exhibiting and Photographing the Other.' In Elizabeth Edwards, ed., *Anthropology and Photography*, 122–31. London: Yale University Press in Association with The Royal Anthropological Institute, 1992.

Sugiman, Momoye, ed. *Japanese Canadian Redress: The Toronto Story*. Toronto: Ad Hoc Committee for *Japanese Canadian Redress: The Toronto Story*, 2000.

Sunahara, Ann Gomer. *The Politics of Racism: The Uprooting of Japanese Canadians during the Second World War*. Toronto: James Lorimer, 1981.

Susman, Warren. *Culture as History*. New York: Pantheon, 1984.

Suzuki, Tessa Morris. *The Past within Us: Media, Memory, History*. London: Verso, 2005.

Sweet, Rosemary. *Antiquaries: The Discovery of the Past in 18th-Century Britain*. London: Hambledon and London, 2004.

Symons, Thomas, ed. *The Place of History: Commemorating Canada's Past*. Ottawa: Royal Society of Canada, 1997.

Taylor, M. Brook. *Promoters, Patriots, and Partisans: Historiography in Nineteenth-Century English Canada*. Toronto: University of Toronto Press, 1989.

Taylor, C.J. *Negotiating the Past. The Making of Canada's National Historic Parks and Sites*. Montreal and Kingston: McGill-Queeen's University Press, 1990.

Terdiman, Richard. *Present Past: Modernity and the Memory Crisis*. Ithaca and London: Cornell University Press, 1993.

Thiesmeyer, Lynn, ed. *Discourse and Silencing: Representation and the Language of Displacement*. Amsterdam and Philadelphia: John Benjamins Publishing Co., 2003.

Thomas, Nicholas. *Colonialism's Culture: Anthropology, Travel and Government*. Cambridge: Polity Press, 1994.

- *Possessions: Indigenous Art/Colonial Culture*. New York: Thames and Hudson, 1999.

Tippett, Maria. *Art in the Service of War*. Toronto: University of Toronto Press, 1984.

- *Making Culture: English-Canadian Institutions and the Arts before the Massey Commission*. Toronto: University of Toronto Press, 1990.

Todorov, Tzvetan. *Facing the Extreme: Moral Life in the Concentration Camps*. New York: Metropolitan Books, 1996.

Tonkin, Elizabeth, et al., eds. *History and Ethnicity*. London: Routledge, 1989.

Toplin, Robert Brent. *History by Hollywood: The Use and Abuse of the American Past*. Urbana: University of Illinois Press, 1996.

Touillot, Michael-Rolph. *Silencing the Past: Power and the Production of History*. Boston: Beacon Press, 1995.

Troper, Harold, and Morton Weinfeld. *Old Wounds: Jews, Ukrainians and the Hunt for Nazi War Criminals in Canada*. Markham, ON: Penguin Books, 1989.

Trouillot, Michel-Rolph. *Silencing the Past: Power and the Production of History.* Boston: Beacon Press, 1995.

Trudel, M., and G. Jain. *L'histoire du Canada: enquête sur les manuels.* Ottawa: Queen's Printer, 1969.

Turner, Louis, and John Ash. *The Golden Hordes: International Tourism and the Pleasure Periphery.* New York: St Martin's Press, 1976.

Urry, John. *The Tourist Gaze: Leisure and Travel in Contemporary Societies.* London: Sage, 1990.

Vance, Jonathan. *Death So Noble: Memory, Meaning, and the First World War.* Vancouver: University of British Columbia Press, 1997.

Vanderhaeghe, Guy. *The Englishman's Boy.* Toronto: McClelland and Stewart, 1996.

Vanderhaeghe, Guy. 'Making History.' In Herb Wyile, *Speaking in the Past Tense: Canadian Novelists on Writing Historical Fiction,* 27–8. Waterloo: Wilfrid Laurier University Press, 2007.

Verdery, Katherine. *The Political Lives of Dead Bodies: Reburial and Postsocialist Change.* New York: Columbia University Press, 1999.

Waiser, Bill. *Park Prisoners: The Untold Story of Western Canada's National Parks, 1914–1946.* Saskatoon: Fifth House Publishers, 1995.

Wallace, Elizabeth Kowalski. *The British Slave Trade and Public Memory.* New York: Columbia University Press, 2006.

Wallace, Michael, 'Visiting the Past: History Museums in the United States.' In Susan Porter Benson et al., eds., *Presenting the Past: Essays on History and the Public,* 137–61. Philadelphia: Temple University Press, 1986.

Warner, Marina. *Joan of Arc: The Image of Female Heroism.* New York: Alfred A. Knopf, 1981.

– *Monuments and Maidens: The Allegory of the Female Form.* New York: Atheneum, 1985.

Wertsch, James V. *Voices of Collective Remembering.* Cambridge: Cambridge University Press, 2002.

Whisnant, David. *All That Is Native and Fine: The Politics of Culture in an American Region.* Chapel Hill: University of North Carolina Press, 1983.

White, Hayden. *Metahistory.* Baltimore: Johns Hopkins University Press, 1973.

Wilson, Alexander. *The Culture of Nature: North American Landscape from Disney to the Exxon Valdez.* Toronto: Between the Lines, 1991.

Wilson, Norman J. *History in Crisis? Recent Directions in Historiography.* New York: Prentice-Hall, 1999.

Wilson, Perry R. *The Clockwork Factory: Women and Work in Fascist Italy.* Oxford: Oxford University Press, 1993.

Wilson, Rob, and Wimal Dissanayake, eds. *Global/Local: Cultural Production and the Transnational Imaginary.* Durham, NC: Duke University Press, 1996.

Wineburg, Sam. *Historical Thinking and Other Unnatural Acts: Charting the Future of Teaching the Past.* Philadelphia: Temple University Press, 2001.

Winter, Jay. *Remembering War: The Great War between Memory and History in the Twentieth Century.* New Haven: Yale University Press, 2006.

– *Sites of Memory, Sites of Mourning: The Great War in European Cultural History.* Cambridge: Cambridge University Press, 1995.

Wright, Patrick. *A Journey through Ruins: The Last Days of London.* London: Radius, 1991.

– *On Living in an Old Counttry: The National Past in Contemporary Britain.* London: Verso, 1985.

Wrobel, David M., and Patrick T. Long, eds. *Seeing and Being Seen: Tourism in the American West.* Lawrence: University Press of Kansas, 2001.

Wyile, Herb. *Speaking in the Past Tense: Canadian Novelists on Writing Canadian Historical Fiction.* Waterloo: Wilfrid Laurier University Press, 2007.

– *Speculative Fictions: Contemporary Canadian Novelists and the Writing of History.* Montreal and Kingston: McGill-Queen's University Press, 2002.

Worrall, Brandy Liên, ed. *Finding Memories, Tracing Routes: Chinese Canadian Family Stories.* Vancouver: Chinese Canadian Historical Society of British Columbia, 2006.

Young, Brian. *The Making and Unmaking of a University Museum: The McCord, 1921–1996.* Montreal and Kingston: McGill-Queen's University Press, 2000.

Young, James E. *The Texture of Memory: Holocaust Memorials and Meaning.* New Haven: Yale University Press, 1993.

– *Writing and Rewriting the Holocaust: Narrative and the Consequences of Interpretation.* Bloomington: Indiana University Press, 1988.

Journal Articles

Allen, Gene. 'Canadian History in Film: A Roundtable Discussion.' *Canadian Historical Review* 82, 2 (June 2001): 331–46.

– 'The Professionals and the Public: Responses to *Canada: A People's History.*' *Histoire sociale/Social History* 34, 68 (November 2001): 381–91.

Anderson, Jay. 'Living History: Simulating Everyday Life in Living Museums.' *American Quarterly* 34 (1982): 290–306.

Appadurai, Arjun. 'Patriotism and Its Futures.' *Public Culture* 5, 3 (1993): 411–30.

Bartov, Omer. 'Intellectuals on Auschwitz Memory, History and Truth.' *History and Memory* 5, 1 (Spring/Summer 1993): 85–129.

Berdahl, Daphne. 'Voice at the Wall: Discourses of Self, History and National Identity at the Vietnam Veterans Memorial.' *History and Memory* 6, 2 (Fall/Winter 1994): 88–124.

Berliner, David C. 'The Abuses of Memory: Reflections on the Memory Boom in Anthropology.' *Anthropological Quarterly* 78, 1 (2005): 197–211.

Blake, Raymond. 'The Canadian 1988 Election: The Nationalist Posture of Prime Minister Brian Mulroney and the Progressive Conservatives.' *Canadian Review of Studies in Nationalism* 30 (2003): 65–82.

Bliss, Michael. 'Privatizing the Mind: The Sundering of Canadian History, the Sundering of Canada.' *Journal of Canadian Studies* 26 (Winter 1991–2): 5–12.

Bodnar, John. 'Power and Memory in Oral History: Workers and Managers at Studebaker.' *Journal of American History* 75, 4 (March 1989): 1200–21.

– 'Symbols and Servants: Immigrant America and the Limits of Public History.' *Journal of American History* 73, 1 (June 1986): 137–51.

Bordo, Jonathan. 'Jack Pine – Wilderness Sublime, or the Erasure of the Aboriginal Presence from the Landscape.' *Journal of Canadian Studies* 27, 4 (1992): 98–128.

Boudreau, Michael. 'A "Rare and Unusual Treat of Historical Significance": The 1923 Hector Celebration and the Political Economy of the Past.' *Journal of Canadian Studies* 28, 4 (Winter 1993–4): 28–48.

Brandt, Susanne. 'The Memory Makers: Museums and Exhibitions of the First World War.' *History and Memory* 6, 1 (Spring/Summer 1994): 93–122.

Buckner, P. '"Limited Identities" and Canadian Historical Scholarship: An Atlantic Provinces Perspective.' *Journal of Canadian Studies* 23 (1988): 177–98.

Burton, Antoinette. 'Who Needs the Nation? Interrogating "British" History.' *Journal of Historical Sociology* 10 (1997): 227–48.

Cameron, Elspeth. 'Heritage Minutes: Culture and Myth.' *Canadian Themes/Thèmes canadiens* 17 (1995): 25–36.

Cameron, Elspeth, and Janice Dickin McGinnis. 'Ambushed by Patriotism: The Wit, Wisdom and Wimps of Heritage Minutes.' *Canadian Forum,* 73, 837 (1995): 12–15.

Cannizo, Jeanne. 'Exhibiting Cultures: "Into the Heart of Africa."' *Visual Anthropology Review* 7, 1 (Spring 1991): 150–60.

Careless, J.M.S. 'Limited Identities – Ten Years Later.' *Manitoba History* 1 (1980).

Carr, Graham. 'Rules of Engagement: Public History and the Drama of Legitimation.' *Canadian Historical Review* 86, 2 (2005): 317–54.

Charland, Maurice. 'Technological Nationalism.' *Canadian Journal of Social and Political Theory* 10, 1–2 (1986): 186–210.

Chevalier, Jacques. 'Myth and Ideology in "Traditional" French Canada: Dollard, the Martyred Warrior.' *Anthropologica* n.s. 21, 2 (1979): 143–76.

Coates, Colin. 'Authority and Illegitimacy in New France: The Burial of Bishop Saint-Vallier and Madeleine de Verchères vs. the Priest of Batiscan.' *Histoire sociale/ Social History* 22, 43 (May 1989): 65–90.

Confessore, Nicholas. 'Selling Private Ryan.' *American Prospect* 12, 17 (September-October 2001): 22–3

Confino, Alon. 'Collective Memory and Cultural History: Problems of Method.' *American Historical Review* 102, 5 (December 1997): 1386–1403.

Connerton, Paul. 'Seven Types of Forgetting.' *Memory Studies* 1, 1 (2008): 60–72.

Conrad, Margaret. 'My Canada Includes the Atlantic Provinces.' *Histoire sociale/Social History* 34, 68 (November 2001): 392–402.

– 'Going Down the Digital Highway.' *CHA Bulletin* 32, 2 (2006): 4–6.

Cook, Ramsay. 'Identities Are Not Like Hats.' *Canadian Historical Review* 81 (2000): 260–92.

Crane, Susan. 'Writing the Individual Back into Collective Memory.' *American Historical Review* 102, 5 (December 1997): 1372–85.

Cupido, Robert. 'Approaching the Past: Pageants, Politics, and the Diamond Jubilee of Confederation.' *Journal of the Canadian Historical Association* 9 (1998): 155–86.

– 'The Medium, the Message, and the Modern: The Jubilee Broadcast of 1927.' *International Journal of Canadian Studies* 26 (2002): 101–27.

Da Breo, Hazel. 'Royal Spoils: The Museum Confronts Its Colonial Past.' *Fuse* (Winter 1989–90): 27–37.

Dawson, Michael. '"That Nice Red Coat Goes to My Head Like Champagne": Gender, Antimodernism, and the Mountie Image, 1880–1960.' *Journal of Canadian Studies* 32, 3 (1997): 119–39.

DeRuyer, Debra, and Jennifer Evans, 'Digital Junction.' *American Quarterly* 58, 3 (September, 2006): 943–80.

Dick, Ernest. 'The Valour and the Horror Continued: Do We Still Want Our History on Television?' *Archivaria* 35, 5 (Spring 1993): 253–69.

Dick, Lyle. 'All's Well That Ends Well.' *Prairie Fire* 7, 1 (1986): 77–82.

– 'A Growing *Necessity* for Canada: W.L. Morton's Centenary Series and the Forms of National History, 1955–1980.' *Canadian Historical Review* 82, 2 (2001): 223–52.

– 'Nationalism and Visual Media in Canada: The Case of Thomas Scott's Execution.' *Manitoba History* no. 48 (Winter 2004–5): 2–18.

– '"A New History for the New Millennium": *Canada: A People's History.*' *Canadian Historical Review* 85, 1 (March 2004): 85–109.

– 'The Seven Oaks Incident and the Construction of a Historical Tradition.' *Journal of the CHA* 2 (1991): 91–113.

Dickenson, Victoria. 'A History of the National Museums from Their Founding to the Present Day.' *Muse* 10, 2/3 (1992): 56–63.

Dodd, Dianne, and Geneviève Postolec. 'Report on the Survey of Women in Public History.' *Canadian Historical Review* 81, 3 (September, 2000): 452–66.

Dorland, Michael. 'A Thoroughly Hidden Country: *Ressentiment*, Canadian Nationalism, Canadian Culture.' *Canadian Journal of Political and Social Theory* 12, 1–2 (1988): 130–64.

Fahrni, Magda. 'Review – Canada: Confederation to Present [CD-ROM].' *Canadian Historical Review* 85, 3 (September 2004): 535–7.

Frank, David. 'Public History and the People's History: A View from Atlantic Canada.' *Acadiensis* 32, 2 (Spring 2003): 120–33.

Frisch, Michael. 'American History and the Structures of Collective Memory: A Modest Exercise in Empirical Iconography.' *Journal of American History* 75, 4 (March 1989): 1130–55.

Furniss, Elizabeth. 'Pioneers, Progress, and the Myth of the Frontier: The Landscape of Public History in Rural British Columbia.' *B.C. Studies* 115/116 (Autumn/Winter 1997/8): 7–44.

Gagnon, Serge. 'L'émergence de l'identité rurale et l'intervention de l'État québécois en tourisme, 1920–1940.' *Téoros* 20, 3 (Autumn 2001): 24–31. Glassberg, David. 'History and the Public: Legacies of the Progressive Era,' *Journal of American History* 73 (1984): 957–980.

– 'Public History and the Study of Memory.' *Public Historian* 18, 2 (Spring 1996): 7–23.

– 'Roundtable.' *Public Historian* 19, 2 (1997): 31–72.

Gordon, Alan. 'Heroes, History, and Two Nationalisms: Jacques Cartier.' *Journal of the Canadian Historical Association* (1999): 81–102.

Gough, P. '"Invicta Pax" Monuments, Memorials and Peace: An Analysis of the Canadian Peace Keeping Monument, Ottawa.' *International Journal of Heritage Studies* 8, 3 (2002): 201–33.

Groulx, Patrice. 'La meilleure histoire du monde.' *Histoire sociale/Social History* 34, 68 (2001): 381–414.

Hall, Jacquelyn Dowd. '"You Must Remember This": Autobiography as Social Critique.' *Journal of American History* 85, 2 (September 1998): 439–65.

Hamel, Natalie. 'Coordonner l'artisanat et le tourisme, ou comment mettre en valeur le visage pittoresque du Québec (1915–1960).' *Histoire sociale/Social History* 34, 67 (May 2001): 97–114.

Hamilton, Paula, and Paul Ashton. 'At Home with the Past: Background and Initial Findings from the National Survey.' *Australian Cultural History*. Special ssue, 22 (2003): 5–30.

Hammerschmidt, Hildegard. 'Images of Canada in Advertising.' *Journal of Canadian Studies* 18, 4 (1984): 154–71

Handler, Richard. 'In Search of the Folk Society: Nationalism and Folklore Studies in Québec.' *Culture* 3, 1 (1983): 103–14.

Hanna, Martha. 'Iconology and Ideology: Images of Joan of Arc in the Idiom of the *Action française*, 1908–1931.' *French Historical Studies* 14, 2 (Fall 1985): 215–39.

Harlan, David. 'Ken Burns and the Coming Crisis of Academic History.' *Rethinking History* 7, 2 (2003): 169–92.

Harrison, Julia. '"The Spirit Sings" and the Future of Anthropology.' *Anthropology Today* 4, 6 (1988): 6–9.

Hart, Susan. 'Lurking in the Bushes: Ottawa's Anishinabe Scout.' *Espace* 72 (Summer 2005): 14–17.

Hein, Laura. 'The Imaginative Power of the "Military Comfort Women" in the 1990s.' *Gender and History* 11, 2 (July 1999): 336–72.

'History and the Public: What Can We Handle – A Round Table about History after the Enola Gay Controversy.' *Journal of American History* 82, 3 (1995).

Hodgins, Peter. 'Our Haunted Present: Cultural Memory in Question.' *Topia* 12 (Fall 2004): 99–108.

Horton, James O. 'Presenting Slavery: The Perils of Telling America's Racial History.' *Public Historian* 21, 4 (Fall 1999): 19–38.

Hoskins, Ian. 'Good Men and Tiger Tanks: "Saving Private Ryan" as History Lesson.' *Public History Review* 7 (1998): 159–62.

Houle, Robert, and Clara Hargittay. 'The Struggle against Cultural Apartheid.' *Muse* 6, 3 (1988): 58–63.

Hoxie, Frederick E. 'Exploring a Cultural Borderland: Native American Journeys of Discovery in the Early Twentieth Century.' *Journal of American History* 79, 3 (December 1992): 969–95.

Hulan, Rénée. 'Historical Method in Canadian Literary Studies: Some Recent Examples.' *Acadiensis* 34, 2 (2005): 130–45.

Hüppauf, Bernd. 'The Emergence of Modern War Imagery in Early Photography.' *History and Memory* 5, 1 (Spring/Summer 1993): 130–51.

Hurtado, Albert. 'Historians and Their Employers: A Perspective on Professional Ethics.' *Public Historian* 8, 1 (Winter 1986): 47–51.

Hutcheon, Linda. 'The Post Always Rings Twice: The Postmodern and the Postcolonial.' *Textual Practice* 8, 2 (1994): 205–38.

Kammen, Michael. 'Public History and the Uses of Memory.' *Public Historian* 19, 2 (Spring 1997): 49–52.

– 'Review of Iwona Irwin-Zarecka, *Frames of Remembrance: The Dynamics of Collective Memory*.' *History and Theory* 34, 3 (1995): 245–61.

Kansteimer, Wulf. 'Finding Meaning in Memory: A Methodological Critique of Collective Memory Studies.' *History and Theory* 41, 32 (May 2002): 179–97.

Kaufman, Eric, and Oliver Zimmer. 'In Search of the Authentic Nation: Landscape and National Identity in Canada and Switzerland.' *Nations and Nationalism* 4 (1998): 483–510.

Kealey, Linda, et al. 'Teaching Canadian History in the 1990s: Whose National History Are We Lamenting.' *Journal of Canadian Studies* 27, 2 (Summer 1992): 129–31.

Klein, Kerwin Lee. 'On the Emergence of Memory in Historical Discourse.' *Representations* 69 (2000): 127–50.

Knibb, Helen. 'Present but Not Visible?: Searching for Women's History in Museum Collections.' *Gender and History* 6, 3 (1994): 352–69.

Knowles, Norman. '"Shall we not raise there again but higher some pyramid piercing the skies?": The Loyalist Tradition and the Adolphustown Centennial Celebrations of 1884.' *Ontario History* 80 (1988): 5–30.

Landsman, Gail H. 'The "Other" as Political Symbol: Images of Indians in the Woman Suffrage Movement.' *Ethnohistory* 39, 3 (Summer 1992): 247–83.

Lattas, Andrew. 'Aborigines and Contemporary Australian Nationalism: Primordiality and the Cultural Politics of Otherness.' *Social Analysis* 27 (1990): 50–69.

Laville, Christian. 'History Taught in Québec Is Not Really That Different from the History Taught Elsewhere in Canada.' *Canadian Social Studies* 31 (1996): 22–42, 42.

Lee, P. 'Making Sense of Historical Accounts.' *Canadian Social Studies* 32, 2 (1998): 52–4.

Létourneau, Jocelyn, and Sabrina Moisan. 'Young People's Assimilation of a Collective Historical Memory: A Case Study of Quebeckers of French-Canadian Heritage.' *Canadian Historical Review* 85, 2 (2004): 325–56.

Litt, Paul. 'The Apotheosis of the Apothecary: Retailing and Consuming the Meaning of a Historic Site.' *Journal of the Canadian Historical Association* (1999): 297–322.

Mackey, Eva. 'Becoming Indigenous: Land, Belonging, and the Appropriation of Aboriginality in Canadian Nationalist Narratives.' *Social Analysis* 42, 2 (1998): 149–78.

– '"Death by Landscape": Race, Nature and Gender in Canadian Nationalist Mythology.' *Canadian Women's Studies* 20, 2 (2000): 125–30.

– 'Postmodernism and Cultural Politics in a Multicultural Nation: Contests over Truth in the "Into the Heart of Africa" Controversy.' *Public Culture* 7, 2 (1995): 403–32.

Maier, Charles S. 'A Surfeit of Memory? Reflections on History, Melancholy and Denial.' *History and Memory* 5, 2 (Fall/Winter 1993): 136–52.

Marquis, Greg. 'Celebrating Champlain in the Loyalist City: Saint John, 1904–10.' *Acadiensis* 33 (2004): 27–43.

Mayo, Edith P. 'Women's History and Public History: The Museum Connection.' *Public Historian* 5, 2 (1983): 63–73.

McGinnis, Janice Dickin. 'Heritage Minutes: Myth and History.' *Canadian Issues/ Themes Canadien* 17 (1995): 13–24.

McGregor, Robert. 'I Am Canadian: National Identity in Beer Commercials.' *Journal of Popular Culture* 37, 2 (2003): 276–86.

McKay, Ian. 'After Canada: On Amnesia, and Apocalypse in the Contemporary Crisis.' *Acadiensis* 28 (1998): 76–97.

– 'Among the Fisherfolk: J.F.B. Livesay and the Invention of Peggy's Cove.' *Journal of Canadian Studies* 23, 1/2 (Spring/Summer 1988): 23–45.

- 'History and the Tourist Gaze: The Politics of Commemoration in Nova Scotia, 1935–1964.' *Acadiensis* 22, 2 (Spring 1993): 102–38.
- 'The Liberal Order Framework: A Prospectus for a Reconnaissance of Canadian History.' *Canadian Historical Review* 81, 3 (September 2000): 617–45.
- 'Tartanism Triumphant: The Construction and Uses of Scottishness in Nova Scotia, 1934–1954.' *Acadiensis* 21, 2 (1992): 5–47.

McKay, Marylin. 'Canadian Historical Murals, 1895–1939: Material Progress, Morality and the "Disappearance" of Native People.' *Canadian Journal of Art History* 15 (1992): 63–83.

McKenna, Katherine. 'Women's History, Gender Politics and the Interpretation of Canadian Historic Sites: Some Examples from Ontario.' *Atlantis* 30, 1 (2005): 21–30.

McKillop, A.B. 'Who Killed Canadian History? A View from the Trenches.' *Canadian Historical Review* 80, 2 (June 1999): 269–99.

McLaughlin, Megan. 'The Woman Warrior: Gender, Warfare and Society in Medieval Europe.' *Women's Studies* 17, 3–4 (January 1990): 193–210.

McPherson, Kathryn. 'Carving Out a Past: The Canadian Nurses' Association War Memorial.' *Histoire sociale/Social History* 29, 58 (November 1996): 418–29.

Melman, Billie. 'Gender, History and Memory: The Invention of Women's Past in the Nineteenth and Early Twentieth Centuries.' *History and Memory* 5, 1 (Spring/Summer 1993): 5–40.

Miles, Roger. 'Museum Audiences.' *International Journal of Museum Management and Curatorship* 5, 31 (1986): 73–80.

Mishra, Vijay. 'Postmodern Racism.' *Meanjin* 55, 2 (1996): 346–57.

Mitchell, Charles. 'Benjamin West's "Death of General Wolfe" and the Popular History Piece.' *Journal of the Warburg and Courtauld Institutes* 7 (1944): 20–33.

Mitchell, Rosemary. '"The Busy Daughters of Clio": Women Writers of History from 1820–1880.' *Women's History Review* 7, 1 (1998): 107–34.

Morgan, Cecilia. 'History, Nation and Empire: Gender and Southern Ontario Historical Societies, 1890–1920s.' *Canadian Historical Review* 82, 3 (2001): 491–528.

Muise, Del. 'Organizing Historical Memory in the Maritimes: A Reconnaissance.' *Acadiensis* 30, 1 (2000): 50–60.

Murton, James. 'La "Normandie du Nouveau Monde": la société Canada Steamship Lines, l'antimodernisme et la promotion du Québec ancien.' *Revue d'histoire de l'Amérique française* 55, 1 (Summer 2001): 3–44.

Neatby, Nicole. 'The Heritage Project 60th Minute Commemorative Video.' *Canadian Historical Review* 81, 4 (December 2000): 668–72.

- 'Meeting of the Minds: North American Travel Writers and Government Tourist Publicity in 1920–1955.' *Histoire sociale/Social History* 36, 72 (November 2003): 465–95.

Nelles, H.V. 'Historical Pageantry and the "Fusion of Races" at the Tercentenary of Quebec, 1908.' *Histoire sociale/Social History* 29, 58 (November 1996): 391–415.

Noppen, Luc, and Lucie K. Morisset. 'À la recherche d'une architecture pour la nation canadienne-française: entre le paysage et la patrie, de la crise à la Seconde Guerre mondiale.' *Les Cahiers d'histoire du Québec au 20ᵉ siècle* 5 (Spring 1996): 9–36.

Nora, Pierre. 'Between Memory and History: Les lieux de mémoire.' *Representations* 26 (Spring 1989): 7–24.

O'Donnell, Terence. 'Pitfalls along the Path to Public History.' *Public Historian* 4, 1 (Winter 1982): 26–40.

Osborne, Brian S. 'From Patriotic Pines to Diasporic Geese: Emplacing Culture, Setting Our Sights, Locating Identity in a Transnational Canada.' *Canadian Journal of Communications* 31 (2006): 147–75.

– 'Landscapes, Memory, Monuments, and Commemoration: Putting Identity in Its Place.' *Canadian Ethnic Studies* 33, 3 (2001): 39–77.

Osborne, Ken. 'An Early Example of the Analysis of History Textbooks in Canada.' *Canadian Social Studies* 29 (1994): 21–5.

– 'Fred Morrow Fling and the Source-Method of Teaching History.' *Theory and Research in Social Education* 31 (2003): 466–501.

– '"Our History Syllabus Has Us Gasping": History in Canadian Schools – Past, Present, and Future.' *Canadian Historical Review* 81, 3 (September 2000): 404–35.

– 'Teaching History in Canadian Schools: A Century of Debate.' *Canadian Issues/ Thèmes Canadiens* (October/November 2001): 4–7.

Owen, Susan. 'Memory, War and American Identity: *Saving Private Ryan* as Cinematic Jeremiad.' *Critical Studies in Media Communication* 19, 3 (2002): 245–82.

Palmer, Bryan. 'Of Silences and Trenches: A Dissident View of Granatstein's Meaning.' *Canadian Historical Review* 80, 4 (December 1999): 676–86.

Phillips, Ruth. 'Re-placing Objects: Historical Practice for the Second Museum Age.' *Canadian Historical Review* 86, 1 (March 2005): 83–110.

Rimstead, Roxanne. 'Cultural Memory and Social Identity.' *Essays on Canadian Writing* 80 (2003): 1–14.

Robert, Davidson J. 'Turning a Blind Eye: The Historian's Use of Photographs.' *BC Studies* 52 (Winter 1981–2): 16–38.

Robert, Jean-Claude, 'L'historien et les médias.' *Revue d'histoire de l'Amérique française* 57, 1 (Summer 2003): 57–69.

Rogers, Nicholas, and Adrian Shubert. 'Introduction: Spectacle, Monument, and Memory.' *Histoire sociale/Social History* 29, 58 (November 1996): 265–73.

Rose, Jonathan. 'Government Advertising and the Creation of National Mythologies: The Canadian Case.' *International Journal of Non-Profit and Voluntary Sector Marketing* 8, 2 (2003): 153–65.

Rosenzweig, Roy. 'Can History Be Open Source?: Wikipedia and the Future of the Past.' *Journal of American History* 93, 1 (June 2006): 117–46.
– 'Scarcity or Abundance? Preserving the Past in a Digital Era.' *American Historical Review* 108, 3 (September 2004): 735–62.
Roy, Fernande. 'Une mise en scène de l'histoire: La fondation de Montréal à travers les siècles.' *Revue d'histoire de l'Amérique française* 46, 1 (Summer 1992): 7–36.
Rudin, Ronald. 'The Champlain–De Monts Tercentenary: Voices from Nova Scotia, New Brunswick and Maine, June 1904.' *Acadiensis* 33 (Spring 2004): 3–26.
– 'Marching and Memory in Early Twentieth-Century Quebec: La Fête-Dieu, la Saint-Jean-Baptiste, and le Monument Laval.' *Journal of the Canadian Historical Association* (1999): 209–36.
Rukszto, Katarzyna. 'The Other Heritage Minutes: Satirical Reactions to Canadian Nationalism.' *Topia* 14 (Fall 2005): 73–92.
Rushing, W. Jackson, III. 'Contrary Iconography: The Submuloc Show.' *New Art Examiner* 21 (Summer 1994): 33–4.
Sangster, Joan. 'Telling Our Stories: Feminist Debates and the Use of Oral History.' *Women's History Review* 3, 1 (1994): 5–28.
Schelereth, Thomas. 'We Must Review History Museum Exhibits.' *History News* 43, 3 (1988): 30–3.
Schildkrout, Enid. 'Ambiguous Messages and Ironic Twists: Into the Heart of Africa and the Other Museum.' *Museum Anthropology* 15, 2 (1991): 16–23.
Schwartz, Barry. 'The Social Context of Commemoration: A Study in Collective Memory.' *Social Forces* 61 (1982): 374–402.
Robert Seiler. 'Selling Patriotism/Selling Beer: The Case of the "I Am Canadian" Commercial.' *American Review of Canadian Studies* 32, 1 (2002): 45–66.
Seixas, Peter. 'Confronting the Moral Frames of Popular Film: Young People Respond to Historical Revisionism.' *American Journal of Education* 102, 3 (1994): 261–85.
– 'Heavy Baggage en route to Winnipeg: A Review Essay.' *Canadian Historical Review* 83, 3 (September 2002): 390–415.
– 'Parallel Crises: History and Social Studies Curriculum in the USA.' *Journal of Curriculum Studies* 25, 3 (1993): 235–50.
– 'The Purposes of Teaching Canadian History.' *Canadian Social Studies* 36, 2 (Winter 2002): 1–7.
Smith, Tori. '"Almost Pathetic ... But Also Very Glorious": The Consumer Spectacle of the Diamond Jubilee.' *Histoire sociale/Social History* 29, 58 (November 1996): 333–56.
Srivastava, Sanjay. 'Postcoloniality, National Identity, Globalisation and the Simulacra of the Real.' *Australian Journal of Anthropology* 7, 2 (1996): 166–90.
Stacey, Robert. '"Salvage for Us These Fragments": C.W. Jefferys and Ontario's Historic Architecture.' *Ontario History* 70 (1978): 147–70.

Stanley, Timothy J. 'Bringing Anti-Racist Theory into Historical Explanation: The Victoria Chinese Students' Strike of 1922–3 Revisited.' *Journal of the Canadian Historical Association* new neries 13 (2002): 141–66.

– 'Why I Killed Canadian History: Towards an Anti-Racist History in Canada.' *Histoire sociale/Social History* (May 2000): 79–103.

Starowicz, Mark. 'The Crucible of History.' *Opinion Canada* 1.2, 15 (20 April 2000).

Staub, Michael. '"Negroes Are Not Jews": Race, Holocaust Consciousness, and the Rise of Jewish Neoconservatism.' *Radical History Review: Histories, Memories, Identities* 75 (Fall 1999): 3–27.

Strong-Boag, Veronica. 'Claiming a Place in the Nation: Citizenship Education and the Challenge of Feminists, Natives and Workers in Post-Confederation Canada.' *Canadian and International Education* 25, 2 (1996): 128–45.

– 'Contested Space: The Politics of Canadian Memory.' *Journal of the Canadian Historical Association* 5 (1994): 3–17.

Sugiman, Pamela. 'Passing Time, Moving Memories: Interpreting Wartime Narratives of Japanese Canadian Women.' *Histoire sociale/Social History* 37 (2004): 51–79.

Tatum, James. 'Memorials of the American War in Vietnam.' *Critical Inquiry* 22, 4 (Summer 1996): 634–78.

Thomas, Jeffrey. 'From the Collections, the Portfolio: Luminance – Aboriginal Photographic Portraits.' *Archivist, Magazine of the National Archives of Canada* 112 (1996): 7–23.

Thomas, William G., III. 'Blazing Trails toward Digital History Scholarship.' *Histoire sociale/Social History* 34, 68 (November 2001): 415–26.

Thompson, Alistair. 'Fifty Years On: An International Perspective on Oral History.' *Journal of American History* 85, 2 (September 1998): 581–75.

Trigger, Bruce G. 'The Historian's Indian: Native Americans in Canadian Historical Writing from Charlevoix to the Present.' *Canadian Historical Review* 67, 3 (1986): 315–42.

Vipond, Mary. 'The Nationalist Network: English-Canada's Intellectuals and Artists in the 1920s.' *Canadian Review of Studies in Nationalism* 7 (1980): 32–52.

Wagman, Ira. 'Wheat, Barley, Hops, Citizenship: Molson's I Am [Canadian] Campaign and the Defence of Canadian National Identity through Advertising.' *Velvet Light Trap* 50 (2002): 77–89.

Weinstein, P.B. 'Movies as the Gateway to History: The History of Film Project.' *History Teacher* 35, 1 (2001): 27–38.

West, Emily. 'Selling Canada to Canadians: Collective Memory, National Identity, and Popular Culture.' *Critical Studies in Media Communication* 19, 2 (June 2002): 212–29.

West, Patricia. 'Gender Politics and the "Invention of Tradition": The Museumization of Louisa May Alcott's Orchard House.' *Gender and History: Special Issue on Public History* 6, 3 (November 1994): 456–67.

Weyeneth, Robert. 'History, He Wrote: Murder, Politics and the Challenges of Public History in a Community with a Secret.' *Public Historian* 16, 2 (Spring 1994): 51–73.

Willems-Braun, Bruce. 'Buried Epistemologies: The Politics of Nature in (Post) colonial British Columbia.' *Annals of the Association of American Geographers* 87, 1 (1997): 3–31.

Wood, Nancy. 'Memory's Remains: *Les lieux de mémoire.*' *History and Memory* 6, 1 (Summer 1994): 123–49.

Wright, Donald. 'W.D. Lighthall and David Ross McCord: Antimodernism and English-Canadian Imperialism, 1880s-1918.' *Journal of Canadian Studies* 32, 2 (Summer 1997): 134–54.

Wright, John, Gregory Millard, and Sarah Riegel. 'Here's Where We Get Canadian: English-Canadian Nationalism and Popular Culture.' *American Review of Canadian Studies* 32, 1 (2002): 11–34.

Wright, Robert. 'Historical Underdosing: Pop Demography and the Crisis in Canadian History.' *Canadian Historical Review* 81, 4 (December 2000): 646–67.

Young, James E. 'The Biography of a Memorial Icon: Nathan Rapoport's Warsaw Ghetto Monument.' *Representations* 26 (Spring 1989): 69–107.

Zimmerman, Larry J. 'Archeology, Reburial and the Tactics of a Discipline's Self Delusion.' *American Indian Culture and Research Journal* 16, 2 (1992): 7–56.

Zelizer, Barbie. 'Reading the Past against the Grain: The Shape of Memory Studies.' *Critical Studies in Mass Communication* 12, 2 (1995): 214–39.

Theses and Unpublished Papers

Bradley, Ben. 'Roving Eyes: Circulation, Visuality, and Hierarchy of Place in East-Central British Columbia, 1910–1975.' MA thesis, University of Victoria, 2003.

Cameron, Ross Douglas. '"Our Ideal of an Artist": Tom Thomson, the Ideal of Manhood and the Creation of a National Icon.' MA thesis, Queen's University, 1998.

Caron, Caroline-Isabelle. 'Se créer des ancêtres. Les écrits historiques et généalogiques des de Forest et des Forest d'Amérique du Nord, 19e et 20e siècles.' PhD thesis, McGill University, 2001.

Dawn, Leslie. 'How Canada Stole the Idea of Native Art: The Group of Seven and Images of the Indian in the 1920s.' PhD thesis, Department of Art History, Visual Art and Theory, University of British Columbia, 2001.

Dawson, Michael. 'Consumerism and the Creation of the Tourist Industry in British Columbia, 1900–1965.' PhD thesis, Queen's University, 2001.

Dyck, Sandra. 'These Things Are Our Totems: Marius Barbeau and the Indigenization of Canadian Art and Culture in the 1920s.' MA thesis, School for Studies in Art and Culture, Carleton University, 1995.

Gordon, Alan. 'Contested Terrain: Public Memory in Montreal, 1896–1929.' PhD thesis, Queen's University, 1997.

Hines, Jessica. 'Art of This Land and the History of Exhibiting Aboriginal Art at the National Gallery of Canada.' MA thesis, School for Studies in Art and Culture: Art History, Carleton University, 2005.

Hodgins, Peter T. 'The Canadian Dream-work: History, Myth and Nostalgia in the Heritage Minutes.' PhD thesis, Carleton University, 2003.

Kicksee, Richard. '"Scaled Down to Size": Negotiating Amerindian Participation in Canada's Centennial Celebrations, 1967.' MA thesis, Queen's University, 1995.

Kines, Gary Bret. '"Chief man-of-many-sides": John Murray Gibbon and His Contributions to the Development of Tourism and the Arts in Canada.' MA thesis, Carleton University, 1988.

MacEachern, Alan. '"No Island Is an Island": A History of Tourism on Prince Edward Island.' MA thesis, Queen's University, 1991.

Marcus, Julie. 'The Erotics of the Museum.' Paper given at the University of Sussex, March 1996. Manuscript in author's possession.

May, Louise Anne. 'Worthy Warriors and Unruly Amazons: Sino-Western Historical Accounts and Imaginative Images of Women in Battle.' PhD thesis, University of British Columbia, 1985.

McNaughton, Janet Elizabeth. 'A Study of the CPR-Sponsored Québec Folk Song and Handicraft Festivals, 1927–1930.' MA thesis, Memorial University of Newfoundland, 1982.

Montgomery, Kenneth E. '"A Better Place to Live": National Mythologies, Canadian History Textbooks, and the Reproduction of White Supremacy.' PhD thesis, University of Ottawa, 2005.

Nurse, Andrew. 'Publishing *The Kingdom of Saguenay*: Marius Barbeau, Hugh Eayrs and the Dynamics of Folklore Publishing in the 1930s.' Unpublished.

– 'Tradition and Modernity: The Cultural Work of Marius Barbeau.' PhD thesis, Queen's University, 1997.

Oikawa, Mona. 'Cartographies of Violence: Women, Memory, and the Subject of "Internment."' PhD thesis, Ontario Institute for Studies in Education, University of Toronto, 1999.

Sackett, Andrew. 'Doing History in the "Great Cyclorama of God": Tourism and the Presentation of the Past in Twentieth-Century St. Andrews, New Brunswick.' MA thesis, Queen's University, 1995.

White, Jay. 'Revisiting the Land of Evangeline: Early Nova Scotia Tourist Literature, 1850–1930.' Paper presented to the Open Conference for the History of the Book in Canada Project, Quebec City, May 2001.

Internet and Other Electronic Resources

Clark, Penney. 'Engaging the Field: A Conversation with Mark Starowicz.' *Canadian Social Studies* 36, 2 (Winter 2002). http://www.quasar.ualberta.ca/css/Css_36_2/ARengaging_the_field.htm.

Conrad, Margaret. 'Public History and Its Discontents or History in the Age of Wikipedia.' Canadian Historical Association Presidential Address, University of Saskatchewan (29 May 2007). http://www.cha-shc.ca/english/info/Conrad_CHA_Address.pdf.

Delagrange, Susan. 'Evolving Sites for the Teaching of Writing: Notes on Hypertextuality.' http://people.cohums.ohio-state.edu/ulman1/courses/E883C/E883C_SP97/Research/delagrange/hypertxt.htm.

Glass, Brent. 'The Importance of Museums to National Identity.' *Canadian American Research Symposium* (Fall 2004). http://www.acs-aec.ca/PastEvents/CARS/Glass-french.pdf.

Melton, Matthew. '"Ken Burns's Civil War": Epic Narrative and Public Moral Argument.' http://www.regent.edu/acad/schcom/rojc/melton.html.

Osborne, Ken.'Voices from the Past.' *Canadian Social Studies* 35, 4 (2001); 36, 1 (2001). http://www.quasar.ualberta.ca/css/.

Rudin, Ronald. 'Celebrating the Origins of French Settlement and the Construction of Canadian Identity.' *Canadian-American Research Symposium* (Fall 2004). http://www.acs-aec.ca/PastEvents/CARS/rudin-french.pdf.

Tate, Marsha. 'Looking for Laura Secord on the Web: Using a Famous Figure from the War of 1812 as a Model for Evaluating Historical Web Sites.' *History Teacher* 38, 2 (February 2005). http://www.historycooperative.org/journals/ht/38.2/tate.html.

Turkel, William. 'Digital History Hacks: Methodology for the Infinite Archive.' http://digitalhistoryhacks.blogspot.com/.

Contributors

Colin M. Coates holds the Canada Research Chair in Canadian Cultural Landscapes at Glendon College, York University, and is currently director of the Robarts Centre for Canadian Studies at York University. He conducts research in the areas of commemoration history, environmental and landscape history, and the history of Canadian utopias. He is the co-author (with Cecilia Morgan) of *Heroines and History: Representations of Madeleine de Verchères and Laura Secord* (2002), which won the Prix Lionel Groulx – Fondation Yves-Saint-Germain of the Institut d'histoire de l'Amérique française. With Geoffrey Ewen, he co-edited *Introduction aux études canadiennes: Histoires, identités, cultures* (2012).

Lyle Dick is the West Coast Historian with Parks Canada in Vancouver and the author of *Muskox Land: Ellesmere Island in the Age of Contact* (awarded Innis Prize, 2003), and *Farmers 'Making Good'* (revised edition, 2008) (co-awarded Clio Prize, 1990). He has presented more than one hundred papers, public presentations, or named lectures across North America and in Europe. He is the president of the Canadian Historical Association.

Peter Hodgins is an assistant professor in the School of Canadian Studies at Carleton University. His research focuses on the politics and poetics of memory in contemporary Canada.

Renée Hulan teaches Canadian literature at Saint Mary's University in Halifax, Nova Scotia. She is the author of *Northern Experience and the Myths of Canadian Culture* (2002) and editor of *Native North America: Critical and Cultural Perspectives* (1999). From 2005 to 2008, she served with Donald Wright as editor of the *Journal of Canadian Studies/Revue d'études canadiennes*. With

Renate Eigenbrod, she edited *Aboriginal Oral Traditions: Theory, Practice, Ethics* (Fernwood, 2008).

Jason F. Kovacs is an assistant professor of geography at Nipissing University, where he teaches courses on cultural and social geography. He is the author and co-author of several articles on cultural and heritage planning practice in Canada.

Eva Mackey is an associate professor in the School of Canadian Studies at Carleton University. She is the author of *The House of Difference: Cultural Politics and National Identity in Canada* and is completing a book manuscript entitled 'Unsettled Expectations: Settler Coloniality, Land Rights, and Decolonizing Strategies' (forthcoming).

Ian McKay has taught history at Queen's University since 1988. His publications include *The Quest of the Folk: Antimodernism and Cultural Selection in Twentieth-Century Nova Scotia* (3rd edition, 2009); *Reasoning Otherwise: Leftists and the People's Enlightenment in Canada, 1890–1920* (2008), winner of the Canadian Historical Association's John A. Macdonald Prize; with Robin Bates, *In The Province of History: The Making of the Public Past in Twentieth-Century Nova Scotia* (2010), winner of the Savard Award from the International Council of Canadian Studies; and with Jamie Swift, *Warrior Nation? Rebranding Canada in an Anxious Age* (2012).

Cecilia Morgan teaches history in the Department of Theory and Policy Studies, University of Toronto. Her publications include *Heroines and History: Representations of Madeleine de Verchères and Laura Secord*, with co-author Colin M. Coates (2002) and *'A Happy Holiday': English-Canadians and Transatlantic Tourism, 1870–1930* (2008). She is currently writing a book on Aboriginal and Métis peoples' travel from British North America to Britain, 1800–1914.

Sasha Mullally is an associate professor of history at the University of New Brunswick, where she teaches courses in the social and cultural history of medicine and health, the history of the Atlantic Provinces, and the history of women and gender. Her research focuses on the history of rural medicine and health care in twentieth-century North America, especially the life narratives and public history renderings of health providers. It was her interest in public history that cultivated an enthusiasm for the digital humanities, and she currently directs a joint honours/graduate course called 'Understanding the Virtual Past/Making Digital History.'

James Murton is an associate professor in the Department of History at Nipissing University. His current research concerns Canada's economic and cultural relationship with the British Empire in the late nineteenth and early twentieth centuries.

Nicole Neatby teaches Canadian History at Saint Mary's University. Her areas of interest include the history of tourism, commemoration, women, and student protest movements. She is the author of *Carabins ou activites? L'idéalisme et la raditicalisation de la pensée étudiante à l'université de Montréal au temps du duplessisme* (1997) and is currently writing a book on the history of Quebec tourism promotion.

H.V. Nelles, the L.R. Wilson Professor of Canadian History at McMaster University and Distinguished Research Professor Emeritus from York University, is the author of *The Art of Nation-Building, A Little History of Canada* (2nd edition) and co-author of *The River Returns, The Painted Valley*, and the forthcoming *Wilderness and Waterpower*.

Brian S. Osborne is Professor Emeritus of Geography at Queen's University, Kingston, and Adjunct Research Professor at Carleton University. His current research considers symbolic landscapes, monumentalism, and performed commemoration as contributors to the construction of social cohesion and national identity, and the role of the commodification of heritage and culture in post-industrial societies as both an economic opportunity and a threat to sustainable communities.

Ken Osborne, a graduate of the Universities of Oxford, Birmingham, and Manitoba, began his career as a high school history teacher in Winnipeg. He joined the staff of the Faculty of Education, University of Manitoba, in 1972 and is now professor emeritus. Over the years he has been actively involved with the teaching of history in schools and has written extensively on issues of history education. Since retirement he has taken a particular interest in the history of history teaching in Canada.

Ruth B. Phillips holds a Canada Research Chair in Aboriginal Art and Culture and is a professor of art history at Carleton University. Her books include *Trading Identities: The Souvenir in Native North American Art from the Northeast, 1700–1900, Native North American Art* for the Oxford History of Art (co-authored with Janet Catherine Berlo), and *Museum Pieces: Toward the Indigenization of Canadian Museums*. She has also curated exhibitions and served as director of the University of British Columbia Museum of Anthropology.

Ian Radforth is a professor of history at the University of Toronto. He has written about a range of topics in Canadian history: immigration and labour, state formation, wartime internment, and public spectacles. He is the author of *Royal Spectacle: The 1860 Visit of the Prince of Wales to Canada and the United States* (2004).

Ronald Rudin is a professor of history at Concordia University. He is the author of numerous publications on the economic, social, and cultural history of French Canada, including the award-winning *Remembering and Forgetting in Acadie: A Historian's Journey through Public Memory*. He is also the producer of the documentary films *Life after Île Ste-Croix* and *Remembering a Memory*.

Timothy J. Stanley is a professor of Education Foundations and Antiracism Education in the Faculty of Education, University of Ottawa. He is the author of *Contesting White Supremacy: School Segregation, Anti-racism, and the Making of Chinese Canadians* (2011).

Ira Wagman is an associate professor of Communication Studies at Carleton University. He researches and writes in the areas of cultural policy, communication theory, and media history.